LEAVING CERTIFICATE
HIGHER AND ORDINARY LEVELS

COMPLETE
HOME ECONOMICS

Leanne Gillick and Laura Healy

PUBLISHED BY:
Educate.ie
Walsh Educational Books Ltd
Castleisland, Co. Kerry, Ireland
www.educate.ie

EDITOR:
Carolyn Dent-Neville

DESIGN AND LAYOUT:
Kieran O'Donoghue

COVER DESIGN:
Kieran O'Donoghue

PRINTED AND BOUND BY:
Walsh Colour Print, Castleisland,
Co. Kerry, Ireland

ISBN: 978-1-910468-60-9

Acknowledgements

I wish to express my deepest gratitude to my family, in particular my parents Charlie and Marie for their unfailing love and encouragement and for helping me to believe in myself. To my partner Daniel, thank you for your unyielding support, reassurance and patience. Without you, this journey would not have been possible. Special thanks to Emer Lennon, my Home Economics teacher, for inspiring me to follow this career path. I hope to instill the same love for Home Economics in my students as you did in me.

Leanne Gullick

I wish to thank my parents, Jim and Lil, for their constant support, love and encouragement. You were my first teachers, instilling in me my love of education and learning. To my husband Ger, thank you for your patience and understanding throughout this process. Behind every great woman is a great man! To my three wonderful girls, Alana, Elissa and Eloise, I hope that I have inspired you to work hard, believe in yourselves and dream big. I attribute my love of Home Economics to my teacher, Frances Guerin. Thank you.

Laura Healy

Finally, both authors would like to thank their students – you are the reason we continue to love to teach and continue to love our subject.

We dedicate this to you.

CONTENTS

INTRODUCTION

Complete Home Economics is a student-friendly, up-to-date and comprehensive package for Higher and Ordinary Level students. Content is fully class-tested and written in line with the requirements of the marking scheme. Fully developed, syllabus-relevant points give students exactly what they need to know.

The *Complete Home Economics* package includes a textbook (with free ebook), a Food Studies Assignment Guide, an Exam Skillbuilder Workbook, a Teacher's Resource Book and digital resources.

Content covered in *Complete Home Economics*

All three Core Areas:

- Core Area 1: Food Studies
- Core Area 2: Resource Management and Consumer Studies
- Core Area 3: Social Studies

The two most popular Electives:

- Elective 1: Home Design and Management
- Elective 3: Social Studies

Key features of *Complete Home Economics*

Learning intentions

Each topic begins with a set of learning intentions (what you will learn) to inform the student and facilitate teacher planning.

Syllabus numbering

All chapters and topics include syllabus numbering for ease of reference and to facilitate subject planning.

Higher Level markers

Complete Home Economics is written with both Higher and Ordinary Level students in mind. Higher-Level-only material is clearly marked.

Exam questions

Relevant exam questions are featured within topics to give students an insight into the wording of exam questions and to test their knowledge.

Up-to-date information

Up-to-date information in areas such as legislation, statutory bodies and initiatives.

Lit Hit and Go Figure boxes

A strong focus on literacy and numeracy, with Lit Hit and Go Figure boxes featured throughout.

Remember Its

The Remember It feature offers handy mnemonics to assist students in learning sets of information, such as essential amino acids.

Complete Home Economics Food Studies Assignment Guide

- A dedicated guide to completing the food studies assignments, written by an experienced corrector.
- Takes into account the recent changes in the journal assignments and is written in line with recent inspection reports.
- Includes recipes, sample answers and blank assignment templates.

Complete Home Economics Exam Skillbuilder Workbook

- Includes learning checklists and past exam questions organised by topic to complement each chapter of the textbook.
- Where a topic has not been examined previously, exam-style sample questions are included.
- All questions include a breakdown of marks (e.g. 20 marks = 5 points @ 4 marks) to focus teaching and learning.

Additional resources for teachers

- Teacher's Resource Book with teaching and assessment for learning strategies included for every chapter, such as demonstration ideas, practical activities and relevant links for extension material.
- Slideshows to accompany every chapter.

We really hope you enjoy using the *Complete Home Economics* package!

Leanne Gillick

Laura Healy

CORE AREA 1

FOOD STUDIES

Chapter 1: Food science and nutrition

1.1.1 FOOD CHOICES

What you will learn:

- Factors that affect food choices

Food is necessary for survival. In our current food environment, we are presented with a wide variety of foods to choose from. Many different factors affect the food choices we make.

Factors that affect food choices

Culture

- Different countries have particular foods associated with them that form part of the country's cultural identity, as these foods have been consumed there for many years. This influences food choices, e.g. rice is a **staple food** in China.
- Religious beliefs influence food choices, e.g. Hindus do not eat beef as they believe the cow to be sacred.
- Travel and immigration influence food choices, as when people visit other places they gain awareness of alternative cuisines.

Lit Hit
A staple food is a food that is eaten routinely and makes up a large portion of a standard diet in a given population.

Nutritional awareness

- People are increasingly nutritionally conscious when making food choices as they understand what a healthy diet is. This may be due to studying subjects such as Home Economics, television programmes about this topic or the work of government agencies, e.g. Bord Bia.
- Nowadays many individuals check nutritional labelling in order to avoid foods that are low in fibre and high in fat, salt and sugar. Several food companies now place specific nutritional information on the front of the pack to make this easier. Some food service outlets, such as Subway, now display calories on their menus.

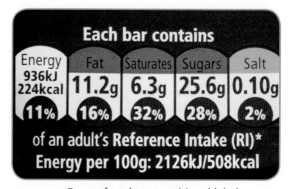

Each bar contains				
Energy 936kJ 224kcal	Fat	Saturates	Sugars	Salt
	11.2g	6.3g	25.6g	0.10g
11%	16%	32%	28%	2%

of an adult's Reference Intake (RI)*
Energy per 100g: 2126kJ/508kcal

▲ Front of package nutritional label

Families

- Children's food choices are influenced by what is made available to eat in the home. It is important that parents avoid purchasing processed foods and provide fresh foods, such as fruit and vegetables, to help children to develop healthy eating patterns of their own.

- Children's food choices are also influenced by watching what their family eats. Parents should choose healthy snacks and meals to set a good example.
- Parents should teach children why good nutrition is important by cooking with them, as well as showing them how to read nutritional labels. This knowledge is especially important in teenage years when parents have less control over the foods their children choose.

Eating patterns

- Eating patterns are influenced by work, school and leisure activities.
- A busy lifestyle can affect food choices as it causes a greater reliance on takeaways or convenience foods, e.g. ready meals, because they take little preparation time and are quick to cook.
- Busy lifestyles can also reduce how frequently families eat dinner together, as family members may have different schedules.

Money available

- Families with less money coming into their household may not be able to spend much on food. This can lead to high quantities of processed food being chosen, as it is seen as more cost-effective. To counteract this, families should plan and shop wisely in order to live within their means while still producing inexpensive, nutritious meals.
- Families with greater incomes can opt for expensive foods frequently, e.g. fillet steak, or eat out more often.

Food availability

- Time of year affects food availability. For example, raspberries are readily available in summer months, as they are in season. However, improved food-processing methods, e.g. freezing and canning, are making many foods more accessible all year round.
- Location also impacts on food availability, as people living in rural areas may not have access to the same choice of food available in urban areas. For example, local shops may not stock coconut milk.
- Improved knowledge of the link between nutrition and health has also increased the availability of healthier foods, such as low-salt products, on supermarket shelves, influencing food choices.

Sensory aspects

- Consumers often have set expectations of a food's appearance, taste, smell and texture, e.g. lettuce should have a crisp texture and should not appear limp. If a particular food appeals to a person's senses, they may choose it over another food.

FOOD CHOICES

- Packaging and advertising that is visual will also attract consumers, making them choose a particular product over its competitor.
- Some food companies make food samples available in stores, as they know consumers will be attracted to taste these foods and, in turn, possibly purchase them.

Emotional influences

- Emotional influences, such as anger, fear or boredom, can cause people to turn to food for comfort. Individuals often make irrational food decisions, e.g. excessive consumption of fatty foods, to provide instant satisfaction and relief from difficult emotions. It is important that people opt for healthier ways to deal with these emotions, e.g. talking to a friend or seeking professional help, to address the real emotional issue or problem.

Health status

- Health status will determine the foods an individual can or cannot consume, e.g. a person with coeliac disease must exclude gluten from their diet.
- If a person wants to lose weight this will also impact on food choices, e.g. they will tend to shop more nutritiously, opting for low-fat and low-sugar foods.

Marketing and advertising

- Marketing strategies, e.g. sweets at the checkout or special offers, influence food choices as they encourage impulse buying.
- Advertising also influences food choices, as it makes consumers aware of new food products available and new developments in food products already on the market, e.g. 30% less sugar.
- Many companies use celebrities to **endorse** their products, as this can influence young people's food choices.

Lit Hit
Endorse means to show approval of product.

REMEMBER IT!

'**C**hoosing **N**utritious **F**oods **E**nsures **M**ore **F**amilies **S**uccessfully **E**at **H**ealthy **M**eals.'
Culture, **N**utritional awareness, **F**amilies, **E**ating patterns, **M**oney available, **F**ood availability, **S**ensory aspects, **E**motional influences, **H**ealth status, **M**arketing and advertising.

❓ Discuss **three** factors that affect the food choices of teenagers. (12) **OL**

Give an account of the factors that affect a consumer's choice of food. (20) **HL**

NUTRITION: AN INTRODUCTION

What you will learn:

- **Key nutrition terms**

Nutrition is a branch of science that deals with food, the nutrients it contains and how the body uses them. To study nutrition it is necessary to understand the following terminology.

What nutrients are

- **Nutrients:** chemical compounds that regulate body processes, provide heat and energy and assist growth and repair. Nutrients are required in varying amounts by the body.
- **Macronutrients:** nutrients required in large amounts, e.g. protein, lipids and carbohydrates. Macronutrients are measured in grams (g).
- **Micronutrients:** nutrients required in small amounts, e.g. vitamins and minerals. Micronutrients are measured in milligrams (mg) and micrograms (µg).

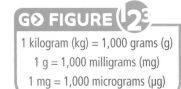

GO FIGURE

1 kilogram (kg) = 1,000 grams (g)
1 g = 1,000 milligrams (mg)
1 mg = 1,000 micrograms (µg)

The science of nutrients

- **Elemental composition:** nutrients are formed from molecules that are made of elements, e.g. protein contains the elements carbon (C), hydrogen (H), oxygen (O) and nitrogen (N), which combine to form a molecule called an amino acid.
- **Chemical formula:** explains how a nutrient is formed by stating the number of elements in each molecule, e.g. the chemical formula for a glucose (carbohydrate) molecule is $C_6H_{12}O_6$ (6 carbon, 12 hydrogen and 6 oxygen elements).
- **Classification:** the arrangement of nutrients into groups, e.g. macronutrients and micronutrients, or according to similarities, e.g. lipids are classified as saturated, monounsaturated and polyunsaturated fatty acids.

Where nutrients are found and what they do

- **Sources:** a food or origin that provides nutrients to the body, e.g. calcium from milk or vitamin D from the action of sunshine on the skin.
- **Properties:** characteristics that are unique to specific nutrients, e.g. lipids are insoluble in water whereas vitamin C is soluble in water.
- **Biological functions:** the function or job a nutrient carries out in the body, e.g. lipids provide insulation.

Nutrients in the diet

- **Recommended Daily Allowance (RDA)/Reference Intake (RI):** the average daily intake level of a nutrient that is sufficient to meet the nutrient requirements of nearly all people (97.5%) in a specific age and gender group, e.g. adults need 800 mg of calcium. The term Reference Intake (RI) is used on food packaging.
- **Deficiency diseases:** diseases that occur when the body is lacking in a particular nutrient over a period of time, e.g. anaemia develops when the diet is lacking iron and vitamin C.
- **Digestion:** the breakdown of food to obtain nutrients.
- **Absorption:** the process of absorbing nutrients into the bloodstream through the villi of the small intestine.
- **Utilisation:** how the body uses the nutrients absorbed into the bloodstream.

PROTEINS

What you will learn:

- **Elemental composition and chemical structure of proteins**
- **Essential and non-essential amino acids**
- **Peptide links**
- **Structure, classification, sources and biological value of proteins**
- **Complementary role/supplementary value of proteins**
- **Properties, biological functions, Recommended Daily Allowance (RDA)/Reference Intake (RI) and energy value of proteins**
- **Digestion, absorption and utilisation of proteins**
- **Deamination**

Proteins are one of the macronutrients. Proteins form the main part of all cells and tissues, making them essential for growth and repair.

Elemental composition of proteins

- Proteins are made up of four elements: carbon (C), hydrogen (H), oxygen (O) and nitrogen (N).
- Proteins are the only nutrients that contain nitrogen, which is essential for growth.
- Some proteins contain small quantities of sulfur (S), iron (Fe) and phosphorus (P).

 List the elements found in protein. (4) **OL**

Chemical structure of proteins

Proteins are large molecules composed of amino acids. Amino acids are joined together by peptide links to form long polypeptide chains that make up proteins.

Basic structure of an amino acid

Each amino acid contains:

- an amino group (NH$_2$) (basic)
- a carboxyl group (COOH) (acidic)
- a central carbon (C)
- a single hydrogen (H)
- a variable group (R): changes with each amino acid.

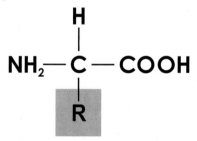

▲ Basic structure of an amino acid

 Give an account of protein and refer to the structure of an amino acid. (8) **HL**

Examples of amino acids

The variable group (R) is different in each amino acid.

When the variable group (R) is hydrogen (H) the amino acid is glycine.	When the variable group (R) is HS-CH₂ the amino acid is cysteine.
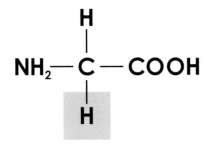	

When the variable group (R) is hydrogen (H) the amino acid is glycine.

$$NH_2 - C - COOH$$

with H above and H below the central C.

When the variable group (R) is HS-CH₂ the amino acid is cysteine.

$$NH_2 - C - COOH$$

with H above and HS-CH₂ below the central C.

HL Essential and non-essential amino acids

The human body uses 20 different amino acids to make all the proteins it needs to function. These are all found in food. They are divided into two groups: essential and non-essential amino acids.

Essential amino acids	Non-essential amino acids
• Cannot be manufactured by the body, therefore must be obtained from food • There are ten essential amino acids. Adults require eight of these and children require ten.	• Can be manufactured by the body, therefore do not need to be obtained from food • There are ten non-essential amino acids
• Valine • Lysine • Leucine • Isoleucine • Phenylalanine • Methionine • Threonine • Tryptophan • Histidine (children) • Arginine (children)	• Alanine • Aspartic acid • Cysteine • Ornithine • Serine • Asparagine • Proline • Tyrosine • Glycine • Glutamic acid

REMEMBER IT!

'**V**ery **L**ong **L**essons **I**n **P**roteins **M**ake **T**ina **T**ired, **HA**!'
Valine, **L**ysine, **L**eucine, **I**soleucine, **P**henylalanine, **M**ethionine, **T**hreonine, **T**ryptophan, **H**istidine (children), **A**rginine (children).

REMEMBER IT!

'**A**mino **A**cids **C**an **O**ften **S**end **A** **P**oor **T**eacher **G**a**G**a!'
Alanine, **A**spartic acid, **C**ysteine, **O**rnithine, **S**erine, **A**sparagine, **P**roline, **T**yrosine, **G**lycine, **G**lutamic acid.

 What is an essential amino acid? (2) **HL**

PROTEINS

⒣ Peptide links

Peptide links are formed when two amino acids join together. This results in the loss of a water (H_2O) molecule and is called a condensation reaction.

Stages in the formation of peptide links

1. The COOH (acidic) group of one amino acid reacts with the NH₂ (basic) group of another.

$$NH_2-\overset{\overset{H}{|}}{\underset{\underset{R}{|}}{C}}-\overset{\overset{O}{\|}}{C}-OH \quad \overset{\overset{H}{|}}{\underset{\underset{H}{|}}{N}}-\overset{\overset{H}{|}}{\underset{\underset{R}{|}}{C}}-COOH$$

2. The COOH (acidic) group loses an OH group. The NH₂ (basic) group loses a hydrogen (H) atom. The hydrogen (H) atom and the OH group join together to form a water (H_2O) molecule that is lost.

$$NH_2-\overset{\overset{H}{|}}{\underset{\underset{R}{|}}{C}}-\overset{\overset{O}{\|}}{C}-OH \quad \overset{\overset{H}{|}}{\underset{\underset{H}{|}}{N}}-\overset{\overset{H}{|}}{\underset{\underset{R}{|}}{C}}-COOH$$

3. The result is a CO-NH bond. This new molecule is called a dipeptide (two amino acids joined together). When more than 20 amino acids join together, a polypeptide is formed. When more than 50 amino acids join together, a protein is formed. Each protein consists of one or more polypeptide chains.

$$NH_2-\overset{\overset{H}{|}}{\underset{\underset{R}{|}}{C}}-\overset{\overset{O}{\|}}{C}-\overset{}{N}-\overset{\overset{H}{|}}{\underset{\underset{R}{|}}{C}}-COOH$$

$$\downarrow$$

$$H_2O$$

The reverse of the condensation reaction is called hydrolysis. Hydrolysis involves the addition of water and enzyme action. It occurs during digestion, when proteins are broken down into individual amino acids.

 Give an account of protein and refer to how a peptide bond is formed. (8) **HL**

Structure of proteins

Primary structure

- Primary structure is the order or sequence of amino acids in protein chains
- Amino acids can be arranged in many different combinations. Insulin, one of the simplest proteins, contains 51 amino acids.

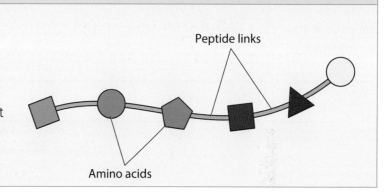

Peptide links

Amino acids

Secondary structure

- Secondary structure involves the folding of the primary structure of proteins into definite shapes
- Polypeptide chains either fold in on themselves or cross-link with another polypeptide chain. This causes the chains to form a spiral shape. Cross-links give proteins their unique properties, e.g. gluten its elasticity
- There are two main types of cross-links: disulfide bonds and hydrogen bonds

Disulfide bonds	Hydrogen bonds
• Disulfide bonds occur when two sulfurs from two amino acids join together from either a single polypeptide chain or two different polypeptide chains • The amino acid cysteine contains sulfur. Two cysteine amino acids can form a disulfide bond. • Insulin contains disulfide bonds	• Hydrogen bonds occur when a hydrogen (H) from the N-H group of one amino acid and an oxygen (O) from the C=O group of another amino acid join together from either a single polypeptide chain or two different polypeptide chains • The amino acids serine and tyrosine are capable of forming hydrogen bonds • Collagen contains hydrogen bonds
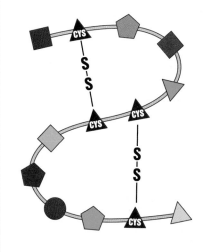	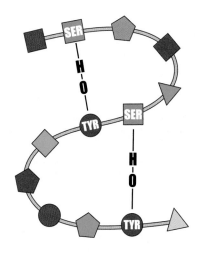

Explain what is meant by primary protein structure. (2) **OL**

Describe (i) the primary structure and (ii) the secondary structure of protein. (24) **HL**

PROTEINS

Tertiary structure

- Involves the folding of the secondary structure of proteins into three-dimensional shapes
- Further cross-linking between amino acids forms definite shapes, which may be fibrous (elongated) or globular (folded over itself to form a compressed unit)

	Fibrous	Globular
Shape	• Polypeptide chains are arranged in straight, spiral or zigzag shapes Straight Spiral Zigzag Cross-link	• Polypeptide chains are arranged in a globular (spherical) shape Cross-links
Properties	• Insoluble in water • Not easily denatured	• Soluble in water • Easily denatured
Examples	• Gluten (wheat) • Elastin and collagen (meat connective tissue)	• Ovalbumin (egg white) • Lactalbumin (milk)

Classification of proteins

Proteins can be classified as simple proteins or conjugated proteins.

Simple proteins			
Group	**Sub-group**	**Examples**	**Sources**
Animal	Fibrous	Elastin	Meat connective tissue
		Collagen	Meat connective tissue
	Globular	Ovalbumin	Egg white
		Lactalbumin	Milk
Plant	Glutenins	Glutenin	Wheat
		Oryzenin	Rice
	Prolamines	Gliadin	Wheat
		Zein	Maize

Conjugated proteins

Conjuated proteins form when proteins combine with a non-protein molecule.

Group	Examples	Sources
Lipoproteins (lipid and protein)	Lecithin	Eggs
Phosphoproteins (phosphate and protein)	Caseinogen	Milk

 Give a detailed account of protein and refer to classification (simple and conjugated). (24) **HL**

Sources of proteins

- **Animal sources:** meat, fish, eggs, milk and cheese.
- **Plant sources:** beans, nuts, lentils, peas and cereals.

 Give one source of each of the following proteins:
- animal
- plant (vegetable).   (2) **OL**

Biological value of proteins

Biological value is a measure of the protein quality in a food and it is displayed as a percentage (%). It is determined by the number of essential amino acids a food contains in proportion to the needs of the body. For example, a 100% biological value protein food contains all the essential amino acids in proportion to the needs of the body.

High biological value (HBV) proteins (complete proteins): contain all essential amino acids. These proteins are mostly found in animal sources, with the exception of soya beans.

Food	Biological value	Proteins present
Eggs	100%	Ovalbumin, vitellin and livetin
Milk	95%	Caseinogen, lactalbumin and lactoglobulin
Meat	80–90%	Collagen, actin, elastin, myosin, globulin
Fish	80–90%	Collagen, actin, myosin
Cheese	84%	Casein
Soya beans	74%	Glycinin

Low biological value (LBV) proteins (incomplete proteins): lack one or more of the essential amino acids. These proteins are mostly found in plant sources, with the exception of gelatine.

Food	Biological value	Proteins present
Rice	67%	Oryzenin
Wheat	53%	Gluten
Maize	40%	Zein
Meat bones	0%	Gelatine

 Name **three** sources of protein under **each** of the following headings:
- high biological value protein
- low biological value protein. (6) **OL**

PROTEINS

Complementary role/supplementary value of proteins

Low biological value (LBV) proteins are deficient in one or more essential amino acids. Consuming two LBV protein foods together (each lacking different essential amino acids) can ensure all essential amino acids are obtained. This is particularly important for vegans and vegetarians.

| Beans + Toast | Hummus + Pitta | Lentil dahl + Naan |

Red = low in methionine and high in lysine
Yellow = low in lysine and high in methionine

▲ Complementary protein foods

> **?** Give a detailed account of protein and refer to supplementary value/complementary role. (8) **HL**

Properties of proteins

Denaturation

Denaturation is a change in the nature of a protein chain. It involves the unfolding of a protein chain, resulting in an irreversible change in shape. It is brought about by physical or chemical means including heat, chemicals, mechanical action and enzymes. This results in the hardening or setting of protein food, known as coagulation.

Causes of denaturation

Heat

Heat causes protein chains to unfold and bond together, causing food to coagulate and set.

🍴 **Culinary application:** egg whites coagulate and change from translucent to opaque at 60°C and egg yolks coagulate at 68°C. Dry heat, e.g. grilling, causes meat fibres to shrink, toughen and lose water, producing a dry texture. Moist heat, e.g. boiling, tenderises meat by converting collagen to gelatine.

Chemicals

Lowering or raising pH levels by the addition of acids and alkalis can denature the structure of proteins.

🍴 **Culinary application:** a vinegar-based marinade tenderises meat by denaturing proteins.

Mechanical action

Mechanical action, e.g. whipping or beating, causes protein chains to unfold and partial coagulation to occur.

🍴 **Culinary application:** meringues, sponges.

Enzymes

Enzymes cause a change to the nature of proteins' structure.

🍴 **Culinary application:** the enzyme rennin in rennet causes caseinogen in milk to coagulate during cheese-making, forming curds and whey. Proteolytic enzymes, e.g. papain (from papaya), tenderise meat.

Elasticity

Some fibrous proteins, e.g. gluten in wheat, are quite elastic.

🍴 **Culinary application:** gluten makes yeast dough elastic enough to trap the CO_2 gas produced by yeast, helping it to rise.

Maillard reaction

The Maillard reaction is the non-enzymic browning of food due to a reaction between certain amino acids and sugars under dry heat. It produces an attractive brown colour and a crust with an appetising flavour.

🍴 **Culinary application:** shortbread biscuits, roast potatoes, roast meat.

▲ Maillard reaction on roast meat

Solubility

Most proteins are insoluble in water, apart from collagen in meat (soluble in hot water) and egg albumin (soluble in cold water).

🍴 **Culinary application:** moist heat tenderises meat by converting collagen to gelatine.

🅗🅛 Gel formation

When collagen (present in the bones and skin of meat) is heated it is converted to gelatine. Gelatine can absorb large amounts of water when heated, as protein chains uncoil and water becomes trapped. This forms a **sol**. On cooling, a sol forms a gel, a semi-solid viscous solution that has a three-dimensional protein matrix in which water molecules become trapped.

🍴 **Culinary application:** cheesecakes, jelly sweets.

> **Lit' Hit**
> A sol is a solution that contains particles that do not dissolve, but are evenly dispersed throughout the liquid.

Foam formation

When an egg white is whisked, protein chains unfold and air bubbles form. The protein chains entrap air, creating a foam. Whisking also creates heat that begins to set the egg albumin. This is known as a temporary foam. It will collapse after a while unless heated to coagulate and set as a permanent foam.

🍴 **Culinary application:** meringues.

▲ Foam formation

❓ Explain the following properties of protein **and** give an example of **each**:
- denaturation
- coagulation. (12) **OL**

Name **two** methods by which protein can be denatured and give an example in **each** case. (6) **HL**

Give an account of protein and refer to properties. (12) **HL**

REMEMBER IT! 💡

'**D**enatured **E**ggs **M**ake **S**tiff **G**lossy **F**oams.'
Denaturation, **E**lasticity, **M**aillard reaction, **S**olubility, **G**el formation, **F**oam formation.

PROTEINS

Effects of dry and moist heat on proteins

Dry and moist heat	• Coagulation, e.g. egg whites coagulate at 60°C and egg yolks at 68°C • Colour change, e.g. myoglobin (red pigment) in meat changes to haematin (brown pigment) • Overcooking causes proteins to become indigestible
Dry heat	• Maillard reaction, e.g. roast beef
Moist heat	• Tenderising meat: collagen in meat converts to gelatine, causing the fibres to tenderise, e.g. pulled pork

Biological functions of proteins

Structural proteins (used to build parts of the body)	• Production of cell membranes, muscle tissue and skin • Cell repair and replacement • Growth
Physiologically active proteins (assist with the normal functioning of the body)	Production of: • hormonal proteins: help to coordinate bodily activities, e.g. production of insulin • enzymes: speed up chemical reactions, e.g. pepsin speeds up the breakdown of proteins in food • antibodies (immunoglobulins): defend the body from harmful substances, e.g. viruses • blood proteins: move molecules around the body, e.g. haemoglobin transports oxygen through the blood • nucleoproteins (DNA): make up the hereditary material in chromosomes
Nutrient proteins (play a nutritional role within the body)	• Provide the body with essential amino acids • Excess can be used as a source of energy when carbohydrate and fat reserves are used

? Give an account of protein under the following heading: functions in the body. (8) **OL**

Recommended Daily Allowance (RDA)/Reference Intake (RI)

The protein requirements of an individual depend on body weight and rate of growth. On average, adults need approximately 0.75 g of proteins per kg of body weight per day. During periods of rapid growth, e.g. childhood, adolescence and pregnancy, more proteins are required.

Group	RDA/RI (g)
Children	30–50 g
Adolescents	60–80 g
Adults and older people	50–75 g
Pregnant and lactating women	70–85 g

Energy value of proteins

1 g of proteins provides 4 kcal of energy (17 kJ).

Digestion of proteins

During digestion, water and enzymes break protein chains into separate amino acids. This process is called hydrolysis.

Mouth: food is chewed into small pieces by the teeth.

Stomach: secretes gastric juice containing:

- hydrochloric acid (HCL), which denatures proteins
- the enzyme rennin, which breaks down caseinogen into casein
- the enzyme pepsin, which breaks down proteins into peptones.

Pancreas: secretes pancreatic juice into the duodenum (the first part of the small intestine). The juice contains the enzyme trypsin that breaks down peptones into peptides.

Small intestine: the ileum (final section of the small intestine) secretes intestinal juice containing the enzyme peptidase that breaks down peptides into amino acids.

The amino acids are now ready to be absorbed and utilised by the body.

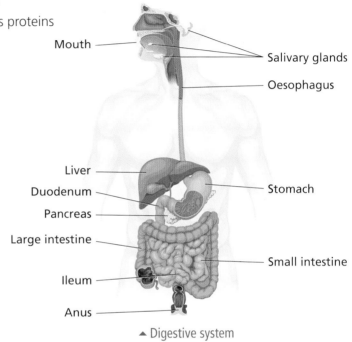

Mouth — Salivary glands — Oesophagus — Liver — Duodenum — Pancreas — Large intestine — Ileum — Anus — Stomach — Small intestine

▲ Digestive system

Organ or gland	Secretion	Enzymes	Substrate	Product
Stomach	Gastric juice	Rennin Pepsin	Caseinogen Proteins	Casein Peptones
Pancreas	Pancreatic juice	Trypsin	Peptones	Peptides
Small intestine (ileum)	Intestinal juice	Peptidase	Peptides	Amino acids

Lit Hit

A substrate is the substance on which an enzyme acts.

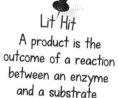

Lit Hit

A product is the outcome of a reaction between an enzyme and a substrate.

? Complete the following statement in relation to the digestion of protein using the words listed below.

enzyme   pancreas   casein

In the stomach the _____ rennin changes caseinogen to

_____.

In the duodenum the enzyme trypsin from the _____ changes peptones to peptides. (6) **OL**

PROTEINS

Absorption and utilisation of proteins

After digestion the amino acids are ready to be absorbed by the small intestine. To enter, they pass through the wall of the **villi** and into the bloodstream.

Next, the hepatic portal vein transports the amino acids to the liver.

HL In the liver, amino acids are:

- used to maintain and repair liver cells
- passed into the bloodstream and body tissues to form new cells, hormones, enzymes and antibodies.

Excess amino acids are deaminated to produce heat and energy.

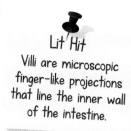

Lit Hit
Villi are microscopic finger-like projections that line the inner wall of the intestine.

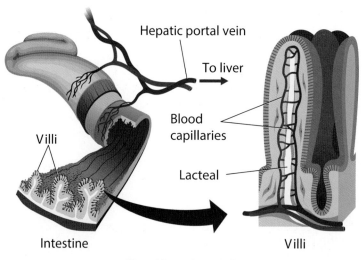

Hepatic portal vein

To liver

Blood capillaries

Lacteal

Villi

Intestine

Villi

▲ Villi and hepatic portal vein

Deamination

Deamination is the process through which excess amino acids are broken down by the body in the liver.

- The NH$_2$ group of the amino acid is removed, converted to ammonia, then to urea and excreted through the kidneys.
- The COOH group of the amino acid is oxidised to produce energy and heat.

❓ Explain protein deamination. (6) **HL**

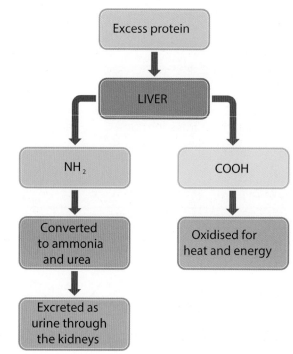

Excess protein

LIVER

NH$_2$

COOH

Converted to ammonia and urea

Oxidised for heat and energy

Excreted as urine through the kidneys

CARBOHYDRATES

What you will learn:

- **Photosynthesis**
- **Elemental composition and classification of carbohydrates**
- **Properties of sugar, starch and non-starch polysaccharides**
- **Effects of heat on carbohydrates**
- **Biological functions, Recommended Daily Allowance (RDA)/Reference Intake (RI) and energy value of carbohydrates**
- **Associated dietary disorders**
- **Digestion, absorption and utilisation of carbohydrates**

Carbohydrates are one of the macronutrients. They provide an essential source of energy. They are mainly found in plants, where they are manufactured by photosynthesis.

Photosynthesis

Photosynthesis is the process by which green plants use sunlight to make sugar (glucose) from carbon dioxide and water.

How photosynthesis occurs

- Plant roots absorb water (H_2O) from the soil.
- Leaves take in carbon dioxide (CO_2) from the air.
- Chlorophyll (green pigment) in leaves absorbs energy from the sun.

Result

- Glucose (sugar) ($C_6H_{12}O_6$) is formed.
- Oxygen (O_2) is released into the air.

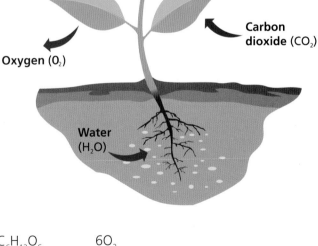

Equation for photosynthesis

$$6CO_2 + 6H_2O \xrightarrow[\text{Chlorophyll}]{\text{Light energy}} C_6H_{12}O_6 + 6O_2$$

Carbon dioxide + Water → Glucose + Oxygen

Elemental composition of carbohydrates

Carbohydrates are made up of three elements: carbon (C), hydrogen (H) and oxygen (O).

 List the **three** elements found in carbohydrates. (3) **OL**

CARBOHYDRATES

Classification of carbohydrates

All carbohydrates are based on simple sugar units. Carbohydrates are classified into three main groups: monosaccharides, disaccharides and polysaccharides.

Monosaccharides

Structure	Chemical formula	Examples	Sources
A simple sugar that contains one single sugar unit. It is the smallest unit of a carbohydrate.	$C_6H_{12}O_6$	Glucose	Fruit
		Fructose	Fruit and honey
		Galactose	Digested milk

HL

Chemical structure

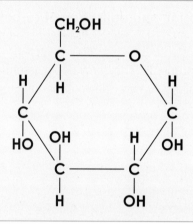

Disaccharides

Structure	Chemical formula	Examples	Sources
Formed when two monosaccharides join, resulting in the the loss of a water (H_2O) molecule (condensation reaction)	$C_{12}H_{22}O_{11}$	Maltose (glucose + glucose)	Barley
		Sucrose (glucose + fructose)	Table sugar
		Lactose (glucose + galactose)	Milk

HL

Chemical structure

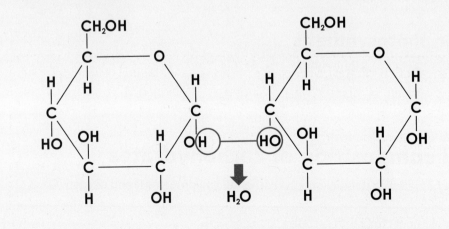

'**S**tarchy **P**otatoes **G**ive **G**reat **C**ellulose.'
Starch, **P**ectin, **G**lycogen, **G**ums, **C**ellulose.

Polysaccharides

Structure	Chemical formula	Examples	Sources
Formed when three or more monosaccharides join together, resulting in the loss of a water (H_2O) molecule with each new link (condensation reaction). Chains can be straight or branched.  Straight chain Branched chain	$(C_6H_{10}O_5)_n$ (n refers to the number of monosaccharides joined together)	Starch	Cereals and potatoes
		Pectin	Fruit
		Glycogen	Meat
		Gums	Plants and seaweed
		Cellulose (dietary fibre)	• Skins of fruit and vegetables • Nuts

HL ## Chemical structure

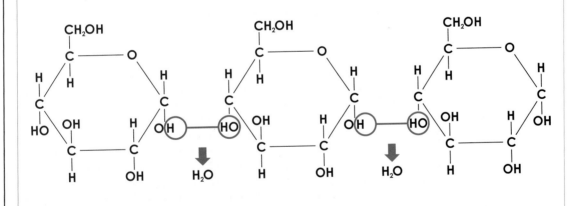

? Give an account of carbohydrates under **each** of the following headings:
- classification
- dietary sources. (18) **OL**

Describe the chemical structure of each of the following:
- monosaccharides
- disaccharides
- polysaccharides.

Give **one** example of each. (24) **HL**

Properties of sugar

Solubility

Sugar is a white crystalline compound. It is soluble in water. A syrup is formed when a large amount of sugar is dissolved in a small amount of water.

🍴 **Culinary application:** used as a preservative in canned fruit, e.g. canned peaches.

Sweetness

All sugars are sweet and give an appetising flavour to food. Some sugars are much sweeter than others. This is measured on a point scale of sweetness. For example, fructose has the highest sweetness rating and lactose has the lowest.

🍴 **Culinary application:** shortbread, cupcakes.

Sugar	Sweetness
Fructose	170%
Sucrose	100%
Glucose	75%
Lactose	15%

Point scale of sweetness ▲

Ability to assist aeration

When sugar is whisked with egg aeration occurs. The sugar helps to denature the egg protein, causing it to unfold and entrap air bubbles. Whisking also creates heat that begins to set the egg albumin. This forms a temporary foam, which will collapse after a while unless it is heated to coagulate and set as a permanent foam.

🍴 **Culinary application:** meringues, sponges.

Maillard reaction

The Maillard reaction is the non-enzymic browning of food due to a reaction between certain amino acids and sugars under dry heat. It produces an attractive brown colour and a crust with an appetising flavour.

🍴 **Culinary application:** shortbread biscuits, roast potatoes, roast meat.

▲ Maillard reaction on biscuits

🅗🅛 Caramelisation

On heating, sugar melts and caramelises. This occurs over ten gradual stages, between 104°C and 177°C. Caramelisation normally occurs at 160°C, resulting in an attractive brown colour and a sweet taste. If overheated (above 177°C), caramel will carbonise or burn.

🍴 **Culinary application:** crème caramel, caramel squares.

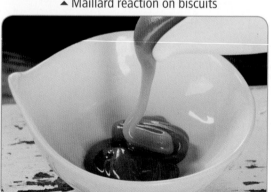

▲ Caramelisation

Crystallisation

When a liquid has dissolved as much sugar as it can, it is saturated. If more sugar is added, crystals of sugar form in the solution and solidify when cooled.

🍴 **Culinary application:** confectionery, fudge.

 Hydrolysis

Hydrolysis (the reverse of the condensation reaction) occurs during digestion. Water and enzymes split disaccharides into two monosaccharides, e.g. lactose into glucose and galactose.

Inversion

Inversion occurs when a liquid sucrose solution is heated in the presence of an acid or enzyme, causing the sucrose (disaccharide) to split in glucose and fructose (monosaccharides). This is known as an invert sugar, and it is sweeter than sucrose.

🍴 **Culinary application:** jam-making. Inversion results in a smooth jam, as invert sugars dissolve easily, preventing sugar crystals from forming.

REMEMBER IT!

> **'S**ugary **S**weets **A**fter **M**eals **C**reate **C**avities, **H**arming **I**ncisors.'
> **S**olubility, **S**weetness, **A**ssists aeration, **M**aillard reaction, **C**aramelisation, **C**rystallisation, **H**ydrolysis, **I**nversion

---

❓ Give an account of carbohydrates under the following heading: properties. (4) **OL**

In relation to carbohydrates, explain each of the following properties:
- caramelisation
- crystallisation. (6) **HL**

Name and explain three properties of carbohydrates that are useful in food preparation. (18) **HL**

Properties of starch

Solubility

Starch is a white non-crystalline powder. It is insoluble in cold water.

Flavour

Starch is not sweet in flavour.

Hygroscopy

Starch has the ability to absorb moisture from the air. This can cause uncovered foods, e.g. biscuits, to soften and lose crunch.

🍴 **Culinary application:** helps to keep cakes moist and prevents them from drying out.

Gelatinisation

When starch is combined with liquid and heated to 55–70°C the grains swell, burst and absorb the liquid around them, increasing the viscosity. As the temperature increases (above 85°C) it becomes even more viscous and forms a sol. When the mixture cools, water molecules become trapped, resulting in a gel.

🍴 **Culinary application:** moist heat – roux sauce, lemon curd; dry heat – popcorn, pastry.

▲ Gelatinisation

CARBOHYDRATES

HL Hydrolysis

Hydrolysis (the reverse of the condensation reaction) occurs during digestion. Water and enzymes split starch (polysaccharide) into the disaccharide maltose.

Dextrinisation

When starch foods are dry-heated, short-chained polysaccharides called dextrins are formed. On further heating these combine to form pyrodextrins. This causes a colour change on the surface of the food, resulting in an attractive brown appearance.

Culinary application: the browning of bread to make toast.

▲ Dextrinisation

REMEMBER IT!

'**S**tarchy **F**oods **H**elp **G**elatinise **H**ot **D**inners.'
Solubility, **F**lavour, **H**ygroscopic, **G**elatinisation, **H**ydrolysis, **D**extrinistation.

?

Explain the term gelatinisation. (3) **HL**

In relation to carbohydrate explain the property dextrinisation. (6) **HL**

Properties of non-starch polysaccharides

Cellulose/dietary fibre

Cellulose/dietary fibre is insoluble in water. It cannot be digested by the body, but it absorbs water as it passes through the intestinal tract and helps stimulate **peristalsis**. This is beneficial to the body as it speeds up the passage of food and waste, preventing bowel disorders, e.g. constipation.

Gums

Gums are soluble in water. They have the ability to absorb large amounts of water to form a thick gel with a firm texture.

Culinary application: salad dressings, ice-cream.

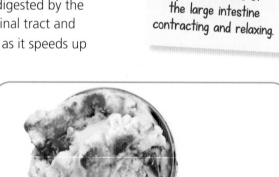

Lit Hit
Peristalsis is a muscular, wave-like movement caused by the muscles of the large intestine contracting and relaxing.

HL Pectin

Pectin is naturally present in plant cells and the cell walls of fruit and vegetables. It is used as a setting agent, as it has the ability to absorb water to form a gel. It is only present in fruits when they are ripe. In underripe fruits it is in the form of protopectin, and in overripe fruits it becomes pectic acid, neither of which can set as they cannot absorb water. For pectin to be extracted it needs heat and acid, e.g. lemon juice.

Culinary application: jam-making.

Effects of heat on carbohydrates

Dry heat	• Dextrinistaion, e.g. toasting bread • Caramelisation, e.g. crème caramel • Maillard reaction, e.g. roast beef
Moist heat	• Syrup formation, e.g. tinned peaches • Gelatinisation, e.g. white sauce • Cellulose softens, e.g. potatoes • Pectin extraction, e.g. jam

 State **two** effects of heat on starch. (6) **OL**

Biological functions of carbohydrates

- Carbohydrates supply the body with heat and energy. This helps to keep the body at 37°C and provides energy for all activities.
- Carbohydrates have a protein-sparing function. By consuming a sufficient amount of carbohydrates, proteins can fulfil their primary function of growth and repair of cells, rather than being used to produce energy.
- Cellulose/dietary fibre absorbs water as it passes through the intestinal tract and helps to stimulate peristalsis. This is beneficial to the body as it speeds up the passage of food and waste, preventing bowel disorders, e.g. constipation.
- Excess carbohydrate intake is converted to glycogen and stored in the liver and muscles as a long-term energy reserve. They may also be converted to fat and stored as adipose tissue under the skin, which insulates the body and acts as another energy reserve.

 Give an account of carbohydrates under the following heading: functions in the body. (8) **OL**

Recommended Daily Allowance (RDA)/Reference Intake (RI)

The carbohydrate requirement of an individual depends on their activity level. On average, adults need approximately 260 g of carbohydrates per day, of which sugars should account for only 90 g. It is also recommended that people consume 25–35 g of cellulose/dietary fibre each day.

Energy value of carbohydrates

1 g of carbohydrates provides 4 kcal of energy (17 kJ).

Associated dietary disorders

Dietary disorders occur when we eat too many sugary and starchy foods and too little cellulose/dietary fibre. Too much sugar and starch can lead to obesity, type 2 diabetes and dental cavities. Too little cellulose/dietary fibre can lead to bowel disorders.

→ For information on ways of reducing sugar and increasing fibre intake see page 81.

CARBOHYDRATES

Digestion of carbohydrates

During digestion water and enzymes break carbohydrate chains into monosaccharides. This process is called hydrolysis.

Mouth: food is chewed into small pieces by the teeth. The salivary glands secrete saliva containing the enzyme salivary amylase, which breaks down starch into maltose.

Pancreas: secretes pancreatic juice containing the enzyme amylase into the duodenum (the first part of the small intestine). This continues to break down starch into maltose.

Small intestine: the ileum (final section of the small intestine) secretes intestinal juice containing:

- the enzyme maltase, which breaks down maltose into glucose
- the enzyme sucrase, which breaks down sucrose into glucose and fructose
- the enzyme lactase, which breaks down lactose into glucose and galactose.

The monosaccharides glucose, fructose and galactose are now ready to be absorbed and utilised by the body.

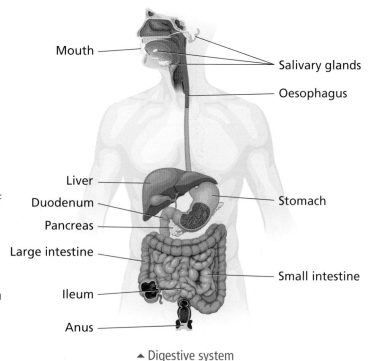

▲ Digestive system

Organ or gland	Secretion	Enzymes	Substrate	Product
Salivary glands (mouth)	Saliva	Salivary amylase	Starch	Maltose
Pancreas	Pancreatic juice	Amylase	Starch	Maltose
Small intestine (ileum)	Intestinal juice	Maltase Sucrase Lactase	Maltose Sucrose Lactose	Glucose Glucose and fructose Glucose and galactose

Absorption and utilisation of carbohydrates

After digestion the monosaccharides glucose, fructose and galactose are ready to be absorbed by the small intestine. They pass through the wall of the villi and into the bloodstream.

Next the hepatic portal vein transports the monosaccharides to the liver via the bloodstream.

HL In the liver, fructose and galactose are converted to glucose. The glucose is then:

- oxidised to produce heat and energy
- converted to glycogen and stored in the liver and muscles as a long-term energy reserve.

Excess glucose is converted to fat and stored as adipose tissue under the skin, insulating the body and acting as an energy reserve.

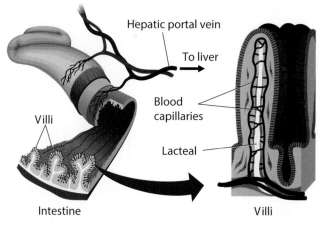

▲ Villi and hepatic portal vein

What you will learn:

- **Elemental composition and chemical structure of lipids**
- **Classification of fatty acids**
- **Distribution of saturated, monounsaturated and polyunsaturated fatty acids in food**
- **Essential fatty acids (EFAs), omega-3 fatty acids and cis and trans fatty acids**
- **Classification of lipids by source**
- **Properties, biological functions, Recommended Daily Allowance (RDA)/ Reference Intake (RI) and energy value of lipids**
- **Associated dietary disorders**
- **Digestion, absorption and utilisation of lipids**

Lipids are one of the macronutrients. Lipids provide a concentrated source of energy. The term 'lipid' refers to both fats (solid at room temperature) and oils (liquid at room temperature).

Elemental composition of lipids

Lipids are made up of three elements: carbon (C), hydrogen (H) and oxygen (O).

> **?** List the **three** elements found in lipids (fats). (3) **OL**

Chemical structure of lipids

Lipids are composed of triglycerides. A triglyceride contains one glycerol molecule and three fatty acid molecules.

Glycerol molecule: glycerol is a trihydric alcohol. It contains three hydroxyl (OH) groups.

CH_2OH

$CHOH$

CH_2OH

◄ Glycerol molecule

Fatty acid molecule: a fatty acid is an organic compound. It is represented by the formula R-COOH (the R represents the **hydrocarbon chain**).

$$H-O-\overset{\overset{O}{\|}}{C}-R$$

◄ Fatty acid molecule

📌 **Lit Hit**
A lipid hydrocarbon chain is a chain of carbon atoms that can vary in length from four to 24 atoms. The R signifies that the amount of carbons present is variable.

Triglyceride formation: each hydroxyl (OH) group of the glycerol molecule combines with hydrogens (H) from three fatty acids, resulting in the loss of three water molecules. This is known as a condensation reaction.

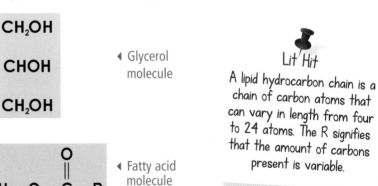
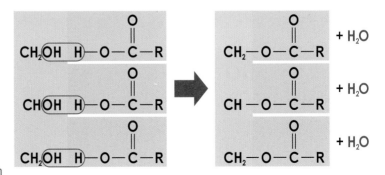

▸ Triglyceride formation

Classification of fatty acids

Fatty acids are long hydrocarbon chains with a carboxyl group (COOH) at one end and a methyl group (CH_3) at the other. The number of carbon atoms differs in each fatty acid. The chemical formula of a fatty acid is $CH_3(CH_2)_nCOOH$. Fatty acids are classified into three main groups, depending on their degree of **saturation**: saturated, monounsaturated and polyunsaturated.

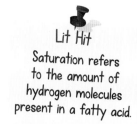

Lit Hit

Saturation refers to the amount of hydrogen molecules present in a fatty acid.

Saturated fatty acids

Structure	Consistency and melting point	Sources	Examples
Each carbon atom is fully saturated with its full quota of hydrogen atoms. No double bonds occur between the carbon atoms.	• Solid at room temperature (18°C) • High melting point	Generally found in animal sources	• Butyric acid in butter • Stearic acid in meat

Chemical structure

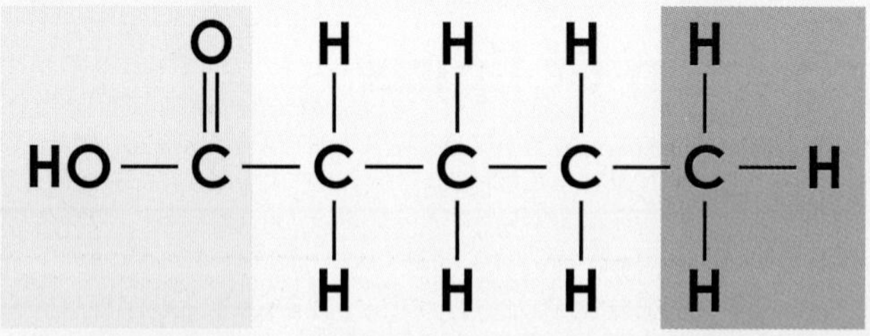

$$HO-C-C-C-C-C-H$$

Carboxyl group
(COOH)

Methyl group
(CH_3)

Monounsaturated fatty acids

Structure	Consistency and melting point	Sources	Examples
Each carbon atom is not fully saturated with a full quota of hydrogen atoms. There is one double bond between the carbon atoms.	• Soft or liquid at room temperature (18°C) • Low melting point	Generally found in plant and marine sources	• Oleic acid in olive oil

Chemical structure

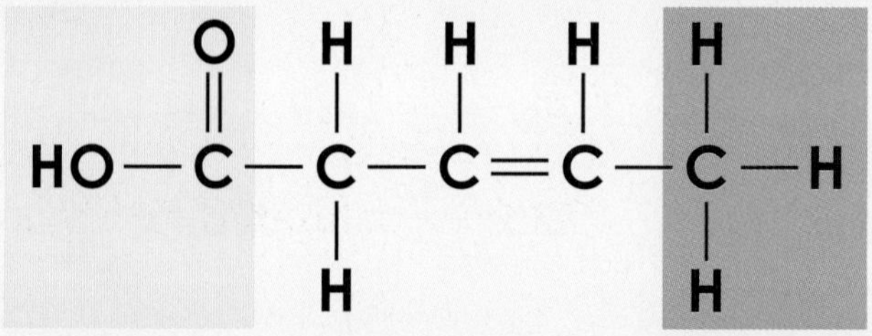

$$HO-C-C-C=C-C-H$$

Carboxyl group
(COOH)

Methyl group
(CH_3)

Polyunsaturated fatty acids (PUFAs)

Structure	Consistency and melting point	Sources	Examples
Each carbon atom is not fully saturated with a full quota of hydrogen atoms. There is more than one double bond between the carbon atoms.	• Soft or liquid at room temperature (18°C) • Lowest melting point of all the fatty acids	Generally found in plant and marine sources	• Alpha linolenic acid (three double bonds) in seed oil • Linoleic acid (two double bonds) in nuts • Linolenic acid (three double bonds) in seeds • Arachidonic acid (four double bonds) in oily fish

Chemical structure

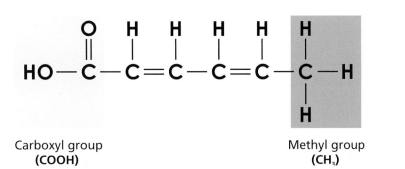

Carboxyl group
(COOH)

Methyl group
(CH₃)

 Describe the structure **and** give **one** example of **each** of the following:
- saturated fatty acids
- monounsaturated fatty acids
- polyunsaturated fatty acids. (24) **HL**

Distribution of saturated, monounsaturated and polyunsaturated fatty acids in food

All fats and oils are made up of a combination of saturated, monounsaturated and polyunsaturated fatty acids. It is this combination of fatty acids that determines the consistency, colour, taste and texture of the fat or oil. The more hydrogen atoms a fatty acid has, the greater the degree of saturation.

Animal fats	Saturated	Monounsaturated	Polyunsaturated
Butter	52%	21%	3%
Lard	40%	43%	10%
Suet	50%	30%	2%
Dripping (from beef)	50%	38%	3%
Vegetable fats	**Saturated**	**Monounsaturated**	**Polyunsaturated**
Olive oil	14%	73%	8%
Sunflower oil	12%	20%	63%
Block margarine	26%	34%	12%

LIPIDS

Essential fatty acids (EFAs)

Essential fatty acids (EFAs) are fatty acids that cannot be manufactured by the body, and therefore must be obtained from food. Linoleic acid, a type of omega-6, and alpha-linolenic acid, a type of omega-3, are both EFAs because they cannot be synthesised by the body. The other polyunsaturated fatty acids, linolenic acid and arachidonic acid, are not essential fatty acids as they can be synthesised by the body in small amounts from linoleic acid.

Sources of EFAs

- Nuts
- Seeds
- Olive oil
- Oily fish

Functions of EFAs

- EFAs aid cell membrane formation, which is essential for growth.
- EFAs reduce the risk of coronary heart disease by raising high-density lipoprotein (HDL), which helps remove cholesterol from the blood, and lowering low-density lipoprotein (LDL), which deposits cholesterol in the blood.

> ❓ What is an essential fatty acid? (2) **OL**

Omega-3 fatty acids

Omega-3 fatty acids have a double bond between the third and fourth carbon atoms along their hydrocarbon chain.

There are two main types of omega-3 fatty acids: eicosapentaenoic acid (EPA) and docosahexaenoic acid (DHA).

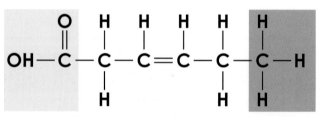

▲ Chemical structure of an omega-3 fatty acid

Sources of omega-3 fatty acids

- Oily fish
- Fish oils, e.g. cod liver oil
- Seeds
- Nuts
- Fortified eggs with added omega-3

Functions of omega-3 fatty acids

- Reduces the risk of coronary heart disease (CHD), heart attacks and strokes by raising HDL and lowering LDL.
- Decreases the viscosity of blood, preventing clots or blockages in the coronary arteries.
- Aids foetal brain development during pregnancy, as well as helping to improve memory and cognitive functioning throughout life.

> ❓ Outline the function of omega-3 fatty acids in the diet.
> Name **two** foods that are rich in omega-3 fatty acids. (6) **HL**
>
> Describe the structure of omega-3 fatty acids. (4) **HL**

🅗🅛 Cis and trans fatty acids

Monounsaturated and polyunsaturated fats can be either cis fatty acids or trans fatty acids.

	Cis fatty acids	**Trans fatty acids**
Chemical structure	Hydrogen atoms are on the same side of the double bond (either above or below) H—C(H)(H)—C(H)=C(H)—C(H)(H)—	Hydrogen atoms are on opposite sides of the double bond —C(H)(H)—C(H)=C(H)—C(H)(H)—
Sources	Naturally occurring in foods such as olive oil and oily fish	• Formed from cis fatty acids during the heating or frying of oils at high temperatures and during industrial processing, e.g. the addition of hydrogen atoms to oil to produce margarine • Also present in foods that contain hydrogenated fats, e.g. pastries and crisps
Health effects	Generally good for health as they raise HDL while lowering LDL, decreasing the risk of coronary heart disease	Generally bad for health as they lower HDL while raising LDL, increasing the risk of coronary heart disease

 Explain **each** of the following and give **one** source in **each** case:
- cis fatty acid
- trans fatty acid. (6) **HL**

Classification of lipids by source

Animal	**Plant**	**Marine**
Mainly saturated	Mainly unsaturated	Mainly polyunsaturated
Meat, meat fats, butter, cream, cheese, egg yolks and milk	Vegetable oils, nuts and nut oils, seeds and seed oils, margarine, avocados, olives and soya beans	Oily fish and fish liver oils

 List **three** sources of lipids (fats) under each of the following headings:
- saturated (animal) lipids
- unsaturated (vegetable) lipids. (6) **OL**

LIPIDS

Properties of lipids

Solubility

Lipids are insoluble in water. They are soluble in solvents such as ether and benzene.

Absorbtion of flavours

Lipids absorb flavours easily.

🍴 **Culinary application:** infused oils, e.g. chilli; flavoured butter, e.g. garlic butter.

▲ Garlic butter

Heating lipids

Melting (slip) point: solid fats melt when heated to 30–40°C.

Smoke point: if lipids are heated to 200°C (fats) or 250°C (oils), they begin to decompose, causing the glycerol to separate from the fatty acids. Glycerol is then broken down into acrolein and produces a blue smoke or haze and an acrid smell.

Flash point: extreme overheating of lipids to 310°C (fats) and 325°C (oils) causes a vapour to be emitted that can spontaneously **ignite**.

Lit Hit

Ignite means to catch fire.

Emulsions

An emulsion is a **colloidal solution**, formed when two immiscible liquids are forced to mix together. Emulsions can be described as water in oil emulsions and oil in water emulsions.

- **Water in oil emulsions:** e.g. butter, margarine. Tiny droplets of water are dispersed throughout the oil or fat.

- **Oil in water emulsions:** e.g. milk, mayonnaise. Tiny droplets of oil are dispersed throughout the water.

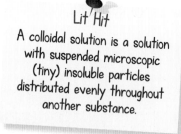

Lit Hit

A colloidal solution is a solution with suspended microscopic (tiny) insoluble particles distributed evenly throughout another substance.

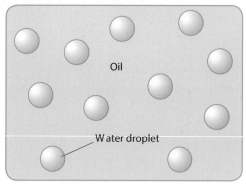
▲ Water in oil emulsion

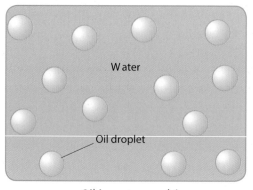
▲ Oil in water emulsion

Emulsions may be temporary or permanent.

- **Temporary emulsions:** formed when the two immiscible liquids, e.g. vinegar and oil, are shaken vigorously. If left to stand they will separate.

- **Permanent emulsions:** formed when an emulsifier, such as lecithin in egg yolk, is added to two immiscible liquids, preventing them from separating, e.g. vinegar and oil in mayonnaise.

ⓗⓛ Emulsifiers

Emulsifiers are molecules that have a hydrophilic (water-loving) head, and a hydrophobic (water-hating) tail. When an emulsifier is added to a mixture of two immiscible liquids the hydrophilic head attaches itself to the water and the hydrophobic tail attaches itself to the oil. This prevents the liquids from separating, creating a permanent emulsion.

🍴 **Culinary application:** lecithin, a natural emulsifier found in egg yolks, is used in the production of mayonnaise. Glycerol monostearate (GMS), a commercial emulsifier, is used in ice cream.

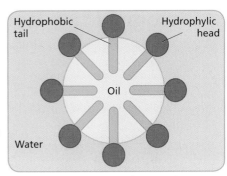

▲ How emulsifiers work

Stabilisers

Stabilisers are long-chained molecules that help to maintain emulsions by separating the oil droplets, and preventing them from coalescing.

🍴 **Culinary application:** gums are used to stabilise yoghurt. Gelatine is used to stabilise ice cream.

Hydrogenation

Hydrogenation is a process whereby hydrogen gas, in the presence of a nickel catalyst, is forced through the double bond of an unsaturated oil, converting the unsaturated oil into a saturated solid fat.

🍴 **Culinary application:** used in the production of margarine.

Rancidity

Rancidity is the spoilage or decomposition of lipids. This results in an unpleasant odour and taste. There are two types of rancidity: oxidative rancidity and hydrolytic rancidity.

- **Oxidative rancidity:** (most common) occurs when oxygen in the air combines with the carbons in a double bond of the unsaturated fatty acid. This results in an unpleasant odour and taste.

- **Hydrolytic rancidity:** occurs when enzymes or bacteria break down lipids into glycerol and fatty acids. This results in an unpleasant odour and taste.

To prevent rancidity, cover lipids, store fats in the fridge and keep oils in a cool, dark place. Manufacturers add antioxidants, e.g. vitamins A, C or E or BHA (butylated hydroxyanisole) or BHT (butylated hydroxytoluene), to foods containing lipids, as they combine with oxygen, making it unavailable to attach to the carbon atom at the double bond.

Plasticity

Plasticity describes how soft, pliable and malleable a fat is at a given temperature. It is determined by the degree of saturation. The more saturated fatty acids present, the more solid the lipid. As a result, butter is solid at room temperature compared to margarine, which is soft and spreadable.

🍴 **Culinary application:** lipids with a low saturation level, e.g. margarine, are used for creaming during cake making.

▲ Creaming during cake making

REMEMBER IT!

'**S**aturation **A**ffects **H**ealth, **E**specially **H**earts, **R**emember **P**lease!'
Solubility, **A**bsorb flavours, **H**eating lipids, **E**mulsions, **H**ydrogenation, **R**ancidity, **P**lasticity.

❓ Explain **two** of the following properties of lipids (fats):
- melting point
- smoke point
- flash point. (6) **OL**

In relation to lipids, explain **each** of the following terms:
- oxidative rancidity
- hydrolytic rancidity. (6) **HL**

Explain the role of emulsifiers in food production. (6) **HL**

LIPIDS

Biological functions of lipids

- Lipids supply the body with heat and energy. This helps to keep the body at 37°C and provides energy for all activities.
- Lipids form a protective layer that surrounds delicate organs, e.g. the kidneys.
- Lipids supply the body with the fat-soluble vitamins A, D, E and K, which are necessary for overall health.
- Lipids provide the body with the essential fatty acids that cannot be made by the body, e.g. linoleic acid.
- Excess lipid intake is stored as adipose tissue under the skin. This insulates the body and acts as an energy reserve.

> **?** Give an account of lipids (fats) and refer to functions in the body. (12) **OL**

Recommended Daily Allowance (RDA)/Reference Intake (RI)

The total fat intake for adults should be no more than 70 g per day. On average, men should eat no more than 30 g saturated fat per day and women should eat no more than 20 g.

Energy value of lipids

1 g of lipids provides 9 kcal of energy (37 kJ).

Associated dietary disorders

Dietary disorders occur when we consume too many saturated fats and too few unsaturated fats. This can result in obesity, coronary heart disease, high cholesterol and strokes.

Digestion of lipids

During digestion, water and enzymes break lipids into one glycerol and three fatty acid molecules. This process is called hydrolysis.

Mouth: food is chewed into small pieces by the teeth.

Stomach: the heat from within the stomach causes some fat to melt.

Liver: secretes bile into the duodenum (the first part of the small intestine) via the bile duct. This emulsifies large fat molecules to produce smaller molecules.

Pancreas: secretes pancreatic juice into the duodenum. The pancreatic juice contains the enzyme lipase, which begins to break down lipids into fatty acids and glycerol.

Small intestine: the ileum (final section of the small intestine) secretes intestinal juice containing the enzyme lipase, which continues to break down lipids into fatty acids and glycerol.

Fatty acids and glycerol are now ready to be absorbed and utilised by the body.

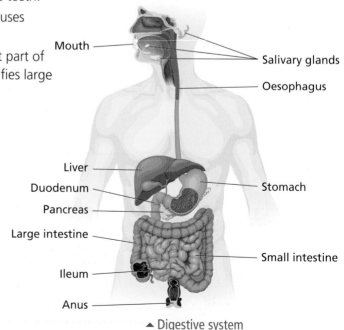
▲ Digestive system

Organ or gland	Secretion	Enzymes	Substrate	Product
Liver	Bile		Large fat molecules	Emulsified fat (small molecules)
Pancreas	Pancreatic juice	Lipase	Lipids	Fatty acids and glycerol
Small intestine (ileum)	Intestinal juice	Lipase	Lipids	Fatty acids and glycerol

Absorption and utilisation of lipids

After digestion the fatty acids and glycerol are ready to be absorbed by the small intestine. They pass through the wall of the villi into lacteals, which form part of the lymphatic system.

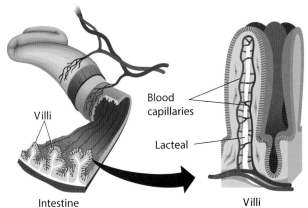

▸ Villi and lacteals

The lymphatic system transports the digested lipids to the thoracic duct, where they are deposited into bloodstream through the subclavian vein (near the left side of the neck).

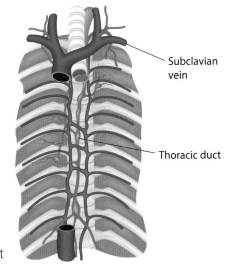

▸ Subclavian vein and thoracic duct

HL
- In the liver and muscles, digested lipids are oxidised to produce heat and energy and form cell membranes.
- Excess digested lipids are stored as adipose tissue under the skin to insulate the body and act as an energy reserve.

? Complete the following table in relation to the digestion of lipids.

Digestive gland	Secretion	Enzyme	Change
Pancreas			

(4) **HL**

Complete the following table in relation to the digestion of lipids.

Digestive gland	Secretion	Enzyme	Product
Small Intestine			

(6) **HL**

What you will learn:

- **Classification of vitamins**
- **Forms, properties, sources, functions, effects of deficiencies and Recommended Daily Allowances (RDAs)/Reference Intakes (RIs) of fat-soluble and water-soluble vitamins**

Vitamins are one of the micronutrients. The human body synthesises few vitamins: they must be obtained from food or manufactured supplements. Each vitamin has its own specific functions. Insufficient amounts of vitamins in the diet may cause deficiency diseases.

Classification of vitamins

Fat-soluble vitamins	Water-soluble vitamins
• Normally found in food that contains fat • Can be stored in the body for several months	• Found in a wide variety of food • Not stored in the body (excess are excreted)
Vitamin A: retinol and beta-carotene **Vitamin D:** cholcalciferol and ergocalciferol **Vitamin E:** tocopherol **Vitamin K:** naphthoquinones	**Vitamin C:** ascorbic acid **B group vitamins:** B1 thiamine B6 pyrodoxine B2 riboflavin B12 cobalamin B3 niacin folate/folic acid

FAT-SOLUBLE VITAMINS

Vitamin A (retinol and beta-carotene)

Forms	
• **Retinol (pure vitamin A):** easily absorbed. Stored in the liver.	• **Beta-carotene (pro-vitamin A):** not easily absorbed. Converted to retinol in the lining of the intestine.
Properties of retinol (pure vitamin A)	**Properties of beta-carotene (pro-vitamin A)**
• A yellow, fat-soluble alcohol • Insoluble in water • Soluble in organic solvents, e.g. acetone • Heat stable, but affected by prolonged high temperatures • Destroyed by oxygen	• A yellow or orange fat-soluble oil • Insoluble in water • Soluble in fat solvents, e.g. alcohol • Heat stable, but affected by prolonged high temperatures • Unaffected by oxygen • A powerful antioxidant that has the ability to counteract the damaging effects of free radicals (chemicals that can damage the human body)

HL

Sources of retinol (pure vitamin A)	Sources of beta-carotene (pro-vitamin A)
Found in animal food sources • Fish liver oils • Offal • Milk • Cheese • Eggs • Margarine • Butter • Oily fish	Found in yellow, green and orange fruit and vegetables (carotenoids) • Carrots • Leafy green vegetables • Tomatoes • Apricots • Red peppers • Sweet potatoes

Functions of vitamin A	Effects of deficiency of vitamin A
Required to manufacture the pigment rhodopsin found in the retina, which helps the eye adapt to dim light	Night blindness, whereby a person will struggle to see in dim light due to a lack of rhodopsin
Helps maintain healthy skin and the mucous membranes of the body, e.g. the eyes	• Follicular hyperkeratosis, a condition that results in rough, dry skin and inflamed hair follicles ▲ Follicular hyperkeratosis • Xerophthalmia can occur on the surface of the eye due to lack of mucous. This causes eyes to dry out and become infected with bacteria and can eventually lead to blindness.
Aids growth and development of children	Stunted or delayed growth in children, leaving them smaller in height than the average for their age
Beta-carotene acts as a powerful antioxidant that can counteract the damaging effects of free radicals	Risk of damage to cells by free radicals, increasing the risk of some cancers, coronary heart disease and strokes

Recommended Daily Allowance (RDA)/Reference Intake (RI) of vitamin A

Group	RDA/RI (µg)
Children	400–500 µg
Adolescents and adults	600–700 µg
Pregnant women	700 µg
Lactating women	950 µg

 Give an account of Vitamin A under **each** of the following headings:
- biological functions
- effects of deficiency
- properties. (18) **HL**

👍 Tip!

If the properties of vitamin A are asked in an exam and the question does not specify which type, answer using the properties of retinol (pure vitamin A).

Vitamin D (calciferol)

Forms

Cholecalciferol D3: an animal form of vitamin D. Created when UV light shines on the skin, converting 7-dehydrocholesterol in the epidermis to cholecalciferol.	**Ergocalciferol D2:** a plant form of vitamin D. Created when UV light shines on fungi and yeasts, converting ergosterol into ergocalciferol. Used in vitamin supplements.

Properties

- The most stable of all the vitamins
- Fat soluble
- Insoluble in water
- Heat stable: unaffected by cooking or preservation methods
- Unaffected by acids, alkalis and oxygen

Food sources	Other sources
• Oily fish • Margarine • Fish liver oils • Fortified milk • Eggs • Butter	Sunlight (humans need approximately 20 minutes of sunshine per day to produce enough vitamin D)

Functions	Effects of deficiency
Controls the absorption of calcium and phosphorus into the blood	Increased risk of bone diseases, such as rickets, osteoporosis and osteomalacia, and tooth decay
Regulates the amount of calcium and phosphorus in the bones and teeth, helping to maintain density and strength	Increased risk of bone diseases and tooth decay
Regulates calcium levels in the blood; if blood-calcium levels are too low, it stimulates the production of a calcium-binding protein needed to absorb more calcium	Increased risk of bone diseases and tooth decay

Recommended Daily Allowance (RDA)/Reference Intake (RI)

Group	RDA/RI (µg)
Children, adults and pregnant or lactating women	10 µg
Adolescents	15 µg

 Oily fish is a good source of vitamin D.

Give an account of vitamin D and refer to (i) properties, (ii) biological functions and (iii) recommended dietary allowance (RDA) *(now known as RI)*. (24) **HL**

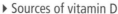 ▶ Sources of vitamin D

Vitamin D deficiency diseases

Rickets	A bone disease that affects children, causing their bones to become soft and weak. This can lead to an increased risk of fractures and bone deformities, e.g. bow legs.
Osteomalacia	A bone disease that affects adults, causing their bones to become soft and weak due to low bone mass. This can lead to an increased risk of fractures and bone pain.
Osteoporosis	A bone disease common in older people or post-menopausal women, causing their bones to become brittle and fragile due to a loss of bone mass. This can lead to an increased risk of fractures, stooped posture and back pain caused by a collapsed vertebra.
Tooth decay	A condition where the tooth enamel, bone and cementum weaken, increasing the risk of dental decay

Did you know

The HSE recommends that all babies, from birth to 12 months, are given 5 µg of vitamin D3 daily, due to an increase in the number of cases of rickets in recent years.

▸ Rickets

REMEMBER IT!

'ROOT!'

Rickets, **O**steomalacia, **O**steoporosis, **T**ooth decay.

Hypervitaminosis

Fat-soluble vitamins are stored in the liver for several months. If a diet contains an excessive intake of vitamins A or D they accumulate in the liver to toxic levels, leading to a harmful condition called hypervitaminosis. This condition is more likely to occur in people who over-use dietary supplements, such as cod liver oil, than those who over-eat foods rich in vitamins A or D.

Did you know

Excessive amounts of beta-carotene are not toxic. They cause the skin and eyes to develop a yellow shade that is reversible.

Symptoms of hypervitaminosis A		Symptoms of hypervitaminosis D	
• Miscarriage	• Birth defects	• Vomiting	• Kidney damage
• Bone pain	• Enlarged liver	• Weight loss	• Can lead to death

Vitamin E (tocopherol)

 HL

Properties		
• Fat soluble	• Unstable to alkalis and light	• Stable to acids
• Insoluble in water	• Antioxidant	• Heat stable

Sources		
• Nuts	• Seeds	• Vegetable oils
• Wheat germ	• Avocados	• Eggs

Functions	Effects of deficiency
A powerful antioxidant that can counteract the damaging effects of free radicals	Risk of damage to cells by free radicals, increasing the risk of some cancers, coronary heart disease and strokes
Protects red and white blood cells from damage	• Anaemia, due to low levels of red blood cells, which are needed to transport oxygen • Reduced immunity, due to low levels of white blood cells, which are needed to fight infection
Protects the retina in the eyes of newborn babies	Eye disorders in premature babies, which can lead to blindness

Vitamin K (naphthoquinones)

Forms		
Phylloquinone K1: made by plants	**Menaquinone K2**: made by intestinal bacteria	**Menadione K3:** a synthetic form

 HL

Properties			
• Fat soluble	• Insoluble in water	• Heat stable	• Destroyed by light

Food sources		Other sources
• Leafy green vegetables • Cereals • Offal • Oily fish • Fish liver oils		Synthesised by bacteria in the small intestine.

Functions	Effects of deficiency
Aids the clotting of blood by synthesising prothrombin	Slow blood clotting of ruptured blood vessels, leading to haemorrhaging. This is common in newborn babies, as their diet lacks vitamin K and their intestines may not have begun to produce it.
Regulates the level of calcium in bones	Increased risk of bone fractures and bone diseases such as osteoporosis

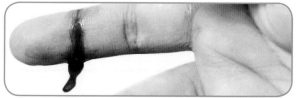

▸ Haemorrhaging due to slow blood clotting

WATER-SOLUBLE VITAMINS

Vitamin C (ascorbic acid)

Properties

- Most unstable of all the vitamins
- Water soluble
- Acidic with a sharp or sour taste
- Insoluble in fat
- Antioxidant
- Destroyed by heat, alkalis, light, oxidase (an enzyme present in the cell walls of fruit and vegetables) and metals, e.g. copper

Sources

- Rosehips
- Blackcurrants
- Kiwis
- Oranges
- Strawberries
- Lemons
- Peppers
- Cabbage
- Potatoes
- Broccoli
- Tomatoes

Functions	Effects of deficiency
Forms healthy gums and prevents inflammation	Scurvy, a severe gum disease. Symptoms include inflamed or receding gums that cause teeth to become loose and fall out and haemorrhaging under the skin. 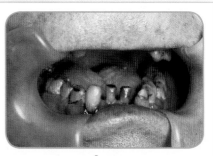 ▲ Scurvy
Forms collagen, which helps to hold cells together to form tissue, e.g. skin or blood vessels	Can lead to weakened body tissues, e.g. blood vessels that rupture easily, leading to bruising and bleeding
Promotes quick wound-healing	Wounds can take longer to heal, increasing risk of infection
Assists with the absorption of iron as it chemically changes ferric iron (non-haem) to ferrous iron (haem)	Anaemia may occur due to reduced absorption of iron needed to make haemoglobin
Maintains the immune system by helping white blood cells to fight illness and infection	Increased susceptibility to illness and infection, such as colds and flu
A powerful antioxidant that can counteract the damaging effects of free radicals	Risk of damage to cells by free radicals, increasing the risk of some cancers, coronary heart disease and strokes

Recommended Daily Allowance (RDA)/Reference Intake (RI)

Group	RDA/RI (mg)
Children	45 mg
Adolescents	50–60 mg
Adults	60 mg
Pregnant or lactating women	80 mg

Give an account of vitamin C under **each** of the following headings:

- main food sources
- biological functions
- effect of deficiency
- role in mineral absorption. (24) **OL**

State **two** functions of ascorbic acid (vitamin C) in the diet. (4) **HL**

VITAMINS

B-group vitamins

There are six main B group vitamins.

- B1 thiamine
- B2 riboflavin
- B3 niacin
- B6 pyridoxine
- B12 cobalamin
- Folate/folic acid

REMEMBER IT!

'**T**aking **R**equired **N**utrients **P**revents **C**onditions **F**orming.'
Thiamine, **R**iboflavin, **N**iacin, **P**yridoxine, **C**obalamin, **F**olate.

Vitamin B12 (cobalamin)

HL

Properties	
• Water soluble	• Destroyed by strong acids, alkalis and light
• Insoluble in fat	• Heat stable, but some loss during cooking

Food sources	Other sources
• Offal • Meat • Eggs • Cheese • Milk • Fish	As vitamin B12 is only found in animal food sources, vegans are strongly advised to take supplements or to consume fortified foods, e.g. soya milk

Functions	Effects of deficiency
Aids the metabolism of fatty acids to release energy	Tiredness and irritability due to a lack of energy
Aids the metabolism of folate/folic acid	Increased risk of neural tube defects in the foetus
Maintains the **myelin sheath**, which speeds up nerve impulses **Lit Hit** The myelin sheath is a protective layer that surrounds the nerve fibres of the nervous system.	Delayed nerve impulses, leading to cognative impairment, e.g. memory loss or slow mental response 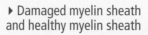 ▸ Damaged myelin sheath and healthy myelin sheath
Aids formation of red blood cells	Pernicious anaemia, due to low levels of red blood cells that are needed to transport oxygen

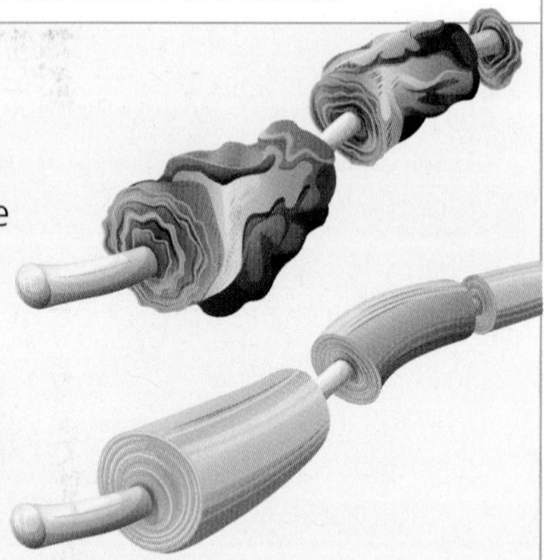

Recommended Daily Allowance (RDA)/Reference Intake (RI)

Group	RDA/RI (μg)
Children	0.7–1 μg
Adolescents and adults	1.4 μg
Pregnant women	1.6 μg
Lactating women	1.9 μg

? Vitamin B12 is sometimes lacking in the diet of vegetarians.

Give an account of **vitamin B12 (cobalamin)** and refer to:
- sources in the diet
- properties
- biological functions. (21) **HL**

Folate/folic acid

Forms

Folate: a natural form found in food	**Folic acid:** a synthetic form used to make supplements

 ## Properties

- Water-soluble
- Insoluble in fat
- Heat stable, but some loss during cooking
- Destroyed by alkalis, oxygen and light
- Unaffected by acids

Food sources | Other sources

Food sources	Other sources
<ul><li>Leafy green vegetables</li><li>Wheat germ</li><li>Wholemeal bread</li><li>Offal</li><li>Fortified breakfast cereals</li></ul>	In pregnancy, women are advised to take daily folic acid supplements (400 µg) for 12 weeks prior to conception and 12 weeks after 

Functions | Effects of deficiency

Functions	Effects of deficiency
Needed during pregnancy to form the brain of a foetus and to close the end of its spinal cord	Neural tube defects (NTD) in the foetus. For example: <ul><li>spina bifida occurs when the base of the spine fails to close, causing paralysis of the lower limbs</li><li>anencephaly occurs when the top of the spine fails to close, and the brain, skull and scalp do not develop. A baby with this condition is not likely to survive.</li></ul> ▲ Spina bifida
Works with vitamin B12 (cobalamin) to form red blood cells	Mild cases of deficiency will lead to feelings of tiredness or fatigue due to a lack of red blood cells. In severe cases anaemia may occur.
Maintains the immune system by helping the white blood cells to fight illness and infection	Increased susceptibility to illness and infection such as colds and flu

Recommended Daily Allowance (RDA)/Reference Intake (RI)

Group	RDA/RI (µg)
Children	100–200 µg
Adolescents and adults	300 µg
Pregnant women	500 µg
Lactating women	400 µg

 Give an account of folic acid/folate and refer to:
- sources in the diet
- properties
- biological functions
- recommended dietary allowance (RDA) *(now known as RI)*. (28) **HL**

Did you know ?

Taking folic acid before and during the early stages of pregnancy may reduce the risk of NTDs by up to 70%.

VITAMINS

Vitamin B1 (thiamine)

 HL

Properties	
• Water soluble	• Destroyed by high temperatures, alkalis and light
• Insoluble in fat	• 70% loss during milling

Food sources		Other sources
• Wholegrain cereals	• Meat	A small amount is synthesised by bacteria in the large intestine
• Fortified breakfast cereals	• Milk	
• Eggs	• Offal	

Functions	Effects of deficiency
Aids the metabolism of carbohydrates and fats to release energy	Tiredness and irritability due to a lack of energy
Aids the correct functioning and maintenance of nerves	Severe deficiency can result in beri beri, a serious nerve disease that causes muscular pain, paralysis and death  ▶ Beri beri
Aids the growth and development of children	Stunted or delayed growth in children, leaving them smaller in height than the average for their age

Did you know ?

Beri beri is a common disease in East Asia due to the high consumption of polished rice. Polishing removes the outer layer which contains much of the vitamin B1 (thiamine).

Vitamin B2 (riboflavin)

 HL

Properties		
• Water soluble	• Unstable at high temperatures	• Sensitive to light
• Insoluble in fat	• Destroyed by alkalis	

Sources					
• Fortified breakfast cereals	• Meat	• Offal	• Milk	• Eggs	• Yeast extract, e.g. Marmite

Functions	Effects of deficiency
Aids the metabolism of carbohydrates, proteins and fats to release energy	Tiredness and irritability due to a lack of energy
Maintains healthy mucous membranes of the body, e.g. eyes and mouth	A swollen, red tongue; sore, cracked lips; dry eyes
Aids growth and development of children	Stunted or delayed growth in children, leaving them smaller in height than the average for their age

Vitamin B3 (niacin)

Properties		
• Water soluble • Insoluble in fat	• Stable to acids and alkalis • 80–90% loss during milling	• Heat stable

Food sources		Other sources
• Fortified breakfast cereals • Meat and offal	• Bread • Nuts	• Produced in the intestine from the amino acid tryptophan

Functions	Effects of deficiency
Aids the metabolism of carbohydrates to release energy	Tiredness and irritability due to a lack of energy
Helps maintain healthy skin	Pellagra, a severe deficiency disease. Symptoms include **D**ermatitis, **D**iarrhoea, **D**epression, **D**ementia, and it can eventually lead to **D**eath.  Remember: pellagra = 5 Ds ▸ Pellagra 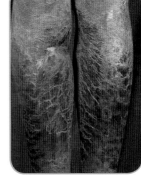
Supports healthy nerve activity	Delayed nerve impulses leading to cognitive impairment, e.g. memory loss or disorientation

Vitamin B6 (pyridoxine)

Properties	
• Water soluble • Insoluble in fat	• Heat stable, but some loss during cooking • Destroyed by oxygen, alkalis and light

Sources					
• Meat	• Fish	• Green vegetables	• Nuts	• Bananas	• Offal

Functions	Effects of deficiency
Aids the metabolism of carbohydrates, proteins and fats to release energy	Tiredness and irritability due to a lack of energy
Relieves symptoms of pre-menstrual tension (PMT) and nausea in early pregnancy.	• PMT symptoms, including mood swings, irritability, depression, anxiety and bloating • Nausea during pregnancy
Supports healthy nerve activity	Delayed nerve impulses leading to cognitive impairment, e.g. memory loss or disorientation
Prevents pyridoxine-dependent epilepsy in babies	Convulsions and seizures in young babies

Did you know

Women who have a high intake of vitamin B6 in their diets are 25% less likely to develop PMT symptoms than those with a low intake.

VITAMINS

MINERALS

What you will learn:

- **Classification of minerals**
- **Sources, Recommended Daily Allowances (RDAs)/Reference Intakes (RIs), functions and effects of deficiencies of minerals**

Minerals are one of the micronutrients. The body requires approximately 20 minerals to protect itself against disease.

Classification of minerals

Minerals are classified into two main types:

- **macro minerals:** required in relatively large amounts, e.g. calcium, phosphorus, potassium and sodium
- **trace minerals:** required in trace amounts, e.g. iron, zinc, iodine and fluorine.

Calcium

Calcium is the most plentiful mineral in the body. Approximately 99% of the body's calcium is in the bones and teeth, the remaining 1% is found in the muscles, nerves and blood.

Sources		Recommended Daily Allowance (RDA)/Reference Intake (RI)	
• Milk • Yoghurt • Sardines	• Cheese • Leafy green vegetables • Sesame seeds	**Group**	**RDA/RI (mg)**
		Children	800 mg
		Adolescents	1,200 mg
		Adults	800 mg
		Pregnant or lactating women	1,200 mg
Functions		**Effects of deficiency**	
Aids the formation of strong bones and teeth		Increased risk of bone diseases, such as rickets, osteomalacia and osteoporosis, and tooth decay ▲ Tooth decay	
Assists blood clotting which is necessary if an injury causes damage to blood vessels		Slow blood clotting of ruptured blood vessels. This can cause haemorrhaging	
Aids normal muscle contraction		Muscles fail to relax after contraction. This can cause muscular spasms, cramps and **convulsions**.	

👍 **Tip!**

If asked about the effects of calcium deficiency in the exam, you must explain the effects of each bone disease you mention. For more information on these see page 37.

Lit Hit

Convulsions are a condition where the muscles contract and relax repeatedly, causing an uncomfortable shaking of the body.

Absorption of calcium

Only 20–30% of calcium intake is absorbed by the body. A variety of factors assist and hinder absorption.

Factors assisting calcium absorption

- Vitamin D stimulates the production of calcium-binding protein, assisting absorption.
- The hormone parathormone, released from the parathyroid gland, controls the levels of calcium in the blood.
- The hormone oestrogen, produced in the ovaries, promotes calcium absorption.
- Phosphorus combines with calcium, creating calcium phosphate, which is easier to absorb.
- An acid environment promotes calcium absorption. Consuming foods high in vitamin C provides this.

Factors hindering calcium absorption

- Tannins present in tea and coffee bind to calcium, inhibiting absorption.
- Excess dietary fibre binds to calcium, inhibiting absorption.
- Excess fat binds with calcium, creating insoluble and non-absorbable calcium soaps.
- As the body burns excess protein for energy it produces sulfate. Sulfate increases the amount of calcium excreted in urine.

- Phytic acid in wholegrain bread and seeds binds to calcium, inhibiting absorption.

- Oxalic acid in rhubarb and spinach binds to calcium, inhibiting absorption.

Did you know

Approximately 37% of girls and 28% of boys aged between 5–12 in Ireland do not get their Recommended Daily Allowance of calcium daily.

MINERALS

List **two** good dietary sources of calcium. (2) **OL**

Set out the results of a study you have carried out on calcium. Refer to **each** of the following:
- sources in the diet
- functions in the body
- effects of deficiency
- factors that affect absorption. (36) **OL**

List **four** different sources of calcium in the diet. (4) **HL**

State **four** possible ill-effects of a diet deficient in calcium. (12) **HL**

Give an account of calcium and include reference to:
- sources
- biological functions
- factors assisting/inhibiting absorption. (18) **HL**

Iron

Over half of the body's iron is found in the blood, as part of the haemoglobin of the red blood cells. The remainder is found in the muscles, bone marrow, cell enzymes and organs, such as the liver and spleen.

Forms			
Haem iron: also known as ferrous iron. Easily absorbed by the body.		**Non-haem iron:** also known as ferric iron. Not easily absorbed by the body, it must be changed into ferrous iron to be easily absorbed.	

Sources		Recommended Daily Allowance (RDA)/Reference Intake (RI)	
Haem iron	**Non-haem iron**	**Group**	**RDA/RI (mg)**
<ul><li>Red meat</li><li>Offal</li><li>Poultry</li><li>Meat products</li></ul>	<ul><li>Cereals</li><li>Pulses</li><li>Eggs</li><li>Leafy green vegetables</li></ul>	**Children and adult males** **Adolescents and adult females** **Pregnant or lactating women**	10 mg 14 mg 15 mg

Functions	Effects of deficiency
Makes red blood cells and forms haemoglobin, a red protein pigment found in red blood cells responsible for carrying oxygen around the body	Anaemia may occur due to lack of haemoglobin and red blood cells, causing a reduction in the oxygen levels in the blood. Symptoms include tiredness, pale skin, shortness of breath, irritability and dizziness.
Normal amount of red blood cells	Anaemic amount of red blood cells
Forms part of myoglobin, which carries oxygen to the muscles for energy	Muscle fatigue due to lack of oxygen. This decreases athletic performance.
Works with enzymes to release energy from food	The body has less energy

Absorption of iron

Only 15% of iron intake is absorbed by the body. A variety of factors assist and hinder iron absorption.

Factors assisting iron absorption

- Consuming haem iron and non-haem iron together increases non-haem iron absorption.
- Consuming food high in vitamin C chemically changes non-haem iron to the more easily absorbed haem iron.
- Acidity from hydrochloric acid (HCL) in the stomach chemically changes non-haem iron to the more easily absorbed haem iron.

Factors hindering iron absorption

- Tannins present in tea and coffee bind to iron, inhibiting absorption.
- Excess dietary fibre binds to iron, inhibiting absorption.
- Phytic acid in wholegrain bread and seeds binds to iron, inhibiting absorption.
- Oxalic acid in rhubarb and spinach binds to iron, inhibiting absorption.

Did you know

Almost 74% of teenage girls and 19% of teenage boys in Ireland do not get enough iron in their diets.

Name **one** nutrient that is necessary for the absorption of iron. (4) **OL**

Give an account of iron under each of the following headings:
- dietary sources
- functions in the body
- effect of deficiency. (24) **OL**

List two biological functions of iron. (4) **HL**

Differentiate between the following and give one food source of each:
- haem iron
- non-haem iron. (6) **HL**

Identify and explain **three** factors which affect the absorption of iron in the body. (15) **HL**

Give an account of iron and refer to:
- sources in the diet
- biological functions
- recommended daily allowance (RDA) for adults. (21) **HL**

MINERALS

HL Zinc

Sources		Recommended Daily Allowance (RDA)/Reference Intake (RI)	
• Meat • Seafood • Pulses • Eggs • Milk • Seeds		Group	RDA/RI (mg)
		Children	4–7 mg
		Adolescents and adults	7–10 mg
Functions		**Effects of deficiency**	
Aids the metabolism of fats, carbohydrates and protein to release energy		Tiredness and irritability due to a lack of energy	
Helps the healing of wounds and repair of tissues		Impaired wound-healing, which can lead to infection	
Helps maintain healthy skin and hair		Hair loss and dry skin conditions, e.g. eczema	

Iodine

Sources		Recommended Daily Allowance (RDA)/Reference Intake (RI)	
• Seafood • Meat • Cod liver oil • Milk • Seaweed, e.g. nori		Group	RDA/RI (µg)
		Children	70–100 µg
		Adolescents and adults	120–130 µg
Functions		**Effects of deficiency**	
Aids the manufacture of the hormone thyroxine in the thyroid gland, which regulates metabolism		Reduced basal metabolic rate (BMR), increasing the risk of obesity due to lack of thyroxine	
Essential for normal growth and development during gestation and childhood		Stunted or delayed physical or mental growth in children	
Maintains the thyroid gland, preventing swelling and breathing difficulties		Goitre, an abnormal enlargement of the thyroid gland in the neck	

Did you know ❓

Nori is dried seaweed that is pressed into thin sheets. It is commonly used as a wrapper for sushi.

▲ Goitre

Sodium (salt)

Sources	Recommended Daily Allowance (RDA)/Reference Intake (RI)	
• Table salt • White bread • Cheese • Cured meats, e.g. bacon • Snack foods, e.g. crisps	**Group**	**RDA/RI (g)**
	Children	1.6 g (4 g salt)
	Adolescents and adults	2.4 g (6 g salt)
Functions	**Effects of deficiency**	
Regulates blood pressure	Low blood pressure (hypotension), reducing oxygen getting to organs as blood flow is slowed down	
Supports healthy nerve activity	Delayed nerve impulses leading to cognitive impairment, e.g. memory loss or disorientation	
Aids normal muscle contraction	Muscles fail to relax after contraction. This can cause muscular spasms, muscle cramps and convulsions.	

> **?** Give **one** main function of sodium in the diet. List **two** good dietary sources of sodium. (6) **HL**

Overconsumption of salt

In Ireland, many people eat more than twice the amount of salt their bodies need. Research shows that overconsumption of salt can increase blood pressure levels and increase the risk of heart attacks or strokes. Salt consumption can be reduced by:

- avoiding high-salt snack foods
- buying reduced salt products
- not adding salt when cooking
- reading nutritional labels carefully when shopping as food may contain hidden sodium, e.g. monosodium glutamate, a sodium salt.

Only 5% of the salt we eat comes from foods naturally containing it, compared to 80% from processed food, takeaway meals and restaurant food.

Potassium

Sources	Recommended Daily Allowance (RDA)/Reference Intake (RI)	
• Meat • Milk • Bananas • Fish • Leafy green vegetables	**Group**	**RDA/RI (g)**
	Children	0.8–2 g
	Adolescents and adults	3.1 g
Functions	**Effects of deficiency**	
Aids the metabolism of carbohydrates and protein to release energy	Tiredness and irritability due to lack of energy	
Supports healthy nerve activity	Delayed nerve impulses leading to cognitive impairment, e.g. memory loss or disorientation	
Aids normal muscle contraction	Muscles fail to relax after contraction. This can cause muscular spasms, muscle cramps and convulsions.	

> Give **one** main function of potassium. List **two** good sources of potassium in the diet. (6) **HL**

MINERALS

WATER

What you will learn:

- **Elemental composition, properties, functions, sources and recommended daily intake of water.**

Water is an essential part of the body. It is the main **component** of cell liquid, blood, lymph and digestive juices.

Elemental composition

Water is made up of the elements hydrogen (H) and oxygen (O) in a 2:1 **ratio** (H_2O).

◀ Water molecule

Lit Hit
A component is a part that combines with other parts to form something bigger.

Lit Hit
A ratio shows the relative size of two or more values.

Properties

- Colourless
- Odourless
- Tasteless
- Boils at 100°C
- Freezes at 0°C
- Neutral pH7
- Excellent solvent
- Can be solid, liquid or gas

Functions

Water:

- quenches thirst
- removes waste products from the body through the kidneys as urine
- makes up 92% of blood plasma, which helps to transport nutrients, oxygen, carbon dioxide, hormones and enzymes around the body
- provides the minerals calcium and fluoride
- regulates body temperature at 37°C
- is involved in the hydrolysis of nutrients during digestion
- prevents constipation, as it makes stools soft and easy to pass.

? List **three** biological functions of water. (6) **OL**

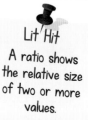

▲ Blood plasma

Sources

- Tap or bottled water
- Beverages, e.g. milk, tea, coffee and juices
- Fruit and vegetables
- Soups

Did you know ?
A person can survive for only three to seven days without water.

Recommended daily intake

Consume two to three litres (eight glasses) per day. Fluid requirements increase in certain circumstances including intense physical activity, lactation, diarrhoea and illness, e.g. a fever.

Chapter 2: Diet and health

1.2.1 ENERGY

What you will learn:

- **Measuring energy**
- **The role of energy in the body**
- **Basal metabolic rate (BMR)**
- **Factors that determine energy requirements/BMR**
- **Average daily energy requirements**
- **Energy balance**

Energy is the body's ability to do work. Everything the body does requires energy. Our body gets the energy it needs from food through a process called metabolism. The amount of energy obtained from a food depends on the nutrients it contains. Proteins, fats and carbohydrates are all good sources of energy.

Measuring energy

The amount of energy a food provides for the body is measured in kilocalories (kcal) or kilojoules (kJ).

Energy content of food	
1 g of protein	4 kcal/17 kJ
1 g of carbohydrate	4 kcal/17 kJ
1 g of fat	9 kcal/37 kJ

GO FIGURE

1 kcal = 4.2 kJ

Ideally, 50% of our energy intake should come from carbohydrates, 35% from fats and 15% from proteins.

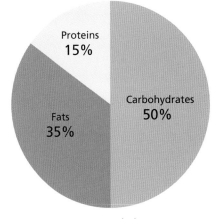

▲ Recommended energy intake sources

The role of energy in the body

Energy is needed in the body for:

- **physical activities**, such as swimming, running and standing
- **growth**, especially among toddlers, children and adolescents, as they are undergoing rapid growth spurts. Pregnant women also require extra energy to support the demands of their developing foetus
- **heat generation** to maintain the body at a constant temperature of 37°C
- **functioning of internal organs**, e.g. the heart
- **cellular activity**, e.g. for nerve cells to transmit nerve impulses to and from the brain.

 List **three** main functions of energy in the body. (6) **HL**

REMEMBER IT!

'**P**eople **G**enerate **H**eat **F**rom **C**alories.'
Physical activities, **G**rowth, **H**eat generation, **F**unctioning of internal organs, **C**ellular activity.

Basal metabolic rate (BMR)

Metabolism is the process through which the body converts the food we eat into energy. This energy is used to maintain bodily functions including breathing, blood circulation, controlling body temperature, cell growth and nerve impulses.

Basal metabolic rate (BMR) is the minimum amount of energy (kilocalories) required to maintain body functions when at rest. BMR differs from person to person. On average, an hourly BMR rate is 70 kcal for adult males and 60 kcal for adult females. BMR accounts for 60–65% of the kilocalories burned every day. It is measured when a person:

- is warm
- is at complete physical and mental rest
- has been fasting for at least 12 hours.

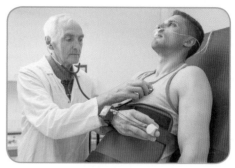
▲ BMR testing

Did you know

The thyroid gland in the neck produces a hormone called thyroxine, which controls metabolism. If a person's supply of thyroxine is inadequate it can cause their BMR to drop, leading to weight gain and, in some cases, obesity.

 What is Basal Metabolic Rate (BMR)? (3) **HL**

Factors that determine energy requirements/BMR

- **Age:** energy requirements gradually rise through childhood and adolescence due to growth spurts and increases in body size. Activity levels are high at this life stage, so additional energy is needed. With increasing age people's energy requirements gradually decline, as individuals stop growing and generally become less active.

- **Occupation:** the more physically active a person's occupation the more energy is required, e.g. an active builder requires more energy than a sedentary office worker.

- **Climate:** a cold climate causes the body to require more energy to keep body temperature constant at 37°C. Less energy is required in warmer climates.

- **Activity level:** the more active a person, the more energy is required, e.g. a person who runs for leisure requires more energy than a person who paints.

▲ Kilocalories burned in 10 minutes

- **Health status:** during times of illness, **convalescents** require less energy due to lack of physical exercise.

- **Pregnancy/lactation:** women require more energy during pregnancy to allow the developing foetus to grow. Extra energy is also required during lactation for milk production.

- **Gender:** generally, males require more energy than females due to different body compositions. Men have a higher proportion of muscle and less body fat than women. This extra muscle requires more energy to maintain.

- **Size:** generally, the larger the body the higher the energy requirement, as more energy is needed to maintain it, e.g. to control body temperature and to mobilise it.

Lit Hit
A convalescent is a person recovering from illness, injury or surgery.

REMEMBER IT!

'**A**void **O**vereating **C**alories **A**s **H**ealth **P**roblems **G**enerally **S**tart.'
Age, **O**ccupation, **C**limate, **A**ctivity level, **H**ealth status, **P**regnancy/lactation, **G**ender, **S**ize.

? Outline **four** factors that determine a person's energy requirements. (12) **OL**

List **three** factors that affect energy requirements. (3) **HL**

Average daily energy requirements

Group	Females	Males
Children and young teenagers (5–13 years)	1,400–2,000 kcal	1,400–2,200 kcal
Adolescents (14–18 years)	1,800 kcal (sedentary) 2,000 kcal (active)	2,200 kcal (sedentary) 2,600 kcal (active)
Adults (19–50 years)	1,800 kcal (sedentary) 2,100 kcal (active)	2,000 kcal (sedentary) 2,600 kcal (active)
Older people (50+ years)	1,600 kcal (sedentary) 1,800 kcal (active)	2,000 kcal (sedentary) 2,300 kcal (active)
Pregnant women	2,400 kcal	
Lactating women	2,800 kcal	

Energy balance

All energy intake should balance energy output to maintain weight. This is known as energy balance.

A balanced diet and sufficient exercise is necessary to maintain energy balance. If energy intake exceeds energy output people gain weight, as excess energy is converted to fat and stored as adipose tissue. If energy output exceeds energy intake people lose weight.

Many people in Ireland experience energy imbalance, as their energy intake is higher than their energy output. This is due to a lack of exercise and overconsumption of empty kilocalorie foods that provide energy but have no other nutritional value, e.g. fizzy drinks and biscuits. This has led to an increase in diet-related diseases, e.g. obesity, type 2 diabetes and coronary heart disease.

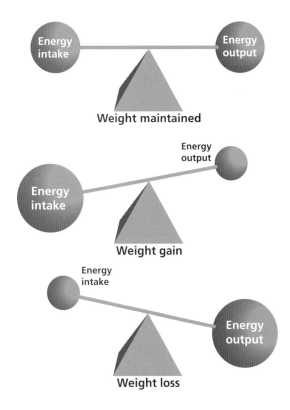

? Explain the term **energy balance**. (2) **OL**

Discuss the importance of balancing energy intake and energy output. (12) **HL**

CURRENT DIETARY GUIDELINES

What you will learn:

- **Formulation of nutritional guidelines**
- **Healthy eating guidelines**
- **Food pyramid**
- **Reference Intake (RI)**
- **Food composition tables**

A balanced diet includes all nutrients in correct proportion to the needs of the body. To achieve this, individuals and families should follow nutritional guidelines, including the healthy eating guidelines and the food pyramid.

Formulation of nutritional guidelines

In order to formulate nutritional guidelines, the dietary practices of the nation are surveyed. The findings are then analysed by nutritional experts to highlight areas of dietary practice that need specific attention, e.g. a lack of fibre or overconsumption of salt. This is then used to compile healthy eating guidelines and to create a food pyramid.

In Ireland nutritional guidelines are established by:

- dietitians and nutritionists
- the Health Service Executive (HSE)
- the Department of Health
- the Food Safety Authority of Ireland (FSAI)
- the Irish Nutrition Dietetic Institute.

Healthy eating guidelines

- Consume foods from the four main food groups on the food pyramid.
- Limit amounts of food and drinks from the top shelf of the food pyramid, e.g. biscuits and cakes, as these are high in calories, fat, sugar and salt.
- Always read nutrition labels to check for high levels of fat, sugar and salt.
- Avoid ready meals and takeaways, as these tend to be high in fat and salt.
- Use fresh ingredients when preparing meals.
- Limit salt intake. Add little or no salt during cooking or at the table.
- Eat cereals, potatoes, wholegrain rice and wholemeal breads and pasta to provide the best calories to fuel the body.
- Eat smaller serving sizes and add plenty of vegetables, salad and fruit.
- Eat five or more portions of a variety of fruit and vegetables daily.
- Use low-fat milks, low-fat or no-added-sugar yoghurts and and reduced-fat cheeses.
- Eat lean meat, poultry and fish (oily is best). Sometimes choose peas, beans and lentils as meat alternatives.
- Opt for polyunsaturated and monounsaturated spreads and oils, and use sparingly.
- Grill, bake, steam or boil food, instead of frying.
- Drink two to three litres (eight glasses) of water daily.
- Adults who choose to drink alcohol should do so sensibly and within the recommended limits.

Food pyramid

The food pyramid illustrates the number and correct portion size of servings of different foods that should be eaten to ensure a diet is balanced.

It is important to adhere to healthy eating guidelines and the food pyramid. Good nutrition, coupled with an active lifestyle, plays a crucial role in the prevention of chronic diet-related health conditions, e.g. obesity, coronary heart disease and type 2 diabetes.

FOOD AND DRINKS HIGH IN SUGAR, FAT AND SALT
(LIMIT TO SOMETIMES, NOT EVERY DAY)
• 1 fun-sized chocolate bar • 1 bag of low-fat crisps • 1 chocolate biscuit

REDUCED-FAT SPREADS AND OILS
(USE AS LITTLE AS POSSIBLE)
• 1 teaspoon of reduced or low-fat spread • 1 teaspoon of oil

MEAT, POULTRY, FISH, EGGS, BEANS AND NUTS (2 SERVINGS)
• 50–75 g of cooked lean meat • 2 eggs (limit to 7 per week)
• 40 g of unsalted nuts, seeds or peanut butter
• 6 dessert spoons of peas, beans or lentils
• 100 g of cooked fish, soya or tofu

MILK, YOGHURT AND CHEESE (3 SERVINGS)
• 1 200 ml glass of low-fat milk • 25 g of low-fat Cheddar or semi-soft cheese
• 50 g of low-fat soft cheese • 125 ml of yoghurt • 200 ml of yoghurt drink

FRUIT AND VEGETABLES (5+ SERVINGS)
• 1 medium-sized fruit, e.g. apples and bananas • 2 small-sized fruits, e.g. plums and kiwis
• 4 dessert spoons of cooked vegetables • 1 100 ml glass of unsweetened fruit juice
• 10–12 berries, grapes or cherries • 1 bowl of salad, e.g lettuce, tomatoes and cucumber

BREAD, CEREALS, POTATOES, PASTA AND RICE (6+ SERVINGS)
• 1 slice of brown or wholegrain bread • 1 medium or 2 small potatoes
• 3 dessert spoons of cooked pasta, rice or noodles • 2 breakfast cereal wheat or oat biscuits • 2–3 crackers or crisp breads

Recommended Daily Allowance (RDA)/Reference Intake (RI)

Recommended Daily Allowance (RDA)/Reference Intake (RI) is the average daily intake level of a nutrient that is sufficient to meet the nutrient requirements of nearly all people (97.5%) in a specific age and gender group. When an individual consumes the recommended RDA/RI of a nutrient a deficiency is extremely unlikely to develop. RDAs/RIs can be used to:

- provide nutritional information on packaging
- evaluate and plan diets for individuals with special dietary needs.

Reference Intake (RI) on nutritional labelling

The RI of nutrients for an average adult can be found on nutritional labelling of foods, so individuals can see the recommended amount of nutrients they should be consuming daily.

The percentage Reference Intake (% RI) may also be displayed. This helps consumers to see what percentage of their Reference Intake of a nutrient a food provides per 100 g or per portion. Nowadays this is also often documented on the front of pre-packaged food. This helps individuals to achieve adequate nutrient intake.

Tells consumers how much energy and nutrients a food provides per 100 g/ml and/or per portion

Tells consumers what % of their Reference Intake of a specific nutrient a food provides per 100 g/ml and/or per portion

Tells consumers what % of their Reference Intake of a specific nutrient a food provides per 100 g/ml and/or per portion

Tells consumers the Reference Intake of nutrients for an average adult

Each muffin contains

Energy 1851kJ 441kcal	22%
Fat 16.5g	24%
Saturates 2.0g	10%
Sugars 53.3g	59%
Salt 0.8g	13%

of the reference intake*

NUTRITION INFORMATION TYPICAL VALUES	100g drained contains	Half of a drained can (120g) contains	%RI*	RI* for an average adult
Energy	536 kJ 128 kcal	643 kJ 153 kcal	8%	8400 kJ 2000 kcal
Fat	2.9g	3.5g	5%	70g
of which: saturates	0.3g	0.4g	2%	20g
Carbohydrate	16.1g	19.3g	-	-
of which: sugars	0.4g	0.5g	1%	50g
Fibre	4.1g	4.9g	-	-
Protein	7.2g	8.6g	-	-
Salt	0.1g	0.1g	2%	6g

*Reference intake of an average adult (8400 kJ/2000 kcal). Portions should be adjusted for children of different ages.

▲ Front of package nutritional label

▲ Back of package nutritional label

Food composition tables

Food composition tables provide information concerning the nutrient and energy content of 100 g of a solid food or 100 ml of a liquid food.

Food composition tables are used:

- by consumers to compare the nutritional value of a wide variety of foods from many different sources
- by dietitians and nutritionists to compile specific diets for a client's individual needs.

Food composition table

Tr = Trace amounts

	Portion weight (g)	Energy (kcal)	Energy (kJ)	Protein (g)	Fat (g)	Carbohydrate (g)	Calcium (mg)	Iron (mg)	Sodium (mg)	Vitamin C (mg)	Vitamin D (µg)	Water
CEREALS												
Bread (white)	100	219	931	7.9	1.6	46.1	177	1.6	400	0	0	38.6
Bread rolls (brown)	100	236	1004	9.9	3.2	44.8	201	2.4	380	0	0	36.4
Rice (white long grain, boiled)	100	131	560	2.8	0.4	31.1	9	Tr	11	0	0	68.2
Pasta (wholewheat spaghetti, boiled)	100	134	569	5.2	1.1	27.5	31	1.5	5	0	0	63.7
MILK												
Whole milk	100	63	265	3.4	3.6	4.8	120	0.02	42	2	Tr	87.6
Skimmed milk	100	34	144	3.5	0.3	4.6	125	0.03	44	1	Tr	90.8
CREAM												
Single (fresh)	100	193	798	3.3	18.0	2.2	89	Tr	29	1	0.3	78.1
Double (fresh)	100	496	2041	1.6	48.0	1.7	49	0.06	22	1	0.3	52.6
YOGHURT												
Whole-milk fruit yoghurt	100	72	306	3.3	2.0	17.7	122	0.12	58	1	0.1	76.0
Low-fat natural yoghurt	100	57	243	4.8	1.0	7.8	162	0.08	63	1	0.1	87.2
Greek-style fruit yoghurt	100	137	572	4.8	8.4	11.2	141	0.16	64	Tr	0.1	73.5
CHEESE												
Cottage	100	103	431	9.4	6.0	3.1	127	Tr	250	Tr	0	80.5
Brie	100	343	1422	20.3	29.1	Tr	256	Tr	556	Tr	0.2	48.7
Cheddar	100	416	1725	25.4	34.9	0.1	739	0.30	723	Tr	0.3	36.6
Parmesan	100	415	1729	36.2	29.7	0.9	1025	0.80	660	Tr	0.3	27.6
EGGS												
Whole egg (boiled)	100	143	595	14.1	9.6	Tr	55	2.0	150	0	3.2	75.4
FATS AND OILS												
Butter (salted)	100	744	3059	0.6	82.2	0.6	18	Tr	730	Tr	0.9	14.9
Low-fat dairy spread	100	354	1457	0.2	39.0	0.7	12	Tr	692	0	3.0	57.5
Margarine	100	688	2827	Tr	76.4	0	1	0	600	0	8.8	22.2
Rapeseed oil	100	899	3696	Tr	99.9	0	Tr	Tr	Tr	Tr	Tr	Tr
MEAT												
Beef rump steak (grilled)	100	177	745	31.0	5.9	0	7	3.6	74	0	0.4	62.9
Lamb loin chops (grilled)	100	213	892	29.2	10.7	0	22	2.1	80	0	0.6	59.6
Chicken breast (grilled, no skin)	100	160	675	28.4	5.2	0	6	0.4	55	0	0.3	67.7
Pheasant (roasted)	100	220	918	27.9	12.0	0	28	2.2	66	0	0.3	59.4
Lamb kidney (fried)	100	188	784	23.7	10.3	0	14	11.2	230	5	0.6	62.8
Bacon rashers (grilled)	100	287	1194	23.2	21.6	0	7	0.6	1390	Tr	0.6	50.4
Pork sausages (grilled)	100	294	1221	14.5	22.1	9.8	110	1.1	640	5	1.1	45.9
FISH												
Cod (baked)	100	100	425	23.9	0.5	0	18	0.2	91	Tr	Tr	76.9
Herring (grilled)	100	181	756	20.1	11.2	0	79	1.6	160	Tr	16.1	63.9
Mussels (boiled)	100	104	438	17.7	2.2	3.5	40	3.3	401	Tr	Tr	75.5
Tuna (canned in brine)	100	109	460	24.9	1.0	0	10	1.5	293	Tr	1.1	74.3
Fish fingers (cod, baked)	100	223	936	14.3	9.2	22.0	32	0.6	317	Tr	Tr	54.5
PROTEIN ALTERNATIVES												
Tofu (steamed)	100	73	304	8.1	4.2	0.7	162	1.2	4	0	0	85.0
Quorn pieces (raw)	100	73	307	14.0	1.4	1.1	42.5	0.6	300	0	0	75.2
FRUIT												
Apples	100	51	215	0.6	0.5	11.6	5	0.09	1	6	0	86.2
Bananas	100	81	348	1.2	0.1	20.3	6	0.3	Tr	9	0	75.0
Plums	100	36	155	0.6	0.1	8.8	13	0.4	2	4	0	83.9
Strawberries	100	30	126	0.6	0.5	6.1	17	0.25	1	57	0	91.6
Oranges	100	36	152	0.8	0.2	8.2	24	0.1	1	52	0	87.0
VEGETABLES												
Carrots (raw)	100	34	146	0.5	0.4	7.7	26	0.2	27	2	0	89.0
Spinach (raw)	100	25	103	2.8	0.8	1.6	170	2.1	140	26	0	89.7
Tomatoes (raw)	100	14	61	0.5	0.1	3.0	8	0.2	2	22	0	94.6
Broccoli (boiled)	100	28	120	3.3	0.5	2.8	35	0.6	6	44	0	90.8
Potatoes (boiled)	100	74	315	1.8	0.1	17.5	6	0.3	1	9	0	78.9
Mushrooms (stewed)	100	9	37	1.4	0.3	0.1	3	0.3	3	Tr	0	93.1
Leek (boiled)	100	21	87	1.2	0.7	2.6	20	0.7	6	7	0	92.2
Peas (frozen, boiled)	100	70	299	5.5	0.7	11.2	37	1.8	4	12	0	76.6

DIETARY AND FOOD REQUIREMENTS THROUGH THE LIFECYCLE

What you will learn:

- **Dietary and food requirements for babies, children and young teenagers (up to 13 years), adolescents (14–18 years), adults (19–50 years), pregnant and breastfeeding women and older people (50+ years)**

Dietary and food requirements vary depending on a person's life stage, body size, age, gender and activity level.

Babies

For the first six months of life, babies grow rapidly. During this time they are fed either breast milk or formula milk, as both contain the correct amounts of nutrients a baby needs to thrive.

Breastfeeding

Health experts believe breast milk is the better choice for infants as it:

- provides natural antibodies from the mother that help boost the baby's immune system
- is always the correct temperature
- is sterile
- has no financial cost and requires no preparation
- contains less fat than formula milk, so babies are more likely to gain the correct amount of weight
- helps the mother and baby to bond.

Despite these benefits, Ireland has one of the lowest rates of breastfeeding in Europe, at 56%, in comparison with the European average of 90%.

▲ Breastfeeding

Did you know

Breastfeeding uses 300–500 kcal per day. Much of this extra energy is taken from fat stores that women lay down during pregnancy. This helps breastfeeding women to lose post-baby weight.

Weaning

After six months a baby's natural reserves of iron are used up, therefore solid food must be introduced to supplement their diet. This is known as weaning. Babies should receive a nutritionally-balanced diet that includes carbohydrates for extra energy, proteins for growth and fresh fruit and vegetables for vitamins and minerals.

Weaning guidelines

- Make homemade meals as they are cheaper than commercial alternatives.
- Purée or mash solid foods, e.g. apples and potatoes, to prevent choking.
- Introduce one food at a time so that food allergies or intolerances can be noted.
- Introduce a variety of solid foods, as this can prevent babies becoming fussy eaters.

- Do not add sugar or salt to a baby's food, as tastes acquired in infancy continue into adulthood.
- Eventually include all five main food groups in a baby's diet in order to provide balanced meals. As a baby grows, more energy and protein will be necessary.

Children and young teenagers (up to 13 years)

Nutritional requirements

Proteins	Proteins are important for rapid growth and to assist with cell and tissue repair and replacement. High biological value (HBV) protein foods, such as meat, fish, eggs, cheese and milk, should be included.
Fats	Fats are required to supply a concentrated source of energy. Essential fatty acids, e.g. omega-3, assist with healthy brain development. Intake should come from saturated sources such as milk and cheese, and unsaturated sources such as seeds, nuts and fish oils. Intake of saturated fat from processed foods should be avoided to reduce the risk of obesity.
Carbohydrates	Carbohydrates are required to provide an essential source of energy. Requirements are determined by gender and activity levels. Intake should come from starchy foods that are high in fibre, e.g. brown rice, as they help prevent bowel disorders and gradually release glucose into the bloodstream, giving the body a steady supply of energy. Sugary foods should be avoided as they release glucose rapidly into the bloodstream, causing a rapid burst of energy followed by a slump. They also increase risk of dental decay, diabetes and obesity.
Vitamins and minerals	• Vitamin C from fruit and vegetables is required to maintain general good health and boost the immune system. It also assists with the absorption of iron. • Iron from meat and green leafy vegetables is required to maintain healthy blood and reduce the risk of anaemia. This is especially important for young teenage girls experiencing menstruation. • Calcium, phosphorus and vitamin D from dairy products and green leafy vegetables are required to maintain healthy bones and teeth. Sufficient intake ensures a high peak bone mass is achieved, reducing the risk of osteoporosis in later life.
Water	On average, 1.3–2 litres of water are required daily to maintain healthy skin and prevent dehydration and bowel disorders, e.g. constipation

Meal planning guidelines

- Eat regular meals that are well balanced.
- Ensure meals have easy-to-manage portion sizes and are attractively presented.
- Enrich food by combining it with other food types to ensure all nutrients are obtained, e.g. add milk and cheese to mashed potato.
- Discourage fussy eating habits by:
  o encouraging children to participate in food preparation
  o introducing new foods with old favourites
  o establishing family meal times, whereby parents eat with their children and set a good example.

DIETARY AND FOOD REQUIREMENTS THROUGH THE LIFECYCLE

Adolescents (14–18 years)

Nutritional requirements

Proteins	Proteins are important for growth, the production of hormones, enzymes and antibodies, and to assist with cell and tissue repair and replacement. HBV protein foods, such as meat, fish, eggs, cheese and milk, should be included.
Fats	Requirements are the same as those for children and young teenagers
Carbohydrates	Requirements are the same as those for children and young teenagers
Vitamins and minerals	Requirements are the same as those for children and young teenagers
Water	On average, two litres of water are required daily to maintain healthy skin and prevent dehydration and bowel disorders, e.g. constipation

Meal planning guidelines

- Eat regular meals that are well balanced.
- Provide nutritious snacks, e.g. fruit and nuts, instead of snacks that are high in fat, sugar and salt. Bringing healthy snacks to school reduces the risk of unhealthy snacking at break times.
- Substitute foods, e.g. cheese, with low-fat options where possible to avoid overconsumption of saturated fat.
- Ensure sufficient quantities of foods rich in calcium and iron are consumed to avoid osteoporosis and anaemia.

? List **four** dietary guidelines that should be considered when planning meals for teenagers. (4) **OL**

Eating disorders

Eating disorders are psychological illnesses defined by abnormal eating habits that may involve either insufficient or excessive food intake. The most prevalent eating disorders are anorexia nervosa and bulimia nervosa.

Eating disorder	Anorexia nervosa	Bulimia nervosa
Description	An eating disorder characterised by the refusal to eat enough to maintain a normal body weight. As a result, both the body and mind are starved of the nutrients needed for healthy, balanced function.	An eating disorder characterised by episodes of secretive excessive eating (binge eating) followed by inappropriate methods of weight control, such as self-induced vomiting (purging) or abuse of laxatives
Symptoms	• Growth of fine, downy hair on the face and body, resulting from the body's efforts to keep warm • Periods may stop (amenorrhoea) • General digestive problems, e.g. cramps, wind and constipation • Dry, thinning hair and discoloured skin	• Inflammation of the oesophagus • Erosion of tooth enamel due to stomach acid • Calluses or scrapes on knuckles if fingers are used to induce vomiting • Irregular periods

Did you know?
About ten times more females than males have eating disorders.

Adults (19–50 years)

Nutritional requirements

Proteins	Proteins are important for the production of hormones, enzymes and antibodies, and to assist with cell and tissue repair and replacement. HBV protein foods, such as meat, fish, eggs, cheese and milk, should be included.
Fats	A small amount of fats are required to supply energy. Intake should come from unsaturated sources, such as seeds, nuts and fish oils. If consuming saturated fat choose low-fat options where possible, e.g. low-fat milk. Intake of saturated fat from processed foods should be avoided to reduce the risk of obesity, high cholesterol and coronary heart disease.
Carbohydrates	Requirements are the same as those for children and young teenagers
Vitamins and minerals	• Vitamin C from fruit and vegetables is required to maintain general good health and boost the immune system. It also assists with the absorption of iron. • Iron from meat and green leafy vegetables is required to maintain healthy blood and reduce the risk of anaemia. This is especially important for pre-menopausal women experiencing menstruation. • Calcium, phosphorus and vitamin D from dairy products and green leafy vegetables are required to maintain healthy bones and teeth. • B-group vitamins are required to help release energy from food.
Water	On average, two litres of water are required daily to maintain healthy skin and prevent dehydration and bowel disorders, e.g. constipation

? Outline **three** healthy eating guidelines for a 30-year-old sedentary worker. (6) **OL**

Meal planning guidelines

- Eat regular meals that are well balanced.
- Keep salt consumption to a minimum by using herbs and spices to add flavour and choosing fresh instead of processed meat. This can reduce the risk of high blood pressure and coronary heart disease.
- Prepare meals that can be frozen to reduce reliance on convenience food.
- Examine nutritional labels on food packaging carefully to make healthy food choices.

Lifestyle guidelines

- Limit alcohol intake. Excessive consumption can cause cancer, epilepsy and cirrhosis of the liver.
- Avoid smoking in order to reduce the risk of lung cancer and coronary heart disease.

▲ Healthy liver and liver with cirrhosis

Pregnant and breastfeeding women

Nutritional requirements

Proteins	Extra proteins are need to help with the formation of maternal and foetal tissue and cells. HBV protein foods, such as meat, fish, eggs, cheese and milk, should be included.
Fats	Requirements are the same as those for all adults. Fatty acids, e.g. omega-3, are especially important for development of the nervous system of the foetus.
Carbohydrates	Requirements are the same as those for children and young teenagers
Vitamins and minerals	• Vitamin C from fruit and vegetables is required to maintain general good health and boost the immune system. It also assists with the absorption of iron. • Iron from meat and green leafy vegetables is required to maintain healthy blood and reduce the risk of anaemia • Calcium, phosphorus and vitamin D from dairy products and green leafy vegetables are required to build the developing baby's bones, teeth, nerves and muscles • Folic acid from offal and green leafy vegetables is required to reduce the risk of neural tube defects. Supplements are also recommended.
Water	Requirements are the same as those for adults. Extra fluids are required by breastfeeding women for milk production.

 Outline **two** healthy eating guidelines for a pregnant woman. (4) **OL**

Meal planning guidelines

• Unpasteurised cheese and pâté should be avoided, as they are possible sources of listeria that can cause listeriosis, an infection that can result in miscarriage, stillbirth or severe illness in a newborn baby.

• Keep salt consumption to a minimum to reduce the risk of high blood pressure and coronary heart disease. Excessive consumption can also lead to oedema, a build-up of fluid causing swelling.

Lifestyle guidelines

• Avoid alcohol consumption, as binge drinking can result in miscarriage, stillbirth, premature birth and foetal alcohol spectrum disorders (FASD).

• Avoid smoking as it can increase risk of miscarriage, stillbirth and premature birth.

Older people (50 years+)

Nutritional requirements

Proteins	Proteins are needed for the production of hormones, enzymes and antibodies and to assist with cell and tissue repair. Proteins also help slow down sarcopenia (loss of muscle mass). Include easily digestible HBV foods, such as poultry, fish, eggs and milk, to provide these.
Fats	Requirements are the same as those for adults
Carbohydrates	Requirements are the same as those for children and young teenagers
Vitamins and minerals	• Vitamin C from fruit and vegetables is required to maintain general good health and boost the immune system. It also assists with the absorption of iron and heals wounds, e.g. bedsores. • Iron from meat and green leafy vegetables is required to maintain healthy blood and reduce the risk of anaemia • Calcium, phosphorus and vitamin D from dairy products and green leafy vegetables are required to maintain healthy bones and teeth • Vitamin A from fish oils and eggs is required for healthy eyes and skin
Water	Requirements are the same as those for adults

Meal planning guidelines

- Eat regular meals that are well balanced. Ideally these should be made using low-fat cooking methods, e.g. steaming and baking, due to decreased energy requirements.
- Finance may be an issue for some older people due to a drop in income on retirement. Expenditure can be reduced when grocery shopping by:
  o choosing cheaper cuts of meat, e.g. stewing beef
  o purchasing own-brand instead of name-brand products.
- Prepare meals with easily-digestible foods, e.g. fish or eggs, as chewing may be difficult if older people are missing teeth or using dentures.
- Ensure meals are easy to prepare, as cooking capabilities may be reduced due to physical illness, e.g. arthritis.
- Avoid spicy foods, as indigestion becomes more common as people age. Symptoms include bloating and heartburn.

Lifestyle guidelines

- Guidelines are the same as those for adults.

Convalescents

Nutritional requirements

Proteins	Proteins are needed to assist with cell and tissue repair to aid the healing of wounds. Include easily digestible HBV foods, such as poultry, fish, eggs and milk.
Fats	Requirements are the same as those for adults
Carbohydrates	Carbohydrate consumption should be reduced, as convalescents are less active due to being in recovery. Intake should come from starchy foods that are high in fibre, e.g. brown rice, as they gradually release glucose into the bloodstream, giving the body a steady supply of energy, and help to prevent bowel disorders which are more likely due to inactivity. Sugary foods should be avoided, as they release glucose rapidly into the bloodstream, causing a rapid burst of energy followed by a slump. They also increase risk of dental decay, diabetes and obesity.
Vitamins and minerals	Requirements are the same as those for older people
Water	On average two litres of water are required daily. More may be needed, especially if a person is suffering from a fever, to prevent dehydration and bowel disorders.

Meal planning guidelines

- Ensure meals have easy-to-manage portion sizes and are attractively presented, especially if the person has an upset stomach.
- Eat regular meals that are well balanced. Ideally these should be made using low-fat cooking methods, e.g. steaming and baking, due to decreased energy requirements.
- Keep salt consumption to a minimum to reduce the risk of high blood pressure and coronary heart disease. However, if the person is suffering from prolonged vomiting and diarrhoea, a saline solution or electrolyte drink may be needed to replace lost salts.
- Ensure strict hygiene rules are followed during food preparation to prevent food poisoning, as convalescents' immune systems are often more susceptible to infection.

What you will learn:

- **Dietary deficiencies**
- **Dietary excesses**
- **Modified diets**

There is a strong link between the food we eat and our overall well-being. It is essential to understand this relationship to ensure long-term health. Despite the wide availability of nutritional information, malnutrition, a condition that develops when a person's diet does not contain the correct amount of nutrients needed, is prevalent in Ireland. This can occur due to not having enough to eat, or by not eating enough of the right foods. In Ireland, not eating enough of the right foods is the main contributor to diet-related health problems.

Diet-related health problems can be classified into two groups: dietary deficiencies and dietary excesses.

- **Dietary deficiencies**, e.g. bowel disorders, osteoporosis, scurvy and anaemia, occur when the diet is lacking essential nutrients.
- **Dietary excesses**, e.g. obesity, coronary heart disease, diabetes mellitus and dental cavities, occur when the diet contains too much of certain nutrients.

As well as food, other factors contribute to the occurrence of these diseases, such as age, weight, gender, genetics, stress and lifestyle, e.g. smoking.

Dietary deficiencies

Bowel disorders

Bowel disorders include constipation, haemorrhoids (piles), diverticular disease, bowel cancer and irritable bowel syndrome (IBS). These disorders are becoming more common in western countries, as dietary fibre is lacking due to high consumption of refined carbohydrates.

Disorder	Description	Causes	Symptoms
Constipation	Stools become hard and difficult to expel	• Lack of dietary fibre which absorbs water, making stools soft and easy to pass • Insufficient water intake. Water is necessary to make stools soft.	• Infrequent bowel movements • Stomach cramps
Haemorrhoids (piles)	Swollen blood vessels are found inside or around the rectum and anus	• Lack of dietary fibre • Insufficient water intake • Excessive pushing when expelling waste, due to constipation • Prolonged sitting down increases pressure on blood vessels in the anus, causing them to swell • Pregnancy, as a growing baby increases pressure on blood vessels in the lower pelvic area causing them to swell	• Pain and discomfort when expelling stools • Itchiness around the anus • Some blood loss passing stools

Internal haemorrhoid

External haemorrhoid

GO FIGURE 1.2.3
Up to 50% of Irish people suffer from haemorrhoids.

Disorder	Description	Causes	Symptoms
Diverticular disease	Small pouches (diverticula) develop in the walls of the intestine. They usually go unnoticed until they fill with food waste. Bacteria acts on the food waste and produces acids and gases that inflame diverticula.	• Lack of dietary fibre • Insufficient water intake	• Pain and discomfort • Bloating • Some blood loss in stools. If severe it may lead to anaemia.

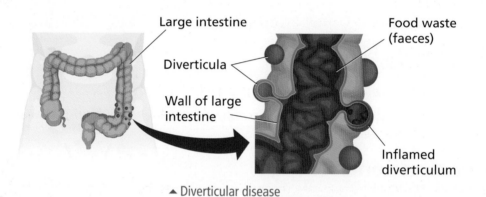

▲ Diverticular disease

Disorder	Description	Causes	Symptoms
Bowel cancer (colon/rectum cancer)	Starts as polyps (growths) on the bowel wall. Most polyps are not cancerous, but over time some can develop into colon cancer, which is often fatal if detected at the later stages.	• Lack of dietary fibre • Insufficient water intake • A diet high in saturated fat **Did you know** The National Screening Service has introduced free bowel screening for people aged between 60–69 to test for bowel cancer and reduce the risk of mortality from this disease.	• Changes in bowel habits, e.g. going to the toilet more often • Some blood loss in stools • Stomach cramps • Bloating • Weight loss
Irritable bowel syndrome (IBS)	The bowel has irregular muscle contractions (spasms)	• The exact cause is unknown. It is often associated with a diet lacking in fibre. • Sufferers may also have trigger foods that heighten symptoms, e.g. spicy food or citrus fruits	• Stomach cramps • Bloating • Diarrhoea • Constipation • Excessive flatulence

How to reduce the risk of developing bowel disorders

• Follow a diet high in dietary fibre.
• Drink approximately two litres of water per day.

 Name **one** diet-related condition associated with nutritional imbalance. Suggest **one** cause of this condition. (2) **OL**

Osteoporosis

Osteoporosis is a skeletal disease in which the bones become thin and porous due to a loss in bone mass. This results in fragile and brittle bones. It is the most common bone disease worldwide. The main bones affected are the hips, spine and wrists.

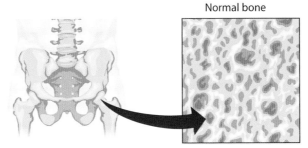

Normal bone   Osteoporosis

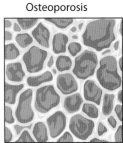

Symptoms of osteoporosis

Symptoms of osteoporosis include:

- fragile and brittle bones
- curvature of the spine resulting in stooped posture or hunching (dowager's hump)
- loss of height (as much as 15 cm) due to curvature of the spine
- neck and back pain
- bone fractures, especially in the wrist and hip.

Risk factors associated with osteoporosis

Heredity: if a person's family has genes responsible for decreased bone mass, risk of oseteoporosis is increased.

Exercise: lack of weight-bearing exercise, e.g. brisk walking, can increase risk, as exercise maintains bone strength.

Age: most prevalent in postmenopausal women (48–55 years) as the female hormone oestrogen decreases, reducing calcium absorption.

Diet: lack of calcium, phosphorus and vitamin D can reduce strong, dense bone formation.

Sex: most prevalent in women as they tend to have smaller, thinner bones than men and oestrogen levels decrease when women reach menopause, reducing calcium absorption.

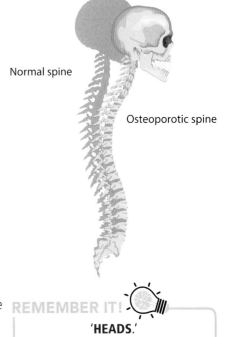

Normal spine

Osteoporotic spine

REMEMBER IT!

'HEADS.'
Heredity, **E**xercise, **A**ge, **D**iet, **S**ex.

GO FIGURE 123

More than 50% of women over the age of 65 suffer from osteoporosis.

How to reduce the risk of developing osteoporosis

- Consume a diet rich in calcium, vitamin D, and phosphorus.
- Avoid calcium absorption inhibitors, such as phytic acid, oxalic acid and tannins.
- Participate in regular weight-bearing exercise, e.g. jogging, to strengthen bones.
- Avoid excessive alcohol consumption as it lowers vitamin D levels in the body, decreasing calcium absorption.
- Women can choose hormone replacement therapy (HRT) to increase oestrogen levels that drop during menopause, increasing calcium absorption.

Peak bone mass

Up to 90% of bone mass is acquired by age 18 in girls and by age 20 in boys. At this point, bones have reached their maximum strength and density, known as peak bone mass. Given that a high peak bone mass reduces osteoporosis risk later in life, it is vital to invest in bone health at an early age.

 Explain (i) what osteoporosis is (ii) the main factors that increase the risk of developing osteoporosis. (18) **HL**

DIET-RELATED HEALTH PROBLEMS AND MODIFIED DIETS

Dietary excesses

Obesity

Obesity is a condition where an individual's weight is 20% or more over their recommended weight, based on their height.

At present 66% of Irish men and 53% of Irish women over 18 are considered overweight or obese.18% of Irish adolescents and 22% of Irish children are considered overweight or obese.

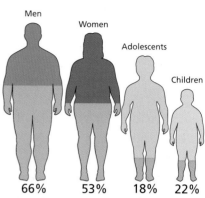

▲ Percentage of overweight or obese people in Ireland

Causes of obesity

- **Incorrect energy balance:** when a person's energy (kilocalorie) intake is greater than their energy output the excess energy is stored as fat. Sedentary lifestyles, greater consumption of processed food and increased portion sizes lead to this.

- **Poor food choices:** choosing excessive amounts of foods high in sugar and fat can cause energy imbalance, leading to weight gain. These choices may be made due to lack of education about healthy eating.

- **Hormonal imbalances:** thyroid hormones from the thyroid gland influence metabolism. Inadequate levels of these hormones can cause a person's basal metabolic rate to drop, leading to weight gain.

- **Medications:** taking steroids, antidepressants, anti-seizure and diabetes medications can cause weight gain.

- **Emotional or psychological issues:** depression, stress or low self-esteem can cause people to turn to foods high in sugar and fat to feel better, leading to weight gain.

- **Lack of physical activity:** inactivity causes energy provided by food to be stored as fat, as it is not burned, causing weight gain.

Health risks associated with obesity

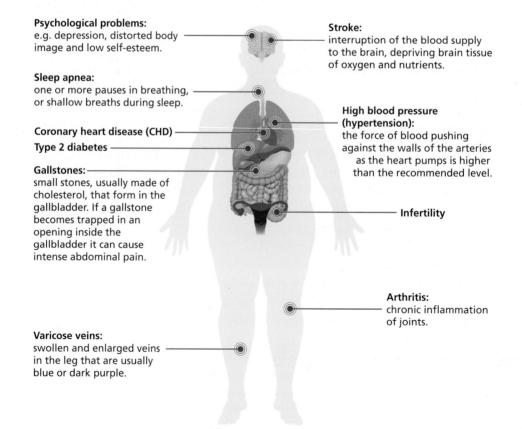

Psychological problems: e.g. depression, distorted body image and low self-esteem.

Sleep apnea: one or more pauses in breathing, or shallow breaths during sleep.

Coronary heart disease (CHD)

Type 2 diabetes

Gallstones: small stones, usually made of cholesterol, that form in the gallbladder. If a gallstone becomes trapped in an opening inside the gallbladder it can cause intense abdominal pain.

Varicose veins: swollen and enlarged veins in the leg that are usually blue or dark purple.

Stroke: interruption of the blood supply to the brain, depriving brain tissue of oxygen and nutrients.

High blood pressure (hypertension): the force of blood pushing against the walls of the arteries as the heart pumps is higher than the recommended level.

Infertility

Arthritis: chronic inflammation of joints.

Treatment of obesity

- Increase daily exercise to a minimum of one hour for children and young teenagers and 30 minutes for older teenagers, adults and older people.
- Follow a balanced, low-calorie diet.

Dietary guidelines to reduce obesity

- Eat a balanced low-calorie diet by following the food pyramid.
- Reduce intake of foods high in saturated fat, e.g. butter and cream. Use low-fat alternatives where possible or choose unsaturated fats, e.g. olive oil.
- Ensure portion sizes are accurate.
- Increase intake of fruit and vegetables, as they are low in fat and have fewer calories.
- Avoid refined carbohydrates, especially those high in sugar, e.g. cakes and pastries, as excess sugar is converted into fat in the body. Replace with high-fibre foods, e.g. wholegrain bread.
- Avoid takeaways and processed foods as they tend to be higher in saturated fat and calories than home-made equivalents.
- Avoid sugar-sweetened fizzy drinks and reduce alcohol consumption as these contain empty kilocalories.
- Grill, bake, steam or boil food instead of frying.

> **?**
>
> Outline **three** current nutritional guidelines (healthy eating guidelines) that are especially relevant for an obese person. (6) **OL**
>
> Discuss **(i)** the causes of obesity **and (ii)** the health risks associated with obesity. (20) **OL**

Coronary heart disease

Coronary heart disease (CHD) occurs when the walls of the coronary arteries narrow due to a build-up of cholesterol. This slowly blocks the flow of oxygen-rich blood through the coronary arteries to the heart. The blockage or hardening of the arteries is called arteriosclerosis.

There may be no symptoms of coronary heart disease in the early stages, but as the narrowing of the arteries continues it may have the following effects:

- **angina:** occurs when cholesterol builds up, restricting the blood supply due to a narrowing of the arteries, causing a lack of oxygen in the heart muscle, which leads to shortness of breath and severe chest pains. Emotional stress can also trigger angina

- **heart attack:** occurs when a blood clot (thrombosis) develops in an already narrowed artery, blocking blood flow and cutting off the oxygen supply reaching the heart, which can cause chest pain, shortness of breath and light-headedness

- **sudden cardiac death (SCD)**.

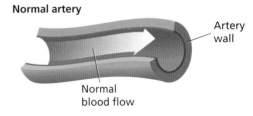

Normal artery — Artery wall — Normal blood flow

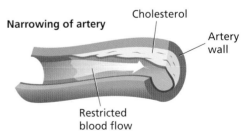

Narrowing of artery — Cholesterol — Artery wall — Restricted blood flow

▲ Artery blocked with cholesterol

GO FIGURE 123

It is estimated that over 5,000 people die of sudden cardiac death in Ireland each year. The risk is 40 times higher in obese adults.

Cholesterol

Cholesterol is a soft, wax-like substance produced by the liver or obtained from foods high in saturated fat. A certain amount is vital for the normal functioning of the body as it:

- forms an essential part of bile that helps emulsify lipids during digestion
- transports fat in the blood around the body
- insulates nerve fibres
- attaches to protein to create lipoproteins
- is an essential component of cell membranes.

There are two types of lipoproteins:

- **low-density lipoproteins (LDLs)** are found in saturated fats. They are harmful, as they lead to a build-up of cholesterol along the coronary arteries, increasing the risk of coronary heart disease (CHD)
- **high-density lipoproteins (HDLs)** are found in unsaturated fats. They are beneficial, as they help remove cholesterol from the blood, reducing the risk of CHD.

Risk factors associated with CHD

Controllable risk factors
- **Smoking:** narrows blood vessels - **Excessive alcohol consumption:** increases the risk of blood clots - **Lack of exercise:** causes LDLs to remain high - **High blood pressure (hypertension):** stresses blood vessels, causing them to narrow - **A diet high in saturated fat:** raises HDLs in the blood - **High cholesterol:** narrows or blocks blood vessels - **Obesity:** strains the heart as an increased area of body tissue needs to be supplied with oxygen - **High stress levels:** trigger reduced blood flow to the heart
Uncontrollable risk factors
- **Age:** more prevalent in men over 45 and women over 55 - **Heredity:** risk is increased if a person's next of kin is diagnosed

Lifestyle guidelines to reduce the risk of CHD

- Reduce weight to within an acceptable range (consult the body mass index (BMI) chart)
- Avoid excessive alcohol consumption
- Exercise regularly
- Do not smoke
- Reduce stress levels

BMI classifications	
Underweight	<18.5
Normal weight	18.5–24.9
Overweight	25–29.9
Obese	>30

Dietary guidelines to reduce the risk of CHD

- Reduce intake of foods high in saturated fat, e.g. butter and red meat. Use low-fat alternatives instead.
- Use unsaturated sources of fat, e.g. rapeseed oil, as they help lower LDLs.
- Choose lean sources of protein, e.g. fish and chicken, instead of red meat.
- Reduce salt intake, as excessive consumption is linked to high blood pressure (hypertension).
- Reduce refined carbohydrates, especially those high in sugar, e.g. cakes and pastries, as overconsumption can result in excess insulin production which can raise LDLs.
  Choose high-fibre foods, e.g. wholegrain bread, as they help lower LDLs.
- Choose functional foods, e.g. Benecol products, as they contain plant sterols that help lower LDLs.

> Describe **three** causes of coronary heart disease. (12) **OL**
>
> Identify and elaborate on (i) the lifestyle changes **and** (ii) the dietary guidelines that should be followed in order to reduce the incidence of coronary heart disease. (16) **HL**
>
> Write an informative account of cholesterol. (12) **HL**

Diabetes mellitus

Diabetes mellitus is an endocrine disorder associated with abnormally high levels of glucose in the blood. This happens because the pancreas does not produce enough insulin, or the insulin produced is ineffective.

Many of the body's cells rely on insulin to attach to them in order to allow glucose to enter from the blood so that the cells can be supplied with energy. If glucose remains in the blood the body will metabolise fats and proteins for energy instead.

High concentration of glucose in the blood can result in:

- blindness or visual impairments
- kidney failure.

Types of diabetes mellitus

There are two types of diabetes mellitus: type 1 insulin-dependent diabetes and type 2 non-insulin-dependent diabetes.

Type 1 Insulin-dependent diabetes (IDD)	Type 2 Non-insulin-dependent diabetes (NIDD)
- The pancreas does not produce insulin - Often hereditary, and develops mainly during childhood, adolescence and young adulthood - Controlled by injectable insulin and by diet and exercise - Cannot be reversed	- The pancreas produces insulin that cannot be used by the body - Develops mainly during later adulthood, especially among overweight adults - Controlled by oral medication or injectable insulin and by diet and exercise, or by diet and exercise alone - Can be reversed when a person loses a significant amount of their body weight
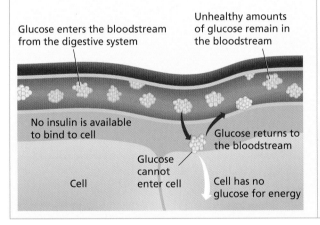	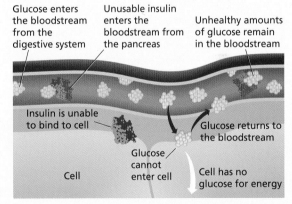

Symptoms of diabetes mellitus

- Frequent urination
- Excessive thirst
- Weight loss
- Tiredness
- Lack of concentration
- Blurred vision

▲ Injecting insulin

> **Did you know** ❓
>
> Approximately 170,000 people in Ireland have a diagnosis of type 2 diabetes, with up to 15,000 new cases diagnosed every year. About 80% of people diagnosed are obese.

HL Dietary guidelines for a person with diabetes mellitus

- Reduce intake of foods high in saturated fat, e.g. butter and cheese, to maintain a healthy weight. This is especially important to control type 2 diabetes.
- Increase intake of high-fibre foods, e.g. wholegrain bread, as they release glucose into the bloodstream slowly and steadily.
- Choose diabetic confectionery, e.g. diabetic chocolate, and artificial sweeteners, e.g. Canderel, instead of sugar to avoid blood glucose levels spiking.
- Choose low glycaemic index (GI) foods, e.g. porridge, rather than high GI foods, e.g. cakes, as low GI foods release glucose into the bloodstream slowly and steadily.
- Eat regular, balanced meals to stabilise blood sugar levels and help avoid hypoglycaemia or hyperglycaemia.

▲ Canderel

▲ Diabetic chocolate

Hypoglycaemia	Hyperglycaemia
Occurs when a person's blood sugar level drops. This can happen if a person with diabetes takes in too much insulin or consumes too few carbohydrates.	Occurs when a person's blood sugar level rises. This can happen if a person with diabetes takes in too little insulin or consumes too many carbohydrates.
• **Glucose** intake is required to prevent a diabetic coma • **Symptoms:** paleness, blurred vision and dizziness	• **Insulin** intake is required to prevent a diabetic coma • **Symptoms:** tiredness, excessive thirst and a frequent urge to urinate

Did you know ?

Normal blood sugar levels are between 4.0 to 7.9 mmol/l. If blood sugar levels drop below this range hypoglycaemia can occur. If blood sugar levels rise above this range hyperglycaemia can occur.

? Write an informative account of diabetes. Refer to:
- types
- symptoms
- specific dietary requirements that should be followed in order to manage the condition. (30) **HL**

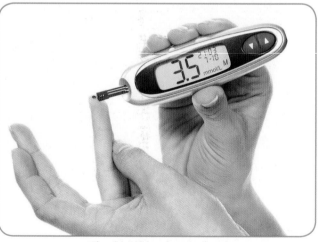

▲ Checking blood sugar level

Dental disease

Plaque is the main cause of dental disease. It is composed of bacteria, food and saliva, which form a coating on the outside of teeth and gums. If plaque is allowed to remain, it can lead to periodontal disease and dental cavities/tooth decay.

Periodontal disease	Dental cavities/tooth decay
• Occurs when plaque builds up along the gum line • Bacteria in the plaque produce toxins, causing inflammation of the gums and destruction of the bone that holds teeth in place • Over time, teeth become loose and may have to be removed	• Occurs when plaque is allowed to remain on teeth • Bacteria in the plaque react with food particles to produce an acid, which attacks the tooth enamel, weakening it • Over time a cavity (hole) will develop in the enamel, which eventually may expose the tooth's nerve, causing a toothache
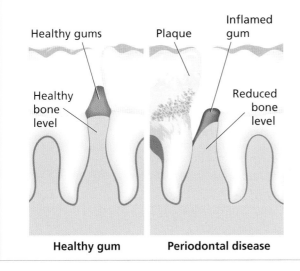	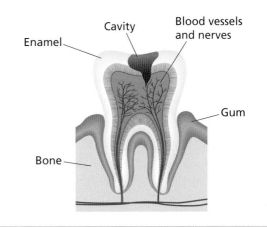

Dietary changes to reduce the risk of dental disease

- Avoid foods with a high sugar content, e.g. confectionery and sugar-sweetened fizzy drinks
- Use artificial sweeteners, e.g. Canderel, instead of sugar
- Choose water over fizzy drinks, dilutable juices and fruit drinks
- Choose high-fibre breakfast cereals, e.g. Shredded Wheat, over processed high-sugar options
- Read ingredient lists on food packaging carefully to avoid hidden sugars, e.g. corn syrup.

Did you know

Periodontal disease is the main cause of tooth loss in Ireland.

Dental care changes to reduce the risk of dental disease

- Visit the dentist at least twice a year.
- Brush teeth at least twice daily, if possible after each meal.
- Floss daily.
- Choose a toothpaste with fluoride, a mineral that strengthens teeth and helps prevent tooth decay.
- Use an antiseptic mouthwash to reduce bacterial build-up and freshen breath.

GO FIGURE

75% of Irish children experience tooth decay by the age of 15.

HL Modified diets

A modified diet is any diet altered to include or exclude certain foods or nutrients. Diets are typically modified for:

- **health reasons:** e.g. bowel disorders, coronary heart disease, obesity, diabetes or food intolerances
- **personal choice:** e.g. vegetarianism.

Coeliac disease

Coeliac disease is an autoimmune condition that causes the immune system to mistake gluten as a threat to the body. This causes the body's defence system to form antibodies that attack the villi on the internal surface of the small intestine. Damage to the villi disrupts the body's ability to absorb nutrients from food, leading to malnourishment.

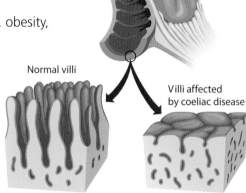

Coeliac disease ▲

Symptoms of coeliac disease

- Diarrhoea
- Bloating and abdominal pain
- Weight loss
- Nausea and vomiting
- Tiredness and fatigue due to anaemia
- Slow growth in children due to lack of nutrients

GO FIGURE 123
One in ten people suffer from coeliac disease.

Dietary guidelines for a person with coeliac disease

- Exclude all foods containing gluten (any food containing wheat, barley and rye).
- Use a range of gluten-free products, e.g. gluten-free bread and breakfast cereals, to maintain a balanced diet.
- Include naturally gluten-free foods, e.g. rice and corn (maize), for a balanced diet.
- Follow dieticians' recommendations to ensure a balanced diet.
- Read ingredient lists on food labels carefully, especially on processed food, to avoid traces of gluten. Check to see if foods carry the gluten-free symbol.

▲ Gluten-free symbol

Unsuitable and suitable foods for a person with coeliac disease

Unsuitable foods containing gluten	Suitable natural gluten-free foods	Suitable gluten-free food products
• Bread • Biscuits • Cakes • Pasta • Sausages • Soups • Sauces, e.g. roux sauce • Breaded or battered fish or poultry products	• Fruit • Vegetables • Meat • Fish • Yoghurt • Cheese • Rice • Eggs	• Commercial gluten-free versions of foods, such as bread, pasta, biscuits and cakes

? Define coeliac condition. Name **three** foods which should be avoided by a person with coeliac condition. (6) **HL**

▲ Gluten-free products

Vegetarian diets

A vegetarian is a person who lives primarily on a plant-based diet.

Types of vegetarian diets

Lacto-vegetarian diets	☑ Include milk and dairy products ☒ Do not include eggs, meat and fish
Lacto-ovo vegetarian diets	☑ Include milk, dairy products and eggs ☒ Do not include meat and fish
Pesco-vegetarian diets	☑ Include milk, dairy products, eggs and fish ☒ Do not include meat
Pollo-vegetarian diets	☑ Include milk, dairy products, eggs and poultry ☒ Do not include red meat or fish
Vegan diets	☑ Include plant-based foods only ☒ Do not include milk, dairy products, eggs, meat and fish

Reasons for choosing a vegetarian diet

- **Religion/culture:** some religions, e.g. Buddhism, follow a vegetarian diet, as they believe killing animals is wrong.
- **Health:** some people choose a vegetarian diet as it is lower in saturated fat and higher in dietary fibre, which is beneficial for reducing the risk of CHD, obesity and bowel disorders.
- **Economic:** vegetarianism is cheaper as meat and fish are omitted from the diet.
- **Sensory factors:** some people choose a vegetarian diet as they do not like the smell, appearance, taste and texture of meat and fish.
- **Ethics:** some people choose a vegetarian diet as they feel it is wrong to kill or harm animals, or may disagree with intensive animal rearing, e.g. caged hens.
- **Family:** a person may follow a vegetarian diet if they were exposed to the practice as a child or because they adapt their eating habits to suit other family members.

Dietary guidelines for a person following a vegetarian diet

- Ensure each meal is nutritionally balanced.
- Replace meat with meat alternatives such as tofu, textured vegetable protein (TVP) and mycoprotein, e.g. Quorn, to ensure sufficient protein intake.
- Include cheese, milk and yoghurt in dishes for vegetarians to increase calcium and HBV protein intake.
- Combine two or more LBV protein foods, e.g. beans with toast, to create complete proteins, ensuring the inclusion of all essential amino acids in the diet.
- Use fortified products, e.g. milk, to increase B12 and calcium consumption.
- Use vegetable stock cubes in soups and sauces instead of chicken, fish or beef.
- Exclude animal fats, e.g. butter, and replace with vegetable oils, e.g. olive oil.
- For vegans, include dairy food alternatives, e.g. soya milk, to ensure adequate calcium and vitamin D intake.

DIET-RELATED HEALTH PROBLEMS AND MODIFIED DIETS

Advantages of a vegetarian diet

✓ A vegetarian diet reduces the incidence of bowel disorders due to higher fibre intake.

✓ A vegetarian diet reduces the risk of obesity and type 2 diabetes due to reduced saturated fat intake.

✓ Less sugar and salt is consumed due to reduced reliance on processed food, reducing the risk of high blood pressure (hypertension) and type 2 diabetes.

✓ More vitamins and minerals are consumed due to a higher consumption of fresh produce, e.g. fruit and vegetables.

Nutrients to consider in a vegetarian diet

There is a risk, particularly in vegan diets, of deficiencies in the following nutrients. Careful consideration needs to be taken during meal planning to ensure sufficient intake.

Protein	**Iron**
• Include soya beans or soya products as they contain HBV protein • Combine two or more LBV protein foods to create complete proteins • Include meat alternatives, e.g. tofu, TVP and mycoprotein	• Include non-haem sources of iron such as cereals, green leafy vegetables and pulses • Include fortified products, e.g. breakfast cereals and soya milk • Include foods rich in vitamin C, e.g. oranges, to enhance iron absorption
Vitamin B12	**Vitamin D**
• Include fortified products, e.g. breakfast cereals and soya milk, to prevent deficiency • Include eggs and dairy products in vegetarian diets • In some cases supplements may also be required	• Include dairy products and eggs in vegetarian diets • Include fortified foods, e.g. breakfast cereals and soya milk • In some cases supplements may also be required
Zinc	**Calcium**
• Include eggs and dairy products in vegetarian diets • Include legumes, green leafy vegetables, wholegrain bread and seeds in vegan and vegetarian diets	• Include dairy products in vegetarian diets • Include green leafy vegetables, seeds, and nuts in vegan and vegetarian diets

? Explain the term *lacto-vegetarian*. Name **two** protein alternatives suitable for the diet of a vegetarian. (6) **OL**

State **two** specific dietary requirements of a lacto-vegetarian diet. (6) **OL**

In relation to each nutrient listed recommend **two** good sources for a vegan diet.
- Protein
- Calcium
- Iron (6) **HL**

Chapter 3:
The Irish diet and the Irish food industry

🔗 THE IRISH DIET
1.2.4

What you will learn:

- **Changes in food and eating patterns in the Irish diet from the beginning of the twentieth century**
- **Changes in nutritional intakes from the beginning of the twentieth century**
- **Investigating the dietary habits of the Irish population**
- **A comparison of the Irish diet with current healthy eating guidelines**
- **Areas of malnutrition within the Irish diet**

The first Irish people farmed, fished and foraged for food in order to survive. Today people can choose from a variety of instantly available foods. This change has had a big effect on Irish eating habits.

Changes in food and eating patterns in the Irish diet from the beginning of the twentieth century

During the twentieth century many changes took place in food and eating patterns in the Irish diet. These changes are attributed to a number of factors and are summarised under the headings: diversity of staple foods, availability of food, national events and cultural changes.

Diversity of staple foods	
1900–1950	• Food was plain and unprocessed. Potatoes, home-made brown soda bread and porridge were the staple foods. • Only the upper classes could afford meat, dairy or eggs, meaning that saturated fat consumption was low.
1950–1990	• White bread, meat and dairy products became more accessible, leading to a decrease in the consumption of potatoes and brown bread. • Bacon and eggs became popular amongst the middle classes.
1990–today	• Rice, pasta and couscous have increased in popularity, reducing potato consumption. • The availability of ciabatta, wraps, baps and panini has reduced other white bread consumption. • Meat consumption has increased across all classes, due to greater wealth and better affordability.

Availability of food

1900–1950	• In the early 1900s sugar consumption increased due to wider availability. • From 1940 onwards fresh fruit and vegetables, e.g. oranges and bananas, began to be imported.
1950–1990	• During the 1970s and 1980s processed convenience foods, e.g. margarine and processed meats, became available due to advances in technology. These were considered superior to home-made food.
1990–today	• Due to developments in importation and increased consumer demand, a wider variety of foods are now available, e.g. spices and sauces from around the world, and exotic fruit and vegetables.

National events

1900–1950	• World War I (1914–1918) led to food shortages and an increase in food prices. • During World War II (1939–1945) food was rationed, especially sugar, tea and flour.
1950–1990	• Rural electrification in the 1950s and 1960s allowed for the refrigeration of perishables, e.g. milk, and instant cooking of food using electric cookers.
1990–today	• The economic recession has meant that people are now price-conscious when buying food. The introduction of discount supermarkets, e.g. Aldi, and increased competition among supermarkets has benefitted the Irish consumer.

MINISTRY OF FOOD
RATION BOOK
1944-45

Cultural changes

1900–1950	• In urban areas there was a move away from home-cooked food to shop-bought goods, e.g. bread and biscuits, as they were regarded as being superior.
1950–1990	• During the 1960s foreign travel became more accessible, exposing people to new cultures and foods. This led to the opening of many new restaurants, e.g. Italian and Chinese restaurants. • Due to their convenience, takeaways increased in popularity in the 1970s and 1980s.
1990–today	• Busy lifestyles mean that people eat 'on-the-go', e.g. in cars. • Meals tend to be irregular, with the main meal in the evening and family members eating at different times due to late working hours and extra-curricular activities. • Travel has continued to influence tastes, with Indian and Thai food gaining popularity. • Immigrants have introduced new foods and dishes, creating a multicultural food society. • People are more nutritionally conscious, leading to better nutritional labelling on food. • Increased awareness of special dietary requirements has increased availability of gluten-, dairy-, nut- and sugar-free products.

? Discuss **four** changes in the eating patterns of Irish adolescents from the beginning of the twentieth century. (16) **OL**

Identify and discuss **two** contemporary trends in Irish eating patterns. (10) **HL**

Changes in nutritional intakes from the beginning of the twentieth century

Nutrient	Early 1900s	1950 onwards	Today
Proteins (15% intake is recommended)	11%	13%	16%
Fats (35% intake is recommended)	24%	30%	36%
Carbohydrates (50% intake is recommended)	65%	54%	48%

Investigating the dietary habits of the Irish population

Surveys are used to gather detailed information about people's eating habits, e.g. the type and amount of food consumed within a set time period. This information is then collated and analysed. Surveys implemented in Ireland include:

- the SLÁN Surveys of Lifestyle, Attitudes and Nutrition 1998, 2002 and 2007, which surveyed over 10,000 people

- the National Adult Nutrition Survey 2011, carried out by the Irish Universities Nutrition Alliance (University College Cork and University College Dublin), which surveyed 1,500 adults

- the Healthy Ireland Survey, commissioned by the Department of Health in 2015 as part of the government Healthy Ireland action plan, which surveyed 7,539 people aged 15 and over.

A comparison of the Irish diet with current healthy eating guidelines

Over the years the eating habits of the Irish population have changed considerably. There is increasing evidence of deficiencies and excesses in dietary practices, leading to many diet-related health problems. The findings from the SLÁN Survey (2007), National Adult Nutrition Survey (2011) and the Healthy Ireland Survey (2015) highlight this, especially when compared with the current healthy eating guidelines.

Healthy eating guidelines	Survey findings
Fat	
• Use low-fat dairy products • Limit amounts of food and drinks from the top shelf of the food pyramid • Avoid ready meals and takeaways	**SLÁN 2007:** 58% of people consumed more than the Recommended Daily Allowance (RDA)/Reference Intake (RI) of fat. **National Adult Nutrition Survey 2011:** 63% of people consumed more than their recommended daily energy intake from fat. **Healthy Ireland Survey 2015:** 62% of people ate snack foods daily, consuming an average of two portions per day.
Salt	
• Limit salt intake • Limit amounts of food and drinks from the top shelf of the food pyramid • Avoid ready meals and takeaways	**SLÁN 2007:** 71% of people consumed more than the RDA/RI of 6 g of salt daily. **National Adult Nutrition Survey 2011:** the average daily intake of salt was 7.4 g.
Sugar	
• Limit sugar intake • Limit amounts of food and drinks from the top shelf of the food pyramid	**SLÁN 2007:** 86% of people consumed more than three servings from the top shelf of the pyramid daily. **National Adult Nutrition Survey 2011:** over three-quarters of the population consumed confectionery on a daily basis. **Healthy Ireland Survey 2015:** Almost 65% of people consumed snack foods or sugar-sweetened drinks daily.
Alcohol	
• Adults who choose to drink alcohol should do so sensibly and within the recommended limits	**SLÁN 2007:** 10% of people consumed more than the weekly alcohol limits. **National Adult Nutrition Survey 2011:** 29% of men and 24% of women consumed more than the weekly alcohol limits. **Healthy Ireland Survey 2015:** 39% of people binge-drank more than the weekly alcohol limits.
Fibre	
• Eat cereals, potatoes, wholegrain rice and wholemeal breads and pasta to provide the best calories to fuel the body	**SLÁN 2007:** 52% of people consumed less than 25 g of fibre daily. **National Adult Nutrition Survey 2011:** fibre intake was found to be 19 g per day.
Calcium	
• Use low-fat milks, low-fat or no-added-sugar yoghurts and reduced-fat cheeses	**SLÁN 2007:** 61% of people consumed fewer than three portions daily from the milk, cheese and yoghurt group. **National Adult Nutrition Survey 2011:** calcium intake was found to be below Estimated Average Requirements in 16% of females aged 18–64
Fruit and vegetables	
• Eat five or more portions of a variety of fruit and vegetables daily	**SLÁN 2007:** 35% of people did not consume the recommended portions of fruit and vegetables daily **National Adult Nutrition Survey 2011:** only 9% of people aged between 18–64 consumed the recommended portions of fruit and vegetables daily. **Healthy Ireland Survey 2015:** only 26% of people consumed the recommended portions of fruit and vegetables daily.

Areas of malnutrition within the Irish diet

Area of malnutrition	Causes	Effects	Corrective measures
Low dietary fibre intake	• Insufficient intake of wholegrain food, fruit and vegetables • Overconsumption of refined foods	• Constipation • Diverticulitis • Irritable bowel syndrome (IBS) • Haemorrhoids (piles) • Bowel cancer	• Choose wholegrain foods instead of refined foods • Where possible, eat fruit and vegetables with skins • Include more pulses • Eat seeds or nuts as snacks
Low iron intake	• Insufficient intake of haem iron and non-haem iron • Insufficient intake of vitamin C • Excessive intake of iron inhibitors, e.g. oxalic acid	• Anaemia • Muscle fatigue	• Increase intake of haem and non-haem iron sources. • Increase intake of vitamin C sources • Avoid excessive intake of iron inhibitors
Low calcium intake	• Insufficient intake of calcium • Insufficient intake of vitamin D • Excessive intake of calcium inhibitors, e.g. phytic acid	• Rickets • Osteomalacia • Osteoporosis • Tooth decay	• Consume three portions of dairy daily • Increase intake of vitamin D • Avoid excessive intake of calcium inhibitors
High saturated fat intake	• Consuming foods high in animal fats • Overconsumption of processed foods and takeaways	• Weight gain and obesity • High cholesterol • Coronary heart disease • Type 2 diabetes	• Use butter and other solid fats sparingly • Use polyunsaturated spreads in place of butter • Choose low-fat dairy products. • Avoid frying food. Grill, bake or steam instead. • Trim excess visible fat from meat
High sugar intake	• Consuming foods high in sugar • Overconsumption of processed foods	• Weight gain and obesity • Dental decay • Type 2 diabetes	• Choose low-sugar products • Choose no-added-sugar breakfast cereals • Use artificial sweeteners or dried fruit to sweeten dishes • Choose fresh fruit instead of canned fruit in syrup

GO FIGURE 123

Between 2010 and 2020 the number of adults with diabetes is expected to rise by 30%, and the number with coronary heart disease by 31%.

THE IRISH DIET

THE IRISH FOOD INDUSTRY

What you will learn:

- **Reasons for the success of the Irish agri-food industry**
- **Food sectors in the Irish food industry**
- **Irish food agencies and government departments**
- **The role of small businesses and home enterprises**
- **Career opportunities in food and related industries**
- **Investigation of a local food business**

The agri-food sector is one of Ireland's most important industries, exporting food and drinks to over 170 countries worldwide. It directly employs around 150,000 people and generates approximately €10.5 billion in annual exports.

Reasons for the success of the Irish agri-food industry

Climate and landscape	• The Irish climate has a high average rainfall, with gentle, mild winters, which benefit Irish horticulture, as grass crops grow in abundance. This has led to a strong livestock industry, making Ireland one of the foremost milk producers in the world. • The availability of rich, fertile soil also enables extensive **tillage** farming of cereal crops.
History and tradition	• Ireland has a rich tradition of local home-made foods, e.g. soda bread, that have become popular as prepared consumer products in recent years. Many of these are produced by small speciality-food businesses. • A strong dairy and livestock farming tradition in Ireland also enables these industries to remain at a high standard.
Government agencies	• Government agencies, such as Bord Bia, provide advice, guidance and support, ensuring success for agri-food businesses. • Many agencies also provide start-up grants to help new food businesses get established. • They also impose regulations around animal health and welfare and traceability. This has assisted Ireland's food export success, as import countries are assured of safe, high-quality food.
Coastline	• Ireland's coastline provides clean, unpolluted seas to fish for seafood, which is used for export or in prepared consumer foods.

Lit Hit
Tillage is the preparation of land for growing crops.

Food sectors in the Irish food industry

The Irish food industry is divided into ten key sectors.

- Prepared foods
- Pig meat
- Seafood

- Beef
- Poultry
- Beverages

- Sheep meat
- Dairy and ingredients
- Edible horticulture and cereals

- Livestock

 Identify **three** major sectors of the Irish Food Industry. (6) **HL**

Major food exports

Exports are products or services produced in a home country and sold abroad. The Irish food and drinks sector has recorded a sixth consecutive year of growth in exports during 2015-2016 due to increasing awareness internationally of Ireland's strong reputation as a producer of safe, high-quality foods.

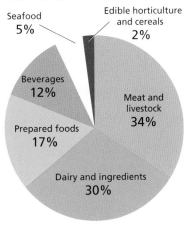

Seafood 5%

Edible horticulture and cereals 2%

Beverages 12%

Meat and livestock 34%

Prepared foods 17%

Dairy and ingredients 30%

▲ Distribution of Irish food and drinks exports by sector 2015–2016

International markets 28%

United Kingdom 41%

Other European Union markets 31%

▲ Main destinations for Irish food and drinks exports 2015–2016

Breakdown of Irish food and drinks exports 2015–2016

Sector	%	Popular exports	Main export markets
Meat and livestock	34%	**Meat**: beef, poultry (chicken, duck, goose and turkey), sheep meat and pig meat. Ireland is the largest beef exporter in the European Union and the fifth largest in the world **Livestock**: cattle, pigs and sheep	United Kingdom (beef, poultry and pig meat), France (lamb)
Dairy and ingredients	30%	Cheese, milk powder, ice cream, infant formula and butter. Ireland is the tenth largest dairy exporter in the world	United Kingdom, China
Prepared foods	17%	Chocolate, chilled foods, ready meals, cooked meats and baked goods	United Kingdom, Netherlands
Beverages	12%	Beer, cream liqueur, whiskey and water	United Kingdom, United States
Seafood	5%	Salmon, trout, mussels, oysters and scallops	France, United Kingdom, Spain, Italy
Edible horticulture and cereals	2%	Mushrooms, potatoes, carrots, cabbage and berries. Mushrooms account for approximately 50% of edible horticulture and cereals exports	United Kingdom

Major food imports

Imports are products or services brought into a home country from abroad and sold.

Food is imported into Ireland:

- to offer a wider variety of foods to consumers
- when certain food products are out of season here, e.g. strawberries
- when there is not enough of a particular food to meet consumer demand, e.g. crisp companies may import potatoes
- to make foods that are not produced here available, e.g. pineapples and tea.

Did you know ?

Irish consumers spend an estimated €1.8 billion on imported food brands per year, even when Irish alternatives are available.

Irish food imports

Sector	Popular imports	Country of origin
Dairy and ingredients	Dairy spreads, e.g. Benecol	United Kingdom
	Cheese, e.g. Port Salut	France
	Yoghurt, e.g. Onken	United Kingdom
Edible horticulture and cereals	Chillies	Zambia
	Pineapples	Costa Rica
	Basil	Israel
Beverages	Tea	Kenya
	Coffee	Costa Rica
	Alcoholic drinks, e.g. Heineken	Holland
	Bottled water, e.g. Volvic	France
Prepared foods	Cakes, e.g. Mr Kipling	United Kingdom
	Confectionery, e.g. Hershey's	United States
Meat	Salami	Germany
	Szynka (ham)	Poland
Seafood	Anchovies	Italy
	Pollock	United States

? Name **two** major Irish food exports and **two** major foods imported into Ireland. (6) **OL**

Irish food agencies and government departments

Numerous food agencies and government departments support the food industry in Ireland.

- Teagasc
- Bord Bia
- Bord Iascaigh Mhara (BIM)
- Enterprise Ireland
- Department of Health
- Food Safety Authority of Ireland (FSAI)
- Department of Agriculture, Food and the Marine

➔ For information on the FSAI and the Department of Agriculture, Food and the Marine see page 253.

Teagasc 	• The agriculture and food development authority in Ireland. Offers training and advice to people within the agriculture and food industry, e.g. advice on animal breeding and sustainable farming • The main provider of further education in agriculture, food, horticulture and forestry. They work in conjunction with Institutes of Technology to run some of these courses
Bord Bia 	• Promotes sales of Irish food, drinks and horticulture in Ireland and abroad. • Offers marketing services to Irish food and drinks manufacturers, enabling them to make consumers aware of their products worldwide • Issues Bord Bia Quality Marks on meat, eggs and horticulture, which highlight that a food is fully traceable and produced with the highest level of care • Runs the Origin Green initiative, enabling Irish food and drinks manufacturers to demonstrate commitment to environmental sustainability in Ireland and abroad 
Bord Iascaigh Mhara (BIM)	• Responsible for developing the Irish marine, fishing and aquaculture industries. • Provides advice to fishers on new fishing and fish farming opportunities • Works in conjunction with national fisheries colleges to run courses that promote careers in the Irish catching, fish-farming and seafood processing sectors • Develops a range of information materials on the health benefits of fish, in order to raise awareness and increase consumption amongst consumers
Enterprise Ireland 	• Responsible for the development and growth of Irish enterprises at home and on the world markets • Works in partnership with Irish entrepreneurs to establish or expand businesses through the provision of advice, mentoring and grants
Department of Health 	• Enforces food legislation through the Food Safety Authority of Ireland • Develops health promotion strategies in conjunction with the Health Service Executive (HSE) • Develops food safety policies

? Name **two** government departments or agencies that have a role in the food and drinks industry. (2) **HL**

State **two** ways that the Food Safety Authority of Ireland (FSAI) supports the work of the food industry (4) **HL**

State **two different** functions of An Bord Bia (Irish Food Board) in the Irish Food Industry. (6) **HL**

The role of small businesses and home enterprises

One of the fastest-growing food sectors in the Irish agri-food industry is the area of speciality foods. Sales of speciality foods are increasing by approximately 12% per year, with the current value of the market at an estimated €450 million.

Speciality foods are niche, high-quality foods produced in limited quantities by small businesses and home enterprises using non-industrial (home-made) artisan techniques. This can result in a superior-tasting product, especially when compared to mass-produced equivalents. The products are also perceived as healthier and more natural, as producers often avoid using additives and may use organic ingredients.

▲ Farmers' market

Many speciality food businesses begin in rural areas and are family run, using traditional cooking methods and recipes that have been passed down through generations.

Speciality foods are available at farmers' markets or food fairs, e.g. Bloom In The Park. Nowadays speciality foods are also appearing on supermarket shelves, as supermarkets such as SuperValu are supporting small local businesses to enable their products to become more widely available.

Advantages of small businesses and home enterprises

✓ Small businesses and home enterprises provide a large amount of direct employment. Jobs created include food management, manufacturing, marketing and advertising. They also create indirect employment, as the business must source ingredients and supplies from local suppliers.

✓ They enhance Ireland's international reputation as a producer of high-quality food and drinks.

Examples of speciality foods

- Ice cream and frozen yoghurt
- Chocolate and confectionery
- Dairy products, e.g. cheese, yoghurt and butter
- Preserves, e.g. chutneys, jams, jellies and relishes
- Beverages, e.g. beer, cider and fruit juices
- Baked goods, e.g. biscuits, cakes and crackers

▶ Irish speciality foods

? Give **two** reasons why food production in small businesses and home enterprises is increasing. (4) **OL**

Comment and elaborate on the growing popularity of foods produced by small business and home enterprises. (20) **HL**

Career opportunities in food and related industries

A wide variety of courses are available in all areas of food and agriculture, as some career opportunities in this field require specific qualifications.

- **Universities and Institutes of Technology (ITs):** offer degrees, diplomas and certificates in the areas of human nutrition, food technology, culinary arts and food science.
- **Fáilte Ireland:** offers degrees, diplomas and certificates through local Institutes of Technology in the areas of travel and tourism management, hospitality management and bar management.
- **Teagasc Agricultural Colleges:** offer degrees, diplomas and certificates in the areas of food, farm management and horticulture. They work in conjunction with Institutes of Technology to run some of these courses.
- **St Angela's College, Sligo:** offers degrees in Home Economics and Food Business Management.

Examples of career opportunities

Supplying	Marketing	Retailing
Farmer Fisher Baker Cheese-maker	Marketing manager Advertising consultant	In-store demonstrator Supermarket worker
Catering	**Food technology**	**Dietetics**
Chef Waiter	Food product developer Food technician	Nutritionist Dietician
Food safety	**Maintenance**	**Transportation**
Environmental health officer Microbiologist	Electrician Plumber	Pilot Sailor Truck driver

▲ Baker

▲ Food technicians

? List **two** career opportunities in the Irish Food Industry. (2) **OL**

INVESTIGATION OF A LOCAL FOOD BUSINESS

Nobó (dairy-free and gluten-free ice cream)

Company name: Nobó

Location: Dublin

Product type: a dairy-free and gluten-free ice cream product made from avocado and coconut milk, and sweetened with pure honey

Flavour range:

- Irish Salted Caramel
- Passion Fruit and Mango
- Vanilla and Coconut
- Fresh Lemon
- Mint Humbug (limited edition)
- Chocolate and Toasted Almond

Did you know ?

Nobó is the world's only commercial dairy-free ice cream made using avocados and coconut milk.

When and why was the business set up?

While living in New York, Brian and Rachel Nolan were exposed to healthy alternatives to foods commonly regarded as being unhealthy, including biscuits, crisps and ice cream. This generated the idea to create a healthy alternative to ice cream, free from refined sugar and commercial stabilisers or gums, and so they established Nobó in 2012 in Dublin.

#FROZENGOODNESS

How was the name for the product decided?

Brian and Rachel were keen to have a name that emphasises their Irish roots, as well as the fact that their product is dairy-free. They came up with Nobó as it highlights these aspects of their product. Bó is the Irish for cow, so the name means 'no cow'.

Who are the main suppliers to the business? Are they local?

Whenever possible, Nobó use local Irish suppliers for ingredients, e.g. Irish Atlantic sea salt is used in their Irish Salted Caramel ice cream. They also use an Irish packaging supplier to source their packaging. It is impossible, however, for the company to solely use Irish suppliers since certain ingredients, e.g. coconut milk and avocado, must be imported, as they are not produced in Ireland.

Does the business contribute to the local area? If so, how?

The business provides direct employment for small numbers of local people, and indirect employment through their use of local suppliers for ingredients, packaging materials and local distribution companies. Nobó also regularly supports local charity events by providing free ice cream.

How many people are employed directly?
What positions do they hold?

Brian and Rachel work full-time as Head of Brand and Head of Sales and Operations respectively. Two other part-time staff members work in Sales and Marketing. A team of people produce the ice cream in a small manufacturing facility in Co. Wicklow.

Are there any plans for expansion of the business?

Brian and Rachel aim to expand the number of Irish, United Kingdom, Dubai and Abu Dhabi stores where Nobó is available and they aim to expand the Nobó product range.

Are there any plans to increase employment within the business?

As of 2016, Brian and Rachel plan to hire two more full-time staff members to join the sales and marketing team, with at least another two employees joining each year after that to keep up with expansion.

What aids or grants were/are available?

Nobó received a Priming Grant (a business start-up grant, available to micro-enterprises within the first 18 months of start-up) from their local Enterprise Office. They partook in the Food Works Programme run by Bord Bia, Enterprise Ireland and Teagasc, which helps small businesses to expand and develop. They completed The SuperValu Food Academy run by the Local Enterprise Office Network and Bord Bia, which provides advice and support to small businesses and opportunities to sell products in a number of SuperValu stores.

Have there been changes in any area of the business since it was established?

Ice-cream production was outsourced to a production team in Co. Wicklow, as consumer demands for the product got too large. This allows Brian and Rachel to focus more on marketing and retailing the product. Distribution of the ice cream was also outsourced to enable the product to be stocked in an increased number of health food stores and SuperValu supermarkets nationwide.

How is the product marketed?

Social media, including Facebook and Twitter. Media, including newspapers, magazines, television and radio. Word-of-mouth is also important: the company works closely with food bloggers and chefs who create awareness of the products. Competitions are also important: in 2014 the Fresh Lemon ice cream won three stars in the Great Taste awards, raising awareness of Nobó products.

What type of quality control is used, e.g. HACCP?

The ice cream production manager manages health and safety controls and implements a strict HACCP plan. A sample of every batch of ice cream produced is tested to ensure quality assurance and health and safety standards are being met. Regular swab tests of the machinery used in production are also sent for microbial analysis.

Chapter 4: Food commodities

1.3.2 MEAT, OFFAL AND POULTRY

What you will learn:

- **Classification, structure, average nutritional composition, nutritional value and dietetic value of meat**
- **Causes of toughness in meat**
- **Methods of tenderising meat**
- **Guidelines for buying and storing meat**
- **Cuts of beef and lamb**
- **Suitable methods for cooking meat**
- **Guidelines for cooking carcass meat**

- **Guidelines for preparing and cooking poultry**
- **Effects of cooking on meat**
- **Meat processing**
- **Meat products**
- **Controlling meat quality in Ireland**
- **Beef and Lamb Quality Assurance Scheme (BLQAS)**

Meat is the flesh of an animal, typically a mammal or bird, consumed as food. It varies in flavour, texture and nutritional composition, depending on the breed of the animal, its environment and feed. The Irish diet includes a wide variety of meat types, and meat is the main source of protein consumed.

Classification of meat

Meat is classified into four main categories.

- **Carcass meat:** e.g. pig (ham, bacon, pork), cow (beef, veal) and sheep (lamb, mutton).
- **Poultry:** domestic birds reared for meat and eggs, e.g. chicken, turkey, duck and goose.
- **Game:** wild birds and animals, e.g. pheasant, rabbit and deer (venison).
- **Offal:** edible internal organs, e.g. kidneys, liver and tongue.

Structure of meat

Meat is made up of meat fibres, connective tissue and fat.

- **Meat fibres** contain the proteins actin, myosin and globulin; minerals, vitamins, water and extractives (substances, e.g. lactic acid, dissolved in water in the meat fibres, that improve the flavour of meat and stimulate gastric juices which aid meat digestion). Fibres vary in length and diameter, which affects the tenderness of meat.

- **Connective tissue** holds meat fibres together in bundles. It contains the proteins elastin and collagen.
- **Fat** is present in two forms:
  - **visible fat**, found under the skin of animals as a layer of adipose tissue or around internal organs, e.g. the rind on rashers
  - **invisible fat**, present in the flesh as globules dispersed between meat fibres and the connective tissues, e.g. fat dispersed throughout mince.

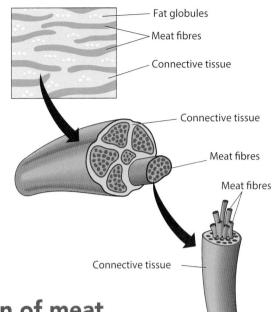

Average nutritional composition of meat

Nutrient	Carcass meat	Offal	Poultry
Proteins	20–30%	20–25%	25–30%
Fat	10–30%	5–10%	2–5%
Carbohydrates	0%	0%	0%
Vitamins	B group	A, B group, C, D, K	B group
Minerals	Iron, zinc, phosphorus, potassium, sulfur	Iron, zinc, potassium, phosphorus, sulfur	Iron, zinc, phosphorus, calcium
Water	50–60%	60–70%	65–75%

Nutritional value of meat

Carcass meat	
Proteins	• An excellent source of high biological value (HBV) protein • The main proteins present are myosin, globulin and actin in the meat fibres and elastin and collagen in the connective tissue
Fat	• A source of saturated fat • The amount of fat present depends on the type of carcass meat, e.g. pork has more fat than beef, and the cut of meat, e.g. striploin steak has more fat than sirloin steak • Fat can be visible or invisible
Carbohydrates	• Lacks carbohydrates, for this reason carcass meat is usually served with a carbohydrate-rich food, e.g. pasta
Vitamins	• A good source of B-group vitamins, particularly thiamine (B1), riboflavin (B2), niacin (B3), pyridoxine (B6) and cobalamin (B12)
Minerals	• A good source of haem iron • Zinc, sulfur, potassium and phosphorus are present in small amounts
Water	• Water content varies depending on the type of carcass meat • The higher the water content the less fat present

Offal

Offal	
Proteins	• An excellent source of HBV protein
Fat	• Low in saturated fat
Carbohydrates	• Lacks carbohydrates, with the exception of a small amount of glycogen (stored glucose) in liver. For this reason, offal is usually served with a carbohydrate-rich food, e.g. potatoes.
Vitamins	• A good source of B-group vitamins, particularly cobalamin (B12) and folic acid • A source of vitamin C • Liver and kidneys have a high content of vitamins A, D and K
Minerals	• A good source of haem iron • Contains small amounts of zinc, potassium, phosphorus and sulfur
Water	• Water content varies depending on the type of offal • The higher the water content the less fat present

▸ Different types of offal

Poultry

Poultry	
Proteins	• An excellent source of HBV protein
Fat	• A source of saturated fat • The amount of fat present depends on the type of poultry, e.g. duck has more fat than chicken, and the meat, e.g. leg meat has more fat than breast meat
Carbohydrates	• Lacks carbohydrates, for this reason poultry is usually served with a carbohydrate-rich food, e.g. rice
Vitamins	• A good source of B-group vitamins, particularly thiamine (B1), riboflavin (B2) and niacin (B3)
Minerals	• A source of haem iron, however it contains less than red meat • Contains small amounts of zinc • Phosphorus and calcium are present in small amounts
Water	• Water content varies depending on the type of poultry • The higher the water content the less fat present

🖒Tip!

If nutritional value of meat appears on the examination paper, remember to include the function of each nutrient in your answer. If you are asked to describe the nutritional value of meat and the question does not specify carcass meat, poultry or offal, use the nutritional value of carcass meat in your answer.

❓ Discuss the nutritional significance of meat in the diet. (20) **HL**

Dietetic value of meat

- Meat is an excellent source of HBV protein that assists with growth and repair. This makes it a valuable food in the diets of children, teenagers and pregnant women.
- As carcass meat is high in saturated fat, it should be restricted in the diets of individuals with high cholesterol and those on calorie-controlled diets. Poultry is a good alternative.
- Meat is a good source of haem iron, which can reduce the risk of anaemia.
- Meat is available in a variety of types and forms, e.g. fresh and processed, to suit different tastes and to add variety to the diet.
- Meat is a versatile food suited to many different cooking methods and flavour combinations, e.g. chilli and garlic.
- Some types and cuts of meat are inexpensive, e.g. round steak, making meat an economical food. Processed meat products, e.g. burgers, are often cheaper than fresh meat.
- Meat lacks carbohydrates, so it should be combined with foods rich in these to balance the diet.

Causes of toughness in meat

▲ Meat hanging

- **Age:** older animals have tougher meat than younger animals because:
  - they have more connective tissue and their connective tissue is stronger
  - their muscle fibres are longer and thicker.
- **Activity:** meat from the active parts of the animal, e.g. the leg, is tougher, as it develops longer muscle fibres and more connective tissue over time.
- **Treatment before and after slaughter:** before slaughter animals should be rested to enable glycogen build-up in their muscles, as after slaughter glycogen converts to lactic acid, tenderising meat fibres during hanging. Failure to do this will result in tough meat. Beef should be hung for 14–21 days and lamb for seven days to ensure sufficient tenderising.
- **Incorrect method of cooking:** tough cuts of meat require slow, moist methods of cooking, e.g. stewing, to convert collagen in connective tissue to gelatine, tenderising meat. If cooked quickly, e.g. grilled, meat will be tough and difficult to chew.

Methods of tenderising meat

- **Meat tenderisers** contain **proteolytic enzymes**, e.g. papain from papayas, which break down meat fibres, making them more digestible.
- **Mechanical breakdown**, e.g. pounding with a meat mallet, piercing with needles or mincing, breaks fibres into shorter lengths, tenderising meat.
- **Marinating** in a mixture of acid (e.g. lemon juice), salt, herbs, spices and fruit or dairy breaks down fibres, tenderising meat.
- **Slow, moist cooking methods**, e.g. stewing and casseroling, tenderise tough cuts of meat, as they convert collagen to gelatine, making meat fibres fall apart and become soft.

> **Lit Hit**
> Proteolytic enzymes are enzymes that promote proteolysis (the breakdown of proteins into smaller polypeptides or amino acids).

▲ Meat mallet

> **?** List **two** factors that affect the tenderness of meat. Suggest **two** ways of tenderising meat. (6) **OL**
>
> Describe **each** of the following:
> - the factors that cause toughness in meat
> - **two** methods of tenderising meat. (15) **HL**

MEAT, OFFAL AND POULTRY

Guidelines for buying meat

- Buy meat from a retailer with a clean and hygienic meat counter. The retailer should have a strict food hygiene and safety policy to ensure any meat being sold is safe and fit for consumption.
- Check the use-by date on pre-packaged meat. After this date meat may be unsafe to eat.
- Buy meat with the Bord Bia Quality Mark. This assures the consumer that best practices were implemented at all stages of meat production, which reduces food safety risks.
- Ensure meat is the correct colour for its type, e.g. beef should be a dark red. The flesh should be firm and elastic.
- To economise, purchase:
  - good-quality cuts of meat, without excessive gristle and fat
  - cheaper cuts of meat, e.g. round steak, as they offer the same nutritional value as expensive cuts.
- Buy meat near the end of the shopping trip to minimise the amount of time it spends at room temperature (optimum temperature for bacterial growth) before being returned to a fridge.
- Buy cuts of meat suitable for the chosen cooking method, e.g. shin beef for beef stew and fillet steak for frying.

> Summarise **five** factors that consumers should consider when buying meat and meat products. (20) **OL**

Guidelines for storing meat

- Store meat in a fridge at 4°C, as room temperature speeds up bacterial growth, increasing the rate of spoilage. If pre-packaged, leave in its original packaging and place on the bottom shelf of the fridge. If purchased loose, remove from the wrapper and place on a plate or in a container that will collect any juices. Cover to prevent from drying out, and place on the bottom shelf of the fridge.
- Minimise the amount of time meat is in storage. Use within two to three days.
- If freezing fresh meat, freeze at −25°C on the day of purchase.

Cuts of beef and lamb

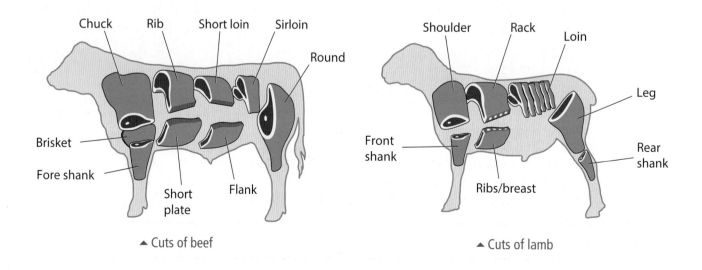

▲ Cuts of beef   ▲ Cuts of lamb

Suitable methods for cooking meat

Roasting, e.g. leg of lamb	**Barbecuing**, e.g. fillet steak	**Frying**, e.g. bacon slices	**Boiling**, e.g. joint of bacon
Grilling, e.g lamb chops	**Stewing**, e.g. beef stewing pieces	**Microwaving**, e.g. minute steak	**Braising**, e.g. beef round roast

▲ Barbecuing meat

Guidelines for cooking carcass meat

- Choose an appropriate cooking method, e.g. frying or braising, suited to the type and cut of carcass meat.
- If baking or roasting carcass meat ensure the oven is preheated, so it will cook meat until it reaches a sufficiently high temperature to ensure all pathogenic bacteria are killed.
- Avoid overcooking carcass meat, as it becomes tough and difficult to digest.

Guidelines for preparing and cooking poultry

- If poultry is frozen, thaw in a fridge at 4°C before cooking.
- Remove giblets (offal), e.g. liver, heart, stomach and neck.
- Avoid stuffing the cavity, as it absorbs the juice from raw poultry, creating an optimum environment for bacterial growth, which may cause food poisoning if the poultry is not sufficiently cooked.
- Thoroughly wash hands and equipment used during the preparation of poultry to prevent cross-contamination and salmonella food poisoning.
- Cook in a preheated oven until the centre of the carcass reaches a sufficiently high temperature, approximately 75°C, to ensure all pathogenic bacteria are killed.
- Cool leftovers quickly to avoid bacterial growth. Cover and store in the fridge and use within two days.

G⊙ FIGURE 123

Meat shrinks by almost 20% in size during cooking.

Effects of cooking on meat

- Protein coagulates at 40–50°C, causing meat to shrink.
- Fat melts, adding flavour to meat.
- Colour changes from red to brown due to the denaturation of myoglobin (red pigment) to haematin (brown pigment).
- Some B-group vitamins are lost, as they are not heat stable. Other vitamins and minerals are also lost, as they as dissolve into the cooking liquid.
- Bacteria are destroyed.
- Flavour develops, as extractives are released from the meat fibres.
- Collagen converts to gelatine, making meat more digestible as the fibres loosen and fall apart.
- Meat can become tough, rubbery and difficult to digest if overcooked.

? Explain **three** effects of cooking on meat. (6) **OL**

Meat processing

Tip!
The processing methods for meat can also be applied to fish.

Freezing

Process	Meat is deboned and some fat is removed. It can then be frozen by commercial methods, e.g. blast freezing at –30°C, or by home freezing at –25°C.
Effects	• No effect on colour, flavour and texture • Microorganisms are inactivated • Some loss of B-group vitamins and extractives during drip loss when thawed • Freezer burn may occur if packaging is damaged • Rancidity of meat may occur if stored in the freezer for too long
Examples	• Pork • Beef • Lamb • Poultry products, e.g. chicken nuggets

Vacuum packing

Process	Meat is deboned, then sealed in polythene packets with the air removed.
Effects	• No effect on nutritional value, colour, flavour and texture • Microorganisms are inactivated • Can be refrigerated for three to four weeks unopened. When opened it must be treated as fresh, and used within two to three days.
Examples	• Rashers • Sausages

Curing

Process	Meat is injected with a preserving solution, e.g. salt and potassium nitrate, and soaked in a brine solution for three to four days. It is then stored for five to six days to allow the flavour develop. At this stage, meat may be smoked.
Effects	• Salt content is increased • Colour and flavour are changed • Microorganisms and enzymes are destroyed
Examples	• Bacon • Ham

Drying

Process	Meat has its moisture removed. This can be completed by fluidised bed drying or accelerated freeze drying.
Effects	• Colour, flavour and texture are changed • Loss of B-group vitamins • Microorganisms and enzymes are destroyed
Examples	• Beef jerky • Meat in packet soups

? Processed meats are popular consumer products. Name **two** types of processed meats and state **one** advantage of each. (16) **OL**

Set out details of **one** process used to extend the shelf life of meat. In your answer refer to:
• name of process
• how the process is carried out to include the underlying principle involved
• the effect of the process on meat. (15) **HL**

Meat products

A number of meat products are made by processing the parts of animals that cannot be retailed as carcass meat. Most processed meat products are made from minced meat, fillers, fat and additives.

- **Fresh sausages:** made from raw meat, fat, water, fillers (wheat flour, **rusk** and corn starch) and flavourings, in a casing that is usually made from synthetic collagen.

Lit Hit
Rusk is a dry biscuit or bread.

- **Cooked sausages:** e.g. black and white pudding and frankfurters. Made with similar ingredients to fresh sausages, but some contain additional ingredients, e.g. oatmeal and pig's blood in black pudding.

- **Dried sausages:** e.g. salami and pepperoni. Made from meat that is cured, minced, mixed with other ingredients, e.g. chilli, and dried.

- **Beef burgers:** made from minced beef, beef fat, wheat flour, water and seasoning, and moulded into a circular shape.

- **Meat extractives:** e.g. stock cubes and gravy powder. Made from meat juice extractives that are dried and mixed with corn flour, salt, yeast extract and flavour enhancers.

- **Pâté:** e.g. chicken liver pate. Made from a mixture of fat, flavouring, cooked ground meat and liver, minced into a spreadable paste.

- **Cold cooked meat:** e.g. ham, turkey, corned beef and luncheon roll. Made from a mixture of meat, fillers and flavourings, e.g. spices.

- **Gelatine:** a colourless, tasteless and odourless setting agent made from the boiled bones, skins and tendons of animals. It is used to thicken and stabilise desserts such as jellies, soufflés and cheesecakes. Gelatine comes in either leaf or powdered form.

▲ Fresh and dried sausages

▲ Pâté

Did you know

Pregnant women should avoid pâté as it can contain listeria, which can cause listeriosis, an infection that increases the risk of miscarriage and premature birth.

▲ Leaf gelatin and powdered gelatin

MEAT, OFFAL AND POULTRY

Controlling meat quality in Ireland

The Department of Agriculture, Food and the Marine enforce food safety within the meat sector throughout Ireland. They ensure that meat purchased is fresh, hygienic and free from disease by:

- enforcing European Union legislation regarding the import of foods of animal origin from outside the European Union
- monitoring the use of antibiotics and growth promoters in animal production
- ensuring the maintenance of abattoirs and meat-processing factories throughout Ireland
- testing animals routinely for diseases such as tuberculosis (TB) and bovine spongiform encephalopathy (BSE)
- ensuring the identification of livestock and traceability of meat.

Did you know

The United States banned the importation of Irish and European Union beef in 1997 following the BSE outbreak. In 2015, Ireland became the first European Union state to be allowed to start importing beef into the United States again.

Beef and Lamb Quality Assurance Scheme (BLQAS)

If beef or lamb products bear the Bord Bia Quality Mark it tells the consumer that the products are quality assured as they have been produced with the highest level of care and attention from primary production through factory processing. To achieve this, the farmer and the processing plant must be certified members of the Bord Bia Quality Assurance Scheme and work in partnership to provide customers with quality-assured beef and lamb products.

For a farmer to become a member of the Quality Assurance Scheme their farm must be audited by Bord Bia to ensure:

- high standards of animal welfare
- accurate records are kept of the origin, sex, age, breed, movement and veterinary treatments of all animals to ensure meat is fully traceable
- farmyards are maintained to a high standard.

For a processing plant to become a member of the Quality Assurance Scheme they must be audited by Bord Bia to ensure:

- slaughter staff demonstrate competence and compassion when handling animals
- the implementation of a cleaning and sanitation programme for the plant, facilities and equipment.
- accurate records are kept on animals to ensure meat is fully traceable.

▲ Beef mince with the Bord Bia Quality Mark

What you will learn:

- Classification, structure, average nutritional composition, nutritional value and dietetic contribution of fish
- Guidelines for buying and storing fish
- Spoilage of fish
- Guidelines for preparing fish

- Suitable methods for cooking fish
- Guidelines for cooking fish
- Effects of cooking on fish
- Fish processing
- Fish products

The natural, clean water around Ireland's 7,500 km of coastline has provided exceptionally good seafood for thousands of years. Turbot, salmon, plaice, cod and sole are some of the most common types of fish found in Irish waters.

The majority of Ireland's fish tends to be exported, as fish consumption in Ireland is low relative to many other countries. Consumption has increased slightly in recent years due to increased availability of fish products and higher awareness of the health benefits associated with fish, such as omega-3.

Classification of fish

Fish can be classified according to their shape, habitat and nutritional value.

> **Did you know** ❓
>
> Round fish are not actually round. Their name comes from the fact that slicing them vertically leaves round pieces of fish.

Shape

- **Flat fish:** e.g. plaice, halibut and sole.
- **Round fish:** e.g. tuna, cod and salmon.

▸ Salmon

▸ Plaice

Habitat

- **Freshwater fish (rivers and lakes):** e.g. salmon, bream and trout.
- **Saltwater fish (sea):**
  - o **demersal fish** (live near the sea bed): e.g. cod, plaice and whiting
  - o **pelagic fish** (live near the surface): e.g. mackerel, tuna and salmon.
- **Farmed fish:** fish farming involves raising fish, e.g. salmon, mussels and oysters, commercially in tanks or enclosures, usually for sale as food.

▸ Fish farm

Nutritional value

- **White fish (round and flat):** e.g. cod, plaice, whiting and monkfish.
- **Oily fish (round):** e.g. mackerel, tuna, herring and salmon.
- **Shellfish:**
  - **molluscs** (hard, unsegmented shell, no claws or legs): e.g. mussels and oysters
  - **crustaceans** (hard, segmented shell with claws and legs): e.g. lobster and crab.

▲ Shellfish

 Classify fresh fish and give one example of each class. (6) **OL**

Structure of fish

Fish is made up of myomeres, connective tissue, fat and an outer layer.

- **Myomeres** are short, thick fibres arranged in broad vertical bands. These fibres are much shorter than those present in meat. They contain the proteins actin and myosin, minerals, vitamins, water and extractives.
- **Connective tissue** holds myomeres in place. The tissue contains the protein collagen. Fish has less connective tissue than meat, and no elastin, therefore it is more tender and easier to digest, and it takes less cooking time.
- **Fat** in oily fish is invisible, as it is dispersed between the myomeres and the connective tissue. The flesh of white fish has no fat, as white fish store fat in their livers. Fish livers are often pressed to form nutritional supplements, such as cod liver oil.
- **Outer layer:** a waterproof, scaly skin covers the flesh of white and oily fish. A shell encloses the flesh of shellfish.

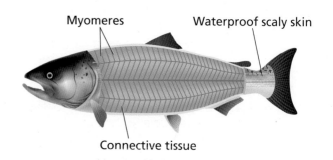

Myomeres

Waterproof scaly skin

Connective tissue

Average nutritional composition of fish

Nutrient	White fish	Oily fish	Shellfish
Proteins	17.5%	18%	16%
Fat	0.5%	15–18%	3%
Carbohydrates	0%	0%	0%
Vitamins	B group	A, B group, D	A, B group, C
Minerals	Zinc, potassium, phosphorus, fluorine, iodine	Zinc, potassium, phosphorus, fluorine, iodine	Iron, zinc, potassium, phosphorus, fluorine, iodine
Water	80.5%	65%	78%

Nutritional value of fish

Proteins	• An excellent source of high biological value (HBV) protein • The main proteins present are myosin and actin in the myomers and collagen in the connective tissue
Fat	• Oily fish are a source of polyunsaturated fat, especially the omega-3 fatty acids eicosapentaenoic acid (EPA) and docosahexaenoic acid (DHA) • No fat is present in white fish as white fish store fat in their livers, which are removed during filleting • Shellfish contain a small amount of cholesterol
Carbohydrates	• Lacks carbohydrates, as any glycogen (stored glucose) is converted to lactic acid during the struggle when fish are caught. For this reason fish is usually served with a carbohydrate-rich food, e.g. potatoes.
Vitamins	• A source of B-group vitamins, particularly pyridoxine (B6) and cobalamin (B12) • Oily fish and white fish livers contain vitamins A and D • Some shellfish, e.g. mussels, are a source of vitamins A and C
Minerals	• Contains small amounts of iodine, zinc, potassium, phosphorus and fluorine • Shellfish, especially mussels and oysters, are good sources of iron • Canned fish are a source of calcium, as the bones are eaten
Water	• Water content varies depending on the fish type • The higher the water content the less fat present

? Evaluate the nutritional contribution fish makes to the diet. (15) **HL**

Tip!
If nutritional value of fish appears on the examination paper remember to include the function of each nutrient in your answer.

FISH

Dietetic value of fish

- Fish is an important source of easily digestible HBV protein, which assists with growth and repair. This makes it a valuable food in the diets of children, teenagers and pregnant women.
- As white fish contains no fat it is low in kilocalories. This makes it an ideal food for individuals following calorie-controlled diets.
- Oily fish contains polyunsaturated fat, especially omega-3 fatty acids, so it is beneficial in low-cholesterol diets, as it helps increase high-density lipoproteins (HDL) that help lower cholesterol levels.
- Fish is available in a variety of types and forms, e.g. fresh and processed, to suit different tastes and add variety to the diet.
- Fish is a versatile food suited to many different cooking methods and flavour combinations, e.g. chilli and lime.
- Some fish is inexpensive, e.g. mackerel, making it an economical food. Processed fish products, e.g. fish fingers, are often cheaper than fresh fish. Fish cooks very quickly, minimising energy costs.
- Fish lacks carbohydrates, so it should be combined with foods rich in these to balance the diet.

? Give an account of the dietetic value of fish. (12) **OL**

State why oily fish is recommended for the diet of a person with coronary heart disease. (6) **HL**

Guidelines for buying fish

- Buy fish from a retailer with a clean and hygienic fish counter. The retailer should have a strict food hygiene and safety policy to ensure any fish being sold is safe and fit for consumption.
- Check the use-by date on pre-packaged fish. After this date fish is unsafe to eat.
- Ensure fish has firm, elastic flesh. The skin should be shiny, moist, unbroken and slime-free, as slime is an indication of bacterial growth. The scales should be tightly attached and not loose.
- Ensure whole fish have bright and bulging eyes. **Gills** should be bright red.
- Ensure cuts of fish have firm, transparent flesh. No discolouration, such as bruising, should be evident.
- Shellfish should feel heavy for their size. Molluscs' shells should be closed or close when touched. Open shells indicate that molluscs are dead and not edible. Crustaceans should be alive to reduce the risk of food poisoning, as they spoil quickly when dead.
- Check fish have a smell of the sea. An unpleasant smell is an indication of bacterial growth. Smoked fish should have a fresh, smoky odour.
- Buy fish near the end of the shopping trip to minimise the amount of time it spends at room temperature (optimum temperature for bacterial growth) before being returned to a fridge.

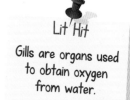

Lit Hit

Gills are organs used to obtain oxygen from water.

? Give an account of six key factors that consumers should consider when buying fresh fish and fish products. (18) **HL**

Guidelines for storing fish

- Store fish in a fridge at 4°C, as room temperature speeds up bacterial growth, increasing the rate of spoilage. If pre-packaged, leave in its original packaging and place on the bottom shelf of the fridge. If purchased loose, remove from the wrapper, rinse under cold water and place on a plate or in a container that will collect any juices. Cover to prevent from drying out and place on the bottom shelf of the fridge.
- Store strong-smelling fish away from foods likely to absorb the flavour, such as milk and butter.
- Minimise the amount of time fish is in storage. Use within 24 hours, as fish spoils quickly.
- If freezing fresh fish, freeze at –25°C on the day of purchase.

Spoilage of fish

Fish is an extremely perishable food, so it must be stored on ice and used or processed as quickly as possible. There are three main causes of spoilage: oxidative rancidity, enzymes and bacteria.

- **Oxidative rancidity:** oils in oily fish react with oxygen in the air. Oxygen combines with the carbons in double bonds along the unsaturated fatty acid chain, causing the fish to become rancid.
- **Enzymes:** naturally present enzymes in fish cause its flesh to deteriorate, even at low temperatures. This can be slowed by placing fish on ice or in the fridge.
- **Bacteria:** when fish are caught they struggle frantically, using up the glycogen in their muscles and liver. This results in little glycogen being left to convert to lactic acid to preserve the fish, which in turn causes rapid deterioration by bacterial action. This produces a strong-smelling nitrogen compound called trimethylamine.

? Explain **two** factors that contribute to the spoilage of fish. (6) **HL**

Guidelines for preparing fish

Fish can be cooked whole or it can be filleted.

Filleting a whole fish

1. Scrape off the scales with the back of a knife.

2. Cut off the head and fins.

3. Cut the underside of the fish and remove the intestines.

4. Wash the cavity by running it under the tap.

The fish is then prepared in one of the following ways:

- **fillets:** long, thin pieces of flesh cut the length of the fish on either side of the bone (round and flat fish)

- **steaks or cutlets:** large slices of fish created by cutting vertically through the round of fish (round fish only).

Suitable methods for cooking fish

▲ Poaching salmon

Baking, e.g. cod

Barbecuing, e.g. trout

Frying, e.g. hake

Poaching, e.g. salmon

Grilling, e.g tuna

Stewing, e.g. monkfish

Microwaving, e.g. salmon

Steaming, e.g. halibut

Guidelines for cooking fish

- Choose an appropriate cooking method, e.g. frying or stewing, suited to the type of fish. Monkfish is one of the only fish suited to slow cooking methods, due to its firm texture.

- Avoid overcooking fish, as it becomes tough, rubbery and difficult to digest.

Effects of cooking on fish

- Protein coagulates at 40–50°C, causing fish to shrink.
- Colour changes from translucent to opaque.
- Some B-group vitamins are lost, as they are not heat stable. Other vitamins and minerals are also lost, as they dissolve into the cooking liquid.
- Bacteria are destroyed.
- Flavour develops as extractives are released out of the fish fibres.
- Collagen converts to gelatine, making fish more digestible as the fibres loosen and fall apart.
- Fish can become tough, rubbery and difficult to digest if overcooked.

Fish processing

Freezing	
Process	Fish can be frozen by commercial blast freezing at –30°C, or home freezing at –25°C.
Effects	• No effect on colour, flavour and texture • Microorganisms are inactivated • Some loss of B-group vitamins and extractives during drip loss when thawed • Freezer burn may occur if packaging is damaged • Oxidative rancidity and enzyme deterioration can occur if fish is stored in the freezer for too long
Examples	• Cod • Salmon • Fish products, e.g. fish fingers

FISH

Canning	
Process	Fish is placed in sterile cans, sealed and heated to high temperatures. Fish may be canned in oil, brine, spring water or a sauce, e.g. tomato sauce.
Effects	• Colour, flavour and texture are changed • Loss of B-group vitamins, particularly thiamine (B1) • Microorganisms and enzymes are destroyed • Canned fish provides calcium, as the canning process fish softens bones so they can be consumed • Vitamins A and D are provided if fish is canned in oil • Calorie and fat content can increase if fish is canned in oil or a sauce
Examples	• Tinned mackerel • Tinned tuna • Tinned salmon

Smoking	
Process	Fish is put in brine or rubbed in salt to give flavour and to act as a preservative. It is then smoked by either cold or hot smoking. • **Cold smoking** involves subjecting fish to smoke from wood chips. The chemicals creosote and formaldehyde in the smoke prevent microorganism growth on fish flesh. The temperature does not go beyond 27°C, so the fish must be cooked before being consumed. • **Hot smoking** follows the same process as cold smoking, but the temperature is gradually increased to approximately 80°C. Fish does not require further cooking to be consumed.
Effects	• Microorganisms and enzymes are destroyed • Colour is changed, e.g. white fish will usually develop a light yellow or brown colour • Flavour is changed to a distinctive, smoky taste • Salt content is increased
Examples	• Haddock • Cod • Salmon

 Name three different types of processed fish products and state why these products are popular. (14) **OL**

🖒**Tip!**

The processing methods for fish can also be applied to meat.

Fish products

A number of fish products are made by processing the parts of fish leftover when cuts, e.g. fillets or cutlets, are removed. Most processed fish products are made from minced fish, fillers, fat and additives.

• **Fish cakes:** made from minced fish, potato, herbs and seasoning. They are shaped into rounds, coated in breadcrumbs or batter, briefly fried and then frozen. Fish cakes usually contain 35–45% fish.

• **Fish fingers:** made from blocks of frozen, filleted white fish, e.g. cod, that are cut into fingers, dipped into a batter or breadcrumbs and refrozen. They usually contain 50–70% fish.

• **Fish extractives:** e.g. fish stock cubes. Made from fish juice extractives that are dried and mixed with cornflour, salt, yeast extract and flavour enhancers.

▲ Fish stock cubes

ALTERNATIVE PROTEIN FOODS

What you will learn:

- Soya protein
- Average nutritional composition and nutritional value of soya beans
- Types of soya products
- Manufacture of textured vegetable protein (TVP)
- Guidelines for preparing and cooking dried TVP
- Advantages and disadvantages of TVP
- Nutritional value and manufacture of mycoprotein
- Quorn
- Advantages and disadvantages of mycoprotein

Alternative protein foods are also known as novel foods. They are obtained from two main non-animal sources:

- **plant sources**, e.g. soya beans.
- **microorganisms**, e.g. fungi, bacteria and yeast.

PROTEIN ALTERNATIVES FROM PLANT SOURCES

Soya protein

Soya protein is the plant protein derived from soya beans. Soya beans are a legume.
The protein in soya beans is unlike most other vegetables as it is of high biological value (HBV).

▲ Soya beans

Average nutritional composition of soya beans

Protein	Fat	Carbohydrates	Vitamins	Minerals	Water
35%	20%	30%	B group	Iron, calcium	14%

Nutritional value of soya beans

Proteins	• A good source of HBV protein; however, the content of the essential amino acid methionine is low in comparison to meat
Fat	• High in polyunsaturated fat • Linoleic fatty acids make up 50% of the fat content
Carbohydrates	• Less than one-third of a soya bean contains carbohydrates. They are present in the form of starch and dietary fibre.
Vitamins	• Contain B-group vitamins
Minerals	• A source of non-haem iron • Contain calcium
Water	• Little water is present

Tip!

If nutritional value of soya beans appears on the examination paper remember to include the function of each nutrient in your answer.

Types of soya products

An extensive range of soya products made from soya beans is now available in supermarkets.

▲ Soya products

- **Tofu:** a soft, cheese-like food made by curdling soya milk and then pressing the resulting curds into blocks. It is used in curries, stews and salads.

- **Tempeh:** made from cooked and slightly fermented soya beans. This fermentation binds the soya beans into a compact cake. It is used in stir-fries, curries and stews.

- **Textured vegetable protein (TVP):** made from soya flour that has been cooked under pressure and then dried. It is frequently used as a meat extender to bulk up a meal. It is used in shepherd's pie, lasagne, spaghetti bolognese and burgers.

- **Miso:** a seasoning paste made from fermented soya beans mixed with rice, salt and water. It is used in sauces, dips, marinades and broth-like soups.

- **Soya milk:** made by soaking soya beans in water and then grinding them with the soaking water. It is used in beverages, baking and sauces.

- **Soy sauce:** made from fermented soya beans, salt, water and barley or wheat flour. It is used as a dipping **condiment** or in stir-fries and marinades.

> **Lit Hit**
> A condiment is a substance used to enhance the flavour of food.

Manufacture of textured vegetable protein (TVP)

1. **Cleaning and preparing:** soya beans are cleaned then dehulled and cracked.

2. **Extraction of oil:** oil is extracted from the soya beans.

3. **Soya flour:** soya beans are ground into soya flour and the remaining carbohydrate is removed.

4. **Addition of ingredients:** soya flour is mixed with ingredients, including vegetable oil, seasoning and flavourings. The flour is also fortified with cobalamin (B12) and iron.

5. **Extruded and shaped:** the mixture is heated and **extruded** through a nozzle into a reduced pressure environment, causing it to expand and achieve a specific texture that is similar to meat. It is then cut into various shapes and sizes, e.g. chunks, flakes, nuggets, grains or strips, depending on the TVP product being produced.

> **Lit Hit**
> Extrude means to force a material through an opening to give it form or shape.

▲ Textured vegetable protein

6. **Dried, packaged and labelled:** TVP is then dried and packaged. The packaging is labelled with details including the ingredients, storage instructions, allergy advice and nutritional information.

 **REMEMBER IT!**

'**C**hildren **E**at **S**oya **A**t **E**ach **D**inner.'

Cleaning and preparing, **E**xtraction of oil, **S**oya flour, **A**ddition of ingredients, **E**xtruded and shaped, **D**ried, packaged and labelled.

Guidelines for preparing and cooking dried TVP

- Follow manufacturer's instructions (listed on the packet).
- Soak in water for 15–30 minutes to **reconstitute** it.
- Drain the water and add it to the dish being made 15 minutes before the end of the cooking time.

> **Lit Hit**
> Reconstitute means to restore something to its original state by adding water.

Advantages and disadvantages of TVP

Advantages of TVP

✓ TVP is a good nutritional alternative to meat, as it is made from soya beans, which are a source of HBV protein. This makes it very useful for vegetarians and vegans who need a high-protein alternative.

✓ TVP is a good source of dietary fibre, as it is made from a plant food source. This helps reduce the risk of bowel disorders.

✓ Little preparation and cooking time is required for TVP. For preparation, it simply needs to be reconstituted by adding water. It can then be cooked in the same manner as meat, but should be added at the end of the cooking time.

✓ TVP is more economical than meat.

✓ During cooking no shrinkage occurs, as TVP has a low water content in comparison to meat.

✓ TVP contains almost no saturated fat and no cholesterol. This makes it ideal for those on low-cholesterol or calorie-controlled diets.

✓ TVP is a versatile food, as it comes in various shapes and sizes, making it suitable for many different culinary uses, e.g. chunks in a stir-fry or mince in a lasagne.

Disadvantages of TVP

✗ TVP has an inferior texture to meat (often softer), so it should be added near the end of the cooking time to avoid disintegration.

✗ TVP is often bland-tasting, so extra flavouring, such as seasoning or spices, may be required.

PROTEIN ALTERNATIVES FROM MICROORGANISMS

Mycoprotein

Increasing demand for protein-based foods to feed the world's growing population has led scientists to investigate ways of obtaining food from microorganisms. Microorganisms such as yeast, fungi and bacteria are being developed into edible protein food sources through fermentation. Mycoprotein is a high-protein food produced from microorganisms. It is made from the fungal **biomass** of a soil fungus called *Fusarium venenatum*.

> **Lit Hit**
> Biomass refers to the total quantity or weight of organisms in a given area or volume.

▲ Mycoprotein

Nutritional value of mycoprotein

Proteins	• A good source of HBV protein; however, the content of the essential amino acid methionine is low in comparison to meat
Fat	• Low in saturated fat
Carbohydrates	• A good source of dietary fibre
Vitamins	• Contains B-group vitamins
Minerals	• Contains small amounts of non-haem iron and zinc
Water	• Little water is present

Manufacture of mycoprotein

1. **Fermented:** the *Fusarium venenatum* fungus is fed into a fermenter and is fermented under ideal conditions to grow the fungus' cells.

2. **Addition of ingredients:** additional ingredients such as sterile glucose syrup, ammonia and oxygen, are added continuously for a period of six weeks to create ideal conditions for fungus cells to grow. Minerals, such as potassium, magnesium and phosphate, are also supplied. A temperature of approximately 30°C remains constant.

3. **Harvested, purified and dried:** during the six-week period the fungal biomass is continually harvested from the fermenter. It is then purified by being heat-treated at 65°C. Lastly, the liquid is drained by spinning the fungal biomass in a **centrifuge**.

> **Lit Hit**
>
> A centrifuge is a machine that rotates at high speed.

4. **Bound:** the fungal biomass is mixed with egg albumin to bind it.

5. **Input additives:** additives, including flavourings and colourings, are inputted.

6. **Textured and shaped:** the mycoprotein is textured to resemble meat. It is then sliced, diced or shredded, depending on what is required.

7. **Steamed:** the mycoprotein is steamed to bind the egg and to set the shape. It is then used to produce mycoprotein products such as burgers or sausages.

REMEMBER IT!

> 'Fungi Are Happiest Burrowing Into Thick Soil.'
>
> Fermented, Addition of ingredients, Harvested, purified and dried, Bound, Input additives, Textured, Steamed.

▲ Mycoprotein sausages

? Complete the following table in relation to alternative (novel) protein foods. (6) **HL**

	Source	Product
Plant		
Micro-organisms		

Quorn

Quorn is a meat-substitute product made from mycoprotein and sold in ready-to-cook forms, such as mince. It is also used in a range of chilled vegetarian meals, including pizzas, lasagnes and cottage pies, and to create products resembling sliced meat, hot dogs and burgers. There are over 100 different Quorn products.

▲ Quorn products

Advantages and disadvantages of mycoprotein

Advantages of mycoprotein

✓ Mycoprotein is a good nutritional alternative to meat as it is made from fungi, which are a good source of HBV protein. This makes it very useful for vegetarians who need a high-protein meat substitute.

✓ Mycoprotein is a good source of dietary fibre. This helps reduce the risk of bowel disorders.

✓ Mycoprotein is low in saturated fat and contains no cholesterol. This makes it ideal for individuals on low-cholesterol or calorie-controlled diets.

✓ Mycoprotein is a versatile food as there are numerous mycoprotein products available, making it suitable for many different culinary uses, e.g. mycoprotein mince for lasagne and mycoprotein cutlets for a stir-fry.

Disadvantages of mycoprotein

✗ Mycoprotein products, e.g. mince, have an inferior texture to meat (often softer), so they should be added near the end of the cooking time to avoid disintegration.

✗ Although they are vegetarian friendly, many mycoprotein products are not suitable for vegans due to the addition of eggs. Vegans should read ingredients lists before purchasing mycoprotein products.

What you will learn:

- Types, structure, average nutritional composition, nutritional value and dietetic value of eggs
- Guidelines for buying and storing eggs
- Labelling regulations for egg boxes and eggs

- Testing the freshness of eggs
- Guidelines for preparing eggs
- Culinary uses of eggs
- Effects of cooking on eggs
- Properties of eggs
- Egg Quality Assurance Scheme (EQAS)

Types of eggs

Eggs are a nutritious, versatile and widely available food. They are easily digestible and suitable for all age groups. There are many different types of eggs.

- **Free-range eggs:** from birds that are able to roam free in large barns and are permitted outdoors for at least part of the day.

- **Barn eggs:** from birds that are able to roam free in large barns.

- **Cage eggs:** from birds kept in enriched cages with slanted floors that allow eggs to roll out onto a conveyor belt.

- **Organic eggs:** from birds that are fed special organic feed that is not treated with chemical pesticides or fertilisers. The birds are also not treated with growth hormones or given antibiotics.

- **Omega-3 eggs:** from birds that are fed a diet high in omega-3. Omega-3 sources may include linseed or seaweed.

▲ Hens in enriched cages

▲ Omega-3 eggs

Structure of eggs

Eggs are composed of three main parts: shell, white and yolk.

- **Shell (10%):** a hard protective layer composed mainly of calcium carbonate. Shells are inedible and porous. They vary in colour, depending on the breed of bird that laid the egg. The colour does not affect the egg's nutritional value or quality. On the inside of the shell is a thin membrane that encloses the white and yolk and leaves an air space at the wider end of the egg.

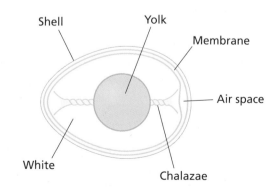

Shell   Yolk

Membrane

Air space

White

Chalazae

- **White (60%):** a viscous, colourless liquid that surrounds the yolk. It is composed of the proteins ovalbumin and globulin; minerals, vitamins and water.
- **Yolk (30%):** a viscous dark-yellow centre that is held in place by a string-like structure called a chalazae. It is the most nutritious part of the egg. The yolk is composed of the proteins vitellin and livetin, saturated fat, cholesterol, lecithin (emulsifier), minerals, vitamins and water.

Did you know

A chicken egg has more than 7,000 pores (holes) in its shell.

Average nutritional composition of eggs

Nutrient	Whole egg	White	Yolk
Proteins	13%	11%	16%
Fat	12%	0.2%	32%
Carbohydrates	0%	0%	0%
Vitamins	A, B group, E, K	B group	A, B group, D, E, K
Minerals	Calcium, phosphorus, zinc, sulfur, iron	Calcium, phosphorus, zinc, sulfur	Calcium, phosphorus, zinc, sulfur, iron
Water	74%	87%	49%

Nutritional value of eggs

Proteins	• An excellent source high biological value (HBV) protein • The main proteins present are ovalbumin and globulin in the white and vitellin and livetin in the yolk
Fat	• Saturated fat is present in the yolk. It is dispersed as a fine emulsion due to the presence of lecithin. • The yolk contains cholesterol • The white is fat-free
Carbohydrates	• Lack carbohydrates, for this reason eggs are usually served with a carbohydrate-rich food, e.g. bread
Vitamins	• A source of B-group vitamins, particularly thiamine (B1), riboflavin (B2), niacin (B3) and cobalamin (B12) • Yolks are a good source of vitamins A, D, E and K. Vitamin A (beta-carotene) gives the yolk its colour. • Eggs lack vitamin C
Minerals	• A good source of calcium, phosphorus, zinc and sulfur • Non-haem iron is present in the yolk
Water	• High water content, with the majority found in the white

EGGS

Describe the nutritive value of eggs. (20) **OL**

In relation to eggs explain **each** of the following:
- albumin
- lecithin. (6) **HL**

Set out the results of a study you have carried out on eggs. Refer to nutritional significance. (8) **HL**

👍Tip!

If nutritional value of eggs appears on the examination paper remember to include the function of each nutrient in your answer.

Dietetic value of eggs

- Eggs are an excellent source of HBV protein, which assists with growth and repair. This makes them an excellent meat alternative in the diets of vegetarians and a valuable food in the diets of children, teenagers and pregnant women.
- Eggs are low in kilocalories (approximately 147 kcal per egg), making them an ideal food for individuals following calorie-controlled diets.
- Eggs are a versatile food suited to many different cooking methods and culinary uses, e.g. baking, sauces and batters.
- Eggs are inexpensive and they cook very quickly, minimising energy costs, making them an economical food.
- Egg yolks are high in saturated fat and cholesterol, so they should be restricted in the diets of people with high cholesterol and at risk of coronary heart disease (CHD). Eating the whites only is a good alternative.
- Eggs lack carbohydrates and vitamin C, so they should be combined with foods rich in these to balance the diet.

 Set out the results of a study you have carried out on eggs. Refer to contribution to the diet. (8) **HL**

Guidelines for buying eggs

- Buy eggs from a retailer with a strict food hygiene and safety policy to ensure any eggs being sold are safe and fit for consumption.
- Check the best before date. After this date eggs may be unsafe to eat, as over time they become stale.
- Buy eggs in small amounts. Buying too many can lead to food waste, as they have a short shelf life.
- Buy eggs with the Bord Bia Quality Mark. This assures the consumer that best practices were implemented at all stages of egg production, which reduces food safety risks.
- Avoid purchasing eggs with cracked shells, as this will quicken the rate of spoilage.
- Ensure eggs feel heavy for their size. If an egg seems light it could be due to a large air space, meaning the egg is stale.

Guidelines for storing eggs

- Store eggs in a fridge at 4°C, as room temperature speeds up bacterial growth, increasing the rate of spoilage.
- Store eggs away from strong-smelling foods, e.g. fish, as the porous shell can absorb odours.
- Ensure eggs are stored with the pointed end downwards to prevent the chalazae from breaking and the egg yolk becoming damaged.
- Leftover whites should be refrigerated in an airtight container for two to four days. Leftover yolks should be refrigerated in water for two to four days to prevent drying out.
- Minimise the amount of time eggs are in storage. Use within the best before date.

Labelling regulations for egg boxes and eggs

Box labelling

Under European Union legislation the following information must be clear and legible on an egg box:

- name and address of packer or seller
- egg packaging centre code
- number of eggs in the pack
- class/quality of the eggs, e.g. 'Class A'
- date of minimum durability, e.g. best before date
- production/rearing method, e.g. organic or free-range
- weight, e.g. extra large (XL), large (L), medium (M) or small (S)
- storage instructions advising to keep eggs chilled after purchase.

Egg labelling

EU legislation also requires that each individual egg for retail sale be stamped with a code to ensure full traceability of the egg to the farm. The code stamped on each individual egg must carry:

- a number to distinguish production/rearing method, e.g. 0 (organic), 1 (free-range), 2 (barn), 3 (caged)
- two letters denoting the country of origin, e.g. IE for Ireland
- a code containing a letter and a number to identify the county and producer the egg came from, e.g. D indicates Cork and 68 indicates the registered producer. This appears as D68 on the egg
- the date of minimum durability (best before date), e.g. 07/04 or 7/APR.

 Explain how food labelling on eggs and egg cartons is beneficial as a source of consumer information. (12) **OL**

Testing the freshness of eggs

As an egg becomes stale its mass decreases. This occurs as the water inside the egg evaporates through the pores in the shell, causing the yolk and white to shrink. The air sac increases in size by filling with air and bacteria, reducing the weight further. This decrease in weight will cause an egg to float when placed in water, so it is a simple test to check for freshness.

Fresh   1 week old   Stale (2-3 weeks old)   Very old

▲ Egg flotation chart

Guidelines for preparing eggs

- Remove eggs from the fridge for one hour before using in order to reduce the risk of the shell cracking during boiling and curdling during cooking. This will also help the eggs to trap more air when being whisked for meringues and sponge cakes.

Culinary uses of eggs

- **Bind:** eggs hold ingredients together to prevent them falling apart, e.g. burgers and fish cakes.

- **Thicken:** eggs change the consistency of a sauce or dish as they coagulate when heated, causing thickening, e.g. custards and quiches.

- **Whole food:** eggs can be eaten on their own or cooked in a variety of ways, e.g. boiled or fried.

- **Emulsify:** eggs enable immiscible liquids, e.g. oil and vinegar, to mix and form an emulsion, e.g. mayonnaise.

- **Garnish:** eggs can be used to add decoration to make a food more visually appealing, e.g. nisoise salad.

- **Glaze:** eggs form a shiny coating on food, giving an attractive finish when baked, e.g. scones and pastry.

- **Aerate:** eggs trap air when whisked, assisting aeration, e.g. sponge cakes and meringue.

- **Coat:** eggs enable a coating to stick to foods, e.g. breadcrumbs on poultry or fish.

- **Enrich:** eggs can make a food taste richer or add to the nutritional value, e.g. rice pudding and mashed potatoes.

▲ Glazing pastry

REMEMBER IT!
'**BTW EGG**s are **ACE**!'
Bind, **T**hicken, **W**hole food, **E**mulsify, **G**arnish, **G**laze, **A**erate, **C**oat, **E**nrich.

? Name **three** uses of eggs in food preparation and give an example of each. (6) **OL**

Effects of cooking on eggs

- Protein coagulates, whites coagulate at 60°C and yolks coagulate at 68°C.

- Egg whites change colour, from translucent to opaque.

- Bacteria are destroyed.

- Some B-group vitamins, particularly thiamine, are lost as they are not heat stable.

- Eggs can curdle if cooked at very high temperatures or overcooked. This causes egg proteins to clump together and squeeze out water, forming lumps of protein and a watery liquid.

- Eggs become tough and difficult to digest if overcooked. The egg yolk becomes dry and crumbly and the egg white becomes rubbery.

▲ Overcooked eggs

- A reaction between iron and sulfur in an egg causes a green ring to form around the egg yolk if it is overcooked.

? List two effects of heat on eggs. (2) **OL**

Properties of eggs

The three main properties of eggs relevant to food preparation are aeration, coagulation and emulsification.

Aeration

When eggs are whisked, protein chains unfold and air bubbles form. The protein chains entrap air, creating a foam. Whisking also creates an amount of heat that begins to set the egg albumin. This forms a temporary foam. It will collapse after a while unless it is heated to coagulate and set as a permanent foam.

🍴 **Culinary application:**
  meringues, sponges, soufflés.

Coagulation

When eggs are heated, protein chains unfold, straighten and bond together around small pockets of water, causing coagulation. Egg whites coagulate and change from translucent to opaque at 60°C and egg yolks coagulate at 68°C. Overcooking causes proteins to clump together and squeeze out water, forming lumps of protein and a watery liquid. This is known as curdling.

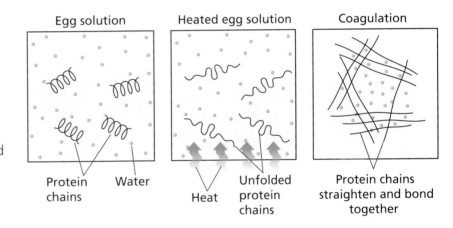

🍴 **Culinary application:**
  cooking, e.g. fried, boiled and poached eggs; binding, e.g. beef burgers and fish cakes; thickening, e.g. custard and hollandaise sauce; and glazing, e.g. pastry and scones.

Emulsification

Lecithin is a natural emulsifier present in egg yolk. It has the ability to join two immiscible liquids, e.g. oil and water, as it has a hydrophilic (water-loving) head and a hydrophobic (water-hating) tail. The hydrophilic head attaches to the water and the hydrophobic tail attaches to oil, preventing them from separating. This creates a permanent emulsion.

🍴 **Culinary application:** mayonnaise and vinaigrettes (oil and vinegar), cakes (fat and sugar), hollandaise sauce (butter and vinegar).

❓ Set out the results of a study you have carried out on eggs. Refer to properties and related culinary uses. (16) **HL**

EGGS

Egg Quality Assurance Scheme (EQAS)

If eggs bear the Bord Bia Quality Mark it tells the consumer that the eggs are quality assured as they have been produced with the highest level of care and attention from primary production through to packaging.

To achieve this, the producer and packager must be certified members of the Bord Bia Quality Assurance Scheme and work in partnership to provide customers with quality-assured eggs.

For a producer to obtain the Bord Bia Quality Mark their farm must be audited by Bord Bia to ensure:

- participation in routine salmonella testing of the hens to prevent the risk of salmonellosis in humans. All hens laying eggs must be certified salmonella-free
- accurate records are kept on the origin, sex, age, breed, movement and vetinary treatments of all hens to ensure eggs are fully traceable
- all feed given to hens is heat-treated to reduce bacterial contamination.

For a packaging plant to obtain the Bord Bia Quality Mark they must be audited to ensure:

- implementation of a thorough sanitation and pest-control programme
- staff who operate or monitor any critical control point (CCP) receive Hazard Analysis and Critical Control Point (HACCP) and food safety training.

▲ Free-range eggs with the Bord Bia Quality Mark

▲ Egg packaging plant

? Explain how quality is assured in egg production in order to minimise food safety risks. (10) **HL**

MILK AND MILK PRODUCTS

What you will learn:

- Types of cow's milk
- Classification of cream, butter, cheese and yoghurt
- Average nutritional composition and nutritional value of milk, cream, butter, cheese and yoghurt
- Dietetic value of milk, cheese and yoghurt
- Milk processing
- Production of cream, butter and cheese
- Guidelines for buying and storing milk, cream, butter, cheese and yoghurt

- Spoilage of milk
- Culinary uses of milk, cream, butter, cheese and yoghurt
- Guidelines for heating and effects of heating on milk
- Controlling milk quality in Ireland
- Guidelines for preparing cream
- Guidelines for cooking with cream, butter and yoghurt
- Effects of cooking on cheese
- Cream substitutes

MILK

Milk is considered an optimal or complete food, as it is easily digestible and contains all six nutrients, with the exception of iron and vitamin C. Milk is the raw material used to manufacture other dairy products such as cream, butter, yoghurt and cheese. The most common milk sold in Ireland is milk from the dairy cow.

GO FIGURE 123

Ireland has the third highest consumption of liquid milk in the world, at 130 litres per person per annum. This compares to China where only nine litres per person are consumed annually.

Types of cow's milk

- **Whole milk:** contains approximately 4% saturated fat and is rich in calcium and fat-soluble vitamins A and D.
- **Low-fat milk (semi-skimmed milk):** contains approximately 1% saturated fat. Fat-soluble vitamins A and D are removed.
- **Skimmed milk:** contains approximately 0.3% saturated fat. Fat-soluble vitamins A and D are removed.
- **Buttermilk:** the sour liquid that remains after the fat in milk has been churned to form butter. It is commonly used in baking.

Average nutritional composition of milk

Nutrient	Whole milk	Low-fat milk	Skimmed milk
Proteins	3.4%	3.4%	3.5%
Fat	4%	1%	0.3%
Carbohydrates	4.8%	4.5%	4.6%
Vitamins	A, B group, D	B group	B group
Minerals	Calcium, phosphorus, potassium, magnesium	Calcium, phosphorus, potassium, magnesium	Calcium, phosphorus, potassium, magnesium
Water	87%	89%	91%

> **?** Name **two** of the main nutrients found in skimmed milk. (2) **OL**

Nutritional value of milk

Tip!
If nutritional value of milk appears on the examination paper remember to include the function of each nutrient in your answer.

Proteins	• An excellent source of easily digestible, high biological value (HBV) protein • The main proteins present are caseinogen, lactalbumin and lactoglobulin
Fat	• Saturated fat is present in small droplets dispersed throughout milk, making it easy to digest • The amount of fat present depends on the type of milk
Carbohydrates	• Contains carbohydrates in the form of the disaccharide lactose (sugar) • Lacks dietary fibre and starch
Vitamins	• A good source of vitamin A. Contains a small amount of vitamin D. Vitamins A and D are removed when fat is skimmed from milk. • A valuable source of B-group vitamins, particularly thiamine (B1), riboflavin (B2) and niacin (B3) • Lacks vitamin C, as the small amount present is lost during processing
Minerals	• An excellent source of calcium • Some phosphorus is present • Contains trace amounts of magnesium and potassium • Lacks iron
Water	• High water content

Dietetic value of milk

- Milk is an excellent source of easily digestible HBV protein that assists with growth and repair. This makes it a valuable food in the diets of children, teenagers and pregnant women.
- Milk is an excellent source of calcium, which is vital for strong bones, especially among children and adolescents.
- Individuals with high cholesterol or on calorie-controlled diets should choose low-fat or skimmed milk as these have a reduced saturated fat content.
- Milk is available in a variety of types, e.g. skimmed, flavoured and fortified, to suit varying tastes and dietary needs.
- Milk is a versatile food suited to many different culinary uses, e.g. drinks, baking and sauces.
- Milk is inexpensive, making it an economical food.
- Milk lacks starch, dietary fibre, iron and vitamin C, so it should be combined with foods rich in these to balance the diet.

> **?** Give an account of the dietetic value of semi-skimmed milk. (15) **OL**
>
> Give an account of the nutritive value **and** the dietetic value of milk. (20) **OL**

Milk processing

Homogenisation

Process	Milk is heated to 60°C. It is then forced under pressure through a machine with tiny holes that break up the large fat globules and disperse them evenly throughout the milk.
Effects	• Improves the texture and flavour of the milk (makes it creamier), as smaller fat globules are evenly dispersed throughout the milk and do not rise to the top as cream

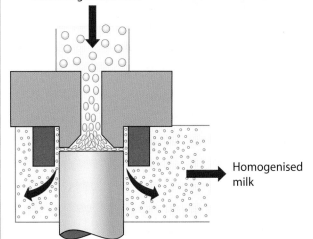

Unhomogenised milk

Homogenised milk

Pasteurisation

Process	Milk is heated to 72°C for 25 seconds and then cooled quickly to 10°C.
Effects	• **Pathogenic** bacteria are destroyed • Shelf life is extended (approximately six to eight days) • Loss of vitamin C and vitamin B1 (thiamine) • No noticeable change in flavour

Lit'Hit

Pathogenic means disease-causing.

Sterilisation

Process	Milk is homogenised. It is then sealed into glass bottles and heated to 110°C for 30 minutes, then cooled.
Effects	• Pathogenic bacteria are destroyed • Shelf life is extended (approximately six weeks if unopened) • Loss of vitamin C and B-group vitamins • Flavour is slightly altered, as lactose becomes sweeter on heating

Ultra heat treatment (UHT)

UHT milk is also known as long-life milk. It is used on aircraft and in hotel rooms.

Process	Milk is heated to 132°C for one to two seconds and then cooled quickly to 10°C. It is then packaged in sterile containers.
Effects	• Pathogenic bacteria are destroyed • Shelf life is extended (approximately six months if unopened) and it does not require refrigeration • Loss of vitamin C and B-group vitamins • Flavour is slightly altered, as lactose becomes sweeter on heating

Condensed milk

Sweetened, concentrated milk used for making caramel.

Process	Milk is homogenised, pasteurised and 15% sugar is added. It is then evaporated to one-third of its volumne, cooled and sealed into cans.
Effects	• Pathogenic bacteria are destroyed • Shelf life is extended (approximately one year if unopened) • Loss of vitamin C and B-group vitamins • Flavour is altered, as lactose becomes sweeter on heating and sugar is added • Increased kilocalorie and carbohydrate content due to sugar added

Evaporated milk

Unsweetened, concentrated milk. Mainly used as a cream substitute.

Process	Milk is pasteurised, evaporated to half its volume then homogenised. It is then sealed into cans and sterilised at 115°C for 20 minutes.
Effects	• Pathogenic bacteria are destroyed • Shelf life is extended (approximately one year if unopened) • Loss of vitamin C and B-group vitamins • Flavour is slightly altered, as lactose becomes sweeter on heating

Dried milk

Process	Milk is homogenised and pasteurised. It is then evaporated to 60% of its volume and dried to form a powdered milk. This can be done by either roller drying or spray drying.	
	Roller drying	**Spray drying**
	Milk is poured onto heated rotating metal rollers that dry the liquid milk to a powder. The milk powder is then scraped off the rollers, cooled and packaged in airtight containers. 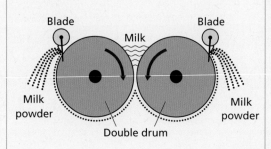	Milk is sprayed into a hot air chamber (165°C) that instantly evaporates the water in the milk, forming a powder that falls to the bottom of the chamber. The milk powder is cooled and packaged in airtight containers. 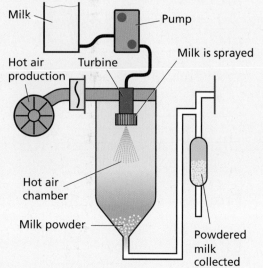
Effects	• Roller-dried milk does not reconstitute easily when stirred with water	• Spray-dried milk reconstitutes easily when stirred with water
	• Pathogenic bacteria are destroyed • Some loss of B-group vitamins and amino acids • Long shelf life due to water extraction (2–10 years)	• Does not taste the same as fresh milk

Name **three** different methods of processing used to make milk safe for consumption. (6) **OL**

State **two** effects of ultra-heat treatment (UHT) on milk. (4) **HL**

State the function of **each** of the following in relation to the processing of milk.
- Homogenisation
- Sterilisation (6) **HL**

Describe **one** process used by manufacturers to prolong the shelf life of milk. In your answer refer to:
- name of process
- how the process is carried out
- the effect of the process on the nutritive value of milk. (12) **HL**

Guidelines for buying milk

- Buy milk from a retailer that has a strict food hygiene and safety policy to ensure any milk being sold is safe and fit for consumption.
- Check the use-by date. After this date milk may be unsafe to consume as bacteria multiply rapidly in high-protein liquid foods.
- Buy milk in small amounts. Buying too much can lead to food waste, as milk has a short shelf life.
- Ensure packaging is properly sealed. Damaged or incorrectly sealed packaging will quicken milk spoilage.
- Buy near the end of the shopping trip to minimise the amount of time milk spends at room temperature (optimum temperature for bacterial growth) before being returned to a fridge.

Guidelines for storing milk

- Store milk in a fridge at 4°C as room temperature can speed up bacterial growth, increasing the rate of spoilage.
- Avoid mixing milks with different use-by dates, as this can cause milk to spoil quicker.
- Keep milk covered and away from strong-smelling foods, such as blue cheese, to prevent it absorbing odours.
- Minimise the amount of time milk is in storage. Use within two to three days.

Spoilage of milk

Spoilage of milk occurs when naturally present lactic acid bacteria breaks down the lactose in milk, forming lactic acid. This causes milk to develop an unpleasant taste and to curdle (form clumps), as the protein caseinogen separates from the liquid part of the milk. This occurs naturally in milk over time, even when stored in the fridge.

Milk may also spoil during food preparation or cooking due to:
- the addition of an acid, e.g. lemon juice
- the addition of enzymes, e.g. rennet is added to milk in cheese-making
- heat, e.g. adding milk to very hot coffee.

▶ Spoiled milk

Culinary uses of milk

- **Drinks:** e.g. milkshakes, lattes.
- **Baking:** e.g. scones, bread.
- **Puddings and desserts:** e.g. bread and butter pudding, crème caramel.
- **Sauces:** e.g. custard, white sauce.
- **Batters:** e.g. **clafoutis**, Yorkshire puddings.
- **Soups:** e.g. cream of chicken soup, mushroom soup.

> **Lit Hit**
> Clafoutis is a type of flan made of fruit baked in a sweet batter.

Guidelines for heating milk

- Keep a watchful eye on milk while heating, as it can quickly boil over.
- Avoid overheating, as it may curdle.

Effects of heating on milk

- Protein coagulates, creating a skin on the surface of milk.
- Bacteria are destroyed.
- Flavour is slightly altered, as lactose becomes sweeter on heating.
- B-group vitamins, particularly thiamine, and vitamin C are lost as they are not heat stable.

▲ Clafoutis

Controlling milk quality in Ireland

The Department of Agriculture, Food and the Marine enforce food safety by implementing measures within the dairy sector throughout Ireland. They ensure that milk purchased is fresh, hygienic and free from disease by:

- ensuring that dairy farms that supply milk to the public are registered with the Department of Agriculture, Food and the Marine
- inspecting herds and milk-producing premises on dairy farms
- testing cattle routinely for diseases such as tuberculosis (TB), as these are easily transmitted to humans from milk
- testing milk routinely for bacterial contamination and residues of antibiotics
- ensuring dairy farms observe strict codes of hygiene when transporting, processing and storing milk.

The majority of milk for sale to the general public in Ireland is heat treated, however raw (unpasteurised) milk can be purchased.

▲ Dairy farm inspection

CREAM

Cream is the fatty liquid that rises to the top of milk. It has a fat content of 18–48%.
It is an oil in water emulsion.

Classification of cream

- **Single/pouring cream:** 18% fat, cannot be whipped.
- **Double cream:** 48% fat.
- **Standard/whipping cream:** 38% fat.
- **Low-fat cream:** 12% fat.
- **Ultra heat treated (UHT) cream (aerosol):** 35% fat. Heated to 132°C for one to two seconds and cooled to 10°C to extend its shelf life. Lasts for several months without refrigeration.
- **Sour cream:** 18% fat. It has a culture of bacteria added that thickens the cream and gives it a sour, tangy taste.

Average nutritional composition of standard/whipping cream

Protein	Fat	Carbohydrates	Vitamins	Minerals	Water
2%	38%	3%	A, B group, D	Calcium	55%

Nutritional value of cream

Proteins	• A small amount of HBV protein is present
Fat	• A source of saturated fat • The amount of fat present depends on the type of cream
Carbohydrates	• Contains a small amount of carbohydrates in the form of the disaccharide lactose (sugar) • Lacks dietary fibre and starch
Vitamins	• Contains small amounts of B-group vitamins • Contains small amounts of vitamins A and D • Lacks vitamin C
Minerals	• A source of calcium • Lacks iron
Water	• Water content varies depending on the type of cream • The higher the water content the less fat present

🖒Tip!

If nutritional value of cream appears on the examination paper remember to include the function of each nutrient in your answer.

Did you know

Whipped cream that has been sweetened or flavoured, e.g. with vanilla, is called chantilly cream.

Production of cream

1. **Warmed:** milk is warmed to 50°C to make its separation easier.

2. **Separated:** cream is separated from milk using centrifugal force. This spins the milk at high speed to separate the upper cream layer from the bottom layer, which is sold as skimmed milk.

3. **Heat treated:** cream is heat treated by pasteurisation, sterilisation or UHT, depending on the type of cream being made.

4. **Packaged and labelled:** cream is packaged in containers of varying size, e.g. 250 ml or 500 ml, made of varying materials, e.g. plastic or metal. The containers are labelled with details including the type of cream, ingredients, storage instructions, allergy advice and nutritional information.

> **REMEMBER IT!**
> **'Whipping Should Happen Promptly!'**
> **W**armed, **S**eparated, **H**eat treated, **P**ackaged and labelled.

Guidelines for buying and storing cream

See guidelines for buying milk and guidelines for storing milk on page 121.

Culinary uses of cream

- **Baking:** e.g. butterfly fairy cakes, sponge cakes.
- **Savoury dishes:** e.g. beef stroganoff, pasta carbonara.
- **Soups:** e.g. cream of vegetable soup.
- **Desserts:** e.g. panna cotta, chocolate ganache tart.
- **Garnish:** e.g. soups (used to create a swirl), cakes (piped on top).

Guidelines for preparing and cooking with cream

- Avoid over-whipping cream as it can separate into butter and buttermilk.
- Avoid overheating cream as it can curdle.

Cream substitutes

For those trying to reduce their saturated fat intake, e.g. those on calorie-controlled diets, there are many cream substitutes that can be used in cooking.

- **Crème fraîche (30% fat):** a type of thick cream made from double cream and buttermilk, sour cream or yoghurt.
- **Fromage frais (3–8% fat):** a soft cheese made with whole or skimmed milk and cream.
- **Natural yoghurt**
- **Greek yoghurt**

➜ For more information on **natural yoghurt** and **Greek yoghurt** see page 130.

▲ Panna cotta

BUTTER

Butter is made from cream, the fatty liquid that rises to the top of milk. It is a water in oil emulsion. By law, butter must contain at least 80% fat. The remaining 20% is made up of water and milk solids.

Classification of butter

- **Salted butter:** 82% fat.
- **Unsalted butter:** 82 % fat.
- **Low-fat butter:** 40% fat.
- **Spreadable butter:** 82% fat.

GO FIGURE

It takes 10 litres of milk to make a pound of butter (454 g).

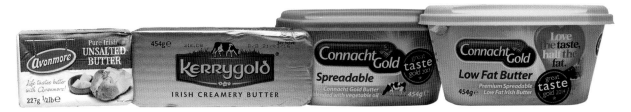

Average nutritional composition of butter

Proteins	Fat	Carbohydrates	Vitamins	Minerals	Water
1%	82%	0.5%	A, D, E	Calcium, phosphorus, sodium chloride	15%

Nutritional value of butter

Proteins	• A small amount of HBV protein is present
Fat	• A source of saturated fat • Butyric acid is one of the main fatty acids present • Contains cholesterol
Carbohydrates	• Contains trace amounts of carbohydrates in the form of the disaccharide lactose (sugar) • Lacks dietary fibre and starch
Vitamins	• A source of vitamin A • Contains trace amounts of vitamins E and D • Lacks vitamin C
Minerals	• Contains trace amounts of calcium and phosphorus • If salt is added, sodium chloride is present. This acts as a preservative. • Lacks iron
Water	• Has a low water content • By law, butter must not contain over 16% water

🖒 **Tip!**

If nutritional value of butter appears on the examination paper remember to include the function of each nutrient in your answer.

Did you know

Butter produced during the summer months contains more vitamin D as cows are exposed to sunlight.

MILK AND MILK PRODUCTS

Production of butter

1. **Pasteurised:** cream is pasteurised.

2. **Chilled:** cream is chilled at 5°C.

3. **Churned:** cream is churned until the fat particles **coalesce** and form butter. This floats in the liquid part of the cream (known as buttermilk).

4. **Drained:** buttermilk is drained off and sold separately for use in baking.

5. **Addition of salt:** butter is washed and 1.5% salt is worked into it.

6. **Weighed:** butter is weighed into retail-size portions, e.g. 227 g or 454 g.

7. **Packaged and labelled:** butter is packaged in varying materials, e.g. plastic or foil. The packaging is labelled with details including the type of butter, ingredients, storage instructions, allergy advice and nutritional information.

> **Lit Hit**
> Coalesce means clump together.

Did you know ?

Approximately 200,000 tonnes of butter were produced in Ireland in 2015.

▲ Butter being packaged

Guidelines for buying and storing butter

• Keep butter covered and refrigerated to prevent oxidative rancidity.

→ For more information on guidelines for buying and storing butter see guidelines for buying milk and guidelines for storing milk on page 121.

Culinary uses of butter

• **Baking:** e.g. shortbread biscuits, flapjacks.

• **Sauces:** e.g. Béarnaise sauce, hollandaise sauce.

• **Desserts:** e.g. apple tart, vanilla cheesecake.

Guidelines for cooking with butter

• Avoid overheating butter as it will decompose. This can cause the fat to reach smoke point and flash point.

▶ Cheesecake

CHEESE

Cheese is a fermented dairy product made from milk by the action of bacteria and enzymes. It is produced in a wide range of flavours and textures, with over 400 varieties of cheese worldwide. Various types of milk are used to make cheese, including milk from cows, sheep, goats and buffalo.

Classification of cheese

The main way cheese is classified is according to its method of production.

• **Hard cheese:** has a dense texture with a low moisture content of 30–40%, e.g. Cheddar, Emmental and Parmesan.

- **Semi-hard cheese:** has a firm texture that is easily sliced, with a moisture content ranging from 40-50%, e.g. Edam, Gouda, Monterey Jack and halloumi.
- **Soft cheese:** has a thin skin and a creamy centre, with a moisture content of 50–80%, e.g. mozzarella, feta, Camembert and cottage cheese.
- **Processed cheese:** made from one or more types of cheese that have been heated and blended with other ingredients including flavourings, colourings and emulsifiers, e.g. Cheestrings, cheese slices, Babybel and Calvita.
- **Mould cheese (blue-veined cheese):** ripened with cultures of the mould *Penicillium*, e.g. Stilton, Roquefort, Danish blue and Gorgonzola.

> **?** Name three classes of cheese and give an example of each. (6) **OL**
>
> Classify cheese and give an example of each class. (6) **HL**

Average nutritional composition of cheese

Nutrient	Cheddar cheese	Cottage cheese
Proteins	26%	10%
Fat	35%	6%
Carbohydrates	0%	3%
Vitamins	A, B group, D	A, B group
Minerals	Calcium	Calcium
Water	36%	80%

Nutritional value of cheese

> **👍Tip!**
> If nutritional value of cheese appears on the examination paper remember to include the function of each nutrient in your answer.

Proteins	• An excellent source of HBV protein • Casein is the main protein present • Hard cheese contains more protein than soft cheese
Carbohydrates	• Lacks carbohydrates, as the lactose (sugar) in milk is converted to lactic acid during cheese production. For this reason cheese is usually served with a carbohydrate-rich food, e.g. bread.
Fat	• A source of saturated fat • The amount of saturated fat depends on the type of milk used to make the cheese. Hard cheese contains more saturated fat than soft cheese, due to a lower water content.
Vitamins	• A good source of vitamins A and D • Lacks vitamin C • A source of the B-group vitamin riboflavin (B2)
Minerals	• An excellent source of calcium • Salt is added during manufacture, so sodium chloride is present. This acts as a preservative.
Water	• The water content varies depending on the type of cheese • The higher the water content the less fat present

Dietetic value of cheese

- Cheese is an excellent source of HBV protein, which assists with growth and repair. This makes it a valuable food in the diets of in children, teenagers and pregnant women.
- Cheese is an excellent source of calcium, which is vital for forming strong bones, especially in children and adolescents.
- Cheese is available in a variety of types and forms, e.g. fresh and processed, to suit different tastes and add variety to the diet.
- Cheese is a versatile food suited to many different culinary uses, e.g. salads, sauces and desserts.
- Some cheeses are inexpensive, e.g. Cheddar, making cheese an economical food. Cheese requires no cooking, eliminating energy costs.
- As cheese can be high in saturated fat it should be restricted in the diets of individuals with high cholesterol and those on calorie-controlled diets. Low-fat and soft cheeses are a good alternative.
- Pregnant women should avoid soft cheeses, as they can contain the food-poisoning bacteria listeria that causes an infection called listeriosis.
- Cheese lacks carbohydrates and vitamin C, so it should be combined with foods rich in these to balance the diet.

Production of cheese

1. **Pasteurised:** raw milk is pasteurised at 72°C for 25 seconds.
2. **Starter culture added:** a starter culture of lactic acid bacteria is added. This changes lactose to lactic acid, which acts as a preservative and adds flavour.
3. **Rennet added:** milk is heated to 30°C and rennet is added. Rennet contains the enzyme rennin that changes the protein caseinogen to casein. This coagulates the milk.
4. **Curds and whey:** the mixture is left for 35–40 minutes until it separates into curds (solid) and whey (liquid).
5. **Cut:** curds are cut to release more whey.
6. **Draining:** whey is drained off. At this point cottage cheese is produced.
7. **Scalding:** curds are heated to 35–40°C for 40–45 minutes and stirred continuously to release more whey and achieve the correct consistency. This process is called scalding.
8. **Cheddaring:** curds are cut into blocks and piled on top of each other to drain more whey. This process is known as cheddaring.
9. **Curd chips:** curds are cut into curd chips by a mill.
10. **Salt added:** 2% salt is added to add flavour and preserve the cheese.

⬆Tip!

Cheese is an example of an added-value food.

Did you know ?

Traditionally rennet came from the stomachs of calves, lambs or goats. Nowadays, it also comes from plant and mould sources. This makes cheese suitable for vegetarians.

▲ Curds and whey

▲ Cheddaring and curd chips

11. **Pressed and ripened:** curds are pressed into moulds. The longer the curds are pressed the harder the cheese. Pressed curds are sprayed with hot water to form a protective rind (skin) on the cheese. The cheese is removed from the mould, date stamped and stored to ripen and mature for 3–15 months. Ripening develops the characteristic flavour, texture and smell of a cheese due to the action of enzymes and bacteria. The longer a cheese is left to ripen the stronger the flavour.

▲ Cheese ripening

12. **Packaged and labelled:** cheese is graded according to quality. It is cut to retail size, e.g. 200 g or 500 g, and packaged in varying materials, e.g. plastic or waxed paper. The packaging is labelled with details including the type of cheese, ingredients, storage instructions, allergy advice and nutritional information.

REMEMBER IT!

'**P**erhaps **S**omeone **R**eliable **C**an **C**hoose **D**elicious **S**crumptious **C**heese, **C**olm's **S**tarving! **P**lease, **P**lease!'
Pasteurised, **S**tarter culture added, **R**ennet added, **C**urds and whey, **C**ut, **D**rained, **S**calded, **C**heddaring, **C**urd chips, **S**alt added, **P**ressed and ripened, **P**ackaged and labelled.

❓ State the role of each of the following in relation to the processing of cheese.
- Lactic acid bacteria
- Rennet (6) **HL**

Write a profile of an 'added value' food you have studied. Give details of each of the following:
- stages of production
- labelling. (26) **HL**
- packaging

Guidelines for buying cheese

- Buy cheese from a retailer that has a strict food hygiene and safety policy to ensure any cheese being sold is safe and fit for consumption.
- Check the use-by date on pre-packaged cheese. After this date cheese may be unsafe to eat.
- Buy cheese in small amounts. Buying too much can lead to food waste, as cheese has a short shelf life.
- Ensure packaging is properly sealed. Damaged or incorrectly sealed-packaging will quicken spoilage.

Guidelines for storing cheese

- Store cheese in a fridge at 4°C and away from heat and light to slow down spoilage.
- Leave cheese in its original wrapping until ready to use. Opened cheese should be sealed well in its original packaging or in polyethylene plastic ziplock bags. Mould cheese (blue veined) should be kept in a box, as it requires moisture and air for mould growth.
- Minimise the amount of time cheese is in storage. Use fresh cheese within two to three days and pre-packaged cheese before its use-by date.

MILK AND MILK PRODUCTS

Culinary uses of cheese

- **Savoury dishes:** e.g. pizza, macaroni and cheese.
- **Baking:** e.g. cheese pastry, cheese scones.
- **Salads:** e.g. caesar salad, Greek salad.
- **Sauces:** e.g. cauliflower gratin.
- **Snacks:** e.g. cheese and crackers.
- **Desserts:** e.g. cheesecake, tiramisu.
- **Dips:** e.g. Gruyère dip, Stilton dip.
- **Sandwiches:** e.g. toasted cheese sandwich, croque monsieur.

▲ Tiramisu

Effects of cooking on cheese

- Protein coagulates, causing cheese to shrink.
- Fat melts. It can be seen as an oily film on the surface of some cooked foods, e.g. lasagne.
- Colour changes as the cheese browns.
- Cheese becomes tough and indigestible if overcooked. It should be added near the end of the cooking time.

? List **two** effects of cooking on cheese. (4) **OL**

▲ Cooked cheese

YOGHURT

Yoghurt is a fermented dairy product made from milk with the addition of a bacterial culture. The most common yoghurts sold in Ireland are made from cow's milk; however, other milks, e.g. goat's milk and soya milk, are becoming more commonly used in yoghurt production.

Classification of yoghurt

- **Set yoghurt:** fermented in individual yoghurt pots that may have fruit or flavourings at the base.
- **Stirred yoghurt:** fermented in bulk, then placed in individual yoghurt pots. It may have fruit or flavourings stirred in.

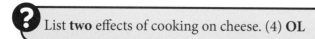

- **Frozen yoghurt:** made by blending sugar or sweeteners, stabilisers, emulsifiers and flavours, then freezing.
- **Drinking yoghurt:** made by diluting stirred yoghurt and mixing it with fruit juices and sugar or sweeteners.
- **Natural yoghurt:** has no added flavours or sugar or sweeteners, giving it a slightly acidic, tart flavour.
- **Greek yoghurt:** has a thicker and creamier texture than stirred yoghurt due to the addition of milk solids and more whey being drained off.
- **Bio yoghurt:** has probiotics (live bacteria), e.g. *lactobacillus acidophilus*, added to aid digestion and strengthen the body's immune system.

? State the benefit to the consumer of adding bacterial cultures, such as acidophilus, to bio yoghurt. (3) **OL**

Average nutritional composition of stirred full-fat yoghurt

Proteins	Fat	Carbohydrates	Vitamins	Minerals	Water
6%	3%	8%	A, B group, D	Calcium, potassium, phosphorus, magnesium	82%

Nutritional value of yoghurt

Proteins	• Contains a small amount of HBV protein • Some yoghurts, e.g. Greek yoghurt, contain more HBV protein, due to the addition of extra milk solids
Fat	• A source of saturated fat • The amount of saturated fat depends on the type of milk used to make the yoghurt
Carbohydrates	• Contains carbohydrates in the form of the disaccharide lactose (sugar) • Can also be high in sucrose and glucose if extra sugar or fruit is added • Lacks dietary fibre and starch unless seeds or granola are added
Vitamins	• A source of the B-group vitamins, particularly thiamine (B1), B2 riboflavin (B2) and niacin (B3) • A small amount of vitamins A and D are present if yoghurt is not made from skimmed milk • Lacks vitamin C, unless fruit has been added
Minerals	• A good source of calcium • Contains trace amounts of phosphorus, potassium and magnesium • Lacks iron, unless cereals, seeds or fruit are added
Water	• The water content varies depending on the type of yoghurt • The higher the water content the less fat present

👍Tip!

If nutritional value of yoghurt appears on the examination paper remember to include the function of each nutrient in your answer.

Dietetic value of yoghurt

- Yoghurt is an excellent source of easily digestible HBV protein that assists with growth and repair. This makes it a valuable food in the diets of children, teenagers and pregnant women.
- Yoghurt is a good source of calcium, which is vital for forming strong bones, especially in children and adolescents.
- Individuals with high cholesterol or on calorie-controlled diets should choose low-fat yoghurts, as these have a reduced saturated fat content.
- The addition of bacteria cultures, e.g. *lactobacillus acidophilus*, to bio yoghurts aids digestion and strengthens the body's immune system.
- Yoghurt is available in a variety of flavours and types, e.g. set, frozen and Greek, to suit different tastes and add variety to the diet.
- Yoghurt is a versatile food suited to many different culinary uses, e.g. drinks, baking and desserts.
- Some yoghurt is inexpensive, particularly when purchased in large tubs or multipacks, making it an economical food.

Production of yoghurt

1. **Homogenised:** milk is homogenised.
2. **Pasteurised:** milk is pasteurised at 90°C for 15–30 minutes.
3. **Cooled:** milk is cooled to 37°C to provide the ideal growth temperature for the addition of the starter culture.
4. **Starter culture:** a starter culture of lactic acid bacteria, e.g. *lactobacillus bulgaricus*, is added.
5. **Fermentation:** the mixture is **incubated** for six to eight hours to allow the starter culture to ferment. During this time milk thickens due to protein coagulation and lactose is converted to lactic acid, which gives yoghurt its distinctive flavour.
6. **Cooled:** yoghurt is cooled at 5°C to stop fermentation. At this point natural yoghurt is produced.
7. **Addition of other ingredients:** other ingredients, e.g. sweeteners, flavourings, colourings, fruit and nuts, are added, depending on the type of yoghurt being produced. Stabilisers such as pectin are also added to prevent the yoghurt separating.
8. **Packaged and labelled:** yoghurt is packaged in containers of varying size, e.g. 125 g or 500 g, made of varying materials, e.g. plastic or cardboard. The packaging is labelled with details including the type of yoghurt, ingredients, storage instructions, allergy advice and nutritional information.

 Tip!
Yoghurt is an example of an added-value food.

 Lit Hit
Incubate means maintain a certain heat.

? Give details of the stages involved in the manufacture of yoghurt. (20) **HL**

REMEMBER IT!
'Happy People Choose Scrumptious Froyo: Convenient And Pleasing!'
Homogenised, Pasteurised, Cooled, Starter culture, Fermentation, Cooled, Addition of other ingredients, Packaged and labelled.

Guidelines for buying yoghurt

See guidelines for buying milk on page 121.

Guidelines for storing yoghurt

- Store yoghurt in a fridge at 4°C, as room temperature can speed up bacterial growth, increasing the rate of spoilage.
- Minimise the amount of time yoghurt is in storage. Use before its use-by date.

Culinary uses of yoghurt

- **In desserts:** e.g. parfaits, cheesecakes.
- **On desserts:** e.g. fruit salads.
- **Dips:** e.g. Greek yoghurt dip, **raita** dip.
- **Savoury dishes:** e.g. chicken tikka masala, pasta carbonara.
- **Drinks:** e.g. smoothies, milkshakes.

Lit Hit
Raita is an Indian side dish made with yoghurt, diced cucumber and spices.

▲ Raita dip

Guidelines for cooking with yoghurt

- Avoid overheating yoghurt, as it can curdle.

What you will learn:

- **Types of cereals**
- **Structure of wheat grain**
- **Types and average nutritional composition of wheat**
- **Nutritional value and dietetic value of cereals**

- **Guidelines for buying and storing cereal products**
- **Effects of cooking on cereals**
- **Wheat processing**
- **Cereal products**

Cereals are the edible grains of cultivated grasses. They are a staple food in many countries as they are easy to grow, economical and nutritious. Cereals are processed through mechanical or chemical operations for ease of use, e.g. wheat is ground into flour for bread and pasta. These are known as cereal products. Cereal products provide the majority of carbohydrate intake in the diet.

Wheat   Rye   Oats

Types of cereals

Types of cereals include wheat, rye, oats, barley, maize and rice.

 Identify the main sources of cereals in the Irish diet. (12) **OL**

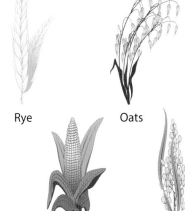

Barley   Maize   Rice

Structure of wheat grain

The wheat grain is composed of three main parts: bran, endosperm and germ. These are surrounded by an outer inedible husk with a tuft of hair on one end known as a beard.

- **Bran (13%):** has a tough outer layer of cellulose that is indigestible in the human body. It contains B-group vitamins, particularly niacin (B3), and the minerals calcium, non-haem iron and phosphorus.

- **Endosperm (85%):** the main part of the wheat grain. It is made up mainly of starch and is used to make white flour. It also contains some B-group vitamins and the protein gluten. The outer layer of the endosperm is called the aleurone layer and it contains low biological value (LBV) protein.

- **Germ (2%):** situated at the base of the cereal grain, the germ is rich in LBV protein. It contains B-group vitamins, particularly thiamine (B1), and vitamin E and non-haem iron. It also contains polyunsaturated fat and some essential fatty acids, e.g. linoleic acid. The thin layer separating the germ from the endosperm is called the scutellum.

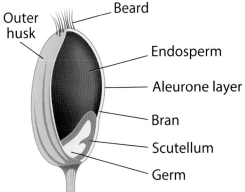

▲ Structure of a wheat grain

 In relation to the wheat grain, explain **two** of the following:
- Endosperm
- Germ
- Bran (6) **OL**

Name the **three** main nutrients found in the endosperm of the wheat grain. (3) **HL**

Types of wheat

The two most common types of wheat grown are winter wheat and spring wheat.

- **Winter wheat:** the main wheat grown. It produces flour with a low protein (gluten) content of less than 10%. It is grown in climates that have milder winters, e.g. Ireland.

- **Spring wheat:** produces flour with a higher protein (gluten) content of 12–14%, making it more ideal for bread-making than winter wheat. It is grown in climates that have cold winters and hot summers, e.g. North America.

▲ Winter wheat

Average nutritional composition of wheat

Proteins	Fat	Carbohydrates	Vitamins	Minerals	Water
12%	2.5%	71%	B group, E	Calcium, iron, phosphorus	12%

Nutritional value of cereals

Proteins	• A source of low biological value (LBV) protein • The main protein in wheat and rye is gluten. The essential amino acids lysine, threonine and tryptophan are lacking in cereal grains. • Cereals should be eaten in combination with other LBV foods to ensure a full complement of essential amino acids
Fat	• The germ is a source of polyunsaturated fat that contains essential fatty acids, e.g. linoleic acid
Carbohydrates	• An excellent source of carbohydrates, particularly starch (64%) • The outer husk contains dietary fibre. This is removed during the refining process.
Vitamins	• A good source of B-group vitamins, particularly thiamine (B1), riboflavin (B2) and niacin (B3) • A small amount of vitamin E is found in the germ • Lacks vitamin C
Minerals	• A source of calcium, iron and phosphorus
Water	• The water content varies slightly between different grains, but it is generally low

 Give an account of the nutritive value of cereals. (15) **OL**

Dietetic value of cereals

- Cereals are an excellent source of starch. This makes them an important energy food for all groups, especially children, active teenagers and pregnant women. They should be consumed in the correct amounts, as excess starch is converted to fat.

- The outer husks of cereals provide an excellent source of dietary fibre, which aids digestion and reduces the risk of bowel disorders.

- Cereals contain polyunsaturated fat, making them beneficial in low-cholesterol diets, as polyunsaturated fat helps increase the production of high-density lipoproteins (HDLs) that help lower cholesterol levels.
- Cereals are a valuable source of LBV protein, which assists with growth and repair. This makes them a valuable food in the diets of vegetarians and vegans.
- Cereals are a versatile food suited to many different culinary uses, e.g. baking, sauces and desserts.
- Cereals are inexpensive, making them an economical food.
- Phytic acid in cereals can inhibit the absorption of calcium and iron, as it has the ability to bind to these nutrients in the digestive tract, inhibiting their absorption.
- Gluten cannot be digested by coeliacs, so they must avoid the cereals wheat, barley and rye.

▲ Gluten allergy warning

 State why some people avoid/limit their intake of cereals. (8) **OL**

Guidelines for buying cereal products

- Buy cereal products from a retailer that has a strict food hygiene and safety policy to ensure any cereal products being sold are safe and fit for consumption.
- Check the best before date. After this date cereal products, e.g. wholemeal flour, may go rancid.
- Ensure packaging is properly sealed. Damaged or incorrectly sealed packaging will cause cereal products to go stale more quickly.

Guidelines for storing cereal products

- Store cereal products, in a cool, dry, well-ventilated space.
- Once opened, store cereal products in an airtight container to prevent staling. Label with the name of the cereal product and best before date.
- Minimise the amount of time cereal products are in storage, as over time they lose their quality. Use within the best before date to ensure maximum quality and freshness.

Effects of cooking on cereals

- Moist heat causes starch grains to swell, burst and absorb the cooking liquid, e.g. roux sauce.
- Dry heat causes starch grains to swell, burst and absorb fat, e.g. pastry and popcorn.
- Cellulose and starch softens, making it easier to digest, e.g. wholegrain rice.
- Protein (gluten) coagulates in dry heat. This sets cakes and breads.
- Some B-group vitamins are lost, as they are not heat stable.
- Dextrinisation of starch and caramelisation of sugar causes browning on the surface of breads and cakes.

▲ Cooked and raw wholegrain rice

CEREALS

Wheat processing

Milling is the term used to describe the processing of wheat to produce wheat flour.

Stage 1: wholemeal flour production

Preparation

1. **Screened:** sieves remove sticks, stones, dust, soil and dirt from the wheat grains.

2. **Cleaned:** wheat grains are **scoured** to remove the beard and washed.

Lit'Hit
Scoured means to clean by scrubbing.

Milling

1. **Conditioned:** wheat is often too dry for milling, so it is conditioned by adding water to make it easier to roll and mill.

2. **Blended:** different wheat types are blended. This blend is referred to as a grist.

3. **Break rolled:** wheat grains pass through rotating metal ridged rollers that peel them open, releasing the endosperm without breaking the outer bran layers into pieces. At this point wholemeal flour is produced.

▲ Wheat flour

REMEMBER IT!
'**S**tarchy **C**ereals **C**an **B**e **B**eneficial.'
Screened, **C**leaned, **C**onditioned, **B**lended, **B**reak rolled.

Stage 2: white flour production (refining process)

1. **Sifted and purified:** the opened wheat grains pass through a series of rotating sieves, starting with a coarse mesh sieve to separate the bran and germ from the rough endosperm (semolina). Air is blown through the grain to help separate the lighter particles (bran) from the heavier particles (rough endosperm). The bran and germ can now be packed and sold separately.

2. **Reducing rollers:** the remaining rough endosperm is ground by smooth steel-reducing rollers. This produces a fine flour.

3. **Air classified:** air is introduced to create a lighter flour.

4. **Addition of additives:** bleaching agents, e.g. calcium carbonate, are added to whiten the flour. Nutritive additives, e.g. calcium, are added to replace the nutrients lost during milling. Improvers, e.g. vitamin C, are added to improve the quality of the gluten in the flour.

5. **Packaged and labelled:** flour is weighed to retail size, e.g. 1 kg or 2 kg, and packaged in varying materials, e.g. paper or cardboard. The packaging is labelled with details including the type of flour, ingredients, storage instructions, allergy advice and nutritional information.

REMEMBER IT!
'**S**uccessful **R**efining **A**lways **A**lters **P**roducts.'
'**S**ifted and purified, **R**educing rollers, **A**ir classified, **A**ddition of additives, **P**ackaged and labelled.

❓ Profile a food of your choice that has undergone extensive processing.
Give details of each of the following:
- stages of production
- packaging
- labelling. (20) **HL**

Cereal products

Wheat

Wheat products

- **Flour**
- **Wholemeal bread**
- **Pasta:** made from the endosperm of durum wheat, which has a high gluten content. The endosperm is ground into semolina flour and mixed with eggs, water, salt and oil to form a dough. The dough is then moulded into various shapes, e.g. penne or spaghetti, that can be purchased dried or fresh.
- **Breakfast cereals:** e.g. Shredded Wheat and Weetabix.

> **Did you know ?**
>
> During pasta making, other ingredients may be added, depending on the type of pasta being made, e.g. spinach to make green pasta or squid ink to make black pasta.

Types of flour

Type	Description	Extraction rate (% wholegrain used)	Uses
Stoneground flour	Made by rolling wheat grains though stone rollers instead of metal. Contains all the wheat grain (high dietary fibre content).	100%	• Bread • Scones
Wholemeal flour	Contains all the wheat grain (high dietary fibre content)	100%	• Bread • Scones
Wheatmeal (brown) flour	Some of the bran has been removed, reducing dietary fibre and B-group vitamin content	83%	• Bread • Scones • Pastry
White (plain/cream) flour	The bran and germ are fully removed, reducing its B-group vitamin and dietary fibre content. Fortified with nutritive additives.	75%	• Bread • Scones • Pastry • Cakes • Biscuits
Self-raising flour	Similar to white flour, but has a raising agent of sodium bicarbonate and cream of tartar added	75%	• Cakes • Biscuits • Scones
Strong flour	Similar to white flour but has a higher gluten content	75%	• Yeast baking, e.g. bread and pizza

> **?** Name **three** types of flour used in home baking and give **one** different culinary use of each. (6) **OL**

CEREALS

Rice

Rice is a staple food in Asian countries, e.g. China. It is becoming increasingly popular among the Irish population due to multicultural influences.

Types of rice

Type	Description	Uses
Short-grain rice	A short, plump rice grain that is sticky and moist when cooked	• Rice pudding
Medium-grain rice	A narrower grain than short-grain rice, which becomes sticky and moist when cooked	• Sushi • Risotto
Long-grain rice	A long and slender grain with all of the bran removed. It stays separate and fluffy after cooking.	• To accompany savoury dishes, e.g. stir-fries
Wholegrain (brown) rice	Similar to long-grain rice, except just some of the bran is removed. It takes a long time to cook.	
Pre-cooked/instant rice	A rice grain that has been fully cooked and then dehydrated. It cooks quickly.	
Basmati rice	A long-grain aromatic rice grown in India and Pakistan	• To accompany savoury dishes, e.g. curries • **Biryanis**

Rice products

- Breakfast cereals, e.g. Rice Krispies
- Rice flour
- Rice pudding
- Rice paper
- Rice cakes

Lit Hit
Biryani is a spicy Indian dish of rice with meat and/or vegetables, flavoured with saffron or turmeric.

Oats, maize, rye and barley

Oat products	Maize products	Rye products	Barley products
• Oat cakes • Flapjacks • Granola • Oat flour • Porridge	• Cornflour • Sweetcorn • Breakfast cereals, e.g. cornflakes • Popcorn	• Rye flour • Rye bread • Rye crispbread	• Malt vinegar • Barley water • Barley flour

FRUIT, VEGETABLES, PULSES AND NUTS

1.3.2

What you will learn:

- Classification and average nutritional composition of fruit and vegetables
- Nutritional value and dietetic value of fruit, vegetables, pulses and nuts
- Guidelines for buying and guidelines for storing fruit and vegetables
- Guidelines for preparing fruit, vegetables and pulses
- Culinary uses of fruit, vegetables, pulses and nuts
- Suitable methods for cooking fruit and vegetables
- Guidelines for cooking fruit, vegetables and pulses
- Effects of cooking on fruit and vegetables
- Fruit and vegetable processing
- Ripening and decaying of fruit
- Grading fruit and vegetables
- Organic fruit and vegetables
- Types of pulses and nuts
- Guidelines for storing pulses

FRUIT AND VEGETABLES

Fruit and vegetables are versatile foods that add a wide variety of colour, texture and flavour to the diet. They are an excellent source of nutrition and are important for overall good health. Unfortunately, only 21% of men and 19% of women in Ireland meet the current World Health Organization target of five portions a day.

Classification of fruit

- **Citrus fruit:** e.g. oranges, satsumas, clementines, lemons, grapefruits and limes.
- **Berry fruit:** e.g. strawberries, cranberries, blackcurrants and gooseberries.
- **Hard fruit:** e.g. apples and pears.
- **Stone fruit:** e.g. plums, peaches, cherries, nectarines and avocados.
- **Dried fruit:** e.g. raisins, sultanas, dates and prunes.
- **Other:** e.g. pineapples, kiwis, grapes and melons.

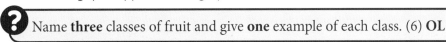

Name **three** classes of fruit and give **one** example of each class. (6) **OL**

Average nutritional composition of fruit

Nutrient	Citrus fruit	Berry fruit	Hard fruit	Dried fruit
Proteins	1%	0.5%	0.5%	2–4%
Fat	0%	0%	0%	0%
Carbohydrates	1%–9%	5–10%	10–12%	40–70%
Vitamins	A, B group, C	A, B group, C	A, C	A, B group
Minerals	Calcium, iron	Calcium, iron	Calcium, iron	Calcium, iron
Water	90–95%	90–95%	88–90%	15–20%

Nutritional value of fruit

Proteins	• Contains trace amounts of low biological value (LBV) protein
Fat	• Lacks fat, due to its high water content. Avocados are an exception, as they contain polyunsaturated fat.
Carbohydrates	• Contains sugar, starch, dietary fibre and pectin in varying amounts • Starch is generally found in unripe fruit, but it changes to sugar on ripening • Sugar is present in all fruit in the form of glucose, sucrose and fructose. Dried fruit has a higher percentage of sugar. • Dietary fibre is mainly present in the skins of fruit, making pears and apples an excellent source • Pectin is present in high amounts in certain fruits, e.g. blackberries and gooseberries
Vitamins	• Fruit, especially berry fruit and citrus fruit, contains an excellent source of vitamin C • Orange or red coloured fruits, e.g. peaches, are an excellent source of vitamin A (beta-carotene) • Contains varying amounts of B-group vitamins, e.g. berry and citrus fruit are a good source of niacin (B3) and folate and bananas are a good source of pyridoxine (B6) • Lacks vitamins D and B12 (cobalamin)
Minerals	• Contains a small amount of calcium • Dried fruits, e.g. prunes, are a good source of non-haem iron • Bananas contain potassium
Water	• High water content • Dried fruit contains much less water

Classification of vegetables

- **Green vegetables:** e.g. spinach, cabbage, kale and brussel sprouts.
- **Flower vegetables:** e.g. broccoli, cauliflower and artichoke.
- **Root vegetables:** e.g. beetroot, carrot, parsnip and celeriac.
- **Tuber vegetables:** e.g. potato, sweet potato and radish.
- **Bulb vegetables:** e.g. white onion, red onion, shallots, leek and garlic.
- **Fruit vegetables:** e.g. pepper, chillis, courgette, aubergine and tomato.
- **Stem vegetables:** e.g. asparagus and celery.
- **Pulse vegetables:** e.g. peas, beans and lentils.
- **Fungi:** e.g. mushrooms and truffles.

Lit Hit
A tuber is a short, thick, round stem that grows underground and is a part of certain plants, e.g. the potato.

? Classify vegetables and give **one** example of each class. (12) **OL**

Did you know ?
Truffles, strong-smelling underground fungi, are considered a culinary delicacy. They are found with the aid of trained dogs or pigs. They are highly priced, with the best-quality truffles costing €10,000 per kilogram.

Average nutritional composition of vegetables

Nutrient	Leafy green vegetables	Root vegetables	Fruit vegetables	Pulse vegetables
Proteins	3%	1%	1%	2–44%
Fat	0%	0%	0%	0-8%
Carbohydrates	2%	5–10%	2–5%	3-60%
Vitamins	A, B group, C	A, B group, C	A, B group, C	A, B group, C
Minerals	Calcium, iron	Calcium, iron	Calcium, iron	Calcium, iron
Water	90–95%	70–90%	90–95%	14–19%

Nutritional value of vegetables

Proteins	• Contain small amounts of LBV protein • Pulses have the highest LBV content • Soya beans are the exception as they contain high biological value (HBV) protein
Fat	• Lack fat, due to their high water content • Olives and soya beans are exceptions as they are a source of polyunsaturated fat
Carbohydrates	• Contain starch, dietary fibre and sugar in varying amounts • Pulse, root and tuber vegetables provide starch in high quantities • Dietary fibre is mainly present in the skins of vegetables, e.g. potatoes. Pulses are also an excellent source of dietary fibre • Carrots, tomatoes, peppers and onions contain small amounts of sugar
Vitamins	• Vitamin C is present in all vegetables, especially green leafy vegetables, tubers, pulses and fruit vegetables • Contain varying amounts of B-group vitamins, e.g. pulses are a good source of thiamine (B1), riboflavin (B2) and pyridoxine (B6); mushrooms are a good source of riboflavin (B2) and niacin (B3); and leafy green vegetables are a source of folate • Leafy green vegetables and orange- or red-coloured vegetables, e.g. carrots and peppers, are an excellent source of vitamin A (beta-carotene) • Lack vitamins D and B12 (cobalamin)
Minerals	• Contain a small amount of calcium, especially leafy green vegetables, root vegetables and pulses • Leafy green vegetables and pulses are a good source of non-haem iron
Water	• High water content

Did you know

Potatoes are one of the best sources of vitamin C in the diet, providing half of an adult's daily Recommended Intake (RI).

FRUIT, VEGETABLES, PULSES AND NUTS

Dietetic value of fruit and vegetables

- Pulse vegetables are a valuable source of LBV protein, which assists with growth and repair. This makes them a valuable food in the diets of vegetarians and vegans.
- Fruit and vegetables provide an excellent source of dietary fibre, which aids digestion and reduces the risk of bowel disorders.
- Most fruit and vegetables contain no fat and are low in kilocalories. This makes them an ideal food for those on low-cholesterol or calorie-controlled diets.
- Soya beans and avocados contain polyunsaturated fat, making them beneficial in low-cholesterol diets as polyunsaturated fat helps increase the production of high-density lipoproteins (HDLs) that help lower cholesterol levels.
- Fruit and vegetables supply the antioxidants vitamin A (beta-carotene) and vitamin C that help reduce free radicals, lowering the risk of coronary heart disease, strokes and some cancers.
- Fruit and vegetables are available in a variety of types and forms, e.g. fresh and processed, to suit varying tastes and add variety to the diet.
- Fruit and vegetables are a versatile food. They can be eaten raw, and are also suited to many different culinary uses, e.g. savoury dishes, baking and sauces.
- Some fruit and vegetables, e.g. bananas and carrots, are inexpensive, making them an economical food.
- Some fruits, e.g. pineapples, can be high in sugar, so they may not be suited to a diabetic diet as they can raise blood sugar levels.
- Fruit and vegetables lack vitamin D and cobalamin (B12), so they should be combined with foods rich in these to balance the diet.

> Discuss **four** reasons why it is important to include an adequate amount of fruit and vegetables in the diet. (16) **OL**
>
> Give details of the nutritional significance **and** the contribution to the diet of either fruit **or** vegetables. (20) **HL**

Guidelines for buying fruit and vegetables

- Buy fruit and vegetables from a retailer that has a strict food hygiene and safety policy to ensure any fruit and vegetables being sold are safe and fit for consumption.
- Buy fruit and vegetables that are fresh, brightly coloured and firm to the touch. Ensure skins are undamaged, as damaged skins will quicken spoilage.
- Buy medium-sized fruit and vegetables, as large fruit and vegetables may lack colour and flavour and be coarse in texture.
- Buy fruit and vegetables in small amounts. Buying too many can lead to food waste, as fruit and vegetables do not have a long shelf life.
- Purchase fruit and vegetables loose or in netted packaging as it allows air circulation, reducing the rate of spoilage compared to plastic packaging.
- Choose fruit and vegetables that are in season, e.g. asparagus from April to June and strawberries from June to August, as they will taste better and be less expensive.

Guidelines for storing fruit and vegetables

- Remove fruit and vegetables from plastic packaging to allow air circulation, reducing the rate of spoilage.
- Remove any discoloured fruit and vegetables before storage, as they can increase the rate of spoilage of nearby fruit and vegetables.

- Store fruit and vegetables in a cool, dry, dark place to slow deterioration, e.g. in a vegetable rack or in the fridge salad drawer.
- Minimise the amount of time fruit and vegetables are in storage, as over time their vitamin levels reduce and they lose their quality, e.g. become soft.

Guidelines for preparing fruit and vegetables

- Prepare fruit and vegetables close to cooking/serving time, as when the cell wall is cut it releases the enzyme oxidase. This reacts with oxygen in the air (oxidation), which causes discolouration (enzymic browning) and reduces the vitamin C levels.
- Avoid soaking in water, as this can cause water-soluble C and B-group vitamins to leach into the liquid.
- If possible, avoid peeling in order to reduce the loss of dietary fibre and the risk of oxidation and damage to vitamin C.
- Use a sharp knive to chop fruit and vegetables as this minimises damage to the cell wall, reducing oxidation and maintaining vitamin C levels.

▲ Chopping vegetables with a sharp knife

Culinary uses of fruit and vegetables

Fruit

- **Drinks:** e.g. juices, smoothies.
- **Baking:** e.g. apple crumble, pear tart.
- **Desserts:** e.g. pavlova, sponge cake.
- **Sauces:** e.g. strawberry sauce (coulis), cranberry sauce.

Vegetables

- **Soups:** e.g. winter vegetable soup, roasted red pepper soup.
- **Salads:** e.g. broccoli salad, coleslaw.
- **Savoury dishes:** e.g. roast vegetable lasagne, mushroom risotto.

▲ Fruit juices

Suitable methods for cooking fruit and vegetables

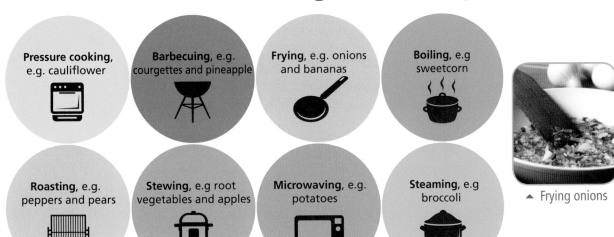

Pressure cooking, e.g. cauliflower

Barbecuing, e.g. courgettes and pineapple

Frying, e.g. onions and bananas

Boiling, e.g sweetcorn

Roasting, e.g. peppers and pears

Stewing, e.g root vegetables and apples

Microwaving, e.g. potatoes

Steaming, e.g broccoli

▲ Frying onions

FRUIT, VEGETABLES, PULSES AND NUTS

Guidelines for cooking fruit and vegetables

- Eat fruit and vegetables raw where possible as no vitamins and minerals are destroyed by heat or lost in the cooking liquid.
- Cook fruit and vegetables quickly in the least amount of water possible, as water-soluble vitamins are lost at high temperatures and can leach into the cooking liquid.
- Cover fruit and vegetables with a tightly fitted lid when boiling to avoid loss of water-soluble vitamins through evaporation. A lid also reduces oxidation as it blocks out air, and it speeds up cooking time.
- Avoid copper or brass saucepans as they react with vitamin C in fruit and vegetables, destroying it.
- Do not discard the water from boiling vegetables as it contains leached nutrients. Use for making the base of soups, stews or sauces.
- Avoid overcooking vegetables, ideally serve **al dente**.
- Do not add bicarbonate of soda to green vegetables to enhance colour, as it depletes vitamin C content.

Lit Hit
Al dente means with a bite, or cooked so as to be still firm when bitten.

Effects of cooking on fruit and vegetables

- Dry heat causes starch grains to swell, burst and become soft. Moist heat causes starch cells to absorb liquid, resulting in softening.
- Cellulose in the cell walls softens, making fruit and vegetables more digestible and easier to eat.
- Some vitamins, especially vitamin C, are lost as they are not heat stable. Some minerals are lost as they dissolve into the cooking liquid.
- Microorganisms and enzymes are destroyed.
- Overcooking vegetables causes them to lose their colour and texture and dilutes their flavour.

▲ Overcooked green beans

❓ State **three** guidelines that should be followed when preparing and/or cooking fruit in order to retain maximum nutrients. (6) **OL**

Identify ways of retaining vitamin C when **(i)** preparing **and (ii)** cooking foods with a high vitamin C content. (12) **OL**

Fruit and vegetable processing

Freezing	
Process	Fruit and vegetables can be frozen by commercial blast methods, e.g. freezing at –30°C, or by being blanched and then home frozen at –25°C.
Effect	• Colour and flavour remains unchanged • Change in texture due to blanching • Microorganisms are inactivated. Enzymes are destroyed if fruit and vegetables are blanched. • Some loss of B-group vitamins and vitamin C due to blanching and through drip loss when thawed
Examples	• Peas • Mixed berries • Frozen fruit and vegetable products, e.g. frozen fruit yoghurt and vegetable burgers

Canning

Process	Fruit and vegetables are placed in sterile cans, sealed and heated to high temperatures. They may be canned in brine, spring water or a sauce, e.g. tomato sauce or sugar syrup.			
Effect	• Microorganisms and enzymes are destroyed • Colour, flavour and texture are altered • Loss of B-group vitamins and vitamin C • Calorie, fat and sugar content can increase, depending on what liquid the fruit or vegetables are canned in			
Examples	• Kidney beans	• Tomatoes	• Strawberries	• Pineapples

Drying (dehydration)

Process	Fruit and vegetables have their moisture content removed. This can be completed by fluidised bed drying, accelerated freeze drying or sun drying.			
Effect	• Colour, flavour and texture are altered • Microorganisms and enzymes are destroyed • Loss of B-group vitamins and vitamin C			
Examples	• Lentils	• Tomatoes	• Raisins	• Banana chips

Irradiation

Process	Fruit and vegetables exposed to low levels of radiation (gamma rays).	
Effect	• No effect on colour, flavour and texture • Microorganisms and enzymes are destroyed • Slows down the ripening and sprouting of fruit and vegetables, so shelf life is extended • Some loss of B-group vitamins and vitamin C	ONE WEEK OLD <u>NOT</u> IRRADIATED ONE WEEK OLD <u>IRRADIATED</u>
Examples	• Onions • Potatoes • Rhubarb	

? In relation to freezing vegetables, explain how loss of vitamin B1 and vitamin C may occur. (6) **HL**

Discuss the options available to consumers when selecting and purchasing fruit and vegetables. (12) **HL**

Did you know ?

At present in the European Union irradiation of fruit and vegetables is not allowed. The only foods authorised for irradiation are dried aromatic herbs, spices and vegetable seasonings.

FRUIT, VEGETABLES, PULSES AND NUTS

Ripening and decaying of fruit

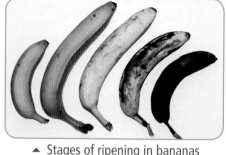

- Enzymic action causes fruit to go through a life cycle from unripe to ripe. Then overripe to decayed.
- Unripe fruit has a high content of starch and is practically inedible and unappealing.
- As enymes ripen:
  - starch is converted to sugars, e.g. fructose, by enzymes. This adds sweetness and juiciness to the fruit
  - colour of fruit changes, e.g bananas go from green to yellow and then to brown
  - texture changes, e.g. plums become soft and easy to digest
  - insoluble protopectin in unripe fruit is changed to pectin
  - ethylene gas is produced by some fruits. This speeds up the ripening process.

▲ Stages of ripening in bananas

- Once ripe, fruit will stay wholesome for a limited time period before decay sets in. Eventually, enzymes, yeasts and mould cause fruit to become overripe and then decay and decompose. Softer fruits, e.g. raspberries, tend to decay quicker than fruits with tough skins, e.g. oranges. Damaged fruits also decay quicker, as juices are released through the blemish, providing an ideal medium for mould and yeast growth.

Grading fruit and vegetables

Under European Union legislation some fresh fruit and vegetables retailed in Ireland must be graded and labelled. Grading involves sorting fruit and vegetables into different classes, according to their size, shape and colour, so that they can be sold at the correct price for their quality. There are three general grades.

- **Class extra:** superior quality. Shape, size and colour must be at an optimum level.

▲ Grading fruit

- **Class I:** good quality. A slight defect in shape, size and colour is permitted.
- **Class II:** reasonable quality. Some minor defects in shape, size and colour are permitted. This category will satisfy consumers for whom price is more important than quality.

 Identify and explain **two** EU grading classes used for fruit and vegetables. (4) **HL**

Organic fruit and vegetables

Fruit and vegetables are labelled organic if they have been grown without the use of any artificial fertilisers, pesticides or preservatives. They tend to be more expensive than intensively **yielded** crops, as organic farmers have a lower yield annually.

Lit' Hit
Yield is the amount of an agricultural or industrial product produced.

▲ Euro Leaf organic logo

To sell organic fruit and vegetables, producers must ensure their farming practices meet EU regulations. Certification bodies, e.g. Irish Organic Farmers and Growers Association (IOFGA), carry out inspections and implement certification.

By law, organic pre-packaged food, including fruit or vegetables, sold in Ireland must display:

- the European Union's Euro Leaf organic logo
- a certification code from the certification organisation, e.g. IE-ORG-O2 is used by the Irish Organic Farmers and Growers Association (IOFGA)
- the place of farming
- the words 'certified organic'.

PULSES AND NUTS

Legumes contain edible seeds in a pod. These seeds include beans, peas and lentils. Normally only the seeds can be eaten, but sometimes the pods can also be consumed, e.g. sugar snap peas. Pulses are the dried, edible seeds of these plants.

Nuts are hard fruits that have only one edible seed enclosed by a shell. They are available whole, shelled, ground, flaked or chopped.

Types of pulses and nuts

Pulses

- **Beans** (oval or kidney shaped), e.g. soya, kidney and pinto beans.
- **Peas** (round shaped), e.g. chickpeas and garden peas.
- **Lentils** (flat discs), e.g. red and yellow lentils.

Nuts

- **Almonds**
- **Pistachio nuts**
- **Pecans**
- **Brazil nuts**
- **Cashew nuts**
- **Hazelnuts**
- **Macadamia nuts**

Nutritional value of pulses

Proteins	• A source of LBV protein
	• Soya beans are the exception, as they contain HBV protein
Fat	• Lack fat
	• Soya beans are the exception, as they are a source of polyunsaturated fat
Carbohydrates	• Contain starch and dietary fibre
Vitamins	• A good source of B-group vitamins, particularly thiamine (B1), riboflavin (B2) and pyridoxine (B6)
	• Pulses contain vitamin C. If pulses have been processed, e.g. canned, vitamin C is lost.
Minerals	• A source of non-haem iron
	• Contain a small amount of calcium
Water	• Water content varies depending on the type of pulse, but it is generally quite low

Dietetic value of pulses

See dietetic value of fruit and vegetables on page 142.

FRUIT, VEGETABLES, PULSES AND NUTS

Nutritional value of nuts

Proteins	• Contain small amounts of LBV protein
Fat	• High in polyunsaturated fat
Carbohydrates	• Dietary fibre is present
Vitamins	• Contain a small amount of B-group vitamins • Lack vitamin C
Minerals	• A source of non-haem iron • Contain calcium
Water	• Low water content

Dietetic value of nuts

- Nuts are a source of LBV protein, which assists with growth and repair. This makes them a valuable food in the diets of vegans and vegetarians.
- Nuts provide a good source of dietary fibre, which aids digestion and reduces the risk of bowel disorders.
- Nuts contain polyunsaturated fat, so they are beneficial in low-cholesterol diets as polyunsaturated fat helps increase the production of high-density lipoproteins (HDLs) that help lower cholesterol levels.
- Nuts are available in a variety of forms, e.g. ground and chopped, to suit different tastes and add variety in the diet.
- Nuts are a versatile food. They can be eaten raw and are also suited for use in a variety of dishes, e.g stir-fries and desserts.

Guidelines for preparing and cooking pulses

- Before cooking, dried pulses must be soaked overnight to rehydrate them and to shorten cooking time.
- Cook in a saucepan of boiling water for the duration specified on the instructions (usually 30–50 minutes).

Culinary uses of pulses and nuts

Pulses

- **Soups:** e.g. pea soup, red lentil soup.
- **Savoury dishes:** e.g. chilli con carne, tarka dahl.
- **Dips:** e.g. refried bean dip.

Nuts

- **Garnish:** e.g. doughnuts, coffee cake.
- **Salads:** e.g. Waldorf salad.
- **Savoury dishes:** e.g. nut loaf, pilaf.
- **Desserts:** e.g. pecan pie, baklava.

▲ Red lentil soup

Guidelines for storing pulses

- Store dried pulses in an airtight container out of direct sunlight.
- Store canned pulses in a cool cupboard.
- Use within the best before date.

▲ Baklava

FATS AND OILS

What you will learn:

- **Classification, average nutritional composition, nutritional value and dietetic value of fats and oils**
- **Manufacture of vegetable oil and margarine**
- **Types of margarine and dairy spreads**
- **Guidelines for storing, culinary uses of and guidelines for cooking with fats and oils**

Fats and oils are classed as lipids. Fats come from animal sources (saturated fat) and are usually solid at room temperature. Oils come from plant or marine sources (unsaturated fat) and are liquid at room temperature. Health experts recommend that people decrease saturated fat and increase unsaturated fat consumption.

> **Did you know** ❓
>
> Due to the health benefits of certain fats and oils when consumed in moderation, a new shelf was created on the food pyramid for them, removing them from the top shelf which contains foods high in fat, sugar and salt.

Classification of fats and oils

Fats and oils consumed in the diet can be obtained from three main sources.

- **Animal fats (saturated):** e.g. cream, suet (fat surrounding organs of cattle, sheep and other animals), lard (fat from the abdomen of a pig), ghee (**clarified** butter), butter and dripping (fat from roasted meat).

- **Plant oils (mainly unsaturated):** vegetable oils, e.g. olive and corn; nut oils, e.g. coconut and peanut; seed oils, e.g. rapeseed and sunflower seed; and margarine.

- **Marine oils (polyunsaturated):** e.g. cod liver oil and herring oil.

📌 **Lit' Hit**
Clarified means to remove impurities..

▲ Suet

Average nutritional composition of fats and oils

Nutrient	Butter	Cooking oil	Margarine	Low-fat dairy spread
Proteins	0.5%	0.2%	0.2%	0%
Fat	82%	99.9%	81.5%	40%
Carbohydrates	0.5%	0%	0%	0.5%
Vitamins	A, D	0%	A, D (fortified)	A, D
Minerals	Calcium	0%	Calcium	Calcium
Water	15%	0.1%	18%	58%

Nutritional value of fats and oils

Proteins	• Butter and margarine contain trace amounts of high biological value (HBV) protein.
Fat	• The fat content present varies depending on the type of fat or oil, e.g. vegetable oil contains 99%, butter contains 82% and low-fat dairy spreads contain approximately 40%
Carbohydrates	• Lack carbohydrates, for this reason fats and oils are usually served with a carbohydrate-rich food, e.g. bread
Vitamins	• Butter and dairy spreads contain trace amounts of vitamins A and D • Margarine is fortified with vitamins A and D
Minerals	• Butter and margarine contain trace amounts of calcium
Water	• Water content varies depending on the fat content • The higher the water content the less fat present

Dietetic value of fats and oils

- Fats and oils delay hunger, as they remain in the stomach for a long period of time, making people feel fuller for longer.
- Fats and oils supply a source of fat-soluble vitamins, especially A and D, necessary for overall health.
- Fats and oils help form a protective layer that surrounds delicate organs.
- Fats and oils help supply essential fatty acids, e.g. linoleic acid, that manufacture and repair cell membranes.
- Plant and marine oils contain polyunsaturated fat, making them beneficial in the diets of individuals on low-cholesterol diets, as polyunsaturated fat helps increase the production of high-density lipoproteins (HDLs) that help lower cholesterol levels.
- Fats and oils provide heat and energy to the body.
- Animal fats, e.g. butter, are a source of saturated fat so they should be restricted in the diets of individuals with high cholesterol or on calorie-controlled diets.

Manufacture of vegetable oil

1. **Seed preparation:** seeds, e.g. rapeseed; nuts, e.g. walnut; and cereals, e.g. corn, are prepared by being cleaned, grinded and crushed through break rollers and heated.

2. **Oil extraction:** oil is removed from seeds by pressing or by the addition of a solvent.

3. **Refined:** oil undergoes a refining process to remove impurities. This includes:

   o **degumming:** the addition of hot water followed by centrifuging (rotating at a high speed), which causes impurities to fall to the bottom, leaving a clear oil

   o **neutralising:** involves mixing oil with an alkali, which changes free fatty acids into insoluble compounds that can be easily removed from oil, leaving it clear.

4. **Bleached:** oil is bleached with Fuller's earth, which removes the deep colour of the oil.

5. **Filtered:** oil is filtered to produce a clear liquid.

6. **Deodorisers added:** deodorisers are added to remove putrid odours.

Did you know ?

Fuller's earth is any clay material that has the ability to adsorb impurities or colouring bodies from fats.

7. **Packaged and labelled:** vegetable oil is packaged in containers of varying size, e.g. 500 ml or 1 litre, and materials, e.g. plastic or glass. The packaging is labelled with details including the type of oil, ingredients, storage instructions, allergy advice and nutritional information.

REMEMBER IT!

'**S**everal **O**ils **R**equire **B**leaching and **F**iltering **D**uring **P**roduction.'
Seed preparation, **O**il extraction, **R**efined, **B**leached, **F**iltered, **D**eodorisers added, **P**ackaged and labelled.

Manufacture of margarine

👍**Tip!**

Margarine is an example of an added-value food.

1. **Oil extraction:** oils from various sources, e.g. olives and rapeseed, are extracted and refined to remove impurities. The oils chosen depend on the desired final properties, e.g. plasticity or low cholesterol.

2. **Hydrogenated:** oil is hydrogenated by forcing hydrogen gas through the double bond of an unsaturated oil in the presence of a nickel catalyst, converting it into a saturated, semi-solid fat. Different oils are blended together.

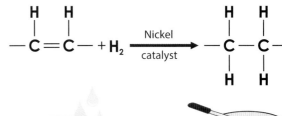

3. **Other ingredients added:** skimmed milk or water is added along with salt, colourings and flavourings. It is also fortified with vitamin A and D.

4. **Emulsification:** an emulsifying agent, e.g. lecithin, is added to prevent the fat and liquid in the margarine from separating.

Vegetable oil

Margarine

5. **Churned:** a machine called a votator churns the oil and water-based ingredients together until they form an emulsion. Mixing is carried out until the desired consistency is reached.

6. **Weighed:** margarine is weighed into retail-size portions, e.g. 250 g or 500 g.

7. **Packaged and labelled:** margarine is packaged in varying materials, e.g. plastic or foil. The packaging is labelled with details including the type of margarine, ingredients, storage instructions, allergy advice and nutritional information.

REMEMBER IT!

'**O**ften **H**ydrogenated **O**ils **E**ndanger **C**oronary arteries **W**ithin **P**eople.'
Oil extraction, **H**ydrogenated, **O**ther ingredients added, **E**mulsification, **C**hurned, **W**eighed, **P**ackaged and labelled.

Types of margarine

Block margarine	Soft margarine
• Made mainly from vegetable oil, but can include marine and animal oils • Wrapped in waxed paper or foil • Generally has a high saturated fat content • Used for baking and frying	• Made mainly from vegetable oil, and is designed to spread straight from the fridge • Sold in plastic tubs • Generally has a high saturated fat content (slightly less than block margarine) • Used for baking and frying

FATS AND OILS

Types of dairy spreads

Dairy spreads have a similar nutritional composition to margarine, but are usually lower in fat. They have a fat content of around 60%, in comparison to margarine, which has a fat content of approximately 80%. Spreads may be fortified with vitamins A and D. Types of dairy spreads include low-fat dairy spreads and functional dairy spreads.

Low-fat dairy spreads	Functional dairy spreads
• Contain approximately half the fat (38–40%) of butter and margarine • Ideal for calorie-controlled diets as they contain approximately 95 kcal per 25 g in comparison to 185 kcal in margarine or butter • Ideal for low-cholesterol diets as they are low in saturated fat and high in monounsaturated fatty acids • Not suitable for baking and frying due to their high water content 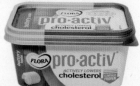	• Scientifically proven to lower cholesterol levels in the body due to the presence of plant sterols (stanol ester) that prevent the absorption of cholesterol in the small intestine • Contain approximately 60% fat • Ideal for calorie-controlled diets, as they contain approximately 131 kcal per 25 g in comparison to 185 kcal in margarine or butter • Ideal for low-cholesterol diets as thet are low in saturated fat and high in polyunsaturated fatty acids • Suitable for baking and frying due to their lower water content

 Differentiate between the following dairy spreads and give **one** example of each.
- Low-fat spreads
- Functional dairy spreads (6) **HL**

Guidelines for storing fats and oils

- Store oils in a cool, dark cupboard and fats in a fridge at 4°C away from heat and light to prevent rancidity.
- Keep covered, as fats and oils go rancid when exposed to air (oxidative rancidity).
- Store fats and oils away from strong-smelling foods, such as blue cheese, to prevent them absorbing odours.
- Minimise the amount of time in storage. Use within the best before date as after this date they could be rancid.

Culinary uses of fats and oils

- **Flavour:** fats and oils add flavour to food, e.g. potatoes and salads.
- **Frying:** oils are suitable for shallow- and deep-frying, due to their high boiling points.
- **Emulsions:** fats and oils create emulsions when mixed with water or vinegar, e.g. mayonnaise.
- **Aeration:** fats assist with the aeration of cakes, as they can entrap air, producing a well-risen end product.
- **Shortening:** fat gives a crumbly texture to pastry, cakes and biscuits by acting as a shortening agent.
- **Anti-staling:** fats and oils act as anti-staling agents, preventing baked goods, e.g. cakes, from drying out.

Guidelines for cooking with fats and oils

- Avoid overheating fats and oils as they will start to decompose, causing them to reach smoke point and flash point.

Chapter 5:
Meal management, planning and recipe adaption

 1.3.3 # MEAL MANAGEMENT, PLANNING AND RECIPE ADAPTION

What you will learn:
- **Benefits of planning meals**
- **Factors to consider when meal planning**
- **Menu design**
- **Recipe adaption**

Whether a person is cooking for one or for an entire family, planning meals will not only save time, effort and money, but will also improve eating habits.

Benefits of planning meals

- Individuals and families are more likely to eat healthy, balanced meals that will meet their nutritional requirements.
- It allows for greater variety in the meals eaten each week.
- Individuals and families tend to shop for groceries more efficiently, as they have a list of the items they need, eliminating impulse buying or overspending.
- It can save money, as dining out and reliance on takeaways is reduced.

Factors to consider when meal planning

Healthy eating guidelines
- Current healthy eating guidelines and the food pyramid should be considered when meal planning, as they help individuals to prepare balanced meals containing the correct proportions of nutrients required.
  For example:
  o eat five or more portions of a variety of fruit and vegetables daily
  o use low-fat milks, low-fat or no-added-sugar yoghurts and reduced-fat cheeses.

Specific dietary requirements

- Consider the dietary needs and nutritional requirements of all individuals when meal planning, as these can vary greatly, e.g. children require a higher carbohydrate intake than older people as children are more active.
- Certain individuals may require specialist foods or modified recipes, e.g. individuals with coeliac disease cannot have gluten and vegetarians cannot have meat or meat products.
- Religious beliefs also need to be considered, e.g. Hindus do not eat beef so a meal will need to be planned in order to suit their needs.

Availability of foods

- Choose foods that are in season when meal planning, as they are cheaper and taste better, e.g. strawberries and tomatoes are in season during summer.
- If people live in rural areas it may be hard to access certain ingredients, such as spices from around the world. This limits the dishes that can be prepared.

Resources

- **Time:** consider the time available to prepare, cook and serve the food when meal planning. Ensure dishes chosen can be completed on time, e.g. a stir-fry may take 30 minutes to prepare and cook compared to a stew that may require three to four hours. Convenience foods can be useful when time is limited, e.g. white sauce for lasagne. However, they should not be used excessively due to their high fat and salt content.
- **Money:** consider the amount of money available. When money is limited use finances wisely by purchasing cheaper cuts of meat, choosing pulses and eggs as cheap protein foods and shopping around for good value.
- **Food preparation and cooking equipment:** certain meals require specific food preparation or cooking equipment. Check what equipment is available before planning meals, e.g. a wok may be needed for a stir-fry. If available, use time-saving equipment, e.g. a food processor, to speed up food preparation processes.
- **Skills and knowledge:** consider existing cookery skills and knowledge. People with competent cooking skills may be able to plan more adventurous meals, whereas less experienced cooks may depend more on convenience food.

Occasion

- If planning a meal for a special occasion, consider the type of occasion, as specific foods may be required, e.g. turkey at Christmas.

People

- Consider the number of people eating when meal planning, as the larger the group the more ingredients needed.
- People's likes and dislikes should be taken into account to ensure everyone enjoys the meal and food is not wasted.

REMEMBER IT!

'**H**appy **S**tudents **A**lways **R**ely **O**n **P**lans.'

Healthy eating guidelines, **S**pecific dietary requirements, **A**vailability, **R**esources, **O**ccasion, **P**eople.

Discuss how the following factors influence the planning and management of family meals:
- money available • equipment • knowledge and skills • dietary considerations. (20) **OL**

Menu design
Guidelines for designing a menu

1. Read the exam question thoroughly. Highlight the specific group of people for whom you have been asked to design a menu. Highlight any special requirements, e.g. high fibre or low fat.
2. Using a full A4 page of your exam paper, draw a box with a ruler.
3. Give the menu a title, e.g. 'Menu for an adolescent'.
4. Divide the menu into courses, as asked for in the exam. For example:
   - Menu for a day (this must include breakfast, lunch, dinner and snacks)
   - Two-course menu suitable for the main meal of the day (this must include starter and main course or main course and dessert).
5. A balanced meal contains at least three out of the four main food groups from the food pyramid. To ensure a menu is balanced, draw a mini food pyramid on the side of the page (for a menu for a day, each of the meals will require a food pyramid). Each time you include a food group, such as fruit and vegetables, tick the shelf on the pyramid. Do not add foods from the top shelf of the food pyramid.
6. Check that the foods selected meet any specific requirements outlined in the exam question, e.g. no meat or animal products if asked to design a menu for a vegan.
7. Explain each food type and cooking method thoroughly in the menu. For example: baked fillet of salmon, served with steamed carrots and broccoli florets, and boiled baby potatoes.
8. Include a drink, e.g. water or milk, with each course or meal.

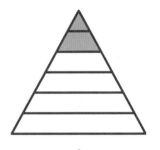

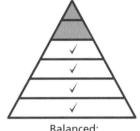

Balanced:
four food groups included

❓ Having regard to current healthy eating guidelines, plan a menu (3 meals) for one day for a person who is obese. (18) **OL**

Having regard to current healthy eating guidelines, and the needs for teenage girls to increase their intake of calcium, plan a menu (3 meals) for one day for a teenage girl. (18) **OL**

Plan a day's menu for a person with coronary heart disease (CHD). Include **one** functional food in the menu and suggest a reason for its inclusion. (22) **HL**

Sample menu

 Having regard to current healthy eating guidelines and the specific dietary needs of adolescents, plan a menu (3 meals) for **one** day for a family with teenagers. (18) **(OL 2012)**

Day menu for a family with teenagers

BREAKFAST

A bowl of warm home-made porridge made with milk, topped with fresh berries.

A boiled egg served with a slice of wholemeal toast and a scrape of butter.

A glass of freshly squeezed orange juice.

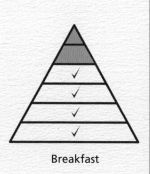

Breakfast

LUNCH

A bowl of home-made vegetable soup (made with carrots, potatoes, onion and celery), served with a wholemeal wrap, filled with lettuce, tomato, tuna and grated cheese.

A carton of strawberry yoghurt.

A glass of water.

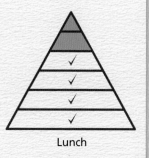

Lunch

DINNER

STARTER

Salmon and potato cakes served with tomato chutney.

MAIN COURSE

Home-made lasagne (minced beef bolognese, pasta sheets and white sauce, topped with grated cheese), served with home-made potato wedges and a side salad.

A glass of milk.

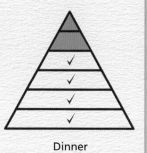

Dinner

DESSERT

Pineapple and mango fruit salad topped with natural yoghurt and seeds.

Recipe adaptation

To adapt a recipe is to substitute, alter quantities or omit ingredients.

Reasons why recipes are adapted

Recipes are adapted to:

- meet current healthy eating guidelines
- cater for specific dietary requirements
- add interest or variety to the diet, e.g. adding nuts to a stir-fry for a crunchy texture
- increase or decrease the quantity served, as most recipes serve four people
- substitute expensive ingredients for less expensive ones, e.g. using textured vegetable protein (TVP) instead of steak mince in a lasagne
- suit personal likes or dislikes, e.g. omitting mushrooms from a curry.

 State the reasons why recipes may be modified/adapted. (12) **HL**

How to adapt a recipe

Original spaghetti Bolognese	Modified recipe	Reason
Knob of butter	1 tablespoon of olive oil	➜ To reduce saturated fat intake
100 g of smoked streaky bacon, finely diced	Omit	➜ To reduce saturated fat intake
250 g of minced beef	250 g of lean (less than 5% fat) steak mince or 250 g of TVP	➜ To reduce saturated fat intake, or to make the dish suitable for a vegetarian diet
1 onion		
1 beef stock cube	250 ml of homemade beef stock	➜ To reduce salt intake and to enhance flavour
1 teaspoon of sugar	Omit	➜ To reduce sugar intake
1 teaspoon of salt	Omit	➜ To reduce salt intake
1 jar of tomato sauce	1 tin of chopped tomatoes	➜ To reduce sugar intake. Tomato sauce has approximately 4 g of sugar per tablespoon.
500 g of spaghetti	500 g of wholewheat spaghetti	➜ To increase dietary fibre intake
50 g of Parmesan cheese	30 g of low-fat cheese	➜ To reduce saturated fat intake
	Add 1 grated carrot, 50 g diced celery and 6 sliced mushrooms	➜ To increase vegetable and dietary fibre intake
	Add fresh parsley	➜ To enhance flavour

Chapter 6: Food preparation and cooking processes

1.3.4 FOOD PREPARATION, COOKING PROCESSES AND APPLIANCES

What you will learn:

- Physical and chemical changes during food preparation and cooking
- Reasons why food is cooked
- Methods of heat transfer
- Factors to consider when choosing a cooking method
- Methods of cooking
- Moist cooking methods, dry cooking methods and frying
- Effects of moist cooking, dry cooking and frying

- Types of household cooking appliances
- Guidelines for the safe use of food preparation appliances and cooking appliances
- Safety features used in food preparation appliances and cooking appliances
- Guidelines for the care of food preparation appliances and cooking appliances

Physical and chemical changes during food preparation

	Physical changes	Chemical changes
Increase in size	When dried fruit and pulses are soaked in water they absorb water and expand	Yeast dough doubles in size during fermentation, as the yeast produces CO_2 bubbles
Tenderising	Meat fibres break up when meat is pounded with a hammer, minced or chopped, tenderising the meat ▲ Meat being marinated	When meat is sprinkled with commercial tenderisers that contain proteolytic enzymes, e.g. papain, they break down meat fibres, tenderising the meat. The acid (vinegar) in a marinade has the same effect. **Did you know** The most common proteolytic enzymes used to tenderise meat are bromelain (made from pineapples) and papain (made from papayas).

	Physical changes	**Chemical changes**
Nutrient loss	When vegetables are soaked in water, B-group vitamins and vitamin C leach into the liquid, decreasing the nutritional value	When vegetables are chopped the enzyme oxidase, present in cell walls, is released and reacts with oxygen in air, destroying vitamin C
Colour change  ▲ Beetroot soaking in water	When beetroot and spinach are soaked in water the colour leaches into the liquid, resulting in a loss of colour	When apples and bananas are prepared too far in advance the enzyme oxidase, present in cell walls, is released and reacts with oxygen in air, causing enzymic browning

Reasons why food is cooked

Food is cooked in order to:

- destroy microorganisms, e.g. salmonella in chicken, making food safer to eat and reducing the risk of food poisoning
- destroy enzymes in food, e.g. fish, lengthening the shelf life
- destroy toxins naturally present in food, e.g. phytohaemagglutinin in kidney beans, which can be harmful if eaten without cooking
- make food, e.g. potatoes, easier to digest
- improve the appearance of food, e.g. red meat becomes an appetising brown color.
- enhance the flavour of food, e.g. meat, as fat melts and extractives are released from the fibres.

Physical and chemical changes during cooking

Physical changes

Physical change	Description
Shrinkage	Protein foods, e.g. meat, shrink, as protein coagulates, water evaporates and fat melts
Tenderising	Collagen in meat connective tissue changes to gelatine, making meat tender and easier to digest
Nutrient loss	B-group vitamins and vitamin C in vegetables are lost, as they leach into the cooking liquid, decreasing the nutritional value 
Colour change	If overcooked, chlorophyll in green vegetables, e.g. green beans, will fade to an olive-green colour
Texture change	Cellulose present in the cell walls of fruit and vegetables softens, making them easier to digest
Thickening	Heat causes starch grains to swell and burst, absorbing liquid present to form a thickened sauce, e.g. roux sauce.

Chemical changes

Chemical change	Description
Maillard reaction	This is the non-enzymic browning of food due to a reaction between certain amino acids and sugars under dry heat. It produces a brown colour that gives an attractive appearance and a crust with an appetising flavour, e.g. the surface of roast meat.
Caramelisation	On heating, sugar melts and caramelises. Caramelisation normally occurs at 160 °C, resulting in an attractive brown colour and a sweet taste, e.g. caramel squares.
Dextrinisation	When starch foods are heated, short-chained polysaccharides called dextrins are formed. On further heating these combine to form pyrodextrins. This causes a colour change on the surface of the food, resulting in an attractive brown appearance, e.g. toast.

? List **two** chemical changes that occur in food during cooking and give **one** example of each change. (6) **OL**

List **two** physical changes that occur during the cooking of food and give **one** example of each. (6) **HL**

Methods of heat transfer

All cooking methods require heat. Heat can be transferred to food by conduction, convection and radiation.

Method	Conduction	Convection	Radiation
Description	The transfer of heat from molecule to molecule until all are heated	The transfer of heat by currents of air or liquid	The transfer of heat directly from the source to the food
Process	A hot cooker ring heats a saucepan. The hot saucepan then heats the liquid or fat present, which cooks the food.	When air or liquid is heated it expands and rises, causing cold air or liquid to fall and take its place. This creates convection currents, resulting in an even temperature which cooks the food	A heating element heats up and radiated heat is transmitted directly from the element to the food, cooking it on one side. Food needs to be turned to cook fully.
Cooking methods	• Frying • Boiling • Stewing	• Boiling • Steaming • Baking • Roasting	• Grilling

? Name **three** methods of heat transfer and give **one** example of a method of cooking that illustrates the use of each. (6) **HL**

Did you know ?

Many cooking methods involve more than one method of heat transfer, e.g. boiling uses conduction and convection.

Factors to consider when choosing a cooking method

- **Density/thickness of food:** this will affect the cooking time and cooking method chosen. For example, a thin cut of meat, e.g. bacon, will be more suited to frying than a thick beef joint.
- **Time:** stewing or braising may not be feasible if time is limited.
- **Quantity of food to be cooked:** fillet steaks may need to be cooked in the oven if they do not fit on a frying pan.
- **Personal likes/dislikes:** individuals may prefer a boiled egg to a fried egg.
- **Equipment:** vegetables may need to be boiled if a steamer is unavailable.

Methods of cooking

There are three cooking methods.
- **Moist cooking methods:** e.g. boiling, poaching, steaming, stewing, braising and pressure cooking.
- **Dry cooking methods:** e.g. baking, roasting and grilling/barbecuing.
- **Frying:** e.g. shallow-, deep-, stir- and dry-frying.

> **?** Listed below are three different cooking methods. Name **two** examples of **each**.
> - Moist cooking methods
> - Dry cooking methods
> - Frying (6) **OL**

Moist cooking methods

Boiling	
Underlying principles	• Food is cooked by conduction and convection in a liquid, e.g. water, at 100°C • Water can be seen rapidly bubbling and evaporating as steam • Simmering is similar to boiling, but occurs at a temperature of 90°C
Advantages	✓ A quick method of cooking
Guidelines	• Monitor closely to prevent food overcooking • Cover the saucepan with a lid and use the minimum amount of water to prevent vitamin loss • Skim off scum that rises to the top when boiling meat • Use the cooking liquid to make stocks or soup bases, as it contains leached nutrients
Suitable foods	• Vegetables • Meat • Starch foods, e.g. pasta, rice, potatoes

Poaching	
Underlying principles	• Food is cooked by conduction and convection in a liquid, e.g. water, wine or stock, just below simmering at 85°C in a saucepan on a hob • Water can be seen barely moving on the surface, not bubbling
Advantages	✓ A quick method of cooking
Guidelines	• It is suited only to naturally tender or delicate foods, e.g. eggs, that require gentle cooking • Ensure the liquid remains at 85°C, otherwise food can fall apart • Use flavoured liquid to impart flavour, e.g. fish poached in white wine or stock
Suitable foods	• Fish • Eggs • Fruit, e.g. pears

Steaming

Underlying principles	• Food is cooked by steam rising from boiling water below which is heated by conduction and convection. The food does not come into contact with the water. • Food can be steamed using a perforated steamer (perforated baskets over a saucepan of boiling water), an electric-tiered steamer (perforated baskets over an element located in the base) or the plate-steaming method (two plates placed over boiling water, with the food in between) 
Advantages	✓ Steaming requires little attention, as it is less likely to overcook compared to boiling ✓ Less nutrient loss compared to boiling, as food does not come in contact with water
Guidelines	• Ensure water is boiling under the perforated baskets before steaming food • Place the densest food, e.g potatoes, in the bottom perforated basket, as dense foods take longer to cook • Leave space around the food so that steam can cook it evenly • Use a tightly fitted lid, so steam can build up and cook the food
Suitable foods	• Fish • Vegetables • Steamed puddings, e.g. plum pudding

Did you know ?

In traditional Chinese cookery a bamboo steamer is placed over a wok with boiling liquid. Meat, fish and vegetables are steamed in this way.

Stewing

Underlying principles	• Food is slowly cooked for two to four hours by conduction and convection in a small amount of liquid at 80–90°C in a covered saucepan on a hob or in an oven
Advantages	✓ Requires little attention, as food cooks slowly ✓ An economical method of cooking, as it tenderises tough cuts of meat ✓ A complete meal can be cooked in one pot, saving time, energy and fuel
Guidelines	• Bring to the boil then reduce heat to 80–90°C, the low simmering temperature is necessary to tenderise tough meat • Use a tightly fitted lid to prevent evaporation of liquid, as this can cause the dish to become dry • Use a well-flavoured stock or wine as a liquid base to enhance flavour
Suitable foods	• Tough cuts of meat, e.g. shin of beef • Fish, e.g. monkfish • Root and tuber vegetables • Fruit, e.g. apples 

Braising

Underlying principles	• Meat is placed on a bed of sautéed diced vegetables called a *mirepoix*, and slowly cooked for one to five hours by conduction and convection in a small amount of liquid, at 80–90°C in a covered saucepan on a hob
Advantages	✓ Requires little attention, as food cooks slowly ✓ An economical method of cooking, as it tenderises tough cuts of meat
Guidelines	• Sear meat in hot fat to give colour and seal in flavour • Use a well-flavoured stock or wine as a liquid base to enhance flavour • Keep at a low simmering temperature to tenderise tough meat • Use a tightly fitted lid to prevent evaporation of liquid, as this can cause the dish to become dry
Suitable foods	• Tough cuts of meat, e.g beef brisket • Chicken • Root and tuber vegetables

> **Did you know**
>
> *Mirepoix* is a combination of chopped carrots, celery and onions used to add flavor and aroma to stocks, sauces, soups and stews. The proportions for making *mirepoix* are 50% onions, 25% carrots and 25% celery.

Pressure cooking

Underlying principles	• A fast, moist method of cooking food at high temperatures by conduction and convection in a vessel with a tightly fitted lid • The boiling point of water is 100°C, however, if pressure is increased inside the pressure cooker it will rise to 108–121°C. Pressure can be increased by manually turning a pressure regulator or adding weights to the lid to prevent the steam from escaping.

Low pressure	Medium pressure	High pressure
5 lb (2.25 kg) **108°C**	10 lb (4.5 kg) **115°C**	15 lb (6.75 kg) **121°C**

Advantages	✓ Food cooks quickly, reducing cooking time, e.g. potatoes cook in 10 minutes instead of 40 ✓ It is energy efficient, as it uses 70–90% less energy than other methods ✓ A complete meal can be cooked in one pot, saving time, energy and fuel

Pressure cooking

Structure

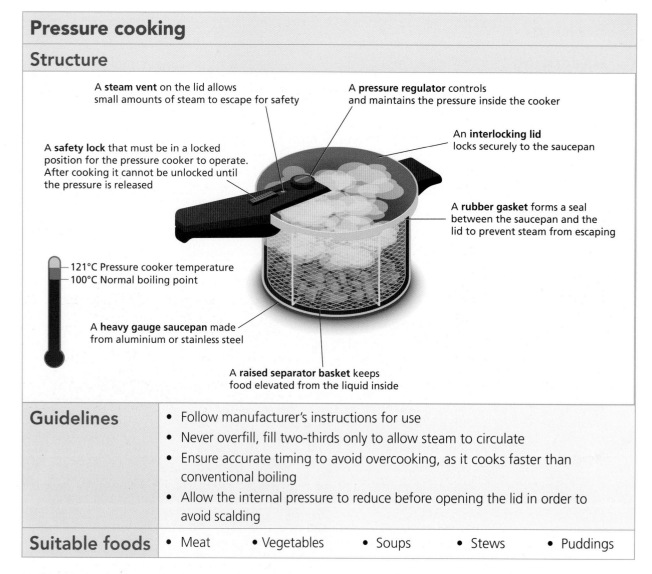

A **steam vent** on the lid allows small amounts of steam to escape for safety

A **pressure regulator** controls and maintains the pressure inside the cooker

An **interlocking lid** locks securely to the saucepan

A **safety lock** that must be in a locked position for the pressure cooker to operate. After cooking it cannot be unlocked until the pressure is released

A **rubber gasket** forms a seal between the saucepan and the lid to prevent steam from escaping

121°C Pressure cooker temperature
100°C Normal boiling point

A **heavy gauge saucepan** made from aluminium or stainless steel

A **raised separator basket** keeps food elevated from the liquid inside

Guidelines	• Follow manufacturer's instructions for use • Never overfill, fill two-thirds only to allow steam to circulate • Ensure accurate timing to avoid overcooking, as it cooks faster than conventional boiling • Allow the internal pressure to reduce before opening the lid in order to avoid scalding
Suitable foods	• Meat • Vegetables • Soups • Stews • Puddings

Effects of moist cooking

Nutritional value	Palatability
✓ No extra fat is added, so it is a low-fat cooking method ✓ If food is steamed or cooked in a pressure cooker, there is a greater retention of nutrients in comparison to other moist cooking methods ✗ If food is boiled or poached there is a high loss of B-group vitamins and vitamin C due to leaching into the cooking liquid	✓ Collagen in meat changes to gelatine, tenderising the meat ✓ Cellulose softens in vegetables, making them easier to digest ✓ Food that is stewed retains flavour, as the liquid forms part of the sauce ✗ Flavour is lost if food is left in cooking water for too long (flavour is not lost when food is stewed or braised) ✗ Fish can fall apart if cooked at too high a temperature or for too long, due to its small amount of connective tissue ✗ Overcooking results in food developing a soggy texture ✗ No extra flavour is added, so food can taste bland

? Define the following method of cooking: poaching. (3) **HL**

Recommend **one** moist method of cooking suitable for fish. In relation to the method recommended:
- state the underlying cooking principle involved
- comment on the palatability of the cooked fish. (10) **HL**

Dry cooking methods

Baking

Underlying principles	• Food is cooked by convection in an oven at 200–260°C. The top shelf is the hottest, as heat rises
Advantages	✓ Food can be batch baked, which saves energy
Guidelines	• Pre heat the oven to ensure food cooks properly • Time food carefully during cooking to avoid drying out or burning • Cover some foods, e.g fish, with tinfoil to retain moisture • Avoid opening the door unnecessarily, as it reduces the temperature and may cause some foods, e.g. cakes, to collapse
Suitable foods	• Bread • Cakes • Meat • Vegetables • Fish 

Roasting

Underlying principles	• **Roasting:** food is cooked by conduction and convection in a little fat in an oven at 175–230°C • **Pot-roasting:** food is cooked by conduction and convection in a little fat in a covered saucepan on a hob • **Spit-roasting:** food is cooked by conduction and convection or radiation on a rotating spit under a grill or in an oven
Advantages	✓ Requires little attention, apart from basting ✓ Numerous foods can be cooked at once in the tray or pot, e.g. roast beef and roast potatoes, saving time, energy and fuel
Guidelines	• Pre heat the oven, as roasting requires a hot oven to ensure food cooks properly • Weigh the meat to calculate cooking times, e.g. beef requires 20 minutes per lb (454 g) with 20 minutes extra • Use a meat thermometer to ensure meat is fully cooked. For beef and lamb it should read 55°C for rare and 75°C for well done • Baste food regularly to add moisture and prevent drying. Use the leftover juices to make a rich, flavoursome gravy
Suitable foods	• Meat, e.g beef, turkey • Root vegetables, e.g. potatoes, carrots 

Grilling/barbecuing

Grilling/barbecuing	
Underlying principles	• **Grilling:** food is quickly cooked under radiant heat, e.g. an electric or gas grill • **Barbecuing:** food is quickly cooked over radiant heat, e.g. burning charcoal
Advantages	✓ A quick method of cooking ✓ The heat from the grill/barbecue seals the surface of the food, which helps to retain nutrients, moisture and flavour
Guidelines	• Some foods, e.g. steak, can be marinated in advance to tenderise and add flavour • Pre heat the grill/barbecue to ensure food cooks properly and to help seal the surface of the food • Use thin pieces of meat or fish, e.g. steak or salmon cutlets, to ensure the food cooks right through • Use a tongs to turn food, so that it cooks evenly • Ensure accurate timing to avoid overcooking or burning food
Suitable foods	• Thin cuts of meat, e.g steaks, rashers • Fish • Vegetables

▲ Barbecuing

Effects of dry cooking

Nutritional value	Palatability
✓ When grilling, fat content is reduced as fat melts and drips away ✗ Loss of B-group vitamins and vitamin C, due to high cooking temperatures ✗ High temperatures can cause meat to shrink, squeezing out juices and resulting in the loss of B-group vitamins	✓ Dry cooking produces an attractive brown surface on food, e.g. meat, due to the Maillard reaction ✓ Steam is produced during baking, preventing food from drying out ✓ Basting food, e.g. meat, with hot fat develops flavour and adds moisture ✓ Collagen in meat changes to gelatine, tenderising meat ✓ Forms a pleasant, crisp texture on food, e.g. roast potatoes

? Define the following method of cooking: pot roasting. (3) **HL**

Recommend **one** dry method of cooking suitable for fish. In relation to the method recommended:
- state the underlying cooking principle involved
- comment on the palatability of the cooked fish. (10) **HL**

Assess grilling/barbecuing as a method of cooking. Refer to:
- cooking/underlying principle
- guidelines to follow in order to ensure palatability of the food
- effect on the nutritive value of the food. (20) **HL**

Frying

Frying	

Underlying principles	• Food is cooked by conduction and convection in hot fat
	• The hot oil or fat seals the outer surface of the food, creating a crisp outer layer
	• There are four main types of frying:
	  o **shallow-frying:** food is cooked in a shallow layer of fat or oil, e.g. in a frying pan
	  o **deep-frying:** food is immersed in hot fat (170–190 °C), e.g. in a deep fat fryer
	  o **stir-frying:** food is tossed in a little oil and cooked quickly, e.g. in a wok
	  o **dry-frying:** foods that contain a high percentage of fat, e.g. sausages, are cooked in a dry pan

Advantages	✓ A quick method of cooking
Guidelines	• Preheat the wok/frying pan before adding oil, otherwise the oil may overheat • Preheat the fat or oil to prevent food from absorbing it and becoming soggy or greasy • Coat delicate foods, e.g. fish, in batter or breadcrumbs to prevent them from falling apart • If shallow-frying, turn food regularly to ensure even cooking • Drain deep-fried food on kitchen paper to remove any excess fat after frying
Suitable foods	• Meat • Fish • Vegetables • Pancakes

Effects of frying

Nutritional value	Palatability
✓ All frying methods, apart from dry-frying, increase the fat and calorie content of the food ✗ Some loss of B-group vitamins and vitamin C, due to high cooking temperatures	✓ Hot fat forms a pleasant, crisp finish on food, e.g. rashers ✓ Fat adds flavour to food, e.g. potatoes, which makes the food more appetising ✗ Some fried foods, e.g. burgers, become greasy in texture, making them difficult to digest

Did you know ?

100 g of boiled potatoes contain approximately 80 kcal, whereas 100 g of deep-fried potato crisps contain approximately 500 kcal.

FOOD PREPARATION APPLIANCES AND COOKING APPLIANCES

Types of food preparation appliances and cooking appliances

- **Food preparation appliances:** e.g. liquidisers, blenders, food processors and carving knives.
- **Cooking appliances:** e.g. cookers, kettles and deep-fat fryers.

Guidelines for the safe use of food preparation appliances and cooking appliances

- Follow the manufacturer's instructions when installing and before using appliances to avoid injury and damage.
- Only use appliances for the function for which they are designed, e.g. a kettle should only be used to heat water.
- Always use the correct attachments in appliances for the function for which they are designed, e.g. a dough hook in a food processor for bread dough. Ensure all attachments are in the correct position on appliances to avoid injury and damage.
- Take special care when handling sharp items, e.g. blades, from appliances, as these can cause injury.
- If using appliances for long periods of time, turn off at intervals to avoid overheating.
- Keep appliances away from water during use and ensure hands are dry when using to avoid electric shock.
- Ensure appliances have correctly wired plugs and flexes are not damaged or frayed, to avoid electric shock.

Safety features used in food preparation appliances and cooking appliances

- Cordless appliances, e.g. electric kettles
- Thermostats, e.g. cookers
- Heat-resistant plastic, e.g. the handles of saucepans
- Fuses, e.g. cookers
- Safety locks, e.g. food processors
- Earth wire in plugs
- Double insulation, e.g. electric kettles

 Name **two** safety features used in electrical appliances and give an example of the use of each. (6) **OL**

Guidelines for the care of food preparation appliances and cooking appliances

- Check the manufacturer's instructions for cleaning guidelines. Improper cleaning of appliances may lead to damage that will not be covered by the guarantee.
- Always disconnect appliances from the electrical source before cleaning, to avoid electric shock.
- Do not immerse appliances in water as it may cause damage. Wash all detachable parts in hot, soapy water. The outer casing should be cleaned thoroughly with a damp cloth.
- Take special care when washing sharp items, e.g. blades, from appliances, as these can cause injury.
- Avoid using harsh abrasives, e.g. steel wool, when cleaning the outer casing of appliances, as they may scratch the surface.
- Dry all attachments and parts of appliances thoroughly, as metal may rust if left damp.
- Never wind the flex around the appliance as this may cause damage.
- Protect appliances from dust by placing a loose covering on top when storing.

SOUP, SAUCES, PASTRY AND RAISING AGENTS

What you will learn:

- **Reasons for including soup and sauces in the diet**
- **Classification of soup, sauces, pastry and raising agents**
- **Stock**
- **Guidelines for preparing and cooking soup, sauces and pastry**
- **Characteristics of well-made soup, sauces and pastry**
- **Garnishes and accompaniments for soup**
- **Commercial soup, sauces and pastry**
- **Ways to serve sauces**
- **Popular sauce- and food-combinations**
- **Types of yeast**
- **Chorleywood processing**
- **Guidelines for baking with yeast**

SOUP

Soup is one of the most nourishing and easily digested foods in the diet. It is often considered a meal in a bowl. It can be served hot or cold.

> **Did you know** ❓
> 'Cream of' soups contain a higher level of saturated fat and calories, due to the addition of cream. These soups are commonly found on restaurant menus.

Reasons for including soup in the diet

- Soup provides nourishment as it is made from vegetables, meat or fish. The nutrients provided vary, depending on the ingredients used, e.g. chicken soup is higher in protein than vegetable soup.
- Soup stimulates appetite and aids digestion when served as a starter course in a dinner menu.
- Hot soups provide warmth on chilly winter days.
- Cold soups, e.g. **gazpacho**, provide refreshment on hot summer days.
- Soup adds interest and variety in the diet by providing a different taste and texture.

Lit'Hit
Gazpacho is a soup made from chopped raw vegetables that is served cold.

Classification of soup

Soup can be classified into two main groups: thin soups and thick soups.

Thin soups

Type	Description	Example
Clear soups	Made from rich, well-flavoured stock and clarified by the addition of egg white	Chicken consommé
Broths	Unclarified soups made from rich, well-flavoured stock containing small pieces of meat, poultry or vegetables and thickened with whole cereals, e.g. barley or pasta	Scotch broth

Thick soups

Type	Description	Example
Puréed soups	Thickened by blending or liquidising the soup ingredients, after they have been cooked, until smooth	Tomato soup
Thickened soups	Thickened by using a liaison. Examples of liaisons include flour, cornflour, arrowroot, roux, eggs, cream and cereals, e.g. pearl barley	Mushroom soup

 Name **two** classes of homemade soup **and** give **one** example of **each** class. (14) **OL**

Stock

Stock is a well-flavoured liquid made by simmering bones, meat/fish and vegetables in water. Once cooked the bones, meat/fish and vegetables are strained and removed. The flavoured liquid can then be used as a base for soups and sauces. Home-made stock is superior to commercial stock cubes as it has a richer flavour, more nutrients and no added salt.

Guidelines for preparing and cooking stock

- Use fresh ingredients to create a rich, well-flavoured stock. Avoid using starchy or fatty foods, e.g. potatoes or milk, as they cause stock to sour more quickly.
- Use a heavy-based saucepan to allow heat to spread evenly throughout the stock, so that it cooks at the same speed without burning.
- Avoid completely covering the pot with a lid, as stock needs to evaporate slightly to develop a rich flavour.
- Allow stock to come to the boil and then simmer gently. If boiled continously it will become cloudy, as impurities, e.g. fat from meat, emulsify into the liquid.
- Skim fat from the top of the stock as it simmers in order to prevent a greasy taste.

Commercial stocks

Due to the time-consuming nature of making stock many people purchase commercially prepared stocks. These are concentrated forms of stock that offer a quick and easy way to add intense flavour to dishes, e.g. soups and risottos. They come in various forms, including granules or powder, cubes or jellies, and in a variety of flavours, e.g. beef, chicken, fish and vegetable. They can be high in salt and additives.

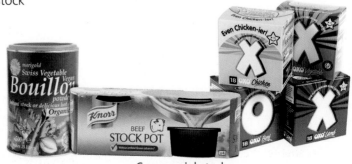

▲ Commercial stocks

Guidelines for preparing and cooking soup

- Use fresh ingredients to create a well-flavoured soup. Fresh ingredients can be substituted with frozen vegetables, but these do not give the same flavour.
- Use a heavy-based saucepan to allow heat to spread evenly throughout the soup, so that it cooks at the same speed without burning.
- Dice or finely chop the ingredients into even-sized pieces to extract maximum flavour and ensure even cooking.
- Sauté vegetables to release flavour and enhance the taste of the final soup.
- Ideally, use fresh stock over commercial for a better flavour. Ensure to add the correct amount, otherwise the soup may be too watery in consistency.
- Allow soup to come to the boil and then simmer gently to extract maximum flavour.
- Season soup at the end, as ingredients may already contain salt, which could be enough to season sufficiently.
- If making a puréed soup, blend thoroughly to remove any lumps and create the correct consistency.

Characteristics of well-made soup

- **Good flavour:** the main ingredients should dominate, e.g. carrot in carrot soup.
- **Correct consistency/texture for its type:** e.g. a puréed soup should be smooth.
- **Appetising and attractive colour:** it should not have a film of grease on top.
- **Well-seasoned:** e.g. with pepper or a **bouquet garni** to enhance flavour.
- **Served at the correct temperature for its type:** e.g. gazpacho should be well-chilled.

Lit'Hit
A bouquet garni is a bundle of herbs tied together.

Garnishes for soup

A garnish is a food item used to decorate and add flavour to another food. Suitable garnishes for soup include:

- **fresh herbs**, e.g. chives or parsley
- **croutons**, pieces of sautéed or re-baked bread, often cubed and seasoned, used to add texture and flavour to soups
- **cream, yoghurt or crème fraîche swirls**
- **grated cheese**, e.g. Parmesan
- **julienne strips of vegetables**, e.g. carrot or courgette
- **lemon or orange zest**.

Lit'Hit
Julienne is food cut into short, thin strips

▲ Julienne garnish

Accompaniments for soup

An accompaniment is a food item served to complement and complete a dish. Suitable accompaniments for soup include:

- **bread**, e.g. soda bread
- **dinner rolls**
- **melba toast**, very thin slices of toasted bread.

Commercial soups

Commercial soups have increased in popularity in recent times due to busier lifestyles. A wide variety are available, including dehydrated soups, canned soups and cook-chill soups.

▲ Melba toast

SOUP, SAUCES, PASTRY AND RAISING AGENTS

Advantages and disadvantages of commercial soups

Advantages	Disadvantages
✓ Quick to make, as they simply need to be heated in the microwave or cooked on the hob for a short period of time ✓ Little skill is needed, so they are ideal for inexperienced cooks ✓ Useful in unforeseen circumstances, as they can be prepared in very little time ✓ Available in a variety of flavours, so many individuals' tastes are met and variety is added to the diet	✗ Expensive compared to homemade alternatives, as conviencience is being paid for ✗ Often high in salt and saturated fat, used to enhance the flavour of the soup and make it more appealing to consumers ✗ Often contain artificial additives, e.g. preservatives and flavourings ✗ Few culinary skills are developed, as the soup is already made

Outline:
- the range of convenience soups available to the consumer
- the advantages **and** disadvantages of convenience soups. (24) **OL**

SAUCES

Sauces are well-flavoured liquids that can be sweet or savoury, thick or thin and served hot or cold.

Reasons for including sauces in the diet

- Sauces provide nourishment. The nutrients present vary, depending on the ingredients used, e.g. a white sauce is higher in calcium than barbecue sauce.
- Sauces add variety and interest in the diet by adding flavour, and enhancing the appearance of food, e.g. cranberry sauce with turkey.
- Sauces moisten foods, making them easier to swallow and digest, e.g. gravy with poultry.
- Sauces garnish and improve the appearance or colour of dishes, e.g. chocolate sauce.
- Some sauces counteract the richness of high-fat foods, e.g. apple sauce served with roast pork.

Classification of sauces

Type	Description	Examples
Roux-based (white) sauces ➜ For more information on how to make a **roux-based sauce** see your Food Studies Assignment Guide.	Made with equal parts fat and flour with the addition of varying amounts of liquid, e.g. stock or milk. Variations can be made to this basic recipe, e.g. addition of onion or parsley.	White, parsley or béchamel sauce ▲ Parsley sauce

Type	Description	Examples
Egg-based sauces	Made from thickened eggs. This can occur by coagulation or emulsification.	Custard, mayonnaise or hollandaise sauce ▲ Hollandaise sauce
Fruit sauces	Made from stewed fruit, often puréed	Apple, cranberry or orange sauce
Cold sauces	Made with a combination of cold ingredients, and involve no cooking	Mint, horseradish or tartar sauce ▲ Tartar sauce
Sweet/sugar-based sauces	Served with desserts to provide colour and enhance flavour	Chocolate or caramel sauce
Miscellaneous sauces	Other sauces that include a wide variety of ingredients and methods	Barbecue, tomato or satay sauce

 Classify sauces and give **one** example in each class. (6) **HL**

Guidelines for preparing and cooking sauces

- Use the correct proportions of ingredients, especially for roux sauces, as they need equal quantities of flour and fat to ensure success.
- Use a heavy-based saucepan to allow heat to spread evenly throughout the sauce, so that it cooks at the same speed without burning.
- If suited to the sauce, use a well-flavoured stock. Ensure to add the correct amount, otherwise the sauce may be too watery in consistency.
- If suited to the sauce, season at the end, as ingredients may already contain salt, which could be enough to season sufficiently.
- Ensure a sauce has the correct consistency associated with its type, e.g. a pouring white sauce should pour easily from a jug.

Characteristics of well-made sauces

- **Good flavour:** the main ingredients should dominate, e.g. a korma curry sauce should taste of coconut and almonds.
- **Correct consistency/texture for its type:** e.g. barbecue sauce should be thick and sticky.
- **Appetising and attractive colour:** it should not have a film of grease on top.
- **Served at the correct temperature for its type:** e.g. gravy should be piping hot.

Ways to serve sauces

- **Hot or cold as part of a dish:** e.g. Thai green chicken curry.
- **Over food:** e.g. cauliflower with cheese sauce.
- **Separately as an accompaniment:** e.g. steak with peppercorn sauce.
- **For decoration:** e.g. strawberry sauce feathered on a cheesecake.

Popular sauce-and-food combinations

- Mint sauce and roast lamb
- Apple sauce and roast pork
- Cranberry sauce and roast turkey
- Orange sauce and roast duck

- Horseradish sauce and roast beef
- Parsley sauce and bacon or gammon
- Tartar sauce and fish

Commercial sauces

Commercial sauces have increased in popularity in recent times due to busier lifestyles. A wide variety are available including dehydrated sauces, canned/jar/bottle sauces and cook-chill sauces.

Advantages and disadvantages of commercial sauces

See advantages and disadvantages of commercial soups on page 172.

▲ Commercial sauces

PASTRY

Pastry is a mixture of fat, flour and water. The proportion of ingredients and how they are incorporated varies from pastry to pastry.

Classification of pastry

Type	Description	Examples
Short crust pastry	Made with half the quantity of fat (butter) to flour and a little water, e.g. 200 g flour and 100 g of butter.	• Steak and kidney pie • Quiche
Rich short crust pastry	Similar to short crust pastry, with the addition of extra fat, eggs and/or icing sugar.	• Lemon meringue pie • Fruit tart
Suet pastry	Similar to short crust pastry except suet is rubbed in as the fat, instead of butter.	• Steamed pudding • Dumplings
Rough puff pastry	Made with flour, water and a large amount of butter, and formed by rolling and folding the dough in layers. Butter is added in lumps.	• Sausage rolls • Chicken and mushroom pie

Type	Description	Examples
Puff pastry	Made with flour, water and a large amount of butter, and formed by rolling and folding the dough in layers. Butter is spread between the layers.	• Croissants • Vol-au-vent ▸ Vol-au-vent
Flaky pastry	Made with butter, flour and water, and formed by rolling and folding the dough in layers. Butter is added in lumps between the layers.	• Mince pies • Eccles cakes ▸ Eccles cake
Choux pastry	Hot pastry made from flour mixed with boiling water, butter and eggs	• Éclairs • Profiteroles
Filo pastry	Paper-thin sheets of pastry made from flour, oil and water. This is a very skilled pastry that is generally only made by pastry chefs.	• Samosas • Spring rolls • Baklava ▸ Samosas

 Name **two** types of pastry. State **one** difference between the types of pastry named. (6) **HL**

Guidelines for preparing and cooking pastry

- Weigh all ingredients accurately. This is especially important when weighing flour as excess makes pastry crumbly and difficult to roll.
- Coldness is essential to avoid the butter melting, causing the pastry to become greasy. This can be achieved by using a metal knife to mix the dough and by not over-handling the pastry.
- Avoid overworking, e.g. excessive kneading, as it will develop the gluten in the flour, making pastry harder to roll. This also makes it more likely to shrink during cooking and have a tough texture once cooked.
- Introduce as much air as possible to ensure light and airy pastry. This can be achieved by sieving the flour and rubbing in the fat.
- Add liquid gradually, as too much will make pastry sticky and difficult to roll.
- Rest and chill pastry in the fridge before baking. This helps relax the gluten in the flour, making the dough easier to roll and less likely to shrink in the oven.
- Avoid using excessive amounts of flour when rolling, as the pastry will become crumbly, making it difficult to roll.
- Complete light, even rolling in one direction to avoid the gluten in the pastry being overstretched, leading to shrinkage during baking.
- Ensure pastry is placed in a hot oven (200°C) as a high temperature is needed to quickly burst the starch grains so that fat can be absorbed. If the oven is too cold pastry will be hard, heavy and greasy.
- After the first ten minutes, reduce the oven temperature to ensure food inside cooks without burning the pastry.

Baking blind method

Baking blind involves baking pastry without any filling. This is completed to crisp the pastry base and prevent it from becoming soggy when moist fillings are added, e.g. egg and milk when making quiche.

Characteristics of well-made pastry

- **Attractive golden-brown colour:** created by the Maillard reaction.
- **Crispy and airy texture:** not soggy or doughy on the base or inside.
- **Rich, buttery flavour**.

→ For information on **how to bake blind** see your Food Studies Assignment Guide.

Commercial pastry

Commercial pastries have increased in popularity in recent times due to busier lifestyles.

A wide variety are available, including short crust pastry, rich shortcrust, puff (all-butter and light versions) and filo pastry.

Advantages and disadvantages of commercial pastry

Advantages	Disadvantages
✓ Quick to make, as it just needs to be rolled out, (may already be done, depending on the pastry purchased), cut to size and have the desired filling added	✗ Expensive compared to home-made alternatives, as convenience is being paid for
✓ Little skill is needed, so it is ideal for inexperienced cooks	✗ Portion size may not suit the consumer's needs, e.g. a block of pastry will be too large for an individual portion
✓ Useful in unforeseen circumstances, as it can be prepared in very little time	✗ Few culinary skills are developed, as the pastry is already made
	✗ Often contain artificial additives, e.g. preservatives

RAISING AGENTS

Raising agents cause baked products to rise, giving a light, spongy and soft texture.

Classification of raising agents

Raising agents can be categorised into three main groups: mechanical raising agents (air), chemical raising agents (bread soda, baking powder) and biological raising agents (yeast).

Mechanical raising agents

Air is an example of a mechanical raising agent. It can be introduced mechanically or physically into a mixture by:

- sieving, e.g. flour
- rubbing, e.g. flour and fat with fingertips
- creaming, e.g. butter and sugar
- whisking, e.g. eggs and sugar
- folding, e.g. flour into eggs and sugar.

▲ Sieving flour

Once cooked, the air bubbles expand and push up the mixture.

Culinary uses: scones and sponge cakes.

Chemical raising agents

Chemical raising agents are based on a chemical reaction between an acid and an alkali. When liquid is added, carbon dioxide gas (CO_2) is produced, which acts as the raising agent.

Chemical formula

alkali + acid + liquid = CO_2

Examples of chemical raising agents include bicarbonate of soda and baking powder.

Bicarbonate of soda (bread soda)

When bicarbonate of soda (alkali) is moistened with an acidic liquid, e.g. buttermilk, it produces CO_2.

Chemical formula

bicarbonate of soda	+ buttermilk	= CO_2
alkali	+ acidic liquid	= gas

🍴 **Culinary uses:** soda bread.

Baking powder

Baking powder contains bicarbonate of soda (alkali), cream of tartar (acid) and flour (absorbs moisture and prevents a premature reaction between the alkali and acid before use). This produces CO_2 when mixed with a liquid, e.g. milk.

Chemical formula

bicarbonate of soda	+ cream of tartar	+ water/milk	= CO_2
alkali	+ acid	+ liquid	= gas

🍴 **Culinary uses:** cakes and muffins.

Biological raising agents

Baker's yeast (saccharomyces cerevisiae) is used as a biological raising agent in bread-making.
Yeast is type of fungi that produces CO_2 by a process of fermentation.

Fermentation

Fermentation is the breakdown of carbohydrate (starch and sugar) by microorganisms (yeast and bacteria) to produce CO_2, alcohol and energy. For this to occur in bread-making, yeast requires food (provided by the carbohydrate in flour or sugar), warmth and moisture.

Fermentation occurs in stages, and works on the action of a series of enzymes. These enzymes are present in flour and yeast.

▲ CO_2 bubbles in bread dough, produced by yeast

Chemical formula

Yeast + $C_6H_{12}O_6$ (glucose) + moisture + warmth = $2CO_2$ (carbon dioxide) + $2C_2H_5OH$ (alcohol) + energy

Stages of fermentation

- Diastase in flour converts starch to maltose.
- Maltase in yeast converts maltose to glucose.
- Invertase in yeast converts sucrose to glucose and fructose.
- Zymase in yeast ferments the glucose and fructose to CO_2 and alcohol.

Enzyme	Substrate	Product
Diastase (in flour)	Starch	Maltose
Maltase (in yeast)	Maltose	Glucose
Invertase (in yeast)	Sucrose	Glucose + Fructose
Zymase (in yeast)	Glucose + Fructose	CO_2 + Alcohol

During proving, yeast cells feed on sugar to produce carbon dioxide, alcohol and energy. The CO_2 bubbles expand and raise the dough (it can double in size). While bread is baking in the oven:

- yeast is killed and fermentation stops
- alcohol, CO_2 and water evaporate from the bread during baking
- gluten coagulates, causing the bread structure to become firmer
- Maillard reaction occurs between the sugars and amino acids present, giving bread a brown colour
- pyrodextrins form, adding to the brown colour on bread.

 Name a suitable raising agent for **each** of the following dishes.
- Bread
- Sponge cake
- Muffins (6) **OL**

Define fermentation. Name **two** by-products of fermentation. (6) **HL**

Types of yeast

The main types of yeast available are fresh yeast and fast-action dried yeast.

Type	Description	Guidelines for use	Storage
Fresh yeast	• Creamy/beige colour with a soft, crumbly texture. • Beer-like smell. • 15 g will raise 450 g of flour.	• Blend with a little warm water and sugar. • Allow the mixture to stand for 10–15 minutes until frothy.	• Store in the fridge for three to four days, or in the freezer for up to three months.
Fast-action dried yeast	• Most popular yeast available to consumers. • Granular, dried fresh yeast with the addition of flour improvers, e.g. enzymes and ascorbic acid (vitamin C), that speed up fermentation. • Sold in individual packets (7 g). • 7 g will raise 450 g of flour.	• Add directly to the bread mix without rehydrating in liquid first.	• Store in a cool, dry place for up to one year.

Chorleywood processing

Chorleywood processing is a process of bread-making that involves the addition of vitamin C to the yeast bread mixture, which speeds up fermentation, reducing proving time. Vitamin C also strengthens the gluten present in flour, making the dough more elastic.

Guidelines for baking with yeast

- Weigh all ingredients accurately. This is especially important when weighing sugar and salt, as excess can kill yeast cells.
- Use good-quality yeast and always ensure it is in date, as yeast loses its potency over time, resulting in longer rising times.
- Use strong flour, as it has a higher gluten content, this enables dough to stretch so it can hold more CO_2 gas produced by yeast. This gives a more airy, spongy texture to bread when baked.
- Provide warmth to encourage yeast to ferment. This can be done by using warm utensils and by warming liquid ingredients.
- Knead dough thoroughly to enable the gluten in the strong flour to develop. Developed gluten forms an elastic network that traps CO_2 giving bread an even rise. Without kneading, bread will be flat and tough.
- Allow dough to prove to give the yeast cells an opportunity to produce CO_2 gas to raise the dough. This can be completed quickly, by placing dough in a warm environment (26°C), e.g. over a warm oven; or slowly, by leaving the dough overnight in the fridge (4°C).

▲ Fresh yeast

▲ Fast-action dried yeast

▲ Kneading dough

SOUP, SAUCES, PASTRY AND RAISING AGENTS

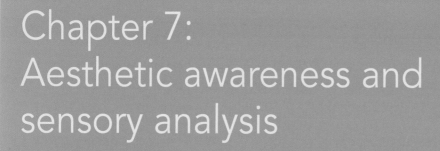

Chapter 7: Aesthetic awareness and sensory analysis

🔗 1.3.4 AESTHETIC AWARENESS OF FOOD

What you will learn:

- **The five senses**
- **Aesthetic awareness when choosing, preparing and cooking food**
- **Aesthetic awareness in food presentation**

Food is not only necessary for human survival, it is also something that can stimulate the senses and give pleasure. The look, smell, taste and texture of a food will influence whether or not people buy, prepare or eat it. This is known as aesthetic awareness.

The five senses

Humans have five senses.

Sense	Sight	Sound	Smell	Taste	Touch
Organ	Eye	Ear	Nose	Taste buds	Nerve endings

When stimulated, senses send messages to the brain through the nervous system. These messages create a response that can be positive or negative, influencing whether or not we choose or reject a food. The senses influence food choice, preparation, cooking and presentation.

Aesthetic awareness when choosing, preparing and cooking food

Sight (appearance)

Choosing food

Sight is used to analyse the size, shape and appearance of a food, and this influences consumers' food choices.

▲ Imperfect carrots

- Consumers often have predetermined ideas about a food's appearance, e.g. carrots should be free from **imperfections** and dirt.

> 📌 **Lit Hit**
> An imperfection is a fault or blemish.

- The appearance of the food is a sign of freshness. Food that appears spoilt, e.g. wilted or covered in mould, may not be chosen by consumers. However, mould growth is accepted on certain foods, such as blue-veined cheese.

- Consumers have predetermined expectations of the colour a food should be, e.g. peas are expected to be green. The canning process often removes the colour from canned peas, leaving them grey and unappetising. In order to meet expectations, manufacturers of canned peas add a green food colouring.

▲ Blue-veined cheese

- The colour of food is a good indication of how ripe or fresh it is, e.g. unripe bananas are green, whereas yellow bananas are ripe.

- Certain flavours are often associated with colours, and form an expectation of the taste, e.g. yellow is associated with a lemon flavour (sour) and red is associated with a strawberry flavour (sweet).

Preparing and cooking food

- Food should be cooked correctly, as underdone or overcooked food is visually unappealing.
- Vegetables that are steamed tend to hold their colour more than those that are boiled, and therefore look more appetising.
- During cooking a number of reactions take place that make food more attractive to the consumer, e.g. the Maillard reaction creates a brown colour on the surface of food, such as roast beef or potatoes.

Sensory terms to evaluate appearance (sight): burnt, greasy, colourful, attractive, moist.

Sound

Choosing, preparing and cooking food

Sound has a part to play in the appreciation of food being prepared and consumed.

For example:

- the sound of a food sizzling, e.g. frying rashers, prepares people for the food to come by stimulating the appetite
- the sound of a crunchy bread roll creates an impression of freshness

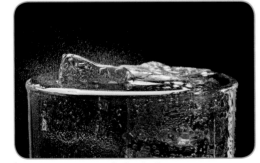

▲ Soft drink, fizzing

- the fizzing sound from a soft drink gives an impression of a rehydrating beverage.

Sensory terms to evaluate sound: bubbling, sizzling, crunchy.

AESTHETIC AWARENESS OF FOOD

Smell (aroma)

Choosing food

The sense of smell is controlled by nasal receptors in the lining of the nose. It is vital to our experience of taste and enjoyment of food.

- Foods that have a pleasant aroma are often enjoyable to eat so will be chosen by consumers. Other foods that produce pungent, strong odours may be off-putting to some, e.g. the smell of blue cheese.
- When choosing food, smell can help consumers to detect if a food is fresh and safe to eat, e.g. fresh fish should smell of the sea, if it smells rancid or sour it is a sign of spoilage.

Preparing and cooking food

When preparing and cooking food, aromas are released that stimulate the appetite and cause the salivary glands to release saliva. Overcooked food smells burnt and unpleasant, whereas undercooked food releases very few aromas. If food is left for too long before consuming aromas can be lost.

Sensory terms to evaluate smell: burnt, fruity, spicy, aromatic.

Did you know

The durian fruit from South East Asia has a smell similar to sewage. For this reason it is banned in many hotel rooms.

Taste (flavour)

Choosing food

The sensation of taste is linked to our sense of smell, the mouthfeel of the food and the taste buds on the tongue. The taste buds help determine the flavour of food.

- **Smell:** when chewing food, volatile aromas and chemicals released travel up into the nose and are detected by smell receptors in the lining of the nasal cavity. This intensifies the flavour of food.

- **Mouthfeel:** mouthfeel refers to the chemical and thermal interactions of food, e.g. cold ice cream or spicy hot chillies, with the nerves in the mouth. These interactions create sensations by stimulating the nerves. Some manufacturers use physical conditioning agents in order to create a pleasant mouthfeel, e.g. gums are added to soups to make them creamier and smoother.

- **Taste buds:** taste buds are sensory organs found on the surface of the tongue. Each taste bud has very sensitive microscopic hairs called microvilli that send messages to the brain about how something tastes. There are four specific tastes that they can detect: sweet, sour, bitter and salty. A fifth taste known as umami is now being used to describe foods that have a pleasant, savoury taste, e.g. soy sauce or Parmesan cheese. If consumers enjoy the overall taste and flavour they get from foods they will choose them.

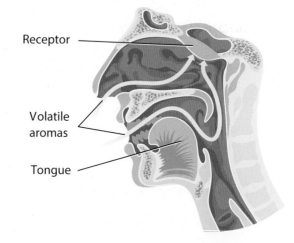

Receptor

Volatile aromas

Tongue

Did you know

The average person has around 10,000 taste buds. Some people have up to twice the average amount of taste buds. They are known as supertasters, and they can get a much stronger taste and flavour from foods.

Did you know

It was originally believed that different parts of the tongue detect different tastes. A recent study has proven that this idea of a 'tongue map' is a myth. Instead, it found that the brain has specialised neurons that interpret signals sent by each taste bud.

Preparing and cooking food

When preparing and cooking food, flavour can be introduced in many ways, e.g. by serving complementary flavours together, like chocolate and orange or by contrasting flavours, like sweet and sour chicken. It is important to be cautious when using strong flavours in cooking, e.g. chillies or garlic, as they can overpower a dish.

Manufacturers often add natural flavourings or flavour enhancers, e.g. MSG, to food to replace flavours lost during cooking, or to enhance flavour.

▲ Chilli and garlic

Sensory terms to evaluate taste: spicy, sweet, sour, salty.

Texture

Choosing food

When choosing food, texture is determined by our sense of sight and our sense of touch.

- **Sight:** our eyes can tell if food has the expected texture, e.g. consumers expect salad leaves to be crisp in texture, not wilted or soft, influencing food choices.
- **Touch:** nerve endings in the mouth send messages to the brain in relation to the texture of the food being eaten, e.g. the soft, squeaky texture of a cooked mushroom is pleasant for some but unpleasant for others. Ideally, choose ripe, fresh, in-season fruit and vegetables, as their texture is at its best.

Preparing and cooking food

- The cooking of food will affect the texture, e.g. overcooked steak will become difficult to cut or chew, making it unappetising.
- Sauces should be the correct consistency, e.g. free from lumps, not too thick or thin.
- If food lacks flavour, texture becomes even more important, e.g. lettuce has no distinctive flavour, but is enjoyed due to its crisp texture.
- Dishes that are soft in texture, such as casseroles, should be served with contrasting textures to add interest, e.g. a crispy bread roll.

Sensory terms to evaluate texture: dry, moist, lumpy, chewy, soft.

Aesthetic awareness in food presentation

When serving food on a plate it should be arranged to look attractive. Include a garnish to decorate. Garnishes can be sweet or savoury.

Savoury garnishes		**Sweet garnishes**	
• Herbs, e.g. parsley and chives • Cream • Lemon wedge • Spring onion tassels		• Icing sugar or cocoa • Whipped cream • Chocolate • Nuts • Fruit • Spun sugar	

 Discuss the importance of aesthetic awareness in relation to the choice and presentation of food. (12) **HL**

Discuss the influence of any **three** of the senses when choosing, buying or eating food. (15) **HL**

AESTHETIC AWARENESS OF FOOD

SENSORY ANALYSIS TESTING

What you will learn:

- **Why sensory analysis is used in the food industry**
- **Conditions necessary for sensory analysis testing**
- **Categories of sensory analysis tests**
- **Methods of presenting sensory analysis results**

HL **Sensory analysis** is a scientific discipline used to measure, analyse and interpret reactions to the characteristics of food, as perceived by our sense of sight, sound, smell, taste and touch.

Organoleptic properties are the sensory properties of food that are detected by the sense organs. These include appearance, flavour, texture, aroma, mouthfeel and aftertaste.

Using the five senses, it is possible to gain an insight into consumers' likes or dislikes. This information helps food producers and manufacturers gauge consumer reactions to their product, and make improvements where necessary.

▲ Sensory analysis test

Why sensory analysis is used in the food industry

- **New products:** sensory analysis is used to determine if customers like new food products before launching the foods into the market place. This saves food companies time and money.

- **Modifications:** food producers use sensory analysis to see if consumers can notice a **detectable** difference between an original and a modified food product. Recipes are often modified by food companies to make a nutrition change, e.g. to modify the fat content, to use a cheaper ingredient to save on costs or to remove an ingredient, e.g. nuts, to make the products safe for allergy sufferers.

- **Own brand:** food producers use sensory analysis to develop own-brand food products to compete with the branded market leaders. If the difference is too noticeable the recipe may need to be altered.

- **Quality assurance:** sensory analysis is used to determine if a food product is manufactured correctly, if the taste profile matches the description, e.g. creamy soup, and if any odd flavours or tastes are present. This ensures a high standard of quality is maintained. If a problem is highlighted the food batch may be discarded.

▲ Original and low-fat crisps

Lit Hit

Detectable means a difference that is noticed by the senses.

▲ Branded and own-brand cereal

 State, giving examples, when sensory analysis tests are used in the food industry. (8) **HL**

Conditions necessary for sensory analysis testing

Testing conditions must be strictly followed to ensure the validity of results obtained.

- **Location:** in industry, sensory analysis must take place in special testing booths with dividing walls to prevent sharing of information. In the classroom, desks should be separated to allow adequate space between testers.
- **Lighting:** correct lighting is essential, as a dark room may affect the colour of food or hide any imperfections. In the classroom, desks should be moved to a window so that food is tested in natural light.
- **Ventilation:** ventilation is necessary to remove any lingering odours. In the classroom, windows should be opened one hour before testing.
- **Silence:** silence should be maintained during the tasting session to prevent the sharing of information.
- **Timing:** tests should be carried out around mid-morning as at this time testers are neither too full or too hungry. Testers should not eat for 30 minutes before the test, as tastes may linger in their mouths.
- **Test organisers:** test organisers should not be involved in the tasting session, as they know the foods being tested and the coding of samples.
- **Special dietary conditions:** test organisers should check if any testers have a special dietary condition. Failure to do so could cause harm.
- **Hygiene and food safety:** test organisers involved in the setting up of the tests should practise strict hygiene standards to reduce the risk of food poisoning. For example, wearing gloves and cleaning all surfaces. They should ensure the food to be tested is fresh and in date.
- **Containers:** test organisers should ensure all containers are the same size and shape. Clear or white containers should be chosen, as coloured containers can affect the appearance of the food.
- **Food samples:** all food samples should be of uniform shape, colour and amount. Test organisers should weigh samples for accuracy and ensure a sufficient quantity of a sample is used to gain an accurate test result.
- **Temperature:** test organisers should ensure all food samples are served at the same temperature. This is especially important for foods such as milk, yoghurt, juices and soup.
- **Coding of samples:** a coding system using shapes, letters or three-digit numbers should be used by test organisers to identify food samples. This prevents any bias amongst the testers. Careful selection of letters and numbers is important. For example, using 'A' or 'B' could cause the taster to perceive 'A' as superior. The arrangement of samples can be random (used for large number of samples), balanced (every possible order occurs an equal number of times) or a combination of balanced and random sequencing.
- **Number of samples:** in industry, a large number of samples should be tested to ensure the results obtained are a true representation of the views of the general population. In the classroom, a smaller sample is sufficient (usually six).
- **Setting the trays:** when setting trays, test organsiers should ensure that:
  o each tray is identical, with the same number of samples and containers
  o each tray has a glass of water or dry cracker to cleanse the palate between tastings. This ensures there is no transference of flavours from one sample to the other
  o each tester has a record sheet and pencil to record results
  o each tester has clear instructions as to how to use the record sheet and taste samples.

Set out the conditions necessary for conducting sensory analysis testing to ensure accurate results. (20) **HL**

Categories of sensory analysis tests

There are three categories of tests used in sensory analysis: preference, difference and descriptive.

Preference tests

Purpose: to find out which food product is preferred, or if a food product is acceptable.

Paired preference tests	Two different samples of a food product are given, e.g. full-fat and low-fat biscuit. The tester is asked: *Taste the samples and identify which you prefer.* 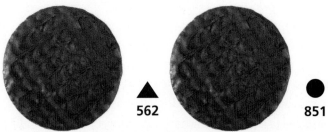
Hedonic rating scale  *Lit Hit* Hedonic refers to pleasure. 	One or more samples of a food product are given. The tested is asked: *Taste the sample and rate how much you like or dislike it on the accompanying verbal or pictorial scale.* 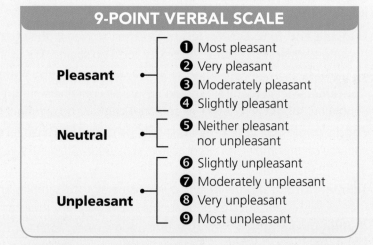 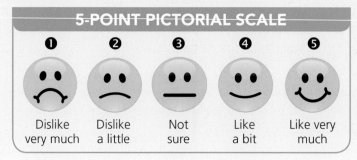
Preference ranking test	Two or more samples of a food product are given. The tester is asked: *Taste the samples and rank your preference by placing 1st choice beside the sample that you prefer the most, 2nd choice beside your next preference and 3rd choice beside the sample you least prefer.*

Difference tests

Purpose: to find out if a difference can be detected between food samples.

Simple paired test	Paired comparison test	Triangle test
Two samples of a food product are given. The tester is asked: *Taste the samples and identify if they are both the same or if one sample is different.*  **432** **769**	Two different samples of a food product are given. The tester is asked to state the difference between the samples based on a particular characteristic. For example: *Taste the samples and identify which sample is sweeter.* **671**  **398**	Three samples of a food product are given. Two of the three are identical. The tester is asked: *Taste the sample and identify which sample is different.* 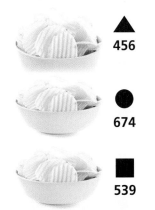 **456** **674** **539**

Descriptive tests

Purpose: to rank or rate the organoleptic properties of a food product, e.g. appearance, flavour and texture.

Descriptive ranking test	Descriptive rating test
Two or more samples of a food product are given. The tester is asked to rank the samples by preference or according to a particular characteristic. For example: *Taste the samples and rank the soups by placing* 1st choice *beside the sample that you consider to be the saltiest,* 2nd choice *beside the next saltiest* and 3rd choice *beside the least salty.*	One sample of a food product is given. The tester is asked to rate the sample for pre-selected attributes in order to create a sensory profile of the food product. An example of pre-selected attributes are: sweet, fruity, attractive appearance, nutty, crunchy texture, golden brown. The tester is asked: *Taste the sample and rate the sweetness on the accompanying line scale.*

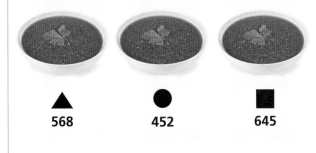

▲ **568**   ● **452**   ■ **645**

1	2	3	4	5
Not very sweet				Very sweet

▲ 5-point line scale

? Name **three** main categories of sensory analysis tests and state the main purpose of the tests in each category. (18) **HL**

Methods of presenting sensory analysis results

Once the sensory analysis test has been carried out test organisers should collect the scorecards from each tray, transfer the results onto a main record sheet, calculate the overall results and present the results. Test results can be presented on a pie chart, bar chart or star diagram.

Pie chart

Results of a paired preference test, comparing two biscuits.

Bar chart

Results of a preference hedonic ranking test showing which of the two crisps is preferred.

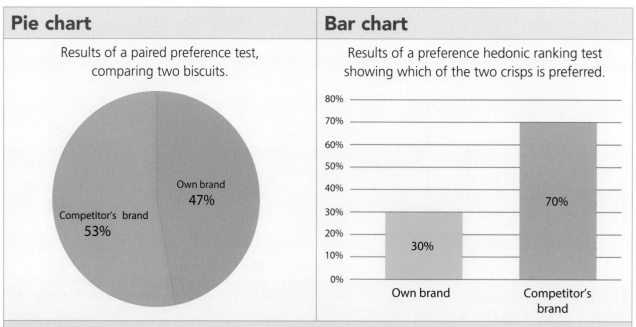

Star diagram

Star diagrams are used by the food industry to outline the results of descriptive rating tests. They can show the result of one test or many tests on the one diagram.

They have many benefits:

✓ they allow for an easy comparison of products, as differences and similarities are clearly evident, e.g. which product is the sweetest

✓ many attributes can be included in one diagram

✓ they provide information to enable manufacturers to create a sensory profile for a product; these are used in advertising and marketing campaigns.

➜ For more information on how to create a **star diagram** see your Food Studies Assignment guide.

Results of a descriptive rating test on a chocolate chip cookie.

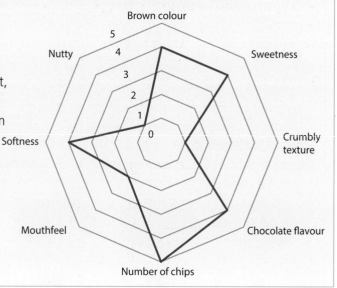

Chapter 8:
Food processing

🔗 1.3.5 FOOD PROCESSING

What you will learn:

- **Why food is processed**
- **Types of food processing**
- **Convenience foods**

- **Cook-chill food production**
- **Functional foods**
- **Genetically modified (GM) foods**

Food processing involves taking raw ingredients and changing them, either physically or chemically, into new food products. The extent of processing on foods varies greatly. Many processed foods can contain large amounts of salt, fat and sugar, e.g. ready meals, crisps and soft drinks. It is important, however, for consumers to recognise that not all processed foods can negatively impact health. Pre-chopped vegetables and fruit, wholegrain breakfast cereals and pasta are examples of nutritious processed foods.

▲ Processed foods

Why food is processed

Food is processed to:

- preserve food and extend its shelf life, e.g. canning vegetables extends their shelf life to one to five years
- make it safe for consumption, e.g. pasteurising milk kills pathogenic bacteria
- make it suitable for use, e.g. pressing rapeseeds to make rapeseed oil. A consumer would not have the skills or equipment to do this themselves
- create new food products, e.g. using milk to make yoghurt or potatoes to make crisps
- reduce time and energy used when preparing and cooking food, e.g. using a jar of white sauce when making a lasagne
- allow for the fortification of food to improve its nutritional value, e.g. the addition of vitamin D to breakfast cereals
- ensure variety and choice of products for consumers all year, e.g. frozen strawberries in winter when they are out of season.

? State **two** reasons why food is processed. (4) **OL**

FOOD PROCESSING

Types of food processing

There are two main types of food processing: primary processing and secondary processing.

Type	Procedure	Examples
Primary processing	Primary processing involves changing or converting a raw food material into a food that lasts longer, is fit for sale and is ready to eat and cook.	• Milling of wheat into flour (extensive processing) • Processing of raw milk (processing to extend shelf life) • Extraction of oil from vegetables, e.g. rapeseed oil • The preparation of fish and meat for sale and consumption
Secondary processing	Secondary processing involves changing or converting primary processed foods into other food products. This produces added-value foods (foods with higher economic value).	• The manufacture of margarine from oil • The production of cheese from milk • The production of cook-chill foods, e.g. vegetable and chicken soup

Convenience foods

Convenience foods are partly or totally prepared to make them easier for the consumer to use, therefore saving time and energy. A number of processed foods are classified as convenience foods. Ideally these foods should be served with fresh foods to help ensure a nutritionally balanced diet.

Classification of convenience foods

Cook-chill foods	Frozen foods	Canned/bottled foods	Ready to serve/instant foods	Dried foods
• Soup • Ready meals • Fresh pasta	• Meat • Fish • Vegetables • Pizzas	• Jams • Marmalades • Jellies • Vegetables, e.g. pickles • Fish, e.g. tuna	• Prepared salads, e.g. potato salad • Prepared fruit and vegetables, e.g. chopped mango • Biscuits • Crisps	• Packet sauces and soups • Cake and pancake mixes • Pasta • Potatoes

REMEMBER IT!

'**C**onvenience **F**oods **C**reate **R**apid **D**inners'

Cook-chill foods, **F**rozen foods, **C**anned/bottled foods, **R**eady to serve/instant foods, **D**ried foods.

Advantages and disadvantages of convenience foods

Advantages	Disadvantages
✓ Save time, labour and energy, e.g. ready meals only need to be microwaved. This is convenient for individuals with busy lifestyles	✗ Can be more expensive than similar home-made versions, as people pay for the convenience of having foods already prepared
✓ Few cooking skills and little knowledge is required, e.g. dried potato mixes just need the addition of water or milk	✗ Often high in fat, sugar and salt, which can lead to health problems if over-consumed
✓ Less waste occurs, as many convenience foods have an extended shelf life. Waste is also prevented as many come in usable portion sizes	✗ May have an inferior taste and texture to similar home-made versions, e.g. packet soup tends to be high in salt
✓ Add variety and interest to the diet	✗ May contain additives such as preservatives and flavourings
✓ Often fortified with vitamins and minerals.	✗ Tend to be low in dietary fibre, e.g. ready meals usually contain refined pasta or rice
✓ Health-conscious consumers are provided for, as low-fat, low-sugar and low-salt options are available	
✓ Easy to store, e.g. canned foods can be stacked	

> **?** List **two** advantages and **two** disadvantages of convenience foods (packet/tinned foods). (4) **OL**
>
> Outline the range of processed foods available **and** discuss the merits of including processed foods in the modern diet. (24) **HL**

Cook-chill food production

Cook-chill foods are made by secondary processing. This involves foods being prepared, cooked and portioned, then chilled to 3°C and packaged for sale. The cook-chill process preserves food for up to four days. Examples include pasta, salads, chilled desserts, e.g chocolate mousse, and fresh soups.

Cook-pasteurise-chill food production: fresh vegetable soup

- **Prepared:** ingredients are prepared, e.g. vegetables are washed and chopped, and stock is made.

Tip!
Cook-chill foods are an example of added-value foods.

- **Cooked:** vegetables are cooked under controlled conditions until the core temperature reaches a minimum of 72°C. Thickening agents, e.g. cornflour or cream, are added if necessary. The vegetables are blended to form a smooth mixture.

- **Portioned and packaged:** soup is portioned into retail-sized portions, e.g. 500 ml or 1 litre, and packaged in varying materials, e.g. plastic or cardboard. Containers are heat sealed.

- **Pasteurised:** soup is pasteurised at 80°C for 10 minutes.

- **Chilled:** soup is rapidly chilled by blast chilling at 3°C.

- **Quality control:** soup is tasted and tested for quality.

- **Labelled:** soup is labelled with details, including the type of soup, ingredients used, storage instructions, allergy advice and nutritional information.

- **Stored:** soup is stored between 1°C and 3°C. before transportation.

- **Distributed:** soup is transported in cold conditions and then stored in chilled cabinets in shops between 1°C and 3°C.

> **?** Write a profile of an 'added value' food you have studied. Give details of **each** of the following:
> - stages of production
> - labelling.
> - packaging
> - (26) **HL**

REMEMBER IT!

> '**P**icky **C**onsumers **P**refer **P**urchasing **C**ountless **C**ook-chill **L**eek **S**oups **D**aily.'
>
> **P**repared, **C**ooked, **P**ortioned and packaged, **P**asteurised, **C**hilled, **Q**uality control, **L**abelled, **S**tored, **D**istributed.

Functional foods

Functional foods contain an added ingredient that gives the food health benefits over and above their basic nutritional value. Greater consumer awareness that health problems, e.g. high cholesterol, can be reduced by the consumption of functional foods has increased their sales in recent years. These foods look, smell and taste the same as their regular counterparts.

▲ Functional foods

Examples of functional foods

Added ingredients	Food sources	Health benefits
Probiotics (live cultures of good bacteria, e.g. *Lactobacillus acidophilus*)	• Bio yoghurts, e.g. Danone Activia • Yoghurt drinks, e.g. Yakult	• Improve the functioning of the digestive system, e.g. reduce bloating • Strengthen the immune system and reduce susceptibility to infection
Omega-3 fatty acids (fatty acids found in oily fish and fish oils)	• Golden Irish omega-3 eggs • Yoghurt drinks, e.g. Flora Omega-3 Plus	• Lower levels of cholesterol in the blood, reducing the risk of coronary heart disease • Aid brain functioning, e.g. assist concentration
Plant stanols and sterols (plant extracts)	• Dairy spreads, e.g. Benecol • Milk, e.g. Avonmore Heart Active	• Lower levels of cholesterol in the blood, reducing the risk of coronary heart disease
Folic acid	• Breakfast cereals, e.g. Kellogg's Cornflakes	• Reduces the incidence of neural tube defects, e.g. spina bifida, in babies

> **?** Explain the term functional food. Outline **two** health benefits of including functional foods in the diet.(6) **HL**

Genetically modified (GM) foods

Genetically modified (GM) foods are foods produced from plants that have had changes introduced into their DNA. Foreign genes (genes from other plants or animals) are inserted into the genetic codes of plants. This potentially can create plants that:

- are disease- and drought-resistant
- require fewer pesticides
- grow faster
- have increased nutritional benefits, e.g. wheat with increased levels of folic acid.

A wide variety of GM foods are available in the United States, including tomatoes, potatoes, corn and soya beans. GM foods must undergo strict tests, e.g. allergy tests, prior to being authorised for entry into the European Union market. Under current European Union regulations manufacturers must label any food where GM ingredients make up more than 0.9% of the total ingredients.

At present, food ingredients obtained from six types of GM crops may be found in foods on the European Union market, including:

- soya beans that are resistant to herbicides
- maize (corn) that is resistant to pest attack and/or resistant to herbicides.

In Ireland, the Food Safety Authority of Ireland (FSAI) ensures that the only GM foods available on Irish shelves are those with European Union authorisation and appropriate labelling.

▲ Genetically-modified tomato purée

FOOD PROCESSING

FOOD PACKAGING AND LABELLING

What you will learn:

- **Functions of food packaging**
- **Characteristics of good packaging**
- **Materials used to package food**
- **Government initiatives to reduce the impact of packaging**
- **Ways consumers can reduce the environmental impact of packaging**
- **Modified atmospheric packaging (MAP)**
- **General food labelling requirements for packaged and non-packaged foods**

- **Labelling requirements and nutritional labelling requirements for packaged food**
- **Front-of-pack nutritional labelling on packaged food**
- **Labelling requirements for non-packaged food**
- **Food claims**
- **Love Irish Food logo**
- **Barcoding**

FOOD PACKAGING

Food packaging is made from materials such as glass, metal, paper and plastic. Ideally, packaging must protect what it sells and sell what it protects. Most food products nowadays have some form of packaging.

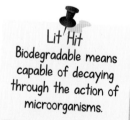

▲ Different types of food packaging

Functions of food packaging

- Food packaging protects food from becoming damaged or contaminated, ensuring that consumers buy products in the best possible condition.
- Food packaging makes the transport and storage of foods easier, as foods can be stacked on top of each other.
- Food packaging advertises a food product, making it more appealing to the consumer, increasing sales and profit.
- Food packaging provides consumer information, e.g. cooking instructions and nutritional information to help consumers make informed food choices.
- Packaging, e.g. vacuum packaging, can preserve food, increasing its shelf life. This reduces food waste and risk of food poisoning.

Characteristics of good packaging

- Hygienic and safe
- Increases shelf life
- **Biodegradable** or recyclable
- Hard-wearing and tamper-resistant
- Moisture or vapour proof

- Easy to open and reseal, e.g. pull rings on tinned cans
- Economical to make
- Attractive, e.g. has eye-catching colours and clear logos

> **Lit Hit**
> Biodegradable means capable of decaying through the action of microorganisms.

? List **two** desirable characteristics (qualities) of food packaging materials. (4) **OL**

Materials used to package food

Glass

Examples of use	• Jars, e.g. mayonnaise and jams • Bottles, e.g. salad dressings and fizzy drinks
Advantages (suitability of purpose)	✓ Protects food from contamination ✓ Easily moulded into a variety of shapes and sizes ✓ Available coloured or transparent, so contents can be examined ✓ Can withstand heat processing without cracking
Disadvantages	✗ Heavy to lift and transport. This increases transport costs ✗ Easily broken or damaged ✗ Expensive to produce ✗ Cannot be printed on, so labelling is required to display consumer information
Environmental impact	• 100% recyclable. This reduces greenhouse gas emissions, pollution and landfill, and conserves raw materials. Glass can be recycled repeatedly without loss of purity or quality. • Reusable, e.g. glass jars can be used for home-made preserves • Consumers should avoid careless disposal of glass as it can be dangerous for animals, e.g. glass can damage their flesh • Non-biodegradable, as it cannot be broken down by microorganisms

Did you know ?
One recycled glass jar saves enough energy to run a television for 15 minutes.

Metal (aluminium and tin)

Examples of use	• Steel cans, e.g. cans of tuna and cans of beans • Aluminium cans, e.g. soft drink cans • Aerosols, e.g. ultra-heat treated whipped cream cans • Foil containers, e.g. ready meal and takeaway containers • Aluminium foil wrap, e.g. margarine wrappers
Advantages (suitability of purpose)	✓ Protects food from contamination ✓ Easy to stack for convenient storage ✓ Can withstand heat processing
Disadvantages	✗ Heavy to lift and transport. This increases transport costs ✗ Easily punctured or dented ✗ Expensive to produce
Environmental impact	• Recyclable. This reduces greenhouse gas emissions, pollution and landfill, and conserves raw materials. • Reusable, e.g. tin cans as pen holders • Non-biodegradable, as it cannot be broken down by microorganisms

Did you know ?
Aluminium cans can be recycled, turned into a new can and be back on shop shelves within 60 days.

Paper

Examples of use	• Paper, e.g. flour and sugar bags • Cardboard, e.g. cereal and egg boxes • Waxed paper, e.g. bread packaging and takeaway burger wrappers • Waxed cartons, e.g. milk and smoothie cartons • Greaseproof paper, e.g. meat wrappers
Advantages (suitability of purpose)	✓ Protects food from contamination ✓ Cheap to produce ✓ Lightweight, so it does not increase transport costs ✓ Can be printed on, so it does not need additional labelling
Disadvantages	✗ Does not reseal well ✗ Easily damaged, e.g. paper bags can rip or tear ✗ Not very durable and can disintegrate when wet
Environmental impact	• Recyclable. This reduces greenhouse gas emissions, pollution and landfill, and conserves raw materials. • Reusable, e.g. using cereal boxes for magazine storage • Biodegradable, as it is made from plant fibres that can be broken down by microorganisms. If paper contains any polyethylene plastic (applied to make it waterproof), it will be resistant to biodegradation.

GO FIGURE 123
One tonne of recycled cardboard and paper saves 17 trees.

Plastic

Examples of use	• Polystyrene (PS), e.g. styrofoam cups and burger boxes • Polyethylene terephthalate (PET), e.g. water bottles • Low-density polyethylene (LDPE), e.g. pasta packets
Advantages (suitability of purpose)	✓ Moisture-proof ✓ Cheap to produce ✓ Lightweight, so it does not increase transport costs ✓ Can be durable and strong, depending on the type, e.g. PET is stronger than polystyrene ✓ Can be printed on, so it does not need additional labelling
Disadvantages	✗ Some plastics may contaminate food. Research highlights that reusing bottles made of PET can be dangerous, as PET breaks down over time, releasing dioxins that may be **carcinogenic**. ✗ Some plastics are easily damaged, e.g. polystyrene can tear
Environmental impact	• Recyclable. This reduces greenhouse gas emissions, pollution and landfill, and conserves raw materials. Only certain types of plastic can be recycled in Ireland, due to a lack of recycling facilities. • Reusable, e.g. using old plastic bottles as plant pots • Non-biodegradable, as it cannot be broken down by microorganisms • Consumers should avoid careless disposal of plastic as it can be dangerous for animals, e.g. plastic bags can suffocate • Made from crude oil which is a limited and non-renewable resource

Lit Hit
Carcinogenic means cancer-causing.

Name **three** different types of packaging materials used in the food industry and give **one** different example of the use of each. (6) **OL**

Assess the use of plastics as a packaging material having regard to:
- types
- suitability for purpose
- environmental impact. (16) **HL**

Government initiatives to reduce the impact of packaging

- **Levy on plastic shopping bags:** introduced on 4 March 2002. Its primary purpose was to reduce the use of disposable plastic bags. It has led to a drop in plastic bag usage from approximately 328 bags per person in 2001 to approximately 18 bags per person in 2012.
- **Landfill levy increase:** on 1 July 2013 the landfill levy was increased by €10, making it €75 per tonne. The increase was introduced to encourage Irish people to recycle and move away from using landfills for disposing of household waste.

Ways consumers can reduce the environmental impact of packaging

- Use a travel mug when visiting a coffee shop.
- Buy fresh, loose fruit and vegetables instead of packaged produce.
- Buy large volumes of food instead of individually packaged items.
- Bring reusable shopping bags when shopping.
- Choose eco-refill products, e.g. Kenco coffee.
- Use a compost bin for food and paper waste so that waste can biodegrade and be used as compost.
- Buy products in recycled packaging, e.g. Kellogg's cereals.

 **Did you know**

Many independent coffee shops and coffee chains, e.g. Starbucks, offer discounts on beverages purchased if consumers bring their own mug.

Identify **one** initiative implemented to reduce the impact of excess packaging on the environment. (2) **HL**

Modified atmospheric packaging (MAP)

Modified atmospheric packaging (MAP) is a food-packaging method in which the proportions of carbon dioxide, nitrogen, and oxygen in a sealed package are different from those in normal air. By surrounding food with different proportions of carbon dioxide, nitrogen and oxygen, this slows down the growth of bacteria, yeasts and moulds that spoil food. This enhances the food's shelf life. Food with this type of packaging must be labelled 'packaged in a protective atmosphere'. Foods packaged using MAP include meat, cheese and salad leaves. Once opened, these foods should be treated as fresh, and used within two to three days.

▲ Salad leaves packaged in MAP

Explain modified atmospheric packaging and give an example of its use. (3) **HL**

FOOD PACKAGING AND LABELLING

FOOD LABELLING

Food labelling aims to provide consumers with key information about food, such as the ingredients and instructions for use, enabling them to make more informed choices when shopping. Food labelling is found on packaged food, e.g. breakfast cereals, biscuits and milk or near non pre-packaged food, e.g. fruit and vegetables, salad bar foods and freshly baked goods.

All food labelling in Ireland must follow European Union (EU) legislation outlined by the Food Information to Consumers (FIC) Regulation 2011. The Food Safety Authority of Ireland (FSAI) is responsible for the enforcement of all EU food labelling regulations in Ireland.

General food labelling requirements for packaged and non-packaged foods

Under the FIC Regulation 2011, the following labelling requirements for packaged and non-packaged food products must be adhered to:

- information provided must be clear and **unambiguous**, and must not mislead the consumer
- information must be easy to understand and be clearly legible. It must also be **indelible**
- information must be in English. The food may be labelled in both English and another language, but it is not sufficient to label a food without providing an English translation.

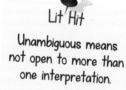

Lit Hit

Unambiguous means not open to more than one interpretation.

Lit Hit

Indelible means easy to see and not obscured in any way.

 Outline the protection provided to the consumer by Labelling Regulations (1982, 1991 and 2002). *(now known as the FIC Regulation 2011)* (8) **HL**

Labelling requirements for packaged food

Under the FIC Regulation 2011 the following labelling requirements must appear on packaged food.

- **Name of the food**.
- **List of ingredients in descending order of weight:** this enables consumers to see exactly what ingredients are used in foods.
- **Declaration of allergens:** e.g. nuts, celery and wheat. Allergens must be declared in the ingredients list, with the names emphasised to enable consumers to clearly distinguish them. This enables consumers to reduce their risk of suffering an allergic reaction.
- **Quantity of certain ingredients:** e.g. pork in pork sausages. This helps consumers compare the composition of the main ingredients in similar food products. It should be in percentage terms and appear beside the name of the food or in the ingredients list.
- **Net quantity:** this is the weight or volume of a food that does not include the packaging material. It enables consumers to determine how many portions or servings the food product will yield.
- **Date of minimum durability:** this is the date until the quality of a food that has been properly stored can be guaranteed. It is indicated by either a use-by date or a best before date.
  - **Use-by date:** found on food that is highly perishable, e.g. milk. Food that has gone past its use-by date is dangerous for human consumption.
  - **Best before date:** found on non-perishable food, e.g. dried rice. This is the date up until which a food can reasonably be expected to retain its optimum quality.

These enable consumers to compare dates on food and ensure they are choosing the freshest products.

- **Special storage instructions:** e.g. refrigerate after opening or store in a cool, dry place. This enables consumers to reduce the rate at which the food they purchased spoils.
- **Name and address of the food business.**
- **Country of origin:** this is currently only mandatory for certain foods, such as poultry, beef, fish and honey. In other cases, it is only necessary if leaving it out might mislead the consumer as to the true origin of a food. For example, 'American-Style Cookies' could imply that the biscuits came from the United States, rather than being made in Ireland.

Chicken risotto

Ingredients

Water, Cooked White Rice (30%), Cooked Chicken (30%), Salt, Yeast Extract, Maize Starch, Tomato, Lemon, Onion, Sugar, Egg, Garlic, Skimmed **Milk** Powder, **Milk**, Flavourings (contain Sugar, Salt, Flavourings, **Celery**, Sunflower Oil, Chicken Fat), Turkey and Chicken Stock (contains **Egg**), Sugar, Basil.

Ⓥ **Allergy advice**

Contains milk, **celery** and **egg**.
Recipe: no nuts
Ingredients: **cannot guarantee nut-free**
Factory: no nuts

Nutrition

Serves 1

Typical values	Per 100g	Per Meal 320g	%RI* Per Meal
Energy - kJ	405 kJ	1296 kJ	15%
- kcal	96 kcal	307 kcal	15%
Fat	1.6g	5.1g	7%
- of which saturates	0.6g	2.0g	10%
Carbohydrate	13.8g	44.3g	17%
- of which sugars	0.8g	2.6g	3%
Fibre	0.6g	1.9g	
Protein	6.3g	20.0g	40%
Salt	0.5g	1.6g	27%

*Reference Intake of an average adult (8400kJ/2000kcal)

STORAGE INSTRUCTIONS

Food freezer	until best before end
Star marked frozen food compartment	Until best before end
***	1 month
*	1 week
Ice making compartment	3 days

Should be –18°C or colder. Do not refreeze once thawed.

Cooking instructions
Cook from frozen.
Before serving check that the food is hot throughout, if not cook further.
Do not defrost before cooking.

Microwave cooking
Pierce film lid before cooking.
| 750 W | 7 minutes | Stir before serving |
| 850 W | 6 minutes | Stir before serving |

Oven cooking
1. Preheat the oven to 200°C (400°F), fan 180°C or gas mark 6.
2. Pierce film lid and place on baking tray.
3. Cook for 40 minutes in the top half of the oven.
4. Take out of the oven and let stand for one minute.
5. Remove lid.
6. Stir gently before serving.

These are for guidance only. Cooking times may need to be adjusted to account for variations in storage conditions, oven performance, and the number of trays being heated.

Produced in Ireland   **320 g**

| Frozen Bites LTD, Green Tree Road, Wexford | **BEST BEFORE END** 12. 2018 |

▲ Food label

- **Instructions for use:** e.g. preparation or cooking instructions. This enables consumers to purchase food products that suit their cooking appliances and equipment.
- **Alcoholic strength:** required for beverages with more than 1.2% alcohol by volume.

Nutritional labelling requirements for packaged food

Nutritional labelling provides consumers with information relating to calories (energy) and nutrients present in a food product. Under the FIC Regulation 2011 the following nutritional labelling requirements for packaged food must be adhered to:

- nutritional information must be displayed per 100 g or per 100 ml
- nutritional information provided must relate to the foodstuff as sold, e.g. if the product is sold uncooked the manufacturer must state the nutritional content of the uncooked food. The nutritional information may be provided for the product after preparation, once sufficient preparation instructions are also labelled
- nutritional information must be presented together in one place, in a table with the numbers aligned.

All packaged food must provide minimum mandatory nutrition information from 13 December 2016. The minimum mandatory information that must be included is energy, fat, saturates, carbohydrates, sugars, protein and salt. These mandatory nutrients can be supplemented with certain additional nutrients, such as monounsaturated and polyunsaturated fat, polyols (sugar-free sweeteners), starch, fibre, vitamins and minerals, however, this is not compulsory.

Did you know

'Sodium' is now changed to 'salt' on food labelling to make it easier for consumers to determine the amount of salt in the foods they are choosing.

Due to increased consumer demand for nutritional information, some food companies voluntarily choose to provide the following information on their packaging:

- **nutritional information per portion,** e.g. two biscuits, or per consumption unit, e.g. per biscuit
- **percentage Reference Intake (% RI) values for energy and nutrients,** including fat, saturates, carbohydrate, sugars, protein and salt, per 100g/ml and/or per portion/consumption unit. If vitamins and minerals are declared in the nutrition table, the % RI per 100 g/ml for each one is compulsory.

Front-of-pack nutritional labelling on packaged food

Many food companies participate in front-of-pack nutritional labelling, presenting the amount of energy, fat, saturates, sugar and salt per 100 g/ml and/or per portion, and % RI values. Although this is not compulsory, the information is displayed as it enables consumers to quickly see the essential nutritional information a food provides without having to read the back of the pack.

Many food companies are also adopting a traffic light version of front-of-pack food labelling to make it even easier for consumers to make healthier food choices. If a nutrient is shaded:

* **red:** the food contains high levels of that particular nutrient per 100 g/ml or per portion
* **amber:** the food contains medium levels
* **green:** the food contains low levels.

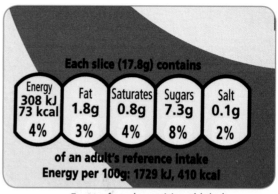

▲ Front-of-pack nutritional label

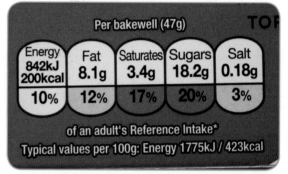

▲ Traffic light front-of-pack nutritional label

Labelling requirements for non-packaged food

Under the FIC regulation 2011 the following labelling requirements must be displayed near non-packaged foods:

* a declaration of allergens, e.g. nuts, celery and wheat.

Additional legislation requires retailers to provide:

* name of the food
* country of origin
* class
* variety
* unit price per kilogram. This enables consumers to compare prices with other products of the same weight.

Did you know ❓

On packaged food of varying weights, e.g. cheese, the unit price must be displayed as well as the price per pack.

▲ Declaration of allergens sign

❓ Name four items of consumer information found on food packaging. Explain the importance of each. (20) **OL**

The following items of information are generally included on food packaging. Explain the benefit to the consumer of each item:
  • list of ingredients   • weight   • country of origin.
  • nutritional information   • best before date   (20) **OL**

Identify **three** different items of nutritional information that are generally included on pre-packed foods. (6) **HL**

Evaluate the role of food labelling in assisting the consumer when selecting foods. (20) **HL**

Food claims

A food claim is a declaration regarding the properties of a foodstuff. There are two types of food claims that can be found on foods: nutrition claims and health claims.

Nutrition claims	Health claims
These are claims that state, suggest or imply that a food has particular nutritional properties due to the energy or nutrients it either provides, does not provide or provides at reduced or increased proportions. For example: *low in fat* or *sugar-free*.	These are claims that state, suggest or imply a relationship between a food or one of its constituents and health. For example: *plant sterols in dairy spreads contribute to the maintenance of normal blood cholesterol levels*. These health claims are often found on functional foods.

All claims on food labels must be 100% true. Food producers cannot claim to cure or prevent any disease and they must not mislead the consumer.

Did you know

For a company to claim that their product is low in fat the foodstuff must contain no more than 3 g of fat per 100 g for solids, or 1.5 g of fat per 100 ml for liquids. For a company to claim that their product is sugar free the foodstuff must contain no more than 0.5 g of sugars per 100 g or 100 ml.

Love Irish Food logo

Love Irish Food was established to help Irish consumers make informed choices about buying Irish-manufactured food and drink brands, and to safeguard the future of food and drink manufacturing in Ireland.

For a brand to be eligible to carry the Love Irish Food logo, the producer must:

- source their ingredients from Ireland where possible. Ingredients that are not grown in Ireland, e.g. tea leaves and cocoa beans, can be imported and used
- manufacture at least 80% of the brand in Ireland.

Examples of brands that carry the Love Irish Food logo include Avonmore, Ballygowan and Kilmeaden.

G> FIGURE 12.3

If one-third of households in Ireland spent an average of €1.67 more on an Irish item each week for a year we would generate €35 million for the Irish economy.

Barcoding

A barcode is a series of black lines and spaces that contain information about a product, such as the product's name, price and description. Barcodes can be read by an electric scanner, and the information is printed on the till receipt, so consumers have an itemised list of what they purchased. Barcoding also enables shops to maintain stock levels, as when an item is scanned it is reduced from the stock list, so shops know to reorder the item.

▲ Barcode

FOOD ADDITIVES

What you will learn:

- **Classification of food additives**
- **Advantages and disadvantages of food additives**
- **Legal controls on the use of food additives**

Additives are substances intentionally added to food in relatively small amounts to improve its colour, flavour, texture, nutritional value and shelf life. These substances can be natural or artificially made.

? Explain the term *food additive*. (2) **OL**

Classification of food additives

| Colourings (E100–E199) | Sweeteners (E900–E999) | Antioxidants (E300–E399) | Nutritive additives | Preservatives (E200–E299) |

| Flavourings | Flavour enhancers (E600–E699) | Physical conditioning agents (E400–E499) |

Colourings (E100–E199)

Functions

- Improve the colour of foods, e.g. soft drinks
- Replace colour lost during processing, e.g. during canning peas change from bright green to olive green
- Add colour to colourless foods, e.g. ice pops

▶ Dried cochineal beetles and cochineal powder

Colourings (natural)

Example	Origin	Uses
Chlorophyll (green)	Green pigment present in plants	• Lime-flavoured jelly • Green-coloured fruit gum sweets
Carotene (yellow/orange)	Carrots	• Orange-coloured soft drinks • Orange-coloured fruit gum sweets
Caramel (brown)	Heated carbohydrates	• Gravy powder/granules • Cola-flavoured soft drinks
Cochineal (red/crimson)	Cochineal beetles (dried and ground)	• Processed meat, e.g. sausages • Pink-coloured fruit gum sweets

Did you know ?

70,000 cochineal beetles must be crushed to produce 1 lb (454 g) of red dye.

Colourings (artificial)

Example	Origin	Uses
Tartrazine (yellow colouring)	Coal tar, a black, thick, opaque liquid obtained from the distillation of coal	• Orange-coloured fruit drinks
Sunset yellow (yellow/orange colouring)	Coal tar	• Yellow/orange-coloured soft drinks
Ponceau 4R (red colouring)	Coal tar	• Red-coloured soft drinks
Green S	Coal tar	• Canned peas

? Name **two** types of food additives used in processed fruit/vegetables. (6) **OL**

Sweeteners (E900–E999)

Functions

• Sweeten food, e.g. biscuits
• Sweeten specialist foods for consumers with diabetes, e.g. sugar-free chocolate
• Intense sweeteners are used to sweeten low-calorie foods, e.g. diet drinks

▶ Sugar cane

Sweeteners (natural)

Example	Origin	Uses	
Fructose	Fruit, honey and vegetables	• Canned vegetables	
Table sugar	Sugar cane and sugar beet	• Biscuits	• Canned fruit
Glucose syrup	Fruit and honey	• Sweets	• Jelly

Sweeteners (artificial)

Type	Example	Origin	Uses
Intense sweeteners (low in kilocalories; used in small amounts as they are much sweeter than sugar)	**Aspartame**	Derived by chemically combining two naturally occurring amino acids: aspartic acid and phenylalanine	• Sweetening tablets or powder, e.g. Canderel
	Saccharin	Coal tar	• Sweetening tablets or powder, e.g. Hermesetas • No-added-sugar canned vegetables

Did you know **?**
Aspartame is approximately 200 times sweeter than sucrose (table sugar).

FOOD ADDITIVES

| Bulk sweeteners (high in kilocalories; used in same amounts as sugar due to similar sweetness strength) | Sorbitol | Lichens, a plant found on rocks or trees made of fungus and algae | • Sugar-free confectionery |
| | Mannitol | Lichens
▲ Lichens | • Sugar-free biscuits
• Sugar-free chewing gum |

? Outline the uses of sweeteners in food manufacture. (8) **HL**

Classify artificial sweeteners and give **one** example of each. (12) **HL**

Antioxidants (E300–E399)

Functions

- Inhibit the oxidative rancidity of foods, especially those high in fats or oils
- Reduce food waste, as food does not go off as quickly

Antioxidants (natural)

Example	Origin	Uses
Vitamin C (ascorbic acid)	Fruit and vegetables	• Fruit juices
Vitamin E (tocopherol)	Nuts and seeds	• Vegetable oils

Antioxidants (artificial)

Example	Origin	Uses
Butylated hydroxyanisole (BHA)	Laboratory-produced chemical	• Instant noodles • Instant soups
Butylated hydroxytoluene (BHT)	Laboratory-produced chemical	• Crackers

Nutritive additives

Foods that have nutritive additives added to them are referred to as fortified foods.

Functions

- Replace nutrients lost during processing, e.g. calcium lost during the milling of wheat to make flour
- Enhance the nutritional value of food, e.g. margarine is fortified with vitamin D

Nutritive additives

Example	Uses
Vitamin D	• Margarine
Calcium	• Flour • Milk
Iron	• Breakfast cereals

Preservatives (E200–E299)

Functions

- Prevent the growth of microorganisms, preventing food spoilage
- Reduce food waste, as food does not go off as quickly
- Reduce the risk of food poisoning, as bacteria growth is inhibited
- Provide out-of-season foods all year, e.g. strawberry jam

Preservatives (natural)

Example	Origin	Uses	
Sugar	Sugar cane and sugar beet	• Jam	• Sweets
Salt	Sodium chloride	• Cured meats	• Butter
Alcohol	Fermentation of yeast	• Fruit cake	
Vinegar (acetic acid)	Fermentation of alcohol	• Pickled vegetables	• Chutney

Preservatives (artificial)

Example	Origin	Uses
Sulfur dioxide	Laboratory-produced chemical	• Dried fruit • Fruit-based breakfast cereals
Sorbic acid	Laboratory-produced chemical	• Baked goods
Benzoic acid	Laboratory-produced chemical	• Energy drinks
Sodium nitrate	Laboratory-produced chemical	• Cured meats • Spreadable cheeses

Flavourings (no E numbers)

Functions

- Add flavour to food
- Replace food flavour lost during processing

Flavourings (natural)

Example	Origin	Uses
Sugar	Sugar cane and sugar beet	• Breakfast cereals • Yoghurts
Salt	Sodium chloride	• Butter • Cheese
Herbs	Plants	• Stock cubes
Spices	Plants	• Sauces • Seasonings

▲ Seasoning

Flavourings (artificial)

Example	Origin	Uses
Esters, e.g. amyl acetate (pear flavouring)	Chemical reaction resulting from heating acetic acid and ethyl alcohol	• Pear-flavoured sweets
Esters, e.g. ethyl acetate (rum flavouring)	Chemical reaction resulting from heating acetic acid and ethyl alcohol	• Rum essence
Aldehydes, e.g. benzaldehydes (almond/cherry flavouring)	Oxidation of benzyl alcohol	• Almond essence • Almond-flavoured cakes • Cherry-flavoured sweets
Aldehydes, e.g. maltol (adds the smell of freshly baked bread to food)	Larch tree bark	• Bread • Cakes

▲ Battenburg (almond-flavoured cake)

Flavour enhancers (E600–E699)

Function

- Enhance the existing flavour of food and make it seem stronger

Flavour enhancers

Example	Origin	Uses
Monosodium glutamate (MSG) (sodium salt)	Glutamic acid (amino acid)	• Stock cubes • Snack foods, e.g. crisps

HL Physical conditioning agents (E400–E499)

REMEMBER IT!

'HEAPS!'

Humecants, **E**mulsifiers, **A**nti-caking agents, **P**ectin, **S**tabilisers.

▲ Chocolate milk powder

Physical conditioning agents

Type	Functions	Example	Origin	Uses
Humectants	Prevent food from losing moisture, drying out and hardening	**Sorbitol and mannitol**	Lichens	• Marzipan • Cakes
Emulsifiers	Form emulsions	**Lecithin** **Alginates**	Egg yolks Seaweed	• Mayonnaise • Dairy spreads
Anti-caking agents (polyphosphates)	Prevent lumping (anti-caking) in a dried food	**Magnesium carbonate**	Laboratory-produced chemical	• Cake mixes • Chocolate milk powder
Setting agents	Act as a setting agent	**Pectin**	Fruit	• Jams • Marmalade
Stabilisers	Prevent emulsions from separating	**Carrageenan** **Guar gum**	Seaweed moss Guar plants	• Ice cream • Yoghurts

▲ Carrageenan

?

State the function of **two** of the physical conditioning agents named below.
• Humectants • Polyphosphates • Stabilisers (6) **HL**

State **one** function and give an example of **each** of the food additives listed below.
• Flavour enhancer • Emulsifier • Antioxidant. (6) **HL**

Name and state the function of **two** different types of physical conditioning agents used in processed foods. (18) **HL**

▲ Guar plant

FOOD ADDITIVES

Advantages and disadvantages of food additives

Advantages

✓ Additives increase the variety of foods available.

✓ Preservatives and antioxidants reduce the rate at which food spoils, extending the shelf life.

✓ Preservatives reduce the risk of food poisoning, as bacterial growth is inhibited.

✓ Preservatives and antioxidants prevent food waste, as food does not go off as quickly.

✓ Colourings enhance the colour of food and make its appearance more appetising.

✓ Flavourings improve the overall taste of food.

✓ Nutritive additives enhance the nutritional value of foods.

✓ Physical conditioning agents improve the texture of foods.

Disadvantages

✗ Some people, particularly children, have negative reactions to additives, e.g. hyperactivity or migraines.

✗ Little is known about the 'cocktail' effect of a combination of additives on health.

✗ Additives can deceive consumers about the colour or flavour of food. For example, some commercial carrot cake mixes contain no carrots. Instead, they contain carrot-flavoured pieces.

✗ Additives, e.g. aspartame, may be carcinogenic.

✗ Some additives destroy the nutrient content of foods, e.g. sulfur dioxide destroys B-group vitamins in food.

> State **two** disadvantages of using additives in food. (4) **OL**
>
> Explain why food additives are used in the manufacture of food. (8) **OL**

Legal controls on the use of food additives

The use of food additives is controlled by European Union (EU) legislation and all EU countries share the same list of permitted additives. Additives undergo rigorous testing by the European Food Safety Authority (EFSA) before being approved for addition to foods. This involves:

- a safety evaluation
- determining the ADI (acceptable daily intake) of an additive. This is the estimated amount of a food additive that can be consumed daily over a lifetime, without any adverse effect on health.

If approved, the food additive is identified with a unique E number (except flavourings).

Food additives must be listed in the ingredient lists of foods either by stating the appropriate E number or its name, e.g. E220 or sulfur dioxide.

Under EU regulations additives cannot be added to food to:

- disguise faulty processing
- deceive the consumer
- present a hazard to consumers' health
- reduce the nutritional value of foods.

Additives, including colourings, preservatives, antioxidants (BHA and BHT) and sweeteners, are also prohibited from commercial baby foods.

In Ireland, the FSAI (Food Safety Authority of Ireland) monitors the use of additives in food.

> Explain how European Union law regulates the use of food additives. (8) **HL**

Chapter 9: Microbiology

MICROBIOLOGY

1.3.8

What you will learn:

- Classification of microorganisms
- Conditions necessary for the growth of microorganisms
- Fungi: moulds, large fungi (basidiomycetes) and yeast
- Bacteria
- Uses of microorganisms in food production

Microbiology is the study of microorganisms (tiny living organisms). Some microorganisms are beneficial to humans, e.g. yeast for bread production, while others can have a negative impact, e.g. salmonella can cause food poisoning and mould can cause food spoilage.

MICROBIOLOGY

HL Classification of microorganisms

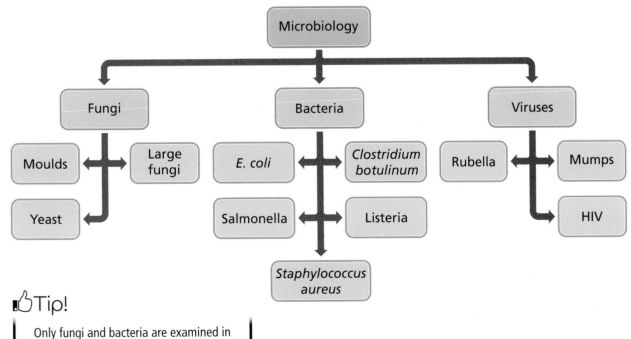

👍 Tip!

Only fungi and bacteria are examined in detail on the Leaving Certificate syllabus.

Conditions necessary for the growth of microorganisms

Food	All microorganisms require food for growth, the source of which can vary. • **Saprophytic microorganisms:** feed on non-living matter, e.g. decaying plants. • **Parasitic microorganisms:** feed on living matter, e.g. animals or humans.
Oxygen	The presence or absence of oxygen influences the growth of microorganisms. • **Aerobic microorganisms:** require oxygen for growth. • **Anaerobic microorganisms:** do not require oxygen for growth. • **Facultative microorganisms:** can grow with or without oxygen.
Temperature	All microorganisms have an optimum temperature at which they grow best. • **Psychrophilic microorganisms:** grow best at low temperatures of –5°C to 20°C. • **Mesophilic microorganisms:** grow best at medium-warm temperatures of 20–45°C. Most microorganisms prefer this temperature range. • **Thermophilic microorganisms:** grow best at hot temperatures of 45–80°C. • **Hyperthermophilic microorganisms:** grow best at hot temperatures of 65–105°C.
Moisture	All microorganisms require moisture for growth. The availability of moisture in food is measured on a water activity (aw) scale that extends from 0 (bone dry) to 1.0 (pure water). The typical water activity of some foods include: • fresh meat (0.99) • bread (0.95) • jam (0.80) • biscuits (0.30). Most microorganisms grow best in foods with an aw level of 0.80 or higher.
pH level	All microorganisms have their own prefered pH level for growth. Certain microorganisms prefer: • **an acidic environment:** pH of 1–6 • **a neutral environment:** pH of 7 • **a basic (alkaline) environment:** pH of 8–14.
Time	Microorganisms require time to grow and multiply.

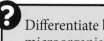 Differentiate between **each** of the following microorganisms.
• Aerobic micro-organisms
• Anaerobic micro-organisms
• Facultative micro-organisms (6) **HL**

 **REMEMBER IT!**

'**F**or **O**rganisms **T**o **M**ultiply **P**rovide **T**ime.'
Food, **O**xygen, **T**emperature, **M**oisture, **p**H level, **T**ime.

FUNGI

Fungi are simple plants that do not make their own food, as they have no chlorophyll to carry out photosynthesis. Instead, fungi obtain food by:

• feeding on non-living matter (saprophytic), e.g. mushrooms feed on soil and mucors feed on bread
• feeding on living matters (parasitic), e.g. animals and humans, and causing ringworm or athlete's foot.

 **Did you know**

Athlete's foot and ringworm are contagious fungal infections.

Fungi are classified into three main types:

- moulds
- large fungi (mushrooms)
- yeast.

Moulds

Moulds are **multicellular** fungi, their basic unit is a mould spore. Some moulds cause food spoilage, but others can be used in the manufacture of foodstuffs, e.g. cheese, and the manufacture of medicine, e.g. penicillin.

Lit Hit

Multicellular means consisting of many cells.

▲ Mould on bread

Conditions necessary for the growth of moulds

Food	Most moulds are saprophytic, feeding on foods such as bread, jam, cheese and fruit. This causes food spoilage.
Oxygen	Moulds are aerobic. For this reason they tend to grow on the surface of solid foods, e.g. strawberries and cheese, and throughout open-structure foods, e.g. bread.
Temperature	Most moulds are mesophilic (20–45°C). Temperatures below 15°C slow down mould growth, freezing temperatures inactivate it and temperatures above 75°C destroy moulds.
Moisture	Moulds require moisture to grow. For this reason they grow best in **humid** conditions on foods with a high water activity, above 0.8 aw.
pH level	Moulds grow best in slightly acidic environments (pH 4–6). Extreme acidic or alkaline conditions inhibit mould growth.
Time	Moulds require between 24 and 48 hours to grow and multiply.

Lit Hit

Humid means high amounts of water vapour in the air.

? List **five** conditions required for the growth of moulds. (6) **HL**

Discuss **four** conditions necessary for the growth of moulds. (16) **HL**

Structure of moulds

1. A mould spore is a single cell. When a mould spore lands on suitable conditions, e.g. moist food in warm temperatures, it produces a thread-like strand called a hypha.

2. The hypha grows down into the food source to absorb nutrients for growth. As the hypha grows, it branches into many hyphae across the food.

3. As the hyphae grow, they become intertwined and form a branched mass called a mycelium.

4. When the mycelium is well established on the food source, some hyphae will grow upwards and produce sporangium or conidia.

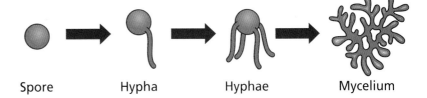

Spore　　　Hypha　　　Hyphae　　　Mycelium

Reproduction of moulds

Asexual reproduction

1. When the mycelium becomes well established in the food source and when conditions for growth remain favourable some hyphae begin to grow upwards from the surface of the food.

2. The tip of the hyphae develop one of two spore-forming structures:
   - **sporangium:** a round structure that contains spores
   - **conidia:** a chained structure made of unprotected spores.

3. When the structure is ripe:
   - the sporangium bursts, releasing spores into the environment; or
   - the conidia breaks away, releasing spores into the environment.

4. These spores can be dispersed by air or water. When the spores find suitable conditions, the asexual reproduction cycle begins again.

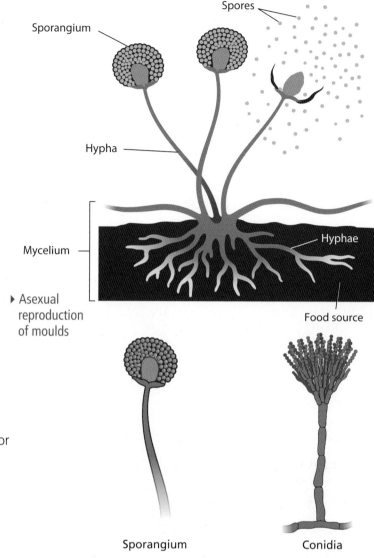

▶ Asexual reproduction of moulds

Sexual reproduction

1. Two hypha grow towards each other and fuse together.

2. The dividing wall between the hyphae breaks down, fertilisation occurs and a zygospore develops. The zygospore produces and houses spores. It has a thick wall that protects the internal spores until conditions are favourable for growth. It can remain dormant for months.

3. When conditions for growth are suitable, the zygospore germinates and a hypha grows vertically, forming a sporangium at the tip.

4. When the structure is ripe the sporangium bursts, releasing spores into the environment.

5. These spores can be dispersed by air or water. When the spores find suitable conditions, the sexual reproduction cycle begins again.

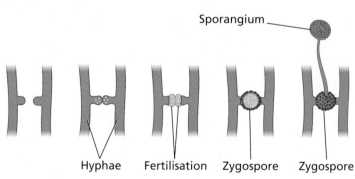

▲ Sexual reproduction of moulds

Classification of moulds

Moulds can be classified as phycomycetes or ascomycetes.

Phycomycetes

- Have an optimum temperature of 30–40 °C
- Reproduce sexually and asexually
- Produce sporangia at the tip of hyphae

Example	Mucor	Rhizopus
Grows on	• Starchy foods, e.g. bread, pasta, rice • Meat • Cheese • Soil	• Bread • Soil • Soft rot (watery decay) on fruit and vegetables
Characteristics	• Saprophytic • Reproduces sexually and asexually • Has white hyphae with grey sporangia	• Saprophytic • Reproduces asexually • Has white hyphae with black sporangia

Ascomycetes

- Have an optimum temperature of 20–25°C
- Reproduce asexually
- Produce conidia at the tip of the hyphae

Example	Penicillium	Aspergillus
Grows on	• Bread • Cheese • Fruit	• Cereal grains • Dried fruit • Black rot on fruit and vegetables
Characteristics	• Saprophytic • Reproduces asexually • Has a green-blue powdery mould	• Saprophytic • Reproduces asexually • Has a black or green mould

Did you know ?

Penecillium is used to make the antibiotic penicillin. It was discovered in 1928. It was the first antibiotic to be discovered.

Certain penicillium and aspergillus species produce toxins, e.g. aflatoxins, that are toxic to humans and animals. Some may also be carcinogenic. These may contaminate food or animal feed.

 Write a detailed account of **one** type of mould with reference to the following:
- name
- description/characteristics
- reproduction. (22) **HL**

Large fungi (basidiomycetes)

Large fungi, e.g. mushrooms, are visible to the naked eye. Some are edible, e.g. field mushrooms such as button, oyster and truffles, and others are poisonous, e.g. destroying angel mushrooms (*amanita virosa*), fly agaric mushrooms (*amanita muscaria*) and death cap mushrooms (*amanita phalloides*).

▲ Truffles

> ### Did you know
>
> Death cap mushrooms are responsible for 90% of all fatal mushroom poisonings. The average death cap is weighs 30–90 mg, and just 5–10 mg can kill the average person.

▲ Fly agaric mushrooms

Reproduction of mushrooms/large fungi (basidiomycetes)

1. Mushrooms start as a single spore.
2. When a spore lands on suitable conditions, e.g. nutrient-rich, warm soil, it produces a thread-like strand called a hypha. As the hypha grows it branches into many hyphae.
3. The hyphae eventually become intertwined and form a branched mass called a mycelium.
4. Tightly packed hyphae begin to grow upwards from the mycelium in the soil, and this forms a stalk.
5. A tightly closed cap forms at the top of the stalk.
6. On the underside of the cap, gills can be seen. Between the gills, spore-forming structures called basidia are found.
7. When the mushroom is ripe the basidia releases spores into the atmosphere.
8. These spores can be dispersed by air or water. When the spores find suitable conditions, the reproduction cycle begins again.

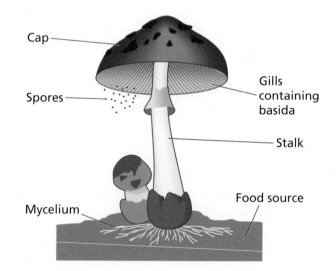

Cap

Spores

Mycelium

Gills containing basida

Stalk

Food source

Yeast

Yeast is a **unicellular** fungi that can only be clearly seen using a microscope, but becomes visible to the eye when large groups of yeast cells form. Yeast is present in the air, soil and on fruit. It causes food spoilage, but can also be used in the manufacture of many foodstuffs, including vinegar, bread and beer.

Lit Hit

Unicellular means consisting of a single cell.

Conditions necessary for the growth of yeast

Food	Yeast cells are saprophytic, feeding on high-carbohydrate foods, e.g. jams, honey, fruit. This causes food spoilage.
Oxygen	Yeast cells are facultative organisms.
Temperature	Yeast cells are mesophilic. They have an optimum temperature of 25–30°C. Temperatures below 15°C slow down yeast growth, freezing temperatures inactivate it and temperatures above 60°C destroy yeast cells.
Moisture	Yeast cells require moisture to grow, for this reason they grow best in humid conditions and on foods with a high water activity (aw), above 0.85 aw.
pH level	Yeast cells grow best in a slightly acidic environment (pH 4–6). Extreme acidic or alkaline conditions inhibit yeast growth.
Time	Yeast cells require time to grow and multiply.

Structure of yeast

- Yeast cells are usually round or oval in shape.
- They have a thin cell wall and cell membrane that encloses a dense cytoplasm.
  The cytoplasm contains:
  o food storage granules (store food)
  o a nucleus (control centre of the cell)
  o a vacuole (cavity containing air or fluid).

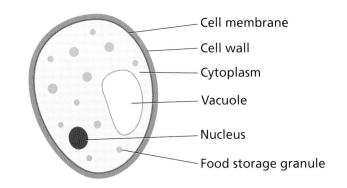

Reproduction of yeast

Yeast cells reproduce asexually by a process known as budding.

1. When conditions are favourable, a parent yeast cell develops a bud. A bud is an outward bulge from the side of the parent cell.
2. The nucleus of the yeast cell moves towards the bud.
3. The nucleus divides in two, resulting in two nuclei. One nucleus enters the bud and the other remains in the parent cell.
4. As the bud develops, a wall forms that separates the bud from the parent cell.
5. When the bud finds suitable conditions the asexual reproduction cycle begins again. During periods of rapid growth, a growing bud will produce a bud of its own before it breaks from its original cell. This can form a colony of yeast cells that is visible to the human eye.

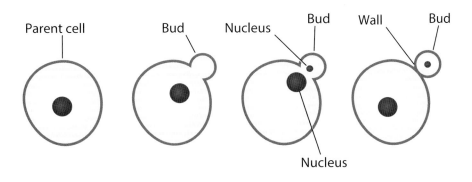

Advantages and disadvantages of fungi

Advantages	Disadvantages
✓ Fungi are used in production of protein-alternative foods, e.g. the fermentation of *Fusarium venenatum* to make Quorn ✓ Many fungi are edible, e.g. button mushrooms and truffles ✓ Some moulds are used in cheese production, e.g. *Penicillium roqueforti* is used to make Stilton cheese ✓ Some moulds are used in the production of antibiotics, e.g. penicillium is used to make penicillin ✓ Yeast is used in bread production and the brewing of alcohol, e.g. beer ✓ Yeast is used in the production of vitamin supplements due to being rich in vitamin B	✗ Can cause food spoilage, e.g. mucor on bread ✗ Can be poisonous, e.g. fly agaric mushroom (*amanita muscaria*) ✗ Can cause human diseases, e.g. ringworm and athlete's foot ✗ Can cause plant diseases, e.g. potato blight ▲ Potato blight

BACTERIA

Bacteria are microscopic unicellular microorganisms. They are found almost everywhere, e.g. in water, soil, plants, animals and humans. Bacteria can be:

- pathogenic (disease-causing)
- non-pathogenic.

Did you know?

One billion bacteria can fit on a pinhead.

Conditions necessary for the growth of bacteria

Food	Bacteria can be: • **saprophytic:** feed on non-living matter such as food, causing spoilage (non-pathogenic), e.g. lactic acid bacteria spoils milk • **parasitic:** feed on living matter such as animals or humans, causing disease (pathogenic), e.g. *Staphylococcus aureus* causes staph infections on the skin.
Oxygen	Bacteria can be: • **aerobic:** e.g. *Mycobacterium tuberculosis* • **anaerobic:** e.g.*Clostridium botulinum* • **facultative:** e.g. *E. coli*
Temperature	Bacteria can be: • **psychrophilic:** e.g. listeria • **mesophilic:** e.g. *E. coli*. Most bacteria prefer this temperature range • **thermophilic:** e.g. *Thermus aquaticus* • **hyperthermophilic:** e.g. *Thermotoga maritima*. Temperatures below 15°C slow down most bacteria, freezing temperatures inactivate most bacteria and temperatures above 70°C destroy most bacteria.
Moisture	Bacteria require moisture to grow. For this reason they grow best in humid conditions and on foods with a high water activity (aw), above 0.90 aw.
pH level	Most bacteria grow best in a slightly acidic or neutral environment (pH 6–7). Extreme acidic or alkaline conditions inhibit bacterial growth.
Time	Bacteria require time to grow and multiply. In ideal conditions, bacteria will double in number every 20 minutes.

Structure of bacteria

- A bacterial cell has a rigid cell wall that gives it structure.
- Inside the cell wall is a cell membrane that encloses a colourless liquid called cytoplasm. The cytoplasm contains:
  o nuclear material (DNA)
  o ribosomes (allow protein synthesis to occur)
  o food vacuoles (store food).
- Some bacteria have a thick, gel-like protective layer called a capsule that surrounds the cell wall.
  The capsule protects bacterial cells from **engulfment** by white blood cells as it makes bacteria slippery so that they can escape easily. White blood cells attack bacteria to protect the body from infection.
- Some bacteria also have flagellae, long thread-like structures that assist the movement of bacterial cells.

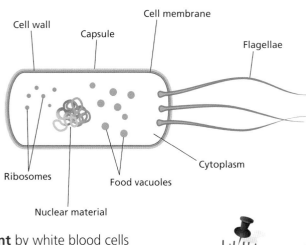

Lit Hit
Engulfment means to swallow up.

Reproduction of bacteria

Bacterial cells reproduce asexually by a process known as binary fission.

1. When conditions are favourable, a bacterial cell elongates and its nuclear material (DNA) duplicates.
2. A cell wall and cell membrane develop to separate the bacterial cell into two halves.
   This forms two cells.

Bacterial cells double every 20 minutes. During periods of rapid growth, bacterial cells will produce a colony of bacterial cells with thousands to millions of bacterial cells, visible to the human eye.

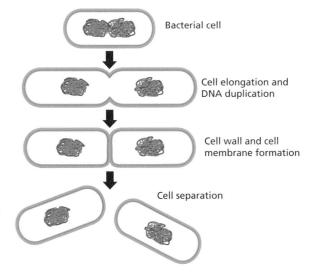

MICROBIOLOGY

Growth phase of bacteria

Binary fission results in a rapid increase in the number of bacteria when conditions are favourable. This growth can be divided into four phases.

- **Lag phase:** bacteria are adapting to their new environment. There is little increase in bacterial numbers.
- **Log phase:** bacteria begin multiplying quickly in ideal conditions and a rapid increase in bacterial numbers can be seen.
- **Stationary phase:** there is no increase in bacterial numbers. The production of new bacteria is compensated for by the death of equal numbers of bacteria, causing the number to **plateau**. The multiplying of bacteria slows due to reduced food, space, moisture and oxygen, leading to competition between bacteria, and a build-up of toxic waste products that cause bacteria to pollute their own environment.
- **Decline phase:** the number of bacteria dying is greater than the reproduction rate (caused by the same factors as in the stationary phase), so a constant decrease in bacterial numbers is evident. A small number of bacteria survive this stage by remaining dormant as endospores.

Lit Hit
A plateau is a state of little or no change.

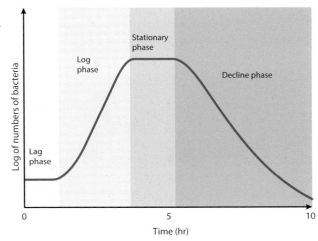

Endospore-forming bacteria

During the decline phase, when conditions for the growth of bacteria are unfavourable, some bacteria die and others, e.g. some rod-shaped bacteria, survive, as they can form endospores.

1. Endospores are tough, dormant cells that form around a duplicated DNA strand that forms inside a bacterial cell.

2. The bacteria cell then disintegrates and the endospore remains dormant.

3. When conditions are favourable again the endospore breaks down its tough wall.

4. The DNA duplicates itself, and a normal bacterial cell forms again.

5. This bacterial cell can then reproduce by binary fission.

Endospores can be destroyed by:

- **moist heat** (heating food to 121°C for 15 minutes)

- **dry heat** (heating food to 150°C for one hour).

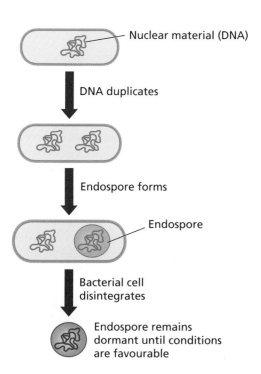

Bacterial toxins

During periods of rapid growth, pathogenic bacteria produce waste toxins. These toxins are poisonous and are a frequent cause of food poisoning. Bacterial toxins include endotoxins and exotoxins.

Endotoxins	Exotoxins
• Toxins made inside bacteria cell walls as they grow • Released when the bacterial cell dies • Easily destroyed by normal cooking temperatures • Can cause infectious food poisoning (long incubation period, over 12 hours) if not destroyed • The toxin only affects the area of infection • **Examples:** salmonella, listeria and *E. coli*	• Toxins secreted by bacteria and released outside the cell as they grow • May be produced before or after food is eaten • Difficult to destroy. Can be destroyed by boiling for 30 minutes • Can cause toxic food poisoning (short incubation period, around two hours) if not destroyed • The toxin can affect parts of the body away from the area of infection • **Examples:** *Staphylococcus aureus* and *Clostridium botulinum*
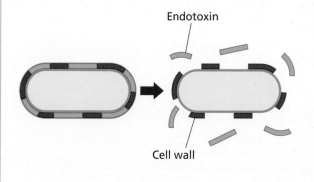	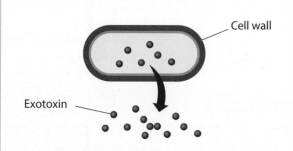

Classification of bacteria

Bacteria are classified in two main ways: by shape or by gram staining.

Classification by shape

Bacteria are classified as coccus (spherical), bacillus (rod shaped) or curved.

Coccus (spherical)

Type		Examples
Single (coccus)	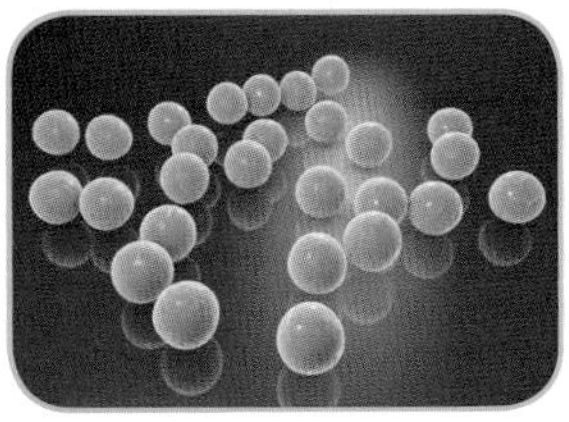	Bacterial meningitis
Pairs (diplococci)		Pneumonia
Chains (streptococci)		Tonsillitis
Clusters (staphylococci)		*Staphylococcus aureus* infection (impetigo) Food poisoning

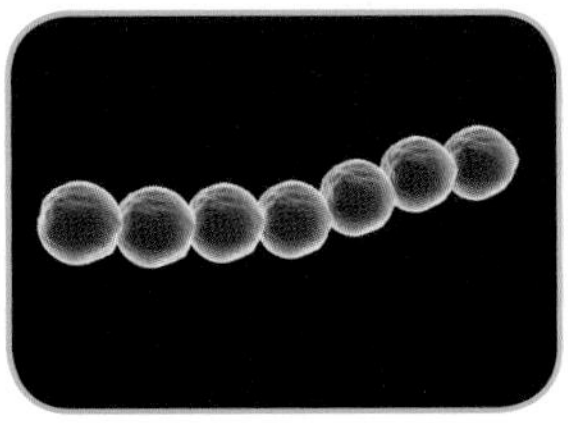

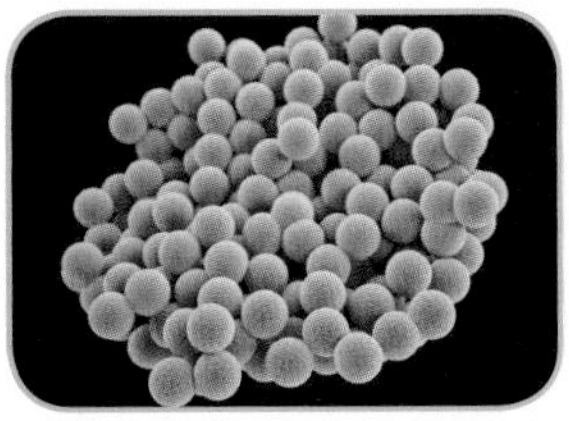

Did you know ?
Ireland has the second-highest death rate from pneumonia in western Europe.

Bacillus (rod-shaped)

Type		Examples
Bacilli	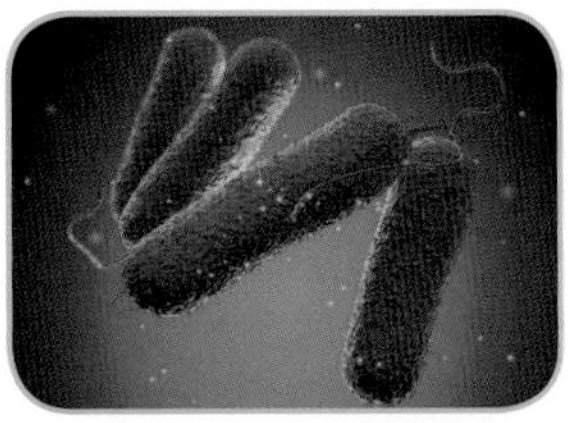	Food-poisoning bacteria, e.g. salmonella, listeria and *E. coli*
Clostridia	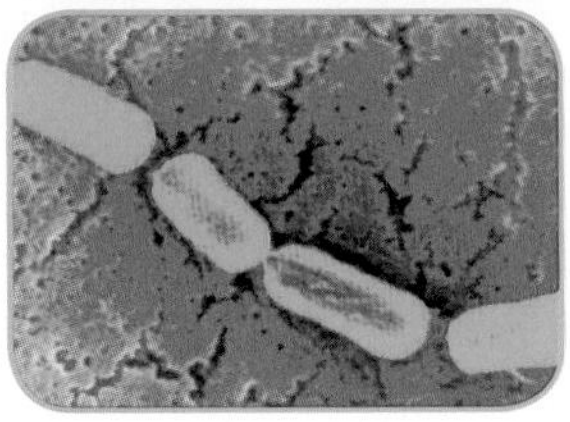	Food-poisoning bacteria, e.g. *Clostridium botulinum*

MICROBIOLOGY

Curved	
Type	**Examples**
Spirilla (spiral)	Sexually transmitted diseases, e.g. syphilis

> **Did you know** ?
> During 2013, there were 576 recorded incidences of syphilis in Ireland. The majority of cases occurred in males, with a male to female ratio of 16:1.

Vibrio (comma-shaped)	Cholera

Classification by gram staining

Gram staining is a laboratory test used to differentiate between two bacterial groups: gram-positive bacteria and gram-negative bacteria.

These two bacterial groups have a different reaction to the stain used in this process. Knowing whether a bacteria is gram positive or gram negative can be important for doctors in determining appropriate treatment for humans who are infected with an unknown pathogenic bacteria.

- If bacteria are gram positive they stain blue/purple.
- If bacteria are gram negative they stain pink.

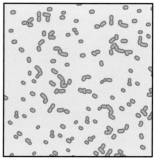

Gram positive   Gram negative

Characteristics of gram-positive and gram-negative bacteria

	Gram positive	**Gram negative**
Structure	The cell wall is one thick layer	The cell wall contains two thin layers
Flagella	No flagella	Has flagella
Reproduction	Produces spores	No spore-production
Resistance	Low resistance to antibiotics	High resistance to antibiotics
Examples	*Clostridium botulinum* and *streptococci*	*E. coli* and salmonella

Advantages and disadvantages of bacteria

Advantages	Disadvantages
✓ Some are used in the production of: ○ **cheese**, e.g. lactic acid bacteria converts lactose into lactic acid, adding flavour ○ **yoghurt**, e.g. *Lactobacillus bulgaricus*, converts lactose to lactic acid, causing the milk to coagulate into the thick consistency of yoghurt ○ **vinegar**, e.g. acetic acid bacteria converts alcohol into vinegar ✓ **Enteric** bacteria, e.g. *E. coli*, produce vitamins B and K in the intestine, which are needed for overall good health ✓ Help decompose organic matter, e.g. raw food waste to make compost ✓ Used in the production of food supplements, e.g. lactic acid bacteria (probiotic) are added to supplements to improve the functioning of the digestive system	✗ Can cause food spoilage, e.g. lactic acid bacteria sours milk ✗ Can contaminate food and cause food poisoning, e.g salmonella and *E. coli* ✗ Can cause human diseases, e.g. cholera and pneumonia ✗ Can cause plant diseases, e.g. blister spot ✗ Can cause animal diseases, e.g. mastitis (inflammation of udder tissue on cows) ✗ Bacteria in the mouth can cause tooth decay as it changes sugar to acid, which erodes enamel on teeth

> **Lit Hit**
> Enteric means naturally occurring in the intestines.

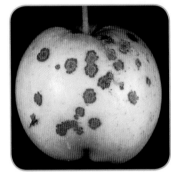

▸ Blister spot

Uses of microorganisms in food production

Food	Microorganism	Process
Cheese	Bacteria (lactic-acid bacteria)	See page 126.
Yoghurt	Bacteria (*Lactobacillus bulgaricus* and *Lactobacillus acidophilus*)	See page 130.
Mycoprotein	Fungi (*Fusarium venenatum*)	See page 107.
Bread	Yeast (*Saccharomyces cerevisiae*)	See page 178.
Vinegar	Yeast and bacteria (acetic-acid bacteria) ▲ White wine vinegar	Vinegar is the acidic liquid obtained from a two-stage fermentation process. Initially, alcohol is produced by yeast fermentation. This process involves the conversion of sugar into carbon dioxide (CO_2) and alcohol. Next, this alcohol is further fermented by the addition of acetic acid bacteria to produce acetic acid. This acetic acid is mixed with water to make vinegar. White wine vinegar is made from the fermentation of wine. Cider vinegar is made from the fermentation of cider.

? Outline **two** uses of micro-organisms in food production. (10) **OL**

State **one** use of each of the following fungi in food production.
- Moulds
- Yeast
- Large fungi (6) **HL**

Outline the uses of microorganisms in food production. (12) **HL**

MICROBIOLOGY

1.3.8   FOOD SPOILAGE

What you will learn:

- **Causes of food spoilage**
- **Types of food poisoning**
- **Common symptoms of food poisoning**
- **Groups vulnerable to food poisoning**
- **Profiles of infectious food-poisoning bacteria**
- **Profiles of toxic food-poisoning bacteria**

FOOD SPOILAGE

Food naturally goes through a cycle of decay that eventually results in spoilage. The rate of food spoilage is quicker among perishable foods, e.g. milk and bread. When food is spoiled it becomes inedible.

Causes of food spoilage

The main causes of food spoilage are enzyme action, moisture loss and microbial contamination.

Enzyme action

Enzymes are protein catalysts that speed up chemical reactions without being destroyed or changed. They are naturally present in food and play a role in food spoilage, as they bring about:

- ripening of food
- browning of food (enzymic browning)
- enzymic deterioration.

This type of spoilage is known as enzymic spoilage.

Ripening of food

All fruit and vegetables naturally contain enzymes responsible for their ripening.
As enzymes ripen the:

- taste (sweetness) improves, as the high starch content is converted to sugars, e.g. fructose
- colour changes, e.g. tomatoes change from green to red
- texture changes, e.g. hard bananas become soft and easy to digest.

Enzymes continue to work after ripening, and eventually cause fruit and vegetables to become overripe and then to decay and decompose.

▲ Stages of ripening in bananas

Browning of food (enzymic browning)

Some fruit and vegetables, e.g. apples, turn brown when cut, as this releases an enzyme, oxidase, from the cell wall, which reacts with oxygen in the air (oxidation). This eventually results in food spoilage.

Enzymic deterioration

Fish naturally contain enzymes that speed up spoilage and deterioration of the flesh, even at low temperatures. This releases a putrid odour.

Vegetables also naturally contain enzymes that cause deterioration, even at low temperatures. This is why vegetables must be blanched before freezing.

Did you know

The enzyme oxidase not only causes some fruit and vegetables to go brown, but it can also reduce their vitamin C content.

▲ Apple with enzymic browning

 Discuss the causes of food spoilage in relation to the action of enzymes. (15) **HL**

HL How to prevent/control enzymic spoilage

Acids	The addition of acids lowers pH levels, inactivating enzymes, as they generally work best at a neutral pH. For example: squeezing a lemon over a cut apple will prevent enzymic browning.
Heat	Enzymes are sensitive to high temperatures and become inactivated by cooking. This stops the browning and ripening of food, e.g. stewing apples.
Additives (preservatives)	The preservative sulfur dioxide inactivates enzymes, reducing the rate of spoilage. It is used commercially to prevent enzymic spoilage of dried fruit and juices.
Cold temperatures	Cold temperatures slow down enzyme activity in food, reducing the rate of spoilage and lengthening shelf life, e.g. refrigerating fish at 4°C.
Blanching	Vegetables, e.g. broccoli, must be blanched before freezing to prevent enzymatic spoilage, as cold temperatures only slow down enzyme activity. Blanching involves immersing food in boiling water (usually for one to four minutes) to kill enzymes, and then plunging them in ice-cold water before freezing.

 Explain how the action of enzymes can be controlled in order to prevent food spoilage. (20) **HL**

REMEMBER IT!

'After **H**arvesting **A**lways **C**onsider **B**lanching.'

Acids, **H**eat, **A**dditives (preservatives), **C**old temperatures, **B**lanching.

Moisture loss

Moisture loss affects fruit and vegetables once they have been harvested, as they lose the ability to absorb moisture from the soil through their roots. This causes them to become dehydrated, resulting in:

- shrinkage, e.g. mushrooms shrivel
- wrinkling, e.g. on the skin of peppers and apples
- a limp appearance, e.g. celery and asparagus become limp.

High-protein foods, e.g. cheese, can also experience moisture loss, which causes the surface to go hard when exposed to air.

▲ Wrinkling on the skin of a pepper

FOOD SPOILAGE

Microbial contamination

Microorganisms are the principal cause of food spoilage. Food can provide microorganisms with ideal conditions for growth, e.g. food, moisture and suitable pH. The main microorganisms responsible for food spoilage are yeasts, moulds and bacteria. They spoil food in different ways.

Yeasts and moulds	Bacteria
• Cause visible food spoilage on the exterior of food • Generally do not cause food poisoning, as people avoid consuming when they see the spoilage on food • Certain mycotoxins (toxins produced by mould), e.g. aflatoxin produced by the mould *Aspergillus flavus*, are considered carcinogenic  ▲ Mould on jam	• Cause food spoilage on the exterior and interior of food. Bacterial cells produce toxins that are not visible • Commonly cause bacterial food poisoning, as toxins are invisible to the eye so are often consumed unknowingly

? Give an account of the main causes of food spoilage. (16) **OL**

FOOD POISONING

Food poisoning is an illness caused by eating food contaminated with harmful substances.

Types of food poisoning

HL

There are three types of food poisoning: chemical, biological and bacterial.

Chemical food poisoning	Caused by eating food contaminated with metal residues, e.g. lead and cadmium, or antibiotics, pesticides or herbicides from agriculture.
Biological food poisoning	Caused by eating foods that naturally contain poisonous substances, e.g. solanine in green potatoes, amatoxin in poisonous mushrooms and haemagglutinin in raw red kidney beans.  ▶ Solanine in a green potato
Bacterial food poisoning	Caused by eating food contaminated with pathogenic bacteria from unhygienic food handlers, pests, water or cross-contamination. There are two types of bacterial food poisoning: infectious food poisoning and toxic food poisoning.

Infectious food poisoning	Toxic food poisoning
• An illness caused by eating food containing pathogenic bacteria that produces endotoxins (toxins made inside pathogenic bacteria cell walls as they grow) • Endotoxins are released when the bacterial cells dies • Easily destroyed by normal cooking temperatures • Long **incubation** period, over 12 hours **Examples:** salmonella, listeria and *E. coli*.	• An illness caused by eating food containing pathogenic bacteria that produces exotoxins (toxins secreted by pathogenic bacteria and released outside the cell wall as they grow) • Exotoxins may be produced before or after the food is eaten • Difficult to destroy. Can be destroyed by boiling for 30 minutes • Short incubation period, around two hours. **Examples:** *Staphylococcus aureus* and *Clostridium botulinum*.

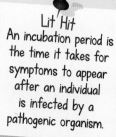

Lit Hit
An incubation period is the time it takes for symptoms to appear after an individual is infected by a pathogenic organism.

> ? In relation to food poisoning explain **each** of the following:
> - incubation period
> - toxic food poisoning
> - infectious food poisoning. (18) **HL**

Common symptoms of food poisoning

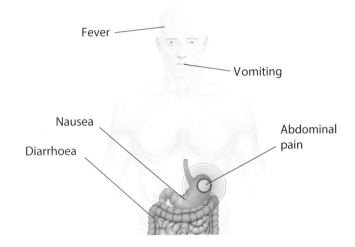

Fever

Vomiting

Nausea

Abdominal pain

Diarrhoea

Groups vulnerable to food poisoning

The following groups are more vulnerable to food poisoning due to reduced immune systems:

- babies and children
- pregnant women
- convalescents
- older people.

Profiles of infectious food-poisoning bacteria

HL Salmonella

Description	• Rod-shaped
Lit Hit Contagious means easily spread from one person to another.	• Gram negative • Non-spore forming • Reproduces asexually by binary fission • **Contagious** • Causes infectious food poisoning
Environmental factors	• Facultative: can grow with or without oxygen • Prefers an optimum temperature of 37°C • Prefers a neutral pH
Sources/habitat	• Human and animal intestines and faeces • Unwashed hands • Rodents and pests
High-risk foods	• Raw or undercooked eggs, meat, fish and poultry • Unpasteurised (raw) milk and cheese
Symptoms	• Nausea and vomiting • Abdominal pains • Diarrhoea • Fever
Incubation period	• 12–36 hours
Duration of food poisoning	• 1–7 days

> **Did you know** ?
> Salmonella is the number one cause of bacterial food poisoning, with over 85,000 cases of salmonellosis reported every year in the European Union.

Escherichia coli (E. coli)

Description	• Rod-shaped • Gram negative • Non-spore forming • Reproduces asexually by binary fission • Causes infectious food poisoning • Contagious
Environmental factors	• Facultative: can grow with or without oxygen • Prefers an optimum temperature of 30–40°C • Prefers a neutral pH
Sources/habitat	• Human and animal faeces • Unwashed hands • Polluted water
High-risk foods	• Unpasteurised (raw) milk and cheese • Raw or undercooked meat
Symptoms	• Nausea and vomiting • Abdominal pains • Diarrhoea • Fever • Kidney failure • Death
Incubation period	• 12–24 hours
Duration of food poisoning	• 1–5 days

Listeria monocytogenes

Description	• Rod-shaped • Gram positive • Non spore forming • Reproduces asexually by binary fission • Causes infectious food poisoning. • Not contagious
Environmental factors	• Facultative • Prefers an optimum temperature of 30°C • Prefers a neutral pH
Sources/habitat	• Human and animal faeces • Unwashed hands • Soil
High-risk foods	• Unpasteurised (raw) milk and cheese • Soft cheese, e.g. Camembert • Raw or undercooked meat • Pâté • Cook-chill foods, e.g. lasagne • Pre-packed salads, e.g. coleslaw
Symptoms	• Nausea and vomiting • Muscle aches • Diarrhoea • Convulsions • Chills • Meningitis in babies
Incubation period	• 1–70 days
Duration of food poisoning	• Several days

Profiles of toxic food-poisoning bacteria

Clostridium botulinum

Description	• Rod-shaped • Gram positive • Spore-forming • Reproduces asexually by binary fission • Causes toxic food poisoning • Not contagious
Environmental factors	• Anaerobic • Prefers an optimum temperature of 30–37°C • Prefers a slightly acidic environment
Sources/habitat	• Soil • Vegetables • Pig intestines
High-risk foods	• Unpasteurised (raw) cheese • Canned food • Vacuum-packed food
Symptoms	• Diarrhoea • Slurred speech • Double vision • Paralysis of the throat • Dizziness • Can lead to death
Incubation period	• 12–36 hours
Duration of food poisoning	• 1–8 days

Staphylococcus aureus

Description	• Spherical • Gram positive • Non-spore forming • Reproduces asexually by binary fission • Causes toxic food poisoning • Not contagious
Environmental factors	• Facultative • Prefers an optimum temperature of 30–40°C • Prefers a neutral pH
Sources/habitat	• In the nose, throat and infections on the skin, e.g. boils • Unwashed hands
High-risk foods	• Unpasteurised milk and cheese • Sliced cold meats, e.g. ham and turkey
Symptoms	• Nausea and vomiting • Abdominal pains • Diarrhoea • Fever
Incubation period	• 2–6 hours
Duration of food poisoning	• Up to 24 hours

? Name **and** give details of **one** type of food poisoning bacteria. Refer to:
- conditions necessary for growth
- source
- reproduction/growth of bacteria
- high risk foods. (20) **HL**

Name and give a detailed account of any **one** type of food poisoning bacteria. Refer to:
- sources of infection
- high-risk foods
- symptoms. (20) **HL**

FOOD PRESERVATION

What you will learn:

- Principles and advantages of food preservation
- Methods of home preservation and commercial preservation
- Home freezing, heat treatments, chemical preservation and dehydration
- Commercial freezing, heat treatments, chemical preservation, dehydration, fermentation and irradiation
- Effects of preservation on food
- Comparative evaluation of freezing and canning strawberries

All foods contain microorganisms and enzymes that cause food spoilage, which can make the food unsafe to eat. If food is preserved it can prevent food spoilage, as preserving methods remove one or more of the conditions that microorganisms and enzymes require for survival. These conditions include moisture, suitable pH, oxygen and temperature.

Principles of food preservation

Preservation:

- inhibits the microbial activity that causes spoilage and food poisoning
- inactivates the enzyme activity that causes food spoilage
- prevents microorganisms re-entering food, by sealing it
- maintains colour, taste, texture, flavour and nutritional value of food as much as possible.

Advantages of food preservation

✓ Preservation avoids food waste, as foods can be preserved before they spoil, e.g. apples can be made into chutney, extending their shelf life.

✓ Preservation makes out-of-season foods available all year around, e.g. frozen strawberries during winter.

✓ Preservation adds variety to the diet, as it enables new foods to be produced, e.g. pickles.

✓ Preservation saves money, as preserved foods have a longer shelf life, so consumers can stock up when foods are on special offer.

✓ Preserved foods, e.g. frozen vegetables, are useful in unforeseen circumstances, as they can be prepared in little time.

HOME PRESERVATION

Methods of home preservation

- **Freezing:** e.g. vegetables and bread
- **Heat treatments:** e.g. jam and chutney
- **Chemical preservation:** e.g. pickling
- **Dehydration:** e.g. drying herbs

Home freezing

Freezing is one of the most common methods of home preservation due to its simplicity. Home freezing retains the colour, texture, flavour and nutritional value of food better than any other home preservation method.

Underlying principle of freezing

Freezing preserves food by:

- using low temperatures (below 0°C) to inactivate microorganism growth and slow down enzyme activity
- converting water in food into ice, making it unavailable to microorganisms.

Before freezing, food should be wrapped well. This stops freezer burn and creates a barrier to prevent the re-entry of microorganisms.

Methods of home freezing

Quick freezing	Slow freezing
• Food is quickly frozen at −25°C in the fast-freeze section of the freezer • Forms small ice crystals in food, causing little damage to the cell walls as the crystals do not tear or puncture them • Nutritional value, texture, colour and flavour are retained on thawing Frozen food cell Thawed food cell	• Food is frozen at 0 to −18°C in the ice box in a fridge or storage section of a freezer • Forms large ice crystals in food, causing large damage to the cell walls as the crystals puncture or tear them • Loss of nutritional value, texture, colour and flavour occur on thawing Frozen food cell Thawed food cell

 In relation to freezing explain **each** of the following.
- Quick freezing
- Slow freezing (6) **HL**

Suitable and unsuitable foods for home freezing

Suitable foods for freezing	Unsuitable foods for freezing
• Most fruit and vegetables • Meat, fish and poultry (raw and cooked) • Soups and sauces • Bread, cakes and pastries • Convenience foods, e.g. pizza and ready meals	• Mayonnaise: causes the emulsion to separate and oil to float on top • Whole eggs (in shell): causes the egg white to expand, cracking the shell • Foods with a high water content, e.g. cucumbers and lettuce: causes damage to the cell walls, leaving them mushy and limp when thawed • Soft cheeses, e.g. cream cheese: causes them to become dry and crumbly

FOOD PRESERVATION

Advantages and disadvantages of freezing

Advantages	Disadvantages
✓ Retains the nutritional value and sensory characteristics of food, e.g. texture, colour and flavour ✓ Saves time, as individuals can bulk-purchase perishable foods, e.g. bread, avoiding numerous supermarket visits ✓ Saves money, as individuals can bulk-freeze meals for busy days, avoiding the need for takeaways ✓ Makes out-of-season foods available all year ✓ Avoids food waste, as foods can be frozen before they spoil, extending shelf life	✗ The initial cost of a freezer can be expensive ✗ Bulk-freezing meals can be time-consuming, as large quantities of food have to be prepared and cooked ✗ Packaging is needed for freezing, which can be costly ✗ Defrosting the freezer can be time consuming and laborious

Guidelines for home freezing food

1. Preparation

- Turn on the fast-freeze button 3–4 hours in advance to reduce the temperature from −18°C to −25°C. This results in quick freezing that retains the nutritional value and sensory characteristics of food.
- Cool food before freezing to avoid the internal temperature of the freezer increasing, causing other food to defrost.
- Avoid freezing greater than one-tenth of the freezer capacity within any 24-hour time period, as it puts pressure on the motor. If over-packed, the internal temperature can increase, causing foods to defrost.
- Freeze foods in usable quantities to avoid having to defrost more food than is needed.
- Blanch vegetables before freezing to avoid enzymic spoilage over time.

Method for blanching and freezing vegetables

1. Bring one litre of water to boil in a large saucepan.
2. Wash, peel and chop 100 g of carrots.
3. Place carrots into the boiling water for three to five minutes. Drain using a colander.
4. Immediately place carrots in one litre of cold water with ice for three to five minutes. Drain using a colander.
5. Place the carrots in freezer bags in usable portions and label with the food and date of freezing.
6. Place in the fast-freeze section of the freezer.

2. Packaging

- Use good-quality packaging that is strong, airtight and moisture-proof. Remove as much air as possible to save space in the freezer.
- Seal packaging well, otherwise freezer burn may occur, resulting in discolouration, toughening and drying out of protein foods, e.g. chicken.

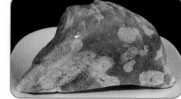

▲ Freezer burn

- If freezing liquids, make sure to leave room for expansion in packaging to prevent tearing.
- Label packaging with the name of the food, quantity and date of freezing so a first-in-first-out (FIFO) system can be followed.

Packaging materials suitable for home freezing

- Polythene freezer bags
- Cling film
- Aluminium foil and containers
- Ceramic or glass containers
- Freezer paper

3. Freezing

- Place food in the fast-freeze compartment (-25°C) to allow for quick freezing to retain the nutritional value and sensory characteristics of food. After 24 hours place in the storage section of the freezer.
- Open freeze foods that will stick together, e.g. berries. Place in a container after freezing.

▲ Open-frozen berries

4. Storing

- Store similar foods together to avoid unnecessary searching and to make it easier to determine when additional food needs to be purchased.
- Use foods in rotation by following the first-in-first-out (FIFO) system.
- Foods should only be stored for their recommended storage time, as frozen food can deteriorate over time. For example, beef, chicken and vegetables should be used within 12 months, lamb and white fish within six months, oily fish within four months, soups and sauces within three months and bread within one month.
- Keep the freezer full to capacity, as the majority of the energy a freezer uses is spent cooling air between foods.
- Avoid keeping the freezer door open for long periods or opening the door too frequently in order to reduce the amount of warm air getting in and, in turn, reduce the amount of energy the freezer needs to maintain a cool internal temperature.

5. Thawing

- Read cooking instructions on packaged foods before thawing, as many do not require thawing prior to cooking, e.g. pizza and waffles. Vegetables better retain their nutritional value and sensory characteristics if cooked from frozen.
- Thaw food in the fridge, as thawing at room temperature can provide optimum temperatures for bacterial growth.
- Place meat or fish to be thawed on a plate at the bottom of the fridge to avoid drips onto other foods, leading to cross-contamination.
- Never refreeze thawed food, unless cooked first. On thawing, food-poisoning bacteria begin to multiply. Food that is refrozen and rethawed therefore contains higher levels of bacteria, increasing the risk of food poisoning.

> **?** Freezing is one method of storing fish for a period of time. Outline the general rules to be followed when freezing fresh food. (16) OL

FOOD PRESERVATION

Home heat treatments

Foods can be preserved at home by exposing them to very high temperatures to destroy microorganisms. There are two main ways of preserving foods through heat treatments: jam making and chutney making. A chemical preservative is also used in each of these methods to assist with preservation: sugar in jam making and vinegar in chutney making.

Jam making

Jam is made by boiling fruit with a high percentage of sugar.

Underlying principle of jam making

Jam making preserves fruit by:

- boiling fruit at 100°C to destroy microorganisms and inactivate enzymes. This also helps to soften the fruit by breaking down its cell walls
- adding sugar (65%). This acts as a preservative as it creates a concentrated sugar solution, causing water to be drawn out of the microbial cells by osmosis to equalise the low water solution. This dehydrates microbial cells, causing them to die.
- the presence of pectin and acid. Most fruits contain pectin and acid, which help to change the watery fruit liquid to a set jam. If fruits are lacking in acid or pectin, extra can be added.

At the end of jam making it is important to seal the jam to prevent re-entry of microorganisms.

Ingredients needed for jam making

Fruit	Sugar
• Fruit aids the setting of jam due to its pectin and acid content. • The acid and pectin content varies in different fruits: **Pectin content of fruits** 	High	Medium	Low
---	---	---
• Apples	• Plums	• Pears
• Blackcurrants	• Apricots	• Cherries
• Oranges	• Blackberries	• Raspberries | • Fruit should be clean and free from blemishes or bruises, otherwise an inferior-quality jam can result. Good-quality, ripe, high-pectin, acidic fruits produce the best results.	• Sugar acts as a preservative and sweetener in jam making. • Sugar preserves jams as it creates a concentrated sugar solution, causing water to be drawn out of the microbial cells by osmosis to equalise the low water solution. This dehydrates microbial cells, causing them to die. • Weigh sugar accurately, as 65% sugar is necessary to inhibit microbial growth. • Use granulated sugar or a jam sugar (sure-set) that contains pectin and fruit acid, which assists the setting of the jam.
Pectin	**Acid**

• Pectin is a polysaccharide found in the cell walls of ripe fruit, which helps the successful setting of jam.
• In underripe fruit, pectin is in the form of protopectin which can be converted to pectin by the addition of acid.
• In overripe fruit it is in the form of pectic acid, which has no setting abilities.
• If using underripe or low-pectin fruits, add extra pecin by:
  o mixing them with a high-pectin fruit, e.g. apples
  o adding commercial pectin, e.g. Certo
  o using sure-set sugar.
	• Acid releases pectin from the cell wall of fruits, which helps the successful setting of jam.
	• Some fruits, e.g. oranges, already have a high acidic content, so extra acid is not needed.
	• Fruits with a low acid content require the addition of extra acid, e.g. lemon juice.
	• Acid improves the colour and flavour of jams and helps to prevent crystallisation.

> **Did you know**
>
> A test can be completed to find out the pectin content of fruit by boiling fruit in water and then adding three tablespoons of methylated spirits to one tablespoon of the created fruit juice. This will cause clots of form.
> - 1 firm clump = high pectin content
> - 3–4 firm clumps = medium pectin content
> - Numerous small clumps = low pectin content

Method for making jam

Ingredients

See your Food Studies Assignment Guide.

Equipment

- Large, heavy-based saucepan
- Chopping board
- Large plate
- Cellophane discs
- Soup ladle
- Sharp knife
- Pot stand
- Glass jars
- Elastic bands
- Small plate
- Wooden spoon
- Waxed discs
- Labels

Method

1. **Weigh:** weigh out ingredients accurately.
2. **Jar preparation:** wash jars in hot, soapy water and dry. Place on a baking tray and sterilise in the oven at 140°C for 20 minutes to remove microbes.
3. **Fruit preparation:** remove bruised or damaged fruit. Wash, peel, remove stalks and leaves and cut (if necessary).
4. **Cooking:** place fruit in a greased saucepan and simmer gently to soften and release pectin from the cell walls.
5. **Sugar addition:** warm sugar in the oven at 140°C for five minutes to help it dissolve quicker, reducing the risk of crystallisation. Add the sugar to the fruit and stir until it is fully dissolved.
6. **Boiling:** bring to the boil and boil rapidly, stirring occasionally. Check if the jam has reached its setting point.
7. **Potting:** if jam is set, skim the scum from the top. Using a ladle, spoon into the sterilised jars, leaving a 1.5 cm head space at the top.
8. **Covering:** cover with a wax disc, removing any air bubbles with the back of a spoon. Apply a cellophane cover over the top of the jar to form an airtight seal. This prevents the growth of microbes. Hold the cellophane cover in place with an elastic band. Place a lid on top.
9. **Labelling:** label the jar with the date of potting and type of jam.
10. **Storing:** store in a cool, dry place.

REMEMBER IT!

> 'Wonderful Jam From Colourful Sweet Berries Pleases Children's Little Stomachs.'
>
> Weigh, Jar preparation, Fruit preparation, Cooking, Sugar addition, Boiling, Potting, Covering, Labelling, Storing.

Characteristics of a good jam

Clear, not cloudy | Good colour | Strong fruit flavour | Well set | 1-year year shelf life

FOOD PRESERVATION

Setting tests for jams

Wrinkle test	Flake test	Thermometer test
Place a small plate in the refrigerator. When cool, spoon one teaspoon of jam onto the plate and let it cool for one minute. Push the jam with a fingertip. If the jam is set it will wrinkle.	Dip a spoon into the jam and allow it to cool for a minute. Tilt the spoon and allow the jam to run off. If set, the jam will fall from the spoon in one large flake.	Place a sugar thermometer into the pot of jam. When the thermometer reads 105°C, the jam is set.

Problems that can occur when jam making

Problem	Causes
Crystallisation (sugar crystals throughout the jam)	• If too much sugar is added (above 65%) • If the jam is not boiled for long enough • If the sugar is not stirred continuously to ensure it is dissolved fully before boiling
Unset jam (runny consistency)	• If insufficient pectin or acid is present • If jam is not boiled for long enough to release pectin from the cell walls of the fruit • If jam is poured into pots before the setting point is achieved
Fermentation (breakdown of jam by microbes, producing an off-flavour)	• If insufficient sugar is added (less than 65%) • If poor-quality fruit is used, e.g. mushy berries • If jam is not boiled for long enough

Chutney making

Chutney is made by boiling fruit and vegetables with a mixture of sugar, vinegar and spices. Chutneys have a characteristic sweet and sour flavour that mellows with age.

Underlying principle of chutney making

Chutney making preserves fruit and vegetables by:

▲ Mango chutney

- boiling fruit and vegetables at 100°C and then simmering to destroy microorganisms and inactivate enzymes. This also helps to soften the fruit and vegetables by breaking down their cell walls
- adding sugar. this acts as a preservative as it creates a concentrated sugar solution, causing water to be drawn out of the microbial cells by osmosis to equalise the low water solution. This dehydrates microbial cells, causing them to die
- adding vinegar. this acts as a preservative as it lowers the pH level, making the environment more acidic and inhibiting microbial growth and inactivating enzymes, as they prefer a neutral pH of 7.

At the end of chutney making it is important to seal the chutney to prevent re-entry of microorganisms.

Method for making chutney

Ingredients

See your Food Studies Assignment Guide.

Equipment and method

Use the same equipment and method as jam making, with the following exceptions.

- Use a wooden spoon to stir the chutney and a plastic funnel to place chutney into the sterilised jars. Avoid using metal utensils as metal reacts with the acid in the vinegar, leaving chutney with an unpleasant taste.
- Do not use cellophane covers as they allow evaporation to take place inside the jar, causing chutney to shrink.
- Use plastic-coated lids as the acid in vinegar can easily corrode metal-coated lids.
- Opt for brown sugar instead of white as it gives a richer colour to chutney.

 Name **one** method of home preservation that involves the application of heat and explain the principle involved. (16) **HL**

Home chemical preservation

Underlying principle of chemical preservation

Chemical preservation preserves food as:

- the chemical preservatives create a concentrated solution, causing water to be drawn out of the microbial cells by osmosis to equalise the low-water solution. This dehydrates microbial cells, causing them to die
- the acids lower the pH level, making the environment more acidic, inhibiting microbial growth and inactivating enzymes, as they prefer a neutral pH of 7.

Types of home chemical preservation

Method of preservation	Chemical used	Underlying principle
Jam making	Sugar	See page 232.
Chutney making	Sugar and vinegar	See page 234.
Pickling	Brine and vinegar	Brine acts as a preservative as salt dehydrates microbial cells by osmosis, causing them to die.

Home dehydration

Dehydration is an uncommon method of home preservation. It is usually carried out in a low-temperature oven or a hot-press.

Underlying principle of dehydration

Dehydration preserves food by removing moisture, inhibiting microbial growth and inactivating enzymes.

▲ Dried apple slices

Suitable foods for home dehydration

- Herbs, e.g. basil and rosemary
- Fruit, e.g apple slices and banana chips
- Vegetables, e.g. chillies, parsnip crisps and tomatoes

Give an account of **one** method of food preservation used in the home. Refer to:
- method of preservation
- how this method of preservation is carried out
- suitable foods
- packaging. (24) **OL**

Suggest **one** method of food preservation which could be used to preserve a surplus of home-grown fruit or vegetables. Explain the underlying principle of the method of preservation you have selected. (15) **HL**

FOOD PRESERVATION

COMMERCIAL PRESERVATION

Methods of commercial preservation

- **Freezing**
- **Heat treatments:** e.g. canning, bottling, pasteurisation, sterilisation and ultra heat treatment (UHT) of milk.
- **Dehydration:** e.g. dried soup and sauces.
- **Chemical preservation:** e.g. sulfur dioxide in dried fruits.
- **Fermentation:** e.g. wine production.
- **Irradiation**

Commercial freezing

Underlying principle of freezing

See underlying principle of freezing on page 229.

Methods of commercial freezing

Commercial methods of freezing include blast freezing, plate/contact freezing, cryogenic freezing and fluidised bed freezing.

Blast freezing

- This is the most common method of commercial freezing
- Food is subjected to a blast of cold air (-30°C to -40°C) that circulates around food as it travels through a specially designed tunnel on a conveyor belt
- It takes approximately two and a half hours to freeze food
- **Uses:** freezing fruit, vegetables and meat

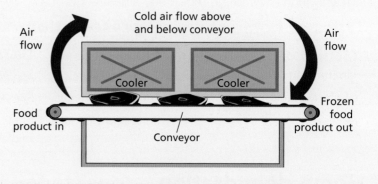

Plate/contact freezing

- Food is placed on or between cool metal plates in an insulated cabinet and frozen by direct contact with the metal surfaces that have been cooled by the circulation of a refrigerant, e.g. ammonia, at -30°C to -40°C
- It takes approximately one hour to 90 minutes to freeze food
- **Uses:** freezing thin pieces of meat and fish, and fish and meat products, e.g. fish fingers and burgers

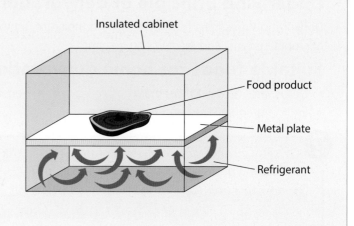

Cryogenic freezing

- This is the most expensive method, but it produces the most superior product due to its low temperature, which results in tiny ice crystals
- Food is placed on a conveyor belt and moved into the insulated chamber where it is cooled by spraying with liquid nitrogen (-196°C)
- It freezes food within minutes
- **Uses:** freezing small fruits, e.g. strawberries, and shellfish, e.g. prawns

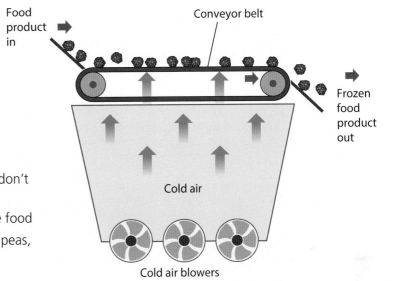

Fluidised bed freezing

- This is similar to blast freezing
- Food is subjected to a blast of cold air (-30°C to -40°C) from underneath a perforated conveyor belt as it travels through a specially designed tunnel. This freezes the pieces of food separately, so that they don't stick together.
- It takes 10–15 minutes to freeze food
- **Uses:** freezing small foods, e.g. peas, sweetcorn and raspberries

 Name **two** commercial methods of freezing and suggest a food suitable for each method. (6) **HL**

Commercial heat treatments

Commercial methods of heat treatment include: pasteurisation, sterilisation, ultra heat treatment (see page 119) and canning and bottling.

Canning and bottling

Underlying principle of canning and bottling

Canning and bottling preserves food by:

- using high temperatures to destroy microorganisms and inactivate enzymes
- sealing food in airtight containers to prevent the re-entry of microorganisms.

Stages in the canning process

1. **Prepared:** food is prepared, e.g. vegetables are washed and bones are removed from meat and fish. Meat and fish are cooked and vegetables are blanched.

2. **Filled:** lacquered cans (coated with a varnish to prevent a reaction between the metal and acidic food) are filled with food and either syrup or brine is added, depending on the food being canned.

3. **Air removed:** air is removed from the can.

4. **Sealed:** cans are hermetically sealed (air tight seal) in a sterile environment.

5. **Sterilised:** cans and food are sterilised and cooled.

6. **Labelled:** cans are labelled.

REMEMBER IT!

'**P**reserving **F**ood **A**lways **S**tretches **S**helf **L**ife.'
Preparing, **F**illing cans, **A**ir removal, **S**ealing, **S**terilising, **L**abelling.

Methods of canning

Aseptic canning	High-acid food canning	Low-acid food canning
• Cans and food are sterilised separately at high temperatures. Food is heated to 120–150°C • Sterilised food is placed into cans and hermetically sealed. Cans are then cooled and labelled • As this method has a short processing time the nutritional value and sensory characteristics of food are retained	• High-acid foods, e.g. fruit, require a short processing time due to their acidic pH of 4.5 or less, which already destroys many bacteria • They are heated to 100°C for less than 30 minutes to destroy remaining bacteria	• Low-acid foods, e.g. meat, fish and vegetables, require a long processing time due to their low acidic pH • They are heated to 115°C for more than 30 minutes to ensure that bacteria are destroyed

Suitable foods for canning

- Fruit
- Soup
- Fish
- Vegetables
- Meat
- Milk

Commercial chemical preservation

Underlying principle of chemical preservation

See underlying principle of chemical preservation on page 235.

Common commercial chemical preservatives

- Sugar, e.g. jam making
- Salt, e.g. pickling, preserving meat
- Vinegar (acetic acid), e.g. chutney making
- Sulfur dioxide, e.g. dried fruit
- Sorbic acid, e.g. fruit yoghurts
- Antioxidants, e.g vegetable oils
- Alcohol, e.g. pickling

Commercial dehydration

Underlying principle of dehydration

See underlying principle of dehydration on page 235.

Methods of commercial dehydration

Commercial methods of dehydration include spray drying and roller drying, fluidised bed drying, accelerated freeze drying and sun drying.

→ For information on spray drying and roller drying see page 120.

Fluidised bed drying	• Food is subjected to a blast of hot air that circulates around, dehydrating it • Food is continuously moved around so it does not stick together • It takes approximately 20-40 minutes to freeze food • **Uses:** drying fruit, vegetables and flat pieces of meat 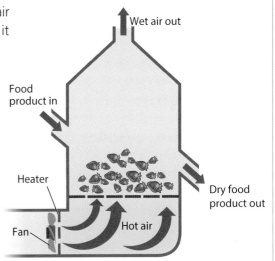
Accelerated freeze drying **Lit Hit** Sublimation is a chemical process where a solid turns into a gas without going through a liquid stage.	• Food is initially frozen at very low temperatures to form small ice crystals. The ice crystals are then evaporated from food in a vacuum chamber by **sublimation**. This produces a dried, lightweight product. • It takes 9–24 hours to dry food • **Uses:** drying coffee, soup, meat, fruit and vegetables 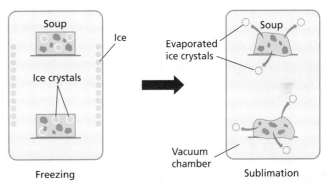
Sun drying	• Food is exposed to direct sunlight in hot climates, e.g. California. Water is evaporated from the food by the heat • **Uses:** drying tomatoes, figs and peppers 

? Name **three** different methods of preserving food and give an example of a food preserved by **each** method. (6) **OL**

Fermentation

Underlying principle of fermentation

Fermentation is the breakdown of carbohydrates (starch and sugar) by microorganisms (yeast and bacteria) to produce carbon dioxide, alcohol and energy.

- Fermentation is used to preserve yoghurt, e.g. lactic acid bacteria converts lactose into lactic acid.
- Yeast fermentation is used in baking and brewing.
- The by-products of fermentation, e.g. alcohol and vinegar (acetic acid) are used as chemical preservatives.

> **?** Define fermentation. Name **two** by-products of fermentation. (6) **HL**

Irradiation

Underlying principle of irradiation

Irradiation preserves food by exposure to low levels of radiation (gamma rays), which passes through food and destroys microorganisms, kills pests, e.g. whiteflies, and prevents sprouting on vegetables and ripening on fruit.

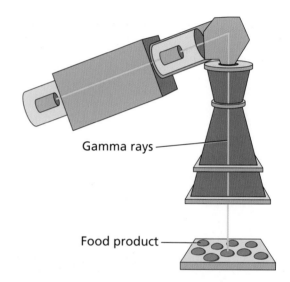

Gamma rays

Food product

> **Did you know ?**
>
> The quantity of radiation necessary to stop sprouting on vegetables is 10–20 times higher than the quantity that would kill humans.

> **?** What is irradiated food? State **two** effects of irradiation on food. (6) **HL**

Irradiation legislation

At present, irradiation is used on more than 60 food types, including herbs, spices, fruit and vegetables in over 40 countries worldwide, including the United Kingdom, the United States and France. In Ireland, there are currently no irradiation facilities. Any irradiated food products for sale on the Irish market are imported. Strict legislation governs these foods and ensures that any imported irradiated foods or foods containing irradiated ingredients must carry the words *irradiated* or *treated with ionising radiation* on them and may also (optionally) carry the international icon for irradiated foods, the Radura symbol.

▲ Radura symbol

> **?** What does this symbol convey to the consumer? (2) **HL**

Advantages and disadvantages of irradiation

Advantages	Disadvantages
✓ Extends shelf life, as it destroys microorganisms ✓ Kills insect pests ✓ Delays the ripening of fruit and the sprouting of vegetables ✓ Retains sensory characteristics of food, including texture, colour and flavour	✕ Vitamins, including B1 (thiamine) and C, are reduced or eliminated ✕ Can cause the chemical composition of high-fat foods to change, e.g. lipids become rancid ✕ May mislead consumers, as it can make food appear fresher by slowing microbial and enzymatic decay ✕ Can cause large numbers of free radicals to form within food, which can increase risk of cancer and coronary heart diseases

 Assess irradiation as a method of food preservation. (15) **HL**

Effects of preservation on food

Freezing	Canning
• Microorganisms are inactivated due to low temperatures and the conversion of water into ice • Enzymes are inactivated if vegetables are blanched before freezing • Incorrectly packaged protein foods can be subject to freezer burn • Slow freezing can cause a change in texture • Some loss of B-group vitamins and vitamin C through blanching and thawing	• Microorganisms are destroyed and enzymes are inactivated due to the use of high temperatures • Loss of B-group vitamins and vitamin C due to high temperatures • If foods are canned in brine, oil or syrup it can increase the salt, fat and sugar content of food • Loss of colour, texture and flavour of food can occur
Chemical preservation	**Dehydration**
• Microorganisms are destroyed and enzymes are inactivated due to the addition of preservatives that lower pH levels • Loss of B-group vitamins and vitamin C • Change in colour, texture and flavour of food can occur	• Microorganisms are destroyed and enzymes are inactivated due to lack of moisture • Loss of water-soluble B-group and C vitamins due to removal of moisture • Loss of colour, texture and flavour of food can occur

Comparative evaluation of freezing and canning strawberries

	Freezing	**Canning**
Ingredients	Strawberries	Strawberries, water, sugar, colouring (allura red: E129)
Underlying principle and method of processing	See underlying principle of freezing and methods of freezing on page 229	See underlying principle of canning and methods of canning on pages 237 and 238
Effects of processing	• Microorganisms are inhibited due to the use of low temperatures and the conversion of water into ice • Enzymes are inactivated if strawberries are blanched before freezing • Some loss of B-group vitamins and vitamin C through blanching and thawing	• Microorganisms are destroyed and enzymes are inactivated due to the use of high temperatures • Loss of B-group vitamins and vitamin C due to high temperatures • As strawberries are sometimes canned in syrup it can increase the sugar content of the food • Loss of colour, texture and flavour of food can occur
Shelf life	• Can be stored in the freezer for 8–10 months	• Can be stored unopened for 1–2 years
Types of packaging	• Packaged in a plastic container with cardboard sleeve or in a plastic bag	• Packaged in aluminium cans
Risk of spoilage	• Repeated thawing and refreezing can encourage microbial multiplication, which can cause food poisoning • Seal packaging well to avoid freezer burn, which may result in discolouration, toughening and drying out of strawberries	• If cans are dented, leaking or bulging, food may be spoiled with *Clostridium botulinum*, which, if eaten, could cause botulism
Labelling	Information on the label includes: • name of the product • list of ingredients • nutritional information • date of minimum durability, e.g. best before • declaration of allergens	
Price	Approximately €0.92 per 100 g	Approximately €0.37 per 100 g
Uses	• Baking, e.g. cupcakes • Sauces, e.g. coulis	• Drinks, e.g. smoothies • Desserts, e.g. cheesecake

 Set out details of the findings of a comparative evaluation you have carried out on a food which can be preserved using **two** different methods of preservation. In your answer refer to:

- name of food
- the underlying principle of each method
- suitable methods of preservation
- risk of food spoilage. (26) **HL**

Chapter 11:
Food safety and hygiene

1.3.10

FOOD SAFETY AND HYGIENE AND HAZARD ANALYSIS AND CRITICAL CONTROL POINT (HACCP)

What you will learn:

- **Safe food preparation guidelines**
- **Hazards and contaminants**
- **Hazard Analysis and Critical Control Point (HACCP)**
- **Procedure for setting up a HACCP system**

- **A basic HACCP system for a hot meat dish (spaghetti bolognese)**
- **Advantages of a HACCP system**
- **International Organization for Standardization (ISO)**

To reduce the risk of food contamination and food poisoning, strict standards of hygiene must be implemented at home and in industry.

Safe food preparation guidelines

Safe food preparation involves strict monitoring of:
- **personal hygiene**
- **kitchen hygiene** (structure and practice)
- **food hygiene** (preparation, cooking, reheating and storage).

Personal hygiene guidelines

- Wash hands frequently with hot water and antibacterial soap, particularly after using the toilet, touching one's hair and face or coughing or sneezing, to prevent the transfer of bacteria.
- Ensure nails are cleaned thoroughly and kept short to avoid harbouring bacteria underneath. Keep nails polish-free to avoid nail polish chipping and falling into food.
- Remove jewellery, as it harbours bacteria and may fall into food.
- Wear protective clothing to protect clothes from getting dirty and to reduce the spread of bacteria.

> **Did you know**
>
> Chefs' uniforms are generally white, as white is a symbol of cleanliness. It is also the most reflective colour, so it repels heat instead of absorbing it, keeping chefs cooler than if they were wearing a darker colour.

- Tie hair up and wear a hairnet or chef's hat to avoid loose hairs falling into food.
- Securely cover cuts or wounds with a waterproof bandage or dressing that is brightly coloured so that it can be seen clearly if it falls into food.
- Do not dip fingers into food to taste. Use a clean spoon each time to taste food throughout preparation.
- If suffering from illness, avoid preparing food.

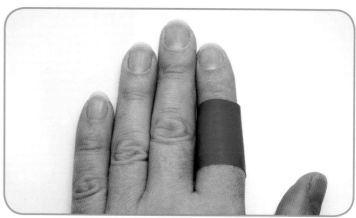

▲ Waterproof, brightly coloured bandage

Kitchen hygiene guidelines

Structure guidelines	Practice guidelines
• Ensure kitchen surfaces are easy to clean, non-absorbent and free from **crevices** to avoid food getting lodged • A good lighting system is necessary to show up dirt and ensure effective cleaning • Sufficient ventilation is vital to keep the kitchen cool and to prevent condensation and microbial growth • Ensure rodents cannot access the kitchen, as they can contaminate food, kitchen surfaces and equipment • A clean water supply is required to maintain hygiene standards when preparing food and cleaning surfaces	• Wash and disinfect kitchen floors, work surfaces and chopping boards frequently to remove bacteria • Disinfect cloths, sponges and scrubbers regularly and change them frequently. To avoid cross-contamination, different cloths should be used for different jobs, e.g. one for cleaning up meat juices and another for wiping countertops. • Keep waste in covered bins and empty regularly. Bins should have a foot pedal for opening to avoid having to touch the lid. • Wash and dry kitchen equipment thoroughly to minimise the potential for microbial growth • Keep pets out, as they can contaminate food, kitchen surfaces and equipment

Lit Hit
Crevices are narrow openings.

▲ Hygienic kitchen structure

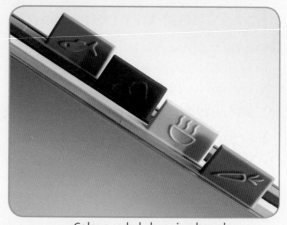

▲ Colour-coded chopping boards

 Compile a set of **four** procedures that a restaurant manager should put in place in order to ensure a high standard of food safety and hygiene. (12) **OL**

Food hygiene guidelines

Preparation guidelines	Cooking guidelines
• Keep food covered until just before use to prevent insects contaminating it • Avoid over-handling food, especially ready-to-eat foods, e.g. salad. Wear gloves or use tongs to reduce the risk of bacterial contamination. • Avoid cross-contamination by keeping raw food and cooked ready-to-eat food apart. This risk can be prevented further by using separate chopping boards and cleaning cloths and by cleaning equipment, countertops and hands between preparation. • Avoid washing hands in the sink used for the preparation of food, as contamination may occur. • Frozen meat and poultry should be completely thawed before cooking. If cooked from frozen the centre may not cook fully, increasing the risk of food poisoning. • Avoid having foods out of the fridge for too long during preparation, as room temperature (approximately 18°C) is within the temperature danger zone for bacterial growth (5–63°C)	• Cook poultry until a core temperature of 75°C is achieved. This ensures pathogenic bacteria are destroyed. • Turn food regularly, especially meat, as it browns on the outside quickly but may still be undercooked on the inside • Stir stews and gravies frequently while cooking to ensure that they are heated through and harmful pathogenic bacteria are destroyed. When cooked, serve as soon as possible. • Wear gloves or use tongs to reduce the risk of bacterial contamination • When cooked, serve food on clean plates and use clean serving tools to avoid bacterial contamination • Serve food straight away after cooking. If it is not being consumed immediately, it should be kept hotter than 63°C. Lukewarm (25–40°C) food is dangerous as it is within the temperature danger zone for bacterial growth.

▲ Housefly contaminating food

▲ Temperature probe

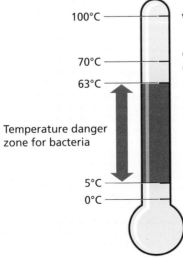

Did you know?

It is strongly suspected that house flies can transmit at least 65 different diseases, including salmonellosis and cholera.

100°C — Water boiling point

70°C — Cooking temperatures (destroy most bacteria)

63°C

Temperature danger zone for bacteria

5°C

0°C — Water freezing point
Freezing temperatures (inactivate bacteria)

FOOD SAFETY AND HYGIENE AND HAZARD ANALYSIS AND CRITICAL CONTROL POINT (HACCP)

Storage guidelines	Reheating guidelines
• Cover food before storage to prevent insects from contaminating it and to avoid food drying out • Cool cooked foods before storage to avoid raising the internal temperature of the fridge and risking bacterial growth • Store perishable and chilled cooked food in the fridge so that bacterial multiplication is slowed. If perishable foods are to be frozen they should be frozen at –25°C and stored at –18°C. • Store cooked ready-to-eat food separately from raw food to reduce the risk of cross-contamination. Raw food should be stored on the base of the fridge to avoid drip-contamination. • Keep fridges clean and do not over-pack to allow air circulation around food to keep it cool	• Reheat cooked food to 100°C for approximately five minutes to ensure food is heated thoroughly • If using the microwave to reheat food, set at the highest power setting so that food is thoroughly heated. Stir periodically to evenly distribute heat. • Reheat food once only, as the more times food is cooled and reheated the greater the potential for food poisoning 

 List **five** guidelines that should be followed to ensure the safe preparation and storage of food in the home. (10) **HL**

To ensure that food is safe to eat, discuss the importance of each of the following:
- food storage
- cooking and reheating procedures
- kitchen hygiene. (24) **HL**

Hazards and contaminants

Hazards are any potential source of harm or adverse health effects on a person. Within the food industry, major hazards may be introduced into the food supply chain at any time during harvesting, processing, transporting, preparing, storing and serving food. Hazards occur in food production processes due to contaminants.

Contaminants are substances that can enter into the food chain either unintentionally or illegally and can adversely affect the human body.

Classification of contaminants

Contaminants can be classified as biological, chemical or physical.

Biological contaminants		
Type	**How contamination occurs**	**Effects**
Microorganisms (for example bacteria and fungi)	• Consumption of food subjected to poor hygiene practices during storage and preparation • Consumption of undercooked meat or eggs • Cross-contamination	• Food poisoning

Chemical contaminants

Type	How contamination occurs	Effects
Pesticides and insecticides (used to kill weeds and pests on crops)	• Consumption of food with pesticide or insecticide residue • Consumption of water contaminated with pesticide and insecticide run-off	• Circulatory problems and respiratory problems • Cancer • Nervous system damage
Antibiotics (used to treat animal diseases and infections, e.g. mastitis)	• Consumption of meat or milk with antibiotic residue	• Allergic reactions to antibiotics • Resistance to antibiotics
Industrial residues (for example, dioxins found in emissions from burning fuels)	• Consumption of meat, fish, eggs and milk from animals who have consumed crops grown in soil contaminated by emissions from the air or rainwater **Did you know** In 2008, pork samples in Ireland were found to have up to 200 times the safe limit of dioxins. This led to one of the largest Irish food recalls related to a chemical contamination, as tonnes of pork meat and products were recalled. The cause was traced back to contaminated feed.	• Cancer • Immune system damage
Metal residues (for example, lead and cadmium found in old pipes and emissions from burning fossil fuels)	• Consumption of crops grown in soil contaminated by emissions falling from the air or carried in rainwater • Consumption of water contaminated with lead or cadmium traces from old piping	• Nervous and immune system damage • Liver and kidney damage

Physical contaminants

Type	How contamination occurs	Effects
Foreign bodies (for example, human or animal hair, dirt, broken glass or metal)	• Consumption of food subjected to poor hygiene practices during storage, preparation or cooking	• Food poisoning

 Identify **two** contaminants that may enter the food chain and in each case state a likely source and the possible effect on the body. (6) **HL**

Ⓗ Hazard Analysis and Critical Control Point (HACCP)

In food production, hazardous contaminants are unacceptable due to their potential damaging effects on the consumer. A Hazard Analysis and Critical Control Point (HACCP) system aims to prevent these contaminants. HACCP is a food safety management system that identifies and controls hazards that could pose a threat to the production of safe food. Since 1998, this system has been a legal requirement for all food businesses.

Procedure for setting up a HACCP system

1. **HACCP team:** establish a HACCP team. Members should have training in food hygiene and safety. The team should compile a flow chart outlining the entire food production process, including purchasing, delivery, storage, preparation, cooking and serving.

2. **Potential hazards:** identify all potential hazards that could pose a threat to the safety of food during the production process, e.g. contamination of cooked food with raw food during preparation or an incorrect fridge temperature (above 5°C) during storage.

3. **Critical control points (CCPs):** decide on critical control points (CCPs). CCPs are points in the food production process where hazards can be controlled or eliminated, e.g. keeping a fridge at a low temperature.

4. **Critical limits:** set critical limits to identify when a CCP is out of control, e.g. a fridge temperature must always be below 5°C.

5. **Monitoring system:** establish a monitoring system to record what happens at each CCP to ensure food is kept safe. Monitoring procedures can include visual inspections and physical measurements, e.g. temperature readings. Written documentation should be kept as proof of monitoring. For each CCP determine the following.
   - **What is to be done?** For example, check the temperature is below 5°C in a dairy fridge.
   - **When it is to be done?** For example, every two hours.
   - **How it is done?** For example, place the digital temperature gauge inside the chilled shelf, check and document the temperature.
   - **Who is to do it?** For example, the deli manager.

6. **Corrective actions:** compile corrective actions to be implemented if monitoring procedures identify that CCPs were not met or are not under control, e.g. if a fridge temperature rises above 5°C due to a technical fault, the food should be discarded and a technician should be called to implement repairs.

7. **Verification process:** establish a verification process to prove that the HACCP system is functioning correctly, e.g. completing microbial tests on food to ensure that the refrigeration system is functioning correctly. This should be reviewed regularly.

8. **Record system:** keep a record system containing detailed, accurate records of monitoring CCPs, corrective actions, etc. These should be available as evidence of compliance with legislation.

 REMEMBER IT!

'**H**ACCP **P**revents **C**hildren **C**onsuming **M**ouldy **C**hicken **V**ery **R**egularly.'
HACCP team, **P**otential hazards, **C**ritical control points (CCPs), **C**ritical limits, **M**onitoring system, **C**orrective actions, **V**erification process, **R**ecord system.

A basic HACCP system for a hot meat dish (spaghetti bolognese)

Steps	Potential hazards	Control measures
1. Purchasing ingredients	⊙ Contamination of food with physical contaminants, e.g. glass, insects, hair or dirt ⊙ Perishable foods, e.g. meat, may not be stored at the correct temperature leading to bacterial growth ⊙ Vegetables may have mould growth ⊙ Damaged packaging, e.g. dents on cans leading to biological contamination	✋ Buy raw ingredients from a shop with a strict food safety management system, e.g. HACCP ✋ Ensure the temperature of the fridge used for perishable foods is below 5°C ✋ Choose loose vegetables and examine them for mould ✋ Examine packaging to ensure it is intact and check the best before or use-by date
2. Transportation of raw materials (ingredients)	⊙ Contamination of food with physical contaminants ⊙ Multiplication of bacteria caused by a rise in temperature (above 5°C) ⊙ Cross-contamination between raw meat and other foods ⊙ Damaged packaging	✋ Ensure perishable foods are packaged and transported in a cool bag to maintain a low temperature. If being delivered, food should be transported in a refrigerated vehicle. ✋ Ensure raw meat and other foods are separated during transportation to avoid cross-contamination ✋ Pack ingredients carefully to avoid damage
3. Storage of food before use	⊙ Contamination of food with physical contaminants ⊙ Perishables may not be stored at the correct temperature, leading to bacterial growth ⊙ Cross-contamination between raw meat and other foods	✋ Store meat and vegetables in a clean fridge below 5°C to inhibit bacterial growth ✋ Place raw meat on the bottom shelf of the fridge to avoid drip-contamination
4. Preparation	⊙ Contamination of food with physical contaminants ⊙ Cross-contamination between raw meat and other foods ⊙ Multiplication of bacteria caused by a rise in temperature (above 5°C)	✋ Keep all ingredients covered until just before use ✋ Follow good personal hygiene practice ✋ Wash all equipment thoroughly before use and disinfect work surfaces ✋ Use separate preparation equipment for raw meat and other foods to avoid cross-contamination ✋ Avoid having foods out of the fridge for too long, as bacteria thrive at room temperature

FOOD SAFETY AND HYGIENE AND HAZARD ANALYSIS AND CRITICAL CONTROL POINT (HACCP)

Steps	Potential hazards	Control measures
5. Cooking	① Survival of pathogenic bacteria due to not cooking food to a sufficiently high temperature	⚕ Bolognese should be cooked until a core temperature of 75°C is reached
6. Serving	① Contamination of food with physical contaminants ① Multiplication of surviving bacteria	⚕ Follow good personal hygiene practice ⚕ Wash all equipment and serving dishes thoroughly before use ⚕ Serve cooked food straight after cooking, as bacteria thrive on lukewarm food

REMEMBER IT!

'**P**erfectly **T**asty **S**paghetti **P**leases **C**ustomers' **S**enses.'

Purchasing ingredients, **T**ransportation of raw materials (ingredients), **S**torage of food before use, **P**reparation, **C**ooking, **S**erving.

> ❓ Describe the stages in a basic HACCP system for making a hot meat dish. Refer to (i) possible hazards and (ii) the corresponding control measures to be implemented. (24) **HL**
>
> Outline a HACCP system that should be followed when preparing and barbecuing food. Refer to potential hazards **and** the corresponding control measures that should be implemented. (24) **HL**

Advantages of a HACCP system

✓ **Confidence:** a HACCP system enhances consumer confidence that the food they are receiving is safe.

✓ **Reduced risk:** a HACCP system reduces the risk of food contamination, as hazards in food production, CCPs and corrective measures are established.

REMEMBER IT!

'**CRUEL**'

Confidence, **R**educed risk, **U**nites workers, **E**vidence, **L**egal requirements.

✓ **Unites workers:** a HACCP system unites workers, as a team is required to implement a successful system, in turn increasing their awareness of the importance of food safety during food production.

✓ **Evidence:** if a false claim is made about a food product, a HACCP system provides evidence that all reasonable precautions were taken by a business to ensure a food was produced safely.

✓ **Legal requirements:** a HACCP system ensures businesses meet legal requirements stipulated by food hygiene and safety regulations.

> ❓ Outline **three** benefits of implementing a HACCP system. (6) **HL**
>
> Explain how a hazard analysis critical control point (HACCP) system can benefit a catering business in the prevention of food poisoning outbreaks. (12) **HL**

International Organization for Standardization (ISO)

International Organization for Standardization (ISO) is an association that describes requirements necessary for businesses to establish effective and efficient quality management systems.

ISO 22000 specifies the requirements for a food safety management system to enable food companies to control food safety hazards and ensure food they produce is safe at the time of human consumption.

The National Standards Authority of Ireland (NSAI) provide accredited ISO 22000 certification to food companies when their food safety management system is working effectively.

FOOD LEGISLATION AND NATIONAL FOOD SAFETY AGENCIES

What you will learn:

- Food Hygiene Regulations 1950–1989
- Food information to Consumers (FIC) Regulation 2011
- European Communities (Hygiene of Foodstuffs) Regulations 2006 (amended 2009 and 2010)
- Sale of Food and Drugs Acts 1875, 1879, 1899 and 1936
- Health Acts 1947, 1953 and 1970
- Food Safety Authority of Ireland (FSAI)

- Department of Agriculture, Food and the Marine
- Department of Health
- Department of the Environment, Community and Local Government
- Health Service Executive (HSE)
- Public analyst laboratories
- Local authorities
- Safe Food (the Food Safety Promotion Board)

FOOD LEGISLATION

The Irish food industry has a responsibility to produce safe food for consumers. National and European food legislation outlines regulations that ensure the provision of safe food from food manufacturers and retailers. Failure to follow these can lead to companies being fined or closed down.

Food Hygiene Regulations 1950–1989

These regulations:

- ban the sale of food that is diseased, contaminated or unfit for human consumption
- require precautions to be taken to prevent the contamination of food at all stages of manufacture, packaging and distribution
- require food premises to maintain hygienic conditions
- require food handlers to maintain the highest standard of hygiene and safety and adhere to a Hazard Analysis and Critical Control Point (HACCP) system
- require mobile food stalls where food is prepared and cooked/heated to obtain a licence.

When there is an immediate threat to public health, closure orders can be issued to food premises and unfit food can be destroyed.

Food Information to Consumers (FIC) Regulation 2011

For information on the Food Information to Consumers (FIC) Regulation see page 198.

European Communities (Hygiene of Foodstuffs) Regulations 2006 (amended 2009 and 2010)

These regulations:

- outline general hygiene standards that food premises must follow
- require all staff to be trained in food hygiene
- require a food safety management system, e.g. HACCP, to be in place and adhered to.

When there is an immediate threat to public health, closure orders can be issued to food premises and unfit food can be destroyed.

Sale of Food and Drugs Acts 1875, 1879, 1899 and 1936

These acts protect the consumer against fraud and **adulteration** of food. Under these acts it is an offence to:

- mix, colour or stain a food with an ingredient or material that makes it hazardous to human health
- sell any food that is not of the nature and quality demanded by consumers, e.g. chicken breasts injected with brine solution or beef proteins to increase weight.

> **Lit Hit**
> Adulteration means to make impure by adding inferior ingredients.

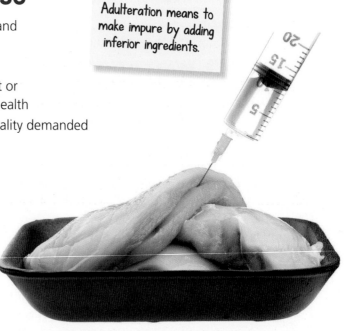

? Outline the protection provided to the consumer by the Sale of Food and Drugs Acts (1875, 1879, 1899 and 1936). (10) **HL**

▲ Chicken injected with brine solution

Health Acts 1947, 1953 and 1970

These acts:

- prevent danger to public health arising from the importation, manufacture, distribution or sale of food
- control compositional standards of foods that are of particular importance to consumers' health, e.g. dairy spreads.

NATIONAL FOOD SAFETY AGENCIES

The control and enforcement of food safety requires the combined activities of numerous government departments and agencies. Their standards, regulations and codes of practice all ensure that high standards are maintained.

Food Safety Authority of Ireland (FSAI)

The FSAI aims to ensure that food produced, distributed and marketed in Ireland meets the highest standards of food safety and hygiene by:

- enforcing food safety legislation through a number of official agencies including local authorities, the Health Service Executive (HSE) and the Department of Agriculture, Food and the Marine

Did you know

Consumers can register on the FSAI website to receive rapid-alert email notifications about food products that are being recalled.

- providing advice to ministers, the food industry and consumers on food safety matters
- ensuring food companies are committed to the production of safe food and comply with all relevant food law
- coordinating rapid-alert systems to recall food that has the potential to cause adverse health effects to consumers
- taking action against food establishments in breach of food safety legislation by issuing:
  - **improvement notices** when the handling and preparation of food or condition of the premises is likely to pose a threat to public health
  - **closure orders** when a food establishment is, or is likely to be, a serious and immediate danger to public health. Closure orders lead to immediate closure. They can be lifted when improvements are made.

 Give a brief account of the role of the Food Safety Authority of Ireland (FSAI). (8) **HL**

Department of Agriculture, Food and the Marine

Department of
**Agriculture,
Food and the Marine**

An Roinn
**Talmhaíochta,
Bia agus Mara**

The Department of Agriculture, Food and the Marine aims to ensure the highest possible standards of food safety and consumer protection in Ireland. It monitors and controls food safety in the following areas.

Meat and meat products	• Ensure the maintenance of abattoirs and meat processing factories throughout Ireland • Routinely test animals for diseases, e.g. tuberculosis (TB) and bovine spongiform encephalopathy (BSE) • Monitor the use of antibiotics in animal production • Ensure animals are not being given illegal substances, e.g. growth hormones • Ensure the identification of livestock and the traceability of meat

Milk and milk Products	• Ensure that all dairy farms that supply milk for public consumption are registered with the Department • Test cattle routinely for diseases, e.g. TB • Test milk routinely for bacterial contamination and residues of antibiotics • Ensure dairy farms observe strict codes of hygiene when transporting, processing and storing milk
Eggs	• Enforce European Union regulations, e.g. all food given to hens is heat treated to reduce bacterial contamination • Ensure farmers complete routine salmonella testing of the hens
Fruit and vegetables	• Monitor fruit, vegetable and cereal crops for pesticide and insecticide residue

 Outline the role of the Department of Agriculture Food and the Marine in food safety. (10) **HL**

Department of Health

The Department of Health is responsible for:
- creating food safety policies
- dealing with issues such as genetically modified foods, food hygiene and contaminants in foodstuffs to ensure a high standard of food hygiene and safety is maintained nationwide
- educating consumers on food safety guidelines to ensure that they can maintain high hygiene standards at home.

An Roinn Sláinte
DEPARTMENT OF HEALTH

Health Service Executive (HSE)

The HSE implements a range of legislation in relation to food safety and hygiene. This is carried out by Environmental Health Officers (EHOs) from various health boards employed by the HSE who:

- carry out routine inspections of establishments where food is handled to ensure high hygiene standards
- deal with complaints about food businesses or products or a suspected case of food poisoning
- respond to rapid food alerts, e.g. mycotoxins in food
- issue improvement notices and closure orders to businesses that are not adhering to food safety legislation
- provide education and advise businesses on how to ensure compliance with food safety and hygiene laws.

 Outline the role of the Environmental Health Officer in relation to food safety. (10) **HL**

Public analyst laboratories

Public analyst laboratories are modern food safety facilities that play an important role in ensuring food available to consumers is safe and wholesome by:

- analysing food and water samples to detect for the presence of biological contaminants, e.g. salmonella, and chemical contaminants, e.g. cadmium. This is often completed on food samples gathered by EHOs from various food businesses. The general public can pay a fee to have food and water tested
- testing foods to ensure compliance with food legislation and labelling, e.g. testing to ensure legal limits of colourings were used.

▲ Food test in a public analyst laboratory

Local authorities

Local authorities aim to ensure high standards of food safety are maintained by vetinary officers who:

- carry out inspections of domestic **abattoirs** to ensure high hygiene standards
- monitor practices in meat-processing plants for hygiene and safety.

Lit Hit

Abattoirs are slaughterhouses.

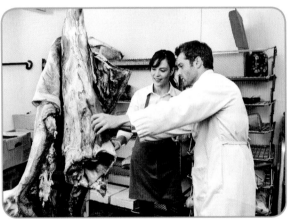

▲ Inspection of an abattoir

Safe Food
(the Food Safety Promotion Board)

Safe Food aims to promote awareness and knowledge of food safety and nutrition issues by:

- implementing public awareness and educational campaigns
- creating food safety and hygiene resources for teachers.

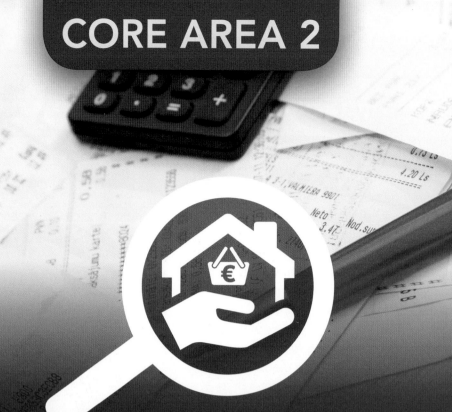

CORE AREA 2

RESOURCE MANAGEMENT AND CONSUMER STUDIES

Chapter 12:
Family resource management

2.1
2.1.1
2.1.2

FAMILY RESOURCE MANAGEMENT AND COMPONENTS OF MANAGEMENT

What you will learn:

- Purpose of family resource management
- Types of resource management systems
- The family as a managerial unit
- Components of management
- The decision-making process and communication
- Factors affecting management
- Case study sample answer

Family resource management is a system that assists a family in planning and achieving goals by making skilful use of available resources. In simple terms, it means the family using what it has in order to get what it wants. Resources include anything that can help to achieve goals, e.g. time, human resources, equipment and money.

Purpose of family resource management

Family resource management:

- improves the quality of family life, e.g. ensures bills are paid, which reduces stress and worry
- assists individuals and families to achieve goals, e.g. going on a holiday
- makes full use of available resources and minimises waste, e.g. reduces food and money waste, as meals and shopping trips are well planned
- allows for unexpected changes in circumstances, e.g. loss of a job.

 State the purpose of family resource management. (2) **OL**

Explain why a good management system can contribute to a well run home and the well being of all family members. (16) **HL**

Types of resource management systems

Open system	Closed system
• Families avail of other systems outside their own boundaries to achieve goals, e.g. children participate in government educational systems to obtain an education. • The majority of families use this system.	• All activities occur within the system boundaries (the family). • The Amish community use this system as they function by living self-sufficiently and do not avail of outside systems to achieve goals, e.g. they do not participate government educational systems to obtain an education.

▲ Members of the Amish community

The family as a managerial unit

Efficient family resource management contributes to the smooth running of a household. Areas of family life that can managed include:

Household finances	Cleaning
Families can create a plan for spending to meet financial goals, e.g. bills. • **Skills used:** money management, IT and organisational skills. • **End result:** family needs will be met, debt is avoided and savings are made.	Families can organise a cleaning schedule with specific jobs for each family member. • **Skills used:** organisational, planning and time management skills. • **End result:** homes will be cleaner for all family members. The risk of health problems, e.g. asthma attacks, will be lessened.
Meal planning	**School/activities schedule**
Families can organise a weekly meal plan and shopping list. • **Skills used:** organisational, planning and budgeting skills. • **End result:** family meals are planned a week ahead and all the necessary ingredients are available. This leads to less food waste and less reliance on ready meals.	Families can organise routines for school drop-offs and extracurricular activities. • **Skills used:** planning and time management skills. • **End result:** children will be dropped to and collected from school and extracurricular activities on time.

Give **one** example of efficient family resource management (2) **HL**

Give an example of when the Management Process may be used. (3) **HL**

Components of management

There are three components of management: inputs, throughputs and outputs.

Inputs	Throughputs	Outputs
Demands	Planning	Goals
Needs		Needs/wants
Wants		Resources
Goals	Organising	Changes in values
Values		Satisfaction
Resources		Feedback
Time	Implementing	
Human skill		
Environmental		
Material		

Feedback

? List the **three** components of management. (3) **HL**

Inputs

Inputs include anything brought in to the management system. Inputs are made up of demands and resources.

Demands

- **Needs:** basic requirements for survival. For example, physical needs, e.g. water, basic nutrition, shelter and clothing; and emotional needs, e.g. security, support and love.
- **Wants:** specific things that a person desires but can survive without, e.g. designer clothes or holidays abroad.
- **Goals:** something a person works towards achieving. To achieve goals individuals must use resources wisely. Goals can be short term, medium term or long term. For example:
  - **short term:** open a savings account
  - **medium term:** save the deposit for a house
  - **long term:** take out a mortgage and buy a house.
- **Values:** a person's unique beliefs about what is important or worthwhile to them, e.g. vegetarianism or learning how to play an instrument.

Resources

- **Time:** individuals need time in order to plan and carry out tasks. Time needs to be managed wisely to make the most of it.
- **Human skill:** all the things a person can offer to the management system, e.g. I.T. skills or budgeting skills. This varies from person to person, depending on factors such as age and skill set.
- **Environmental**
  - Physical resources, e.g. available space and climate.
  - Social systems, e.g. health, education and welfare systems.
- **Material:** money and equipment, e.g. household appliances, mobile phones, laptops and books.

REMEMBER IT!
'THEM'
Time, Human, Environmental, Material.

? List **two** factors that affect the management of family resources. (4) **OL**

Tony is the father of two school going children and has recently lost his job. His wife Julie works part-time in an office and earns €100 per week. Tony is now receiving social welfare benefit for his family. Tony and Julie manage the home together.

List **three** resources, other than money, available to Tony and his family. Explain how **each** resource contributes to a good management system. (24) **OL**

Throughputs

This is the active or 'doing' stage. Throughputs involve the processes of planning, organising and implementing.

Planning

- **Identify the goal:** what is hoped to be achieved?
- **Identify available resources:** money, time, equipment and human skill.
- **Collect relevant information:** information can be collected by researching online, asking others for their opinions and comparing prices in shops.
- **Consider the alternatives:** consider various options, e.g. option A or option B.
- **Consider the consequences of each alternative:** what are the positives or negatives of each option?
- **Make a decision:** choose one option.
- **Design a logical plan:** the plan should have tasks in the correct order to ensure success.

Organising

- **Appoint appropriate individuals to tasks: delegate** jobs, taking into account the skills of each person.
- **Allocate available resources:** divide out the available money and equipment, e.g. cars or laptops.

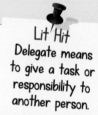

Lit Hit
Delegate means to give a task or responsibility to another person.

Implementing

- **Put the plan into action:** begin to implement the steps of the plan in a logical order.
- **Take control of the plan:** control of the plan is important to improve effectiveness.
- **Ensure flexibility:** flexibility is necessary to allow for unforeseen circumstances, as adjustments may need to be made if the plan is not working or if something disrupts it.

Outputs

These are the end result of the inputs and throughputs. Outputs are evaluated in the following terms.

- **Goals:** have the goals been reached? Have individuals or families achieved what they set out to do in the planning process, e.g. created and followed a weekly cleaning schedule? It is easy to identify whether or not goals have been achieved by looking at the outcome.

- **Needs and wants:** have the needs been met, e.g. did the family have nutritious meals? Have the wants been satisfied, e.g. did the family go on holiday?
- **Resources:** were all resources, e.g. money, used to maximum effect? Were any resources, e.g. time, wasted? Will some of the resources used, e.g. car fuel, need to be replaced?
- **Changes in values:** have the values changed, e.g. have the family decided it is better to keep savings for a rainy day, rather than spending them on material things for Christmas?
- **Satisfaction:** was the outcome satisfactory, e.g. did everyone feel the plan worked? Was any person stressed or under pressure? If dissatisfaction occurred changes will need to be made for next time.
- **Feedback:** one of the most important parts of the outcome process is to recognise improvements that can be made the next time. For example, if parents were under pressure dropping children to extracurricular activities, e.g. football and scouts, the family may need to consider asking the children to give up one activity. This is determined by feedback.

REMEMBER IT!

'**G**ood News! **R**eviewing **C**an **S**upply **F**eedback'
Goals, **N**eeds and wants, **R**esources, **C**hanges in values, **S**atisfaction, **F**eedback.

? In relation to the management process explain and give an example of **each** of the following.
- Input
- Output (6) **HL**

You have been elected as chairperson of your school's graduation committee. Using the management framework (inputs, throughputs and outputs), set out the plan for the event. (18) **HL**

The decision-making process and communication

Decision-making process

Decision-making is the process of deciding between two or more options when working towards achieving a goal.

Steps in the decision-making process

1. **Define** the decision (goal).
2. **Identify** available resources
3. **Collect** relevant information.
4. **Consider the alternatives.**
5. **Consider the consequences** of each alternative.
6. **Make a decision.**
7. **Put a plan in place.**
8. **Implement the plan.**
9. **Evaluate** and use feedback when making similar decisions in the future.

Decision making can be influenced by primary reference groups, e.g. family and peers, or secondary reference groups, e.g. guidance counsellors and work colleagues. The decision-making process relies on communication.

REMEMBER IT!

'**D**ecisions, **I**f **C**arefully **C**onsidered, **C**an **M**ake, **P**laning **I**mmensely **E**asy.'
Define, **I**dentify available resources, **C**ollect, **C**onsider the alternatives, **C**onsider the consequences, **M**ake a decision, **P**ut a plan in place, **I**mplement the plan, **E**valuate.

Communication

Communication is a two-way process that involves the sharing of ideas, information and emotions. Communication is vital in order for a management system to run effectively and achieve goals. Communication is necessary to:

- understand the values of each family member. For some this could be spending time together as a family, for others it could be learning a new skill
- identify each family member's goals, e.g. a child may want to go to a summer camp or a parent may want to return to university
- make family decisions together. By doing so, each member feels listened to and a valuable part of the family
- allocate tasks based on individuals' skill sets. This enables family members to be clear about the role they have been assigned
- evaluate the management process. This enables family members to express their satisfaction or dissatisfaction with a management system and provide feedback for improvement for the future
- resolve conflict, as family members can express their unhappiness or anger with a situation.

? Give an account of the importance of decision making in family resource management. (12) **HL**

Factors affecting management

Employment patterns

- A different management system is required in households where two parents are employed compared to families with a full-time homemaker.
- The income received from employment affects management systems. For example:
  - **single-income families** may need to manage their income wisely to cover the household's needs
  - **dual-income families** may have greater financial resources to meet the household's needs and wants. However, this extra income can mean restricted family time, as working parents may struggle to find time to spend with their children due to long hours at work.
- Duration of commutes and patterns of employment, e.g. job-sharing and shift work, influence a family's routines and management systems. Shift work, in particular, impacts on management, as it can mean one parent has to take on more responsibilities during the day. It may also affect mealtimes and sleeping patterns.

Management of dual roles

- When both parents are employed, they have dual roles: earner and family manager. Management systems within these families will differ greatly from those of families where one parent is a full-time homemaker. To ensure all household tasks are completed both parents should take equal responsibility.
- In one-parent households a parent is often the earner and the home manager without the support of another person. This can be challenging and stressful as it puts a strain on resources such as money and time.

Socio-economic status

- Priorities vary between families of different socio-economic status. For example:
  - **families of lower socio-economic status** may prioritise meeting basic needs before wants in their management systems, to ensure they live within their means
  - **families of higher socio-economic status** often have income left over after their basic needs are met. They may prioritise this to be spent on wants.
- Children from families of higher socio-economic backgrounds are more likely to have supports that allow them to access third-level education. This will affect family management.
- Families of higher socio-economic status can have more opportunities available to them, e.g. summer camps and theatre trips. These will also affect family management.

Lit Hit
Socio-economic means a person's social and economic position within society. It depends on a combination of variables, including occupation, education, income, wealth and place of residence.

Stages in the family life cycle

- Management systems within a family are changed by the:
  - **arrival of children:** money and time can no longer all be spent on parents' wants as the child's needs are now a priority
  - **number of children:** the more family members the more money and time required to manage the family
  - **age of children:** younger children will often cost more due to childcare costs. They also require more time and attention than older children.

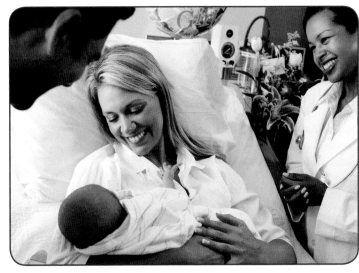

- As children get older and move into their teenage years their input may be considered more in family decision-making and in how the family management process is carried out.
- Older people may have reduced income and decreased agility, which will affect their management system.

Values and standards

- A family's values and standards will influence their choices, thereby affecting management systems. For example, some families' concern for animal welfare will influence decisions, e.g. to buy free-range eggs or products not tested on animals.
- When a family's circumstances change, e.g. a child becomes ill, it can cause family members to re-evaluate their values and, in turn, change their management systems.

Composition of family

- The number of dependents and number of providers within a family will affect management systems.
- Dependents can include:
  - **older family members:** may need constant care due to illness
  - **children:** need constant care at a young age. This can be provided at home or through outside childcare
  - **family members with special needs:** may require 24-hour care or frequent hospital visits. This may require a special management approach.

- Providers are usually parents. Within a two-parent household, responsibilities can be shared. This is more difficult in a one-parent household as the parent may have to rely on others, e.g. friends or their own parents, for support. Financially it is often easier to manage in a two-parent household, as these families are often dual-income.

Culture

- Cultural aspects can affect family management due to the impact of culture on areas such as diet and the role of women. For example:
  - Jewish people keeping **kosher** must refrain from eating pork
  - women are forbidden from driving in Saudi Arabia.

> **Lit Hit**
> Kosher refers to food that has been ritually prepared or blessed, to satisfy Jewish dietary laws.

- Religious ceremonies impact on family management systems, e.g. Catholic families allocate resources to religious ceremonies such as First Holy Communion.
- Changes in Irish women's work practices also affect management systems. In the past, Irish women had few opportunities for working outside of the home, whereas now it is common for women to have careers.

Gender roles

- Management systems within modern families are no longer greatly affected by traditional gender roles. Equal partnerships and shared roles are a feature of everyday life. Women are not expected to be the sole homemaker anymore, and men are involved in childrearing and household tasks.

- Every family member should contribute to household management, with tasks being allocated fairly based on skills, availability of time and preferences, rather than gender.
- Parents should participate equally in all household tasks regardless of gender, to highlight the importance of gender equality to children.

 Discuss how **each** of the following may affect a family when managing the home:
- stage in life cycle
- employment patterns
- sex/gender roles. (18) **OL**

Discuss **four** factors that can influence the management of family resources. (20) **HL**

REMEMBER IT!

'**E**very **M**anagement **S**ystem **S**hould **V**alue **C**hildren's **C**riticism **G**reatly.'
Employment patterns, **M**anagement of dual roles, **S**ocio-economic status, **S**tages in the family life cycle, **V**alues and standards, **C**omposition of family, **C**ulture, **G**ender roles.

CASE STUDY SAMPLE ANSWER

Colm and Jane Brown live with their two teenagers – David aged fifteen and Yvonne aged seventeen. Monday is a hectic day in the household. Colm leaves for work at 7.30 am and returns at 5.30 pm. Jane works from 9.00 am to 4.00 pm. David and Yvonne have training for the local swimming team from 4.30 pm to 5.30 pm. Yvonne also goes to guitar lessons at 6.30 pm. As they live in a rural area transport is necessary for all activities. The family try to apply a management system to ensure that everything runs smoothly.

Using the components of management (inputs, throughputs and outputs) explain how the Brown family could apply a management system to ensure that Mondays run smoothly in the household. (18) **(HL 2006)**

🖒Tip!

All of this answer was not required to obtain full marks in this question. It required two points under the headings: inputs, throughputs and outputs.

Management systems are made up of three components: inputs, throughputs and outputs.

Inputs

Inputs are anything brought in to the management system. They are made up of demands and resources.

Demands

- Needs: Colm and Jane need to go to work to earn money to be able to provide for their family.
- Wants: Colm and Jane want their children to attend extracurricular lessons to make new friends and enjoy themselves. David and Yvonne want to attend these lessons.
- Goals: ensure that Colm and Jane attend work for the full day. Ensure that Yvonne and David get to their lessons:
    - a joint swimming lesson from 16.30 to 17.30
    - a guitar lesson for Yvonne at 18.30.
- Values: Colm and Jane value the importance of their children participating in extracurricular lessons, as this enables David and Yvonne to develop as people and learn new skills.

Resources

- Time: Colm and Jane have time:
    - Jane is available after 16.00
    - Colm is available after 17.30.
- Human skill: Colm and Jane have the human skill of being able to drive.
- Environmental: Colm and Jane live with their family in a rural environment. This means they do not have access to public transport.
- Material: Colm and Jane have material resources including:
    - a car as their mode of transport
    - money to send their children to the classes and pay for fuel for the car.

Throughputs

This is the active or 'doing' stage. Throughputs involve the processes of planning, organising and implementing.

Planning

- Identify the goal: ensure that Colm and Jane attend work for the full day in order to earn money. Ensure that Yvonne and David get to their lessons:
  - a joint swimming lesson from 16.30 to 17.30
  - a guitar lesson for Yvonne at 18.30.

- Identify available resources: how much money and time and what equipment and human skills are available to Colm and Jane?

- Collect relevant information: at what time does each lesson start? Where is each lesson located? How much does each lesson cost?

- Consider the alternatives:
  - OPTION A
    Would it be best for Jane to drive both children to the swimming lesson and then drop David home and continue on to the guitar lesson with Yvonne?
  - OPTION B
    Would it be best if they divided up the driving, with Jane taking both of the children to the swimming lesson then coming home and Colm taking Yvonne to guitar?

- Consider the consequences of each alternative:
  - OPTION A
  - ✓ Positive: Colm can get dinner or some household chores done if he does not need to leave the house after returning from work.
  - ✗ Negative: does this option put too much pressure on Jane all evening dropping/collecting her children to/from their lessons?
  - OPTION B
  - ✓ Positive: neither of the parents is under pressure to do all the driving and collecting.
  - ✗ Negative: what if Colm gets delayed at work and is late getting home so he cannot take Yvonne to her guitar lesson?

- Make a decision: decide between OPTION A or OPTION B. In-depth discussion should be completed between Jane and Colm before making a decision. Chosen option: OPTION A.

- Design a logical plan: Jane is to drive both children to the swimming lesson and then drop David home and continue on to the guitar lesson with Yvonne.

Organising

- Appoint appropriate individuals to tasks: ensure that Jane knows she is bringing both children to their swimming lesson and Yvonne to her guitar lesson.

- Allocate available resources: ensure that money is available for Jane to pay for the swimming and guitar lessons. The car needs to be made available, fuelled and ready to drive.

Implementing

- Put the plan into action: Jane and Colm implement their plan in the decided manner.
- Take control of the plan: ensure that Jane has an alarm on her phone reminding her of the time she needs to leave work to collect the children and bring them to their activities.
- Ensure flexibility: if Jane gets delayed at work, Colm and Jane should have a contact number of another parent who may be able to collect/drop the children from their lessons.

Outputs

These are the end result of the inputs and throughputs. Outputs are evaluated in the following terms.

- Goals
  Did the family achieve their goals? For example, did Colm and Jane get to spend all the time they needed to at work while still getting Yvonne and David to their lessons on time?

- Needs and wants
  - Did the family meet their needs? For example, did Colm and Jane get to complete a full day's work?
  - Did the family satisfy their wants? For example, did Yvonne and David attend their activities and did they enjoy them?

- Resources
  - Did the family use their resources to the maximum effect? For example, did David and Yvonne use their time effectively or was time wasted dropping David home before Yvonne's guitar lesson?
  - Did they waste any resources? For example, was fuel wasted dropping David home?
  - Do they need to replace some resources? For example, fuel in the car?

- Changes in values
  Have the values changed, e.g. do Colm and Jane still deem extracurricular activities important in the lives of their children, or are these activities too much effort? Would the time be better spent together as a family?

- Satisfaction
  Was the family satisfied with the outcome? For example, was Jane stressed? Did traffic on the way home from swimming affect Jane getting David home, meaning Yvonne was late to guitar? Would it be easier if Colm could meet Jane at a midway point so that Colm could take Yvonne to guitar and Jane could take David home? If dissatisfaction occurred changes will need to be made for next time.

- Feedback
  One of the most important parts of the outcome process is to recognise improvements that can be made the next time. This is completed through feedback which is used in the next management process. Next Monday the driving could be divided up, with Jane taking both of the children to their swimming lesson then coming home and Colm taking Yvonne to her guitar lesson. If this is still too stressful the family may consider another option, e.g. getting Yvonne to drop her guitar lesson or move it to another day.

Chapter 13:
Household finances

2.1.3

MANAGEMENT OF HOUSEHOLD FINANCIAL RESOURCES

What you will learn:

- **The role of the household as a financial unit within the economy**
- **Social factors affecting household income**
- **Sources of household income**
- **Deductions taken from pay**

- **Social welfare payments**
- **Types of household expenditure**
- **Factors that contribute to varying patterns of household expenditure**
- **Ways to reduce household expenditure**

The role of the household as a financial unit within the economy

- Individuals in paid employment contribute to the country's economy by paying statutory taxes. These provide revenue that the government uses to maintain state services, e.g. An Garda Síochána and the Health Service Executive (HSE).
- Individuals and families contribute to the economy by spending wages on goods and services, generating wealth and employment in the country.
- Many households have mortgages and loans that contribute to the profits of financial institutions, e.g. banks and building societies.
- Many families are financially self-sufficient, using income earned from employment. Others depend on social welfare payments, e.g. Jobseeker's Allowance. If high numbers of families are relying on these payments it puts pressure on the economy.
- Money management skills, e.g. saving or budgeting, should be passed on to children within the family unit. Teaching children these skills benefits the economy, as it reduces the risk of children falling into debt or relying on social welfare benefits in the future.

? Outline the role of the household/family as a financial unit within the economy. (10) **HL**

Social factors affecting household income

Age

- Income tends to increase as individuals get older and move up the payscale. However, monthly outgoings also increase, e.g. mortgage payments and childcare.
- Teenagers may take on part-time jobs, providing a source of income to spend on their wants or to alleviate financial strain in families.
- If individuals do not pay contributions into a private pension when working they may experience a drop in income on retirement, as the State Pension they receive may not be sufficient to maintain their current standard of living.

Gender

- The number of women in the workforce has increased greatly in recent generations, leading to more dual-income families with greater household income.
- Legislation, such as the Employment Equality Act, helps ensure equal pay for equal work, regardless of gender. Despite this, men still often earn more than women and they dominate managerial positions.

Socio-economic status

- Individuals from lower socio-economic backgrounds may have fewer educational opportunities, which can cause them to progress into unemployment or low-paid jobs that provide little opportunity for career advancement or increased income.
- Individuals from higher socio-economic backgrounds tend to have greater educational opportunities, leading to advancement to third-level education and the possibility of obtaining higher-paid jobs.

Culture

- Salaries for the same occupation differ from country to country, e.g. construction workers in Australia are higher-paid than those in India.
- Culture also dictates whether it is acceptable for women to participate in the workplace and earn an income, e.g. in Saudi Arabia less than 15% of the workforce are female.

 Analyse **three** social factors that affect household income. (18) **HL**

Discuss the impact of the following social factors on household income.
- age   • gender   • social class   • culture. (24) **HL**

Sources of household income

- Wages and salaries. A wage is a fixed payment earned for work or services, typically paid on a daily or weekly basis. A salary is a fixed payment, typically paid on a monthly basis, but expressed as an annual sum, e.g. €30,000 per year.
- Social welfare payments, e.g. Jobseeker's Benefit
- Pensions
- Income from rental property
- Interest from savings and returns from investments
- European Union farm subsidies

MANAGEMENT OF HOUSEHOLD FINANCIAL RESOURCES

Gross and net income

- **Gross income:** income earned before any deductions, e.g. income tax, are taken.
- **Net income:** income earned after deductions have been made. This is often called take-home pay.

Explain **each** of the following:
- gross income
- net income. (6) **OL**

Deductions taken from pay

There are two types of deductions taken from a person's gross income: compulsory deductions and voluntary deductions.

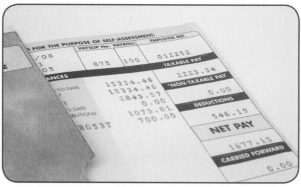

▲ Employee payslip

Compulsory deductions	**Voluntary deductions**
Statutory payments that must be paid to the state	Non-statutory payments or optional deductions
• Income tax/Pay As You Earn (PAYE) • Pay-Related Social Insurance (PRSI) • Universal Social Charge (USC)	• Private health insurance • Pension contributions (superannuation) • Union fees • Savings • Loan repayments

Compulsory deductions

Income tax/Pay As You Earn (PAYE)

- This is a compulsory tax taken from a person's gross pay.
- Under the PAYE system, the employer is legally required to deduct tax owed from a person's gross wage or salary before payment (at source) and pay it directly to the Revenue Commissioners.
- The Revenue Commissioners collect taxes on behalf of the government. This money is used to run the country, e.g. maintaining state services such as road lighting and education.

Rates of income tax

Tax liability refers to the amount of income tax an individual owes the Revenue Commissioners. Income tax is calculated as a percentage of a person's total income. The tax percentage a person is liable to pay depends on individual circumstances, e.g. earnings and marital status. Individuals on a very low income are exempt from paying tax.

Currently there are two rates of tax in Ireland.

- **A standard rate of tax at 20%** applies to income up to a certain limit, called the standard rate cut-off point. This point is calculated by the Revenue Commissioners and varies from person to person, depending on individual circumstances.

- **A higher rate of tax at 40%** applies to any income earned above a person's standard rate cut-off point.

Examples of current standard rate cut-off points

Rate of tax	Personal circumstances	
	Single person	Married couple or civil partners with one income
20%	Up to €33,800	Up to €42,800
40%	Balance above	Balance above

How it works

If a married couple or civil partners with one income earn €50,000 annual gross income they pay:

- 20% tax up to the standard cut-off point of €42,800 = €8,560
- 40% tax on the remaining balance of €7,200 = €2,880.

Gross income tax to be paid: €11,440.

Tax credits

Tax credits reduce the amount of income tax a person has to pay. These are calculated based on a number of factors, including a person's gross income and type of employment. The Revenue Commissioners send each employee an annual tax certificate that lists his or her tax credit entitlements and tax liability. This is called a *notice of determination of tax credits and standard rate cut-off point*.

Examples of current tax credits

Personal circumstances	Tax credit
Single employed person	€3,300

How it works

If a single employed person earns €30,000 annual gross income they receive a tax credit of €3,300. They therefore would pay a total of €2,700 in tax (€6,000 (20% income tax) – €3,300 (tax credit) = €2,700).

Pay-Related Social Insurance (PRSI)

- This is a compulsory contribution taken from a person's gross pay by an employer and paid directly to the Revenue Commissioners. It is calculated as a percentage of a person's total income. The percentage a person is liable to pay depends on individual circumstances, e.g. earnings and profession. Both the employee and the employer share the cost of PRSI payments. Individuals on a very low income are exempt from paying the contribution.

- Income from PRSI is used by the government to pay for social welfare payments, e.g. Jobseeker's Benefit and Maternity Benefit. A minimum number of 39 PRSI contributions in the tax year must have been made by a person in order for them to claim these benefits.

- Self-employed people pay low rates of PRSI and are entitled to a limited number of social welfare benefits.

Universal social charge (USC)

- This is a compulsory tax taken from a person's gross pay by an employer and paid directly to the Revenue Commissioners. It is calculated as a percentage of a person's total income.
- Employees are liable to pay USC tax if their gross income is more than €13,000 annually. Individuals who earn an income that is below this are exempt from paying the tax.

Examples of current USC rates

Rate	Income band
1%	Up to €12,012
3%	€12,012.01– €18,668.00
5.5%	€18,668.01– €70,044.00
8%	€70,044.01+

How it works

A person earning €13,001 will pay 1% on income up to €12,012, and 3% on income between €12,012 and €13,001. Total USC to be paid: €149.79.

P60 and P45

P60	P45
At the end of each tax year all employers send their employees a P60 document that contains details of pay, as well as the income tax, PRSI and USC that have been deducted by the employer and paid to Revenue.	If a person leaves his or her place of employment, their employer must issue a P45. This is a statement of pay, as well as of income tax, USC and PRSI deducted to date by the employer. It is used by the new employer to help work out how much tax the person has to pay.

Voluntary deductions

- **Private health insurance:** paid to a private health insurer, e.g. Vhi Healthcare or GloHealth, to cover medical expenses if a person gets sick, has an accident or needs an operation. Payments can be deducted annually or monthly.
- **Trade union subscriptions:** paid to the person's relevant trade union, e.g. the Services, Industrial, Professional and Technical Union (SIPTU), to protect employees' rights and negotiate terms of pay and working conditions.
- **Loan repayments:** for example, house, car or personal loans.
- **Savings:** for information on savings see page 288.
- **Pension schemes (superannuation):** a pension is a financial plan for retirement.

Types of voluntary pension schemes

- **Private pensions:** a person pays contributions into a private personal pension fund for the duration of their working life. On retirement they will receive a lump sum. The amount depends on contributions made.
- **Occupational pensions:** a pension fund set up by employers in larger companies. Both the employer and the employee contribute to it.

Advantages of pensions

✓ Pensions compensate for the reduction in income when a person retires.
✓ Pensions provide protection to pension holders' dependants in the event of death, as a lump sum will be paid out.
✓ The State provides tax relief on contributions made to pension schemes.

 Net income is take home pay after deductions have been made. Name **two** compulsory deductions and **two** voluntary deductions that may be made from an employee's salary/wage. (6) **OL**

Explain the term PAYE. Give **two** examples of how PAYE contributions are used by the government. (6) **OL**

What is Pay Related Social Insurance (PRSI)? Name **two** PRSI benefits. (6) **HL**

Social welfare payments

The Department of Social Protection provides financial assistance in the form of social welfare payments. There are three types of social welfare payments:

- social insurance payments (contributory benefits)
- social assistance payments (non-contributory benefits)
- universal payments.

Social insurance payments (contributory)

- Payments paid to individuals who have paid the minimum 39 weeks of PRSI contributions
- Not means-tested

Payment	Details	Current rate (per week)
State Pension (contributory)	A weekly payment paid to individuals over the age of 66 who have paid a minimum number of PRSI contributions.	• Under 80 years: €233.30 • Over 80 years: €243.30
Widow's/widower's or surviving civil partner's pension	A weekly payment paid to the husband, wife or civil partner of a deceased person who had paid a minimum number of PRSI contributions.	• Under 66 years: €193.50 • Over 66 years: €233.30
Jobseeker's Benefit	A weekly payment paid to individuals who are out of work and who have paid a minimum number of PRSI contributions. To qualify individuals must: • be fully unemployed or unemployed for at least four days out of seven • be capable, available for and genuinely seeking work. 	€188 for six to nine months
Maternity Benefit	A weekly payment paid to women who are on maternity leave from work who have paid a minimum number of PRSI contributions before the first day of maternity leave.	€230 for 26 weeks

Did you know ?

As and from 2015 people are eligible for the State Pension at 66 years of age. This will increase to 67 years in 2021 and to 68 years in 2028.

Did you know ?

Since September 2016, two weeks' paternity benefit is paid to new fathers at a rate of €230 per week.

Social assistance payments (non-contributory)

- Payments paid to individuals who have insufficient PRSI contributions
- Means-tested

Payment	Details	Current rate (per week)
State Pension (non-contributory)	A weekly payment paid to individuals over the age of 66 who do not qualify for the contributory State Pension.	• Under 80 years: €222 • Over 80 years: €232
Widow's/widower's or surviving civil partner's pension (non-contributory)	A weekly payment to the husband, wife or civil partner of a deceased person who does not qualify for the contributory State Pension and has no dependent children.	€188
Jobseeker's Allowance	A weekly payment to those who do not qualify for, or who have used up their entitlement for Jobseeker's Benefit	• 18–24 years: €100 • 25 years: €144 • 26+ years: €188
Family Income Supplement (FIS)	A weekly payment available to low-income working families with children. Families receive 60% of the difference between their actual weekly income and the income limit that applies to their family size. To qualify individuals must: • be working at least 19 hours per week • have at least one dependent child • have an income that falls below a certain limit for their family's size. **How it works** A family with one child, earning €436 per week have an income limit of €511. Their earnings are deducted from the income limit, leaving a €75 difference. 60% of the difference of €75 is €45. The Family Income Supplement paid to this family is €45 per week.	

Income limits based on family size

Children	Income <€
1	€511
2	€612
3	€713
4	€834
5	€960

Payment	Details	Current rate (per week)
Supplementary Welfare Allowance	A weekly payment paid by the Department of Social Protection to individuals whose means don't meet their or their dependents' needs. To qualify individuals must: • satisfy a means test, e.g. be earning no income or be earning a weekly income below the Supplementary Welfare Allowance rate for the family size • be waiting on social welfare payments that have yet to be processed • have registered for work with their local Intreo office	• 18-24 years: €100 • 25 years: €144 • 26+ years: €186
One-Parent Family Payment	A weekly payment paid to men and women who are bringing up children without the support of a partner. To qualify individuals must: • be under 66 years of age • not be living with a spouse, civil partner or co-habiting • be the main carer of at least one child who lives with them • earn €425 or less per week	€188 plus €29.80 per additional child thereafter.

Did you know ?

Intreo is a service run by the Department of Social Protection, which provides jobseeking advice, information on job vacancies and income support for jobseekers.

Universal payments
- Payments paid to every individual, regardless of PRSI payments
- Not means-tested

Payment	Details	Current rate (per month)
Child Benefit	A monthly payment to the parents or guardians of children under 16 years of age, or under 18 years of age if the child is in full-time education, YouthReach training or has a disability.	€140 per child

Individuals may also be entitled to the following payments, depending on their circumstances:
- medical card
- fuel allowance
- free electricity/telephone rental allowance
- free television licence.

? What is Family Income Supplement (FIS)? (2) **HL**

State **two** conditions that must be fulfilled in order to qualify for FIS. (4) **HL**

Explain **each** of the following state benefits and give **one** example of each.
- Social insurance payments
- Social assistance payments (6) **HL**

What is Supplementary Welfare Allowance? (6) **HL**

MANAGEMENT OF HOUSEHOLD FINANCIAL RESOURCES

Types of household expenditure

Essential expenditure		Discretionary expenditure
Money spent on items necessary to manage family life. This can be fixed or irregular.		Money spent on non-essential items
Fixed	**Irregular**	• Holidays
The same amount is paid at the same time, e.g. weekly or monthly. • Mortgage/rent • Insurance	Different amounts are paid at different times. • Clothing • Educational needs • Food	• Entertainment • Leisure 

 In relation to household budgeting, explain essential expenditure and discretionary expenditure. Give **one** example of each. (6) **HL**

Factors that contribute to varying patterns of household expenditure

- **Socio-economic status:** individuals or families of higher socio-economic status often have more discretionary income for personal spending on items such as holidays or entertainment. Individuals or families of lower socio-economic status, generally have less discretionary income, and instead have to focus spending on essential family needs such as mortgage/rent and food.

Did you know

According to the OECD, an average family in Ireland with two children spends 40% of their income on childcare costs.

- **Family size/stage:** the larger the family the greater the household expenditure, as more money is required for essential items, e.g. food. Household costs are also more expensive, as larger homes are required, incurring greater costs, e.g. heating bills. The stage of the family also impacts on expenditure, as extra money is required for childcare, school and college.

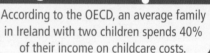

- **Location:** families living in urban homes generally incur a higher cost of living, e.g. larger mortgages/rents, increasing household expenditure. However, travel costs are generally more expensive for rural families, as they have to commute to work.

- **Beliefs/values:** each household has its own set of beliefs or values that impact on household expenditure. For example, if a family values private education, they may pay school fees.

Identify and explain **four** factors that may contribute to varying patterns of household expenditure. (16) **HL**

REMEMBER IT!

'**S**uburban **F**amilies **L**ove **B**uying.'
Socio-economic status, **F**amily size/stage, **L**ocation, **B**eliefs/values.

Ways to reduce household expenditure

When devising or reviewing expenditure, e.g. analysing receipts, many people find that they are overspending in certain areas, which may lead to debt. In order to reduce household expenditure people should try to make savings in the following areas.

Food shopping

- Shop in discount food stores, e.g. Aldi or Lidl
- Buy own-brand instead of branded products in supermarkets.
- Purchase non-perishable foods, e.g. pasta, in bulk, especially when on offer.

Household bills

- Turn down the thermostat on home heating systems by one degree, to reduce heating bills.
- Compare the costs of various utility providers, e.g. Electric Ireland and Airtricity, to avail of the best deal being offered.
- Use the economy setting on washing machines and dishwashers, and only turn machines on when they are full, in order to reduce electricity bills.

Clothing

- Buy clothing from second-hand shops.
- Buy clothes during sales and watch out for special offers.

Travel

- Where possible, walk or cycle to destinations to cut down on fuel or public transport costs, or carpool with another individual.
- Buy a yearly travel pass for public transport, as it is cheaper than paying for individual fares.

? Describe **four** different ways a consumer could reduce expenditure when managing the household budget. (12) **OL**

MANAGEMENT OF HOUSEHOLD FINANCIAL RESOURCES

What you will learn:

- **Reasons for creating a budget (advantages)**
- **Guidelines to follow when preparing a budget**
- **Budget percentages**
- **Money Advice and Budgeting Service (MABS)**
- **Sample budget**

A budget is a plan for spending. It estimates income and expenditure for a set period of time, so that debt can be avoided.

Reasons for creating a budget (advantages)

✓ A budget helps individuals to develop good money management skills by helping to identify total income and focusing spending on priority expenses, e.g. rent and food.

✓ As a budget requires the listing of all expenditure and the reviewing of receipts or bills, areas of overspending will become apparent and debt can be avoided.

✓ Budgeting reduces reliance on credit, e.g. credit cards, to pay for goods and services. This helps avoid debt, as credit can incur high interest rates and repayment costs.

✓ A budget provides financial security for individuals and families as expenses, e.g. bills, will be paid. This alleviates worry and stress.

✓ As a budget has a savings element it ensures that money is available to cover unplanned eventualities, e.g. job loss. Saving regularly also teaches children the value of money and money management skills.

Did you know
Individuals and families should ideally have enough savings to cover household expenses for a redundancy period of three to six months.

Outline **two** advantages of planning a household budget. (4) **OL**

Jack and Jane O'Brien have two children ages five and three, Jack works five days a week and Jane stays at home to look after the children. They currently live in a three bedroomed rented house and are saving to buy a home of their own.

- Explain why it is important for the O'Brien family to set up a budget. (12) **OL**

Guidelines to follow when preparing a budget

Guidelines	Explanation
Estimate total income	• Estimate total annual regular income, including salary/wages, benefits or other sources, e.g. rent from another property. Do not include irregular income, e.g. bonuses or overtime, as these cannot be guaranteed. • If creating a monthly budget, divide annual income by 12. For a weekly budget divide by 52.
List all expenditure	• List all essential expenditure, e.g. mortgage and food, and discretionary expenditure, e.g. entertainment and leisure
Allocate a percentage of income	• Allocate a percentage of the total income to each expenditure listed, e.g. housing 25%
Allocate savings	• Every budget should contain a savings element in case of an emergency or unplanned eventualities, e.g. job loss. This also allows for funds to be available for times of increased expenditure, e.g. occasions such as Christmas or back to school. Savings should be lodged into a separate savings account
Review and evaluate	• Carry out regular reviews of the budget to ensure it is effective, e.g. bills are being paid and overspending is not occurring. Keep all bills and receipts to monitor spending. • Budgets may need to be recalculated to cater for changes in circumstances, e.g. a new baby

BUDGETING

❓ Discuss **four** of the principal guidelines that should be followed when drawing up a budget for a family. (20) **OL**

Suggest some strategies that should be followed when planning family budgets to ensure effective management of financial resources. (20) **HL**

Budget percentages

Item	Standard percentage
Housing (mortgage, rent, household insurance, maintenance)	25%
Food (grocery shopping, eating out)	25%
Household expenses (bills, e.g. electricity, water, fuel, Wi-Fi, TV licence)	15%
Education/childcare (crèche or childminder, uniforms, books, college fees)	10%
Travel (petrol or diesel, car tax and insurance, public transport costs)	5%
Clothing (work or casual clothing, evening wear)	5%
Medical (doctor or dentist fees, prescriptions)	5%
Savings (for emergencies, special occasions, future events)	5%
Entertainment/leisure (cinema, sports activities, holidays)	5%

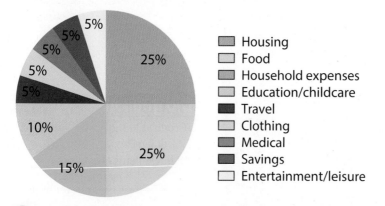

Tip!

These percentages are only a guideline, they may need to be changed depending on the question asked in the Leaving Certificate exam.

? John is 25 years old. His net weekly income is €370. He shares a house with three others and commutes to work each day by bus. He is a member of the local health and fitness club that has an annual membership charge of €350. He is planning to buy a car next year.

Using the information given above, plan and set out a weekly budget for John to ensure that he uses his money wisely. (24) **OL**

Brian and Helen Jones live with their two children, Colm (4) and Niamh (2). Both parents work full time and have a combined net monthly income of €3,250. They also receive child benefit of €250 per month. Their mortgage repayment is €600 per month. They commute to work using the family car. Colm and Niamh attend the local crèche each day.

Using the information given above, set out a monthly budget for the Jones family to ensure efficient management of financial resources. (16) **HL**

Money Advice and Budgeting Service (MABS)

The Money Advice and Budgeting Service (MABS), funded by the Department of Social Protection, is a free, confidential and independent service for people in debt or at risk of getting into debt. It operates within the Citizens Information Board. There are over 60 MABS offices nationwide, staffed by trained money advisers who:

- provide a confidential money advice and budgeting service to clients who are in debt, or who are at risk of getting into debt
- facilitate clients to develop the knowledge and skills they need to avoid getting into debt, and to deal effectively with debt situations that arise
- identify sources of credit that best meet the needs of clients to pay back debt, and facilitate clients to access these sources.

> **?** Explain how MABS (Money Advice and Budgeting Service) assists families who are experiencing financial difficulties. (10) **HL**

Tip!

All of this answer was not required to obtain full marks. It required six points.

Sample budget

 Design a family budget (two adults and two young children) where the net weekly income is €650. Give a reason for the proposed allocation of income for each area of expenditure. (18) **(HL 2015)**

Item	%	Amount	Reason
Housing	25%	€162.50	To cover mortgage or rent repayments, household insurance payments, and the maintenance of the home, e.g. repairs
Food	25%	€162.50	To cover the weekly food shopping bill for the family. It also includes the cost of meals eaten outside the home
Household expenses	15%	€97.50	To cover household bills, e.g. electricity, water, fuel, Wi-Fi and TV licence
Education	5%	€32.50	To cover the costs associated with the education of the two children, e.g. uniforms and books. It is also used for future costs of education, e.g. planning for college
Childcare	5%	€32.50	To cover payment for the services of a childminder or a crèche for the two children
Travel	5%	€32.50	To cover the cost of travelling to work, school or other activities, e.g. petrol or diesel expenses for a car or fares for public transport services. It is also used to cover the cost of car tax and insurance
Clothing	5%	€32.50	To cover the cost of buying work and casual clothing for the adults and casual clothing for the children
Medical	5%	€32.50	To cover doctor and dentist fees and prescriptions
Savings	5%	€32.50	To plan for emergencies such as job loss, special occasions, such as religious holidays and birthdays, and future events, such as college
Entertainment	5%	€32.50	To cover personal expenses, e.g. cinema tickets and sporting activities

BUDGETING

PAYMENT OPTIONS AND CREDIT

What you will learn:

- **Payment options for goods and services**
- **Forms of credit**
- **Factors to consider when choosing credit**
- **Advantages and disadvantages of using credit**
- **Consumer Credit Act 1995**

Payment options for goods and services

Method	Advantages	Disadvantages
Cash	✓ Quick and convenient ✓ No extra charges are incurred from transactions ✓ Less chance of overspending, as consumers can only spend the cash in their possession	✗ Risk of losing cash or of cash being stolen ✗ Not suitable for paying large bills or purchasing expensive items, e.g. a car ✗ Coins can be bulky and heavy to carry
Cheques Written bills of exchange drawn on a bank by a current-account holder to pay out a specific sum of money	✓ Convenient and safe ✓ Useful for postal payments: if a cheque is lost it can be cancelled	✗ A charge is incurred for each cheque used ✗ It takes approximately three days for a cheque to clear (enter a **recipient's** account)
Debit cards Deduct money directly from a consumer's current account to pay for a purchase. Debit cards can only be used if sufficient funds to pay for the goods being purchased are in the account	✓ Safer than carrying cash. If a card is stolen, it can be cancelled. ✓ A contactless payment (up to €30) and cash-back option is available ✓ Less chance of overspending, as an individual can only spend the money available in their account ✓ Can be used to pay bills online and for online shopping	✗ May incur a charge each time the card is used

Did you know ?

Irish people are the second greatest users of cheques in the European Union, behind the French. Around 84 million cheques are used by Irish people annually.

Lit Hit

A recipient is a person who receives something.

Did you know ?

In 2013 Irish customers made almost 420 million payment card transactions.

Method	Advantages	Disadvantages
Direct debits/standing orders • **Direct debts** involve variable sums of money, e.g. phone bills, paid directly out of the consumer account • **Standing orders** involve fixed sums of money, e.g. rent, paid directly out of the consumer's current account	✓ Convenient and safe for regular bills, e.g. electricity bills ✓ Ensures that important bills are not forgotten	✗ A charge is incurred for setting up a standing order ✗ Easy to lose control of spending if there are numerous direct debits or standing orders on a single current account
Credit cards Allow consumers to pay for purchases on credit	✓ Enables consumers to purchase goods that they do not have the cash for straight away, e.g. in the event of an emergency ✓ Useful for paying large bills or purchasing expensive items, e.g. a suite of furniture ✓ Safer than carrying cash. If a card is stolen, it it can be cancelled. ✓ Can be used to pay bills online and for online shopping	✗ The government take an annual stamp duty charge of €30 for the use of credit cards ✗ Encourages impulse buying, as consumers do not need money in their account to purchase goods. This can lead to debt ✗ If credit card bills are not paid back on time, high rates of interest can be charged
	G⊘ FIGURE 123 There are now 1.8 million personal credit cards in Ireland. This is down from 2.2 million in 2007, during the economic boom.	
24-hour phone banking A facility that allows current-account holders to perform banking activities at home 24 hours a day 365 days a year	✓ Convenient, as bills can be paid over the phone at any time ✓ Can be accessed anywhere in the world to pay bills or transfer money	✗ May incur a charge for phone calls
Online banking Banking offered to current-account holders to perform banking activities at home via the internet	✓ Convenient, as bills can be paid over the internet at any time ✓ Can be accessed anywhere in the world to pay bills or transfer money ✓ Consumers can download their bank's app, making banking even more accessible	✗ May incur a charge for each transaction ✗ Current accounts could be hacked if account information is obtained ✗ Internet access is necessary

PAYMENT OPTIONS AND CREDIT

Method	Advantages	Disadvantages
Credit transfer/giro A paper slip addressed to a bank instructing it to debit a specified sum of money from the consumer's account to the named account on the giro. They are commonly found in the form of tear-off strips at the bottom of regular bills.	✓ Convenient, as all relevant details are on the giro at the bottom of a bill, e.g. account details of the recipient, so it saves time having to fill this in	✗ A charge is incurred for each giro transaction ✗ Inconvenient compared to 24-hour banking or online banking, as one must travel to the post office or bank
Billpay A service operated by An Post that enables consumers to pay a variety of bills, including telephone, gas, cable, and electricity bills, free of charge **POST**	✓ No charge by An Post for carrying out the billpay service ✓ Convenient service, as there are many An Post branches nationwide ✓ Accessible online, so consumers can pay certain bills at any time	✗ Not all transactions can be completed online, so it can be inconvenient compared to 24-hour banking or online banking

> **?** Explain **two** of the following methods of payment used for goods and services.
> - Credit Card   • Laser Card *(now known as Visa Debit)*   • Direct Debit/Standing Order (6) **OL**
>
> Name **two** methods of paying for goods and services. State **one** advantage and **one** disadvantage of each method. (6) **OL**

Forms of credit

Credit involves borrowing money to purchase goods or pay for services, and repaying it at a later date. Consumers pay for this privilege in the form of interest: a fee for borrowing, charged on top of the money borrowed.

There are many types of credit available including:

- store cards
- credit cards
- overdrafts
- term loans
- charge cards
- hire purchase.

Store cards	
Description	• Allow consumers to purchase goods when they do not have sufficient funds and repay at a later date, but only in the store associated with the card • Often come with initial discounts, e.g. 10% off purchases for the first three months, or additional extras, e.g. free delivery
Issued by	• Department stores, e.g. Brown Thomas and Arnotts

Interest	• Consumers have approximately 56 days to pay their bill. This can be completed in a lump sum or in staged payments. If the balance is:
	  o paid in full, no interest is charged
	  o not paid in, full interest (18–23%) can be charged.

BROWN THOMAS

Credit cards

Description	• Allow consumers to purchase goods or services when they do not have sufficient funds and repay at a later date • Have a credit limit. This is the maximum amount someone can borrow on a single card. This can be extended once a good credit rating is established.
Issued by	• Lending institutions, e.g. banks and building societies
Interest	• The interest rates are similar to those charged for store cards, however they can sometimes be a little lower (13–23%)

Overdrafts

Description	• An agreed sum of money that a consumer can withdraw from their current account when they have no money in their account • Useful for short-term borrowing of money, e.g. in the case of an emergency • The agreed overdraft sum (often known as the overdraft limit) varies from person to person, depending on their credit rating. A set-up charge may apply.
Issued by	• Lending institutions, e.g. banks and building societies
Interest	• Interest is charged (11–17%) on the amount overdrawn from the account • No interest is charged if the consumer does not use the overdraft facility

Term loans

Description	• A monetary loan that is paid out in a lump sum to consumers and repaid in regular payments over a set period of time • Consumers often obtain term loans to buy a home or car. The duration of term loans varies. • When the loan is granted, the agreed amount is transferred into the consumer's chosen account
Issued by	• Lending institutions, e.g. banks, building societies and credit unions

Interest	• Interest is charged (7–14%) on the amount borrowed. Credit unions generally offer the lowest interest rates.
	• Interest rates may be:
	  o **variable:** fluctuate over the duration of the loan. If the interest rate falls the consumer will benefit and the loan may be repaid earlier than agreed
	  o **fixed:** remain the same for the entire duration of the loan

Charge cards
(for example, American Express and Diners Club International)

Description	• A charge card works in a similar manner to a credit card, except:
	  o consumers must pay their full balance upon receipt of their monthly bill
	  o consumers do not have a credit limit

Issued by	• Lending institutions, e.g. banks and building societies

Interest	• No interest is charged. If the balance is:
	  o paid in full upon receipt, no late fee is applied
	  o not paid in full, a late fee is applied

Hire purchase	
Description	• A combination of hiring and buying goods. Consumers have use of the good while paying weekly or monthly instalments, but they do not fully own it until the final instalment has been paid. • If payment instalments are not met, goods may be repossessed
Issued by	• Lending institutions, e.g. banks and building societies, and credit intermediaries, e.g. retailers such as garages and furniture shops
Interest	• Interest is charged (approximately 8%) on the amount borrowed
Agreement conditions	When a consumer enters into hire purchase they must sign an agreement. Hire purchase agreements were previously protected by the Hire Purchase Acts 1946 and 1960, but these acts were superseded by Consumer Credit Act 1995. The Consumer Credit Act 1995 states that a hire purchase agreement must include: • a description of the goods the agreement refers to, e.g. a car • the cash price and the hire purchase price of the good(s) • the number of payment instalments, the amount of each instalment and the date each instalment is to be paid • the names, signatures and addresses of all the parties involved • a statement that the consumer has the right to withdraw from the agreement within ten days of receiving the agreement. This is known as a cooling-off period • the rights of the parties involved, e.g. repossession of the goods, penalties for missed payments a statement that the hirer (consumer) must inform the owner as to the whereabouts of the goods to which the agreement relates • fees and penalties that apply.

> **REMEMBER IT!**
> **'SCOTCH!'**
> **S**tore cards, **C**redit cards, **O**verdrafts, **T**erm loans, **C**harge cards, **H**ire purchase.

Factors to consider when choosing credit

- **Essential purchase:** credit is generally an expensive way to purchase goods, due to high interest rates charged. Consumers should be certain that purchases are a need or a genuine want before choosing credit to pay for them. This helps consumers to avoid having large repayments with high interest on an item they regret purchasing.

- **Interest rate:** the interest charged on credit varies greatly among lending institutions, so it is important for consumers to shop around. The lower the interest, the cheaper the cost of the credit.

- **Hidden fees:** check the fine print on credit agreements to avoid paying hidden charges, e.g. an overlimit fee on credit cards for exceeding monthly credit limits or a high administration fee to set up a term loan.

- **Penalties for missing credit repayments:** on missed repayments some **creditors** will:
  - charge a late payment fee (usually every 30 days)
  - charge a default interest rate (higher interest rate charged when repayments are overdue)
  - record late repayments on the consumer's credit record, which may make it difficult to obtain credit again in the future, e.g. a mortgage loan.

> **Lit Hit**
> Creditors are people or financial institutions that lend money.

> ❓
> Name **two** forms of credit. (2) **OL**
>
> Explain the term *hire purchase*. State **one** advantage and **one** disadvantage of hire purchase for the consumer. (6) **OL**
>
> State **two** benefits to the consumer of the Hire Purchase Acts (1946, 1960). (6) **HL**

Advantages and disadvantages of using credit

Advantages	Disadvantages
✓ Enables consumers to pay large bills and purchase expensive items, e.g. a new car, which very few could afford to pay for with cash ✓ Useful to meet the cost of unexpected emergencies, e.g. a dental visit ✓ Provides consumers with the option of taking advantage of special sales at short notice, which can save money ✓ Eliminates the need to carry large sums of cash around, which can be easily lost or stolen ✓ Encourages consumers to spend money, which benefits the Irish economy as it generates revenue and creates jobs	✗ May encourage impulse buying and cause consumers to live beyond their means, which can lead to debt, as a planned budget was not followed ✗ Interest rates can be high, causing the item or service paid for to work out more expensive in the long run ✗ Goods can be repossessed if the consumer fails to make repayments 

 State **one** advantage and **one** disadvantage of buying goods on credit. (10) **OL**

State **one** advantage and **one** disadvantage of using credit to pay household utility bills. (6) **HL**

Consumer Credit Act 1995

The Consumer Credit Act 1995 provides protection for borrowers as it:

- regulates various aspects of credit, including hire purchase, mortgages, term loans and credit cards
- monitors credit advertising, ensuring it contains information including the **Annual Percentage Rate** (APR) and restrictions on the availability of credit
- imposes that credit agreements, e.g. hire-purchase agreements, must be in writing and contain information including the cash price and the hire-purchase price of the good, the names, addresses and signatures of all parties involved and the number of payment instalments
- stipulates that lenders who provide credit, e.g. hire purchase, must not visit borrowers in their workplace seeking payment.

Lit Hit

Annual Percentage Rate is a rate, expressed as a percentage, that incorporates the annual interest rate, setting-up fees and management costs placed on credit.

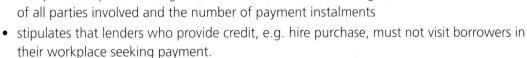 Name **two** items of information, as required by the Consumer Credit Act (1995), that must be included in an advertisement for buying goods on credit. (10) **OL**

Explain how borrowers are protected by the Consumer Credit Act (1995). Give **two** points. (6) **HL**

PAYMENT OPTIONS AND CREDIT

What you will learn:

- **Reasons why it is important to save (advantages)**
- **Factors to consider when selecting a savings scheme**
- **An Post saving schemes**
- **Bank and building society saving schemes**

Saving means to regularly set aside a portion of money for the future. The amount of money saved and the frequency depends on individuals' circumstances. Saving can be short term, e.g. for a holiday, or long term, e.g. for retirement.

Reasons why it is important to save (advantages)

✓ Saving reduces reliance on credit, e.g. credit cards, to pay for goods and services. This helps avoid debt, as credit incurs high interest rates and repayment costs.

✓ Saving ensures money is available for essential expenditure, e.g. rent and food, in the case of an emergency or unplanned eventualities, e.g. job loss. Saving also helps people to prepare for times of the year when there is extra spending, e.g. Christmas.

✓ Saving provides financial security for individuals and families, as future needs such as third-level education or retirement are provided for. This alleviates worry and stress.

✓ Savings will earn interest if invested wisely, increasing their returns. Generally, the longer the savings investment term the greater the interest gained.

✓ Saving builds a good financial reputation with a financial institution, and creates a favourable credit history. This is required when applying for loans, as it shows an ability to meet payments.

 Outline **three** reasons why it is important for a family to save money. (12) **OL**

Factors to consider when selecting a savings scheme

- **Security of savings:** savings schemes with An Post and banks provide a safe saving option, as they are covered by the government Deposit Guarantee Scheme which protects saving deposits up to €100,000 in the case of a financial institution becoming **insolvent**. Despite the possibility of offering a greater return, equity-based schemes (stocks and shares) are less secure, as they are dependent on the performance of the stock market.

Lit Hit
Insolvent means not having enough funds to pay debts.

- **Interest earned:** the interest earned on saving schemes varies between financial institutions, even within the one institution, as different savings schemes have varying interest rates, so it is important to shop around. The annual equivalent rate (AER) shows the amount of interest earned in a year. The higher the AER, the greater the return.

- **Tax payable:** some saving schemes may charge Deposit Interest Retention Tax (DIRT), a form of tax levied by the government on interest earned. DIRT is charged at 41% on all interest earned. Most State saving schemes with An Post are exempt from DIRT, so returns on savings can be greater.

Did you know ?

People aged 65 or over are not subject to DIRT on the interest they earn from savings.

- **Access to funds:** certain saving schemes allow individuals to withdraw money immediately if needed. This is suited to short-term saving, e.g. for holiday spending money. Other schemes are not as accessible, e.g. accounts that require money to be invested for three years, and penalties may be incurred for early withdrawal or encashment.

?

Explain why **each** of the following are important considerations when selecting a saving scheme:
- security of savings
- interest payable
- access to funds
- tax payable. (20) **HL**

REMEMBER IT!

'**S**ave **I**n **T**rusted **A**ccounts.'
Security of savings, **I**nterest payable, **T**ax payable, **A**ccess.

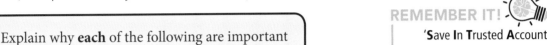

The following financial institutions offer a range of saving schemes:
- An Post
- banks and building societies.

An Post saving schemes

Scheme	Description	Interest earned	Ease of access
Deposit account	• Minimum investment is €1 • No maximum investment	• 0.15% variable interest rate • Interest is calculated daily, and paid at the end of the year • Interest earned is subject to DIRT at 41%	Up to €3,000 can be withdrawn daily at any post office, once individuals have a personal deposit book and proof of identity
Savings bonds	• A fixed lump sum is invested for three years • Minimum individual investment is €50 • Maximum individual investment is €120,000	• 1% fixed interest rate earned over three years; AER: 0.33% • Interest is calculated annually • Lower interest is paid if encashed before the three years are complete • Interest earned is tax free	Seven working days' notice is required for withdrawal
Savings certificates	• A fixed lump sum is invested for five years • Minimum individual investment is €50 • Maximum individual investment is €120,000	• 5% fixed interest rate earned over five years; AER: 0.98% • Interest is calculated every six months • Lower interest is paid if encashed before the five and a half years are complete • Interest earned is tax free	Seven working days' notice is required for withdrawal

SAVINGS

Scheme	Description	Interest earned	Ease of access
Instalment savings scheme	• A fixed amount is invested monthly for one year. This money then remains on deposit for five years. • Minimum monthly investment is €25 • Maximum monthly investment is €1,000	• 5.5% fixed interest rate, earned over five years; AER: 0.98% • Interest is calculated annually • Lower interest is paid if encashed before the six years are complete • Interest earned is tax free	Seven working days' notice is required for withdrawal
National Solidarity Bond (ten year)	• A lump sum is invested for ten years • Minimum individual investment is €50 • Maximum individual investment is €120,000	• 16% fixed interest rate, earned over ten years; AER: 1.5% • Interest is calculated annually • Lower interest is paid if encashed before the ten years are complete • Interest earned is tax free • Has the highest interest rate due to having the longest investment term	Seven working days' notice is required for withdrawal

Bank and building society saving schemes

Scheme	Description
Demand deposit accounts	• A secure account suitable for short-term saving deposits • Access to savings is instant through ATMs • There is no minimum or maximum investment, and money can be invested for any period of time • Offer a low variable interest rate • Interest earned is subject to DIRT at 41%
Notice deposit accounts	• A secure account suitable for short-term savings deposits • Access to savings requires notice, e.g. 31 days, 60 days or 90 days, depending on the type of notice account chosen • The minimum investment is €5,000 and the maximum is €1,000,000. Money can be invested for any period of time. • Offers a variable interest rate: the longer the notice required to access savings the higher the interest rate • Interest earned is subject to DIRT at 41%

Scheme	Description
Special term accounts	• A secure savings account suitable for long-term saving. A lump sum is invested for a fixed term, e.g. three or five years. • Minimum investment is €6,000, maximum investment is €25,000 • Offers a higher fixed-rate of interest. Any interest earned (up to €480 on a three-year account and €635 on a five-year account) is not subject to DIRT. Interest earned above these amounts is subject to DIRT at 41%. • Money must remain in the account for the duration of the term, if withdrawn early, there will be a penalty on the interest paid

? Name **two** saving schemes suitable for a low-income family. (6) **OL**

Describe **one** saving scheme you would recommend to a young person who is saving to buy a car. Refer to **four** of the following:

- name of institution
- type of account
- risk
- ease of access to funds
- interest payable. (20) **OL**

Recommend **one** type of savings scheme suitable for a family. Refer to:

- name of institution
- type of savings scheme
- interest paid
- ease of access to funds
- tax payable. (14) **HL**

SAVINGS

INSURANCE

What you will learn:

- **How insurance works**
- **Factors to consider when choosing an insurance policy**
- **Types of insurance**
- **Life assurance, health insurance and property insurance**
- **Advantages of insurance**

Insurance is a form of financial protection provided by insurance companies against something that might happen, e.g. illness or damage to property. These events can result in serious financial complications for individuals and families. By having insurance, compensation will be paid out to cover these losses.

The term *assurance* applies to protection against something that will happen, e.g. death.

How insurance works

- Individuals pay an insurance company a specified amount of money, called a premium, to take out an insurance policy. This is a document detailing the terms and conditions of the insurance being taken out by an individual. Once obtained, individuals then become known as policyholders.

Did you know

Insurance companies ensure the premiums they charge are high enough to cover compensation payments, while also making a profit.

- A large number of individuals pay premiums to insurance companies. This creates a pool of money, which is used by an insurance company to pay compensation to policyholders to cover financial losses in the event of certain risks, e.g. fires, car accidents or illnesses.

- To receive compensation, a claim must be made to the insurance company asking for a payment based on the terms of the insurance policy. Insurance claims are reviewed for validity and paid out to the policyholder or their family once they are approved.

? In relation to insurance explain the following:
- premium. (3) **HL**

Factors to consider when choosing an insurance policy

- **Cost:** consider an insurance policy that has an affordable premium, so payments can be met. Shopping around can help individuals to obtain a policy that matches their needs and budget.

- **Independent advice:** seek independent advice from consumer services, e.g. consumerhelp.ie, or **insurance brokers**, e.g. Chill Insurance. Avoid relying solely on the advice of insurance salespeople: they may not have the consumer's best interests at heart, as they often earn commission on sales.

Lit Hit

Insurance brokers provide independent advice about the insurance policies available from different companies and arrange insurance policies.

- **Needs and family circumstances:** consider needs and family circumstances, as these influence the amount and type of insurance cover necessary. For example, a woman having a baby may need to ensure the private health insurance policy she chooses has suitable maternity cover.

- **Cover overlap:** avoid cover overlap by carefully reading the fine print on current policies before opting for additional insurance. For example, individuals should check their car insurance policy for breakdown assistance before paying extra for car breakdown insurance cover. This will save money.

- **Extent of cover:** check insurance policies vigilantly for limitations and exclusions before paying a premium. Exclusions are services not covered by an insurance policy, e.g. some house and building insurance policies do not cover flood damage. Limitations refer to services with limited coverage, e.g. a health insurance policy that covers the cost of a semi-private hospital room but not a private room.

> **?** In relation to insurance explain the following:
> - broker. (3) **HL**

REMEMBER IT!

'**C**hoosing **I**nsurance **N**eeds **C**areful **E**xamination!'
Cost, **I**ndependent advice, **N**eeds and family circumstances, **C**over overlap, **E**xtent of cover.

Types of insurance

There is a wide variety of insurance options available to consumers.

Life assurance · Health insurance · Travel insurance · Pay-related social insurance

Motor insurance · Mortgage protection insurance · Pet insurance · Property insurance

Tip!

Only life assurance, health insurance and property insurance are examined in detail in the Leaving Certificate.

> **?** Name **three** different types of insurance that a consumer might require. (6) **OL**

INSURANCE

Life assurance

Life assurance is a form of insurance taken out on a person's life. Compensation is paid out by an insurance company when the policyholder dies. This can be used to provide financial security for dependents, e.g. family members, as they can pay off bills, make mortgage repayments and supplement existing income. The more money paid into a life assurance policy, the higher the lump sum paid out.

Types of life assurance

Term life assurance

- An insurance policy that covers individuals for a specified and agreed length of time, e.g. ten years
- In the event of death during the term of cover, a lump sum of compensation will be paid out to dependents, e.g. family members
- If a person survives the term of the cover, no payment is made. They must renew their policy to ensure continued cover.
- It is the cheapest and simplest form of life assurance, because there is no guarantee a claim will have to be paid, as a person may not die. However, the older the person is when taking out term insurance, the more expensive the premium, as the person has a higher chance of dying within the term.
- Mortgage protection insurance is the most common example of term life assurance

Whole of life assurance

- An insurance policy that lasts for a whole lifetime, and is not limited to a specific time frame. The person's life is covered indefinitely, as long as premium payments are made.
- A lump sum of compensation is paid out to surviving relatives on the death of the policyholder
- It is more expensive than term life assurance, because a claim is **inevitable**

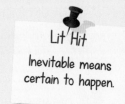

Lit Hit

Inevitable means certain to happen.

Endowment life assurance

- An insurance policy that combines life assurance and a savings element
- Part of the policyholders' payments are used to purchase life assurance. The rest are invested in funds by the insurance company.
- The policy exists for an agreed term, e.g. ten years, or up to an agreed age. When the term is up the insurance company pays out a lump sum.
- If a person dies before the agreed term has lapsed a lump sum of compensation is paid out to surviving relatives
- The policyholder can encash the policy at any time, e.g. on retirement, but they will receive a reduced return
- It is the most expensive form of life assurance

❓ What protection does life assurance give to a person or family? (2) **OL**

Health insurance

Health insurance provides cover to the policyholder in the event of illness or injury. The insurance company can cover medical expenses, including visits to the doctor, hospital stays, surgery and medication, and it can compensate for income loss. The cover provided varies greatly, depending on the health insurance policy chosen.

Types of health insurance

Income protection insurance/permanent health insurance

- An insurance policy that provides a replacement income if a policyholder cannot work as a result of an illness or injury
- On average, a person will receive 75% of their earnings on an ongoing basis if they become ill or disabled
- Cover continues until the policyholder returns to work, or until they reach the age of 66 as they are then eligible for the State Pension

Critical/serious illness insurance

- An insurance policy that pays out a lump sum of compensation if a policyholder is diagnosed with one of the specific illnesses or disabilities that the policy covers. Examples of serious illnesses and disabilities included in these policies are cancer, blindness and dementia.
- The compensation can be used to pay for medical expenses or to supplement income loss
- It is important to check the fine print of these policies carefully, as not all policies cover the same illnesses and disabilities

Private health insurance

- An insurance policy that helps policyholders cover medical expenses if they get sick, have an accident or need an operation
- People generally pay for private health insurance so that they can avail of quicker access to medical treatments and get access to a choice of hospitals, consultants and rooms, instead of having to rely on the public health system provided by the HSE
- Health insurance companies generally offer cover in the areas of:
  - hospital in-patient treatment (medical treatment that requires at least one overnight stay)
  - hospital out-patient treatment (medical treatment that does not require an overnight stay)
  - convalescent care
  - maternity benefit
  - psychiatric and substance abuse treatment
- The premium paid will determine the level of cover provided in respect of each of the above, e.g. some policies will offer semi-private rooms and others will cover private rooms
- Some policies also cover medical treatment abroad, dental and optical treatments and alternative treatments such as homeopathy and acupuncture
- The main providers of private health insurance in Ireland include Vhi Healthcare, Aviva Health and GloHealth

> **Did you know**
> Vhi Healthcare is the largest provider of voluntary private health insurance in Ireland.

? Name **one** provider of private health insurance. State **two** advantages of private health insurance. (6) **OL**
Outline **two** benefits of private health insurance. (6) **HL**

INSURANCE

Property insurance

Property insurance provides compensation to the policyholder in the event of damage to the structure or damage, loss or theft of the contents of their home. Property insurance premiums are generally based on the:

- **value of the house/building/contents:** the higher the value, the more money required to protect them
- **location:** addresses in areas with higher risk of crime, flooding or **subsidence** will often pay higher premiums
- **security level:** if a burglar alarm, fire alarm or a smoke detector is installed in a home, premiums may be lower.

> **Lit Hit**
> Subsidence is the gradual sinking of land.

Types of property insurance

Building insurance

- An insurance policy that covers damage to anything that cannot be moved from the home, including the structure, e.g. the walls and roof; permanent fittings, e.g. kitchen units; and outbuildings, e.g. garden sheds
- It protects against damage caused by burglary, vandalism, fire and certain natural disasters, e.g. lightning and flooding
- In the event of damage compensation will be paid out
- It is important to check the fine print of these policies for exemptions, e.g. protection from flood damage is omitted from some policies
- Public liability is also included in most policies, which covers homeowners' **liability** for injury or loss suffered by another person on their property as a result of an accident
- Building insurance is a necessary requirement to obtain a mortgage

> **Lit Hit**
> Liability means being legally responsible for something.

Contents insurance

- This is an insurance policy that covers all moveable items kept in the home, including personal items, domestic appliances and furniture, against risks like damage, loss or theft
- Compensation will be paid out in the event of damage, loss or theft
- It is important to check the fine print of these policies for exemptions, e.g. protection of antiques
- This can be taken out as an optional extra policy with building insurance, or combined in a single home insurance policy

All risks insurance

- An insurance policy that covers damage to personal valuables, including paintings, computers, tablets and jewellery, against risks like damage, loss or and theft both inside and outside the home
- In the event of damage, loss or theft compensation will be paid out
- This can be taken out as an optional extra policy with building insurance

> **?** Name and describe **two** different types of household insurance. (14) **OL**

Advantages of insurance

✓ Insurance helps provide peace of mind, as there is comfort in knowing measures of protection are in place for unforeseen circumstances.

✓ Property insurance protects assets such as homes and valuable items, as compensation is paid out to repair or replace these if they are damaged, stolen or lost.

✓ Life assurance policies provide financial protection, as compensation is paid out to dependents on death. This can prevent bereaved families falling into debt, especially if the main earner in the household passes away.

✓ Private health insurance provides physical protection, ensuring that individuals or families receive medical treatment quicker than if they were relying on the public health service, and covers their treatment costs.

✓ Income protection insurance/permanent health insurance provides financial support in the event of an illness/injury and loss of income, ensuring an individual or families can still meet their basic needs and avoid debt.

> **?** Outline the advantages to the householder of having adequate insurance cover. (12) **OL**

HOUSING FINANCE

What you will learn:

- **Factors to consider when choosing a mortgage**
- **Types of interest**
- **Conditions to qualify for a mortgage**
- **Types of mortgages**
- **Mortgage protection policy (life assurance)**

HL A mortgage is a loan from a lending agency that is used to purchase a home. Mortgages are available from lending agencies including banks, building societies and local authorities. The lending agency takes hold of the ownership (title deeds) of the property until the final mortgage repayment is made.

GO FIGURE

71% of the Irish population own their own homes. Home ownership figures in Ireland are among the highest in Europe.

Factors to consider when choosing a mortgage

- **Interest rate:** the interest charged on mortgages varies greatly among lending institutions, so it is important for individuals to shop around. The lower the interest the cheaper the cost of the mortgage.
- **Incentives offered:** some lending agencies offer incentives to first-time buyers, e.g. a lower interest rate for the first year or payment of **stamp duty** to the value of 1% of the mortgage.
- **Early repayment charge:** an early-funding fee may be charged by some lending agencies if individuals wish to pay off their fixed mortgage early, e.g. 20 years into a 30-year term. This is a form of compensation, to cover additional costs for the lending institution.
- **Break from repayments charge:** some lending agencies may offer a mortgage payment break for times when individuals cannot afford repayments, e.g. due to job loss. However, this may affect an individual's credit rating, and the total postponed payments will be added onto the mortgage balance, increasing the cost of future repayments.
- **Type of interest:** consider the type of interest offered, as this will affect the total cost of the mortgage. Fixed interest rates are usually higher than variable rates.

> **Lit Hit**
> Stamp duty is a tax payable to the government for changing documents that specify who owns a particular property.

Types of interest

There are three types of interest that apply to mortgages: fixed rate, variable rate and tracker.

Fixed rate	Variable rate	Tracker
• The interest rate is fixed, so it cannot change for a set period of time, e.g. one to five years • No risk is involved: if the European Central Bank (ECB) rates go up the interest will remain the same. This means the borrower knows exactly how much the payments will be monthly. • Fixed interest rates are usually higher than variable rates, so they can be more expensive	• The interest rate varies, as it rises and falls with ECB rates • If the ECB rates fall the borrower will have lower monthly repayments. If the ECB rates increase repayments will be higher. • If the ECB rates fall banks often do not pass the reduction onto the borrower straight away	• The interest rate tracks the ECB rates, and is usually 1% higher • If the ECB rates fall the borrower will have lower monthly repayments. If the ECB rates increase repayments will be higher. • If the ECB rates fall the reduction is passed on to the borrower straight away

? State one advantage of each of the following types of mortgage interest rates:
- fixed rate   • variable rate. (6) **HL**

Conditions to qualify for a mortgage

Each lending institution has a list of requirements that must be fulfilled before approving a mortgage.

- **Amount to be borrowed:** applicants may borrow three and a half times their gross annual income. The lending agency will require proof of income in the form of three recent payslips and a latest P60 form.
- **Deposit**
  - o First-time buyers require a 10% deposit for properties costing up to €220,000. For properties over €220,000, a 20% deposit on the excess is necessary.
  - o Non first-time buyers will require a 20% deposit.
- **Credit history:** applicants need to have a good credit history before they will be considered for a mortgage, e.g. regular savings and no default payments on loans.

GO FIGURE 1 2 3

A €200,000 mortgage over 20 years will cost €304,000, however, over 30 years it will cost €364,000.

- **Length of the mortgage:** mortgage terms can vary between five and 35 years. The length of a mortgage term offered depends on an applicant's:
  - o **age:** an older applicant will have to repay over a shorter term
  - o **ability to afford monthly repayments:** a longer term may be offered to lower the monthly repayments, but this will increase the overall cost due to the interest charged.
- **Good investment:** a lending agency will get a property **surveyed** to check the structural quality before granting a mortgage, to ensure the property is a good investment. This may make obtaining a mortgage for an older property more difficult.
- **Insurance:** applicants legally require:
  - o a mortgage protection policy
  - o building insurance that covers the cost of damage to the home
  - o a mortgage indemnity bond that protects the lending agency against making a loss if the house is repossessed.

Lit Hit
Surveyed means having the value or quality assessed.

? Identify and elaborate on the general terms and conditions that have to be fulfilled before a mortgage is granted. (20) **HL**

REMEMBER IT!
'**A**fter **D**epositing **C**ash, **L**enders **G**rant **I**nvestment.'
Amount to be borrowed, **D**eposit, **C**redit history, **L**ength of the mortgage, **G**ood investment, **I**nsurance.

Types of mortgage

Annuity mortgage/repayment mortgage

- This is the most popular mortgage type
- Each monthly mortgage repayment goes towards:
  - o paying the interest rate on the loan
  - o paying off the principal amount (capital) borrowed
- Little risk is involved with this mortgage type, as at the end of the mortgage term the interest and principal amount borrowed are paid off
- A mortgage protection policy is a compulsory requirement of this mortgage

HOUSING FINANCE

Endowment mortgage

- This mortgage combines borrowing and investing
- Each monthly mortgage repayment goes towards:
  - paying the interest rate on the loan
  - paying a premium into an endowment life assurance policy, which is invested by an insurance company in the stock market
- At the end of the mortgage term the endowment policy is encashed to pay off the principal amount (capital) borrowed. Any surplus money can be used for personal spending.
- This is a less popular mortgage option, as there is a high risk the investment yield will not be sufficient to pay off the mortgage at the end of the term. If this happens, the borrower will need to repay the shortfall.
- A mortgage protection policy is not required, as it is included in the premium

Pension mortgage

- This mortgage combines borrowing and investing. It is a popular option for the self-employed as they are not part of a company pension scheme.
- Each monthly repayment goes towards:
  - paying the interest on the loan
  - paying a premium into a pension scheme investment policy, which is invested in the stock market

- At the end of the mortgage term the pension scheme investment policy is encashed to repay the principal amount (capital) borrowed and provide a pension fund for retirement
- This is a less popular mortgage option as there is a high risk that the investment yield will not be sufficient to pay off the mortgage at the end of the term. If this happens, the borrower will need to repay the shortfall.
- A mortgage protection policy is a compulsory requirement of this mortgage

 Explain **each** of the following:
  - annuity mortgage
  - endowment mortgage. (6) **HL**

Mortgage protection policy (life assurance)

- Under the Consumer Credit Act 1995, a mortgage-lending agency is obliged to ensure that a borrower has a mortgage protection policy in place to cover the balance due on a mortgage in the event of their death, or, in the case of a joint mortgage, in the event of the death of one of the borrowers.
- The insurance company that provides the mortgage protection policy will pay the balance due on the mortgage if the borrower dies, so the mortgage lending agency will not be left with an outstanding balance.

 Explain the term *mortgage protection* and state why mortgage protection is necessary. (10) **HL**

What you will learn:

- **Factors that influence housing choices**
- **Local authority housing schemes**

Factors that influence housing choices

Housing choices are influenced by four main factors:

- socio-economic factors
- National Housing Policy
- modern trends in housing development
- availability of housing.

Socio-economic factors

- **Income:** the amount of available income will greatly influence an individual or family's housing choices. If considering buying, individuals will need to be able to obtain a mortgage and afford the repayments. If renting, they will need to be able to meet monthly rent costs. The running costs of a home will also influence house choice, as larger homes will require more money for heating and maintenance.

- **Size:** the larger the family, the more space required when choosing a home, e.g. a larger kitchen/living space and more bedrooms.

- **Family stage:** a family with young children will have different housing needs from a retired couple, e.g. greater outdoor space, a study area and separate bedrooms for children, affecting housing choice.

- **Personal preferences:** personal likes and dislikes regarding a home's exterior and outdoor space, layout, interior decor or view will influence a person's decision when choosing a home.

- **Special needs:** if a family member has a special need, e.g. a physical disability that causes them to use a wheelchair, it is important to choose a house that meets their needs, e.g. a bungalow with a ramp.

- **Location:** the location of the house will influence individuals' and families' house choices, as it determines the price or rental cost and the future investment value of the property. Homes in towns or cities tend to cost more due to their proximity to work, schools and amenities.

Paul and Geraldine are responsible consumers planning to buy a new home.

Explain how **each** of the following could influence Paul and Geraldine when planning to buy their new home:

- cost
- size and type of house/apartment
- location/environment. (15) **OL**

Discuss how socioeconomic factors influence housing choices. (10) **HL**

REMEMBER IT!

'**I**'ll **S**ave **F**or **P**ersonal **S**pending **L**ater.'
Income, **S**ize, **F**amily stage, **P**ersonal preferences, **S**pecial needs, **L**ocation.

National Housing Policy

The National Housing Policy was introduced in 2011 by the Department of the Environment, Community and Local Government (now known as the Department of Housing, Planning, Community and Local Government). The aim of the policy is to enable all individuals and families to access good-quality housing appropriate to their needs in their community of choice by:

- improving the private rental market by enforcing minimum accommodation standards and supporting tenants' rights
- helping meet the needs of those in society unable to pay for housing by increasing the supply of permanent new social housing, as well as improving the quality of existing social housing through regeneration and improvement works programmes
- supporting individuals with disabilities to live independently within the community, rather than in an institution, by providing housing adaptation grants and financial assistance
- supporting the vulnerable and deprived within society by providing Traveller-specific accommodation and housing supports to help alleviate homelessness
- protecting individuals in mortgage arrears by establishing a code of conduct for all financial institutions to follow when handling such cases.

 Identify **two** features of current National Housing Policy in Ireland. (6) **HL**

Modern trends in housing development

- Due to **negative equity**, many people are choosing to extend, adapt or renovate their existing home rather than sell it at a loss.
- Mixed-development housing estates are a popular choice as they offer a selection of housing styles in one development, e.g. detached or semi-detached houses, apartments and townhouses. These are more commonly found in large towns and cities, due to reduced land space and cost of land.
- Small, exclusive housing estates are popular, as they are gated communities with larger homes, green areas, playgrounds and well-maintained public areas, e.g. green areas, footpaths.
- Apartments continue to be a popular choice for those living in cities, especially young professionals.
- One-off houses are still being built in rural areas due to popular demand, with many becoming increasingly energy efficient, e.g. using solar panels to generate electricity, and including modern design features, e.g. open-plan living.

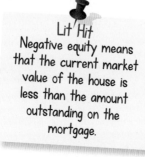
Lit Hit
Negative equity means that the current market value of the house is less than the amount outstanding on the mortgage.

▲ Exclusive housing estate

 Identify **three** recent trends in housing developments in Ireland. (6) **HL**

Discuss how trends in housing development influence housing choices. (10) **HL**

Availability of housing

Private housing

- Some urban areas, e.g. Dublin and Cork, are experiencing a private housing shortage, as demand is exceeding supply. This is causing an increase in house prices.
- In rural areas, demand is much lower and there are still many unoccupied private houses for sale, many of which are located in **ghost estates**. The recession left many of these houses unfinished.

Lit Hit

Ghost estates are developments of ten or more houses, where 50% of the houses are unoccupied or incomplete.

Rental market

- Rent costs have increased dramatically in recent years, particularly in urban areas, due to increased demand for rental properties and a shortage of supply. In the current market, many are finding it difficult to obtain a mortgage or save for the large deposit needed, meaning that they stay renting for longer, which is further reducing supply.
- In order to stabilise the private rental market and ensure security for renters, the Residential Tenancies Act was amended in 2015. Under this, landlords may review the rent only once every two years and they must give 90 days' notice to do so.

Social housing

- There is a severe shortage of **social housing** due to high demand and little or no availability. Currently, over 130,000 people are on the social housing waiting list.

Outline **three** factors that determine (influence) a person's choice of housing. (6) **OL**

Give an account of the factors that affect an individual's choice of housing. Refer to:
- social factors
- economic factors
- availability of housing. (30) **OL**

Lit Hit

Social housing is housing provided to individuals on low incomes or with particular needs by the government or non-profit organisations.

 **GO FIGURE 123**

The social housing strategy 2020 aims to provide 35,000 new social housing units over a six-year period to meet the additional social housing supply requirements.

Local authority housing schemes

Local authorities are the main providers of social housing for individuals and families who cannot afford to buy their own homes or to rent privately. Social housing is allocated according to eligibility and need.

- **Eligibility:** to be regarded as eligible for social housing, individuals or families must satisfy an income criteria by earning below an agreed annual income limit, and show that they do not have suitable alternative accommodation.
- **Need:** the local authority will consider individuals' or families' current accommodation when determining need. For example, if the current home is not fit for human habitation, overcrowded or unsuitable for an individual or a family member with a disability, the family may be considered for social housing. Individuals or families living in institutions, emergency accommodation or hostels have a greater need for accommodation, so they will be given priority.

 **GO FIGURE 123**

In 2013, 72% of the households that qualified for social housing support were dependent on social welfare as their only source of income.

HOUSING

If a person is eligible and in need of local authority housing they are placed on a waiting list (now known as a record of qualified households) and allocated a house as it becomes available. Rents charged are based on the household's ability to pay.

Local authorities offer a variety of options to individuals and families to help provide them with housing, including the Housing Assistance Payment (HAP), Mortgage Allowance Scheme, Home Choice Loan and Incremental Purchase Scheme (IPS).

Housing Assistance Payment (HAP)

- This payment is available to individuals who have a long-term housing need and are approved for social housing support. It aims to enable them to obtain accommodation within the private rental sector.

- Suitable accommodation in the private rental sector must be sourced by the individual in receipt of the HAP. Once approved, the local authority pays the full agreed monthly rent to the landlord on behalf of the individual.

- The individual in receipt of HAP then pays a rent contribution to the local authority, based on their income and their ability to pay.

- A benefit of HAP is that individuals in receipt of the payment are able to take up full-time employment while recieving this payment, so it does not prevent them from seeking work in the fear of payment being lost.

Mortgage Allowance Scheme

- This scheme is available to social housing tenants who wish to take out a mortgage to buy or build a private house.

- It is designed to ease the transition from rented social housing to paying a mortgage, and to ensure mortgage repayments can be met.

- An allowance of up to €11,450 is paid directly to the lending agency by the Department of Housing, Planning, Community and Local Government over a five-year period on a reducing scale.

Home Choice Loan (local authority mortgage)

- A government-based loan provided by four designated local authorities, available to first-time buyers who are unable to obtain a loan from a commercial lending agency.

- The loan offered can be up to 92% of the price of a new or second-hand house, or the pricing of building a new home, with the maximum loan provided being €285,000. This is repaid monthly for a period of up to 30 years.

- To qualify applicants must:
  o earn over €35,000 as a single applicant or over €45,000 as joint applicants
  o be in continuous employment for a minimum of one year
  o provide evidence they could not obtain sufficient finance from two banks or building societies.

Incremental Purchase Scheme (IPS)

- This scheme aims to provide an affordable route to homeownership for households in receipt of social housing support for a minimum of one year and earning at least €15,000 annually.
- It applies to new-build social housing or approved houses only.
- Depending on their annual income, an IPS applicant receives a discount of 40–60% on the total price of the house. For example:

Bands	Household income	Discount applicable
Band 1	€15,000–€19,999	60%
Band 2	€20,000–€29,999	50%
Band 3	€30,000+	40%

This means that an applicant who is eligible for a 60% discount only has to purchase the remaining 40% balance on the house price.

- The applicant must take out a mortgage with a lending agency to purchase the remaining balance and pay it to the local authority.
- The applicant must pay an incremental purchase charge to the local authority on the discounted amount over the next 20–30 years. It stays the same for the first five years, but drops annually until the charge is fully paid.

How it works

For a house worth €180,000 an individual earning €15,000 is entitled to a 60% discount on the price = €108,000 discount.

They take out a mortgage of €72,000 (remaining 40%) and pay this to the local authority.

An incremental purchase charge is then placed on the remaining €108,000 (the discounted amount) and paid to the local authority over 20–30 years.

> **?** Local authorities provide a range of services/schemes in relation to the provision of housing. Name and describe **one** service/scheme provided. (8) **OL**
>
> Name and give details of **one** Local Authority scheme available to people in need of housing. (12) **HL**

HOUSING

Chapter 14:
Household technology

2.1.5 HOUSEHOLD TECHNOLOGY AND APPLIANCES

What you will learn:

- **Technological developments in the home**
- **The contribution of technology to efficient home management**
- **Factors to consider when choosing appliances**
- **Categories of household appliances**
- **A small appliance with a motor: a food processor**
- **A small appliance with a heating element: a kettle**
- **A refrigeration appliance: a standard refrigerator**
- **A microwave oven**

Technology has revolutionised the way people manage the home. Household tasks are easier and less time-consuming than in previous years. Careful consideration should be given when purchasing appliances for the home.

Technological developments in the home

- **Food preparation:** e.g. food processors, blenders, liquidisers, coffee machines.
- **Cooking:** e.g. microwave ovens, dual rings, halogen rings, induction hobs.
- **Cleaning:** e.g. vacuum cleaners, steam mops, dishwashers.
- **Laundry:** e.g. washing machines, tumble dryers, heated clotheshorses.
- **Household surfaces:** e.g. stainless steel worktops, plastic vinyl flooring, ceramic tiles.
- **Automation:** e.g. timers on water/central heating that can be accessed by a mobile phone.
- **Security:** e.g. sensor alarms and lighting, electric gates.
- **Communications:** e.g. smartphones, internet (cloud computing, Skype), email.
- **Entertainment:** e.g. PlayStations, DVDs, Netflix, high-definition televisions.
- **Financial management:** e.g. computer packages such as spreadsheets, Word documents.
- **Outdoor maintenance:** e.g. lawnmowers, hedge trimmers, electric tools such as drills.

The contribution of technology to efficient home management

- In the past, household tasks, e.g. washing clothes, were time-consuming and labour intensive. Nowadays, technological advances, e.g. the washing machine, have reduced the amount of labour required, allowing more time for leisure.

- Homes are now cleaner and more hygienic places to live since appliances, e.g. vacuum cleaners, are more efficient at cleaning compared to doing the job by hand. This has increased standards of living and reduced health problems, e.g. asthma.

- Many appliances, e.g. ovens, now come with automatic timers and pre-programmed tasks, enabling appliances to turn on and off automatically. This is an advantage for individuals and families with busy lifestyles.

- Some heating and lighting systems now can be controlled remotely from mobile phones through downloaded applications. This ensures that homes are warm when individuals return home and enhances security as lights can be switched on when people are away.

- Computers and tablets can be used to carry out household financial tasks, e.g. budgeting or banking online, and may also be used to shop online for food or clothing, saving individuals and families time.

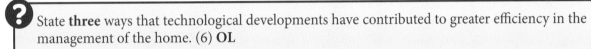

State **three** ways that technological developments have contributed to greater efficiency in the management of the home. (6) **OL**

Discuss how technology has contributed to the efficient management of the home. (16) **HL**

Factors to consider when choosing appliances

- **Information:** source information about appliances, e.g. brands and models available or features included, e.g. auto defrost, before buying to ensure it meets specific needs. This information can be found in showrooms, from salespeople, word of mouth, magazines or consumer websites.

- **Cost:** consider the:
  - **initial cost of the appliance.** Shopping around can help get the best value for money. Reliable brands may be more expensive, but are often superior in terms of quality and lifespan
  - **running cost of the appliance.** The higher the wattage the more electricity it will use, therefore the more it will cost to run
  - **servicing cost of the appliance.** This often excludes the cost of parts.

- **Energy efficiency:** all electrical appliances must display an energy label indicating the energy efficiency of the appliance. Appliances are rated from A to G.
  - A-rated appliances should be chosen as they use the least electricity, making them the cheapest to run. They cause the least harm to the environment.
  - **G-rated appliances** should be avoided as they use the most electricity, making them the most expensive to run. They cause the greatest harm to the environment.

▲ Energy label

- **Cleaning/maintenance:** ensure appliances are easy to clean in order to reduce the time and effort required to maintain them. Try to avoid appliances with too many crevices or grooves, as dirt can get lodged during use.
- **Guarantee:** a guarantee is a written contract between the manufacturer and the consumer which states that if a fault arises within a certain period of time, the manufacturer will repair or replace the appliance free of charge. Consider the terms of the guarantee offered with appliances, e.g. duration (one year to a lifetime), servicing offered, replacement parts provided.
- **Design:** consider appliances that have a design that will coordinate with the existing decor of the home. Check the measurements of the space available in the home to ensure the appliance will fit. The appliance should be easy to operate and should be well designed so that it fulfils its function.

> **?** Explain energy labelling in relation to household appliances. Name two household appliances which carry an energy label. (6) **HL**
>
> Discuss the following factors that should be considered when selecting kitchen appliances for a family home:
> - sourcing consumer information
> - value for money. (12) **HL**
> - design

> **REMEMBER IT!**
> 'Irish Consumers Everywhere Can Get Discounts!'
> Information, Cost, Energy efficiency, Cleaning, Guarantee, Design.

Categories of household appliances

Appliances with a motor	Appliances with a heating element	Refrigeration appliances	Other appliances
• Food processor • Blender • Carving knife • Juicer • Vacuum cleaner	• Kettle • Toaster • Cooker • Deep-fat fryer • Iron	• Standard fridge • Larder fridge • Fridge-freezer • American-style fridge	• Microwave oven

A small appliance with a motor: a food processor

A food processor is designed to save time and energy by completing a number of food preparation functions in one unit, including chopping, slicing and grating.

> **?** Set out the results of a study you have carried out on a household appliance with a motor. Refer to:
> - type of appliance. (3) **OL**

Design and construction of a food processor

- **Base unit:** a base unit made from strong metal or toughened plastic with support legs for stability. It has a:
  o motor with a wattage 200–700 W
  o flex with a three-pin plug that connects to the electricity supply
  o belt that connects the motor and the spindle
  o on/off switch that controls the electricity supply
  o speed control to increase or decrease speed of the food processor.

- **Bowl:** a bowl made of toughened, clear plastic with a capacity between 500 millilitres and 3.5 litres (standard size is 2 litres). It sits on the spindle. It has a safety locking lid with a feed tube and pusher to push food into the bowl.

- **Attachments:** attachments made from steel or toughened plastic sit on the spindle.

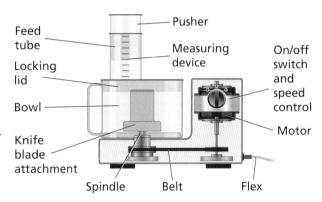

Types of attachments and their uses

Knife blade	**Julienne blade**	**Egg whisk**

Chopping, puréeing or mixing food, e.g. onions, soup or pastry	Cutting food into julienne strips, e.g. julienne potatoes or carrots	Beating or whipping food, e.g. eggs or cream
Fine, medium or coarse shredding/grating discs	**Dough hook**	**Citrus press**

Slicing, dicing or grating food, e.g. cabbage or cheese	Mixing dough, e.g. bread or pizza dough	Extracting juice from fruit, e.g. oranges

> **?** Set out the results of a study you have carried out on a household appliance with a motor. Refer to:
> - design of appliance. (9) **OL**

HOUSEHOLD TECHNOLOGY AND APPLIANCES

ⓗⓛ Working principle of a food processor

- **Motor:** when a food processor is plugged in and switched on, electricity causes the motor to operate, which causes the belt in the base to turn.
- **Attachments:** the belt causes the spindle and attachments to rotate at high speed. Depending on the attachment chosen, it chops, beats, liquidises, slices, grates or whisks the food within the bowl.
- **Bowl/feed tube:** foods can be added to the bowl at the start, or during operation through the feed tube. The pusher is used to push the food through. Liquids can also be poured directly into the bowl through the feed tube, e.g. water if making pastry.
- **Safety locking lid:** a safety lock system prevents the food processor from operating unless the lid is fully locked in position. It will also turn off the motor if the lid is removed during operation.

> **?** Set out details of a study you have undertaken on one type of electrical appliance suitable for a kitchen. Refer to:
> - working principle. (9) **HL**

Guidelines for using a food processor

- Follow the manufacturer's instructions when assembling and using the food processor.
- Use the correct attachment for the function required and ensure it is fitted correctly to avoid damaging the food processor.
- Do not overfill, as this reduces the food processor's efficiency and may cause injury, e.g. hot liquids spilling from the bowl.
- When placing food through the feed tube, ensure the food is cut small enough to avoid it becoming lodged. To avoid injury, always use the pusher and never use fingers to push food through.
- If using a food processor for long periods of time, turn off at intervals to avoid it overheating and damaging the motor.
- Pause at intervals to scrape down the sides of the bowl to avoid uneven blending of foods.

Guidelines for caring for and cleaning a food processor

- Unplug before cleaning, to prevent getting an electric shock.
- Take apart carefully before cleaning. Be especially careful when removing attachments with blades, as they could cause injury.
- Wash the bowl and attachments in hot, soapy water, then rinse and dry carefully. Thorough drying is especially important for metal attachments, as they can rust over time.
- Wipe the outer casing with a damp cloth to remove any splashes. Polish with a dry cloth.
- When not in use, store with the lid off to enable air to circulate and prevent the build-up of odours.

> **?** Set out the results of a study you have carried out on a household appliance with a motor. Refer to guidelines for use. (9) **OL**

A small appliance with a heating element: a kettle

A kettle is designed to heat water quickly and efficiently.

Design and construction of a kettle

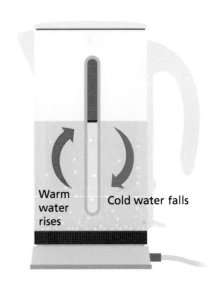

Spout
Lid
Heat-resistant handle
Jug
Water level indicator
Indicator light
On/off switch
Concealed heating element and thermostat
Flex

- **Jug:** a jug made from different materials, e.g. stainless steel or plastic, in a variety of colours and comes in various capacities/sizes, e.g. 1.7 litres. It may be a traditional dome or a modern jug shape.

- **Tightly fitting lid:** a tightly fitting lid can be opened or removed for filling.

- **Spout:** a spout that may have a filter to trap particles of limescale when pouring.

- **Water level indicator:** a water level indicator that shows the minimum and maximum water levels.

- **Handle:** a handle made of heat-resistant plastic.

- **On/off switch:** an on/off switch controls the electricity supply.

- **Indicator light:** an indicator light that shows if the kettle is in operation.

- **Flex and a three-pin plug:** a flex and a three-pin plug connect to the electricity supply. The flex can be connected to the kettle itself or to a removable base.

- **Heating element:** a heating element that heats the water inside the base of the kettle.

- **Thermostat:** a thermostat automatically switches off the kettle when the water reaches boiling point.

🔵 Working principle of a kettle

- **Heating element:** when a kettle is plugged in and switched on electricity flows through the heating element, which offers resistance to the flow of electricity. This causes the element to heat up.

- **Water heats:** the heated element heats the water surrounding it by creating convection currents. As the water heats it begins to rise and the colder water at the top falls down to the base. It continues circulating until all the water reaches the same temperature.

- **Thermostat:** when the water reaches 100°C a thermostat integrated in the base will automatically turn off the flow of electricity to the kettle.

- **Boil-dry device:** most kettles contain a boil-dry device that automatically turns off the flow of electricity to the kettle if there is insufficient water to cover the element. This prevents overheating or an electrical fire.

Warm water rises   Cold water falls

> **?** Set out details of a study that you have undertaken on a household appliance with a heating element. Refer to working principle. (6) **HL**

> **Did you know ?**
> Kettles use a bimetallic thermostat that is made of two metals fused together. One metal expands quicker than the other, which causes the thermostat to change shape and cut off the power supply when it reaches boiling point.

Guidelines for using a kettle

- Follow the manufacturer's instructions when using a kettle.
- Switch off and unplug the kettle before filling to prevent electrical shock. This is especially important if using a corded kettle that remains connected to the electricity supply.
- Ensure the heating element is covered with water before switching the kettle on to avoid the risk of overheating or an electrical fire.
- Do not overfill the kettle past the maximum-fill line, as boiling water could spill out of the spout, causing a scald.
- Allow the kettle time to cool before refilling, otherwise burns or scalds could occur.

> **?** Set out details of a study that you have undertaken on a household appliance with a heating element. Refer to:
> - guidelines for using the appliance. (9) **HL**

Guidelines for caring for and cleaning a kettle

- Only use a kettle for boiling water, as other liquids or foodstuffs can damage the appliance.
- Unplug before cleaning to prevent getting an electric shock.
- Descale regularly, as limescale build-up slows down the kettle's boiling time and causes a scum on the surface of tea or coffee.
- Never immerse the kettle in water when cleaning.
- Wipe the outer casing with a warm, damp cloth to remove splashes. Avoid harsh abrasives, e.g. steel wool, as these may scratch the outer casing. Polish with a dry cloth.

Did you know ?
Limescale can be removed from a kettle by adding white wine vinegar or citric acid, or by using a limescale catcher.

▲ Limescale on kettle heating element

A refrigeration appliance: a standard refrigerator

A refrigerator is designed to keep food fresh. The low internal temperature (3–5°C) reduces bacterial growth, which in turn slows down the rate of food spoilage.

Types of refrigerators

- **Standard refrigerator:** fits neatly under the kitchen counter and has a separate icebox on top.
- **Larder refrigerator:** a tall refrigerator with more space than a standard refrigerator. It has no icebox on top, so a separate freezer is required.
- **Fridge-freezer:** consists of two separate cabinets: a fridge and a freezer, one on top of the other.
- **American-style fridge-freezer:** consists of a large refrigerator and a large freezer side by side and of equal size. It often includes an icemaker and/or juice dispenser.

▲ American-style fridge-freezer

> **?** Set out details of a study that you have undertaken on a refrigeration appliance. Refer to:
> - type of refrigeration appliance. (2) **HL**

Design and construction of a standard refrigerator

- **Outer casing:** an outer casing made of enamelled steel coated with a layer of plastic in a variety of colours. Integrated refrigerators have a door attached that matches the kitchen cabinets.

- **Inner casing:** an inner casing that consists of a layer of moulded polystyrene plastic.

- **Insulating material:** a layer of insulating material between the outer casing and inner casing keeps the fridge cold.

- **Door with rubber gasket and magnetic strip:** a door with a rubber gasket and a magnetic strip that form an airtight seal when the door is closed. It contains adjustable bottle or carton holders and cheese and egg compartments.

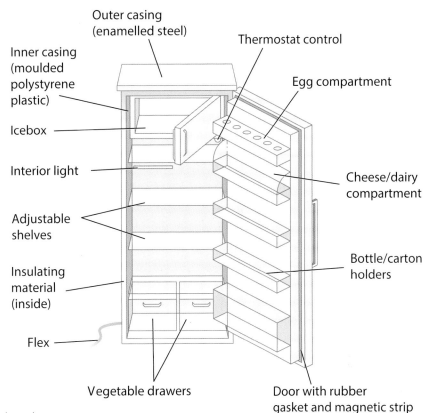

- **Interior light:** an interior light that switches on when the door is open.

- **Adjustable shelves:** adjustable shelves made from moulded polystyrene plastic, glass or metal.

- **Clear plastic vegetable drawers:** clear plastic vegetable drawers are at at the base of the fridge.

- **Icebox:** an icebox is located at the top of the refrigerator with a one- to four-star rating.

➔ For information on **star ratings** see page 315.

- **Thermostat:** a thermostat that controls the internal temperature. Once set, it maintains a constant temperature of 3–4°C, unless changed by the dial control.

- **Flex and three-pin plug:** a flex and a three-pin plug connects to the electricity supply.

Modern design features

Zoned refrigeration	• Not all foods benefit from being kept at the same temperature. Some refrigerators come with a multi-temperature drawer which can be set to different temperatures, e.g. −18°C to 15°C, depending on the foods being stored. • Food stored at the correct temperature lasts longer and is less likely to spoil
Automatic defrost	• This setting regularly defrosts a refrigerator or freezer, removing built-up ice. It is controlled by a timer. • It works by heating the evaporator with an integrated heating element for a short period of time, which melts any ice. Any resulting water drains through a duct at the back of the unit.

HOUSEHOLD TECHNOLOGY AND APPLIANCES

Humidity-controlled drawers	• A low **humidity** setting is used to prevent the rotting of fruit and vegetables that naturally release ethylene gas, e.g. apples or celery. The low humidity setting creates an opening in the drawer that allows the ethylene gas to escape. • A high humidity setting is used for fruit and vegetables prone to wilting or moisture loss, e.g. strawberries or spinach. The high humidity setting keeps the drawer sealed, retaining moisture and keeping fruit and vegetables crisper and fresher for longer.
Humidity control Low ⋅ ι ι ι ι ι ι High	
Ice/water dispensers	• Water is plumbed from the mains water supply, filtered and kept chilled. Some water is taken to form ice cubes or crushed ice. • It is operated by a push lever dispenser on the front of the refrigerator.

? Set out the results of a study you have carried out on a refrigeration appliance. Refer to:
• modern features. (9) **HL**

HL Working principle of a refrigerator

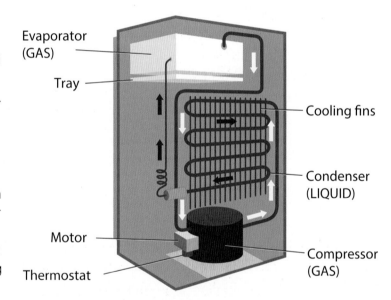

Evaporator (GAS)
Tray
Cooling fins
Condenser (LIQUID)
Motor
Compressor (GAS)
Thermostat

- **Compressor:** the compressor is found at the base of the refrigerator. It contains the gas refrigerant isobutene. A motor or pump connected to the compressor forces the gas refrigerant into the condenser above.

- **Condenser:** the condenser cools the gas refrigerant and condenses it into a liquid. It is then sent to the evaporator above. The cooling fins at the back of the refrigerator radiate or release heat generated during the process, keeping the condenser cool.

- **Evaporator:** the evaporator, found at the top of the refrigerator, rapidly evaporates the liquid refrigerant into a gas by drawing heat from the fridge cabinet. This cools the internal temperature of the refrigerator cabinet to 3–4°C. The gas refrigerant then returns to the compressor and the cycle begins again.

- **Thermostat:** the thermostat is connected to the compressor and maintains the constant internal temperature of 3–4°C within the refrigerator cabinet by turning on and off the motor when needed, e.g. if the door is left open.

? State the function of **each** of the following refrigerator parts:
• compressor   • condenser   • evaporator. (6) **HL**

Set out details of a study that you have undertaken on a refrigeration appliance. Refer to working principle. (12) **HL**

Guidelines for using a refrigerator

- Follow the manufacturer's instructions when installing and using the refrigerator. Do not position the refrigerator beside a heat source, e.g. a cooker, as the motor will have to run continuously to keep the temperature below 5°C, increasing electricity usage.
- Avoid opening the door unnecessarily and do not keep opened for prolonged periods of time, as this raises the internal temperature, speeding up bacterial growth. This also wastes electricity, as the motor has to work harder to keep the refrigerator cabinet cool.
- Avoid overfilling and allow space between foods to enable air to circulate and to keep foods at 3–4°C.
- To avoid raising the internal temperature, cool warm or cooked foods to room temperature (18°C) before placing them in the refrigerator.
- Store raw meat on the bottom shelf of the refrigerator to prevent drip-contamination onto foods below, which could cause food poisoning.
- Keep food, e.g. cooked ham and cheese, covered to prevent it from drying out. Covering also prevents the transfer of odours from strong-smelling foods to other foods, e.g. fish odours to milk.

Guidelines for caring for and cleaning a refrigerator

- Wipe any spills inside the refrigerator immediately, otherwise they will dry onto the surface, making them harder to remove.
- Clean regularly by:
  - removing all shelves or compartments and washing in hot, soapy water, then rinsing and drying
  - cleaning the interior with a solution of warm water and bicarbonate of soda
  - wiping the outer casing with a damp cloth and polishing with a dry cloth. Avoid harsh abrasives, e.g. steel wool, as they may scratch the metal or plastic coating.
- Clean the rubber door gasket to avoid food becoming lodged and preventing the refrigerator from closing properly.
- Clean the back regularly to remove any build-up of dust on the cooling fins, as it reduces their efficiency.
- When not in use, unplug and leave the door open to enable air to circulate and prevent the build-up of odours.

 Set out details of a study that you have undertaken on a refrigeration appliance. Refer to guidelines for use. (12) **HL**

Star ratings on refrigerators

Star ratings on refrigerators indicate the temperature within the icebox (freezer), which affects the length of time food can safely be stored.

The icebox in a standard refrigerator has a one- to three-star rating and is used to store already frozen food for the times stated.

★	-6°C	Stores food for one week
★ ★	-12°C	Stores food for one month
★ ★ ★	-18°C	Stores food for three months
★ ★ ★ ★	-18°C to -25°C	Stores food for one year

A fridge-freezer with a four-star rating can be used to both store frozen food and to freeze fresh food.

 Give a detailed account of the star rating system found on refrigeration appliances. (12) **HL**

HOUSEHOLD TECHNOLOGY AND APPLIANCES

A microwave oven

The microwave oven is a cooking appliance that generates microwave energy, a form of electromagnetic radiation, to heat and cook food.

Types of microwave ovens

- **Conventional microwave oven:** used for cooking, defrosting and reheating.
- **Microwave oven with grill:** works in the same way as a conventional microwave oven, but has a built-in grill to brown food.
- **Combination microwave oven:** combines a microwave, an oven and a grill to brown and cook food.

 Set out the results of a study you have carried out on microwave cookers. Refer to:
- the different types of microwave cookers available. (6) **OL**

Design and construction of a microwave oven

- **Door:** a door with a glass window allows food to be viewed during cooking, and a perforated metal backing redirects the microwaves back into the oven. The door has a safety seal to prevent the loss of microwaves during cooking. If the door is opened during the cooking time, the power automatically turns off.

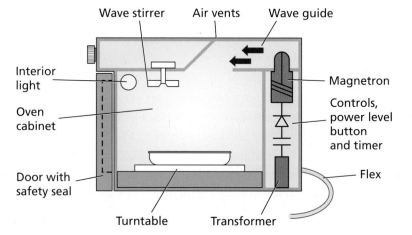

- **Oven cabinet:** an oven cabinet with an enamelled exterior, constructed from steel and lined with metal. Vents are located on the top and back of the cabinet to release steam during cooking.
- **Flex and three-pin plug:** a flex and a three-pin plug connect to the electricity supply.
- **On/off switch:** an on/off switch controls the electricity supply.
- **Interior light:** an interior light switches on when the microwave oven is on.
- **Transformer:** a transformer increases normal domestic voltage from 230 V to a much higher frequency needed to produce microwave (electromagnetic) energy.
- **Magnetron:** a magnetron converts electrical energy into microwave (electromagnetic) energy.
- **Wave guide:** a wave guide distributes guides the microwave (electromagnetic) energy from the magnetron into the oven cabinet.
- **Wave stirrer:** a wave stirrer rotates during cooking or reheating to ensure even distribution of microwaves throughout the oven cabinet.
- **Turntable:** a turntable made from heat-resistant glass rotates to ensure even cooking of the food.
- **Timer:** a timer sets the desired duration of cooking time in minutes or seconds.
- **Power level button:** a power level button changes the wattage, e.g. low (90 W) for defrosting.

 State the function of each of the following parts of the microwave oven.
- Transformer
- Magnetron (6) **HL**

Set out details of a study you have undertaken on microwave ovens. Refer to the following: construction. (8) **HL**

Modern design features

Temperature probe	• A temperature probe is connected to the inside wall of the microwave oven and inserted into the thickest part of the food before cooking. Once the food has reached the required internal temperature, e.g. 75–80°C for poultry, it will automatically turn off the microwave oven. • This eliminates the need to calculate the cooking times of various foods.
Auto weight defrost	• The microwave oven will automatically calculate the correct length of time and power setting needed to defrost foods. This will vary depending on the type of food and weight inputted.
Jet power/jet start button	• Cooks food at full power for a set amount of time, e.g. 1,000 W for 30 seconds. This is often used to heat food quickly and it eliminates the need to set the time or the power level.
Combination microwave ovens	• These modern microwave ovens combine the standard microwave oven with a convection oven and a built-in grill. A convection oven contains a heating element and a fan at the back that circulates hot air throughout. This ensures even cooking and produces a browning effect on baked goods. A grill browns the surface of food, creating a crisp, attractive finish. 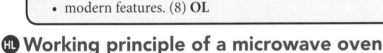

 Set out the results of a study you have carried out on microwave cookers. Refer to:
  • modern features. (8) **OL**

ⓗ Working principle of a microwave oven

- **Transformer:** when a microwave oven is plugged in and switched on, the transformer increases the normal domestic voltage from 230 V to a much higher frequency needed to produce microwave (electromagnetic) energy.
- **Magnetron and wave stirrer:** the magnetron converts the electrical energy into microwave energy, which enters the oven via the wave guide and is distributed evenly by the wave stirrer.
- **Reflected and transmitted:** the microwaves reflect off the metal-lined oven cabinet and transmit through the cooking container to the food inside.
- **Absorbed:** the microwaves penetrate the food two to five centimetres deep, and are absorbed by the particles of water, sugar and fat. The particles begin to vibrate, creating friction or heat. This cooks food by conduction.
- **Standing time:** the water, fat and sugar particles continue to vibrate after the power in the microwave has been switched off, so the food continues to cook during this time. For this reason, food should be left to stand for one to five minutes.

Reflected

Transmitted

Absorbed

 Set out details of a study you have undertaken on microwave ovens. Refer to the following:
  • working principle. (12) **HL**

Suitable and unsuitable foods/cooking processes

Suitable	Unsuitable
• Defrosting frozen foods • Reheating dishes • Heating liquids, e.g. milk • Melting foods, e.g. chocolate and butter • Cooking vegetables • Cooking thin cuts of meat or fish • Snack foods, e.g. popcorn • Porridge	• Large/dense foods, e.g. a leg of lamb, as the microwaves cannot penetrate deep enough to cook the food • Baked foods, e.g. pastry, as a soggy texture occurs • Sausages, as the skin can explode • Whole eggs, as the shell can explode

Suitable and unsuitable containers

Suitable	Unsuitable
• Glass • Pyrex • Heat-resistant plastic • Ceramic • Microwave-grade cling film • Porcelain or china • Paper plates/kitchen paper • Plastic with the microwave-safe symbol	• Aluminium plates • Foil containers • Metal-trimmed dishes • Very thick dishes, e.g. ceramic casserole dishes • Lightweight plastics, e.g. cling film

▲ Microwave-safe symbol

Did you know ?

Very thick ceramic dishes should not be used in the microwave as they absorb microwaves, rather than allowing them to pass through the food, causing the dish to become very hot and the food to barely be heated.

Guidelines for using a microwave oven

- Follow the manufacturer's instructions when installing and using the microwave oven.
- Consider the cooking time of food, as the larger or denser the food the longer the cooking time required. Larger quantities of food will also take longer to cook.
- Cover some foods, e.g. beans, with a suitable lid or microwave cling film to prevent soiling the sides or roof of the microwave cabinet. This also helps to keep food moist and speeds up cooking time.
- Stir liquids frequently during cooking to ensure an even distribution of heat throughout. If this is not completed hot spots may occur, whereby some parts get very hot and others remain cold.
- Pierce the skin of dense foods, e.g. potatoes, to allow steam to escape and to prevent them from exploding.
- Choose appropriate dishes, e.g. glass or Pyrex, in which to cook the food. Avoid foil containers or metal-trimmed dishes, as they will reflect the microwaves and damage the magnetron preventing the microwave from working.
- Allow food to stand for one to five minutes after cooking, as food will continue to cook during this time.

? Set out details of a study you have undertaken on microwave ovens. Refer to the following:
- **guidelines for use. (6) HL**

Did you know ?

Baby bottles should not be heated in a microwave as uneven pockets of scalding milk can form, causing serious mouth burns.

Guidelines for caring for and cleaning a microwave oven

- Wipe any spills immediately, otherwise they will harden onto the surface each time the microwave is used, making them more difficult to remove.
- Avoid moving the microwave, as this can damage the magnetron, preventing the microwave from working.
- Unplug before cleaning to prevent getting an electric shock.
- When cleaning the interior:
  - remove the turntable and wash in hot, soapy water, then rinse and dry
  - place a bowl of water in the cabinet and turn on for two minutes. This creates steam, which softens hardened splashes, making them easier to remove, clean the cabinet with hot, soapy water, then rinse and dry.
- When cleaning the exterior:
  - wipe with a warm, damp cloth
  - avoid harsh abrasives, e.g. steel wool, as these may scratch the metal or plastic coating. Polish with a dry cloth.

Advantages and disadvantages of a microwave oven

Advantages	Disadvantages
✓ Uses considerably less electricity compared to an oven, as it operates on a much lower wattage, reducing electricity bills	✗ Conventional microwaves do not brown food, making certain foods unsuitable for microwave cooking, e.g. pastry
✓ Cooks foods faster than an oven	✗ Unsuitable for cooking large amounts of food, as it takes too long to cook
✓ Retains the nutritional value and sensory characteristics of vegetables, e.g. texture, colour and flavour, as they cook quickly and in very little water	✗ Food reheated in the microwave tends to cool much faster than food from the oven
✓ Reheats food quickly, so it is ideal for people with busy lifestyles	✗ Food poisoning may occur if the appropriate standing time is not observed when heating food, e.g. ready meals. This is especially dangerous for children, the elderly or pregnant women.
✓ Useful for defrosting food, e.g. meat, if it was not taken out of the freezer in time for a meal	
✓ Simple to use, as individuals just have to input the power level and the cooking time required	

Did you know ?

When microwaves were first introduced in the 1980s people were advised to brush their microwaved chicken with marmite to create a brown colour.

> Evaluate the contribution of the microwave cooker to modern food preparation and cooking practices. (12) **HL**

Chapter 15:
Textiles

∞ TEXTILES
2.1.6

What you will learn:

- **Functions of clothing and household textiles**
- **Factors to consider when choosing textiles**
- **Basic scientific principles underlying the care of fabrics**

- **Care labels**
- **Types of fabric**
- **Safety considerations in the selection of household textiles**
- **Fire Safety (Domestic Furniture) Order 1988, 1995**

Textiles are fabrics. They are widely used for clothing purposes, e.g. trousers, and household purposes, e.g. curtains.

Functions of clothing

- **Safety:** clothes offer protection from injury, infection, fire and chemicals, e.g. firefighter uniforms, lab coats.
- **Weather protection:** clothes offer protection from rain, wind and sun, e.g. waterproof jackets, sun hats.
- **Modesty:** society expects people to wear a minimum amount of clothing for modesty. This varies from culture to culture, e.g. in Iran women must wear hijabs in public places.
- **Identification:** particular clothing or uniforms indicate a person's role or profession, e.g. nurses, Gardaí.
- **Hygiene:** in all areas of food production and preparation, protective clothing, e.g. chef's jackets and trousers, is important to prevent contamination and maintain high standards of hygiene.
- **Self-expression:** clothes allow people express their personality, e.g. colourful clothing can express confidence, and interests, e.g. a favourite football team.

▲ Garda uniform

Functions of household textiles

- **Decoration:** a variety of colours, patterns and textures are provided by **upholsteries**, soft furnishings and carpets, adding decoration. These enhance the aesthetics of the home by adding interest and design.
- **Privacy:** soft furnishings, e.g. blinds and curtains, prevent others seeing into homes, providing privacy and seclusion.
- **Comfort:** soft furnishings, e.g. cushions and blankets, provide comfort in the home. Upholstered furniture and carpets also provide this, and are often more comfortable than solid wood alternatives.

Lit Hit

Upholsteries are fabrics and stuffings used to cover and pad furniture.

- **Warmth:** soft furnishings, e.g. blankets and duvets, provide heat. This is particularly important during winter months. Carpets are warm underfoot compared to tiles or wood. Lined curtains also prevent draughts and keep in heat.
- **Protection:** fabric oven gloves can prevent burns in the kitchen. Non-slip mats can prevent slips in bathrooms.

> **?** Describe **four** functions of household textiles. (16) **OL**

Factors to consider when choosing textiles

- **Suitability for purpose:** the properties of fabric must be considered to ensure the fabric chosen is suitable for the purpose intended. Properties of textiles refers to the characteristics of the material, e.g. crease-resistant. For example, fabrics chosen for curtains should drape well and children's nightwear should be made from flame-retardant fabrics.

Desirable properties of textiles	
• Crease-resistant	• Moth-resistant
• Strong when wet (does not stretch out of shape)	• Elastic
• Easy to dye	• Colourfast (colour will not run into other fabrics or fade with frequent washing)
• Durable	

- **Cost:** the amount of money available determines the quality and type of fabric that can be purchased. For example, a silk scarf is generally more expensive than a cotton scarf. A wool carpet will be more expensive than a synthetic polyester one.

- **Aesthetic appeal/personal preferences:** appearance, drape, texture and durability all contribute to the aesthetic appeal of a fabric. What an individual finds aesthetically appealing is informed by personal likes and dislikes. For example, certain consumers will choose fabrics in bold colours in comparison to other consumers who prefer a neutral palette.

- **Care and cleaning:** consider fabrics that can be machine washed, as they are easier and cheaper to maintain than fabrics that must be dry-cleaned. Individuals should also consider stain-resistant fabrics for clothing and home furnishings, especially if they have young children. Careful consideration should also be given to the colour of fabrics chosen, as light colours often require more cleaning and are difficult to maintain.

- **Durability:** the level of durability required by a fabric depends on the amount of use the fabric will receive. For example, carpets for home entrances and stairs need to be more durable than carpets for bedrooms, as these areas endure more footfall.

> **?** Explain **each** of the following fabric properties:
> - Absorbent
> - Colourfast
> - Flammable (6) **OL**
>
> Comment on the importance of each of the following when selecting textiles for clothing:
> - suitability for purpose (use)
> - aesthetic appeal
> - personal choice
> - cost. (24) **OL**
>
> Identify **three** desirable performance properties in textiles. (6) **HL**

REMEMBER IT!

'**S**hould **C**onsumers **A**lways **C**onsider **D**urability?'

Suitability for purpose, **C**ost, **A**esthetic appeal/personal preferences, **C**are and cleaning, **D**urability.

Basic scientific principles underlying the care of fabrics

When cleaning fabrics, the following points need to be taken into consideration to ensure that cleaning is successful and no damage is caused to the fabric being washed.

Detergent

Choose a detergent suitable for the fabric type. Detergents are available in liquid and powder form. Detergents contain surfactants, conditioners, bleach, fluorescents (optical brighteners) and enzymes.

- **Surfactants:** surfactant molecules contain a hydrophilic (water-loving) head and a hydrophobic (water-hating) tail that reduce the surface tension of water. The hydrophilic head attaches to the surface of water, disrupting the bonding of water molecules and enabling them to thoroughly wet fabric. They also loosen dirt from fabric, as the hydrophobic tail attaches itself to the dirt or stain on fabric and keeps the dirt particles suspended in the water.

- **Conditioners:** soften fabric and eliminate static cling, as they coat the fabric fibres with a lubricating finish, preventing static electricity forming when fabrics rub together, e.g. a skirt rubbing on tights.

- **Bleach:** removes stains and brightens clothing, as it releases small amounts of hydrogen peroxide.

- **Fluorescents (optical brighteners):** enable fabrics to absorb ultraviolet light and re-emit it as blue light. This creates a visual whitening effect on fabrics, as it interacts with the yellow light emitted from fabric fibres that gives clothes a grey hue, and it tricks the eye into thinking the clothes are whiter than they are by producing a white light.

- **Enzymes:** break down protein-based stains, e.g. blood or milk, into smaller particles, making it easier for the detergent to clean fabrics.

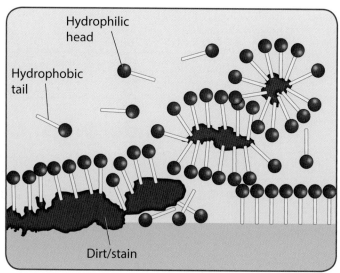

▲ Role of surfactants

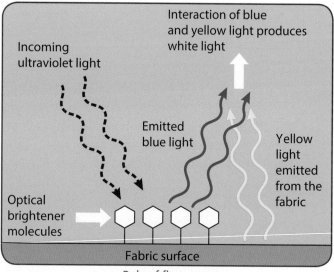

▲ Role of fluorescents

> **Did you know** ❓
>
> Always use a low temperature wash, e.g. 30°C, when using enzyme detergents, as enzymes are denatured at high temperatures.

Water

- The type of water used will affect the efficiency of washing fabrics. For example, hard water does not create a good lather of soap, due to the presence of calcium and magnesium ions, affecting how well clothes are washed.

- Some fabrics cannot be washed with water and must be dry-cleaned with a specific solvent.

Water temperature

- Consideration of the water temperature is important to prevent damage to the structure, colour, finish and shape of fabric when washing. For example, extreme heat (95°C) can cause wool to shrink, compared to cotton which may go undamaged.

Agitation

- Agitation is the movement necessary to dislodge dirt or stains from fabrics.
- The required amount of agitation depends on how dirty a fabric is or the type of fabric. Too much agitation can cause damage. For example, delicate fabrics, e.g. silk and wool, require a minimum action wash with a wool cycle spin, compared to cotton which can withstand a maximum action wash and normal spin.

Fabric softener/conditioner

Fabric softener/conditioner does not assist fabric cleaning. Instead it:

- reduces static electricity
- reduces wrinkling, making ironing easier
- enhances softness
- adds a pleasant smell.

Water removal

Water removal from fabrics can be completed by:

- drip, line or flat drying
- wringing: squeezing or twisting fabric after hand washing
- spin drying: completed at the end of a washing machine cycle by spinning clothes in the rotating drum
- tumble drying: dries washed clothes by spinning them in hot air inside a rotating drum.

▶ Fabric softener

 Explain the purpose of any **two** of the following fabric detergent components:
- Surfactants
- Enzymes
- Fluorescents (6) **HL**

Care labels

All fabrics and garments carry a permanently attached care label with written instructions and internationally recognised symbols that describe how the textile should be washed and cared for. Each care label contains instructions for washing, drying, dry cleaning, ironing and bleaching.

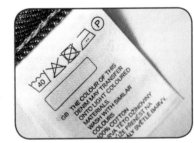

Washing symbols

Symbol	Meaning
95	Wash at 95°C (maximum washing action and normal spin)
40	Wash at 40°C (medium washing action and normal spin)
30	Wash at 30°C (minimum washing action and wool cycle spin)
	Hand wash
	Do not wash

Bar symbols	
	No bar: use a maximum action wash and normal spin
	One bar: use a medium action wash and short spin
	Broken bar: use a minimum action wash and a wool cycle spin

TEXTILES

Tumble drying symbols

Symbol	Meaning
▢	Suitable to tumble dry
⊠	Do not tumble dry

Drying symbols

Symbol	Meaning
▭	Dry flat
▢	Line dry
⫴	Drip dry

Ironing symbols

Symbol	Meaning
🗕	Cool iron
🗕	Warm iron
🗕	Hot iron
🗕	Do not iron

Dry cleaning symbols

Symbol	Meaning
(A)	Dry-cleanable with any solvent
(F)	Dry-cleanable in white spirits or solvent 113
(P)	Dry-cleanable in perchlorethylene, white spirit, solvent 113 or solvent 11
⊗	Do not dry-clean

Bleaching symbols

Symbol	Meaning
△CL	Can be treated with chlorine bleach
⊠	Do not bleach

? Explain **each** of the textile care symbols shown below. (6) **OL**

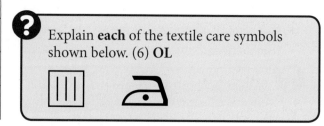

Types of fabric

Fabrics can be divided into two categories: natural fabrics and human-made fabrics.

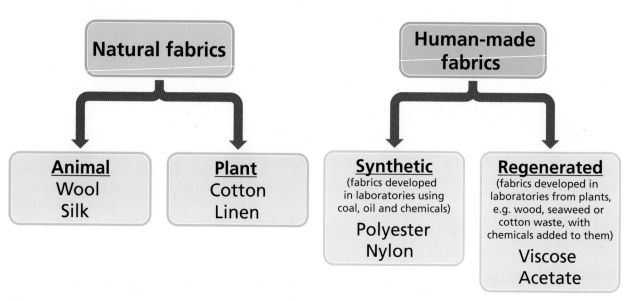

The care of these fabrics depends on their properties.

Natural fabrics

Wool (animal)

Wool fabric examples: tweed, velour, jersey

Properties	Guidelines for care	Uses
• Soft and comfortable • Absorbent: dries slowly • Weak when wet • Shrinks at high temperatures • **Scorches** easily • Pills and felts easily	• Hand or machine washable (30–40°C minimum action) • Gentle agitation (wool cycle spin) • Dry flat • Do not bleach • Cool iron • Do not tumble dry	• Clothes, e.g. jumpers, jackets • Home furnishings, e.g. throws, upholstery, curtains

Lit Hit Scorches means burns.

Cotton (plant)

Cotton fabric examples: denim, towelling, gingham

Properties	Guidelines for care	Uses
• Strong when wet • Easy to dye • Absorbent: dries slowly • Creases easily • Shrinks easily • Scorches easily	• Machine washable (95°C maximum action) • High agitation (normal spin) • Bleach can be used • Hot iron • Suitable for tumble drying	• Clothes, e.g. t-shirts, trousers • Home furnishings, e.g. curtains, cushion covers, bed linen • Household items, e.g. towels, oven gloves

Human-made fabrics (synthetic)

Polyester (synthetic)

Properties	Guidelines for care	Uses
• Good drape • Non absorbent: quick to dry • Strong when wet • Easy to wash • Crease-resistant • Prone to static build-up	• Machine washable (40°C medium action) • Gentle agitation (short spin) • Do not bleach • Cool iron • Not suitable for tumble drying	• Clothes, e.g. hoodies, jackets • Home furnishings, e.g. bed linen, cushion covers

Viscose (regenerated)

Properties	Guidelines for care	Uses
• Good drape • Absorbent: dries slowly • Weak when wet • Creases easily • Shrinks at high temperatures • Prone to static build-up	• Machine washable (40°C medium action) • Gentle agitation (short spin) should be used • Do not bleach • Cool iron • Not suitable for tumble drying	• Clothes, e.g. dresses, suit jackets • Home furnishings, e.g. curtains, rugs

Name **one** natural fibre and **one** synthetic fibre. Explain why natural fibres are commonly used in household textiles. (6) **OL**

TEXTILES

Safety considerations in the selection of household textiles

Safety considerations must be taken into account when selecting household textiles. Many fabrics catch fire and burn easily, which can lead to fatal consequences. Some fabrics and furnishing fillings emit toxic fumes when on fire. In order to reduce the risk when selecting fibres, consumers should:

- opt for fabrics that have been treated with a flame-retardant finish
- ensure all foam fillings are Combustion Modified High Resilience (CMHR)
- choose low-risk flammability fabrics instead of high-risk flammability fabrics.

> **Did you know**
> Chip pans, lit cigarettes, children playing with matches and electrical faults are the main causes of fatal house fires in Ireland.

Low-risk and high-risk flammability fabrics

Low-risk flammability fabrics	High-risk flammability fabrics
• Wool (smoulders and may self-extinguish) • Polyester (ignites slowly and shrinks away from flames)	• Cotton and linen (burn rapidly) • Silk (burns rapidly)

Flame-retardant finishes

Flame-retardant finishes are applied to fabrics to reduce their risk of flammability.

These finishes cause fabrics that have caught fire to self-extinguish when removed from flames (note: they will continue to burn in the flames). Examples of textiles that have flame-retardant finishes applied include children's nightwear and protective work clothing, e.g. firefighter uniforms, military uniforms.

There are two main types of flame-retardant finishes:

- **coated flame-retardant finishes:** a cheap method, as it is only applied on the outside of fabrics and is not permanent
- **inherent flame-retardant finishes:** an expensive method, as it is applied to fabric fibres prior to being woven or knitted into fabric, making it permanent.

PROBAN

PROBAN is an example of a flame-retardant finish.

- PROBAN is applied to fabrics to make them flame-retardant.
- Fabrics are coated with an invisible layer of PROBAN (phosphorus and nitrogen compound) which forms an insoluble polymer trapped within the fabric fibres. This gives fabrics a flame-retardant finish.
- When exposed to fire, the flame retardant in the fabric fibres breaks down and forms an insulating **char** around the fabric, protecting the wearer.

> **Lit Hit**
> Char is to partially burn and blacken a material or surface.

Advantages

✓ PROBAN reduces the risk of fabric igniting.
✓ The fabric self-extinguishes when removed from the flame.

? Name and explain the effect of **one** fire-retardant finish. (10) **OL**

Identify **two** safety considerations that should be considered when selecting textiles for household purposes. (4) **HL**

Name a fire/flame retardant finish used on household furnishings. Outline **two** effects of this finish. (6) **HL**

🅗 Fire Safety (Domestic Furniture) Order 1988, 1995

The purpose of this order is to protect consumers by reducing the risk of accidents related to household fire. The order applies to items including beds, cots, pushchairs, cushions and upholstered furniture such as sofas and pillows. It states that:

- fabrics used must pass fire safety tests, e.g. match tests, cigarette tests
- any foam fillings used must be CMHR foam
- permanent safety labels on all relevant items must be securely attached, clearly legible and durable
- a square or triangle display/swing label must be attached to all relevant items.

Permanent labels	Display/swing labels
These labels are stitched onto fabric and should contain: • the warning message 'Carelessness causes fire' • the name and address of the manufacturer or importer • the manufacturer's identification and batch number • a description of the filling and cover material used • details of the fire-resistant **interliner**, if used	These labels hang from fabric and are removable

Lit Hit
Interliner is a material placed between the fabric on the outside of a piece of furniture and the filling material.

Square label
- Has a green border
- Indicates that the filling and covering fabric have passed a match and cigarette test

RESISTANT

CARELESSNESS CAUSES FIRE

BATCH/.I.D. No.

To comply with the Furniture and Furnishings (Fire) (Safety) Regulations 1988.

This item includes a Schedule 3 interliner.

All foams, fillings and composites have been tested to ensure compliance with the relevant ignitability test.

Covers and fillings are cigarette-resistant.

Covers are not match-resistant.

Further details are available from your retailer.

Filling material(s) and covering fabric(s) meet the requirements for resistance to cigarette and match ignition in the 1988 safety regulations

CARELESSNESS CAUSES FIRE

Triangle label
- Has a red border
- Indicates that the covering fabric has not passed a match test
- Shows that a fire-resistant inner liner is present

COVER FABRIC NOT MATCH RESISTANT

Purpose of fire safety labelling

The purpose of fire safety labelling is to:
- inform the consumer about what fabric/filling was used in the production of an item
- warn the consumer about possible dangers
- provide traceability information, so that the item can be traced back to the manufacturer.

What information does the following label convey to the consumer? (4) **HL**

Identify **two** requirements of the *Fire Safety (Domestic Furniture) Order (1988) (1995)*. (6) **HL**

RESISTANT

TEXTILES

Chapter 16:
Consumer studies

2.2.1– 2.2.3   CONSUMER STUDIES

What you will learn:

- **Factors that influence consumer choices**
- **Classification of retail outlets**
- **Retail psychology**
- **Shopping patterns**
- **Types of consumer research**
- **Benefits of consumer research for the retailer and the consumer**
- **Sources of consumer information**
- **Consumer rights**
- **Consumer responsibilities**
- **Consumer protection legislation**
- **Statutory and voluntary consumer protection agencies**
- **Procedure for making a consumer complaint**
- **Small Claims procedure**
- **Quality, safety and hazard symbols**

CONSUMER CHOICE

A consumer is a person who purchases goods and services for their own use.

Factors that influence consumer choices

- **Income:** disposable income available influences consumer choices. When disposable income is limited, consumers must ensure their needs, e.g. food and bills, are met before wants or luxuries are purchased. Discount stores and own-brand goods enable consumers to get better value for money if finances are limited.

- **Personal preferences:** personal likes and dislikes influence consumer choices. If a product appeals to a consumer's tastes immediately, they will be more inclined to purchase.

- **Advertising:** the purpose of advertising is to introduce new products or services to the market, provide information and increase sales. Advertising influences consumer choices by using techniques including wit and humour, catchy songs, celebrity endorsements and **weasel words**.

Lit Hit

Weasel words are words used to evade or retreat from a direct statement, e.g. saying shampoo 'helps control' dandruff, rather than stopping it.

- **Marketing:** the purpose of marketing is to promote and sell goods or services to increase immediate sales. Marketing influences consumer choices by using techniques including sales promotions, in-store tasting sessions and loyalty cards, e.g. Tesco Clubcard. This often leads to impulse buying.

Did you know ?

Studies show that when consumers shop they make choices in as little as 20 seconds.

- **Packaging:** attractive packaging on products will influence choices consumers make. A distinctive colour palette and graphics, e.g. the iconic K on Special K, clear and simple text, eco-friendly packaging and the provision of detailed nutritional information all influence consumer choices.

- **Values:** strong personal beliefs on the environment and animal rights will influence consumer choice. For example, consumers concerned with animal welfare may decide to purchase products not tested on animals, and consumers with strong environmental beliefs may decide to purchase eco-friendly cleaning products.

- **Other people:** family and friends influence consumers' choices, as consumers will be more inclined to purchase products or services advocated by people they know. Salespeople can also influence choices by giving details about the goods or services, as well as their personal opinion. However, many sales personnel receive commission on sales, so they may be motivated by money rather than consumer interest.

REMEMBER IT!

'**I** **P**urchase **A**ll **M**y **P**recious **V**aluables **O**nline.'

Income, **P**ersonal preferences, **A**dvertising, **M**arketing, **P**ackaging, **V**alues, **O**ther people.

?

Explain how any **two** of the following affect consumers' decision-making when shopping:

- money available
- advertising
- discount offers. (20) **OL**

Discuss three factors that affect consumers' decision-making when selecting goods and services (12) **HL**

ⒽⓁ Classification of retail outlets

Type	Description
Supermarkets (e.g. Tesco, Lidl, Aldi) 	• Large, open-plan stores, making them easy for customers to move around • Offer a wide array of products, including own-brand products, e.g. food, household items and clothing • Offer self-service, allowing customers to shop independently • Some offer internet shopping with home delivery • Offer cheaper prices, as supermarkets can bulk-buy products, due to a large turnover of stock • Often located on the outskirts of cities and towns, which can make them inaccessible for individuals without transport
Hypermarkets (e.g. Carrefour (France), Walmart (United States and Canada) 	• Similar to supermarkets, but much larger in size • Offer a wide array of products, e.g. food, appliances and cleaning products, at much cheaper prices than supermarkets • Offer self-service, allowing customers to shop independently • Often have a café or restaurant • The vast size and wide array of stock can encourage impulse buying • Often located on the outskirts of cities and towns, which can make them inaccessible for individuals without transport
Independent shops (e.g. local bookstores, butcher shops) 	• Tend to be small, family-run businesses • Often specialise in one range of goods, e.g. jewellery or meat • Many offer a counter service, which is deemed a more personal service • Often have a limited stock, as turnover is less than larger stores • Often more expensive than supermarkets because they cannot bulk-buy products to avail of discounts, as they do not have as big a turnover. This means they must charge more to make a profit. • Generally located in cities and towns
Department stores (e.g. Brown Thomas, Arnotts) 	• Large, open-plan stores • Offer a wide array of products, e.g. cosmetics, clothes and electrical items • Offer self-service, allowing customers to shop independently, and a personal service, e.g. by providing personal shoppers • Offer competitive prices and good value for money • Tend to be located in large cities and towns, which can make them inaccessible for individuals who live in rural areas

Type	Description
Multiple chain stores (e.g. Penneys, Lifestyle Sports) 	• Under the management of one company but have numerous branches nationwide • All shops tend to have a similar layout, uniform style and sell the same products • Offer self-service, allowing customers to shop independently • Offer competitive prices and good value for money • Tend to be located in large cities and towns, which can make them inaccessible for individuals who live in rural areas
Discount stores (e.g. Dealz, Euro Giant) 	• Offer goods at a greater discount as they have a high turnover and focus on low-cost items • Offer a wide array of products in store, e.g. cosmetics, food, cleaning products and games • Offer self-service, allowing customers to shop independently • Impulse buying is encouraged due to most products costing €2 or less • Tend to be located in large cities and towns, which can make them inaccessible for individuals who live in rural areas

 Name **two** types of retail outlets where household appliances can be purchased. State **one** advantage and **one** disadvantage of each outlet. (12) **HL**

Other retail outlets

Other retail outlets include:

- auctions
- street markets
- party selling, e.g. Tupperware
- mail-order shopping: involves choosing goods from a catalogue and ordering them by post, phone or through an agent, e.g. Avon
- online shopping: involves purchasing goods via the internet, e.g. Amazon, eBay.

Advantages and disadvantages of online shopping

Advantages	Disadvantages
✓ Goods are delivered by post, so consumers do not have to leave their homes and visit shops ✓ A variety of websites can be searched easily by the click of a button ✓ May be cheaper, as consumers can shop around on various websites ✓ Not restricted by opening hours, so goods can be purchased at any time	✗ Risk of credit card fraud if card details are obtained by other sources ✗ Risk of impulse buying and overspending due to ease of use ✗ The product purchased may not be as expected, e.g. incorrect size, poor-quality fabric ✗ Goods can take three to four weeks to be delivered ✗ Postage charged can increase the overall price of the purchased goods

 Discuss **two** advantages and **two** disadvantages of online shopping when purchasing food and household products. (20) **OL**

Retail psychology

Retail psychology is the study of consumers and the factors that influence how consumers spend. Advertising and marketing techniques use retail psychology to influence consumer spending. Some merchandising techniques are subliminal, while others are more obvious.

- **Shop layout:** shops are usually large, bright and warm, so consumers will remain in the store for longer. Retailers often change the position of products on shelves so consumers have to search for items and may purchase other products while looking.

- **Background music:** soft music is played to relax consumers into wanting to browse for longer. Fast-paced music is played at busier shopping times to encourage consumers to shop faster, to avoid having large crowds in store.

- **In-store smells:** fresh smells, e.g. baked bread, stimulate consumers' taste buds, encouraging them to buy more.

- **Product placement:** essential (destination) goods, e.g. bread and milk, are placed at the back of the store, so consumers are forced to pass by other products, making them tempted to purchase more items. Sweets and toiletries are often placed beside checkouts to encourage impulse buying. Products are placed by association, e.g. wafers next to ice cream, so consumers buying one product may see the other product and buy it also. Special offers are often placed at the end of aisles, encouraging impulse buying. Fresh fruit and vegetables are placed at the front of store, as they are colourful and eye-catching, encouraging sales.

- **Shelf position:** products with the highest profit margin are often placed at eye level on shelves in order to increase sales, e.g. Avonmore milk is placed at eye level while own-brand milk is placed lower down.

- **Pricing:** goods are often priced to make consumers feel they are getting better value for money, e.g. €1.49 instead of €1.50.

- **Food samples:** consumers are more inclined to purchase food products if samples are available for them to taste in store. Demonstrations often include money-off vouchers, making the products even more attractive.

- **Loyalty schemes:** if consumers are part of a shop's loyalty scheme and earn points each time they purchase in a store it may lessen the chance of consumers shopping around, as points they build up can be exchanged for money-off coupons. Examples include Tesco Clubcard and Boots Advantage Card.

? Explain why loyalty schemes, used by retail outlets, encourage consumers to purchase goods. Name **one** shopper loyalty scheme. (6) **OL**

Name **two** merchandising (marketing) techniques. How does merchandising encourage consumer spending? (6) **OL**

Describe **four** in-store techniques that supermarkets use to encourage consumer spending. (20) **HL**

Shopping patterns

Major changes in the retail sector have altered consumer shopping patterns, including how we shop, when we shop and why we make the choices we do.

- **Online shopping:** online shopping enables consumers to purchase goods at any time and have them delivered to homes, reducing the need to go to shops. This service has increased in popularity in recent times due to busier lifestyles.

- **Consumer expectations:** nowadays consumers have very high expectations when shopping. For example, they demand:
  - good-quality products at reasonable prices. This has led to the increased popularity of discount supermarkets, e.g. Aldi and Lidl
  - friendly, helpful and knowledgeable staff
  - access to multicultural foods, e.g. spices, curry pastes and pasta
  - high standards of hygiene in stores
  - well-maintained and well-stocked shelves and rails.

- **Time available:** due to busier lifestyles, time available for shopping can be limited. Shopping is often completed once a week or fortnight. To facilitate families' busier lifestyles, many shops now offer late and early opening times, and some offer 24-hour service.

- **Environmental awareness:** consumers are becoming more environmentally aware when shopping, leading to demand for:
  - A-rated energy efficient appliances
  - products with less packaging or made from recycled packaging
  - eco-friendly products, e.g. LED bulbs.

- **Tradition:** many consumers continue to shop in independent food and service suppliers where they have built up a past relationship, e.g. a local vegetable shop. This is can be due to a sense of loyalty, or because the suppliers are perceived to provide a better-quality product and personal service. The traditional method of payment with cash is generally being replaced by debit or credit card payments.

REMEMBER IT!

'OCTET!'

Online shopping, **C**onsumer expectations, **T**ime available, **E**nvironmental awareness, **T**radition.

CONSUMER STUDIES

HL CONSUMER RESEARCH

Consumer research involves the collection, processing and analysis of information from consumers about their needs and wants. This provides companies, manufacturers and retailers with a greater understanding of what consumers will buy. Marketing techniques and advertising rely heavily on consumer research.

Types of consumer research

Consumer research can be carried out through field research and desk research.

Type of research	Field research	Desk research
Description	• Involves collecting data and information that has not been collected previously • This can be obtained by face-to-face interviews, questionnaires/surveys or observation	• Involves collecting and analysing data and information that already exists • This can be obtained from a variety of informative sources, including the internet, newspapers and company reports

Purpose	• To find out information such as:
	  o how often customers purchase a company's product or service
	  o how likely consumers are to purchase new products or services
	  o what market price consumers expect to pay for a product or service
		• To find out information such as:
		  o competitors
		  o market trends

Advantages	✓ Information obtained is specific and can be as detailed as necessary ✓ Information is current ✓ Information is accurate	✓ Information can be collected quickly ✓ An inexpensive form of research
Disadvantages	✗ Information can be time-consuming to collect ✗ Can be expensive to carry out, as numerous people are needed, e.g. to distribute questionnaires and calculate findings	✗ Information available can be quite general and lacking in detail: it may not be specific to the researchers' needs ✗ Information may not be current

 In relation to consumer research, differentiate between each of the following two methods:
- desk research
- field research. (6) **HL**

Benefits of consumer research for the retailer and the consumer

Benefits for the retailer	Benefits for the consumer
• Provides information about consumers, e.g. expectations, which is used in the development of a product or service to ensure that it sells • Reduces the financial risk of launching a new product or service, as retailers can identify if it is needed on the market. This avoids investing in a product or service that will not sell. • Overproduction is avoided, as retailers can determine the market size for their products • Helps determine a recommended retail price (RRP) for products and services that is acceptable to consumers. • Consumer profiles are established for products and services in terms of age, gender and lifestyle, so retailers know who their target market should be.	• Needs and wants are identified so that retailers can make specific products or services to meet consumer requirements, e.g. milk fortified with omega-3 • If consumer research reveals a competitor's brand is more popular, it may influence retailers to produce a better product or drop their prices. This is beneficial for consumers, as quality is improved and they get better value for money.

> **?** Name three research methods used to gather information on the consumer. Explain how consumer research benefits (i) the retailer and (ii) the consumer. (19) **HL**

Sources of consumer information

- **Magazines, newspapers, television and radio programmes and websites:** provide detailed information about products or services, e.g. price, style and features. They can also offer comparison of products to enable consumers to make more informed choices.
- **Salespeople:** offer in-depth knowledge about products or services available. However, opinions can be **biased** due to commission rates available for sales.
- **Showrooms and exhibitions:** e.g. car showrooms, Ideal Homes exhibitions, offer in-depth knowledge about products on display.
- **Advertising:** provides limited information about products or services. Information tends to be biased in favour of the product or service advertised.
- **Manufacturer leaflets:** often supply detailed information about products, e.g. instructions for use.
- **Other people/word of mouth:** provide unbiased, truthful information based on actual experiences of products or services.

Lit Hit
Biased means unfairly for or against someone or something.

> **?** Identify **two** sources of reliable consumer information. (8) **OL**

CONSUMER STUDIES

CONSUMER RIGHTS AND RESPONSIBILITIES

All consumers should be aware of their rights and responsibilities when choosing goods and services to ensure they are getting value for money and good-quality products or services.

Consumer rights

The right to truthful information

- Consumers have the right to honest and accurate information about goods and services, e.g. price. This enables them to compare goods and services and make wise choices for their individual or family's needs. This right is protected by the Consumer Protection Act 2007 (previously the Consumer Information Act 1978), as it prevents misleading claims being made about goods or services.

The right to choice

- Consumers have the right to choose from a wide range of goods and services. When there is more than one product or service, consumers can choose the one that suits their needs best. This encourages competition between companies, causing them to:
  - o become aware of consumers' needs
  - o enhance the quality of their goods or services
  - o keep prices down.

The right to value for money

- Consumers are entitled to expect value for money. All products or services offered should be of high quality, regardless of price. This is protected by the Sale of Goods and Supply of Services Act 1980. It is important for consumers to remember that value for money does not always mean the cheapest product, e.g. a cheap appliance could end up having high running costs due to not being energy efficient.
- Consumers should receive a high-quality product or service, regardless of whether it is full price or on sale.

The right to safety

- Consumers have the right to purchase goods or services that are guaranteed safe and will not harm their health or put their lives at risk. Goods undergo strict safety and quality testing to ensure that they are of a high standard before being retailed, e.g. cars undergo crash tests to ensure design standards will protect occupants.
- Some goods also carry the following to protect the consumer from harm:
  - o instructions for use, e.g. wear gloves
  - o safety warnings, e.g. poisonous: do not swallow
  - o hazard symbols, e.g. flammable.

▲ Flammable hazard symbol

The right to redress

- Should a consumer find that a good they have purchased is faulty or a service is not as expected, they have the right to complain. If the complaint is legitimate, the consumer is entitled to compensation in the form of a refund, repair or replacement. This is protected by the Sale of Goods and Supply of Services Act 1980.
- A number of factors influence the form of compensation the consumer is entitled to, e.g. how much time has passed since the good was purchased or when the service was availed of.

? Name and explain **four** consumer rights. (16) **OL**

REMEMBER IT!
'Irish **C**onsumers **V**igilantly **S**tudy **R**ights.'
Information, **C**hoice, **V**alue, **S**afety, **R**edress.

Consumer responsibilities

To be well informed

- Consumers should become educated about their rights and consumer law in order to make wise choices when shopping. They should also shop around and gather as much information as possible about products or services, e.g. from the internet or leaflets, before making a purchase.

To be aware of quality and value

- Consumers should be aware of the balance between price and quality when buying goods and services to ensure they receive value for money. Expensive goods or services are not necessarily better quality.

To follow instructions

- After purchasing a product, consumers should read and follow any instructions so they use a product correctly and ensure their own safety. If consumers fail to follow instructions, they may not be entitled to compensation if a problem arises. Safety symbols and hazard symbols should be regarded.

To complain

- Consumers should complain if a product or service fails to meet expectations or is faulty. Complaining will ensure that companies provide a higher-standard product or service in the future.

To avoid waste

- Consumers should take responsibility for preserving the environment by:
  o avoiding products with excess packaging
  o purchasing energy-saving products, e.g. A-rated appliances
  o disposing of products in an environmentally friendly manner, e.g. recycling.

> **Did you know** ❓
>
> An A-rated appliance will use about 55% of the electricity used by a similar appliance with a D rating.

REMEMBER IT!

'**I** **A**lways **F**ollow **C**onsumer **A**dvice.'
Informed, **A**ware of quality and value, **F**ollow instructions, **C**omplain, **A**void waste.

❓ List three consumer responsibilities. (9) **OL**

Give details of **four** consumer responsibilities. (16) **HL**

CONSUMER PROTECTION

Consumer protection legislation

Consumer rights are protected by legislation. Such legislation is necessary to safeguard the consumer from exploitation by retailers and manufacturers by prohibiting retailers and manufacturers from:

- selling products of non-merchantable quality
- providing misleading information
- refusing redress for valid complaints
- providing substandard services.

Consumer protection legislation includes:

- Sale of Goods and Supply of Services Act 1980
- Electronic Commerce Act 2000
- Consumer Protection Act 2007
- Consumer Credit Act 1995.

 Name **one** law that protects the rights of the consumer. (2) **OL**

Sale of Goods and Supply of Services Act 1980

This act protects consumers when they purchase goods, as a legal contract is established between the consumer and the retailer. The act covers goods, services, illegal signs and guarantees.

Goods

The Sale of Goods and Supply of Services Act states that any goods consumers buy from a retailer must:

- **be of merchantable quality:** e.g. fit for sale and in perfect condition
- **be fit for purpose:** e.g. a kettle must boil water
- **be as described:** correspond with the written description on the label or to the salesperson's description, e.g. made with 100% wool
- **correspond to sample:** e.g. paint or flooring received should be direct replicas of the samples displayed to consumers in store.

Services

The Sale of Goods and Supply of Services Act states that all services should:

- **be supplied by a person with necessary skill:** e.g. only a qualified hairdresser should cut hair
- **be supplied with care and diligence**
- **be completed with good-quality materials:** e.g. an attic conversion should be constructed with quality timber.

Under the Sale of Goods and Supply of Services Act, the consumer is entitled to redress if the goods are faulty or a poor service was provided. This redress takes the form of a:

- refund
- repair
- replacement
- repeat service (free of charge).

The amount of compensation received depends on:

- the duration of time between purchasing the good or availing of the service and making a claim, e.g. a consumer cannot return a faulty appliance after 15 years
- how serious the fault is, e.g. if a laptop keyboard loses a letter a consumer cannot expect a new laptop
- how quickly the product was returned once the fault was noticed, e.g. whether or not the consumer continued to use the goods after they noticed a fault.

Illegal signs

- Under the Sale of Goods and Supply of Services Act consumers can ignore illegal signs such as 'No refunds' or 'No exchanges' if they have a valid complaint, e.g. a fault with a product. They also do not have to accept a credit note if their complaint is legitimate.
- If consumers were told at the time of purchase that the goods they were purchasing were damaged, marked as seconds or faulty, then there is no redress. This also

applies if consumers change their mind about a product or if they misuse it, e.g. using a camera under water if it is not waterproof.

Guarantees

- A guarantee is a written contract between the manufacturer and the consumer that states that if a fault arises with the product purchased within a certain period of time the manufacturer will repair or replace the product free of charge.
- A guarantee can vary in time limit. Generally, the longer the guarantee the higher the quality of the product. Some guarantees have conditions, e.g. a manufacturer may provide certain parts to fix an appliance but they may not cover the cost of the labour.
- A guarantee does not affect consumers' rights, and manufacturers are not legally obliged to offer a guarantee.
- Under the Sale of Goods and Supply of Services Act 1980, all guarantees must be clearly legible and include:
  o a description of the product
  o the name and address of the company or manufacturer offering the guarantee
  o the duration of the guarantee
  o the procedure to follow in order to make a claim
  o what the manufacturer or company will do if a claim is made
  o charges the consumer may incur, e.g. postage for parts.

? Complete the following sentence:

A guarantee is a contract between the _____ and the _____. (2) **OL**

State how the Sale of Goods and Supply of Services Act (1980) protects the interests of consumers. (12) **OL**

Outline the role of the Sale of Goods and Supply of Services Act (1980) in protecting the consumer should the product prove faulty. (8) **HL**

Consumer Protection Act 2007 (previously known as the Consumer Information Act 1978)

This act protects the consumer against false or misleading claims about:

- **goods:** e.g. a jumper cannot be labelled 'made in Ireland' if it is manufactured outside the country
- **services:** e.g. a supermarket cannot advertise a 24-hour service if they close for certain hours in the day
- **price, previous price and RRP:** e.g. a dress cannot be marked 50% off if the sale price is not half the original price on the item for 28 consecutive days in the previous three months.

? Outline the protection provided by the Consumer Information Act 1978 (*now known as the Consumer Protection Act 2007*). Give **two** points. (6) **HL**

Electronic Commerce Act 2000

This act provides the same legal recognition of electronic contracts, signatures, documents and evidence in court as written documents. This provides additional safety to consumers when purchasing online.

Consumer Credit Act 1995

For information on the Consumer Credit Act 1995 see page 287.

Statutory consumer protection agencies

Competition and Consumer Protection Commission (CCPC)

The CCPC is responsible for enforcing consumer protection and competition law in Ireland. It does this by:

Coimisiún um Iomaíocht agus Cosaint Tomhaltóirí | Competition and Consumer Protection Commission

- enforcing a wide range of consumer protection legislation and investigating breaches
- enforcing Irish and European competition law in Ireland and investigating breaches
- informing consumers about their rights and personal finance through a consumer helpline, public awareness campaigns and their website
- advising the government, its agencies and public bodies on how proposed legislation or regulations could affect markets in terms of competition and/or consumer welfare.

Office of the Ombudsman

The Office of the Ombudsman investigates complaints made by members of the public against public bodies in Ireland, e.g. government departments, local authorities, the Health Service Executive (HSE), publicly funded third-level education bodies and private nursing homes. An attempt should be made by the consumer to resolve the issue with the public body before involving the Office of the Ombudsman.

**Oifig an Ombudsman
Office of the Ombudsman**

Complaints process

- A consumer lodges a complaint against a public body with the Office of the Ombudsman, which then examines the case and determines if the complaint requires an investigation.
- If an investigation is deemed necessary, the ombudsman will investigate the complaint and inform the consumer of its decision. The ombudsman only has the power to make a recommendation and its findings are not legally binding. It cannot force the public body to accept or act upon the decision. Most public bodies will comply with the ombudsman's recommendation in order to avoid negative publicity.
- If the public body fails to act upon the decision of the ombudsman, the ombudsman may make a report to the Houses of the Oireachtas.

Citizens Information Board

The Citizens Information Board provides information and advice to consumers on a broad range of areas, including consumer rights, social welfare payments, family law and housing. This information is provided on its website, through its phone services or in citizen information centres throughout the country. The Money Advice and Budgeting Service (MABS) is supported and funded by the Citizens Information Board.

Citizens **Information** Board
information · advice · advocacy

National Standards Authority of Ireland (NSAI)

The NSAI works to set and enforce quality and safety standards for goods and services in Irish industry. It runs the ISO 9000 scheme, an internationally recognised award given to companies that achieve high-quality standards with their goods and services.

European Consumer Centre (ECC) Ireland

The ECC provides information and advice on consumer rights when buying goods or services in other European Union countries (including online purchases). It also provides assistance with settling disputes arising between consumers and traders based in different European Union countries.

Voluntary consumer protection agencies

Consumers' Association of Ireland (CAI)

The CAI aims to protect, promote and represent the interests of Irish consumers. Its roles include:

- publishing *Consumer Choice* magazine, which provides consumers with impartial information about their consumer rights and how to get value for money when buying goods and services
- representing consumers on various bodies and international organisations
- lobbying the government for improvements in consumer legislation
- carrying out research to produce reports with objective information for consumers on products and services.

Advertising Standards Authority of Ireland (ASAI)

The ASAI was established and financed by the advertising industry to promote the highest standards in advertising and marketing.

It aims to ensure that all commercial advertisements are:

- legal, decent, honest and truthful
- prepared with a sense of responsibility to the consumer, e.g. do not contain offensive content.

It also investigates complaints made by the public regarding advertisements, and has the authority to instruct the advertisement be modified or removed.

Name **one** statutory body and **one** voluntary body/agency concerned with consumer protection. (6) **OL**

Outline **two** functions of the Citizens Information Board. (6) **HL**

Outline the role of each of the consumer organisations named below.
- Consumer Association of Ireland (CAI)
- Advertising Standards Authority of Ireland (ASAI). (6) **HL**

Name and outline the role of any **one** voluntary agency concerned with consumer protection. (11) **HL**

Procedure for making a consumer complaint

- If a consumer believes a good is faulty, they should return it as soon as possible after the fault is noticed. In the case of a service, a complaint must be made to the supplier immediately.
- Bring relevant documents, e.g. proof of purchase, for the service or good purchased. This can be in the form of a receipt, cheque stub or bank statement.
- Complain initially at the least formal level, by speaking to the retailer or service provider. If the retailer or service provider is co-operative they should offer realistic compensation.
- If the retailer or service provider is unco-operative, the complaint should be put in writing to the retailer or service provider's head office. The letter or email should include:
  - a description of the goods or service
  - the location and date of purchase
  - the action taken to date
  - copies of proof of purchase or guarantee
  - compensation requested.
- If the outcome is still unsatisfactory and the retailer or service provider still fails to accept responsibility for the faulty goods or service, the consumer may seek advice and assistance from consumer bodies, e.g. the Consumers' Association of Ireland. They also can take legal action through the Small Claims Court.

> **?** Outline the procedure that should be followed when making a complaint when a problem occurs with a product or service. (12) **OL**

Small Claims procedure

The Small Claims procedure aims to provide an inexpensive, fast and easy way for consumers to resolve disputes with retailers or service providers without the need to employ a solicitor. It is part of the District Court Office. Claims of up to €2,000 may be resolved by the Small Claims service.

Small Claims procedure

- The **claimant** fills in an application form and pays €25 to have it processed.
- The complaint is registered and a Notice of Claim is sent to the **respondent**.
- The respondent can admit, dispute or ignore the claim, or they can counterclaim. They have 15 days to reply.
- If the claim is disputed with 15 days the Small Claims registrar will try to resolve the issue. If the issue cannot be resolved it may be referred for a court hearing.
- If the respondent does not reply or challenge the claim within 15 days, it is taken that they admitted the claim, and the claim is settled in favour of the claimant. The respondent has 28 days to comply with the judgement.

Lit Hit
A claimant is a person making a claim.

Lit Hit
A respondent is a person or business against whom a claim is filed.

Benefits of the Small Claims procedure

The procedure is:
- inexpensive
- quick
- easy: no solicitor is required.

> **?** State the function of the Small Claims procedure. (4) **OL**
>
> State **two** benefits of the Small Claims procedure. (6) **HL**

Quality symbols

Q mark		Indicates products are produced to the highest standards of quality and excellence. It is awarded by the Excellence Ireland Quality Association (EIQA).
BSI kitemark		Indicates goods are of a high quality standard in terms of performance and safety. It is awarded by the British Standards Institution (BSI).
ISO standards symbol		Indicates goods and services are of excellent quality. It is awarded by the National Standards Authority of Ireland (NSAI).
Guaranteed Irish		Indicates a product has been manufactured in Ireland to a high degree of quality. It is awarded by Guaranteed Irish Limited.

Explain the quality mark which may appear on the label of a small electrical appliance.(2) **OL**

Safety symbols

Conformité Européenne	C E	Indicates goods comply with European safety standards. It can be found on electrical equipment and children's toys.
Double insulated		Indicates goods are double insulated, so they do not require a safety connection to an earth wire. It can be found on small electrical equipment, e.g. hair dryers and toasters.
Irish mark of electrical conformity	Electrical Safety **NSAI** Certified	Indicates electronic goods have achieved a high safety level. It can be found on electrical goods. It is awarded by the National Standards Authority of Ireland (NSAI).

What information does each of the following symbols convey to the consumer: C E   (6) **HL**

Hazard symbols

- These symbols aim to inform the consumer about the damage a particular substance or mixture can cause to our health or the environment.
- They are found on industrial chemicals, cleaning agents and stationery supplies, e.g. Tipp-Ex.

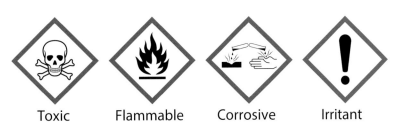

Toxic   Flammable   Corrosive   Irritant

CONSUMER STUDIES

CONSUMER RESPONSIBILITY TO THE ENVIRONMENT

What you will learn:

- Consequences of not managing the environment responsibly
- Renewable and non-renewable resources
- Global warming
- Ways to reduce energy consumption in the home
- Sustainable Energy Authority of Ireland (SEAI)
- Air, water and noise pollution
- Waste management
- Recycling symbols
- Government initiatives to reduce the impact of packaging
- ENFO
- Waste Electrical and Electronic Equipment (WEEE) directive

As consumers we have a responsibility to manage our waste and use energy effectively to ensure minimum damage to the environment. To do this, consumers must adopt a sustainable lifestyle. This is a lifestyle that attempts to reduce use of Earth's natural resources and cause the least amount of environmental damage for future generations.

Consequences of not managing the environment responsibly

- There is a reduction in non-renewable sources of energy, e.g. oil and coal.
- Global warming/climate change increases due to greenhouse gas emissions, such as carbon dioxide from burning fossil fuels.
- There is depletion of the protective ozone layer that absorbs harmful ultraviolet radiation from the sun due to chlorofluorocarbons (CFCs).
- **Deforestation** of rainforests leaves fewer trees to remove carbon dioxide from the atmosphere.
- There is an increase in air, water and soil pollution.

▲ Deforestation

▲ Water pollution

Lit' Hit
Deforestation is the cutting down and clearing away of trees or forests.

GO FIGURE 123

Over 32 million acres of tropical rain forest were cut down each year between 2000 and 2009.

Renewable and non-renewable resources

Renewable resources

Renewable resources are resources that are always available naturally, and are not depleted despite constant use. They cause no harm to the environment. Examples include:

- **solar energy:** created by solar panels, that convert radiant light and heat from the sun into electricity.
- **biomass energy:** created by burning wood and crops to release the energy captured by them from the sun during photosynthesis
- **wind energy:** created by windmills or wind turbines harnessing wind to turn their blades. This drives a generator, producing electricity.
- **geothermal energy:** created by obtaining energy from water reservoirs under the earth's surface. The hot water that rises emerges as steam, which drives a generator, producing electricity
- **hydropower energy:** created by using the power of falling water. This drives a generator, producing electricity.

▲ Wind energy

▲ Hydropower energy

Advantages of renewable resources

✓ Renewable resources generate electricity for general heating and water heating in domestic homes.
✓ Renewable resources have little effect on the environment, as they do not deplete natural resources and they produce little or no waste products, e.g. carbon dioxide.
✓ Renewable resources are sustainable, so they will not to run out.
✓ Renewable resources bring economic benefits to rural areas, as some projects, e.g. wind farms, tend to be away from urban centres due to the large land space necessary.

Non-renewable resources

Non-renewable resources are resources that are in limited supply and cannot be replaced once they have been depleted. They can cause harm to the environment. Examples include:

- **fossil fuels:** e.g. coal, oil and natural gas are formed in the earth from dead plants or animals. When burned they drive a generator to produce electricity, but release greenhouse gases as a result
- **nuclear energy:** created by a nuclear reaction (splitting uranium into two atoms to give off heat) in a nuclear power plant reactor. This drives a generator, producing electricity.

> **Did you know**
>
> In 1986 the world's worst nuclear power disaster occurred at Chernobyl in Ukraine. Studies show that nearly one million people have died, mainly of cancer, due to this disaster.

? Name **two** renewable energy resources and **two** non-renewable energy resources. (4) **OL**

State **one** advantage of using renewable energy sources. Name **two** forms of renewable energy. (6) **HL**

In relation to the environment explain and give an example of each of the following:
- Renewable resource
- Non-renewable resource (6) **HL**

Global warming

Global warming is the gradual increase in the overall temperature of the earth's atmosphere, caused by increased levels of greenhouse gases. These greenhouse gases come from burning fossil fuels, deforestation, industrial processes and some agricultural practices.

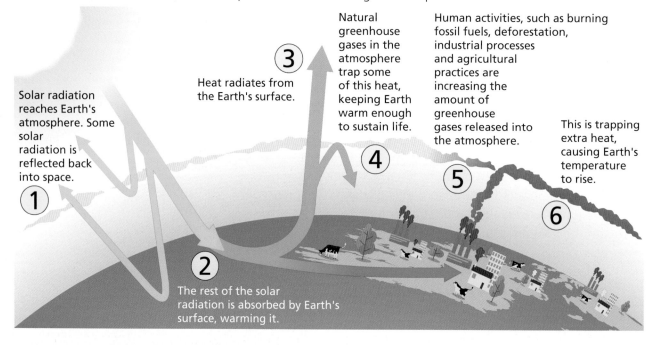

1 Solar radiation reaches Earth's atmosphere. Some solar radiation is reflected back into space.

2 The rest of the solar radiation is absorbed by Earth's surface, warming it.

3 Heat radiates from the Earth's surface.

4 Natural greenhouse gases in the atmosphere trap some of this heat, keeping Earth warm enough to sustain life.

5 Human activities, such as burning fossil fuels, deforestation, industrial processes and agricultural practices are increasing the amount of greenhouse gases released into the atmosphere.

6 This is trapping extra heat, causing Earth's temperature to rise.

Effects of global warming

Global warming causes temperatures to rise, leading to:

- more frequent heatwaves, causing increased droughts and wildfires
- melting ice caps in polar regions, causing sea levels to rise
- heavier precipitation, causing flooding
- reduced habitats and potential extinction of animals that depend on cooler environments, e.g. polar bears
- disruption in food supplies, due to changes in weather patterns.

Ways to reduce energy consumption in the home

Energy used in the home is responsible for 30% of energy-related carbon dioxide emissions, which are a primary contributor to global warming. Energy consumption can be reduced by:

- choosing energy-efficient appliances, e.g. A-rated appliances
- avoiding leaving appliances on standby
- using compact fluorescent lamp (CFL) light bulbs instead of incandescent
- filling the washing machine and dishwasher fully before putting on, or using the half load wash option
- putting a lagging jacket on the hot water cylinder to retain heat
- ensuring homes are insulated well, e.g. double-glazed windows

G> FIGURE 12.3

The average global temperature on Earth has increased by about 0.8°C since 1880. Two-thirds of the warming has occurred since 1975, at a rate of roughly 0.15–0.20°C per decade.

Did you know ?

A lagging jacket can save a consumer up to 30% on water heating costs.

- fitting a timer on the immersion, in case family members forget to switch it off
- turning off lights in rooms when not in use
- taking a shower rather than a bath.

State **two** different methods of reducing energy consumption in the home. (4) **OL**

Compile a set of guidelines outlining how the consumer can protect the environment. (12) **OL**

Sustainable Energy Authority of Ireland (SEAI)

The Sustainable Energy Authority of Ireland (SEAI) is Ireland's national energy authority. It aims to transform Ireland into a society based on sustainable energy by:

- promoting a move towards renewable energy resources
- improving energy efficiency in homes, e.g. by providing homeowners with grants under the Better Energy Home scheme
- advising and providing the government with information about sustainable energy.

seai SUSTAINABLE ENERGY AUTHORITY OF IRELAND

Air, water and noise pollution

Air pollution	
Causes	• Domestic and commercial burning of fossil fuels • Transport emissions • Chlorofluorocarbon (CFC) emissions, e.g. from old refrigerators • Cleaning products, e.g. window sprays emit ammonia • Solvent-based painting supplies, e.g. oil-based paints emit volatile organic compounds (VOCs)
Effects	• Respiratory problems, e.g. asthma, and bronchitis • Global warming • Ozone layer depletion, leading to exposure to higher levels of ultraviolet rays, increasing risk of skin cancer and **cataracts** • Acid rain (precipitation that contains high concentrations of the pollutants that have been released into the atmosphere and combined with water vapour), which can acidify lakes, rivers and soils, killing animals and plants
How to reduce	• Use renewable energy sources, e.g. wind power, or hydropower • Use a bike, public transport or car pool to reduce transport emissions • Use local recycling centres to dispose of old refrigerators containing CFCs • Choose eco-friendly cleaning products made from plant-based ingredients • Use water-based paints containing either low levels or no VOCs

Lit Hit

Cataracts is the clouding of the normally clear lens of the eye, leading to blurred vision and blindness.

Water pollution	
Causes	• Industrial waste, e.g. chemical solvents • Marine dumping • Oil leakage/spillages • Run-off of chemical fertilisers and pesticides • Leakage from sewer lines

▶ Marine dumping

Water pollution

Effects	• Makes water unsafe for human consumption • Death of aquatic animals. This affects tourist and fishing industries • Increase in algae bloom, which depletes the oxygen in the water, causing aquatic animals to suffocate
How to reduce	• All industries should implement environmentally friendly waste management systems, and avoid illegal dumping of industrial waste • Ensure heavy fines are imposed for illegal rubbish dumping and oil spillages • Reduce the use of fertilisers and pesticides or choose eco-friendly versions

Noise pollution

Causes	• Transportation • Construction activities	• Security systems • Social events	• Household chores
Effects	• Hearing problems, as constant exposure to loud noise can damage eardrums and cause hearing loss • Health issues, e.g. stress, fatigue, hypertension and headaches		
How to reduce	• Insulate homes, e.g. install soundproof windows • Avoid purchasing homes near social venues, e.g. pubs, or transportation locations, e.g. motorways • Organise local committees to ensure residents do not use loud music or have loud parties after certain hours		

 Identify **two** different types of pollution. In relation to **each** type of pollution state (i) the possible causes and (ii) the effects on the environment. (20) **OL**

Waste management

Waste management involves the collection, removal, processing and disposal of materials considered as waste.

Waste produced in the home can be categorised as:

- **organic waste:** waste that is biodegradable (decomposes over time due to microorganisms), e.g. food waste
- **inorganic waste:** waste that is non-biodegradable (does not break down, as microorganisms cannot feed on it), e.g. glass, clothing and metal.

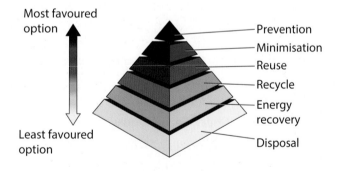

▲ European Union waste hierarchy

Historically in Ireland, waste has been sent to landfills or burnt. This has an extremely negative impact on the environment, as both methods produce greenhouse gases that deplete the ozone layer and give rise to global warming. To divert consumers from using this form of disposal, waste management plans based on the European Union waste hierarchy have been developed by local authorities and put in place in Ireland. The waste hierarchy is a list of approaches to manage waste in order to reduce environmental impact, and it is arranged in order of the most desirable option to the least desirable option.

Prevention	Consumers should: • ask themselves whether or not they really need a product or service • avoid disposable products, e.g. coffee cups • avoid plastic carrier bags and use canvas bags or bags for life

▲ Bag for life

Minimisation	Consumers should: • repair broken goods rather than replacing them • choose concentrated goods, e.g. washing detergent • purchase second-hand goods rather than new goods • choose products with less packaging, e.g. one large bag of rice rather than individual boil in the bag packs

Reuse	Consumers should:
	• reuse products that can be used more than once, e.g. plastic bottles and ink cartridges
	• reuse products for something different (upcycling), e.g.
	   o jam jars as tea-light holders
	   o old clothes as cleaning cloths

Recycling

GO FIGURE 123

Ireland has raised its recycling rate from 11% to 36% since 2006.

Consumers should:
• recycle a range of items, including paper, plastic, metal, glass, batteries, textiles and old appliances
• recycle organic waste for compost, e.g. vegetable peelings and eggshells
• purchase products made from recycled goods, e.g. paper bags and stationery

Advantages of recycling

Did you know?

Recycling just one plastic bottle will save enough energy to power a 60 watt light bulb for three hours.

✓ Conserves natural resources, e.g. oil and water
✓ Reduces pollution
✓ Reduces harmful emissions from e.g. methane gas
✓ Reduces waste disposal costs
✓ Creates employment, e.g. jobs in recycling centres
✓ Lowers production costs, as it takes less money to make something with recycled materials than it does to make something new

▲ Recycling organic waste for compost

Lit Hit
An incinerator is an apparatus for burning waste.

Energy recovery	Consumers' non-recyclable waste materials can be converted into usable energy for electricity and heat. This can be done by: • the combustion of waste in an **incinerator** • harnessing gases produced from landfill or animal waste, e.g. methane

Disposal	Consumers should avoid disposal as a method of waste management, as it causes waste build-up in landfills and increased levels of methane in the air

? Explain how consumers/householders can contribute to sustainable waste management. Give **two** points (6) **HL**

REMEMBER IT!

'**P**eople **M**ust **R**eally **R**ecycle **E**ach **D**ay.'
Prevention, **M**inimisation, **R**euse, **R**ecycling, **E**nergy recovery, **D**isposal.

CONSUMER RESPONSIBILITY TO THE ENVIRONMENT

Recycling symbols

Green Dot		PET	
Indicates that the packaging suppliers have contributed to the funding for recovery and recycling of packaging waste. Repak (packaging compliance scheme) is the sole registered licenser of the Green Dot trademark for Ireland, so only companies that are members of Repak carry the symbol.		Indicates bottles are made of polyethylene terephthalate (PET) plastic. Soft drink and mouthwash bottles are made from this type of plastic. PET bottles have the identification number one on the bottom, which makes them easier to identify in the recycling stream.	
Recycling		**Ecolabel**	
The universal recycling symbol. It indicates that goods and packaging contain recyclable materials or are recyclable.		Indicates that products and services are kinder to the environment. It is a voluntary scheme. To receive the symbol, products must be audited on the energy or materials used during manufacture and their potential to pollute.	

> **?** Explain this symbol which may be found on packaging material.
> (2) **OL**
>
> What information does each of the following symbols convey to the consumer?
> (6) **HL**

Government initiatives to reduce the impact of packaging

For information on government initiatives to reduce the impact of packaging see page 197.

ENFO

The main public resource for environmental information in Ireland, including waste management. Information is available from www.enfo.ie and at various ENFO points in local libraries.

Waste Electrical and Electronic Equipment (WEEE) directive

This directive requires producers to finance the collection, treatment, recovery and environmentally-sound disposal of waste electrical and electronic equipment. This enables consumers of household electrical and electronic equipment to leave them back free of charge, either to retail outlets or to other authorised collection points, e.g. civic amenity sites.

> **?** State how the consumer should dispose of electrical appliances. (2) **OL**
>
> Identify and give details of **one** initiative aimed at promoting a clean green environment. (10) **OL**

SOCIAL STUDIES

Chapter 17: The family in society

3.1.1 SOCIOLOGICAL TERMS AND CONCEPTS

What you will learn:

- Key sociological terms and concepts

Sociology involves the scientific study of the organisation and functioning of society. It is the study of people and how they behave and interact. The following sociological terms and concepts are associated with this area of study.

- **Society:** a group of people who share a common way of life, e.g. Irish society.

- **Social groups:** subgroups of people within society who share a common purpose. For example:
  - **primary social group:** a small group of people with permanent relationships and close personal ties, e.g. family or close friends
  - **secondary social group:** a large group of people with less permanent relationships and impersonal ties, e.g. school community or work colleagues.

- **Kinship:** a blood relationship that exists between family members.

- **Norms:** the normal patterns of behaviour individuals are expected to follow within society, e.g. saying please and thank you.

- **Values:** the attitudes and beliefs held by a society regarding what is right and wrong. These are reinforced by the laws of a country.

- **Mores:** the norms, values and customs that are considered important by society, e.g. showing respect to elders.

- **Socialisation:** the process whereby an individual learns appropriate norms, values, behaviour and social skills in order to behave in a manner acceptable to society. This is achieved by:
  - o **primary socialisation:** within the family
  - o **secondary socialisation:** outside the family, e.g. school or work.

- **Culture:** the way of life of a society, which includes language, music, customs, norms, values and skills passed on from one generation to the next.

- **Role:** the expected pattern of behaviour of an individual according to their status or position in society, e.g. a judge should be fair and impartial when in court.

▲ Secondary socialisation

- **Status:** the position held by individuals relative to others within society. It is often defined by the amount of respect and prestige shown to them by others. Status can be:
  - o **ascribed:** given at birth, e.g. members of a royal family
  - o **achieved:** gained through an individual's own effort, e.g. educational achievements.

- **Socio-economic grouping:** the classification of individuals according to their economic and social position in relation to others, based on income, education and occupation. In Ireland these groups are usually classified as: lower, middle and higher class.

- **Social mobility:** the movement of individuals between socio-economic groupings, e.g. from middle class to higher class. This may occur due to educational progression.

- **Social institutions:** organised social arrangements found in many societies, e.g. family and marriage.

- **Social change:** changes that take place in society due to major developments. For example:
  - o changes in technology, e.g. social media
  - o national or international events, e.g. the Troubles in Northern Ireland
  - o law reform, e.g. divorce was legalised in Ireland in 1996.

? Explain the following sociological terms:
  - culture
  - norms
  - values
  - role. (12) **HL**

THE FAMILY IN SOCIETY

What you will learn:

- **Defining the family**
- **The universality of the family**
- **Modern family structures**
- **Historical development of the family in Ireland from the beginning of the twentieth century**
- **Social, economic and technological changes affecting modern family structures**
- **Family functions**

Defining the family

The family is a group of people related to each other by blood, marriage or adoption.

The Irish Constitution (article 41) describes the family as *the natural primary and fundamental unit group of Society*. The United Nations (1994) describes the family as *the basic unit of society, which acts as a support for its members and which transmits values from one generation to the next*.

 ? Define the term *family*. (5) **HL**

The universality of the family

The family is a group that exists, in some form, in all societies throughout the world. The form may change due to variations in culture, but the family is still the fundamental cornerstone of society.

The family is considered to be one of the most important social institutions. It is through the family that children learn how to behave and fit into society. Over a lifetime people may belong to three types of family.

- **Family of orientation:** the family individuals are born into, made up of parents and siblings.

- **Family of procreation:** the family created when individuals have or adopt children.

- **Family of affinity:** also known as a family of choice, whereby people with or without legal or blood ties feel they belong together as a family, e.g. close friends.

? Explain what is understood by the universality of the family. (5) **HL**

Modern family structures

Modern family structures include nuclear families, extended families, one-parent families and blended families.

Nuclear families

Nuclear families consist of parents and their children.

Characteristics

- Nuclear families are small in size, nowadays, the average number of children in a nuclear family is 1.4.
- Nuclear families are mobile due to the small number of people in the family, so they can easily move from place to place. This is often necessary for employment opportunities.
- Nuclear families are often dual-income households, with both parents working outside of the home to earn an income in order to meet the high cost of living.
- Nuclear families are often economically self-sufficient, meaning that they do not rely on other family members for financial support.
- Democratic decision making between parents in nuclear families is common, meaning that both parents have equal say.
- Egalitarian roles exist between parents in nuclear families. Household tasks are shared equally, regardless of gender.
- Feelings of isolation and loneliness can occur in nuclear families, especially in times of crisis if they live far away from extended family members.

Extended families

Extended families consist of grandparents, aunts, uncles and cousins. There are two types of extended families: classic extended families and modified extended families.

- **Classic extended families:** extended families related by blood, marriage or adoption that live in the same home or close to one another.
- **Modified extended families:** extended families related by blood, marriage or adoption who are separated geographically from one another, but keep in close contact.

Characteristics

- Extended families are large in size, as more than one generation lives in the same home or nearby.
- Extended families are immobile, due to the large numbers of people in the family, so they cannot move easily from place to place.
- Extended families are often economically interdependent and reliant on a family business, e.g. a farm, to provide all family members with financial support. This is not as commonplace nowadays, due to a decline in agriculture.
- Extended families are long-lasting families, as children of extended families usually remain beside the family home or in the local area after they marry and establish their own family of procreation. This maintains connections for further generations and creates a close-knit family community.
- Historically, patriarchal-style decision making was evident in extended families, meaning the male(s) of the household often had full control over decision making. This is not as commonplace nowadays.
- Historically, segregated roles existed between parents in extended families. Males were the breadwinners and worked outside the home, whereas females worked inside the home. This is not as commonplace nowadays.
- Support is provided by other family members in extended families during times of crisis.

One-parent families

One-parent families consist of one parent with his or her children. One-parent families may be the result of the death of a spouse/partner/civil partner, separation, divorce, an unplanned pregnancy or may be by choice.

Characteristics

- Approximately 87% of one-parent families are headed by females.
- Lone parents often live with their own parents, for financial reasons or for support, e.g. childminding.
- One-parent families are often dependent on social welfare payments, e.g. the One-Parent Family Payment, for financial support, as the high costs of childcare may prohibit them from accessing work, education or training opportunities, increasing their risk of poverty.
- Emotional difficulties, e.g. depression or stress, may be experienced by single parents when trying to cope with the demands of parenting and sole responsibility for all decisions. Lone parents may feel isolated from others, especially peers.

GO FIGURE

Figures show that nearly a quarter of Irish children live in one-parent homes (23.2%). This is much higher than the European average of 13.6%. This makes one-parent families the second most common family type in Ireland, after nuclear families.

GO FIGURE

In 1986 there were 104,713 one-parent families in Ireland. In 2011 this figure had increased to 215,315.

Blended families

Blended families consist of two parents from previous relationships or marriages, and their children.

Characteristics

- Blended families are increasingly common due to greater numbers of separations and divorces.
- Family size increases when two families come together, combining both sets of children as well as extended families.
- Conflict can occur between stepsiblings if they do not bond or get along, or between step-parents and stepchildren due to a change in family rules or discipline structure.
- Children's relationships with the absent biological parent may be difficult.
- Financial strain may be experienced in blended families, as two families need to be supported.

Explain each of the following family structures:
- nuclear family
- extended family
- blended family. (15) **OL**

Identify and describe **three** types of modern family structures in today's society. (18) **HL**

Historical development of the family in Ireland from the beginning of the twentieth century

The historical development of the family is evident through changes in structure, marriage, size and children, standard of living, and roles.

THE FAMILY IN SOCIETY

Structure

Pre industrial (1900–1960)	The extended family structure was the norm, with more than one generation living under the same roof or within the same area.
Post industrial (1960–1990)	There was a move away from the rural extended family to the urban nuclear family, as many families had to move from rural locations to industrial towns and cities in order to find employment.
Modern day (1990–today)	The nuclear family is still the main type of family in Ireland today. However, many new types of families are now evident, e.g. one-parent and blended families, due to increased social acceptance of separation and divorce.

Marriage

Pre industrial (1900–1960)	Marriages were often arranged by parents for economic benefit rather than romantic love and compatibility. The bride was frequently much younger than her future husband, and often her parents had to provide a **dowry**.
Post industrial (1960–1990)	Generally, people chose their own partners based on romantic love and compatibility. Couples were much closer and focused on fulfilling their partner's emotional needs.
Modern day (1990–today)	Today couples continue to base their choice of companion on romantic love. Cultural changes and a more **secular** society have made it more acceptable for couples to cohabit rather than marry, and to separate, divorce and remarry. Same-sex couples can now marry.

> **Lit Hit**
> A dowry is an amount of property or money brought by a bride to her husband on their marriage.

> **Lit Hit**
> Secular means not bound by religious rule.

Size and children

Pre industrial (1900–1960)	Families were large, with seven to nine children on average. This occurred as Ireland was strongly influenced by the Catholic church and contraception was not permitted. Children were seen as an economic asset, as they worked on the family farm or in the family business.
Post industrial (1960–1990)	Families became smaller, with the average family size in the 1970s falling to four to six children. This occurred due to the availability of contraception and decreased influence of the Catholic church.
Modern day (1990–today)	Families are much smaller, with the average family having 1.4 children. This is occurring as contraception is now widely available and society is increasingly secular. This may also be attributed to the fact that more women are now establishing careers, and childcare costs are high.

> **Did you know ?**
> The average age of a first-time mother in Ireland is 31 years, making Irish women the oldest first-time mothers in Europe.

Standard of living

Pre industrial (1900–1960)	Families' standards of living were poor as wages were low. Many homes were damp, cold and unhygienic and lacked proper sanitation facilities. Infant mortality rates were high, with nearly 10% dying due to disease, infection and poor nutrition.
Post industrial (1960–1990)	The standard of living improved, as people earned a regular, dependable wage from industry. Homes had electricity and better sanitation facilities. Increased health services and the introduction of the medical card in 1970 caused infant mortality rates to drop and extended the lifespan of families.
Modern day (1990–today)	Standards of living are high, as many families are dual income. Homes are better insulated and have a high standard of sanitation facilities. Health services have greatly improved due to new treatments and improved facilities.

Roles

Pre industrial (1900–1960)	Families were usually patriarchal, with men having full control over all family decision making and discipline. Wives were expected to be submissive and follow their husbands' wishes.
	Segregated roles were evident between parents, e.g. men were the bread winners and worked outside the home, whereas women worked inside the home.
Post industrial (1960–1990)	Families became less patriarchal as the rights of women improved, meaning that women had more say on parenting, finances and discipline. Despite increased educational opportunities for females, segregated roles were still evident between parents during this time. Many women were still expected to work inside the home while men were the breadwinners and worked outside the home.
Modern day (1990–today)	Few families today are patriarchal. Families are more egalitarian with both parents now having an equal say on parenting, finances and discipline. Integrated roles are evident between parents, with both now playing an equal role in household tasks, e.g. cleaning and childminding, regardless of gender.

? Outline the historical development of the family in Ireland from the beginning of the twentieth century to the present day. (16) **HL**

Social, economic and technological changes affecting modern family structures

Social changes

Marital breakdown

Since the introduction of the Family Law (Divorce) Act 1996, the stigma surrounding marital breakdown has reduced in Ireland. A more liberal and secular society has also made it more socially acceptable to separate or divorce if a couple no longer wishes to remain together.

Effects on modern family structure

- There has been an increase in the number of one-parent and blended families.

Changing role of women

More women are advancing to third-level education, due to increased educational opportunities. This has improved their career prospects, causing many women to shift roles from working in the home to working outside the home.

Effects on modern family structure

- Families tend to be smaller, as women are having fewer children because they have the opportunity to establish careers.
- In some families role reversal has occurred, with fathers staying at home to mind children, as mothers have higher-paid occupations.
- In dual-income households, symmetrical roles are common, with household tasks shared equally between partners, as they are both working.

Same-sex marriage and adoption

The introduction of the Children and Family Relationships Act 2015 enabled same-sex couples to jointly adopt children. Previously, only one person could become the legal adoptive parent. This was followed by the Marriage Act 2015, which legalised same-sex marriage in Ireland, allowing two people of the same sex to marry and benefit from the same status under the Constitution as couples of opposite sex. The introduction of these acts has resulted in a more inclusive and tolerant society in Ireland, willing to acknowledge the greater variety of family forms.

Effects on modern family structure

- Children may now legally have two adoptive parents of the same sex.
- Families may now legally be headed by married couples of the same sex.

Economic changes

High cost of living

An increase in the cost of living has left Ireland in the top ten most expensive countries in the world to reside, therefore many families must budget carefully to meet needs, e.g. rent, food and childcare. After these needs have been met, there is often little money left for families, especially if on a low income.

Effects on modern family structure

- The number of dual-income families has increased, as both parents need to work to earn sufficient income to meet needs.
- Families are having fewer children due to the high cost of childcare.
- Stress and worry surrounding finances within the family are increased. In severe cases this may lead to marital breakdown.

The economy

When the Irish economy was in recession, unemployment rates increased to a high of 15% in 2012, which put huge financial strain on families. In recent times, the Irish economy has begun to recover and unemployment rates have begun to steadily drop. This has allowed many unemployed people to re-enter the workplace and move away from social welfare payments.

Effects on modern family structure

- There is an increase in dual-income families due to greater access to employment.
- There is a reduced number of families reliant on social welfare payments, e.g. Jobseeker's Benefit, to meet basic needs.

State benefits

The state provides social welfare payments, e.g. Jobseeker's Allowance or Supplementary Welfare Allowance, to unemployed families struggling to pay for basic needs. One-parent families can obtain the One-Parent Family Payment.

Effects on modern family structure

- Enables one-parent or unemployed families to provide for their children's basic needs.
- Reduces stress and worry surrounding finances among one-parent families and unemployed families, enhancing stability.

Technological changes

Automated household appliances

The increased availability of automated household appliances, e.g. washing machines and dishwashers, allow housework to be completed quicker and more efficiently.

Effects on modern family structure

- Increases leisure time for families, as the amount of time and effort spent cleaning and maintaining the home is reduced.

Communication

Developments in communication technologies, e.g. email, Skype and WhatsApp, have enabled families to have greater communication with family or friends all over the world. People can share conversations, messages, images or videos instantly.

Effects on modern family structure

- Closer bonds and relationships can form between family members, as it is easier for people to keep in contact with their extended family.

Entertainment

Developments in entertainment technology, e.g. smart-televisions, online streaming services such as Netflix, and gaming apps, have greatly influenced pastimes participated in by families.

Effects on modern family structure

- Familial bonds are affected, as families spend less time interacting with one another.
- There is a reduction in participation in physically active pastimes, which increases the risk of obesity.

 Discuss the social, economic and technological changes that affect families in Ireland today. (24) **HL**

Family functions

Family functions may be classified as:
- physical
- emotional
- social
- economic
- educational.

The state supports the family in meeting these functions.

Physical function

- The family should provide for the basic physical needs of its members, including shelter, food, warmth and clothing, ensuring that family members grow and develop in a healthy environment.
- The family is required to provide a safe environment for its vulnerable members, e.g. children, elderly people and people with a disability.
- The family unit has an important role in procreation, ensuring the survival of the human race. It also allows for the regulation of sexual behaviour, i.e. having one partner.

How the state supports/assists the family

- The state social welfare system provides Child Benefit to help parents to meet the needs of the child.
- The HSE employs public health nurses to carry out developmental examinations on all children under the age of three, ensuring that children are growing and developing as they should.
- The HSE runs the Community Mothers Programme, which trains experienced mothers from the local community to visit first-time mothers, mainly in disadvantaged areas, to provide necessary support and parenting skills.
- If a family cannot provide for their children's basic physical needs, or provide a safe environment, a social worker from the Child and Family Agency (Tusla) may place the children in foster care.

Emotional function

- The family should provide a loving, caring and secure home for their children. All children should be able to express their emotions, feelings, fears or desires and know that they are being listened to. This allows children to develop a healthy self-esteem, enabling them to grow in confidence, form healthy relationships later in life and fit into society in the future.

How the state supports/assists the family

- The HSE runs parenting courses, e.g. Parent Plus Programmes, to help parents develop positive parenting skills and support their children so that they grow up happy and emotionally secure.

Social function

- The family should provide an environment where children can learn acceptable social behaviours to fit into society; this is known as socialisation. This can be done by parents displaying society's norms, values and customs, e.g. having manners and respecting others. Children then observe and imitate their parents' behaviour from an early age.
- The family must act as an agent of social control. Through effective discipline by parents, children learn what is right and wrong. This helps them learn appropriate behaviour and become moral individuals.

How the state supports/assists the family

- Pre-schools and state-funded primary and secondary schools continue the process of socialisation through the hidden curriculum (knowledge conveyed to students without ever being explicitly taught). For example, children learn how to respect others and follow rules. This helps produce socialised people prepared for the world of work.
- If children do not display acceptable social behaviours and if they break the law, the state will intervene through the judicial system. Children may be placed in detention centres if the crime committed is of a very serious nature.

Economic function

- The family should economically support children until they reach the age where they are self-sufficient, i.e. 18 years or 23 years if in full-time education.
- In order for the family to fulfil its economic function, usually one or both parents work to earn an income.

How the state supports/assists the family

- If a family is unable to meet its economic function, financial support is available from the state social welfare system, e.g. Family Income Supplement and Back to School Clothing and Footwear Allowance.

Educational function

- The family should act as the child's primary educator for the first five years of their lives until they begin school. During this time, family norms, values and customs should be passed on.
- Games, books and jigsaws provide a stimulating environment that helps children develop intellectually. Children should be praised, encouraged and challenged in order to help them reach their full potential.
- Once children start school, parents should play a supportive role by supervising homework, monitoring progress and showing an interest in their schoolwork.

Did you know ?
Research shows that 90% of a child's brain develops in the first five years.

How the state supports/assists the family

- The state provides the Early Childhood Care and Education Scheme (ECCE), which offers free pre-school education to children aged three, until they start primary school.
- The state provides free full-time primary and post-primary education to all children. It also provides access to supports for children with special educational needs, including special classes, resource teachers and special needs assistants for children, or access to special schools, e.g. for the visually or hearing impaired.

? Explain, giving examples, how the state provides support to children who are disadvantaged. (15) **OL**

Describe **four** main functions of the family in modern society **and** outline how the state supports the family with these functions. (24) **HL**

3.1.5 MARRIAGE

What you will learn:

- Marriage customs and cultural variations
- Legal requirements for marriage in Ireland
- Rights and responsibilities within a marriage in Ireland
- Marriage preparation
- Marriage in Ireland today
- Factors that affect marital stability
- Marriage counselling
- Family mediation
- Separation
- Nullity of marriage
- Divorce
- Reasons why marital breakdown is increasing in Ireland
- Effects of marital breakdown

Marriage is the socially and legally acceptable union between two persons, without distinction as to their sex, with the exclusion of all others.

Prior to 2015, only couples of the opposite sex could legally marry in Ireland. This changed in May 2015 when the Irish public voted 62.1% in favour of same-sex marriage in the Marriage Equality Referendum. The requirement for a couple to be of opposite sex in order to marry is now removed in Ireland under the Marriage Act 2015.

Marriage is made official by either religious or civil ceremonies, and the union is legally binding.

> **Did you know**
> Up until 1993, it was illegal to be homosexual in the Republic of Ireland.

> **?** Define marriage as it exists in Irish law. (5) **HL**

Marriage customs and cultural variations

Minimum age

- The minimum age for marriage in Ireland is 18 years of age. The age rule is the same irrespective of a religious or civil ceremony.
- The minimum age restriction is not the same for all countries, e.g. in Sudan the legal marriage age is ten years old.

> **Did you know**
> In 2015 the Irish government announced its intention to disallow court exemptions granting permission for 16–17 year olds to get married.

Choice of partners

- All societies place some form of restraint on an individual's choice of marriage partner. These constraints can be based on religion, socio-economic background or close family relationship.
- In Ireland, individuals are prohibited from marrying based on close family relationships including:
  - **consanguinity:** blood relationships, e.g. a woman cannot marry her son
  - **affinity:** a relationship by marriage, e.g. a man cannot marry his son's spouse
- In some cultures, individuals do not choose their partners, as marriages are arranged. For example, in India parents often find a spouse for their son or daughter who is of the same socio-economic status in accordance with the **caste system**, so they will share similar values, beliefs and norms.

▲ An Indian wedding

Lit Hit
The caste system is a class structure that is determined by birth.

> **GO FIGURE 123**
> It is estimated that 95% of Indian marriages are arranged.

Number of spouses

Depending on the culture, marriages may be: monogamous or polygamous.

Monogamy

- Monogamy is a form of marriage that allows a person to have one husband or wife.
- It is the most common form of marriage in western society and Christian communities.
- In monogamous relationships it is a criminal offence to enter into a second marriage while still legally married. The act of marrying another person while legally married to another is known as bigamy.
- In many societies serial monogamy is common. This involves individuals marrying and divorcing different people many times.

Polygamy

- Polygamy is a form of marriage that involves having more than one partner at the same time. People who participate in this are known as polygamists.
- There are two types of polygamy: polygyny and polyandry.

Polygyny	Polyandry

- A form of marriage that involves a man having two or more wives at the same time
- These marriages are often patriarchal, with the male making decisions and supervising all of the family's finances. The more wives a man has, the wealthier he is considered within some societies.
- Polygyny is practised in some:
  o **Islamic countries:** the Quran states *marry of the women, who seem good to you, two or three or four*
  o **African communities**
  o **Mormon communities**
	- A form of marriage that involves a woman having two or more husbands at the same time
	- This practice is rare but it exists in some poor agricultural societies, where more than one man is needed to support the family financially.
	- Polyandry is practised in some:
	  o **Tibetan communities:** fraternal polyandry is the most common form. This involves two or more brothers marrying one woman. It occurs when families want to prevent land being subdivided among all their sons
	  o **Marquesas communities:** this occurs as there are more men than women on the islands

Location

In some cultures, couples are expected to live in certain locations after they marry.

- **Matrilocal residence:** live in proximity to the wife's extended family.
- **Patrilocal residence:** live in proximity to the husband's extended family.
- **Neolocal residence:** live separately from both families in a neutral location.

Customs during marriage ceremonies

Marriage ceremonies have a rich history of varied cultural traditions around the world. For example:

- at the end of some Jewish wedding ceremonies a glass is broken under the groom's foot to symbolise the destruction of the ancient Jewish temple in Jerusalem, to remind the couple that a marriage can break

- during some Hindu wedding ceremonies the bride and groom are led around a ceremonial fire in seven steps. A wedding vow and prayer is said at each step. Participants pray for food, wealth, strength, children, good luck, seasons and friendship.

?
> Explain **three** ways in which marriage customs may differ between cultures. (18) **OL**

REMEMBER IT!
> 'Marriage Creates New Loving Couples.'
> Minimum age, Choice of partners,
> Number of spouses, Location, Customs.

Legal requirements for marriage in Ireland

- **Over 18:** both partners must be over 18 years of age.

- **Mental capacity:** both partners must have the mental capacity to understand the nature of marriage. This may not be present if either party is intoxicated, mentally impaired due to drugs or mentally ill.

- **Notification:** three months' notification of the marriage must be given to:
  - o a registrar for a civil marriage ceremony
  - o a registrar and the local priest/pastor/vicar of a church for a religious marriage ceremony.

- **Registered venue:** marriages must take place in a registered venue, e.g.:
  - o civil ceremonies in a registry office or any other venue that is approved by a registrar, e.g. a hotel
  - o religious ceremonies in a church.

- **Free to marry:** both partners must be free to marry, i.e. single, widowed or divorced.

- **Voluntary basis:** both partners must enter marriage on a voluntary basis. They cannot be forced to marry against their wishes.

- **Wedding registration:** after the ceremony the couple and two witnesses must sign a marriage registration form to register the marriage.

- **Not closely related:** partners must not be closely related by blood (consanguinity) or marriage (affinity).

Did you know ?
The average age of grooms in Ireland has changed from 26 years in 1962 to 35 years in 2014. The average age of brides has changed from 26 years in 1962 to 33 years in 2014

Did you know ?
Licences to temporarily register a venue, e.g. a hotel, for the purpose of a marriage only became available in Ireland in November 2007. Outdoor venues, e.g. beaches, were only added in 2014.

?
> Outline four conditions that are necessary to make a marriage legally valid in Ireland. (20) **OL**
>
> Set out the legal requirements for marriage in Ireland. (16) **HL**

REMEMBER IT!
> 'On Marrying, Numerous Regulations
> For Verification Were Needed.'
> Over 18, Mental capacity, Notification,
> Registered venue, Free to marry, Voluntary basis,
> Wedding registration, Not closely related.

MARRIAGE

Rights and responsibilities within a marriage in Ireland

All married couples in Ireland have the following rights and responsibilities.

- To cohabit together and keep each other company.
- To have sexual relations with each other during the marriage.
- To show commitment to the marriage and remain faithful and loyal in a monogamous relationship.
- To provide financial support for dependent spouses and children as set out in the Family Law (Maintenance of Spouses and Children) Act 1976.
- To share joint guardianship of any children born within the marriage, and to meet their children's physical, moral, emotional, intellectual and social needs. Children may be taken into care if parents do not fulfil this right.
- To inherit from each other under the Succession Act 1965, e.g. if a spouse dies and there is no will and no children the surviving spouse is entitled to all of the **estate**.

Lit Hit

An estate is all of the valuable things an individual owns, e.g. land, jewellery, investments.

Discuss the (i) rights and (ii) responsibilities of a couple within the marriage relationship. (24) **OL**

Identify and elaborate on the rights and responsibilities of a couple within a marriage relationship. (20) **HL**

Marriage preparation

Marriage is a big life decision that people should be prepared for. Preparation is usually provided informally at home and in school, and formally through pre-marriage courses.

Home

Home life provides children with their first experience of marriage. Parents are the role models that children base their future relationships on.

- If children are raised in a household where there is a stable, loving relationship between parents this will provide a positive image of what forms a happy marriage. Such children may form similar relationships in their own lives.
- If children are raised in a household where there is a tension-filled relationship between parents, this is more likely to develop a negative image of married life. Such children may have difficulty in forming loving, lasting relationships.

The skills and qualities needed to form and maintain healthy marital relationships are also learned within the family, e.g. communication, trust, compromise, respect and faithfulness.

School

Various subjects studied at school provide marriage preparation, including:

- Social Personal and Health Education (SPHE), as it examines relationship building skills
- Home Economics, as it explores the roles and responsibilities of married spouses and legal requirements for marriage
- Religious Education (RE), as it examines different religions' views on marriage.

Pre-marriage courses

Pre-marriage courses offer couples the opportunity to reflect on their hopes and expectations of each other as partners in a marriage. These courses are provided by:

- **denominational** groups, e.g. Accord Catholic Marriage Care Service
- non-denominational groups, e.g. Relationships Ireland.

Topics covered at pre-marriage courses include:

- family planning
- finance
- role expectations
- parenthood
- communication
- potential problems, e.g. alcoholism.

ACCORD
CATHOLIC MARRIAGE CARE SERVICE

Advantages of pre-marriage courses (aims)

✓ Pre-marriage courses allow couples to discuss what marriage means to them and their expectations of married life, e.g. does one partner believe that it is the other's responsibility to work at home and mind their children?

✓ Pre-marriage courses allow couples to discuss each other's positive personal qualities, e.g. honesty and generosity. Negative qualities that can have an unsettling effect on a marriage, e.g. jealousy and anger, are also examined to prevent future arguments.

✓ Pre-marriage courses help couples to strengthen their listening and communication skills, which will allow partners to feel heard and understood within married life, reducing the likelihood of conflict.

✓ Pre-marriage courses allow couples to discuss specific issues that may be worrying them, e.g. alcohol problems, financial issues or conception difficulties. The marriage preparation counsellor helps find ways to resolve these issues, and provides couples with practical advice to resolve future issues that may arise.

> **?** Outline the role of **each** of the following in relation to marriage preparation:
> - the school
> - marriage preparation courses. (12) **OL**
>
> Outline the benefits of a young couple attending a pre-marriage course. (16) **OL**
>
> Discuss the benefits of pre-marriage courses for couples preparing for marriage. (18) **HL**

Marriage in Ireland today

In the past, children were expected to be born into a loving marriage between a man and a woman. Society assumed that children needed this stability in order to thrive. Irish society has changed, and so have attitudes towards the institution of marriage.

At present, one in three families in Ireland depart from the traditional model of a married couple. Alternative family structures are dominated by:

- **cohabiting couples:** 6% of children in Ireland live with cohabiting parents
- **one-parent families (never married, divorced or separated):** 23% of children in Ireland live with single parents
- **blended families:** 2.5% of children in Ireland live in blended families
- **same-sex parents**.

These family structures are becoming more prevalent due to a decline in the number of people getting married, an increase in separation and divorce and the introduction of the Marriage Act 2015.

MARRIAGE

Factors that affect marital stability

- **Young age:** marriages entered into in early adulthood are more likely to break down due to:
  - o lack of maturity to respond to difficult situations, e.g. responding to conflict by ignoring it rather than communicating
  - o lack of adequate financial support, leading to conflict around financial difficulties.
- **Unrealistic expectations:** many partners enter marriage with unrealistic expectations, e.g. a romantic fantasy, which can lead to breakdown when this idealism is not fulfilled. Romance in the media often feeds this fantasy.

- **Different role expectations:** when partners have different role expectations, e.g. one partner believes they should be the breadwinner and their partner should be the homemaker, while the other partner wants to work and to share the household tasks, marital instability can occur. This issue is common if partners are from different cultures, as role expectations many differ.
- **Dissimilar interests:** lack of common interests between spouses can make it difficult to bond and enhance marital relationships, affecting stability.
- **Social problems:** alcoholism, gambling and drug abuse can cause marriage instability, as they can lead to broken communication, economic instability and physical violence among spouses.
- **Infidelity:** spouses have an expectation of sexual **fidelity** in marriage. If one partner is unfaithful, trust can be lost, affecting marital stability.
- **Unemployment:** loss of employment can create financial insecurity, placing strain on marital relationships, affecting stability.

Lit Hit
Fidelity means faithfulness to a person.

Marriage counselling

A couple experiencing marital difficulties should avail of professional counselling in order to prevent marital breakdown where possible. This is provided confidentially by trained counsellors from organisations such as ACCORD or Relationships Ireland. Counsellors must remain impartial and demonstrate good listening skills.

At counselling sessions, the counsellor helps couples express their feelings, concerns, problems or any personal issues. They also offer couples guidance and support on adjustments required in their marriage. Counselling can only be successful if:

- both spouses attend and are serious about preventing separation
- the couple's problems are not so far advanced that the best solution for both parties is separation.

If couples have more specific problems, e.g. alcohol addiction issues, they may be referred to a more specialised counsellor.

Family mediation

Family mediation is a service provided for free through the state-funded Family Mediation Service to couples who have decided to separate or divorce. It helps couples to make arrangements for the future in the presence of an impartial mediator. Arrangements include:
• custody of children • parenting of children • division of finances • issues concerning the family home.
If the mediation process results in an agreement acceptable to both spouses, the mediator will draw up a mediated agreement that includes all the decisions made, and is signed by both parties. This agreement is not legally binding, so couples must take it to their solicitors to draw up in a Deed of Separation to give it legal standing.

Benefits of mediation

✓ Mediation encourages co-operation and communication between spouses, which may reduce or resolve conflicts.
✓ Mediation enables joint decisions to be made, rather than one spouse feeling a decision is being forced on them.
✓ Mediation avoids involving children in conflict.
✓ Mediation helps spouses to come to terms with the reality of their separation.

Separation

Couples who separate are not legally entitled to marry again. They may separate legally by legal separation or judicial separation.

Lit Hit
A decree is an official order enforced by law.

Legal separation (separation agreement/Deed of Separation)	Judicial separation
• When a couple can agree the terms on which they will live separately, they may enter into a separation agreement. This is a legally binding written contract between partners, setting out their future rights and duties as agreed. • The agreement will include: 　o an agreement to live apart 　o arrangements regarding the responsibility for and care of dependent children 　o the amount of **maintenance** to be paid for the support of the dependent spouse and children 　o arrangements regarding home ownership and who will live in the family home 　o arrangements regarding succession and inheritance • A trained mediator can help a couple negotiate the terms of their separation without involving lawyers or going to court • A Deed of Separation, including all decisions made and signed by both parties, must be drawn up by a solicitor to make it legally binding	• When a couple cannot agree the terms of a legal separation an application to the courts for a **decree** of judicial separation is made under the Judicial Separation and Family Law Reform Act 1989 as amended by the Family Law Act 1995 • An application for a judicial separation must be based on one of the following grounds: 　o one spouse has committed adultery 　o unreasonable behaviour, e.g. alcoholism 　o desertion for at least one year at the time of application 　o no normal marital relationship for at least one year 　o the couple have not cohabited for one year before the application (where both consent to separation) or three years (where one spouse does not consent) • If an application meets one of the above grounds, the case is heard by a judge. If the judge is satisfied that a spouse has grounds for a judicial separation, they will grant a decree of judicial separation • The judge may also make additional orders in relation to: 　o custody of children and access 　o payment of maintenance 　o allocation of property 　o extinguishment of succession rights

Lit Hit
Maintenance means provision of financial support.

MARRIAGE

Nullity of marriage

Nullity of marriage is a declaration by a court that a supposed marriage is null and void, and that no valid marriage ever existed between two partners. There are two types of nullity available.

- **Legal (annulment) nullity:** obtained by couples who married in civil and church ceremonies. Legal nullity is required in order for either spouse to remarry and avoid bigamy.
- **Church (annulment) nullity:** obtained by couples who married in the church. It is important to note that this annulment has no legal standing, and so from a legal perspective the couple are still married.

Grounds for nullity of marriage

A marriage may be declared null if:

- one partner was under 18 or already legally married
- there was non-observance of formal requirements, e.g. not giving three months' notice to a registrar
- one partner did not give free and full informed consent due to reasons such as **duress**, e.g. from parents, insanity or intoxication
- one partner is unable to engage in consummating the marriage due to physical and/or psychological reasons
- normal marital relationships could not be achieved due to one partner having psychiatric problems, including bipolar disorder or schizophrenia.

Lit' Hit
Duress means to force someone into doing something against their will.

Effects of nullity of marriage

- Partners are free to marry.
- Under the Succession Act 1965 partners have no legal entitlements to their former partner's estate if they die.

Divorce

Divorce was introduced in Ireland in 1996 under the Family Law (Divorce) Act 1996. A decree of divorce allows both partners to terminate their existing marriage legally so they can remarry. When a court grants a decree of divorce, the court may also make orders in relation to:

Did you know
In 1997 93 divorces were granted in Ireland, in comparison to 2,949 in 2013.

- custody of children and access
- payment of maintenance
- allocation of property
- extinguishment of succession rights.

When a decree of divorce is granted, it cannot be reversed.

Grounds for divorce

- Spouses must have been living apart from one another for four out of the previous five years.
- There is no reasonable possibility of reconciliation between spouses. Solicitors are legally obliged to discuss this possibility before proceeding and to recommend counselling.
- Adequate provisions have been made for the spouse and any dependent members of the family.

Explain how the Family Mediation Service helps couples who are experiencing difficulties in their marriage. (10) **OL**

Explain **each** of the following options that couples, who are experiencing relationship difficulties, may consider:
- marriage counselling
- legal separation
- divorce.

State one advantage and one disadvantage of each option. (15) **OL**

Identify and give an account of the options that are available to couples that are experiencing difficulties in their marriage. (24) **OL**

Set out the conditions required for granting a divorce under the Family Law (Divorce) Act 1996. (8) **HL**

Reasons why marital breakdown is increasing in Ireland

Marital breakdown is on the increase in Irish society. This can be attributed to a variety of factors.

- Separation and divorce are now more socially acceptable than in the past.
- The process to obtain a divorce is easier.
- Women are less likely to be financially dependent on their husbands, due to increased qualifications and established careers.
- Social welfare payments are available for one-parent households.
- An increase in unemployment and social problems, e.g. alcoholism, which can place undue strain on marital relationships.

> **Did you know**
> Marital breakdown in Ireland is up 500% since 1986.

> **Did you know**
> Marital breakdown in Ireland is highest in the age group 50-54. In this age group, over one in five marriages have ended in divorce or separation.

Effects of marital breakdown

Effects on spouses	Effects on children	Effects on society
• May experience a sense of guilt for not being able to make the marriage work, or for how the separation or divorce has affected their children • May feel rejected by their spouse when a marriage breaks down, which can lead to feelings of poor self-worth or failure • May experience a decline in their standard of living due to the loss of one income. They may struggle to pay bills, which leads to stress	• May feel responsible for the marital breakdown, resulting in feelings of guilt • May exhibit behavioural or emotional problems, e.g. anxiety, due to feeling sad or rejected • May experience feelings of loneliness due to the absence of a mother or father after marital breakdown	• Increases the number of one-parent families and blended families • Increases the need for accommodation, as families often split into two homes • In certain circumstances, families may become dependent on social welfare payments, e.g. the One-Parent Family Payment

MARRIAGE

THE FAMILY AS A CARING UNIT

What you will learn:

- **The roles and responsibilities of family members through the life cycle**
- **Gender issues in relation to family roles**
- **Social and economic factors affecting the changing roles of the family**
- **Child-parent relationships**
- **The rights of children within the family**
- **Adolescent-parent relationships**
- **Importance of good communication within the family**
- **The role of older people within the family**
- **Importance of independence for an older person within the family**
- **Generation conflict**
- **Response of the family unit to those with special needs**
- **Statutory and voluntary services available to those with special needs**

The family is a unit where all members should feel loved, cherished and cared for. Each member has a role and responsibilities in the running of the family in order to fulfil its function as a caring unit. If a family member has special needs, the family must respond to their needs with the help of various statutory and voluntary services.

The roles and responsibilities of family members through the life cycle

A role is the expected pattern of behaviour of an individual according to their status or position in society. A person's role within the family will depend on their position, e.g. father, mother, partner, sibling, son, daughter or grandparent. People play different roles towards different family members, e.g. father to child, husband to wife. Different roles bring different responsibilities. Responsibilities are the duties or tasks people are required to carry out as part of their role, e.g. a parent has a responsibility to keep their child safe.

Role overload

In life, a person may have to play many roles at one time, each with a different expected behaviour. For example, a woman may have to play the role of an employee, a wife and a mother.

When a person attempts to play many roles at the same time it can lead to role overload, causing feelings of stress and anxiety. Women, in particular, suffer from role overload, as they may struggle to find the balance between their careers and being the main homemaker.

Role conflict

Role conflict may occur when the person is playing many roles at one time and the expectations of one role clashes with the expectations of another, e.g. a parent who has to work but their child is ill. This dilemma can lead to stress, feelings of guilt and worry.

Family roles

The life cycle of the family includes children, adolescents, parents and grandparents. Each family member has roles and responsibilities that are expected of them. These change as people age.

Children

A child may be a son/daughter, sibling or grandchild. The roles and responsibilities of a child are influenced by their age.

Roles and responsibilities

- Learning to behave in a socially acceptable way, e.g. having manners and showing respect for others. Parents pass on this knowledge either formally by instruction, or informally by example, e.g. by mirroring parents' behaviour
- Following family rules and carrying out simple chores
- Understanding the difference between right and wrong and following the rules of society, e.g. do not steal. Such morals are passed on by parents and are vital to ensure a child's successful integration into society.

Adolescents

An adolescent may be a son/daughter, sibling or grandchild. Adolescence is a period of change, when roles and responsibilities change from that of a child to an adult.

Roles and responsibilities

At home

- Taking on extra responsibilities around the home, e.g. babysitting, cooking family meals or laundry
- Having more of an input in family decisions and family rules. This teaches adolescents to learn to moderate their own behaviour in preparation for adulthood.
- Acting as role models for younger siblings, passing on positive behaviours and attitudes

In school

- Following school rules and behaving in a socially acceptable way, e.g. treating fellow students and staff with respect. Peer pressure can sometimes compromise this.
- Working hard to achieve their best at school to reach their full academic potential

 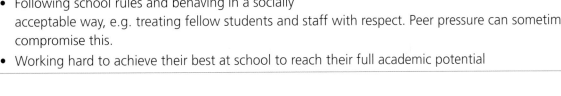

Each family member has a role and a number of responsibilities within the family unit. Describe **one** role and **two** responsibilities of teenagers/adolescents. (12) **OL**

THE FAMILY AS A CARING UNIT

Parents

A parent may be a mother/father, spouse or son/daughter. Parents' roles and responsibilities are extensive, as they must ensure that the needs of family members are fulfilled. Nowadays, both parents take on the roles and responsibilities of managing the home and caring for their children.

Roles and responsibilities

- Caring for and looking after their spouse/partner
- Reproducing to create a family
- Providing financially for family members so that their physical needs are met
- Providing a safe, loving and caring environment for family members so that their emotional needs are met
- Teaching children the norms, values, morals, behaviours, and social skills appropriate to behave in a manner approved of by society. This helps a child to integrate successfully into society.

Grandparents

A grandparent may be a parent, grandparent or spouse. Nowadays grandparents carry out a number of important roles and responsibilities in the life of the family, as they are living to an older age and often have more time to spend with family members.

Roles and responsibilities

- Helping their children financially, e.g. paying a deposit for a house, due to the high cost of living
- Passing on values, knowledge and wisdom to younger generations
- Helping out with child-minding, which can reduce the expense of childcare for parents
- Providing emotional support to their children and grandchildren. Often grandchildren may find it easier to discuss matters with their grandparents, as the relationship has fewer rules and regulations.

As grandparents get older, they may have to depend on others for care or financial support to meet their own needs. This often becomes the responsibility of their children.

? Describe how roles within the family change as parents get older. (20) **OL**

Assess the role of grandparents in modern family life. (9) **HL**

Discuss the roles and responsibilities of family members **and** explain how these roles change through the life cycle of the family. (24) **HL**

Gender issues in relation to family roles

Gender roles are the behaviours expected of an individual by society because of their sex. Traditionally, roles within the family were segregated into male and female gender roles. Men were the breadwinners and worked outside the home, whereas women worked inside the home and were responsible for minding children and doing housework.

Changes in modern society have altered these gender roles.

Change in society	Effect on gender roles
Improved equality laws and changing attitudes towards women	Less gender-specific roles are evident within the home. Integrated roles are now common between parents, with both now playing an equal role in household tasks and childminding, regardless of gender. Household responsibilities are shared between siblings of either gender.
Increased educational and job opportunities for women	Men are no longer the sole breadwinners in many households, as women are shifting roles from working in the home to working outside the home. In some families role reversal has occurred, with fathers staying at home to mind children as mothers have higher-paid occupations.
Increased one-parent families	Gender roles have become less defined, as one parent has to take on the roles and responsibilities of mother and father.

 Outline **three** changes in modern society that have affected gender roles in the family. (12) **OL**

Social and economic factors affecting the changing roles of the family

Social factors

- In the past, the traditional extended family was the norm, with segregated roles between partners. Today, the self-sufficient nuclear family is the norm. In this family type integrated roles are evident, with both partners playing an equal role in parenting and managing the home.

- Due to an increased number of women obtaining third-level qualifications, many women are now shifting roles from working in the home to working outside the home. This has led to shared duties in the rearing of children and managing the home, instead of these duties being the sole responsibility of the mother.

- Older people are less dependent on their children, as they have better health due to improved health care and knowledge of nutrition. They can also continue to live independently due to social welfare payments, e.g. the State Pension. The longer lifespan of older people has meant that they now play a large part in the rearing and minding of grandchildren.

THE FAMILY AS A CARING UNIT

Economic factors

- In many families both parents are required to work outside the home to meet high living costs, so they must pay for childcare. However, high childcare costs may prohibit both parents in some families from working. This has led to an increase in the number of stay-at-home fathers in recent years.

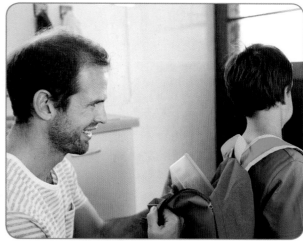

- Many adolescents are choosing to attend third-level education due to higher minimum education requirements for many jobs. This has meant that children are dependant financially on their parents for longer, which can put a financial strain on the family.

- The state provides social welfare payments, e.g. Children's Allowance and Back to School Clothing and Footwear Allowance, to help parents fulfil their economic function, especially if they are struggling to meet their basic needs. The state also provides the State Pension, free travel and a Fuel Allowance for older people, helping them maintain their independence.

 Explain how the role of older people within the family has changed as a result of social and economic factors. (12) **HL**

Describe how changing roles within the family have impacted on individuals and/or society. (18) **HL**

Analyse how (i) social factors and (ii) economic factors affect parenting roles within the family unit. (20) **HL**

Child-parent relationships

The relationship between a child and his or her parents is the first, and perhaps the most **formative**, relationship a child has. It should meet the physical and psychological needs of the child. The fulfilment of these needs will create a close relationship between a child and his or her parents, which will help the child grow into a balanced, secure and confident adult, capable of forming his or her own relationships.

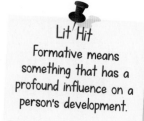

Lit Hit

Formative means something that has a profound influence on a person's development.

Physical needs

- Children are completely dependent on their parents for all their physical needs, especially in the first year of life. To meet these needs parents must provide:
  - food for growth and development
  - shelter for safety and warmth
  - clothing for modesty and protection.

- A child that is well cared for will be happy, content and will develop physically to their full potential.

Psychological needs

- Children's psychological needs include security, love, encouragement and protection. These are important to enhance confidence and self-esteem.
- The bond and relationship between a child and their parents has a profound effect on a child's psychological well-being. To meet these needs parents must:
  - provide a loving, open and supportive environment for their child, helping the child to feel safe and able to express his or her feelings
  - pass on norms, values, morals, behaviours and social skills, e.g. sharing, listening and manners, through their relationship with their child, so that the child can learn the social skills required to fit into society
  - act as role models for their child to base his or her future behaviour on. Effective, non-violent discipline can help children behave in an acceptable way
  - create a fun learning environment to help their child's education. Learning with parents in a positive way, with encouragement and praise, engages a child in learning for life.

> Explain how parents provide for (i) the physical and (ii) the psychological needs of young children. (12) **OL**

The rights of children within the family

Within the family, all children (under the age of 18), have the following rights.

- The right to life
- The right to have a name and be granted a nationality
- The right to live with their parents, unless it is against their best interests
- The right to basic physical needs, including food, shelter and clothing for a basic/adequate standard of living
- The right to develop physically, mentally, socially, morally and spiritually
- The right to access medical care in order to gain the highest standard of health
- The right to protection from abuse and neglect
- The right to education, leisure, recreation and cultural activities
- The right to special care, education and training for those with a disability

> Outline **four** rights of children within the family. (12) **HL**

THE FAMILY AS A CARING UNIT

Adolescent-parent relationships

Adolescence is the stage in life where a young person is no longer regarded as a child, but is not yet old enough to be considered an adult. This can be a time of conflict with parents.

Causes of conflict between adolescents and parents

- **Independence:** adolescents may feel ready to make their own choices and seek more independence from their families. This can lead to conflict, as parents may be afraid to relinquish control as they worry about their child's safety.

- **Peers:** adolescents are no longer solely influenced by their parents, as peers play an ever-increasing role in influencing beliefs, behaviours and attitudes. If an adolescent begins to behave in a negative way, e.g. smoking or not studying, as a result of peer influence, parents can become frustrated, as they know the long-term **repercussions** of this behaviour. This can lead to conflict.

- **Relationships:** dating and the formation of romantic relationships occurs during adolescence. This can cause conflict as parents may feel their son or daughter is too young to be in a relationship and may worry about teenage pregnancy or sexually transmitted diseases.

- **Social media:** adolescents often begin to use social media, e.g. WhatsApp and Snapchat to interact with peers. Parents may worry their child will not behave in a safe way online or may become a target for online bullying or predators, leading to conflict.

- **Employment:** Adolescents may take on a part-time job in the evenings or weekends in order to earn extra income. This may cause conflict if parents feel children are spending too much time working and not enough time on schoolwork.

> Lit Hit
> A repercussion is something that happens as a consequence of an action.

REMEMBER IT!

'Infuriating Parents Raise Strong Emotions.'
Independence, Peers, Relationships, Social media, Employment.

Dealing with conflict

- Avoid angry confrontations. If this is occurring, both sides should take time out and wait until they have calmed down before attempting a resolution.

- When communicating, ensure both sides are given a fair chance to speak and explain their viewpoint in a calm way.

- Display empathy. This is important in helping to understand the other person's point of view.

- A compromise may have to be reached if a decision cannot be made on either side, in order to reduce future conflict.

- Parents should involve adolescents in the setting of new boundaries and rules, as this joint decision making will make them feel involved and that they have a say. A set of consequences should be established in case the new rules are broken.

? Identify **two** factors, outside the family, which may influence a teenager's behaviour. (8) **OL**

Outline how relationships with family members change during adolescence. (12) **OL**

Discuss **three** ways of dealing with conflict. (15) **OL**

Describe one strategy for resolving conflict within the family. (12) **HL**

Importance of good communication within the family

Communication is a big factor in determining the success or failure of family relationships. Effective communication involves the sharing of ideas, information and emotions. This is beneficial as it:

- **helps clarify rules and expectations:** without communication, family members do not know what is expected from them, which may lead to conflict
- **helps to build trust among family members:** if family members feel able to express their opinions, views, worries or anxieties, they will build trust between one another
- **develops listening skills:** if parents can communicate by listening and speaking without shouting, it teaches children to do the same, which can benefit their relationships in the future.

 Explain why good communication is important between family members. (10) **OL**

Discuss the merits of good child-parent communication. (12) **HL**

The role of older people within the family

For information on the role of older people within the family see page 374.

Importance of independence for an older person within the family

Being independent is important as it helps older people to:

- **develop friendships:** after retirement, older people have more time to join active retirement associations, carry out voluntary work or take part in various leisure activities. Through this they meet new people, form friendships and develop a sense of belonging
- **maintain self-worth:** an older person who helps the family with childminding will develop feelings of self-worth and confidence, as they feel they have a valuable role and a place in the family and society.

Factors that enable older people to maintain their independence

Community supports

- Supportive family and neighbours can help older people maintain independence by calling regularly and offering help if needed, e.g. to do their grocery shopping. This provides company and companionship, which prevents loneliness and isolation.
- Housing options, e.g. sheltered housing schemes, can help older people maintain independence if they are no longer able to live alone, as they will still have some level of independence.
- Voluntary services, e.g. meals on wheels, offer services to ensure that older people can continue to live independently for longer and avoid feeling that they are a burden on others.

Did you know

Sheltered housing schemes are groups of small houses built with the needs of older people in mind. There is a nurse/manager on call and a community centre to meet and socialise with others.

THE FAMILY AS A CARING UNIT

State supports

- Social welfare payments, e.g. contributory or non-contributory pensions and the Fuel Allowance, allow an older person be financially independent within the family.
- Community care services, e.g. public health nurses, focus on keeping older people in their homes, e.g. by calling to their home to dress wounds rather than taking older people into hospitals for care, maintaining independence.
- Medical cards enable an older person over 70 years of age to obtain necessary medication, allowing them to be financially independent within the family.
- Free travel from the age of 66 maintains independence as it allows older people to travel and keep in touch with friends and family when they may no longer be able to drive a long distance.

> **?** Discuss **three** reasons why people are living longer. (18) **OL**
>
> Comment on (i) the importance of independence for elderly people in the family **and** (ii) how the state supports the independence of elderly people. (20) **OL**
>
> Give an account of **four** factors that enable older people to maintain their independence. (16) **HL**

Generation conflict

Generation conflict occurs when the opinions, views and morals of one generation clash with those of the next generation, e.g. between parents and children.

Causes of generation conflict

- **Behaviours:** older people may disapprove of behaviour or norms that are different from that of their generation, e.g. changes in the ways adolescents socialise, leading to conflict.
- **Control:** parents often find it difficult to **relinquish** control of their children, no matter what age the children are. For example, grandparents can become too involved and interfere with the rearing of grandchildren, causing conflict.
- **Generalisations:** older people can make generalisations about younger people, e.g. they all have bad manners, causing conflict. Younger people may also make generalisations about older people, thinking they are 'past it', or losing respect for them as they age and physically and mentally slow down.
- **Lack of privacy:** families and older people may resent the lack of privacy that results from cohabiting if a grandparent has to move into the family home, creating conflict.

Lit Hit

Relinquish means let go.

> **?** Explain what you understand by *generation conflict* **and** state **two** ways of dealing with conflict. (15) **OL**
>
> Discuss the reasons why conflict may arise between adult children and their parents. (18) **OL**
>
> Give an account of the advantages **and** the disadvantages of grandparents living with a family member who has young children. (20) **OL**

Response of the family unit to those with special needs

When a family member has special needs, it is the duty of the other family members to care for that person. Outside assistance can be availed of from voluntary and statutory services throughout Ireland.

Examples of special needs include:

- **physical disabilities**, e.g. mobility impairments, visual impairments, hearing impairments
- **intellectual disabilities**, e.g. Down syndrome
- **mental health disorders**, e.g. depression, schizophrenia, obsessive-compulsive disorder (OCD), addiction
- **neurodevelopmental disorders**, e.g. autistic spectrum disorders, attention deficit disorder (ADD), attention deficit hyperactivity disorder (ADHD).

Difficulties faced by a family member with special needs

- Lack of mobility may be a difficulty experienced by a person with a physical disability. Even with aids such as wheelchairs, walking sticks or guide dogs, they may feel they lack the freedom to move about or access transport in the same way as able-bodied people.

- Lack of independence can affect people with special needs, especially those who need constant care from others. This reliance on others can lead to feelings of inadequacy and resentment.
- Social isolation may be experienced by those with a physical disability, as their disability may make it difficult for them to get out and to meet new people. Wanting to be alone and avoiding social contact can be a characteristic of certain cognitive impairments, e.g. autistic spectrum disorder. This can lead to loneliness, low self-esteem and difficulties in forming relationships.
- Children with special educational needs may have to travel long distances daily to attend a special school, e.g. a school for the visually impaired. This can create feelings of isolation, as their school friends may not live in their locality.
- Fewer employment opportunities may be available to those with special needs due to discrimination, access problems or lack of facilities, e.g. a wheelchair-suitable lift. This can lead to a reliance on social welfare payments and increased incidences of poverty.

Difficulties faced by the family unit when a family member has special needs

- Isolation and exhaustion may be experienced by parents who are the primary carers for family members with special needs, as they may not get a break or a day off.
- Reduction in income is common if one parent chooses to give up work and stay at home to look after a family member with special needs. Meeting financial obligations may become difficult, as disposable income is reduced.

THE FAMILY AS A CARING UNIT

- Increased expenditure, e.g. on special equipment, carer's visits, doctor's appointments and home conversions, may affect the family's finances. Applying for social welfare payments and grants, e.g. Carer's Allowance or the Housing Adaptation Grant, can be time-consuming and stressful for parents.
- Feelings of stress and guilt are experienced by parents who are finding it hard to split their time between all of their family members. Other family members may feel left out or resentful.

How the family can respond to the needs of a family member who has special needs

- Adapt the home to suit the requirements of the family member with special needs, e.g. a sensory room can provide stress relief and assist with **sensory processing difficulties** for those with autistic spectrum disorders.
- Encourage independence whenever possible, e.g. teaching the family member with special needs to dress themselves, cook or use computers. This will allow them to care for their own needs rather than relying on others in the future.
- Provide emotional support by being there to listen, care for and show understanding and love. This is important, as it can be difficult for the member with special needs to cope with the challenges they experience.
- Ensure all social welfare payments and supports available are availed of, e.g. Disability Allowance or medical card. This may need to be completed for the family member with special needs throughout their life if they are incapable of applying for their own entitlements.
- One parent may choose to stay at home to look after the family member with special needs, so that they are not reliant on others or state care to meet their needs.

> **Lit Hit**
>
> Sensory processing difficulties mean that the brain has trouble receiving and responding to information that comes in through the senses, e.g. common sounds may be painful or overwhelming.

? Identify and elaborate on the difficulties that the family unit may experience when a member of the family has special needs. (18) **HL**

Discuss how a family might respond to the needs of a member who has a disability. (20) **HL**

Discuss **each** of the following:
- the difficulties that the family unit may experience when a child has special needs **and**
- the difficulties that the family unit may experience when a parent has special needs. (24) **HL**

Statutory and voluntary services available to those with special needs

Statutory services

National Disability Authority (NDA)
- The NDA provides expert advice to the government on disability policy in Ireland, e.g. on disability services and supports, employment opportunities and housing.
- As part of the NDA, the Centre for Excellence in Universal Design promotes the universal design of buildings, products, services and ICT so that they can be easily accessed and used by everyone, including people with disabilities.

Special schools
- The state provides over 140 special schools in Ireland that cater for particular types of special needs, e.g. visual or hearing impairments.
- In these schools children benefit from smaller classes, specially trained teachers and specialised facilities and equipment to suit their particular needs.

Other statutory services
- The Equality Authority
- Citizens Information Board
- Health Service Executive (HSE)

Voluntary services

Rehab
Rehab is a charity that promotes diversity and inclusion for people with a disability or disadvantage. It provides services including:
- National Learning Network, which provides a range of training programmes, e.g. certified courses in catering or computers, and support services for people who need specialist support, enabling them to take up employment or go on to further education
- Rehab Enterprises, which employs people with disabilities in a range of businesses, e.g. recycling or retail services
- RehabCare, which provides health and social care services, e.g. resource centres, supported accomodation and **respite care**, all over Ireland.

RehabGroup
Investing in People, Changing Perspectives

Lit'Hit
Respite care is the provision of short-term accommodation in a facility outside the home. This provides temporary relief to those who are providing continual care and assistance to family members with special needs.

Enable Ireland
Enable Ireland provides services to children and adults with disabilities to enable them to achieve maximum independence and inclusion in their communities. Services provided include:
- an Early Services Team that provides a range of services for children up to the age of six with physical disabilities and/or developmental delays, e.g. cerebral palsy. Each child receives an individual programme to maximise their mobility, play, communication, and social skills
- respite breaks in an Enable Ireland respite facility, to give children and adults with special needs further opportunities to participate in mainstream, community-based activities, e.g. swimming.
- literacy and computer training for adults with disabilities, which helps them to build on and develop skills.

enable ireland
Empower · Include · Enable
Action on Disability

Other voluntary services
- Irish Wheelchair Association
- DeafHear
- National Council for the Blind in Ireland

 Outline the role of the *Rehab Group*. (12) **HL**

THE FAMILY AS A CARING UNIT

What you will learn:

- Family Law (Maintenance of Spouses and Children) Act 1976
- Family Home Protection Act 1976 (amended by the Family Law Act 1995)
- Domestic Violence Act 1996
- Judicial Separation and Family Law Reform Act 1989
- Childcare Act 1991 (by the Children and Family Act 2013)
- Making a will

Family law is necessary to ensure the rights of the family and the child are protected.

Family Law (Maintenance of Spouses and Children) Act 1976

Maintenance is a financial support paid by a person for the benefit of a dependent child/children or spouse/civil partner.

Under this act, if a relationship breaks down maintenance must be paid to a:

- dependent spouse/civil partner if they do not have the financial resources to support themselves
- parent with custody of the dependent child/children. A child is considered dependent if they are under 18 years of age, are under 23 years of age in full time education or have a disability.

This act states that if a relationship breaks down, maintenance must be paid to the parent with custody of the children, even if both parties are sharing the same house.

Maintenance may be agreed between spouses/civil partners or parents, however, if an agreement cannot be reached they will have to attend the District Court and apply for a maintenance order. A maintenance order outlines the amount a spouse/civil partner or parent has to pay the other. The amount awarded depends on individual cases.

> **Did you know** ❓
>
> The maximum that the District Court can order for maintenance of a child is €150 per week. The maximum they can order for maintenance of a dependent spouse/civil partner is €500 per week.

> ❓ Explain how the Family Law (Maintenance of Spouses and Children) Act, (1976) protects the family. (10) **OL**

Family Home Protection Act 1976 (amended by the Family Law Act 1995)

The family home is defined as a dwelling in which the married couple/civil partners ordinarily live. This may be owned by one, or both partners (joint tenancy).

This act protects the family home from being sold, mortgaged, leased or transferred without the **consent** of both spouses/civil partners, regardless of who owns the family home. If a court finds that the withholding of consent to sell the family home by one spouse/civil partner is unreasonable, they can choose to dismiss this.

> *Lit Hit*
> Consent means permission or agreement between two people.

> ❓ State how the family is protected by the Family Home Protection Act (1976). (6) **HL**

Domestic Violence Act 1996

Domestic violence is any form of physical, sexual or psychological violence that puts the safety or welfare of a person at risk.

This act protects any person who lives in a domestic relationship, e.g. spouses, civil partners, cohabiting couples, parents, children or any others living together, from violence, threatening behaviour or creation of fear.

Under the law there are three main kinds of protection a person experiencing domestic violence can apply for: a safety order, a barring order or a protection order.

- **Safety Order:** prevents the alleged offender from committing further violence, or threatening violence, against the applicant and their dependents. The offender is not required to leave the family home. This can last for a period of up to five years.
- **Barring Order (Section 22, Family Law Act 1976):** requires the alleged offender to leave the family home for a specified time outlined by the court, and prevents them from committing further violence or threats of violence against the applicant and their dependents. They also are prohibited from watching or being near the applicant's home. This can last for a period of up to three years.
- **Protection Order:** a temporary safety order issued to an applicant if they have to wait for the district court to hear their case for a safety or barring order. It offers protection that is similar to a safety order.

> **Did you know**
>
> If any of these orders under the Domestic Violence Act are breached by the offender, an Garda Síochána have immediate powers of arrest. The matter will come before the courts as a criminal matter, and an offender may receive a prison term of 12 months.

Judicial Separation and Family Law Reform Act 1989

For information on the Judicial Separation and Family Law Reform Act 1989 see page 369.

Childcare Act 1991 (amended by the Children and Family Act 2013)

An Ghníomhaireacht um
Leanaí agus an Teaghlach
Child and Family Agency

This act makes provision for the care and protection of all children, and is enforced by an Garda Síochána and the Child and Family Agency (Tusla).

These enforcement services believe that it is generally in the best interests of a child to be reared in his or her own home. However, if an Garda Síochána or Tusla fear for a child's safety, e.g. if a child is deemed to be at risk of being assaulted or sexually abused, or if they have concerns that a child is not receiving adequate care and protection, they have the power to intervene in family situations.

To intervene they must apply to the courts for a Care Order or a Supervision Order.

- **Care Order:** facilitates the removal of a child from the family home to be placed in care. An Emergency Care Order covers a maximum of eight days in care, a standard Care Order may last until the child is 18 years.
- **Supervision Order:** allows personnel from Tusla to visit a child in their home periodically to monitor their health and welfare for a maximum of 12 months.

> **?** Write an informative note on the Childcare Act, 1991. (14) **HL**
>
> Comment on the protection afforded to children under current Irish family law. Refer to **two** acts. (14) **HL**

FAMILY LAW

Making a will

A will is a witnessed document that sets out in writing the deceased's wishes for his or her estate after death.

Why it is important to make a will (advantages)

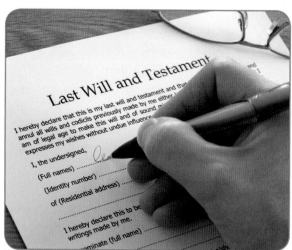

✓ A will ensures that the wishes of the **testator** are carried out, e.g. their estate is divided among people as listed on the will. This can provide peace of mind and also avoid conflict arising on the event of their death.

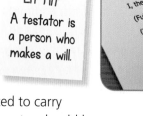
Lit Hit
A testator is a person who makes a will.

✓ A will ensures an executor is appointed to carry out the wishes of the testator. An executor should be someone the testator trusts to comply with their wishes and do their best to alleviate any disputes.

✓ A will ensures that guardians and trustees are appointed to look after children should a situation arise where both parents become deceased. These should be people the testator trusts completely to look after the needs of their children.

Did you know

Ireland has the highest inheritance tax rate in the world, at more than three times the international average.

✓ A will raises a testator's awareness of Capital Acquisition Tax (inheritance tax) limits that are placed on beneficiaries' inheritance, e.g. surviving children can receive an inheritance of up to €280,000 tax free, but they must pay 33% inheritance tax on the remainder to the government. An awareness of these limits can help a testator to distribute their estate in a way that limits the amount of inheritance tax their beneficiaries will have to pay.

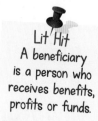
Lit Hit
A beneficiary is a person who receives benefits, profits or funds.

Succession Act 1965

If an individual dies without making a will, any money or estate is distributed in accordance with the rules set out in the Succession Act 1965.

The family of the deceased	How the estate is distributed
Surviving spouse/civil partner (no children)	• Surviving spouse/civil partner receives the complete estate
Surviving spouse/civil partner and children	• Surviving spouse/civil partner receives two-thirds of the estate • Surviving children receive one-third of the estate
Surviving children (no spouse/civil partner)	• Surviving children receive the complete estate
No spouse/civil partner or children	• Surviving parents receive the complete estate • If the deceased's parents have passed away their surviving siblings receive the complete estate • If the deceased's parents and siblings have passed away the next surviving blood relative receives the complete estate

Procedure for making a will

- **Employ a solicitor** to advise in relation to the legalities and taxation issues that apply to making a will. An individual can draw up a will without a solicitor, but they may not fully understand the legal requirements needed, which could **render** the will null and void.

- **List all assets**, e.g. property and savings. State their location and possible value.

- **Appoint an executor** to ensure that any requests or wishes stated on the will be carried out. A minimum of two executors are normally recommended.

- **List beneficiaries**, e.g. a spouse, children and relatives. Include their names, addresses and contact details.

- **Divide the estate** between the listed beneficiaries, with due regard for the limitations imposed by the Succession Act. Under this act a spouse/civil partner is entitled to half of their spouse/partner's estate if they do not have children together or one-third of the estate if they do have children together.

- **Outline funeral arrangements**, e.g. a church or a humanist ceremony, burial or cremation.

- **Validate the will** by getting it drawn up in writing and signed by the testator in the presence of two witnesses (witnesses cannot be beneficiaries), and signed by the two witnesses.

- **Store in a safe place**, e.g. a safety deposit box in a bank. The executor should be made aware of this location.

A will may need to be reviewed from time to time due to changes in life situations, e.g. divorce.

Lit Hit

Render means to cause something to become.

Did you know

Approximately 34% of adults in Ireland have a will.

Features of a valid will

- An individual making a will must be over 18 years.
- An individual making a will must be of sound mind. This means having understanding of their actions and reasonable knowledge of their family, possessions and surroundings.
- The will must be in writing, signed and dated in the presence of two witnesses.

Explain why it is particularly important for divorced parents to make a will. (5) **OL**

Outline **three** important features of a valid will. (12) **OL**

Outline the procedure for making a will. (12) **OL**

State why it is important for parents to make a will and outline the procedure involved. (14) **HL**

FAMILY LAW

HOME DESIGN AND MANAGEMENT

Chapter 18: Housing styles

🔗 HOUSING STYLES
4.1.1

What you will learn:

- Historical housing styles in Ireland
- Historical development of housing styles in Ireland from the nineteenth century
- Popular housing styles in Ireland today
- Social, cultural, economic and environmental factors that influence the choice of housing style

As the culture of a country changes, so too does the architecture. Housing styles in Ireland have changed in many ways since the beginning of the nineteenth century. Housing style refers to the overall look of the house: its shape, features, design and appearance. Throughout history, a number of different housing styles have emerged, each with its own unique features. Housing styles include Georgian, Gothic, Tudor, Arts and Crafts, Italianate and modern.

Historical housing styles in Ireland

Did you know ❓
Gargoyles, towers and rose windows are all typical features of Gothic-style churches.

Georgian
- Shallow roof
- Square or rectangular windows
- Feature door with fanlight and columns
- Steps up to door
- Quoin stones

Gothic
- Pointed, steep roof
- Arched windows
- Bay windows
- Decorative moulding in eaves

Tudor
- Pointed gables
- White plaster panels
- Black timber framing
- Leaded windows
- Bay windows
- Red brick

Arts and Crafts
- Romantic and picturesque style
- Small windows
- Projecting porch
- High roof

HOUSING STYLES

Italianate

- Classical formal style, popular in towns
- Low-pitched roof
- Decorative mouldings over windows and doors
- Arch-headed windows
- Balconies

Modern

- Post-war buildings 1920–1930
- Flat roof
- High rise
- Steel and concrete construction with lots of glass
- Simple design
- White plaster/paintwork

Historical development of housing styles in Ireland from the nineteenth century

The historical development of housing styles in Ireland can be examined across five periods, spanning from the 1800s until the present day.

Early nineteenth century (1800–1850)

During the early nineteenth century 70% of the Irish population lived in rural areas, with the remaining 30% living in urban towns and cities.

Rural areas

- Single-storey thatched cottages were the usual home of poor farm labourers. They consisted of two rooms: a kitchen/living area and a bedroom. Some cottages had another small bedroom in the loft for children to sleep in. The walls were made of stone and mud and were whitewashed. The roof was thatched with reeds, straw or hay. Windows were small to keep in heat. A half-door opened onto the kitchen. An open turf fire was used to heat the kitchen and for cooking.

▲ Single-storey thatched cottage

- Prosperous farmers built stone two-storey farmhouses with slate roofs. They had four or five bedrooms and a room called a parlour that was used on special occasions.
- Wealthy landowners lived in large estate houses with many bedrooms and servants' quarters in the basement.

Urban areas

- The Georgian-style house was popular in towns and cities. Houses were terraced with three to four storeys and a basement below street level. Walls were constructed of stone and covered with lime plaster. Roofs were slated. The door was the focal point, with steps leading up to it and a fanlight above. Rooms had high ceilings with ornate, decorative cornices. Doorways had architraves as a decorative frame.
- Poorer families lived in urban tenements, originally designed as large Georgian homes for the wealthy. These were subdivided into flats or single rooms, housing many families in poor conditions.

▲ Georgian door

Late nineteenth century (1850–1900)

The pace of housing development and building slowed during this time.

Rural areas

- Housing styles were similar to those in the early nineteenth century, with small thatched cottages and farmhouses remaining popular. Stone two-storey farmhouses with slate roofs increased in popularity with those who could afford them.

▲ Stone two-storey farmhouse with a slate roof

Urban areas

- Many wealthy families moved out of their inner-city Georgian homes and into newly built homes in the suburbs.
- There was a move away from Georgian style to the more ornate and decorative Gothic and Tudor styles. Gothic style featured pointed windows and arches, steeply-pitched roofs and decorative mouldings. Tudor style featured plaster panels with black timber frames, leaded bay windows and red bricks.
- Better infrastructure and transport meant that materials, e.g. bricks, became more widely available for use in house building.
- Many working people lived in small terraced houses that were cramped and had small gardens. Poorer families continued to live in tenement, inner-city housing.

Early twentieth century (1900–1950)

Rural areas

- Government grants were used to upgrade rural homes, e.g. replacing thatch with slate or tiles, or building extra rooms onto the side. Others built new two-storey homes and used the old cottage as an outhouse for animals.
- In 1946 the government introduced the Rural Electrification Scheme, which greatly improved the standard of living in rural areas, e.g. electric lights replaced oil lamps.

▲ Upgraded single-storey cottage

Urban areas

- People began to move away from terraced, city-centre houses to detached or semi-detached homes in the suburbs. Houses were simpler in design than the ornate Tudor and Gothic styles seen previously. Many council and housing estates were also built on the outskirts of towns and cities.
- Houses were built from newly improved building materials, e.g. steel windows instead of timber, concrete blocks or brick instead of stone, and tiles instead of slate for roofing.

▲ Semi-detached houses

- For those who remained in towns and cities, houses tended to be two storeys or more, as land became more expensive. Local authority housing schemes were introduced, which led to the building of small, utilitarian homes.

HOUSING STYLES

Late twentieth century (1950–2000)

Rural areas

- One-off housing, particularly the modern bungalow, increased in popularity during the 1970s and 1980s, and the style was replicated across the country.
- Housing estates were built in rural areas on the outskirts of villages and towns.

Urban areas

- High-rise housing, e.g. the Ballymun tower block in Dublin, was built in inner cities, due to high cost of land. These housed hundreds of families in cramped conditions and were often poorly maintained with few amenities.
- Small plots of land were used to build private housing estates. Many houses were built in the same small plot. This resulted in smaller-sized homes. These were often built quickly with poor insulation.
- New building materials were used, e.g. double glazing, fibreglass insulation and PVC window frames.

▲ High-rise flats

Twenty-first century (2000–present)

Today 62% of the Irish population live in urban areas and 38% live in rural areas. Building regulations and planning guidelines have greatly improved building standards, e.g. insulation and soundproofing, in both rural and urban areas.

Rural areas

- During the economic boom a large number of housing developments and estates were built in villages and towns, many with few amenities or services. Many remain unfinished as ghost estates due to economic downturn. Some are currently in the process of being demolished or completed.
- One-off custom-designed buildings on private land are still being built. These include bungalow, dormer or two-story dwellings.

Urban areas

- The majority of Irish people now live in urban areas. The difference between rural and urban housing is slowly disappearing, with more houses being built on the outskirts of towns.
- Land for building is limited and expensive, leading to high-density housing. Houses are compact, with small living spaces and outdoor areas. Apartments are increasing in popularity in cities and towns.

> **?** Outline the historical development of housing styles in Ireland since the nineteenth century to the present day. (20) **HL**

Popular housing styles in Ireland today

- Modern-style, one-off homes are popular as they are bright, minimalist and easy to care for.
- Renovated rural cottages or old houses are popular with those who wish to preserve Irish heritage.
- Due to **negative equity**, many people are choosing to renovate, extend or adapt their existing homes rather than sell them at a loss. A popular method of extending a home is to convert the attic space.
- Mixed-development housing estates are popular as they offer a selection of housing styles, e.g. semi-detached houses and apartments in one development. These are more commonly found in large towns and cities due to reduced land space. Smaller, exclusive housing estates in gated communities are also popular, with bigger, better-quality homes, larger green areas and playgrounds.
- Apartments are popular, especially among those living in cities who wish to be near work and amenities.

Lit Hit

Negative equity is when the value of a house falls below the outstanding balance on the mortgage.

▲ Apartment block

? Identify three housing styles commonly found in Ireland today and suggest reasons for the popularity of each. (24) **HL**

Social, cultural, economic and environmental factors that influence the choice of housing styles

Social and cultural factors

- **Personal preferences:** some people prefer privacy, so will choose a detached home on private land, compared to others who may prefer a semi-detached house in an estate near other people. A modern, minimalist housing style appeals to some, but others may opt for older period homes for their timeless features.
- **Availability:** the availability of houses to buy will determine choice of housing style, as if there is high demand for a particular style of house, e.g. three-bedroomed semi-detached family homes, availability to buy will be reduced.
- **Location:** where the house is located, e.g. urban or rural, will influence choice of housing style, as planning regulations dictate housing styles in different areas. Houses within a certain distance from towns and cities or close to services and amenities are in higher demand.
- **Family requirements:** a large family with young children will require more space, e.g. more bedrooms and a large garden, influencing preferred housing styles. If a family member has a special need this will limit choice, as many property styles may not suit specific needs, e.g. a two-storey home for an individual in a wheelchair.
- **History/tradition:** the style of the traditional Irish cottage, e.g. thatched roof and whitewashed walls, appeals to many, as it is seen as a symbol of Irish culture and heritage. For this reason, many people are choosing to renovate and restore traditional houses.

REMEMBER IT!

'People Always Love Family Homes.'
Personal preferences, Availability, Location, Family requirements, History/tradition.

HOUSING STYLES

Economic factors

- **Income:** available income will determine if individuals or couples can buy or rent their chosen style of house. Local authority housing schemes, e.g. the Incremental Purchase Scheme, are available to those on low incomes wishing to buy their own home.

- **Fees and costs:** many fees and costs associated with choosing a new home, e.g. stamp duty, council fees, solicitor fees or site costs, affect the overall price and therefore the style of house chosen.

- **Cost of materials:** when building a home the cost of materials has an impact on the style chosen. For example, a stone-finish exterior will be more expensive than plaster. Locally sourced materials, e.g. timber, are often less expensive than materials that must be imported.

- **Investment potential:** the possible future returns should be considered when choosing a house style if there is a possibility that the house will be resold. People should research local development plans to see if future developments could impact on the price, e.g. improved transport links that could increase the house resale price.

REMEMBER IT!
'**I**ndividual **F**amilies **C**an **I**nvest.'
Income, **F**ees and costs, **C**ost of materials, **I**nvestment potential.

Environmental factors

- **Building regulations:** when building, the building regulations and planning guidelines will influence housing styles, as local authorities aim to ensure that the house style chosen is in keeping with the local environment. Regulations can dictate the site location, shape of the house, materials chosen and landscaping.

- **Energy efficiency:** when selecting a housing style to build, energy efficiency is an important influence. This can be achieved by installing renewable sources of energy such as solar panels, insulating the home or installing double-glazed windows.

- **Surroundings:** it is important when building that the chosen house style fits in with the surrounding area and follows the gradient of the land, e.g. built in a hollow rather than on an exposed hill. This will protect the home from climate conditions, e.g. wind.

- **Aspect:** the direction that the site faces will influence the housing style chosen, as the main living areas should preferably be positioned facing south or west so that they benefit from natural light and passive solar energy, reducing heating costs.

▲ House fits in with its environment, and is protected from climate conditions, e.g. wind

REMEMBER IT!
'**B**e **E**nvironmentally **S**avvy **A**lways.'
Building regulations, **E**nergy efficiency, **S**urroundings, **A**spect.

? Comment on the factors that may influence a person's choice of housing style. (20) **OL**

Discuss (i) the economic and (ii) the environmental factors that influence the choice of housing styles. (24) **HL**

Chapter 19:
Housing provision

4.1.2

HOUSING PROVISION

What you will learn:

- **Housing requirements**
- **Housing provision in Ireland: distribution and adequacy**
- **Quality of accommodation**
- **The comparative costs of buying and renting**
- **Social housing provision**
- **Provision of local amenities and services**

Housing requirements

An individual's and family's housing requirements will vary significantly, depending on their physical and social requirements or stage in life.

Single people

- Single people require less space than other groups, but enough to live in comfort, e.g. a bedroom and living area.
- Proximity to an urban area is usually important, so single people can be close to college, work, leisure facilities and social outlets.
- An outdoor area is not a high priority.
- Access to public transport, e.g. bus or Luas routes, is important, especially for people who do not own a car.

Suitable accommodation: bedsits, apartments or flats. House-shares are also popular, as rent and expenses are shared among all tenants.

Families

- Families require more space than other groups, especially families with younger children.
- Suburban areas are a preferred choice for many, as homes cost less than in urban areas.
- Proximity to work, schools, shops or leisure facilities is usually important.
- Sufficient living space is required for the whole family to live comfortably, e.g. large, open-plan kitchens and an adequate number of bedrooms.
- Families with younger children may need a separate playroom and extensive storage space, e.g. in bedrooms. Families with older children may require a study space.
- An outdoor area, e.g. an enclosed garden, is a requirement of many families.
- Public transport or access to a good road network is a necessity for travelling to work. Children may need to be on a bus route for school.

Suitable accommodation: a semi-detached or detached home with two or more bedrooms (depending on size of family).

Older people

- Older people require less space than other groups, but enough to live in comfort, e.g. a bedroom and living area.
- Older people may prefer living in a small village or town for ease of access to local services and amenities.
- Adapted kitchen facilities, e.g. specially adapted taps and lower countertops, may be needed for those with physical ailments.
- Older people may require a downstairs bedroom, as well as a wheelchair-accessible bathroom with non-slip floors, handrails and shower seats for safety.
- An efficient and safe heating system and a well-insulated home is important to reduce the risk of **hypothermia**.
- Security, e.g. alarm systems or emergency buttons, is very important, especially for those living alone.
- A small outdoor area or patio is sufficient, as they may not have the mobility to maintain a large outdoor space.
- Access to public transport is important to help prevent loneliness and isolation, especially among those who do not drive.

> **Lit'Hit**
> Hypothermia is the condition of having a dangerously low body temperature.

Suitable accommodation: a compact, single-storey dwelling with one or two bedrooms, or **sheltered housing**, depending on the person's level of mobility and health.

People with disabilities

- People with disabilities may require more open space than other groups, e.g. wider hallways and larger bedrooms.
- Proximity to an urban area allows for greater access to local amenities and services, e.g. Enable Ireland.
- People with disabilities may require the following home modifications:
  - o a ramp or lift to the main door
  - o wider doorways for ease of access
  - o a downstairs wheelchair-accessible bathroom with non-slip floors, handrails and a shower seat for safety
  - o kitchen facilities, e.g. countertops, may need to be adapted for people in wheelchairs
  - o handrails may be needed to aid movement throughout the home for people with visual impairments
  - o flashing alarm bells may be needed to alert those with hearing disabilities when visitors call.
- The surface of the outdoor area should be made smooth and easy to move on.
- Access to public transport links can help maintain independence.

> **Lit'Hit**
> Sheltered housing consists of small, private independent homes with some shared facilities and a warden or nurse who provides assistance if necessary.

Suitable accommodation: a single-storey dwelling with one or two bedrooms or a ground-floor apartment. The type of accommodation chosen will depend on the extent of the person's disability.

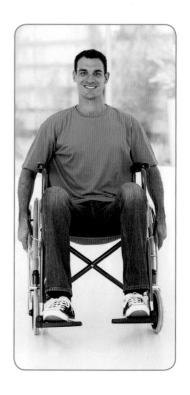

People who are homeless

- People who are homeless are those without temporary or permanent shelter, who live on the streets, in hostels or shelters.
- In Dublin and Cork, the local authorities and the Department of Social Protection provide dedicated services for people who are homeless, in an effort to find them accommodation and provide them with advice.
- Voluntary organisations, such as the Simon Community, provide support for homeless people.

🏠 **Suitable accommodation:** homeless people have the same accommodation requirements as all other people. They require shelter, e.g. a hostel, emergency bed and breakfast or private accommodation with:
  o bathroom or shower facilities
  o secure storage for belongings
  o privacy, e.g. a bed of their own and a private place to change
  o communal facilities, e.g. a shared kitchen or television room
  o access to laundry facilities.

❓ Identify **four** modifications (changes) that should be made when designing a house for a person who uses a wheelchair. (12) **OL**

Give details of the housing requirements for **each** of the following:
- a young single person
- a retired couple
- a family with young children. (18) **OL**

Give an account of the specific housing requirements of the following groups:
- families
- single people
- elderly people. (18) **HL**

🅗🅛 Housing provision in Ireland: distribution and adequacy

Housing provision refers to the supply of housing in the Irish market, and whether it is sufficient to meet the supply and demand at that time. When evaluating housing provision, distribution and adequacy must be considered.

- **Distribution of housing:** refers to how housing is distributed or spread among the Irish population, e.g. privately owned, privately rented or social housing. It can also refer to the location of these homes, e.g. urban or rural areas.

- **Adequacy of housing provision:** refers to whether there is enough of each type of housing available. Is the supply adequate, or should more be provided? Is the housing provided in good condition?

Distribution of housing in Ireland 2011

- Private housing (71%)
- Private rental sector (19%)
- Social housing (9%)
- Other (1%)

→ For more information on rural and urban housing distribution see page 392.

HOUSING PROVISION

Private housing sector

Distribution

Ireland has a high level of private home ownership at 71%.

Why? Ireland has a tradition of homeownership, which peaked at 80% of households in 1991. This continued (at a slightly lower rate) during the economic boom (1994–2007), due to increased economic prosperity and low mortgage interest rates. Since then, private home ownership has decreased due to the economic recession, increased house prices and difficulty accessing a mortgage. Currently the economy is showing signs of recovery, so it is expected that the purchase of private homes will rise again as house prices stabilise and demand increases.

Adequacy

Currently there are private homes available to purchase; however, a shortage of three-bedroomed semi-detached homes is evident in some urban areas due to increased demand and lack of supply. The quality of private homes can vary, depending on the year in which they were constructed. Homes built in recent years tend to be of a high standard, due to strict building regulations.

Private rental sector

Distribution

The number of Irish people renting from private landlords has increased dramatically in recent years to 19%, compared to 8% in 1991.

Why?

- Young, single workers do not want the burden of mortgage repayments, or they have been refused mortgage approval.
- Increased numbers of students are moving to urban areas for third-level education and require accommodation to rent.
- Improved security of tenure for tenants has left people feeling more secure when renting, reducing the need to own their own home.

Adequacy

Currently, demand for private rental properties is outstripping supply, especially in urban areas such as Dublin, Cork and Galway, leading to high rental costs that are unattainable for many. Legislation sets down minimum standards for rental accommodation, but in certain cases accommodation offered is of poor quality and is not good value for money.

Social housing sector

Social housing is provided for people on low incomes, or those who are unable to afford a private house or unable to pay rent in the private rental sector. It is provided mainly by local authorities or by voluntary or co-operative housing groups.

Distribution

The number of Irish people in receipt of social housing is at 9%, down from 10% in 1991.

Why? The numbers in receipt of social housing are low as there are not enough social housing units to meet current demand.

> **Did you know**
>
> In 2015 the Department of the Environment, Community and Local Government announced that local authorities are to receive €312 million to build 1,700 houses in order to counteract the lack of social housing.

Adequacy

Currently over 130,000 individuals and families are on the local authority waiting list (now known as a record of qualified households), as the supply of social housing is inadequate. The quality of social housing units can vary, depending on the age of the house and its location.

> **?**
>
> Evaluate the adequacy of social housing provision in Ireland. (12) **HL**
>
> Write an informative note on the private rented accommodation sector. Give three points. (15) **HL**
>
> Comment on the adequacy of housing provision in Ireland to meet the variation in housing needs. (15) **HL**
>
> Discuss the adequacy of housing provision in Ireland today. (18) **HL**

Quality of accommodation

The quality of housing in the Irish market has improved in recent years, mainly due to the introduction of stricter rental and building regulations.

Rental accommodation

Housing (Standards for Rented Houses) Regulations 2008 (amended 2009)

These regulations ensure that properties for rent meet minimum physical standards. The regulations require the landlord to:

- ensure that the rental property is in a proper state of structural repair, e.g that the roof does not have any leaks
- provide fire-safety equipment, e.g. a wired smoke alarm and a fire blanket
- ensure that electricity or gas supplies are safe and in good repair
- ensure that every room has adequate heating, ventilation and lighting.

Residential Tenancies Act 2004 (amended 2015)

This act controls the standard of private rental properties. It states that every landlord must register with the Private Residential Tenancies Board and comply with the following regulations:

- buildings must be structurally sound
- hot and cold water must be provided
- bathrooms and showers need to be in good working order
- sufficient cooking facilities must be in place
- electricity, lighting, ventilation and heating must be provided.

> **Did you know**
>
> If a tenant feels their rental accommodation does not meet the quality standards, they can make a complaint to the Private Residential Tenancies Board (PRTB) which was set up under the Residential Tenancies Act 2004.

New builds and extensions

Building Energy Rating (BER)

The Building Energy Rating (BER) system was introduced in 2009. It stipulates that all homes available to rent or buy must display their BER certificate, which rates the house from A–G. A-rated homes are the most energy-efficient, and so are easier and cheaper to heat. G-rated homes are the least energy-efficient, and more expensive to heat. Grants are available from the Sustainable Energy Authority of Ireland (SEAI) to improve the energy efficiency standards in older homes.

Building Control Regulations 1997–2015

For information on Building Control Regulations 1997–2015 see page 411.

National House Building Guarantee Scheme (HomeBond)

For information on the National House Building Guarantee Scheme (HomeBond) see page 412.

Comparative costs of buying and renting

When deciding whether to buy or rent, people need to examine all the costs involved.

	Buying	**Renting**
Initial costs	• A 10% deposit is needed on properties costing up to €220,000 • For properties over €220,000 the borrower will need a deposit of 20% on the excess	• A deposit of one month to six weeks' rent is required in advance

Fees	• Lending agency fees, including:
	  o an application fee
	  o a fee for property searches
	  o a lender's survey cost
	  o an **indemnity bond** fee
	• Legal fees, which may be a fixed amount or a percentage of the total cost of the house
	• Stamp duty, a tax payable to the government, e.g. 1% on houses priced up to one million
	• Buyer's survey fee to ensure second-hand properties are a good investment
		• If the services of a letting agency are used to find a rental property, fees may be charged

Lit Hit

An indemnity bond insures the lender against making a loss if the property is repossessed and the house with worth less than the outstanding amount on the mortgage.

	Buying	**Renting**
Continuous costs	• Monthly mortgage repayments, the amount paid depends on the sum borrowed • Monthly or yearly mortgage protection/life assurance policy fees • Monthly or yearly home or contents insurance fees • Maintenance and repair costs to keep the property in good condition • Service charges, e.g. refuse collection • Household bills, e.g. electricity	• Monthly rent payments, the amount paid depends on the location, size and type of home rented • Contents insurance, e.g. for laptops or sound systems • Service charges, e.g. refuse collection • Household bills, e.g. electricity
Advantages	✓ The value of the property may go up, so a profit may be made if reselling in the future ✓ Security is provided in knowing the property will belong to the individual once the final mortgage payment is made ✓ Individuals can design the interior to suit their own tastes	✓ A smaller deposit is required, making it more affordable ✓ Offers mobility for those who may wish to change jobs, move to another area or emigrate ✓ The landlord is responsible for maintenance, e.g. replacing broken appliances
Disadvantages	✗ A mortgage is a commitment that lasts for many years, e.g. 35 years ✗ The value of the property can fall, so if reselling in the future a loss may be made ✗ The property may be repossessed if individuals fail to meet mortgage repayments ✗ The owner is responsible for maintenance, e.g. replacing broken appliances	✗ The quality of some accommodation can be poor, especially in urban areas ✗ Facilities, e.g. a kitchen, may have to be shared ✗ An expensive option that is seen as 'dead money' (money invested with no return) ✗ During the first six months of tenancy the landlord can ask the tenants to leave without giving a reason (28 days' notice is required)

GO FIGURE 123

In 2014, AA Ireland calculated that the cost of running a home worth €170,000 was €16,000 a year.

State (a) the advantages and (b) the disadvantages of renting a house/apartment. (12) **OL**

Discuss why renting a home is currently a popular housing option. (12) **OL**

State **three** advantages of buying a home of your own. (12) **OL**

Discuss the comparative costs of buying versus renting a house for a family. (15) **HL**

Social housing provision

There are three main housing providers within the social housing sector in Ireland: local authorities, voluntary housing associations and co-operative housing associations.

In the past, local authorities provided nearly all social housing. However, in recent years voluntary and co-operative housing associations have increased provision, supplying a quarter of all new social housing.

Local authority housing

For information on local authority housing see page 303.

Voluntary housing associations

Voluntary housing associations are non-profit organisations, formed to meet the housing needs of people already on a local authority housing list. They provide housing in the form of houses, flats, sheltered housing, group homes and hostels for individuals and families on low incomes who cannot afford to buy their own home and vulnerable groups of people in society, e.g. the elderly and people with disabilities.

All tenants of voluntary housing bodies pay rent based on an affordable proportion of their available income.

Examples of voluntary housing associations include Respond! Housing Association and Clúid Housing Association.

Did you know

Many voluntary housing associations also offer non-housing services such as group meals, social activities and welfare advice.

Funding for voluntary housing associations

All voluntary housing organisations must be approved by the Department of Housing, Planning, Community and Local Government. Once registered and approved, the government provides financial aid under two schemes: Capital Advance Leasing Facility (CALF) and Capital Assistance Scheme.

Capital Advance Leasing Facility (CALF)	Capital Assistance Scheme
• Provides funding through the Department of Housing, Planning, Community and Local Government to purchase or construct new social housing • A loan is provided to cover 30% of the costs. The remaining 70% must be privately sourced. Once the 70% has been repaid, the 30% CALF loan must then be repaid.	• Provides funding through the local authorities to purchase or construct housing for people with special needs, e.g. accommodation for the elderly, physically disabled, intellectually challenged or homeless individuals • A loan is provided to cover 100% of the costs, and does not need to be repaid

Co-operative housing

A co-operative (co-op) is an organisation that is owned and run jointly by its members, who share all the profits or benefits.

Housing co-operatives are non-profit organisations governed by Co-operative Housing Ireland. They endeavour to relieve housing needs in communities by building and managing houses or apartments for co-operative members to own or rent.

Co-operative members come from the local authority waiting list (now known as a record of qualified households) from areas where the houses are located. From these, a management committee is established, which works together to provide accommodation for all its members. They can form a home ownership, social rental or shared ownership housing co-operative.

- **Home ownership co-operatives:** made up of members who have the finances to build. Members combine their finances to build 10–30 houses and share all related costs and fees, e.g. the cost of the site, building materials and legal fees. Sites for building are often provided by the local authority at a reduced price.
- **Social rental co-operatives:** provide housing for rent to people on the local authority waiting list (now known as a record of qualified households). The rent to be paid is based on an individual's or family's income and household circumstances, e.g. number in the family. It is generally 15–17% of income.
- **Shared ownership housing co-operatives:** help members to part-purchase their own homes while the remainder of the property continues to be owned by the co-operative.

> **?** Name and give details of any **one** house purchase scheme offered by local authorities to persons who are unable to finance a home of their own. (15) **OL**
>
> Differentiate between *Local Authority Housing* and *Co-Operative Housing*. (10) **HL**
>
> Name and give details of **one** type of social housing. (12) **HL**

Provision of local amenities and services

Amenities, e.g. parks, are desirable, pleasant local features or facilities. They are provided for leisure and form an integral part of any community. Services, e.g. schools, are provided by trained professionals or service providers within the community.

Many local amenities and services are provided by the Department of Housing, Planning, Community and Local Government, and supplied through local authorities to ensure towns and cities are attractive places to live. Local area development plans set out planning guidelines for houses, roads, schools, leisure facilities and playgrounds.

Amenities and services available

Schools

Pre-schools and Montessoris are privately-run services located within or near housing developments. Local primary and secondary schools are provided by the Department of Education and Skills. The size and number of schools provided depends on the number of children in the **catchment area**.

Importance: pre-schools and Montessoris help to develop social skills in a fun, stimulating environment. Primary and secondary schools provide a vital educational service, helping children achieve their academic potential.

Lit Hit
Catchment area means the area around a school, from which the pupils are drawn.

Play areas and green areas

Play areas and green areas now form an important part of all new housing developments, as they are attractive for families.

Importance: play areas provide a fun outdoor space for children to play and socialise together.

Green areas with landscaping help to give a housing development a sense of space and add to the visual appeal.

HOUSING PROVISION

Community centres

Community centres provide a venue for local classes, events and activities, e.g. art classes and parent-and-baby groups. They are funded by the Department of Housing, Planning Community and Local Government and by the community itself.

Importance: provide a place for individuals and families to meet and socialise. Community centres help develop a sense of community spirit, as people get to know each other.

Transport

Proximity to public transport links is often a selling point for housing developments. Planning will only be granted for housing developments when the local authority approves the layout of road infrastructure.

Importance: a well-planned road network in housing developments ensures the safety of the residents. Nearby public transport links enable people to travel easily to and from work, or to other amenities.

Shops

Proximity to shops is important to most individuals and families. The type and number of shops is generally based on demand.

Importance: enables easy access to essential items without having to travel to urban areas.

Refuse collection

Refuse collection is a weekly or fortnightly service provided by either the local authority or private refuse companies.

Importance: keeps homes and housing developments clean and hygienic and prevents littering.

Street lighting

Street lighting is provided on public streets and in housing estates by the local authority and energy companies such as Airtricity. Street lighting operates by light-sensitive sensors.

Importance: makes people feel safer when driving or walking within a housing development or public area.

 Discuss the provision of amenities in new housing developments. (12) **OL**

Susan and Joe have two children, a boy aged eight and a girl aged ten.
Identify four local amenities/services which you consider essential for this family and state one reason why you think each amenity/service is important. (16) **OL**

Evaluate the importance of local amenities and services in housing developments. (16) **HL**

Chapter 20:
House building

4.2 **HOUSE BUILDING AND DESIGN**

What you will learn:

- **Factors that influence choice of location when designing and building a house**
- **Factors that influence choice of house style when designing and building a house**
- **Planning requirements**

- **Professional services available for the design and building of a house**
- **Factors that influence the design and construction of a house**
- **Regulation of house building standards**

Many people choose to build their home, as they can design a home layout that suits their particular needs and choose styles and design features that appeal to them. Standards in relation to house building have improved greatly in recent years due to improved planning guidelines and building regulations.

Factors that influence choice of location when designing and building a house

- **Available budget:** money available will affect a person's choice and location of site, as costs vary depending on the size of the plot of land, the affluence of the area, whether it has a desirable view, and its access to amenities.

- **Personal preference:** the location chosen is influenced by a person's preferences. People may choose urban sites to build a house on to be closer to work, transport links or amenities, e.g. schools or shops. Rural sites have the advantage of a beautiful setting and views, which appeal to many.

- **Site specifications:** site specifications will influence the choice of location. A site should ideally be easy to access from the road, and it should be well drained and slightly raised to avoid flooding or water damage. It should have access to a water supply and a safe sewerage system. A south-facing site will get more sunlight.

- **Suitability for building:** sites on zoned agricultural land or in areas with little or no possibility of obtaining planning permission should be avoided. The local area development plan provides information on any future building or developments, e.g. a factory, that may affect the resale value of the home in the future.

> ? Elaborate on the factors that influence the design and building of a house under the following heading: location. (6) **OL**
>
> Describe **three** factors that might influence a person's choice of location when building a house. (15) **OL**

Factors that influence choice of house style when designing and building a house

- **Available budget:** cost directly influences the size and style of a house. The larger the house, the more expensive it will be due to the added labour and material costs. Elaborate design features, e.g. large windows, will also add to the cost.
- **Personal preferences:** the layout and style of a house will be dictated by personal preferences. For example, some people prefer modern buildings with glass and open-plan living, compared to others who prefer a more traditional style with stone and timber.
- **Family requirements:** specific needs or requirements will influence the house style chosen. For example, a modern, minimalist style may be unsuitable for families with young children as it is difficult to keep clean. If a family member has a physical disability this will have to be considered when choosing a style, e.g. an open-plan bungalow may be suitable.
- **Surrounding landscape/area:** the style of house chosen will be influenced by its surroundings. For example, if all the houses nearby are bungalows it is unlikely that the person will be given planning permission to build a two-storey house. Planning guidelines state that homes should blend into the local environment and not detract from it, especially in a rural setting.
- **Aspect of the site:** the direction of the site, e.g. south-facing, will dictate the style and layout of the home. House styles should take full advantage of the light and heat provided by the sun by incorporating large glass windows.

> ? Elaborate on the factors that influence the design and building of a house under the following heading: house style. (6) **OL**

Planning requirements

Planning permission is required for:

- a new building
- an extension to an existing building that is over 40 square metres.

Planning permission must be sought from the local planning authority, e.g. county councils or urban district councils.

If planning an extension under 40 square metres, a commencement notice without documentation (short commencement notice) must be submitted to the local building authority before any building work begins.

If a development or extension has been built without planning permission, the person may have to apply for **retention planning permission** to prevent the building being demolished.

> **Did you know**
>
> Before the Building Control Act 1990, all extensions under 23 square metres required bye-law approval.

> **Lit Hit**
>
> Retention planning permission allows the owner to retain an existing structure or a partially constructed structure.

> **?** Why is it necessary to obtain planning permission? (6) **OL**

> **Did you know**
>
> According to the CSO, in 2004 27,512 planning permissions were granted. This fell dramatically to 3,606 in 2014.

Planning permission

Types of planning permission

There are two main types of planning permission: outline planning permission and full planning permission.

Outline planning permission	Full planning permission
• Sought from the local planning authority to find out whether a site may be developed and granted planning permission • No house plans are needed, but some outline details are required, e.g. a site map with the proposed location and general type of proposed dwelling • The local planning authority may agree that the site is suitable for future development, or the application may be refused • If outline permission is granted, building cannot begin until full planning permission is obtained	• Sought from the local planning authority before starting building work on the site • Applicants must send in a detailed submission including: o site layout maps marking the position of the proposed house o house plans with front, side and rear **elevations**, as well as interior layouts o details of materials to be used during construction o an application form o the relevant planning fee, e.g. €65 to build a house. o copies of planning application notices published in the local papers and those erected on the site • The local planning authority may agree that the site is suitable for building, or the application may be refused. If permission is granted, building can begin.

> **Lit Hit**
>
> Elevations means the exterior look of the building.

General procedure involved in obtaining full planning permission (12 weeks)

Start

- **Notice of application/site notice:** a notice of application for planning permission must be placed in a local newspaper and a site notice must be erected in clear view near the proposed entrance. Both must identify the name of the person applying for permission, the type of permission applied for and details of the proposed development.

2 weeks later

- **Detailed application:** after two weeks a detailed application must be made to the local planning authority, including site maps, plans, an application form, a planning fee and copies of planning application notices.

▲ Site notice

2–5 weeks later

- **Planning register:** the application is placed on the planning register where, for the next two to five weeks, any member of the public can inspect it. Any objections must be formally lodged with the local planning authority. Planning officials inspect the site during this time.

5–8 weeks later

- **Decision:** during this time the local planning authority will inform the applicant of their decision. This is called a notice of intention. The planning authority can grant permission, seek further information or refuse permission.

Final 4 weeks

- **Appeals:** if permission has been refused the applicant may lodge an appeal with An Bord Pleanála during the final four weeks. If permission is granted and a member of the public has an objection, they can lodge a written appeal with An Bord Pleanála. If there is no appeal, the planning authority will formally grant permission.

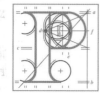

An Bord Pleanála

A commencement notice with documentation (long commencement notice) must be submitted to the local building control authority between 28 to 14 days prior to commencement of works. On completion of building, a Certificate of Compliance should be lodged with the Building Control Authority before the building is occupied or used. As of 2015, owners of new single dwellings or domestic extensions may opt out of this certification.

? Why is it necessary to obtain planning permission when building a house? (7) **OL**

State the difference between outline and full planning permission **and** describe the procedure involved in obtaining full planning permission. (24) **OL**

Describe the procedure involved in obtaining planning permission to build a house. (12) **HL**

Did you know ?

The standard duration for planning permission is five years before it expires. After this time, a new application will need to be made.

Professional services available for the design and building of a house

Architects

- Architects advise on the choice of site and whether it is suited to the proposed building. If the site has issues, e.g. restricted road visibility, the plans can be altered to suit.
- Architects produce computer-aided design (CAD) drawings of the exterior elevations and interior floor plan of the house to suit an individual's requirements. These are submitted as part of the planning application.
- Architects carry out site visits to oversee the house construction and advise constructors.

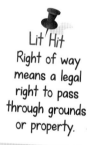

Site engineers

- Site engineers assess the house plans before building begins to ensure that the plans meet current building guidelines structurally, and will not pose health or safety problems.
- During construction, site engineers call to site to assess the quality of the work and ensure the building standards are being complied with. If any problems occur the site engineers advise the builders on how to rectify these.

Surveyors

- Surveyors carry out detailed and extensive surveys of sites to highlight any potential problems that could affect the future design and building of the house, e.g. poor drainage. They then advise on how to rectify the problems and provide solutions.

Lit'Hit
Right of way means a legal right to pass through grounds or property.

Solicitors

- Solicitors deal with the legal matters relating to the purchase or building of a new home. They check the land register to confirm ownership and check **right of way**.
- They provide advice on building regulations and the procedure involved in obtaining planning permission.

Builders

- Builders produce a detailed contract with prices for each stage of building as well as a list of dates for completion.
- Builders prepare the site for building. e.g. by installing **foundations.** Once the foundations are in place, they then construct the house according to the architect's drawings and engineer's guidelines.
- Builders may hire subcontractors for various specialist jobs, e.g. an electrician to wire the house.

Lit'Hit
Foundations are the prepared ground on which a structure rests.

Books of house plans

- High-quality house plans, including exterior and interior floor plans, can be ordered from book publishers. These can be modified to suit individual housing requirements. This is a cheaper alternative to employing an architect. The plans include details about the planning permission process and the stages that need to be followed.

 In relation to house building and purchase explain the role of **each** of the following:
(a) the architect, (b) the surveyor and (c) the solicitor. (15) **OL**

Describe the role of three professional services available to assist people who are designing/building their own home. (18) **HL**

HOUSE BUILDING AND DESIGN

Factors that influence the design and construction of a house

- **Cost:** the available budget influences the design and construction of a house. The larger the house and the more elaborate the design, the greater the building costs. Consider how much money will be required to maintain the home in the future, e.g. a plaster-finished exterior will require regular painting in comparison to natural stone, which needs no maintenance.

- **Aesthetic requirements:** both the exterior and interior design of a house should be aesthetically pleasing to the eye. The exterior should blend in with the surroundings, and with houses in the area. Obtrusive features, e.g. a high-pitched roof, should be avoided. The interior should be planned to make maximum use of space and light, as well as incorporating attractive design features.

- **Family requirements:** when designing and constructing a house there needs to be adequate space for all members, e.g. sufficient bedrooms, large kitchen/living area. If a family member has a special need this should take priority when planning the layout and materials chosen. Ensure the house can be adapted for possible future needs, e.g. a downstairs office that can be converted into an extra bedroom.

- **Ergonomics:** ergonomics is the study of people's efficiency in their environment. When planning the design of a home, the layout should be arranged in such a way that people can move freely and live comfortably. For example, the work triangle in the kitchen ensures that the least amount of human time and energy is wasted walking from the cooker to the fridge and the sink. Adequate storage space, low-maintenance kitchen surfaces and appliances positioned at a comfortable height are also elements of ergonomic design.

- **Environmental factors:** a house should be designed and constructed to reduce its impact on the environment, both in relation to its effect on the surroundings and in the materials chosen to build it. For example:
  - by using timber and natural stone rather than synthetic or high carbon footprint materials, e.g. concrete
  - by installing a radon barrier in the foundations, which prevents radon seepage into the house
  - by installing a bio tank to ensure that sewage from the home is treated to make it environmentally safe.

> **Did you know**
>
> Naturally occurring radioactive radon gas is a known carcinogen and poses a chronic toxicity hazard to humans. It is responsible for around 250 avoidable deaths from lung cancer every year in Ireland.

- **Energy efficiency:** consider energy efficiency when designing and constructing a home to reduce environmental impact. For example:
  - a zoned heating system using renewable energy sources such as geothermal energy will save on energy usage and fuel costs
  - insulating the home, e.g. walls, to the minimum standard or higher will reduce the heat loss
  - installing energy-efficient appliances reduces environmental impact and electricity costs
  - orientating the main living areas facing south or west makes use of passive solar energy, reducing heat and light costs.

- **Technological developments:** advances in technology, e.g. new materials, systems and appliances, influence the design and construction of homes. For example:
  - computer-aided design (CAD) has made it easier to implement alterations to plans during the design stage and to visualise the final design using 3D images and virtual-reality tours
  - modern heating systems can be incorporated at the design stage, allowing for efficient and comfortable home heating, e.g. thermostats, zoned heating
  - sensor-operated cameras, gates and lighting installed during construction have made homes safer.

▲ 3D CAD image

REMEMBER IT!

'**C**ould **A**ll **F**amilies **E**verywhere **E**mploy **E**ngineers? **T**hanks!'

Cost, **A**esthetics, **F**amily requirements, **E**rgonomics, **E**nvironmental factors, **E**nergy efficiency, **T**echnological developments.

Elaborate on the factors that influence the design and building of a house under **each** of the following headings:
- family requirements (present/future)
- technological developments. (14) **OL**

Give a brief account of **four** factors that should be considered when designing a family home. (16) **OL**

Describe **three** ways in which the design and construction of a house can help reduce energy consumption. (15) **HL**

Discuss how aesthetic and environmental factors influence the design of modern housing. (16) **HL**

State, giving examples, how (i) ergonomics, (ii) technological developments and (iii) environmental factors influence house design/construction. (18) **HL**

Regulation of house building standards

Regulations are necessary to ensure all new buildings, or changes to an existing building, are carried out to a high standard. This protects individuals from poor workmanship on their homes, and protects the environment from damage.

Building Control Regulations 1997–2015

- The Building Control Regulations are a set of legal requirements for the design and construction of new buildings. These regulations are based on the Building Control Acts 1990–2014, and are enforced by local authorities (Building Control Authorities).
- These regulations cover all aspects of building design, including materials and workmanship, waste disposal, heating, lighting, ventilation, insulation, fire safety and access for people with disabilities.
- An assigned certifier, e.g. an architect, oversees the building process. On completion, a certificate of compliance must be lodged with the Building Control Authority, verifying that the regulations have been complied with.

National House Building Guarantee Scheme (HomeBond) Certificate

HomeBond is operated by the National House Building Guarantee Scheme and the Department of Housing, Planning, Community and Local Government. This scheme was established to provide protection for the consumer against faulty building work.

To take part in this scheme, builders pay a fee to register the house they plan to build. The house is then inspected by a department official three times during its construction. On completion, if the home meets all the regulations and passes each inspection, a HomeBond certificate is awarded.

If a buyer purchases a HomeBond-registered home they are covered for ten years if:

- the builder goes out of business during that time (the deposit or stage payments made will be returned to the purchaser)
- a structural fault occurs (it will be rectified free of charge by the builder).

Most mortgage lenders require a HomeBond guarantee before granting a mortgage to ensure the home being purchased is a good investment and good quality.

Certificate of Compliance

A Certificate of Compliance is required for new-build works, extensions over 40 square metres or for work to an existing property, e.g. internal alterations. It is provided by an assigned certifier, e.g. an architect, surveyor or engineer, to certify that they have supervised the construction project and that it was built in compliance with building and planning regulations.

Grants

The Better Energy Warmer Homes Scheme (BEWH) operated by the Sustainable Energy Authority of Ireland (SEAI) is available to homeowners whose homes were built prior to 2006 and who are in receipt of either the Fuel Allowance, Family Income Supplement or Jobseeker's Allowance. Work funded under the scheme includes attic or cavity wall insulation, draught proofing and lagging jackets.

▲ Builder adding attic insulation

State the benefits of the National House Building Guarantee Scheme. (8) **HL**

Set out details of **one** piece of current legislation which regulates house building standards. (14) **HL**

Explain how house-building standards are regulated. Refer to at least **two** different methods. (14) **HL**

Chapter 21: Designing the house interior

4.3 DESIGNING THE HOUSE INTERIOR

What you will learn:

- Elements of design
- Principles of design
- Factors that influence the interior design of the home
- Room floor plans
- Sample answer: how to draw a living room floor plan
- How to evaluate and modify the layout of a home
- Sample answer: how to modify a ground-floor layout

The interior of a home is not only a reflection of the era in which it was designed, but the taste or personality of the owner. A well-designed interior makes the home aesthetically pleasing and more enjoyable to live in.

Elements of design

The three elements of design are colour, pattern and texture.

Colour

Benefits of colour in the home

- Colour adds interest and character to a room, e.g. a bright red wall in a cream room will catch the eye and grab attention.
- Colour prevents interior spaces from being bland and uninteresting, e.g. an all-beige room.
- Colour can express a person's personality or interests, e.g. red for a person's favourite team.
- Colour can complement external surroundings, e.g. neutral colours in a conservatory will complement the green tones outside.

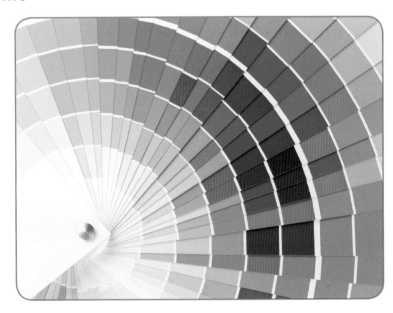

Types of colour

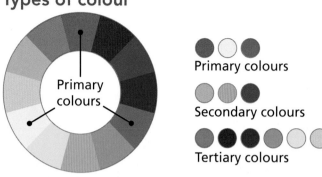

Primary colours

Secondary colours

Tertiary colours

📖 The colour wheel

Primary colours	Secondary colours	Tertiary colours
Primary colours cannot be created by mixing other colours **Red** Yellow **Blue**	Secondary colours are created by mixing two primary colours **Red** + Yellow = Orange **Red** + **Blue** = **Purple** **Blue** + Yellow = Green	Tertiary colours are created by mixing a primary and a secondary colour **Blue** + Green = Turquoise **Red** + Purple = Mauve Yellow + Green = **Olive**

Shade	Tint
Shade is achieved when black is added to a colour, e.g. red + black = burgundy. This darkens the **tone** of the colour.	Tint is achieved by adding white to a colour, e.g. black and white = grey. This lightens the tone of the colour.

Lit' Hit
Tone refers to the lightness or darkness of a colour.

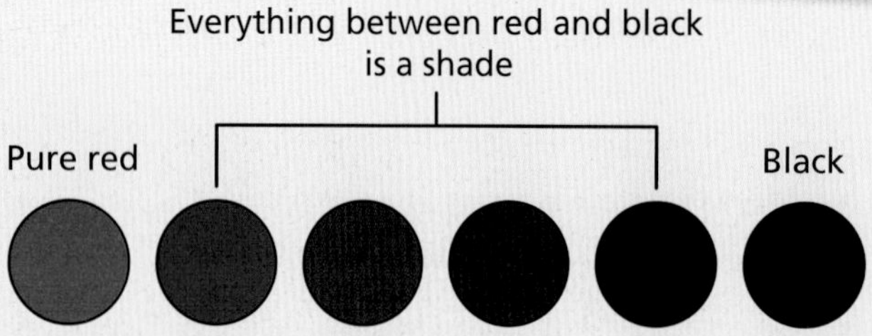

Everything between red and black is a shade

Pure red   Black

Classification of colour

Warm	Cool	Pastel	Neutral
Red	Blue	Baby pink	White
Yellow	Green	Duck-egg blue	Cream
Orange	Turquoise	Lemon	Beige

Colour schemes

Complementary colours	Harmonious colours
Complementary colours are colours that are opposite each other on the colour wheel, e.g. yellow and purple	Harmonious colours are colours that are beside each other on the colour wheel, e.g. green and blue

▲ Shades of primary red with neutral black and tertiary olive

🖹 Neutral tints of grey with secondary blues

> ❓ In relation to room design describe the following: colour scheme. (8) **HL**

Factors to consider when choosing colour

- **Function of the room:** consider the overall function of the room and specific requirements before choosing colour. For example, bedrooms are used to sleep or study in so use relaxing colours, e.g. blue or green, whereas kitchens are used to socialise and entertain in, so use bright, vibrant colours, e.g. yellow or red.

- **Size of the room:** room size should always be taken into account when planning a colour scheme. Painting a small room a dark colour will only make it appear even smaller, as dark tones absorb light. These are best suited to large spaces. Light colours can alter the proportion of a room, making it appear higher or wider, as they reflect light. Painting a feature wall a striking colour will make it appear closer and alter the proportions of the room, e.g. make it appear smaller and cosier.

- **Aspect:** consider the aspect or direction in which the room is facing when considering colour. This is important as north-facing rooms can be cold with little natural light, and therefore should be painted in warm colours, e.g. yellow. South-facing rooms get lots of yellow-toned natural light, so they can be painted any colour.

- **Features:** if chosen wisely, colour can be used to highlight positive features, e.g. an alcove or cornicing around the ceiling, by painting them a contrasting colour to that of the rest of the room. Colour can also disguise negative features of a home, e.g. radiators, by painting them the same colour as the wall.

- **Mood:** colour can influence an individual's moods or thoughts, so should be chosen wisely. For example, a red wall in a bedroom could prevent sleep as it is a stimulating colour, but red works well in a dining room as it stimulates conversation.

▲ Black feature wall suits the large, open space

> ❓ Give an account of the factors that should be considered when choosing colour for a sitting room in a family home. (18) **OL**

DESIGNING THE HOUSE INTERIOR

Pattern

Benefits of pattern in the home

- Pattern adds interest and character to a room, e.g. polka dot wallpaper.
- Pattern provides contrast against plain items, e.g. a vertical-striped sofa against a white room.
- Pattern is a simple way to update a room and, if used wisely, it can be changed regularly in line with trends, e.g. patterned cushions.
- Pattern can express a person's personality or interests, e.g. a floral pattern to display an interest in vintage decor.

Examples of pattern

Vertical stripe

Horizontal stripe

Geometric

Polka dot

Floral

Check

Factors to consider when choosing pattern

- **Function of the room:** consider the overall function of the room and specific requirements before choosing pattern. For example, patterns used in a bedroom should be subtle to allow for relaxation and sleep.
- **Style of the room:** patterns considered should fit into the existing style of the room, e.g. French vintage, modern contemporary. They should also correspond with the colours and furnishings already used in order to create rhythm.
- **Size of the room:** room size should always be taken into account when considering which patterns to use. If the room is large in size, then large, bold patterns can be used. If the room is small, large patterns should be avoided, as they can make the room appear smaller and cluttered. Pattern can also be used to alter the perception of the proportions or size of the room. Vertical-striped wallpaper draws the eye upwards, making a room appear higher. Horizontal-striped wallpaper draws the eye around, making a room appear wider.
- **Amount:** pattern must be used carefully, as if too much is used it can overpower a room, making it appear fussy. On the other hand, too little pattern can make a room look bland and bare. If using more than one pattern, they should be linked by using coordinating colours.

▲ Geometric pattern rug

▲ Sofa with various patterned cushions to add interest and variety

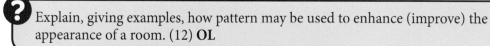

? Explain, giving examples, how pattern may be used to enhance (improve) the appearance of a room. (12) **OL**

Texture

Benefits of texture in the home

- Texture adds interest and contrast to a room, e.g. a fluffy rug on a wooden floor.
- Texture satisfies the sense of touch, e.g. a soft blanket.
- Texture can add warmth to a clinical, cold room, e.g. a mat in a tiled bathroom.

Examples of texture

Rough texture	Smooth texture
Rough textures create a sense of cosiness and warmth, e.g. wool carpets or rugs, fur throws, knitted cushions, upholstered sofas, stone walls, wooden furniture	Smooth textures create a clean, streamlined finish, e.g. mirrors, stainless steel, polished porcelain tiles, glass, gloss paintwork

Factors to consider when choosing texture

- **Function of the room:** consider the overall function of the room and specific requirements before choosing texture. For example, kitchens and bathrooms require smooth textures that are water-resistant, easy to clean and hygienic, e.g. tiles. Sitting rooms and bedrooms should use rough textures, e.g. carpets and throws, as they create a sense of comfort and warmth.
- **Texture combinations:** consider combining rough and smooth textures to create interest and add variety to an interior decor scheme, e.g. a wool rug on a tiled floor. If too many smooth textures are used a room can feel clinical and cold.
- **Sound:** texture can influence sound levels in a room, so it should be chosen wisely. Smooth textures reflect sound, causing echoing and making rooms feel empty, e.g. a tiled hallway. Rough textures absorb sound, preventing echoing, e.g. carpet on a stairs.
- **Lighting:** texture can influence lighting, so it should be chosen wisely. Smooth textures reflect light, making the space appear bigger and brighter. Rough textures absorb light, making the room seem smaller and more intimate. Lighting can be used to highlight variations in texture, e.g. an uplight on a stone wall.

> **Did you know**
>
> Cinema theatres use rough textures to absorb sound and prevent echoing or a sound delay during films, e.g. carpets, upholstered seats and fabric-cushioned walls.

> **?** Texture is an important element of design. Give **two** examples of the use of smooth textures and **two** examples of the use of rough textures in interior design. (12) **OL**
>
> Explain two elements of design and give an example of the application of each in interior design. (12) **HL**

Principles of design

There are four principles of design: balance, emphasis, proportion and rhythm.

Balance  ▲ Symmetrical balance	Balance is created when the elements of design (colours, patterns and textures) and the items of furniture in a room work well together and in harmony. For example, symmetrical balance occurs when one object is a mirror image of another in terms of size/shape, colour, pattern or texture.
Emphasis 	Emphasis involves drawing attention to a particular object or feature, e.g. a feature wall in a room, by using strong/contrasting colours, pattern, texture, shape or lighting. Emphasis adds interest and variety to a room, giving it a focal point.
Proportion 	Proportion is achieved when the pieces of furniture in a room relate to one another in size and relate to the size of the room they are in, e.g. the size of a sofa in a sitting room
Rhythm 	Rhythm is used to link various objects in a room to create a harmonious, unified look. It can be achieved by repeating colours, patterns or textures.

? Explain three principles of design and give an example of the application of each in interior design. (18) **HL**

Factors that influence the interior design of the home

- **Function:** the overall function of a room and its specific requirements should influence the interior design of a home. For example, a kitchen should have hygienic easy-to-clean surfaces and sufficient space to work. A sitting room should have comfortable seating and be warm and inviting.

- **Aesthetics:** the elements and principles of design should be used to create visually attractive rooms. Aesthetics are largely influenced by personal taste or current fashion trends. Care should be taken when choosing bold-statement items, as they can date very quickly.

- **Comfort:** interior design should be planned to ensure that rooms are comfortable spaces for people to live, e.g. soft flooring in a bedroom, sufficient space in a kitchen to work, comfortable seating in a sitting room. Efficient heating and warm, soft lighting also create a comfortable environment.

- **Special needs:** if a member of the family has a special need, e.g. requires a wheelchair, this will need to be considered when planning the interior. For example, floor coverings and room layouts chosen should allow for ease of movement, e.g. a tiled, open-plan living area.

- **Cost:** the available budget should always be considered when planning interior design, as interior finishes, e.g. wooden flooring, can be expensive. Cheaper alternatives, e.g. laminate flooring, may need to be considered for those on a lower budget. Quality, well-made items are often more expensive, as they tend to last longer and withstand greater wear and tear.

- **Family size and circumstances:** the size and stage of the family will influence interior design. For example, large families with young children will require greater living and sleeping space, extensive storage and finishes that can withstand wear and tear.

- **Environmental awareness:** materials used in interior decor can have a significant impact on the environment so should be considered carefully. For example, plastic is not regarded as being environmentally friendly due to the production of greenhouse gases during its manufacture. It is also difficult to recycle. On the other hand, local, naturally sourced stone and timber or organic paints have little impact on the environment.

▲ Playroom with storage

Did you know ?

Organic paints are more environmentally friendly, as only 10% waste is produced during manufacture compared to 90% from standard paints.

- **Ergonomics:** this refers to the relationship between people and their surroundings. Interiors should be ergonomically planned in order to save on human time and energy. This can be achieved by:
  - planning the layout of furniture to allow for ease of movement, e.g. sofas and armchairs in a sitting room
  - arranging the cooker, sink and fridge in the work triangle so that the least amount of time and energy is wasted walking between them
  - choosing surfaces and finishes that are quick and easy to clean, e.g. tiles instead of carpet in a kitchen.

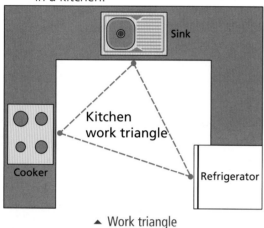

▲ Work triangle

REMEMBER IT!

'**F**abulous **A**nd **C**reative **S**paces **C**ome **F**rom **E**legant **E**tchings.'
Function, **A**esthetics, **C**omfort, **S**pecial needs, **C**ost, **F**amily size and circumstances, **E**nvironmental awareness, **E**rgonomics.

Lit Hit
Etchings are sketches or drawings.

? Identify and discuss three factors that should be considered when planning the interior design of a house. (15) **OL**

Mary and John Ryan have two teenage boys. They live in a semi-detached, two storey house in a small town. They have decided to carry out some re-decoration on their 20-year-old home.

Describe how **each** of the following might influence the Ryan family when planning the redecoration of their house:
- environmental factors
- family size and circumstances
- special needs of family members/friends. (20) **OL**

State, giving examples, how **each** of the following may impact on the interior design of the home:
- function of the room
- cost
- environmental awareness. (18) **HL**

Explain how **each** of the factors listed below can influence the interior design of the home:
- aesthetic and comfort factors
- ergonomics
- family size and circumstances. (20) **HL**

Room floor plans

A floor plan is a representation of what the home or a single room will look like. Floor plans:

- are drawn from overhead-view
- are drawn to scale, meaning that the features of the room are reduced down in proportion to fit on a piece of paper
- show the position of permanent fixtures, e.g. walls, stairs, doors, windows, radiators and electrical power points
- include temporary/moveable objects, e.g. tables, sofas, bookcases and lamps.

Floor plans can be drawn freehand, but modern plans are created using computer-aided design (CAD) software.

Sample answer: how to draw a living room floor plan

? Design and sketch the layout of any **one** room in the house. (10) **(HL 2005)**

A

l. Draw the outline of the room and insert the permanent fixtures.

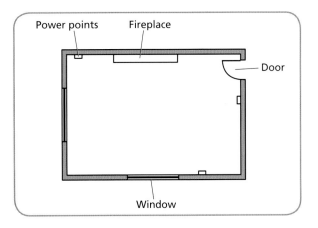

2. Add the temporary/moveable objects.

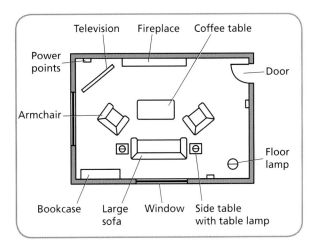

3. Add and describe the interior finishes.
  - State the type of flooring, e.g. wooden floor, carpet, rug.
  - Label the wall covering, e.g. wallpaper, paint.
  - Add soft furnishings, e.g. curtains, cushions, throws.
  - Colour in the design and add pattern.

How to evaluate and modify the layout of a home

In the exam you may be asked to analyse a floor plan and discuss its suitability, or to carry out modifications to the layout.

- **Suitability:** when analysing the suitability of a plan for a particular group, e.g. a couple or a family with young children, consider the layout and evaluate whether it suits their specific needs and requirements.

- **Modify:** modifying the layout may involve changing the use of a room, e.g. a garage into a playroom, or moving internal walls, e.g. to make an open-plan kitchen. Modifications are made to cater for existing or future needs.

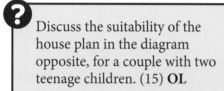

Discuss the suitability of the house plan in the diagram opposite, for a couple with two teenage children. (15) **OL**

The diagram opposite shows the floor plan of a two-bedroom house.

Assess the suitability of the house plan, shown opposite, for a family of one parent and two children aged 13 and 4 years. (20) **OL**

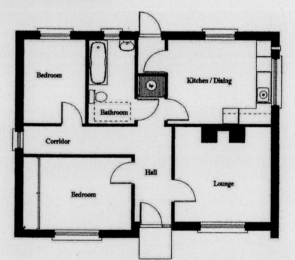

Sean and Julie have three young children and are planning to build a new house. The diagram opposite shows the floor plan for the house.

- Evaluate the suitability of this house plan for Sean, Julie and family.

- Suggest **two** modifications (changes) that could be made to the house plan in order to cater for family needs in the future. (25) **OL**

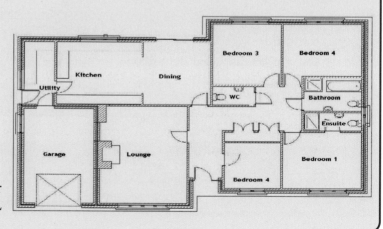

Sample answer: how to modify a ground-floor layout

?

Lifestyle and fashion trends are increasingly influencing design in the home. Many new houses are smaller, so the key requirement is to create a sociable living space that works efficiently for the modern family.

Suggest **three** changes you would make to the house plan shown in the diagram in order to accommodate the needs of a couple with two young children. In **each** case give a reason for your recommendation. (18) **(HL 2008)**

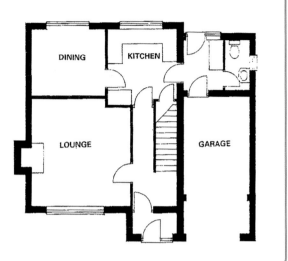

A

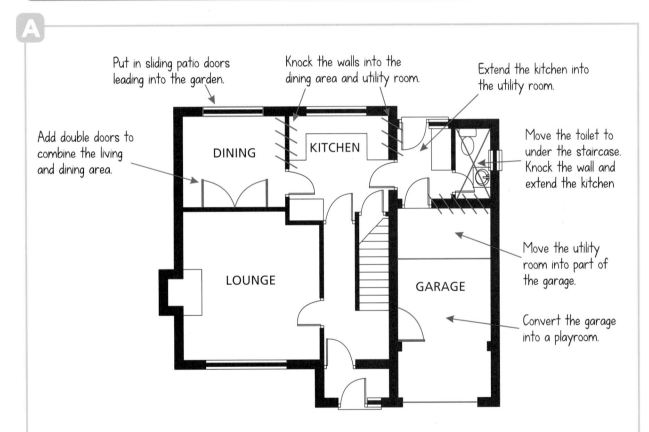

Put in sliding patio doors leading into the garden.

Knock the walls into the dining area and utility room.

Extend the kitchen into the utility room.

Add double doors to combine the living and dining area.

Move the toilet to under the staircase. Knock the wall and extend the kitchen

Move the utility room into part of the garage.

Convert the garage into a playroom.

1. Knock the walls into the dining area and utility room: this will make the kitchen area bigger and more open plan. This larger space will suit the needs of a family with two young children, and allow for communal living.

2. Add double doors to combine the living and dining area: these can be opened to extend the space if the family are entertaining a crowd, and closed for privacy if needed.

3. Convert the garage into a playroom: this will create a space for the two young children to play, as well as providing an area to store their toys. This space would be more beneficial to a family with young children than a garage.

FLOORING AND FLOOR COVERINGS

What you will learn:

- **Solid and suspended floors**
- **Factors to be considered when selecting floor coverings**
- **Classification of flooring**
- **Hard flooring**
- **Semi-hard flooring**
- **Soft flooring**

Flooring is one of the more expensive finishes for the home interior. It is often a permanent fixture that is difficult to change, therefore, it is important to choose flooring wisely.

Solid and suspended floors

Floors may be solid or suspended.

Solid floors	Suspended floors
A solid concrete floor is usually found on the ground floor of a house. It consists of: <ul><li>a hard core base with a layer of damp-proof course/membrane on top</li><li>a concrete slab followed by a layer of insulation</li><li>a thin, smooth layer of concrete or **screed** poured on top</li><li>flooring, e.g. tiles, is laid on top</li></ul>	A wooden, concrete or steel floor usually found on the first floor of a house. A wooden suspended upper floor consists of: <ul><li>joists of wood that are covered by wooden tongue-and-groove floorboards</li><li>an air space between the joists that allows air to circulate, preventing dampness. A layer of insulating material can be inserted in the air space to conserve heat and absorb sound</li><li>a layer of damp-proof course/membrane</li></ul>

Lit Hit
Screed is a level layer of concrete with no hollows or bumps. It is suitable to lay a floor covering onto.

Solid floor diagram labels: Tiles; Concrete/screed; Insulation layer; Concrete slab; Hard core base; Damp-proof course/membrane

Suspended floor diagram labels: Wooden tongue-and-groove floorboards; Insulation layer; Air space; Wooden joists; Damp-proof course/membrane

?

Explain **each** of the following:
- solid floors
- suspended floors. (12) **HL**

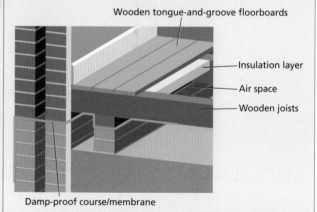

Did you know ?

A damp-proof membrane prevents rising damp in a home. Rising damp causes walls to absorb moisture from the ground, resulting in black mould and peeling wall surfaces.

Factors to consider when selecting floor coverings

- **Cost:** the available budget should be considered when selecting floor coverings, as the price of flooring can vary greatly. For example, lino wood-effect flooring may be a good alternative to solid-wood flooring for those with a lower budget. Floors are usually sold with a price per metre squared; therefore, the larger the room the greater the cost.

▲ Solid-oak wooden flooring

- **Function of the room:** consider the overall function of the room and the specific requirements before choosing flooring. For example, kitchen flooring needs to be easy to clean and hard-wearing, compared to a bedroom which requires comfortable flooring that is warm underfoot.

- **Cleaning:** flooring chosen should be easy to clean and suit the purpose and use of the room. For example, carpet would be an impractical choice in a kitchen compared to tiles, as floors need to be easily cleaned. The colour of flooring chosen will also affect the ease of cleaning, e.g. white carpets may be unsuitable in a hallway due to a large footfall.

- **Aesthetics:** the colours, patterns and textures of flooring chosen should coordinate with the existing interior design scheme to enhance the aesthetics of a room. Ideally, it is best to choose neutral, unpatterned flooring, as it will not date or be visually overpowering.

- **Safety:** flooring should be chosen with safety in mind, especially if children, the elderly or a person with a disability lives in the home. For example, bathrooms should be covered with non-slip tiles to reduce the risk of falls.

REMEMBER IT!

'**C**hoosing **F**looring **C**auses **A**wful **S**tress!'
Cost, **F**unction, **C**leaning, **A**esthetics, **S**afety.

❓ Discuss the factors to be considered when selecting floor coverings for a family home. (12) **OL**

FLOORING AND FLOOR COVERINGS

Classification of flooring

Flooring may be classified as hard, semi-hard or soft.

Hard flooring

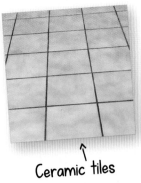

Ceramic tiles

Marble

Terracotta

Slate →

Stone (limestone)

Semi-hard flooring

Wood

Sheet flooring: vinyl

Natural flooring: coir

Lit Hit

Coir is the fibre from the outer husk of a coconut, woven to create a floor covering.

Soft flooring

Carpet

Hard flooring

Two examples of hard flooring are ceramic tiles and marble.

Ceramic tiles

Properties (advantages and disadvantages)

✓ Durable and hard-wearing, as they can withstand wear and tear in high-traffic areas of the home

✓ Easy to clean due to their smooth surface

✓ Available in a wide range of colours, patterns, sizes and designs. Can be cut to size, so are suited to any room shape. Texturally, they can be bought with a natural finish (unglazed) or highly polished (glazed).

✗ Relatively expensive per square metre

✗ Hard and cold underfoot, as they absorb heat from the body

✗ May crack or chip easily if a heavy item is dropped on them

✗ Replacing a broken tile is difficult

Uses

- Kitchens   - Bathrooms   - Hallways

Marble (natural stone)

Properties (advantages and disadvantages)

✓ Aesthetically beautiful, creating an elegant appearance that suits most styles of homes

✓ Durable and hard-wearing and can withstand wear and tear in high-traffic areas of the home

✓ Available in a wide range of natural colours, e.g. cream, brown and green. Texturally it can be bought with a natural finish (unglazed) or highly polished (glazed).

✗ Very expensive due to high importation costs and the need for a specialist tiler to lay it

✗ Hard and cold underfoot, as it absorbs heat away from the body

✗ A porous stone, so if not sealed regularly it can stain easily

Uses

- Kitchens
- Bathrooms
- Hallways

? State the advantages **and** the disadvantages of ceramic floor tiles. (12) **OL**

Describe **one** hard flooring that you would recommend for the hallway. Refer to:
- type of flooring
- properties. (9) **HL**

FLOORING AND FLOOR COVERINGS

Semi-hard flooring

Two examples of semi-hard flooring are wooden flooring (solid wood) and sheet flooring (vinyl).

Wooden flooring: solid wood

Solid-wood flooring, e.g. oak, is sold in planks or strips with a tongue-and-groove construction. Strips of solid wood can vary in thickness. They can also be cut into blocks and laid in a pattern, e.g. herringbone or basket weave.

▲ Tongue-and-groove flooring   ▲ Herringbone pattern

Properties (advantages and disadvantages)

✓ Aesthetically attractive: the variations in the **natural grain** and colours create a warm and welcoming finish to homes

✓ Stronger and more durable than softwoods, e.g. pine

✓ Comfortable underfoot and warmer than tiles or marble, as it does not draw heat from the body

✗ Expensive per square metre

✗ Can be noisy underfoot

✗ Scratch and mark easily, e.g. from high heels

> **Lit Hit**
>
> Natural grain refers to the patterns, lines and knots created by the wood as it was growing.

Uses

- Sitting/living rooms
- Kitchens
- Bedrooms

Sheet flooring: vinyl

Vinyl flooring is made from a sheet of polyvinyl chloride (PVC) or plastic developed from petroleum. It is purchased from a roll and it comes in a variety of thicknesses. To lay, it is normally glued to the solid floor using a glue or resin.

Properties (advantages and disadvantages)

✓ Thick vinyl is durable, waterproof and easy to clean

✓ Available in a wide range of colours, patterns and finishes. They can be made to look like wood or natural stone.

✓ Warm and soft underfoot, especially foam-backed vinyl

✗ Can scorch and melt if heat is applied

✗ Can mark easily, e.g. by heavy furniture legs

✗ Over time it can show signs of wear and tear, e.g. rips

> **Did you know**
>
> Linoleum (lino) is another type of sheet flooring. It is made from natural linseed oil, whereas vinyl is made from petroleum.

Uses

- Kitchens
- Bathrooms

Soft flooring

Carpet

Carpet is an example of soft flooring.

How carpet is made

Carpet can be woven or tufted.

Woven carpet

Woven carpet has fibres or threads woven into a canvas backing. There are two main types of woven carpet: Axminster and Wilton.

Did you know

Placing a thick, good-quality underlay beneath a carpet will make it feel softer, thicker and more luxurious underfoot. It also increases the lifespan and provides extra insulation and warmth.

Axminster	Wilton
• Has short **pile** threads woven into the canvas, which can be left uncut or cut into various lengths	• Has a long thread woven into the canvas in one continuous strand. The strand may be left in loops, twisted or cut, creating different piles.
• Comes in a wide variety of colours and designs	• Comes in a limited number of colours and designs
• Durable, soft and easy to clean	• Durable, soft and easy to clean

> *Lit Hit*
> Pile refers to visible surface of the carpet, made up of fibres or threads.

Short pile threads

Canvas backing

Long thread in loops

Canvas backing

Tufted carpet

- Tufted carpet has tufts of pile inserted into a canvas backing using needles. The canvas backing is then coated with latex to anchor and hold in the tufts.
- Tufted carpet is generally cheaper than woven carpet, as synthetic fibres are used.
- Tufted carpet comes in a wide variety of colours.
- Tufted carpet is soft, durable and easy to clean.

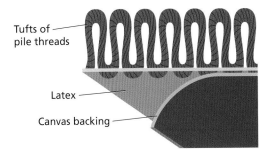

Tufts of pile threads

Latex

Canvas backing

Types of fibres used in carpet production

Natural and human-made fibres are used in carpet making.

Tip!

The term human-made may be referred to as man-made in the Leaving Certificate exam papers.

Natural fibres

Example	Properties
Wool	✓ Warm and soft ✓ Resilient ✓ Very good insulator ✓ Easy to clean ✓ Fire-retardant × Expensive

FLOORING AND FLOOR COVERINGS

Human-made fibres

Example	Properties
Nylon	✓ Warm ✓ Very hard-wearing ✗ Affected by **static** ✗ Can compact over time
Acrylic	✓ Similar to wool in texture and appearance ✓ Durable ✗ Can pill
Polypropylene	✓ Tough and hard-wearing ✓ Water-resistant ✓ Cheap ✗ Melts under direct heat, e.g. cinders from an open fire

> **Lit Hit**
> Static is a stationary electric charge, typically produced by friction, which causes sparks or crackling or the attraction of dust or hair.

Properties (advantages and disadvantages)

✓ Blended carpet fibres, e.g. 80% wool and 20% nylon, combine the softness and resilience of wool with the strength and value of nylon

✓ Available in a wide range of colours, patterns and textures

✓ Insulating, so rooms with carpet tend to be warmer

✓ Warm and soft underfoot

✓ Quiet underfoot

✗ Can be expensive, especially if it has a high wool content. Woven carpet is more expensive than tufted carpet, but it will stand the test of time.

✗ Prone to fading if placed in a room that gets a lot of sunlight

✗ Can gather dust if not thoroughly cleaned, making it unsuitable for asthma sufferers

Classification and uses

Carpets are classified depending on how much wear and tear they can withstand.
The three main classes are:

* **heavy domestic** (high-traffic wear and tear): used for hallways and stairs
* **general domestic** (general wear and tear): used in living rooms
* **light domestic** (little use, light wear and tear): used in bedrooms.

Tip!
In the exam be specific when naming the soft flooring chosen, e.g. a woven, wilton, heavy domestic carpet with 80% wool and 20% nylon.

? Recommend **one** type of floor covering for a kitchen. Give **two** reasons for your choice. (14) **OL**

Suggest **two** types of flooring suitable for a sitting room. State **two** properties of each. (18) **OL**

Name and describe **one** soft flooring that you would recommend for a family living room. State the main advantage **and** the main disadvantage of this flooring. (9) **HL**

▲ Sitting room with a general domestic carpet

∞ WALL FINISHES
4.3

What you will learn:

- **Factors to consider when selecting wall finishes**
- **Paints**
- **Wallpaper**
- **Wall tiles**

Choosing a wall finish is an important part of creating an aesthetically pleasing interior decoration scheme in the home. Walls may be finished with paint, wallpaper or tiles.

Factors to consider when selecting wall finishes

- **Cost:** consider the available budget before choosing a wall finish, as the price can vary greatly. For example, paint is relatively cheap compared to tiles, so it may suit a lower budget.

- **Function:** consider the overall function of the room and its specific requirements before choosing wall finishes. For example, kitchens and bathrooms require a wall finish that is moisture-resistant and durable, as moisture is created here. The wall finish in a sitting room should be aesthetically pleasing.

- **Cleaning:** wall finishes in bathrooms and kitchens need to be washable and easy to maintain. Many paints now come with an easy-clean finish that is easy to wipe and does not stain. Tiles are also easy to clean, but grouting may become dirty over time.

- **Aesthetics:** consider the desired effect of the wall finish and how it can be used to enhance the aesthetics or appearance of the room. Paint is a cheap way of transforming a room with colour. Wallpaper can be used to add pattern and create a feature wall.

- **Room specifications:** room size should always be taken into account when choosing wall finishes, as large patterns or dark colours in a small room will make it appear even smaller. These are best suited to large spaces. If the room has a north-facing aspect, avoid choosing blues or greens, as these are cool colours and will make the room feel even colder.

REMEMBER IT!
'**C**olourful **F**inishes **C**an **A**lter **R**ooms.'
Cost, **F**unction, **C**leaning, **A**esthetics, **R**oom specifications.

? Give an account of **four** factors that should be considered when choosing wall finishes for the interior of the home. (16) **OL**

Identify and discuss **three** factors to be considered when selecting wall finishes for a kitchen in a new house. (18) **OL**

Paints

Paints can be classified as water-based or oil/solvent-based.

GO FIGURE 123

Water-based paints account for roughly 80% of paints sold.

Water-based paints

- Have paint pigments dispersed in a liquid that consists mainly of water
- Take two to four hours to dry

Types

Emulsion	Kitchen/bathroom	Thixotropic/ceiling
Matt vinyl emulsion • Gives a matt finish • Good for hiding imperfections on walls, e.g. cracks **Silk vinyl emulsion** • Gives a slight sheen finish, which reflects light • May make rooms appear larger **Uses:** sitting rooms, living rooms, bedrooms, hallways	• Designed for use in high-moisture areas with condensation from cooking/ showering, as it contains an anti-fungicide to prevent mould growth • Easy to wipe clean **Uses:** kitchens, bathrooms	• Designed for painting ceilings, as it does not drip • One coat is normally sufficient for coverage **Uses:** ceilings

Properties (advantages and disadvantages)

- ✓ Easy to apply and covers walls well
- ✓ Dries quickly
- ✓ Available in a wide range of colours
- ✓ Inexpensive
- ✓ Durable, so can withstand general wear and tear
- ✓ Matt-finish paint masks minor imperfections on walls, e.g. cracks
- ✗ Not as hard-wearing as oil/solvent -based paints

Oil/solvent-based paints

- Have paint pigments dispersed in oil and solvent
- Take 12–24 hours to dry

Types

Gloss

- Gives a high-gloss, attractive finish

Uses: doors, skirting boards, window frames and windowsills

Satin finish

- Gives a semi-sheen finish

Uses: walls, ceilings, woods and metals

Properties (advantages and disadvantages)

- ✓ Hard-wearing and durable, suited for areas that require maximum protection, e.g. skirting boards
- ✓ Suitable for outdoor use, as they are water-resistant once dry
- ✓ Available in a limited range of colours
- ✓ Create a glossy, reflective finish that is attractive to look at
- ✗ Slow to dry
- ✗ Gives off a strong odour, so rooms need to be ventilated for many hours after use
- ✗ Unsuitable for unsmooth surfaces, e.g. cracked walls, as they can highlight imperfections

Did you know ❓

When oil/solvent-based paints evaporate, they release volatile organic compounds (VOCs) into the atmosphere. These are potentially hazardous to both human health and the environment.

Specialised paints

- **Flame-retardant paint** for high-risk areas, e.g. kitchens or caravans
- **Floor and step paint**, e.g. for a garage
- **Textured paint** to hide minor imperfections on a wall surface

Paint effects

Paint can be used to achieve various effects, patterns or finishes, including:

- rag rolling, colour washing, sponging and stencilling
- suede or metallic finish
- blackboard paint.

🖼 Sponge effect

WALL FINISHES

Wallpaper

Types

General purpose	Vinyl
• Designs are machine- or hand-printed onto paper of varying thicknesses **Uses:** sitting rooms, living rooms, bedrooms, hallways	• Designs are printed on the paper backing then treated with a vinyl topcoat • Durable, waterproof and easy to clean **Uses:** kitchens, bathrooms, bedrooms
Embossed	**Flock**
• Designs are pressed onto a paper backing, creating a raised, textured effect • Can hide most wall imperfections **Uses:** sitting rooms, living rooms, bedrooms	• A fuzzy, velvet-like texture design is printed onto a paper backing, which creates a three-dimensional effect and adds a textural element to the room **Uses:** feature walls in sitting rooms or bedrooms

Properties (advantages and disadvantages)

✓ Available in many different colours and designs that can enhance a home's interior design scheme and add a focal point in the form of a feature wall

✓ Flock wallpaper adds texture to a room, creating a contrast from smooth finishes

✓ Embossed wallpaper hides imperfect walls, making it especially suited to older houses

✓ Vinyl wallpaper is thicker than standard papers, making it durable and hard-wearing. The vinyl finish makes it washable.

✗ Can be difficult and time-consuming to hang, especially if it is not pre-pasted

✗ Can tear easily

▲ Bedroom with general-purpose wallpaper

Wall tiles

For information on tiles see page 427.

Describe **one** type of wall finish suitable for a young child's bedroom. Give **two** reasons for your choice. (14) **OL**

Describe **two** different wall finishes suitable for use in the house interior and state **two** properties of each finish. (14) **HL**

FURNITURE, SOFT FURNISHINGS AND FABRICS

4.3

What you will learn:

- **Factors to consider when choosing furniture**
- **Types of furniture**
- **Soft furnishings**
- **Fabrics**

Furniture has many practical uses in the home, but it should also be aesthetically pleasing.

Factors to consider when choosing furniture

- **Cost:** consider the available budget before choosing furniture, as the price can vary greatly. For example, handcrafted furniture is more expensive than flat-pack furniture, due to the time and skill level required to make it.
- **Function of the room:** consider the overall function of the room before choosing furniture. For example, a family living room requires robust pieces of furniture that can withstand wear and tear. Bedrooms require comfortable beds and sufficient storage.
- **Aesthetics:** the style of furniture considered should fit into the existing interior decor of the room, e.g. rustic country, modern contemporary. Pieces chosen should be **balanced** with other objects in the room. A strikingly coloured or patterned piece of furniture used in a neutral-coloured room can add to the design and create **emphasis** in a neutral palette.
- **Space available:** furniture chosen should be the correct **proportion** for the room. Take measurements of the room, e.g. the length and width, to ensure that furniture being considered will fit.
- **Comfort:** ensure that furniture chosen for sitting or sleeping is comfortable and relaxing. Comfort can be a matter of preference, as some people prefer firm support whereas others prefer softness.

➜ For more information on the principles of design, including **balance**, **emphasis** and **proportion**, see page 418.

- **Personal preference:** consider personal likes and dislikes when choosing furniture. There are many styles available to suit every taste.
  - o **Antique furniture**, e.g. Georgian furniture, is over 150 years old and handcrafted from high-quality materials. It is commonly sold in auction rooms or antique salvage yards and can be very expensive.
  - o **Traditional furniture**, e.g. cottage dressers, is about 100 years old. It is homely and simple in design and used to create a traditional cottage look.
  - o **Modern furniture is often sleek**, simple and contemporary in style. It uses metal, glass and plastics as well as fabrics and wood. It provides a simple and modern feel.

▲ Antique chest of drawers

▲ Traditional cottage dresser

▲ Modern chest of drawers

Mark and Emma have recently purchased a two-bedroomed bungalow in a large town.
The bungalow consists of a small kitchen, a bathroom, a large sitting room and two bedrooms. It has no heating system and little insulation.

Outline **four** factors that Mark and Emma should take into consideration when selecting furniture for the bungalow. (16) **OL**

Outline the factors to be considered when choosing furniture for a family living room. In your answer include reference to **two** principles of design. (18) **HL**

REMEMBER IT!

'**C**omfortable **F**urnishings **A**re **S**eldom **C**heap **P**urchases'

Cost, **F**unction, **A**esthetics, **S**pace, **C**omfort, **P**ersonal preference.

Types of furniture

Types of furniture include:
- upholstered furniture
- bedroom furniture
- storage furniture
- soft furnishings.
- dining furniture

Upholstered furniture

Upholstered furniture consists of:
- a wooden frame for structure
- a filling made from springs and padding (foam) for support and comfort
- an outer fabric cover, e.g. cotton, wool or polyester.

Types of upholstered furniture

- Sofas
- Armchairs
- Dining-room chairs

Factors to consider when choosing upholstered furniture

Ensure that:
- the outer fabric and inner filling are fire-resistant
- it is well constructed and well finished to ensure durability
- the covering is easy to keep clean; it may be treated with a stain-resistant finish
- the filling provides good back support and is comfortable to sit on.

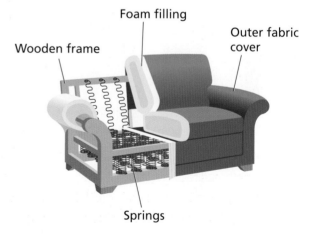

Foam filling

Outer fabric cover

Wooden frame

Springs

Storage furniture

Storage is designed to prevent clutter and save space.

Types of storage furniture

Built-in wardrobes 	• Consist of hanging rails, drawers and open shelving • Available in a wide variety of shapes, sizes and materials, e.g. solid wood or medium-density fibreboard (MDF) • May be custom-built to suit the space in a room. This is often more expensive. • Cannot be moved or rearranged after they are installed
Basic shelving 	• Consists of open shelving units • Available in a wide variety of shapes, sizes and materials, e.g. solid wood or MDF • Useful to store everyday items and prevent clutter • A cheap form of storage
Modular units 	• Consists of a single wall unit designed with open shelving, cupboards, display areas, a television unit or a desk • Useful to store everyday items, display decorative pieces and prevent clutter • Useful for confined spaces, e.g. apartments
Free-standing units 	• Inexpensive, flat-pack furniture, e.g. IKEA furniture • Consists of open shelving units and drawers • Can be moved or changed to suit the room • Useful to store everyday items, e.g. toys

> **Did you know ?**
> A kitchen is another type of built-in storage unit.

Factors to consider when choosing storage furniture

Ensure that it:

- is made from good-quality materials so it is durable and strong
- functions efficiently, e.g. drawers open smoothly
- is large enough to provide sufficient storage space for the purpose of the room, e.g. toys in a playroom
- will fit into the room without dominating it

 Name and describe **two** items of storage furniture suitable for a modern living room. Give reasons for your choice. (18) **OL**

FURNITURE, SOFT FURNISHINGS AND FABRICS

Dining furniture

Dining furniture consists of a large table and chairs made from wood, glass, plastic or metal. Some chairs may be upholstered.

Factors to consider when choosing dining furniture

Ensure that:

- it is sturdy, strong and suitable for everyday use
- it has enough chairs and table space to accommodate all the family
- the table surface and chairs are easy to clean and stain-resistant
- the seating provides good back support and is comfortable to sit on.

Bedroom furniture

A bed may be single, double, king size or super king size. Sofa beds and bunk beds are also available. Beds consist of two parts: a divan/base and a mattress. Some may have a headboard.

Types of divans/bases

Spring-edge		• Springs go all the way to the edge of the divan/base and are covered with a layer of fabric • Comfortable to sleep on as the springs offer extra support • Can be expensive
Solid-top		• Solid wood top with no springs. This provides a firmer, orthopaedic feel to the bed. • Cheap to buy
Stretch wire/ wooden plank Wooden planks		• Commonly used for bunk beds or camping beds • Cheap to buy

Types of mattresses

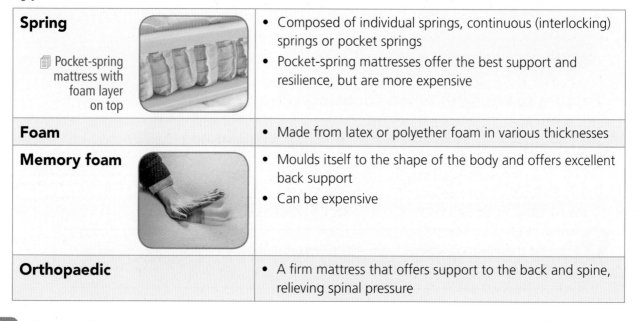

Spring 📄 Pocket-spring mattress with foam layer on top		• Composed of individual springs, continuous (interlocking) springs or pocket springs • Pocket-spring mattresses offer the best support and resilience, but are more expensive
Foam		• Made from latex or polyether foam in various thicknesses
Memory foam		• Moulds itself to the shape of the body and offers excellent back support • Can be expensive
Orthopaedic		• A firm mattress that offers support to the back and spine, relieving spinal pressure

Headboards

- Headboards protect the wall behind the bed and add a decorative feature to a bedroom.
- They can be made from a variety of materials, e.g. wood or metal, or may be upholstered for comfort.

Factors to consider when choosing a bed

Ensure that it:
- is comfortable to lie on
- offers good back support
- is well made using high-quality materials and is well constructed.

Soft furnishings

Soft furnishings are decorative items made of textiles or fabrics, used in interior design to enhance the appearance of a room. Examples include:

- curtains
- blinds
- bed linen
- cushions.

Curtains

- Curtains come in various lengths: to the windowsill, below the windowsill, full/floor length and puddle length (sits on floor).
- Curtains can be unlined or lined with standard, heavy or blackout lining. Lining makes the curtain drape well and appear thicker/more luxurious.
- Headings on curtains include pencil pleat, French pleat, box pleat, tab top and eyelet.

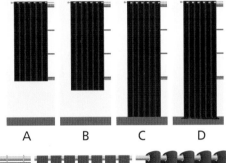

A. To the windowsill
B. Below the windowsill
C. Full/floor length
D. Puddle length (sits on the floor)

A   B   C   D

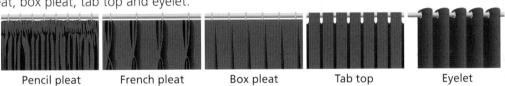

Pencil pleat   French pleat   Box pleat   Tab top   Eyelet

Functions of curtains (reasons for choice)

- **Privacy:** curtains provide privacy by preventing others from looking in the windows of the home.
- **Aesthetics:** curtains enhance the aesthetic appearance of a room, as they add colour, pattern and texture, creating an attractive look.
- **Insulation:** heavy, lined curtains provide insulation, both in terms of heat and sound. Closing curtains also ensures heat is not lost through the window.
- **Light:** curtains block out light and darken a room. This is especially important during the summer months or for people who work night shifts.

REMEMBER IT!

'PAIL!'
Privacy, Aesthetics, Insulation, Light.

Factors to consider when choosing curtains

- **Cost:** consider the available budget before choosing curtains, as the price varies greatly, e.g. silk curtains cost more than cotton curtains.
- **Style of room:** the choice of curtains should reflect the existing interior decor. Avoid fussy styles, which date.
- **Size of windows:** ensure curtains fit the dimensions of the windows. When measuring for curtains, the width of the window should be multiplied by two to ensure fullness. Choose height A or height B.
- **Care and cleaning:** consider curtains that can be machine washed, as they are easier and cheaper to maintain than curtains that must be dry cleaned.

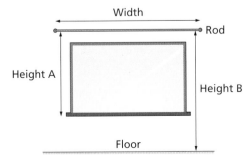

Width

Rod

Height A

Height B

Floor

FURNITURE, SOFT FURNISHINGS AND FABRICS

Fabrics suitable for curtains

- Cotton   • Polyester   • Velvet   • Silk

Desirable properties of curtains

Curtains should:

- drape well and hang with attractive pleats
- be pre-shrunk, so that when washed they will remain the same length
- be colourfast, so colours do not run in the wash
- complement the existing decor and style of the room
- be flame-resistant
- insulate the room.

Blinds

Blinds are a decorative window-dressings that can be used in addition to curtains or on their own.

Types of blinds

Roller	• Made from stiffened fabric, e.g. linen, fixed onto a roller that can be pulled down to cover the window
	• Available in a wide variety of colours and patterns
	• **Vinyl-coated** roller blinds are best suited to areas of high moisture. e.g. bathrooms
Roman	• Made from fabric, e.g. cotton, with wooden slats at the back of the blind
	• Designed to fold neatly at the top of the window when pulled up
	• Available in a wide variety of colours and patterns
Venetian	• Made with overlapping horizontal wooden or plastic slats
	• May be opened or closed by pulling a cord. When opened, they allow light through but still keep the room private.
	• Tend to gather dust between the slats

Lit Hit
Vinyl-coated means that the fabric is treated with a layer of PVC which makes it waterproof and more hard-wearing.

Did you know ❓

Every blind should be fitted with a child-safety device that keeps the cord secured to the wall, as a child can die within 50 seconds of becoming entangled in a cord.

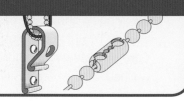

Bed linen

There are various types of bed linen, including sheets, pillowcases and duvet covers. Bed linen is available in a wide variety of colours and patterns, and can create a pleasing look in rooms.

Sheets

Sheets can be fitted, flat or **valance**.

> **Lit Hit**
> A valance is a type of sheet that is used to cover the divan/base of the bed.

Desirable properties of sheets

- Smooth and soft to sleep on
- Easy to launder, as sheets need to be washed weekly
- Absorbent
- Shrink-resistant

Suitable fabrics for sheets

- Cotton
- Polyester
- Silk
- Linen

Duvets

Duvets consist of two outer layers of closely-woven cotton or polyester fabric, sewn together with a filling inside. Fillings include:

- **down:** heavy filling from the breast of ducks and geese; this is expensive
- **feather and down:** not as heavy as pure down duvets; expensive
- **pure cotton:** ideal for summer months, as it is cool
- **synthetic filling:** e.g. polyester, a cheap filling option.

A duvet's insulating value (warmth) is measured in tog:

- 1.5–4.5 tog = light summer duvet
- 12–15 tog = heavy, warm winter duvet.

▲ Feather and down duvet filling

Pillows

Pillows consist of an outer cotton covering filled with down, down and feather or a synthetic filling, e.g. polyester. Pillows should provide good head and neck support.

Cushions

Cushions consist of a fabric outer layer stuffed with a filling of soft material. The outer covering can be made from a variety of fabrics, e.g. cotton, velvet or polyester. The filling is usually down, feathers, foam or polyester wadding. They are used to make seats more comfortable and add back support. They are available a wide variety of colours, patterns, textures, shapes and sizes, to add an aesthetically pleasing look to rooms.

> **?** Recommend **two** types of soft furnishings that would enhance the appearance of a sitting room. Give reasons for your choice. (12) **OL**

FURNITURE, SOFT FURNISHINGS AND FABRICS

HL Fabrics

Fabrics are classified as natural or synthetic.

- **Natural fabrics** (from plants or animals): e.g. cotton, linen, silk and wool.
- **Synthetic fabrics** (human-made from coal, oil and chemicals): e.g. polyester, viscose and acrylic.

Natural fabric

Type	Properties	Uses
Cotton (from the cotton plant) ▲ Cotton plant	• Strong and durable • Absorbent • Easy to launder • Cool against the skin, as it allows air to pass through • Easy to dye, making it available in a wide variety of colours and patterns • Inexpensive • **Examples:** chintz, towelling, gingham	• Curtains • Bed linen • Upholstered furniture fabric • Cushions

Synthetic fabric

Type	Properties	Uses
Polyester (derived from coal, air and chemicals)	• Strong and hard-wearing • Crease-resistant • Stain-resistant • Good drape • Available in a wide variety of colours and patterns • Inexpensive • Often blended with cotton to combine the best qualities of both, e.g. bed linen that is soft and does not crease	• Bed linen • Cushions • Filling for duvets ▲ Polyester bed linen and duvet

? Recommend **one** type of fabric suitable for household soft furnishings. Give reasons for your choice. (12) **HL**

MATERIALS USED IN THE HOME

What you will learn:

- **Types, properties and uses of metals, plastics, glass and wood**

HL All household furniture, appliances and equipment are made from materials, including metal, plastic, glass, wood and fabric. The materials influence how an item should be used and cared for and how long it will last. A mixture of materials used in a home provides interest.

Metals

There are four main types of metals that may be used in the home: stainless steel, copper, aluminium and tin.

Type	Properties	Uses
Stainless steel (an **alloy** of iron and chromium) **Lit Hit** An alloy is a mixture of two elements, one of which is a metal.	• Resistant to rust/corrosion • Strong and durable, can withstand constant use • Easy to clean • Comes in a shiny or brushed (satin) finish • Poor conductor of heat • Shiny finish can show up marks, e.g. fingerprints or water spotting	• Cutlery • Utensils • Saucepans • Sinks • Countertops • Appliances, e.g. fridge casing • Furniture
Copper	• A soft and **malleable** metal • An excellent conductor of heat, making it a popular metal for chefs' saucepans **Lit Hit** Malleable means able to be hammered or pressed permanently out of shape without breaking or cracking. • An excellent conductor of electricity, which is why it is used in electrical wiring and appliances • Easy to clean • Reacts with oxygen in the air to form a green layer (verdigris) • Highly reactive with foods, which is why saucepans are lined with tin or steel • Expensive	• Domestic water pipes and cylinders • Professional saucepans • Electrical wires ▲ Copper domestic water pipes

Aluminium	• A lightweight metal • A good conductor of heat, so it retains heat well • Resistant to corrosion, as it does not react with oxygen • Can react with acidic/alkaline foods or cleaning agents, resulting in a darkening of the metal. A non-stick enamelled layer prevents this.	• Cooking utensils • Saucepans • Foil wrap • Window frames 
Tin	• A lightweight metal • Hard-wearing • Inexpensive • Can react with acidic/alkaline foods or cleaning agents, resulting in a darkening of the metal. A non-stick enamelled layer prevents this.	• Baking tins and trays 

Plastics

Plastics are now one of the most widely used materials in the home. Plastics are made by combining natural products, e.g. cellulose, coal, natural gas and salt, with crude oil.

The two main types of plastic available are thermosetting and thermoplastic.

Type	**Properties**	**Examples and uses**
Thermosetting Thermosetting plastic is a hard plastic that has very strong bonds between molecules. Very strong bonds between molecules Once the plastic is moulded it sets. Further heating cannot break these strong bonds, therefore thermosetting plastic remains hard when heated and cannot be remoulded.	• Hard, rigid plastics • Can withstand very high temperatures • Damaged by strong acids and alkalis • Not damaged by solvents	**Melamine formaldehyde** • Mixing bowls • Children's plates • Worktop surfaces • Trays **Polyester** • Oven bags • Boil-in-the-bag rice bags **Phenolics (Bakelite)** (brown/black colour, heat resistant to 150 °C) • Handles of saucepans/grill pans

Type	Properties	Examples and uses
Thermoplastic Thermoplastic is a soft plastic that has very weak bonds between molecules. 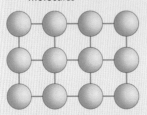 Weak bonds between molecules Once the plastic is moulded it can be remoulded and melted several times by heating it. When thermosetting plastic is heated it softens and changes shape.	• Soft and flexible plastics • Soften further when heated, harden on cooling • Acid- and alkali-resistant • Damaged by solvents	**Polytetrafluoroethylene (PTFE)/Teflon** • Non-stick frying pans • Saucepans  **Polystyrene** • Containers • Tumblers • Disposable cutlery  **Polyethylene** • Bottles • Chopping boards • Toys 

General properties of plastics (advantages and disadvantages)

✓ Plastics can withstand wear and tear or constant use.

✓ They do not transfer toxic chemicals to food.

✓ They are easy to clean, due to their non-stick surface.

✓ Thermosetting plastics, e.g. phenolics, can withstand high temperatures, which is why they are used as saucepan handles to prevent burns.

✓ Plastics are waterproof.

✓ Plastic is a cheap material to produce, due to low production costs.

✗ Some plastics can blister and crack when heated.

✗ Strong acids and alkalis can cause damage.

 Differentiate between thermoplastic **and** thermosetting plastics. Refer to:
- properties
- examples
- uses. (20) **HL**

Name the **two** main types of plastic used in the home. In relation to **each** list (a) its uses and (b) its properties. (20) **HL**

Glass

There are three main types of glass used throughout the home: heat-resistant, soda lime and stained glass.

Type	Properties	Uses	
Heat resistant (Pyrex)	• Can withstand high temperatures (up to 230°C) without shattering or breaking • Hard and strong • Can be transparent or coloured • Can chip easily	• Pyrex jugs • Casserole dishes	
Soda lime	• Transparent • Cheap to manufacture • Can be recycled • Breaks easily • Can crack at high temperatures	• Jars • Glasses • Light bulbs	
Stained	• Available in a wide variety of colours • Attractive • Expensive	• Windows • Fanlights	

Wood

Wood can be classified as natural wood and human-made wood.

Natural wood

Two types of natural wood used in the home are hardwood and softwood.

Hardwood (solid wood) (from slow-growing, deciduous trees)		
Examples	**Properties**	**Uses**
• Oak • Maple • Walnut • Mahogany • Beech • Ash • Cherry	• Strong and durable • Has an attractive appearance and is available in many colours with a fine grain. Darkens with age. • Resistant to rot, damage and decay, so it lasts longer than softwood • Expensive to buy • Can **warp** or swell if it comes in contact with moisture	• Floorboards • Furniture • Fitted kitchens ▲ Walnut dresser Lit Hit Warp means bend or twist out of shape.

Softwood
(from fast-growing, coniferous trees)

Examples	Properties	Uses
• Pine • Spruce • Fir	• Cheap • Easy to work with, as it is soft and easy to cut • Easily marked and scratched, e.g. flooring from high heels • Can warp and swell if it comes into contact with moisture	• Doors • Skirting boards • Furniture

Did you know ?
The wood from softwood trees is collectively known as 'deal'.

▲ Pine door

Human-made wood

Three types of human-made wood used in the home are plywood, medium-density fibreboard (MDF) and chipboard.

Type	Properties	Uses
Plywood (made from thin sheets of softwood glued together)	• Strong, due to the gluing of many layers • Laminated or veneered to create a moisture-proof finish • Inexpensive • A versatile material as it has many uses	• Flooring, e.g. suspended floors • Furniture
Medium-density fibreboard (MDF) (made from wood fibres glued together and compressed under heat and pressure)	• A very stiff, durable material • Easy to work with and easily machined • Inexpensive • Can be easily painted or laminated • Can release formaldehyde when cut, which can irritate the lungs and eyes	• Storage cabinets • Skirting boards • Furniture
Chipboard (made from softwood chips glued together under heat and pressure)	• Inexpensive • Available in various thicknesses and strengths • Damaged by moisture, so it degrades easily • Unattractive	• Laminated kitchen counters • Flooring

 Describe **one** solid wood used in the home and refer to:
- type of wood
- properties
- uses. (12) **HL**

MATERIALS USED IN THE HOME

Chapter 22:
The energy-efficient home

4.4 THE ENERGY-EFFICIENT HOME

What you will learn:

- Energy supplies to the home
- Emissions from burning fuels and the effects on the environment
- How to reduce emissions
- Energy inefficiencies in the home and improvement strategies
- Building Energy Rating (BER) system

Energy supplies to the home

Energy is supplied to the home from non-renewable and renewable resources.

Non-renewable sources	Renewable sources
Non-renewable sources are resources that are in limited supply and cannot be replaced once they have been depleted. They can cause harm to the environment. For example, fossil fuels including: • gas • oil • solid fuels, e.g. coal and peat.	Renewable sources are resources that are always available naturally, and are not depleted by constant use. For example: • solar energy • geothermal energy • hydropower energy • wind energy • biomass energy.

Electricity (non-renewable and renewable)

Sources
Electricity is created from: • non-renewable sources: burning fossil fuels, e.g. coal, peat, oil and gas • renewable sources: e.g. solar energy, wind power and hydropower

Uses		
• Domestic heating and lighting	• To power appliances	• Cooking food

Advantages	Disadvantages
✓ A reliable, readily-available energy source delivered to every home and business in Ireland ✓ An efficient form of energy	✗ Electrical power can be interrupted due to storms, improvement works or damaged lines ✗ Currently there is too much dependence on fossil fuels to generate electricity

Sustainability
The use of non-renewable resources to generate electricity is unsustainable, as fossil fuel supplies are limited and cannot be replaced. They also create harmful greenhouse emissions that cause air pollution, which increases global warming and causes acid rain. For this reason, targets have been set to increase the use of renewable energy sources to create electricity, e.g. Ireland has a target to create 16% of its energy from renewable energy sources by 2020.

Gas (non-renewable)

Source

Gas was formed from the compressed remains of aquatic plants and animals, whose remains settled at the bottoms of oceans and lakes millions of years ago. As layers of sediment built up, pressure and heat increased. When combined with bacteria, a hydrocarbon (gas) field was created.

There are two main types of gas:

- **natural gas:** piped ashore in a series of underground pipes to homes located on the national grid
- **liquefied petroleum gas (LPG):** sold in bottles or delivered to a domestic tank. Useful for those not on the gas grid.

Uses

- Domestic heating and hot-water systems
- Cooking food

Advantages	Disadvantages
✓ An efficient fossil fuel that heats homes and cooks food quickly	✗ Natural gas can be dangerous if used carelessly
✓ Natural gas is cleaner than other fossil fuels, as it produces no soot or ash	✗ Burning releases emissions, e.g. carbon monoxide, which are harmful to the environment
✓ Produces 70% less carbon dioxide emissions than oil or coal	✗ LPG can be impractical, as it can run out and is difficult to transport

Sustainability

Gas is a non-renewable resource. Supplies are limited and cannot be replaced. Consumption currently outweighs the amount being discovered. If current consumption levels continue, it is predicted that gas reserves will run out by 2050.

Guidelines for safe use of gas in the home

- Ensure that the gas boiler and gas appliances are serviced regularly
- Avoid installing gas cookers in draughty areas, as the flame may extinguish and gas will continue to leak
- Ensure a balance flue is fitted with all gas appliances, as this carries gases away from the appliance and expels them outside, preventing a build-up in the home that can cause carbon monoxide poisoning
- Fit an audible carbon monoxide alarm to alert when high levels of carbon monoxide are produced by unsafe gas appliances

Did you know ?

Since 1 September 2014, a change in building regulations requires householders to install carbon monoxide alarms when new or replacement boilers, fires, heaters and stoves are installed.

Outline **four** guidelines for the safe use of gas in the home. (20) **OL**

THE ENERGY-EFFICIENT HOME

Oil (non-renewable)

Source
Oil was formed from the compressed remains of aquatic plants and animals, whose remains were buried between layers of earth and rock millions of years ago. As layers built up, pressure and heat increased, eventually transforming them into crude oil. Crude oil must be refined before use. 

Uses

- Domestic heating and hot-water systems
- Cooking food

Advantages	Disadvantages
✓ One of the most abundant fossil fuels ✓ Has a high heating value, so it produces more heat than other fossil fuels ✓ A relatively clean fuel compared to burning solid fuels, as it produces little waste	✗ Oil-fired heating systems need regular maintenance, otherwise carbon monoxide may be produced ✗ Oil prices are continuing to rise, making it an expensive energy source ✗ Oil spills cause environmental and ecological damage

Sustainability
Oil is a non-renewable resource. Supplies are limited and cannot be replaced. If current consumption levels continue, it is predicted that oil reserves will run out by 2040.

Solid fuels

Solid fuels are used to heat homes in open fires, stoves or range cookers. Examples include coal, peat and wood.

Coal (non-renewable)

Source
Coal was formed from the remains of plants and trees that sank to the bottom of swamps. Over time, pressure caused by the weight of rocks and soil compressed the remains, and the heat that was generated gradually changed the material to coal. 

Uses

- Domestic heating
- Electricity generation

Advantages	Disadvantages
✓ An economical fuel compared to other sources ✓ Easy to burn and generates a lot of heat	✗ Releases large amounts of smoke and carbon dioxide emissions on burning, which are harmful to the environment ✗ Creates waste in the form of ash and soot

Sustainability
Coal is a non-renewable resource. Supplies are limited and cannot be replaced. The most recent coal mine found is over one million years old.

Peat (non-renewable)

Source
Peat was formed from the remains of plants and trees that sank to the bottom of swamps, forming a soggy, dense material and resulting in a blanket bog. Peat is cut by hand on privately owned land by individuals for private use, or by Bord na Móna, which supplies briquettes and machined turf for retail. 

Uses
• Domestic heating   • Electricity generation

Advantages	Disadvantages
✓ A relatively cheap fuel source	✗ Smoulders when burned, releasing smoke and carbon monoxide ✗ Creates waste in the form of ash and soot

Sustainability
Peat is a non-renewable resource, as it takes thousands of years to form. Cutting turf destroys the natural habitat created in Irish blanket bogs. For this reason, restrictions have been put in place to limit the number of bogs used for fuel.

GO FIGURE

It is estimated that 2–4% of bogland is being lost every year, mainly as a result of turf-cutting.

Wood (non-renewable and renewable)

Source
Wood in Ireland comes from over one million acres of state forests grown by Coillte.

Uses
• Domestic heating

Advantages	Disadvantages
✓ Burns quickly ✓ Attractive to look at, e.g. stacked beside the fire ✓ Not as harmful to the environment, as the carbon dioxide emissions released on burning only contain carbon that was absorbed from the atmosphere by the tree when it was growing	✗ Does not produce as much heat as other fossil fuels

Sustainability
Wood is both a renewable and non-renewable source, as trees cut do not regrow, but new trees may be planted. If new trees are planted, the renewing period takes a number of years due to the slow rate at which trees grow, e.g. conifer trees take 40 years to reach maturity. Coillte plants over 15 million trees annually to compensate for trees harvested, making wood one of the more sustainable sources of energy.

? Discuss **one** non-renewable source of energy used in the home. Refer to:
- source
- advantages/disadvantages
- sustainability. (15) **HL**

Solar energy (renewable)

Source

Solar energy is created using radiant light and heat from the sun. There are three main methods of utilising the sun's energy for domestic use: passive solar architecture, active solar heating/solar panels and solar photovoltaic system (PV).

▲ Active solar heating/solar panels

- **Passive solar architecture:** orientating a house south or south-west with large glass windows ensures that the home receives the maximum benefit of heat from the sun. This can reduce heating requirements by up to 80%.

- **Active solar heating/solar panels:** the sun's heat is absorbed by solar panels on the roof and converted into energy to heat the home water system. This process can supply 50–60% of hot water requirements for the home, and in some cases it is used for home heating.

- **Solar photovoltaic system (PV):** the sun's heat is absorbed by solar panels on the roof and converted into electricity using semiconductor materials, supplying the home with its own electricity supply. If not enough energy is generated, electricity can be imported from the grid e.g. from ESB sources.

> **Did you know** ?
>
> Excess electricity generated by an individual's solar panels can be sold back to the national grid, providing an income.

Advantages	Disadvantages
✓ Grants are available from the Sustainable Energy Authority of Ireland (SEAI) for the installation of all solar energy systems	✗ Solar panels and photovoltaic systems are expensive to purchase and install
✓ Solar panels provide a plentiful supply of hot water for washing, showering and for space heating	✗ There is a limited, undependable supply of sunshine in Ireland, so other forms of energy may be required as a back up
✓ No smoke or carbon dioxide emissions are released	✗ To achieve maximum passive solar gains, the house must be orientated to the sun. If the house is facing north or blocked by trees, solar energy may be unsuitable.

Sustainability

The sun is a renewable source of energy. It can supply a large proportion of the world's energy for an infinite period.

?

State the advantages/the disadvantages of solar energy. (12) **OL**

Name **and** set out details of **one** renewable energy source you have studied. Include reference to:
- source
- advantages/disadvantages
- sustainability. (14) **HL**

Emissions from burning fuels and the effects on the environment

The burning of fossil fuels releases harmful emissions into the atmosphere, these include:

- carbon dioxide CO_2
- sulfur dioxide SO_2
- nitrogen oxide NO_2
- smoke.

Effects of emissions on the environment

Greenhouse effect/climate change

The average temperature of Earth's surface is 15°C. This temperature is maintained by natural greenhouse gases in the atmosphere which trap some of the heat from the sun and allow about 30% to be reflected back out into space. Burning fossil fuels releases greenhouse gases, such as carbon dioxide. These act like a blanket in Earth's atmosphere, preventing excess radiation from the sun escaping.

> **GO FIGURE**
> Atmospheric carbon dioxide levels have increased by more than 40% since the beginning of the Industrial Revolution in the eighteenth century.

Effects

- **Temperature increase:** there has been a gradual increase in the overall temperature of Earth's atmosphere. Temperatures have increased by 0.8°C since 1880. By 2020 they are expected to increase by 1.5–4.5°C.
- **Rising sea levels:** sea levels are rising, as glaciers are melting from the increase in Earth's temperature, leading to flooding of low-lying areas. This also causes animals, such as polar bears, to lose their natural habitat and face extinction.

> **GO FIGURE**
> Sea levels are expected to rise by over 1.5 metres in the next 40 years.

- **Climate change:** increasing temperatures are causing more extreme unpredictable weather patterns worldwide, such as increased rainfall in some areas with drought in others.

Acid rain

Normal rain has a pH of 5.6, which is naturally slightly acidic. When fossil fuels are burned they release harmful emissions such as carbon dioxide and sulfur dioxide that combine with water vapour and result in acidic precipitation with a pH of 4.1.

Effects

- **Damage to plants and crops:** acid rain reduces the pH of the soil and removes essential nutrients, e.g. calcium, necessary for plant and crop growth.
- **Kills fish:** some species of fish cannot survive in acidic water, so many die and ecosystems are destroyed.
- **Destroys limestone:** acid rain dissolves the calcium carbonate present in limestone. This is slowly destroying many historic buildings and monuments.

Smog

When fossil fuels are burned they release smoke into the atmosphere. This combines with fog, forming a substance called smog. This is common in industrialised cities, e.g. Beijing.

▲ Smog

Effects

- **Respiratory problems:** smog increases the risk of respiratory problems such as asthma and bronchitis. It also causes irritation of the nose, throat and mouth.
- **Reduced sunshine:** thick smog can block out the rays of the sun, making an area appear darker or dim. This affects plant growth, as sunshine is needed for photosynthesis to occur.

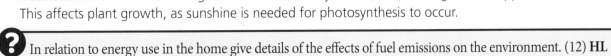
? In relation to energy use in the home give details of the effects of fuel emissions on the environment. (12) **HL**

How to reduce emissions

- Choose natural gas or liquid petroleum gas in preference to coal or oil, as they produce approximately 50% less carbon dioxide and no smoke during combustion.
- Choose smokeless fuels, e.g. smokeless coal nuggets, as they produce less smoke and 20% less carbon dioxide when burned in comparison to traditional coal.
- Switch to renewable sources of energy, e.g. solar panels or wind energy. Customers can opt to obtain their electricity from an electricity company that produces some of its electricity from renewable source, e.g. SSE Airtricity.
- Buy A-rated energy-efficient appliances and equipment as they use less energy during operation.
- Dispose of fridges and freezers correctly, as per the Waste Electrical and Electronic Equipment (WEEE) legislation. Its purpose is to prevent the release of CFC gases by ensuring that old electrical and electronic equipment is recycled rather than disposed of in landfill sites.

> **Did you know**
>
> In 1990 a smoky coal ban was introduced in Dublin, meaning people could only burn smokeless coal. Research indicated that the ban resulted in over 350 fewer annual deaths. Currently, 29 areas in Ireland are under the smoky coal ban.

> **?** Describe **three** different methods of reducing harmful emissions in the environment. (12) **HL**

Energy inefficiencies in the home and improvement strategies

Heating	
Inefficiency	**Strategy for improvement**
Boiler	• Install a condensing boiler • Have the boiler serviced regularly to ensure it is working efficiently
Central heating system	• Install a zoned heating system, so heat is only supplied to the areas in the home where it is needed • Install thermostats on every radiator and turn down the temperature by one degree • Install a timer to turn on the heating when needed
Open fires	• Install a stove to prevent heat being lost up the chimney • If an open fire is preferred, add a back boiler, as it heats the household water system at the same time • Change to smokeless coal or timber

▲ Thermostat

GO FIGURE

80% of the heat from an open fire is lost up the chimney.

Water heating

Inefficiency	Strategy for improvement
Immersion	• Install a timer on an electric immersion to prevent electricity being wasted • Install solar panels to heat the water
Hot water cylinder	• If not insulated with foam, fit an insulating lagging jacket on a hot water cylinder, as this keeps the hot water inside hotter for longer
Baths	• Take a shower instead of a bath, as showers require less hot water

Water

Inefficiency	Strategy for improvement	
Toilet systems	• Install a dual-flush toilet. This saves water, as the small flush uses less water. • Install a rainwater harvesting system. The water it collects is stored in a tank and forms part of the water system, e.g. it can be used to flush toilets	
Appliances	• Choose A-rated appliances, e.g. an A-rated washing machine, as they are more efficient in terms of energy and water use • Wait until the washing machine or dishwasher is full before switching on, to avoid wasting electricity	
Leaking taps	• Repair leaking taps, as they can waste up to 90 litres of water per day	

? Describe **three** methods of conserving water in the home. (15) **OL**

Electricity

Inefficiency	Strategy for improvement	
Standby	• Always switch off appliances after use, as they still use 20% electricity on standby **GO FIGURE 123** A typical house could save up to €47.00 per year by turning off appliances on standby at night.	
Tumble drying	• Hang clothes on a clotheshorse or on an outdoor line before tumble drying. This reduces the time needed to dry clothes.	
Bulbs	• Install CFL bulbs. These are 80% more efficient than incandescent bulbs. • Switch off lights when not in use	

Insulation	
Inefficiency	**Strategy for improvement**
Attic	• Insulate the attic with fibreglass or cellulose insulation to save heat from being lost through the roof
Draughts	• Fit draught-excluders around windows and doors, as this can cut heat loss by as much as 20% in winter • Install double- or triple-glazed windows

? Identify **three** areas in the home where energy inefficiencies may occur and in relation to each suggest **one** method of improving efficiency. (18) **OL**

In relation to energy use in the home give details of potential energy inefficiencies and strategies for improvement. (18) **HL**

Building Energy Rating (BER) system

The Building Energy Rating (BER) system used for homes is similar to the energy label on appliances, with a scale of A to G. A-rated homes are the most energy efficient, while G-rated homes are the least efficient.

Since 1 January 2009, a BER certificate is compulsory for all homes being sold or rented and must be included in commercial advertisements. The home must be assessed by a registered BER assessor in order to determine a BER rating and obtain a certificate. During the survey they assess the:

• area of the rooms and windows
• thickness of the walls and the levels of insulation
• heating system
• floor and the wall types.

? Write an informative note on the Building Energy Rating (BER) system. (12) **HL**

Chapter 23:
Systems and services

⊂⊃ ELECTRICITY
4.5.1

What you will learn:

- Household electricity supply
- Types of circuits
- Electrical terms
- Charges on a domestic electricity bill

- Electrical safety devices
- Guidelines for the safe use of electricity in the home.
- Wiring a plug

Electricity is a form of energy, created from renewable or non-renewable processes and supplied to the home for a variety of tasks, e.g. lighting and heating.

Household electricity supply

1. **Electricity generation:** electricity is generated in a power plant and sent to the home via overhead distribution lines.

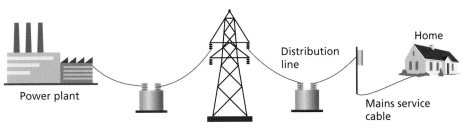

Power plant • Distribution line • Home • Mains service cable

2. **Mains service cable:** a mains service cable carries electricity to the home from the nearest distribution line via an underground duct.

3. **Meter cabinet:** the mains service cable enters a sealed meter cabinet, normally located on an outdoor wall of a home. A meter inside the cabinet records electricity consumption. A night-rate meter may also be installed to record night-rate/off-peak consumption.

4. **Consumer unit/main fuse board:** electricity is brought into the home from the outdoor meter box via cables to the indoor consumer unit/ main fuse board. It contains a main switch that can be used to turn off the electricity supply to the home and a Residual Circuit Device (RCD) to protect from electrical faults.

> **Did you know** ❓
>
> An underground duct is red in colour so that it is easily seen. It must be covered with a yellow ESB warning tape, which alerts people digging that dangerous electricity cables are underneath.

> **Did you know** ❓
>
> Meter cabinets are placed on an outdoor wall so that the meter can be read by ESB Networks meter readers.

ELECTRICITY

5. **Circuits:** electricity is supplied to the whole house from the consumer unit/main fuse board via individual circuits. Each circuit is fitted with a miniature circuit breaker (MCB), which is a safety device that protects the consumer and the circuit if a fault occurs.

> **?** Explain how electricity enters the home. Include reference to the meter box and the miniature circuit breakers. (18) **OL**

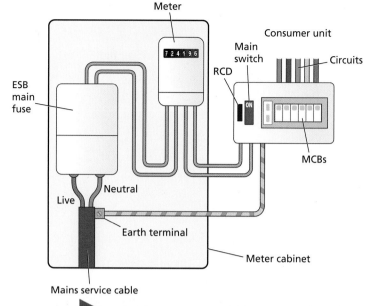

Types of circuits

There are two types of circuits found in the home: ring circuits and radial circuits.

> **Did you know ?**
>
> Older houses use porcelain fuses instead of MCBs. Once blown, these fuses must be removed and replaced.

HL Ring circuits

Ring circuits consist of an electrical wire that leads from the consumer unit/main fuse board to sockets all around the house, and back to the consumer unit again.

- In a two-storey house, one ring circuit is used for downstairs sockets and another for upstairs sockets. Each has its own MCB.
- It carries 35 amps of **current**, so must be fitted with a 35-amp MCB.
- An extra socket can be added to the circuit at a later date. This is called a spur.
- A socket circuit is an example of a ring circuit.

> Lit Hit
> Current refers to the flow of electricity.

Radial circuits

Radical circuits consist of an electrical wire that leads from the consumer unit/main fuse board but does not return, as it ends at the last point on the circuit, e.g. the last light on a lighting circuit.

- Each radial circuit only carries a certain amount of current, therefore each must be fitted with an appropriate MCB, e.g. a cooker circuit carries 35 amps of current so must be fitted with a 35-amp MCB.
- Lighting circuits, cooker circuits and immersion heaters are examples of radial circuits.

> **?** In relation to household electricity supply describe the following: ring circuit. (6) **HL**

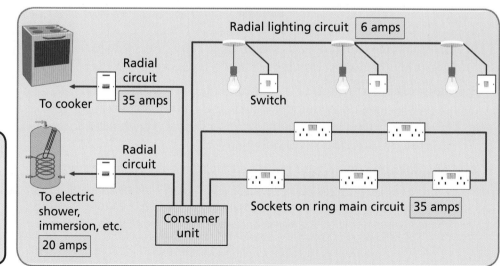
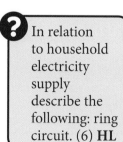

▲ Ring and radial circuits in the home

Electrical terms

Voltage (V)	• A measure of the electrical force required to drive the electrical current through the wire • Measured in volts (V) • In Ireland the standard domestic voltage is 230 V
Wattage (W)	• A measure of the amount of electrical power used by an appliance • Measured in watts (W) • The higher the wattage the more electricity used wattage = voltage × amperage
Amperage (A)	• A measure of the rate at which electricity (current) flows into an appliance • Measured in amps (A) • The higher the amp the more electricity flows to the appliance, e.g. a vacuum cleaner is 1 A, an electric cooker is 35 A amperage = wattage ÷ voltage
Kilowatt per hour (kWh)	• A measure of electrical consumption, also known as a unit of electricity • A one kWh (1,000 watt) appliance used for one hour will use one unit of electricity

> **Did you know** ?
>
> The standard domestic voltage in the United States is 120 V. If an American appliance is plugged in in Ireland, it can damage or burn out the appliance, as the voltage is too strong.

GO FIGURE

1000 watts (W) = 1 kilowatt (kWh)

Appliance	Time taken to use 1 unit/1 kWh
Electric shower	8 minutes
Tumble dryer	30 minutes
100 W bulb	10 hours

GO FIGURE

For homes that use electricity as their only energy source, an annual electricity usage of 7000 kWh is common. This costs approximately €1,300 per year.

ELECTRICITY

? In relation to electricity explain **each** of the following:
  • kilowatt per hour (kWh)   • voltage. (8) **OL**

A name plate attached to a vacuum cleaner includes the following information:

220-230 v	1800 w max.

Why are each of the above items of information important for the consumer? (14) **OL**

Charges on a domestic electricity bill

Electricity bills are issued every two months. Costings on a domestic electricity bill include the following.

1. **Unit charge:** this is the charge for the amount of electricity used by a household over the two-month period, recorded in units by the meter. The new meter reading is compared with the last reading taken in order to calculate the number of units used. The total units used are charged at the unit price.

2. **Standing charge:** this charge covers the cost of maintaining the electricity network, reading meters and issuing bills. This is a yearly figure, but paid as a daily rate on each bill. Rural standing charges are higher than urban standing charges, due to the additional cost of maintaining supply to rural customers.

Did you know ?

A meter is either:
- read by a meter reader (a = actual reading)
- estimated based on previous bills (e = estimated)
- submitted by the customer (c = customer reading).

Your electricity bill in more detail

Your last bill		Total €
Your last bill		€180.00
Payments / Transactions		€180.00 cr
Balance Brought Forward		€00.00

Your Electricity usage Tariff Domestic

meter num	current reading	previous reading	unit usage	unit price	unit type	Amount	
XX	48046a	47046a	**1000**	0.1680	General	168.00	(1)
Total electricity charges						168.00	

Standing charges and other items		Total €
(2) Standing charge	60 days at €0.3379 per day	20.27
(3) PSO Levy Oct/Nov		7.14
(4) VAT	13% on €195.41	25.40

Payments/Other Transactions		Total €
Payment received thank you		220.81 cr

Your energy consumption on this bill amounts to approximately XXkg of carbon emissions

▲ A domestic electricity bill

3. **Public service obligation (PSO) levy:** this levy covers the cost of buying electricity from generating stations using renewable forms of energy.

4. **Value-added tax (VAT):** each bill is subjected to VAT at 13.5%.

> **?** Explain two of the following terms in relation to electricity/natural gas bills:
> - standing charge • unit charge/general units • public service obligation (PSO). (14) **OL**
>
> Name and explain **three** charges shown on a domestic electricity bill. (12) **HL**

Electrical safety devices

The following electrical safety devices prevent electrocution, damage to appliances or circuits, 63.7.1 or the risk of electrical fires.

Fuse

A fuse is a deliberate weak link found in the plugs of most appliances, used to protect the circuit from:
- faulty appliances, e.g. a kettle with a faulty thermostat
- overloading, i.e. too many appliances plugged in
- faulty or damaged wiring.

How it works

A fuse consists of a porcelain casing (cover) with a thin wire inside. If a fault is detected the wire will heat up and melt. This breaks the circuit, stopping the flow of electricity. A blown fuse must be replaced with a fuse of the same strength, e.g. 5 amps.

Miniature circuit breaker (MCB)

An MCB is a modern safety device used in an electrical circuit instead of a traditional porcelain screw-in fuse. MCBs come in varying strengths, e.g. 6 A, 20 A and 35 A.

How it works

If a fault is detected on the circuit the MCB will trip, flicking down to the off position. This breaks the circuit, stopping the flow of electricity. Once the fault is found and rectified the MCB can be switched back to the on position.

Residual circuit device (RCD)

An RCD is an additional safety device used in an electrical circuit to protect against electrical shocks and fires. It is found in:

- the main consumer unit/fuse board
- a plug-in unit, which can convert any socket into a protected circuit, e.g. for electric lawnmowers.

Did you know

New domestic installations must be provided with an RCD on all socket, water heater and electric shower circuits.

How it works

If a fault is detected on a circuit, e.g. an electric shower, the RCD will trip, flicking down to the off position. This breaks the circuit, stopping the flow of electricity. Once the fault is found and rectified the RCD can be switched back to the on position.

Earth wire

An earth wire (yellow/green wire) is found in most plugs and appliances to prevent electrocution.

How it works

If a fault develops, allowing a damaged live wire (brown) to come in contact with a metal casing of an appliance the casing becomes 'live'. If touched, this can cause electrocution. The earth wire prevents this by carrying the current from the damaged live wire down to a metal plate in the ground and away from the appliance.

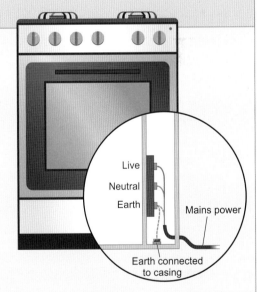

Live
Neutral
Earth
Mains power
Earth connected to casing

In relation to electricity explain the following: fuse. (4) **OL**

Explain how each of the following impact on electrical safety:
- fuses
- miniature circuit breakers (MCBs)
- earth wire. (18) **HL**

In relation to household electricity supply describe the following: miniature circuit breakers (MCBs). (6) **HL**

ELECTRICITY

Guidelines for the safe use of electricity in the home

Appliance safety

- Ensure plugs are wired correctly and have the correct-size fuse, to prevent the appliance overheating.
- Hire an electrical contractor to replace any damaged or worn flexes.
- Avoid dragging an appliance by the flex or pulling on the flex to remove a plug from the socket.
- Avoid using multiple outlet adaptors in plug sockets for appliances. Instead use fused multi-socket boards, as they are safer.

Kitchen safety

- Unplug an electric kettle before filling it, otherwise electrocution may occur.
- Avoid handling plugs, switches or appliances with wet hands, as electrocution may occur.
- Avoid trailing appliance flexes near a cooker or sink, as they may melt or become wet.

Bedroom safety

- Check electric blankets regularly for wear or damage, e.g. scorch marks, otherwise they may overheat and cause an electrical fire.
- Keep portable electric heaters away from bedding or curtains to avoid catching fire.
- Never drape clothes over electric heaters, as they may catch fire.

Bathroom safety

- Only install shaver outlets, as other sockets may become affected by the wet surroundings.
- Never bring portable electrical appliances, e.g. hair dryers, into a bathroom, as it may result in electrical shock.
- Only pull-cord switches are suitable for strip lights or wall heaters. The main light switch must be positioned outside the door.

 Outline **four** guidelines for the safe use of electricity in the home. (20) **OL**

Wiring a plug

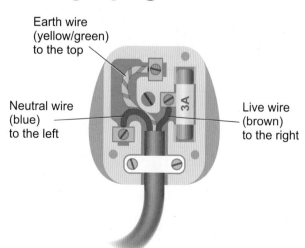

Earth wire (yellow/green) to the top

Neutral wire (blue) to the left

Live wire (brown) to the right

3A

Tip!

BRown goes to the Right.
BLue goes to the Left.

WATER SUPPLY AND STORAGE

What you will learn:

- **Water source**
- **Water treatment**
- **Household cold water supply and storage**
- **Hard water**
- **Water charges**
- **Methods of conserving water in the home**

Over 70% of Earth's surface is covered in water, most of which is found in the oceans and seas. Water must first be treated to make it fit for human consumption. Most people in towns and cities are connected to a public water supply.

GO FIGURE 123

Only 1% of Earth's water is suitable for drinking.

Water source

Water supply to the home begins as precipitation, e.g. rain.

- The sun causes the water from oceans, lakes and streams to evaporate as water vapour.
- As it rises, the vapour cools and condenses to form clouds. Water then falls from the clouds as precipitation, e.g. rain, sleet, hail or snow, on high ground.
- This creates streams and rivers that run off into lakes. Lakes form natural reservoirs, storing water as part of the local authority water supply. Human-made reservoirs can also be created by blocking rivers, allowing water to accumulate.
- Some rainwater percolates through the ground and comes into contact with non-porous rock. Here it accumulates and forms a spring.

Water for urban and rural homes is provided in the following ways:

Did you know ❓

Examples of human-made reservoirs include Ardnacrusha on the River Shannon and Poulaphouca on the River Liffey.

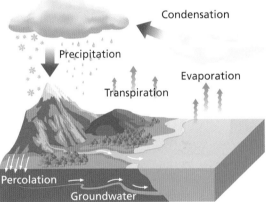

Condensation
Precipitation
Evaporation
Transpiration
Percolation
Groundwater

Urban water supply

Most urban homes are supplied with clean water through public water services. Much of this water is sourced from either natural or human-made reservoirs in the surrounding area. Once treated by the local authority, it is piped to every home where a meter records consumption.

Rural water supply

Many rural homes are supplied with clean water through public water services; however, some rural homes source their water by drilling wells to underground springs. Wells are lined with steel or concrete to prevent contamination from the surrounding soil. The water may have to be treated to make it fit for consumption. An electric pump brings the water into the home.

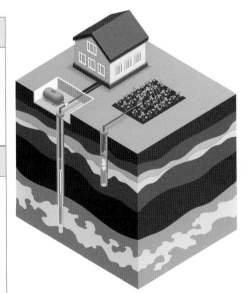

▲ Rural underground well

 Write an informative note on water with reference to the following: sources of domestic water in rural or urban areas. (5) **HL**

WATER SUPPLY AND STORAGE

Water treatment

The water in reservoirs must be treated to make it safe for human consumption, as it may contain impurities or bacteria. Local authorities carry this out in a treatment plant through the following processes.

1. **Screening:** water is passed through coarse and fine mesh screens to remove any floating debris, e.g. leaves or twigs.

2. **Sedimentation:** water is left in holding tanks where large suspended particles settle to the bottom, as they are denser than water. Chemicals, e.g. alum, are added to cause smaller particles to clump together and settle to the bottom.

3. **Filtration:** water is passed through layers of sand and gravel to remove any remaining particles, as they become lodged in the layers.

4. **Chlorination:** chlorine is added to kill bacteria, making the water safe to drink. Ozone and ultraviolet light may also be used to destroy bacteria.

5. **Fluoridation:** fluoride is added to strengthen teeth and reduce tooth decay.

6. **Softening:** in hard water areas, chloride of lime is added to soften water by removing calcium and magnesium ions present.

7. **Testing:** water is distributed to the general public, it is tested for quality and pureness to ensure it is fit for human consumption. It is then stored in a high storage reservoir until it is pumped to homes.

> **Did you know** ❓
>
> If a water supply constitutes a danger to human health, Irish Water must take action to protect consumers by issuing a Drinking Water Restriction Notice or a Boil Water Notice.

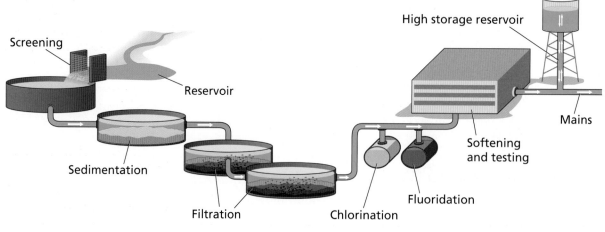

> **REMEMBER IT!**
>
> 'Streams Send Fountains Colourless Fluid, Satisfying Thirst.'
> **S**creening, **S**edimentation, **F**iltration, **C**hlorination, **F**luoridation, **S**oftening, **T**esting.

❓

Explain **four** of the stages involved in the treatment of water to make it safe for human consumption and domestic use. (20) **OL**

Write an informative note on water with reference to the following: water quality. (5) **HL**

Describe the processes carried out at water treatment plants to ensure household water supply is fit for human consumption. (15) **HL**

Household cold water supply and storage

- Water is stored in high storage reservoirs. Mains pipes carry water from these reservoirs to towns and cities.
- A service pipe coming from the mains pipe brings the water to each home and building. It usually enters the home under the kitchen sink.
- A stopcock is a special valve found on a service pipe that can be used to switch off the water supply in the event of an emergency. One is found outside the home on a public footpath and the other is located beside the kitchen sink.
- The service pipe enters the home at the kitchen sink and splits in two. One branch supplies cold, fresh water to the kitchen sink, while the other, called the rising mains, brings a supply of cold water to the storage tank/cistern in the attic.
- The storage tank/cistern can hold 230 litres of water. It uses the force of gravity to create pressure to supply water to cold taps and toilet cisterns in the home. It should be covered in order to prevent any dust, mice or flies entering the water. During the winter, the tank should be well insulated to prevent water inside freezing. All pipes should be insulated.
- The storage tank/cistern contains a ball valve and an overflow pipe.
  - **Ball valve:** controls the water level in the tank. When the ball is floating on the surface of a full tank, it cuts off the flow of water. If water is used, e.g. for a bath, the ball drops, turning on the main water flow and allowing it to fill up again.
  - **Overflow pipe:** prevents flooding if the ball valve fails. If the tank fills beyond its maximum capacity it allows excess water to flow out the side of the house.

> **Did you know** ?
> When water freezes it expands, causing pipes to crack. When ice thaws water flows from cracked pipes and causes flooding.

WATER SUPPLY AND STORAGE

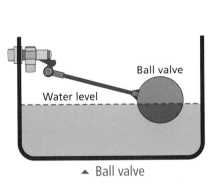

▲ Ball valve

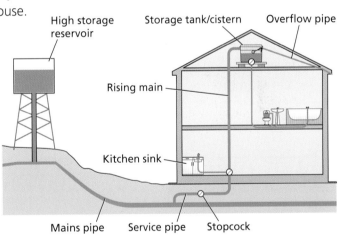

In relation to the cold water supply system in a house, state the function of each of the following:
- ball cock/valve
- mains pipe. (10) **OL**

(i) Using the diagram describe the domestic cold water supply. (16) **OL**

(ii) Explain: (a) why the storage tank is situated in the attic
(b) why the mains water is supplied directly to the kitchen sink. (10) **OL**

(iii) State the function of (a) the overflow pipe **and**
(b) the stopcock. (8) **OL**

(iv) State **two** precautions that should be taken to prevent the cold water supply freezing in winter. (8) **OL**

Describe the cold water system in a house. (15) **HL**

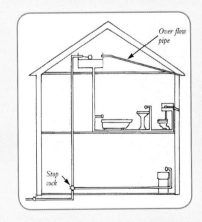

Hard water

Hard water contains dissolved calcium and magnesium ions that cause two types of hardness: temporary hardness and permanent hardness.

- **Temporary hardness:** temporary hardness is caused by calcium and magnesium bicarbonates. It is removed by boiling.
- **Permanent hardness:** permanent hardness is caused by calcium and magnesium sulfates. It is removed by the addition of washing soda or a commercial water softener, e.g. Calgon, or by installing a softening system.

Effects of hard water

- Limescale builds up in kettles, washing machines, hot-water pipes and boilers, reducing their efficiency.
- Hard water causes difficulty producing a lather from soap, which can lead to inefficient cleaning.
- Scum forms on baths and sinks.
- Hair becomes dull and coarse and skin can dry out.

▲ Limescale build-up on a washing machine element

Water charges

Irish Water was established by the Irish government in 2013 as the sole supplier of public water and public **wastewater** services. Homes were fitted with water metres to record water consumption, measured in cubic metres (m³). One cubic metre is equal to 1,000 litres. Bills issued to homes were based on consumption.

> **Lit Hit**
> Wastewater means waste material including sewage waste and used bath/shower/sink water that is collected and treated at wastewater plants.

> ? Write an informative note on water with reference to the following: water charges. (5) **HL**

Methods of conserving water in the home

For infomation on methods of conserving water in the home see page 455.

> ? Describe three methods of conserving water in the home. (15) **OL**

Nº 0642571

▲ Water meter

HEATING

What you will learn:

- Thermal comfort in the home
- Controlling thermal comfort
- Types of heating
- Factors to consider when choosing a heating system
- Home central heating systems

Thermal comfort in the home

Thermal comfort refers to whether a person feels too hot, too cold or comfortable in their environment. It varies from person to person. General guidelines are in place for each room of the house, to ensure that most people feel comfortable.

Room	Temperature	Function/activities
Sitting room	19°C–23°C	Used for relaxation: little activity takes place here. The temperature needs to be warm to allow for this.
Bathroom	23°C	Used for washing, showering and personal hygiene. The temperature needs to be higher here to keep the body warm.
Kitchen and living room	17°C–21°C	Kitchens are used for cooking, which generates heat. The temperature should be slightly lower, as an overly warm kitchen may speed up the rate of food spoilage. Living rooms are often an extension of the kitchen, used to dine and relax. A warmer temperature is preferable here.
Bedroom	10°C–16°C	Used to sleep and relax. The temperature does not need to be as warm, as duvets or blankets insulate the body during the night.

> **?** Discuss levels of thermal comfort in relation to **two** rooms in the home. (12) **HL**

Controlling thermal comfort

The thermal comfort of rooms can be controlled in three ways: timers, thermostats or zoned heating.

Timers

Timers are electronically operated devices used to switch the heating on or off at predetermined times. They ensure that rooms are warm when required, e.g. early in the morning, and less energy is wasted as the heating is automatically turned off.

Thermostats

Thermostats are devices that automatically regulate temperature. There are three types of thermostats that may be used in the home: an electric thermostat, a gas thermostat or a thermostatic radiator valve (TRV).

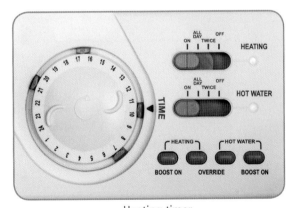

▲ Heating timer

> **Did you know** **?**
>
> The word *thermostat* is based on two ancient Greek words: *thermo*, meaning heat, and *statos*, meaning to stay the same.

HEATING

Electric thermostats

Electric thermostats are found on the central heating boiler, room thermostats, large appliances, e.g. ovens, and small appliances, e.g. kettles.

Working principle

The working principle of the thermostat is based on the principle of thermal expansion, i.e. when objects are heated they expand. Electric thermostats consist of two pieces of different metals – brass and **invar** – joined together to form a bimetallic strip. When heat is applied, the brass expands faster than the invar, causing the strip to bend. Eventually, it bends so much that it breaks the electrical circuit, causing the electricity flow to switch off.

A room thermostat detects the surrounding temperature of a room and maintains it at a set temperature, e.g. 18°C. When the temperature of the room reaches the required temperature it switches off the heating. As the room cools it switches the heating back on.

Lit Hit
Invar is an alloy of iron and nickel.

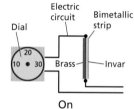
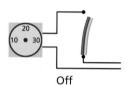

On   Off

Gas thermostats

Gas thermostats are found on gas boilers, gas water-heating appliances and gas ovens.

Working principle

Gas thermostats consist of a brass tube with an invar rod inside. As the temperature increases, the brass tube expands, which pulls the invar rod. A valve at the end of the invar rod closes, restricting the gas flow and switching off the heating. As the room cools, the brass contracts, causing the valve to open once more, allowing the gas to flow and switching the heating back on.

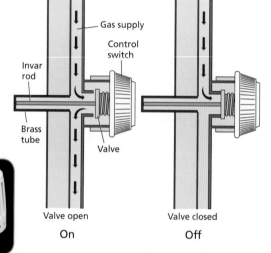

Valve open   Valve closed
On   Off

Thermostatic radiator valves (TRV)

A TRV is fitted to each individual radiator.

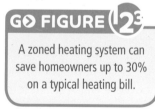

Working principle

The head of the TRV senses the air temperature around it and regulates the flow of water through the radiator. When the radiator has achieved the desired temperature, e.g. 18°C, the TRV closes the valve, stopping the flow of hot water. As the room cools, the valve opens, allowing hot water into the radiator.

Zoned heating

Zoned heating systems use thermostats and timers to independently heat certain areas of the home, e.g. upstairs or downstairs, rather than heating the whole house at once. It is an energy-efficient way of heating the home and controlling the temperature.

GO FIGURE (123

A zoned heating system can save homeowners up to 30% on a typical heating bill.

 Name **two** types of controls used on heating systems and explain how **each** helps to ensure efficient use of energy. (16) **OL**

Explain, giving examples, how levels of thermal comfort in the home can be controlled. (10) **HL**

Explain the working principle of a thermostat **and** give examples of the use of thermostats in the home. (18) **HL**

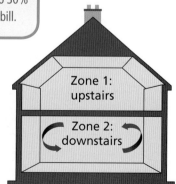

Zone 1: upstairs

Zone 2: downstairs

Type	Description	Advantages
Full central heating 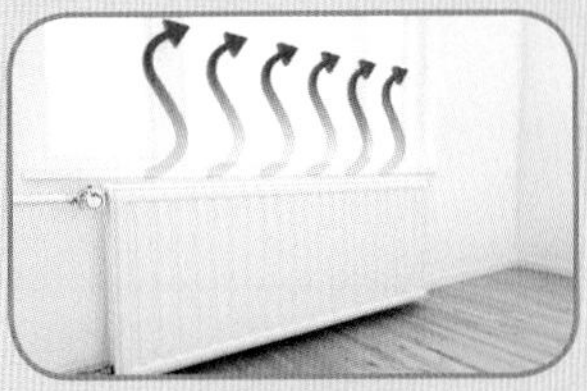	• Heats the whole house from a central source, e.g. a boiler • Water is heated by the boiler and sent to radiators in the home. Boilers may be fuelled by oil, gas or solid fuel.	✓ Ensures that all rooms achieve the same level of thermal comfort ✓ Easy to operate once installed ✓ Heats the household water supply
Partial central heating 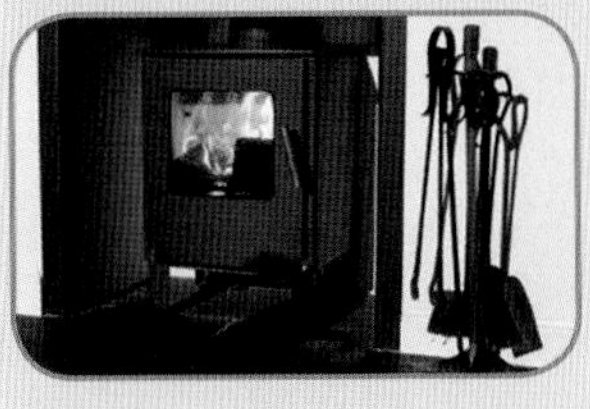	• Heats one area of the home, usually from a central point, e.g. a stove • Normally in the most frequently used rooms, e.g. living rooms. Other areas, e.g. bedrooms, rely on overflow heat, or require another heat source.	✓ Achieves good thermal comfort in frequently used rooms ✓ Heat rises, so this form is suited to two-storey homes, as the upper floor receives residual heat
Background heating 	• Provided by storage heaters that heat the whole house, but at a lower temperature of 13°C • Must be supplemented with other heating forms, e.g. an open fire or individual heater, to achieve thermal comfort	✓ The whole house is heated enough to take the chill out of the air ✓ Storage heaters may be turned up in cold weather to give an extra boost of heat
Local heating 	• Heats one room locally, e.g. the living room by an open fire or electric/gas heater • Other areas, e.g. bedrooms, will require another heat source	✓ The room achieves good thermal comfort ✓ Suited to times when rooms are particularly cold
Passive solar heating 	• Uses the natural heat from the sun to heat south- and west-facing rooms • Large glass windows are necessary to maximise heat gain	✓ Causes no harm to the environment, as it is a renewable energy source ✓ No fuel is required, so energy bills are reduced
Active solar heating/solar panels 	• Uses the heat of the sun to heat the home and water	✓ Causes no harm to the environment, as it is a renewable energy source ✓ Heats the household water supply

HEATING

Factors to consider when choosing a heating system

- **Cost:** consider the:
  - **installation cost:** a wet central heating system is a more complicated and expensive system to install compared to a dry heating system
  - **running cost:** solid fuel is cheaper than oil or gas, renewable sources have low or no running costs
  - **maintenance cost:** both gas and oil boilers need regular servicing.
- **Environmental impact:** renewable heating sources, e.g. solar, do not harm the environment, compared to non-renewable fossil fuels e.g. oil, which release harmful greenhouse gases during combustion. An efficient heating system, e.g. a condensing boiler, is also less damaging than older conventional systems.
- **Water heating:** some heating systems, e.g. wet central heating systems or back boilers behind open fires, may heat the household water supply as well as the room. Other heating systems, e.g. storage heating, will require a separate immersion to heat water.
- **Size of house:** larger houses will require a more efficient and elaborate heating system, e.g. a wet central heating system, to heat the whole home at the one time. It can also be zoned to allow for heating various areas.
- **Reliability:** the heating system chosen needs to be reliable, work efficiently and be easy to maintain, so that it provides even, controlled heat when required.

> **?** Explain the factors which should be considered when choosing a heating system for a family home. (20) **HL**

> **REMEMBER IT!**
> 'Couples Enjoy Warm Sitting Rooms.'
> Cost, Environment, Water heating, Size of house, Reliability.

Home central heating systems

There are two main types of home central heating systems that may be chosen to heat the home:

- **wet central heating system:** uses hot water from a boiler to heat radiators in each room
- **dry heating system:** uses hot air from storage heaters to heat each room.

Wet central heating system

Wet central heating is the most common type of central heating as it heats space and water. A boiler heats water, which is then pumped through small bore (narrow diameter) pipes to radiators in every room.

Working principle and method of heat transfer

- **Boiler:** the boiler heats cold water by convection. As the water heats it rises and colder water falls to take its place. This creates convection currents until all the water reaches the required temperature.
- **Hot water cylinder:** due to thermal expansion, the hot water leaves the top of the boiler and travels in a narrow pipe up to the hot water cylinder, whereby it passes through a heat exchanger (coiled pipe). This heats the water in the tank indirectly through a process of convection, and is used to provide hot water for baths and sinks. When the water in the heat exchanger cools, it returns to the boiler.

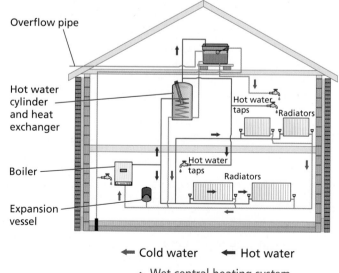

◄ Cold water ◄ Hot water

▲ Wet central heating system

- **Radiators:** hot water is sent from the boiler to each of the radiators through a series of narrow pipes. The radiators and pipes heat the rooms by:
  - o **radiation:** metal radiators and pipes radiate heat into the rooms
  - o **convection:** as the air above the radiator heats up it begins to rise and cold air falls to take its place, creating currents until all the air reaches the required temperature; when the water in the radiators gets cold it returns to the boiler and the cycle starts again.
- **Expansion vessel:** as the temperature of water increases, so does the pressure inside the boiler. The expansion vessel, a safety device located near the boiler, helps to relieve the build-up of pressure and prevents damage to the system.

> **Did you know**
> In the past, an expansion tank was placed in the attic. Nowadays, an expansion vessel is placed near the boiler to help relieve pressure.

Fuel/energy source and the effect on the environment

Boilers can use the following fuels to generate heat.
- **Non-renewable sources,** e.g. fossil fuels including oil, gas and solid fuel. When burned they release greenhouse gas emissions which damage the atmosphere, leading to global warming or acid rain.
- **Renewable energy sources,** e.g. solar energy and geothermal energy. They cause no harm to the environment and will never run out.

Efficiency/convenience

Modern wet central heating systems with condensing boilers are extremely efficient and convenient as the boiler heats the water quickly for radiators, heating rooms in a short period of time. It is an easy system to use. It should, however, be regularly serviced.

Dry heating system (storage heaters)

Working principle and method of heat transfer

- The electrical elements of a storage heater are embedded in thermal blocks of fireclay or concrete that are surrounded by insulating material.
- The elements are heated by electricity at off-peak periods at night, causing the thermal blocks to heat up.
- Through conduction, the fire clay blocks absorb the heat and gradually release heat during the day. Most systems have an afternoon boost of heat option.
- Some of this heat is radiated and most is transferred by convection through the front grill, creating space heating.

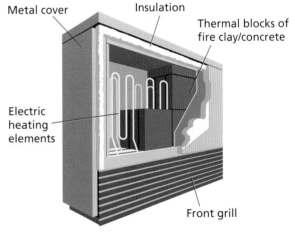

Metal cover   Insulation

Thermal blocks of fire clay/concrete

Electric heating elements

Front grill

▲ Storage heater

Fuel/energy source

A storage heater runs on off-peak electricity.

> ? Describe one type of home heating system under the following headings:
> - type of heating system
> - fuel / energy source
> - method of heat transfer. (14) **OL**
>
> Set out details of **one** domestic central heating system you have studied. Include reference to: efficiency and convenience. (7) **HL**
>
> Describe **one** type of central heating system suitable for a family home and include reference to:
> - fuel/energy source
> - working principle to include methods of heat transfer
> - impact on the environment. (24) **HL**

HEATING

What you will learn:
- **Underlying principle of insulation**
- **Advantages of insulation**
- **Methods of insulating the home**

Insulating a house helps to reduce heat loss and to keep down the cost of heating bills.

Underlying principle of insulation

Insulation materials are poor conductors of heat, as they do not allow it to travel through them, thus reducing the loss of heat from a house. Examples of insulating materials include air, polystyrene, fibreglass and wool.

Advantages of insulation

✓ Insulation reduces heat loss in the home. An uninsulated house can lose heat through the walls, roof, floor, windows and doors.

✓ Insulation reduces fuel/energy bills, as less oil, gas or electricity is required to heat the home.

✓ Insulation reduces damage to the environment, as less fuel is required to heat the home, reducing the amount of greenhouse gases released.

✓ Insulation creates homes that are warm and comfortable places to live, as the room temperature is constant and draughts are reduced.

✓ Insulation reduces noise levels due to its soundproofing qualities.

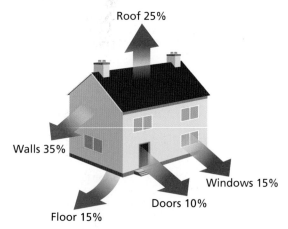

Roof 25%

Walls 35%

Windows 15%

Doors 10%

Floor 15%

▲ Average heat loss from a house

? State **three** advantages of having a well insulated home. (12) **OL**

Methods of insulating the home

The Building Regulations 2011 (part L: Conservation of Fuel and Energy) require that all new buildings achieve minimum standards of insulation. Standards apply to attics, walls, floors, windows and airtightness (draughts).

Attic insulation

To meet the requirements of the Building Regulations 2011 a minimum of 250–300 mm of attic insulation is needed.

Types of attic insulation

- **Fibreglass roll insulation:** composed of bundles of very thin strands of glass that trap heat. It is rolled out between the joists in the attic.

 Fibreglass roll insulation

G⊙ FIGURE 123

Insulating the attic space of a typical house costs around €400 and saves approximately €130 a year on fuel bills, so it would pay for itself in about three years.

Did you know ?

Fibreglass insulation can cause eye, skin and lung irritation when handling and installing it, so protective eyewear and gloves should be worn.

- **Foam insulation:** a type of synthetic resin sprayed between the roof rafters. After it is sprayed it expands and completely fills all cavities and voids, eliminating warm air leakages and the **infiltration** of cold air. It is ideal insulation for difficult-to-reach areas and tight spaces in the attic.

- **Blown cellulose insulation:** composed of 75–85% recycled paper (usually post-consumer waste newsprint) and 15% fire-retardant, e.g. boric acid. It is blown between the joists in the attic using hoses connected to a special pressurised machine. It has the highest recycled content of any insulation available, making it one of the most environmentally friendly types of insulation.

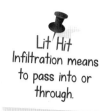
Lit Hit
Infiltration means to pass into or through.

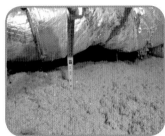

▲ Blown cellulose insulation ▲ Foam insulation

Underlying principle of attic insulation

In homes, 25% of all heat is lost through the attic as heat rises. Fibreglass, foam and cellulose are all poor conductors of heat, meaning that they do not allow heat to pass through. When heat comes into contact with attic insulation it is directed back into the rooms below.

> Recommend **one** method of insulation suitable for the following area of the home: attic. State the underlying principle of the method of insulation. (8) **HL**

Wall insulation

To meet the requirements of the Building Regulations 2011, 80 mm thermal insulating material should be placed in concrete walls and 150 mm in timber-frame walls.

Types of wall insulation

- **Bonded beads:** polystyrene bonded beads coated with an air-drying adhesive are pumped through an opening, either on the outer or inner wall, into the cavity space. The adhesive then sets and the beads form into a bonded mass, creating an effective barrier to prevent heat loss through the outer wall.

- **Aero board/polystyrene sheets:** 80 mm or 150 mm sheets of aero board/polystyrene are slotted into the cavity space between the inner and outer wall during building.

- **Insulated slabs:** consist of a sheet of plasterboard with a layer of thick polystyrene fixed to the back. They are fixed to internal solid walls and plastered afterwards.

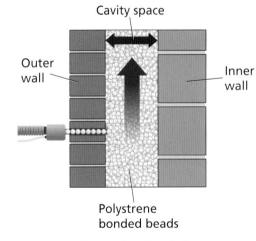

▲ Bonded-bead insulation

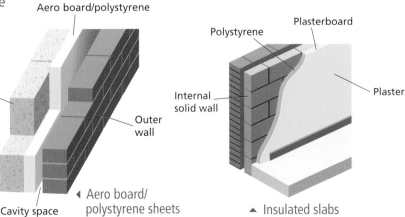

◄ Aero board/polystyrene sheets ▲ Insulated slabs

Underlying principle of wall insulation

In homes, 35% of heat is lost through the walls. Bonded beads, aero board/polystyrene sheets and insulated slabs are all poor conductors of heat, meaning that they do not allow heat to pass through. When heat comes in contact with wall insulation it is directed back into the room.

 Name **and** describe the method of insulation you would recommend for the following: walls. (8) **OL**

Floor insulation

To meet the requirements of the Building Regulations 2011, 100 mm of insulating material should be used on ground floors and 150 mm on upper floors.

Types of floor insulation

- **Ground floor insulation:** a 100 mm rigid polystyrene board is positioned over the solid concrete base and covered with a final concrete/screed layer.
- **First floor insulation:** 150 mm of sub-floor insulation, e.g. fibreglass, is laid between the ceiling joists of a suspended timber floor.
- **Underlay and carpets:** if carpeting an upper floor, an underlay laid underneath will provide additional insulation and assist with soundproofing. Wool carpets, in particular, are excellent natural insulators, due to their heat-retaining properties.

▲ Ground floor insulation

Underlying principle of floor insulation

In homes, 15% of heat is lost through the floor. Polystyrene slabs, fibreglass, underlay and carpets are all poor conductors of heat, meaning that they do not allow heat to pass through. When heat comes in contact with floor insulation materials it is directed back into the room.

Window insulation

Types of window insulation

- **Double glazing:** consists of two panes of glass with air or argon gas in between.
- **Triple glazing:** consists of three panes of glass with air or argon gas in between.

To meet the requirements of the Building Regulations 2011, double-glazed and triple-glazed windows should have a gap of 6–12 mm, which is filled with either air or argon gas. Argon gas is a mixture of oxygen and nitrogen and is 30% more effective at preventing heat loss than air alone. A low-emissivity coating/layer is often applied to the inner pane of glass, which allows light in but further reduces heat escaping through the windows.

Underlying principle of window insulation

In homes, 15% of heat is lost through the windows. A layer of dry air/argon gas acts as an insulator, as it is a bad conductor of heat. Warm air is reflected back into a room.

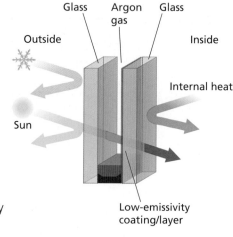

Glass   Argon gas   Glass

Outside

Inside

Internal heat

Sun

Low-emissivity coating/layer

▲ Double glazing

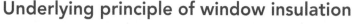 Explain the underlying principle involved in double glazing as a method of reducing heat loss through windows. (10) **HL**

Draught insulation

Draughts are caused by cold air forcing its way into the house through vents or cracks around windows and doors. This lowers the temperature of the room and displaces warm air. Draught insulation is one of the cheapest and most efficient ways to save energy and money in a building, as it reduces heat loss.

▲ Polyurethane-foam strips

Types of draught insulation

- **Doors:** draught excluders can be fitted around a door frame and to the threshold (space underneath). Types of draught excluders suitable for doors include:
  - **polyurethane-foam strips** for the openings around doors
  - **brush excluders** or **fabric snakes** for the base of doors.
- **Windows:** types of draught excluders suitable for windows include:
  - polyurethane-foam strips for openings
  - silicone sealants between the frame and the wall.
- **Letterboxes:** brush excluders can be used to keep draughts from coming through letterboxes.

Underlying principle of draught proofing

In homes, 15% of heat is lost through the windows and 10% is lost through doors due to cold air entering through cracks and openings. Draught excluders block the entry of cold air, helping to keep the warmer air inside and an overall even temperature.

> **Did you know** ❓
>
> As part of the 2008 building regulations, every new home must carry out an air tightness test to determine the level of uncontrolled air flow through gaps or cracks in the fabric of a building. The results of the test highlight areas of the home that will require further insulation or draught-proofing.

❓

(i) State, giving a reason, the **two** areas of this house that should be prioritised for insulation. (12) **OL**

(ii) Name **and** describe the method of insulation you would recommend for **each** of the following:
- attic/roof   • walls. (16) **OL**

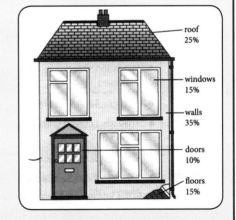

roof
25%

windows
15%

walls
35%

doors
10%

floors
15%

Identify **three** areas of the house that should be insulated in order to reduce heat loss. Recommend a method of insulation for each area **and** explain the underlying principle of each method. (24) **HL**

INSULATION

VENTILATION

What you will learn:

- **Underlying principle of ventilation**
- **Importance of adequate ventilation**
- **Humidity**
- **Condensation**
- **Methods of ventilation**

Air often contains some invisible water vapour, stale odours, waste gases and bacteria. Ventilation is the removal of stale air and the introduction of fresh air, without causing a drop in temperature or creating draughts.

Underlying principle of ventilation

Ventilation is based on the principle of thermal expansion. When air is heated it expands and rises. Ventilation outlets (vents) are placed high up on walls, so that when warm, stale air rises it can be easily removed. Cold, fresh air is drawn in lower down, e.g. through windows or from under doors, to replace the lost air, creating a convection current. This is known as air exchange.

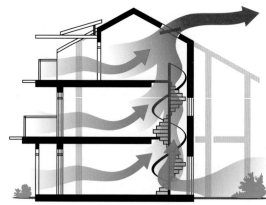

Stale air out
17% oxygen,
4% carbon dioxide
- Body odours
- Cooking odours
- Water vapour
- Dust
- Smoke
- Excess heat
- Bacteria

Fresh air in
21% oxygen,
0.4% carbon dioxide

▲ Air exchange

Importance of adequate ventilation

- Ventilation provides oxygen-rich fresh air for respiration. A lack of oxygen can result in poor concentration, headaches, drowsiness and fainting.
- Ventilation removes stale air full of impurities including:
  - **waste gases**, e.g. carbon dioxide
  - **odours**, e.g. cooking odours
  - **bacteria**, which can lead to greater susceptibility to illness and infection
  - **dust**, which can aggravate respiratory conditions, e.g. asthma or bronchitis.
- Ventilation allows combustion to occur, e.g. in an open fire/stove, by providing oxygenated air for fuel to burn.
- Ventilation prevents condensation by removing water vapour created by showering, bathing, cooking and exhaling. This prevents structural damage, e.g. mould growth on walls.
- Ventilation reduces room temperature, as stale air is generally warmer than fresh, making it stuffy and uncomfortable.

Explain the importance of good ventilation. (12) **OL**

Discuss the importance of adequate ventilation in a house. (15) **HL**

Humidity

Humidity is a measure of the amount of water vapour in the air. It is measured as a percentage on a hygrometer. The ideal relative humidity in a home is 50–55%. Humidity is created in the home by:

- breathing
- showering/bathing
- cooking
- washing/drying clothes
- heaters, e.g. portable gas heaters.

GO FIGURE 12³

A typical four-person household produces 5–12 kg of water vapour per day.

High humidity levels (above 55%) in the home can cause drowsiness, sleeping problems and aggravate the respiratory system. An appliance called a dehumidifier can be used if humidity levels become too high. It draws in air high in water vapour, condenses it and collects the water in a container at the base, emitting the dry air. If humidity levels are too low (below 50%) due to heating systems, a humidifier may be used to add back moisture to dry air.

▲ Dehumidifier

Condensation

Condensation occurs when warm, humid air meets cold air or a cold surface and changes into liquid water. It can appear as:

- surface condensation, e.g. mist or droplets, on single-glazed windows and mirrors.
- internal condensation on uninsulated external walls. Warm, moist air from rooms passes through gaps on the surfaces of walls and condenses inside the block work.

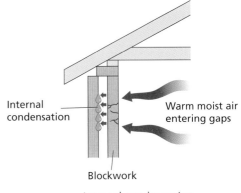

Internal condensation

Warm moist air entering gaps

Blockwork

▲ Internal condensation

Effects of condensation

- Internal condensation can result in mould growth on the inside of walls and ceilings.
- A damp, musty smell in the home can occur, which is difficult to remove.
- Construction materials, e.g. wood and metal, may decay, rot or rust, giving rise to structural damage to the home.
- Wall coverings, e.g. paint or wallpaper, can peel or flake off walls.
- Respiratory problems can develop, as mould emits particles that may aggravate respiratory conditions such as asthma and bronchitis.

How condensation may be reduced/prevented

- Open windows and doors daily, especially in rooms with high humidity, e.g. bathrooms.
- Install artificial ventilation systems, e.g. extractor fans, in the kitchen and bathrooms to remove humid air.
- Install an efficient heating system, as cold rooms and surfaces are more likely to experience condensation and, in turn, mould growth.
- Insulate the home well, especially external walls, floors and ceilings.
- Avoid too many cold, smooth surfaces, e.g. tiles, as they encourage condensation. Use hygroscopic materials in soft furnishings, e.g. rugs, to reduce condensation build up.

▲ Mould growth due to condensation

Outline the effects of condensation in the home **and** state how condensation may be reduced/prevented. (12) **HL**

VENTILATION

Methods of ventilation

There are two main types of ventilation in the home: natural ventilation and artificial ventilation.

Natural ventilation

Natural ventilation involves introducing fresh, cool air from outside through openings on the walls, to replace the stale, warm air in rooms.

Natural ventilation methods

- **Doors:** a 10 mm gap at the bottom of a closed door and an open doorway will efficiently ventilate a room.
- **Windows:** open windows will ventilate rooms. Trickle vents in windows can ventilate rooms with a continuous air supply without the window having to be opened.
- **Open fireplace:** when wind blows over a chimney it creates a suction that draws warm, stale air through an open fireplace and up through the chimney, ventilating a room.
- **Wall air vents:** air vents high on the wall of a room remove warm air as it rises and draw in colder, fresher air in its place, ventilating a room. The most common vents are hit-and-miss vents that can be opened and closed to let air through.

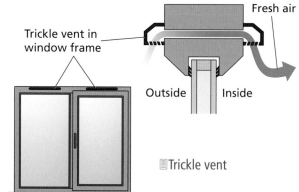

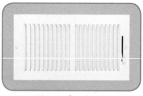

▲ Hit-and-miss vent

Artificial ventilation

Artificial ventilation involves the use of electrical or mechanical fans, e.g. extractor fans and cooker hoods, to bring about air change.

Artificial ventilation methods

Artificial ventilation methods include extractor fans and cooker hoods.

Extractor fans
Construction
<ul><li>Have an outer casing made of plastic or metal</li><li>Internally it contains a set of rotating blades and an electric motor</li><li>Louvre shutters in front of the blades close when the fan is not in use, preventing draughts</li></ul> 
Working principle
An extractor fan is positioned high up on an outside wall so that it can remove stale, moisture-laden air. When the fan is turned on by a switch or pull cord, the shutters open and the electric motor rotates the blades. The high-speed rotation creates suction, drawing stale air up out of the room. This is naturally replaced by fresh air from underneath doors or through windows/vents. 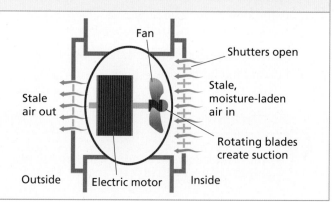

Cooker hoods

Construction

- Have a metal canopy, a mesh screen, filters and a centrifugal fan. There are two types of cooker hoods: ducted and ductless.
  - o **Ducted cooker hoods:** have a duct connected to an outside wall, which completely removes stale, moisture-laden air and expels it outside through an opening in the external wall. Ducted hoods contain a grease filter to remove grease.
  - o **Ductless cooker hoods:** used when a cooker may be too far from an outside wall. They work in a similar manner to ducted cooker hoods, except stale moisture-laden air is not expelled outside, instead it is cleaned and recirculated back into the room. Ductless hoods contain both a grease and charcoal filter to remove grease and odours.

▲ Ducted cooker hood

Working principle of a ducted cooker hood

When a ducted hood is turned on, the electric motor rotates the blades of the fan. This creates suction, drawing air containing airborne grease, combustion products, fumes, smoke, odours, heat and steam up and out of the room. As the air passes through the grease filter, grease is trapped.

The air is expelled outside and naturally replaced by fresh air from underneath doors or through windows/vents.

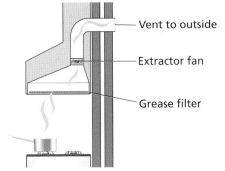

Vent to outside

Extractor fan

Grease filter

VENTILATION

?

Name **one** natural method and **one** artificial method of ventilating a home. Describe **one** of the methods mentioned. (18) **OL**

Explain how natural ventilation is provided in a modern house. (9) **HL**

Recommend **one** method of artificial ventilation suitable for a kitchen **and** describe the working principle of the method recommended. (15) **HL**

∞ LIGHTING
4.5.6

What you will learn:

- **Importance of good lighting**
- **Classification of lighting**
- **Contemporary lighting developments**
- **Properties of light**
- **Principles for planning lighting systems**

Importance of good lighting

An efficient lighting system in the home is needed to:

- provide light to carry out essential tasks and activities, e.g. preparing food
- prevent accidents, e.g. tripping on stairs
- prevent eyestrain by allowing items to be viewed clearly, e.g. reading in a study
- create atmosphere and mood, e.g. soft lighting creates a cosy atmosphere
- highlight and emphasise attractive features or focal points in the home, e.g. downlights on paintings.

Classification of lighting

Lighting can be classified into two categories: natural lighting and artificial lighting.

Natural lighting

Natural light enters the home through:

- windows
- doors
- glass bricks
- sun tunnels.

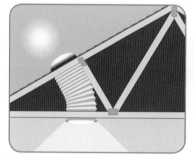

▸ Sun tunnel

Did you know ?

Studies have shown that people exposed to natural light are more productive, achieve a better sense of well-being, and are more positive.

Ways to maximise natural light entering the home

- **Aspect:** when building a home, position the main living areas facing south or west to ensure the maximum amount of natural light enters the home.
- **Windows:** the number and size of windows will dictate the amount of natural light entering. Skylights can provide additional light in dormer homes or attic conversions.
- **Sun tunnels:** natural light is carried through a sun tunnel from the roof into rooms below. They are often used in rooms that have no windows or are positioned far away from a natural light source.
- **Colour scheme:** light, pale colours, e.g. white, will reflect natural light, making the room look bigger and brighter, compared to dark colours, which absorb light, making rooms appear smaller and darker.

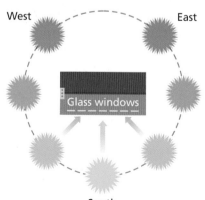

West   East

Glass windows

South

▲ Aspect

- **Materials used:** smooth, shiny textures, e.g. mirrors or polished porcelain tiles, reflect natural light, making a room appear brighter. Rough textures, e.g. carpets, absorb natural light, making a room appear darker.

 Describe **three** ways by which the amount of natural light entering a home may be maximised (increased). (15) **OL**

Artificial lighting

Artificial lighting can be provided by tungsten bulbs or fluorescent bulbs.

Tungsten bulbs

Type	Structure and underlying principle	Advantages and disadvantages
Tungsten filament bulb ▲ Screw-in tungsten filament bulb **Did you know** Under a European Union directive as of September 2013, manufacturing of tungsten filament light bulbs has been banned, making way for new, more energy-efficient bulbs, e.g. CFL and LED bulbs.	• Made of pearl, clear or coloured glass and filled with a mixture of argon and nitrogen gas • A coiled filament of tungsten wire is found inside the bulb. As electricity flows through the thin filament it meets resistance, causing the filament to glow white and produce light. Argon and nitrogen gas — Clear, coloured or pearl class Coiled filament of tungsten wire — Supports Fuses Contacts ▲ Bayonet tungsten filament bulb	✓ Provides instant, warm light ✓ Inexpensive to buy and available in varying strengths (25–200 W) ✗ Only last approximately 1,000 hours ✗ Expensive to run and not energy efficient **Did you know** An average home with incandescent light bulbs will spend up to €292 per year on light bulbs.
Tungsten halogen (quartz) bulb	• Made of quartz glass filled with halogen gas. • Produces light in the same way as a tungsten filament bulbs • Provides instant light (similar to sunlight)	✓ Last three times longer than a tungsten filament bulb, approximately 3,000 hours ✓ Generates a lot of heat during use ✗ Expensive to run and not energy efficient

LIGHTING

Fluorescent bulbs

Type	Structure and underlying principle	Advantages and disadvantages
Fluorescent tube bulb	• Made of a glass tube coated on the inside with a layer of phosphor and filled with argon gas and mercury. • As electricity flows into the tube, electrodes at each end heat up, causing the mercury to vaporise in the argon gas. These gases react with the phosphor coating on the inside of the tube and create a glow. Electrodes Argon gas Mercury Contact Glass tube lined with phosphor	✓ Inexpensive to run, energy efficient. ✓ Last eight times longer than tungsten filament bulbs, approximately 8,000 hours ✗ There is a delay between turning on the light and the light coming on ✗ Provides a cold light and can produce a humming noise during operation ✗ Contains a mercury component, so it needs to be disposed of carefully, as mercury is toxic

Energy-efficient lighting

All bulbs are given a rating to indicate their efficiency. Compact fluorescent lights (CFLs) and light-emitting diode (LED) bulbs are the most efficient bulbs available, with an A rating. These are approximately 85% more efficient than the incandescent equivalent.

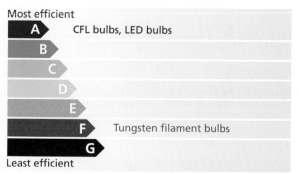

Most efficient

A — CFL bulbs, LED bulbs
B
C
D
E
F — Tungsten filament bulbs
G

Least efficient

Type	Structure and underlying principle	Advantages and disadvantages
Compact fluorescent light (CFL bulb)	• Made of a glass tube coated with a lining of phosphor and filled with argon gas and mercury • As electricity flows into the tube, electrodes at each end heat up, causing the mercury to vaporise in the argon gas. These gases react with the phosphor coating on the inside of the tube and create a glow.	✓ Inexpensive to run: use approximately 80% less electricity than standard tungsten bulbs ✓ Last 15 times longer than tungsten filament bulbs, approximately 15,000 hours ✓ Suited for difficult to reach areas, e.g. double-height rooms, due to their long lifespan ✗ Expensive ✗ Can take a few minutes to reach full brightness, and cannot be dimmed ✗ Contains a mercury component, so it needs to be disposed of carefully, as mercury is toxic

? Name and describe **one** modern energy efficient light fitting. (12) **OL**

Explain the underlying principle of one type of energy efficient lighting. (12) **HL**

GO FIGURE

A standard CFL bulb costs approximately €15.00, compared to a tungsten bulb, which costs approximately €0.89.

Contemporary lighting developments

- **LED rope lighting:** often used to highlight contemporary interior design features, e.g. a recess in a ceiling.

- **LED step lighting:** often used on stairs as a decorative feature, making them attractive to look at, and as a safety feature, making steps easier to see at night.

- **Sensor/motion activated lighting:** detects movement by picking up the heat that radiates from an object or person, causing the light to automatically turn on. Often used as a safety device to alert homeowners of intruders.

▲ LED rope lighting in a recess

- **Colour-changing lighting:** e.g. bulbs that can be connected to an app that wirelessly changes their colour. Often used to create mood lighting in the home.

- **Outdoor lighting:** e.g. solar lights containing a solar panel with a **photovoltaic** cell that converts sunlight to an electrical current. Energy is stored during the day and released at night. Often used to light up pathways and decking in the garden.

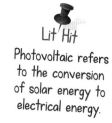

Lit Hit

Photovoltaic refers to the conversion of solar energy to electrical energy.

◄ Outdoor solar lighting

> **?** Recommend **two** modern light fittings for a student's bedroom. (6) **OL**
>
> Give details of **three** contemporary developments in lighting technology. (18) **HL**
>
> Identify **two** types of contemporary lighting and in each case evaluate its use in interior design. (18) **HL**

LIGHTING

Ⓗ Properties of light and their application

Property	Explanation	Application in the home
Reflected	When light falls on a shiny or pale surface it is reflected back.	• Mirrors • Polished porcelain tiles • Light colours, e.g. white walls
Diffused	When light falls on an uneven or dull surface it is scattered or dispersed in many directions. This can also occur when light passes through a translucent substance.	• Net curtains • Frosted glass windows • Translucent lampshades
Absorbed	When light shines on matt surfaces and dark colours it is absorbed.	• Dark painted walls
Dispersed	When light shines through a glass prism or crystal it is broken into its component colours.	• Chandeliers/crystal light fittings
Refracted	When light rays shine through a thick layer of glass they bend.	• Glass bricks

In the Dispersed diagram: Sunlight, Glass prism, Red, Orange, Yellow, Green, Blue, Indigo, Violet

❓ Name and explain **three** properties of light. In **each** case give an example of its application in the home. (18) **HL**

Describe **three** properties of light. (12) **HL**

REMEMBER IT!

'**R**ain **D**rops **A**nd **D**aylight = **R**ainbows!'
Reflected, **D**iffused, **A**bsorbed, **D**ispersed, **R**efracted.

Principles/guidelines for planning lighting systems

- **Building:** when creating house plans and building a home the living areas should be facing south or west, with large windows to avail of maximum natural light gain. The plans should clearly mark the position of the light fixtures, sockets and feature lighting.

- **Function of the room:** consider the overall function of the room and its specific requirements when planning lighting, as this will affect the layout and types of light fittings chosen, e.g. a kitchen will require more lighting than a bedroom.

- **Each room:** when choosing lighting, each room in the home should include:

  o **general lighting:** a centre light or recessed lights

  o **task lighting:** for a specific task, e.g. a desk lamp for study, over-counter lights for food preparation

  o **accent lighting:** to add interest and design, e.g. spotlights on paintings.

- **Safety:** include efficient lighting in areas where accidents are most likely to occur, e.g. on the stairs. Install outside lighting to provide security. All wiring and installation of light fittings should be carried out by a qualified electrician to ensure safety and avoid accidents.

- **Aesthetics:** consider lighting when planning the interior decoration scheme of a room, as it can influence the aesthetics by adding a focal point to a room. It can also add to the overall mood and ambience of the home.

- **Energy efficiency:** use energy-efficient lighting in the home, e.g. CFL or LED bulbs, to save energy and reduce electricity bills.

▲ A kitchen with task and accent lighting

REMEMBER IT!

'**B**right **F**ittings **E**nsure **S**paces **A**re **E**ngaging.'

Building, **F**unction, **E**ach room, **S**afety, **A**esthetics, **E**nergy efficiency.

Discuss three important points that should be considered when planning lighting systems for the home. (18) **OL**

Give an account of the factors that should be taken into account when planning the lighting system for a teenager's study bedroom. (15) **OL**

Discuss the principles that should be considered when planning a lighting system for a family home. (12) **HL**

LIGHTING

ELECTIVE 3

SOCIAL STUDIES

Chapter 24:
Social change and the family

🔗 6.1 SOCIAL CHANGE AND THE FAMILY

What you will learn:

• **Social and economic changes in Ireland**

Social and economic changes in Ireland

Many social and economic changes have occurred in Ireland over the past number of years which have had a significant effect on family life, including:

- changes in settlement patterns from rural to urban areas
- reduction in working hours and increase in leisure time
- improvements in the provision of education
- improvements in the provision of social welfare
- changing attitudes to marriage
- changing attitudes to parenting and traditional roles within the family
- improved pay and working conditions
- increased participation of women in the workforce
- legislation on equal pay and employment opportunities
- unemployment
- modern communications technology development.

Changes in settlement patterns from rural to urban areas

In the early twentieth century the majority of the Irish population resided in rural areas. The urban population in Ireland has increased dramatically in recent years, with 62% of the Irish population now living in urban regions. This can be attributed to:

- technological developments within the agricultural industry, causing fewer people to be required to work on rural farms, as machines can now carry out most of the work
- an increase in multinational companies being attracted to urban areas, due to a highly educated workforce and good infrastructure, e.g. roads, airports and internet services, causing individuals to move for new employment opportunities
- a greater array of services, e.g. hospitals, shops and banks, that are easily accessible
- a greater offering of amenities, e.g. cinemas, gyms and playgrounds, that are easily accessible. This is attractive for many, as they feel it offers a better social life and reduces the risk of isolation
- a greater selection of educational opportunities. Many families nowadays want a choice of schools, and this is often not an option in rural towns or villages.

Impact on family life

Rural areas	Urban areas
• Rural depopulation occurs, as young people leave to seek employment opportunities in urban areas. This leads to a population imbalance, as older people are left behind, increasing feelings of social isolation.	• Greater provisions of services are available to accommodate the rapid growth in population. However, over time educational and health services can become inadequate due to overpopulation and increased demand.
• Services are cut back due to lack of use. Many schools and garda stations have had to close or **amalgamate** due to declining numbers.	• Amenities are more readily accessible due to high numbers availing of them. This enhances social life.
• Amenities are reduced due to declining numbers availing of them. This causes social life to decline.	• Employment opportunities are reduced due to overpopulation, leading to higher competition for a smaller number of jobs. This can lead to high rates of unemployment and an increase in social problems, e.g. theft.
• Marriages and birth rates decline, as young families establish their families in urban areas beside their employment. This further impacts on population imbalance.	• Traffic congestion is more prevalent, as roads are not sufficient to deal with the ever-increasing traffic using them on a daily basis. For long-distance commuters this can further decrease family time.
• Less government funding is put into developing rural infrastructure, leaving rural areas a less attractive option for multinational investors, causing the cycle of unemployment to continue.	• Pollution, including air pollution from car fumes and noise pollution from construction, is increased.

> **Lit Hit**
> Amalgamate means combine.

? Discuss **two** effects of the following on family life in Ireland: more people living in urban areas. (10) **OL**

Give an account of the reasons why more people in modern Ireland are living in urban areas. (16) **OL**

Discuss how changes in settlement patterns from rural to urban areas have impacted on family life. (18) **HL**

Efforts made to halt/reverse population decline in rural areas

- **Rural Resettlement Programme:** this programme is run by Rural Resettlement Ireland (RRI). It assists families to leave urban areas and resettle permanently in rural areas. This has led to the survival of many rural communities and their amenities. All services, e.g. advice on housing and furniture removal, are provided free of charge to families.

- **Improved infrastructure:** infrastructure is central to rural economic prosperity, as roads, rail, ports and broadband connections encourage business investment. Recent infrastructure improvements in rural areas include:
  - o the opening of the M6 motorway between Dublin and Galway
  - o the opening of the Irish rail train route between Galway and Limerick.

These have helped attract foreign businesses to rural areas, and, in turn, created jobs, causing families to move and settle in these locations and surrounding areas.

> **?** Name **and** give details of **one** initiative that has helped maintain the population in rural areas. (10) **OL**
>
> Why, in your opinion, has there been an increase in the number of people living in rural areas between 1991 and 2006? (15) **OL**
>
> *'Almost 60% of the Irish population now live in urban areas.'*
> Comment on efforts being made by the Government to reverse this trend and halt population decline in rural areas. (12) **HL**

Reduction in working hours and increase in leisure time

The change to shorter working hours and increased availability of leisure time has come about due to:

- European and Irish legislation governing maximum working hours, ensuring employees work no more than 48 hours a week. Any extra time worked beyond these hours is now viewed as overtime and must be paid accordingly
- legislation governing statutory entitlements to paid holidays of at least four weeks per year and paid leave, e.g. sick, maternity and parental leave
- the introduction of more flexible working hours, such as flexi-time, shift work, part-time work and job-sharing
- the economic recession, which led to a reduction in working hours or unemployment as many businesses closed.

Impact on family life

- An increase in leisure time enables families to spend more quality time together, as parents have more free time away from work.
- Increased leisure time reduces stress among parents and allows for relaxation. This can benefit mental health and reduce the risk of depression.
- Participating in active leisure activities improves the families' physical well-being, as it enhances fitness and muscular strength and controls weight.
- Reduced working hours or unemployment has resulted in many families seeing a drop in disposable income, leading to a reduced standard of living. This can cause financial stress and worry.

> **?** Discuss the impact of the following on family life: reduction in working hours. (10) **OL**

Improvements in the provision of education

A number of measures have improved the Irish education system and made it more accessible for all. These include:

- the introduction of free post-primary education in the 1960s. Every child in Ireland is entitled to free, state-run primary and post-primary education
- the development of school transport systems, particularly in rural areas. This provides subsidised school transport for students who live away from their local school
- government investment in education. This pays for the upkeep of school buildings and equipment, staffing and running costs
- increased resources in the area of special needs education. Resources available include special needs assistants and resource teachers
- the introduction of a new range of courses such as Leaving Certificate Applied (LCA) and the Leaving Certificate Vocational Programme (LCVP) at second level. These aim to accommodate the varying learning styles and ability levels among students, and to encourage them to remain in full-time education for longer
- a greater range of third-level courses and adult education courses to meet the demands of a skills-based job market
- easier access to third-level education through the elimination of third-level fees, the provision of state financial assistance, e.g. the student grant scheme and the provision of admission schemes, e.g. Disability Access Route to Education (DARE) scheme.

> **Did you know**
>
> Despite third-level fees being eliminated, prospective students are still expected to pay a student services charge at a maximum rate of €3,000 per year. This covers student services and examinations.

Impact on family life

- The provision of free education as well as financial assistance for third level has made education more accessible for all. This eases the financial burden education can have on families.
- Increased resources available for students with special educational needs in schools helps alleviate stress on families, as they can ensure their child's individual needs are catered for.
- The provision of new courses at second level for a range of abilities and learning styles enhances students' self-esteem, causing them to achieve their full academic potential and remain in education for longer. This also improves their future family life, as they are more likely to obtain employment due to their educational qualifications, leading to a higher standard of living.
- Parents can avail of adult and second-chance education, enabling them to enhance their self-esteem and improve their chances of obtaining work or an internal promotion, which can lead an improved standard of living for their family.

 Discuss how social and economic change has affected family life. Refer to the following: improvements in the provision of education. (8) **OL**

Improvements in the provision of social welfare

Before the introduction of the social welfare system, members of the family had sole responsibility for caring for and protecting vulnerable family members. Nowadays the state has taken over much of the protective role of family members by the provision of social welfare payments including:

- pensions, e.g. Non-Contributory State Pension
- allowances, e.g. Disability Allowance, Fuel Allowance
- benefits, e.g. Child Benefit.

These payments help families with their day-to-day living expenses.

Impact on family life

- The family may feel less financial responsibility for certain family members, e.g. older people, and people with disabilities, since the introduction of social welfare payments.
- The provision of payments, including the State Pension, Fuel Allowance and medical cards, helps alleviate financial hardship among older people, as they can afford to meet their basic needs. These payments also prevent older people feeling as if they are a burden on the family, since they can maintain their independence.
- Child Benefit helps families meet their children's needs and ensures that their well-being is maintained. In low-income households it can help families from falling into poverty.
- The provision of payments, including the Family Income Supplement and the Back to School Clothing and Footwear Allowance helps alleviate financial hardship among low-income families, as they can provide for the basic needs of their family.
- The One-Parent Family Payment helps alleviate financial hardship among one-parent families, as they can provide for the basic needs of their family.

? Discuss the impact on family life of improvements in social welfare entitlements. (12) **OL**

Changing attitudes to marriage

Traditionally people married at a very young age and remained in this marriage for the duration of their life. Marriages were also only between males and females. In recent times attitudes to marriage have changed. This has occurred due to:

- women no longer seeing marriage as a means of securing their future, as they are more educated and are establishing their own careers
- the diminishing influence of the Catholic Church, meaning some couples are opting for civil marriage ceremonies instead of religious ceremonies
- cohabitation becoming more commonplace
- divorce and separation becoming more socially acceptable, so spouses are no longer expected or prepared to remain in an unhappy or abusive marital relationship
- the introduction of The Marriage Act 2015, enabling same-sex marriages to take place in Ireland.

Impact on family life

- Divorce and separation has led to a breakdown in the traditional nuclear family unit and an increase in blended families, as individuals are remarrying.
- There has been an increase in one-parent families, generally headed by females, due to marital breakdown and divorce.
- As numerous couples are cohabitating before getting married, there is an increase in the number of children born outside marriage. There is no longer a stigma attached to this.
- There has been an increase in same-sex marriages due to the introduction of the Marriage Act 2015. Same-sex couples are expanding their families by adoption, *in vitro* fertilisation (IVF) and surrogacy.

? Discuss **two** effects of the following on family life in Ireland: changing attitudes to marriage. (10) **OL**

Social change has had a major impact on family life in Ireland today.
Discuss this statement in relation to changing attitudes to marriage. (10) **HL**

Changing attitudes to parenting and traditional roles within the family

In the past, parenting and childcare was chiefly the domain of the mother, as mothers tended to work as homemakers. Fathers were the breadwinners in households, and they upheld the parenting role of the disciplinarian, implementing a strict discipline regime. Nowadays there has been a move towards equal partnership in the home. This has led to integrated roles being evident in homes, with parents taking joint responsibility for parenting, discipline, childcare and household tasks. Roles are no longer segregated, as many households are dual-income, with both parents working. These changes have been acknowledged by the provision of parental leave and paternity leave for relevant parents.

Impact on family life

- In some households men are staying at home to mind their children, as women are the breadwinners. This enables children to create closer relationships with fathers than in previous decades.

- More democracy is evident between parents when decision making, with men no longer being the sole decision makers. Children have also been given a greater say in family matters.

- As both parents take a more egalitarian approach to childcare and household tasks, children are exposed to gender equality from a young age. This makes children aware that everyone is equal and can fulfil the same roles, regardless of gender.

- Each parent now has an equal say in the provision of discipline. This generally takes the form of consequences. In some families discipline can be too **lenient**. This lack of parental control can increase social problems, e.g. alcohol abuse, among children, as they have more freedom than is advisable.

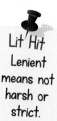

Lit Hit
Lenient means not harsh or strict.

- As many families are now dual-income households they can experience role conflict. This occurs when the expectation of one role clashes with another, e.g. a parent who has to work but their child is ill. This can cause parents to experience feelings of guilt.

- When parents attempt to play several roles at one time, role overload can occur. Women, in particular, may struggle to find the balance between their careers and their responsibilities at home. This can cause feelings of guilt if work duties begin to interfere with their role as a parent.

- As both parents in some households are working outside the home, children must spend more time in childcare, reducing the amount of child–parent bonding that occurs in families.

? Discuss how social and economic changes have affected family life. Refer to the following: traditional roles within the family. (8) **OL**

Discuss **two** effects of the following on family life in Ireland: changing attitudes to parenting. (10) **OL**

Social change has had a major impact on family life in Ireland today.
Discuss this statement in relation to changes in traditional roles within the family. (10) **HL**

Improved pay and working conditions

Pay and working conditions have improved greatly for all employees. This has occurred due to:

- the introduction of legislation governing working conditions, minimum wage, employment equality and working hours
- the establishment of trade unions to protect employees by seeking to improve working conditions and pay.

Impact on family life

- Due to shorter working hours, families have more leisure time to bond or take up a leisure activity together.
- Minimum wage enables most families to have sufficient income to meet basic needs. Some families have more disposable income and therefore enjoy a higher standard of living.
- Parents can be happier and healthier at work. This reduces the risk of mental health issues, e.g. depression, which can impact on home life.

 Discuss the impact of the following on family life: improved conditions of work. (5) **OL**

Increased participation of women in the workforce

For information on increased participation of women in the workforce see page 518.

Impact on family life

- As many families are now dual income, disposable income has increased, enabling them to enjoy a higher standard of living.
- Women can experience role overload as they struggle to find the balance between their careers and being a homemaker. This can cause feelings of guilt if work duties begin to interfere with their role as a mother.
- As both parents are working, children must spend more time in childcare, reducing the amount of child–parent bonding that occurs in families.
- Families tend to be smaller as many women are establishing careers.
- Older children may be required to take on extra responsibilities when they get home from school, e.g. caring for younger siblings or making dinner in the absence of parents. This can be good for developing a work ethic and independence, but it should not impact on school work.
- Working mothers can be positive role models for their children, particularly their daughters.

 Discuss **four** factors that have contributed to 56% of women being in paid employment in Ireland today. (20) **OL**

Give an account of the reasons why the number of women in paid employment has increased in recent years. (20) **OL**

Legislation on equal pay and employment opportunities

The Employment Equality Acts 1998–2015 protect the rights of workers, ensuring equal pay and access to employment regardless of gender, civil status, family status, age, race, religion, disability, sexual orientation or membership of the Travelling community. These acts have helped to prohibit discrimination in the workplace.

Impact on family life

- Many jobs have become less gender specific, as legislation prevents gender discrimination.
- Ensures workers receive equal pay for equal work, enabling all individuals to have the same chance at a decent standard of living.
- Increased participation of women in the workforce has occurred. Despite this increase women still tend to be:
  - concentrated in low-paid jobs with little room for promotion. However, this is on the decline, as women are better educated than before
  - holding jobs with little authority, while men hold more powerful managerial positions, e.g. in government, finance and law enforcement.

GO FIGURE

23.6% of women are in low-paid jobs compared to 17.6% of men.

- Increased participation of people with disabilities and members of the Travelling community in the workforce has occurred. Despite this, many still experience discrimination when seeking employment.

> **?** Discuss how social and economic change has affected family life. Refer to the following: employment opportunities. (8) **OL**

Unemployment

The unemployment levels in a country reflect the state of the economy. When a country's economy is in recession, unemployment figures tend to be high, in comparison to unemployment levels being low in a strong economy. At present, despite the economy showing signs of recovery, Ireland has an unemployment rate of approximately 8.5%.

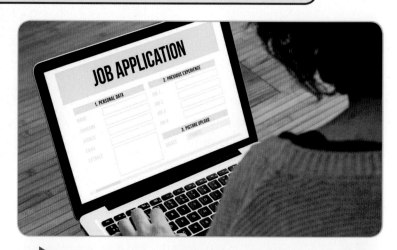

JOB APPLICATION

1. PERSONAL DATA
2. PREVIOUS EXPERIENCE
3. PICTURE UPLOAD

Impact on family life

For information on the impact of unemployment on family life see page 528-529.

> **Did you know ?**
> Unemployment rates in Ireland reached a record high of 17.3% in 1985 due to economic recession, and a record low of 3.7% in 2000 due to economic prosperity.

Modern communications technology development

Technological progress, e.g. the development of smartphones and tablets, is a considerable driving force behind the development of modern communication technology. Examples of communication technology include:

- email
- short message services (SMS)
- video conferencing and chat services, e.g. Skype, FaceTime, WhatsApp and Snapchat
- social media, e.g. Twitter and Facebook.

Impact on family life

- Closer relationships between family members may form as it is easier to keep in contact, especially with those living far away.

> **Did you know** ?
> Over one billion people are monthly active users of WhatsApp.

- Children's IT skills, e.g. the ability to send an email, develop. This can enhance their prospects for future employment.
- Children's education can be enhanced, as communication technologies, e.g. Twitter, can act as a resource to support learning activities.
- Family relationships are affected if members develop an unhealthy desire to spend hours checking social media sites. In severe cases this can lead to addiction.

> **Did you know** ?
> Almost half of all internet users aged between 50 and 64 use social media.

> **?** Discuss the impact of (a) social change and (b) economic change on family life. (20) **OL**
>
> **Social change has had a major impact on family life in Ireland today.**
> Discuss this statement in relation to the impact of modern communications technology. (10) **HL**
>
> Discuss the impact of social change on family life. (20) **HL**

Chapter 25: Education

EDUCATION

6.2

What you will learn:

- **The purpose of education**
- **Factors that influence educational achievement**
- **Provision of education in Ireland**
- **Factors that influence equality of opportunity in education**
- **Groups that experience inequality of opportunity in education**
- **Initiatives for improving access to education**

Education is a fundamental right. In Ireland it is compulsory for children to participate from the ages of six to sixteen, or until they have completed three years of second-level education. The Department of Education and Skills oversees the provision of education in Ireland.

The purpose of education

Education has an important role to play in individuals' socialisation, development and preparation for work.

Socialisation

Socialisation is the process whereby an individual learns the norms, values, customs and social skills appropriate to behave in a manner acceptable to society, e.g. patience and respecting authority. It begins at home (primary socialisation), but continues and is reinforced during schooling (secondary socialisation). Socialisation at school can be:

- **formal:** in the classroom, e.g. developing moral values through the Social Personal and Health Education (SPHE) curriculum

- **informal:** through the hidden curriculum (knowledge conveyed to students without ever being explicitly taught), e.g. developing the ability to share and be punctual. Rewards and sanctions are used to encourage children to conform.

A well-planned system of education can produce socialised individuals. Socialisation is especially important during formative years, as it enables a child to fit into society.

? Outline the contribution of education to the socialisation of young children. (12) **HL**

Development of individuals

The education system plays a key role in contributing to the physical, emotional, intellectual and moral development of individuals.

Physical development

Education assists physical development as it:

- provides opportunities for children in early education to play with toys, e.g. shape sorters and jigsaws, which can develop hand–eye coordination and dexterity
- provides practical subjects, e.g. Science and Home Economics, which can enhance coordination and motor skills
- provides Physical Education (PE), which develops balance and **agility**.

Lit' Hit
Agility is the power to move quickly and gracefully.

Emotional development

Education encourages emotional development as it:

- helps children gain emotional independence from parents
- provides opportunities to develop relationships outside the home. This interaction with peers helps students to become more aware of the feelings of others, so they can develop empathy
- promotes emotional health and well-being by providing coping skills for life, e.g. techniques to manage stress through SPHE classes.

If children attend mixed-sex schools it encourages friendships between the sexes, enabling them to be emotionally accustomed to relate to people of both genders. This will be of benefit in future workplaces.

Intellectual development

Education contributes to intellectual development as it:

- provides access to educational resources, e.g. computers, that may not be accessible at home
- challenges and tests intellect by providing an array of subjects and extracurricular activities
- provides examinations and homework assignments that motivate students to achieve their full intellectual potential. Healthy competition between peers also instils the motivation to do well.

Moral development

Education encourages moral development as schools:

- have an ethos outlining their beliefs, values, customs and moral thinking, which students are expected to conform to
- have rules, which teach students how to function well in society and live by its laws and norms
- examine moral dilemmas in SPHE and Religious Education, instilling in students the difference between right and wrong.

? Discuss the role of education in contributing to the development of the individual. Refer to **each** of the following:

- physical development
- emotional development
- moral development
- intellectual development. (24) **OL**

Outline **three** ways in which education contributes to the development of the individual. (15) **OL**

Preparation for work

Education has an important role to play in the preparation of students for working life as it:

- provides basic education, e.g. numeracy and literacy, a minimum requirement in most employment nowadays
- supports the attainment of educational qualifications through various subject levels and educational programmes, e.g. Leaving Certificate Applied (LCA) and Leaving Certificate Vocational Programme (LCVP). These aim to accommodate the different learning styles and abilities of students, ensuring academic success for all
- develops specialised skills, e.g. woodwork, necessary for those seeking employment in specialist jobs
- provides work experience, e.g. during Transition Year, so students obtain an insight into the working world. This can help students decide on their future profession
- develops qualities through the hidden curriculum, e.g. punctuality and respect for authority, which are vital to obtain and hold on to employment.

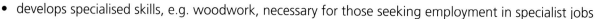

? Outline the purpose of education as a preparation for work. (10) **HL**

Explain, giving examples, how education prepares students for participation in employment. (15) **HL**

Factors that influence educational achievement

- **School environment:** enthusiastic teachers encourage children to be more engaged and interested in learning, enhancing educational achievement. Schools with large class numbers, discipline issues and fewer resources can hinder students' progression at school. Bullying can also affect educational achievement, as children can become unfocused in class or skip school.
- **Family size:** parents with large families often have less time to spend assisting children with school work, which can affect educational achievement. Extra financial pressure can also reduce resources, e.g. books and laptops, available in the home to assist with education progression.
- **Parental attitude:** a positive attitude towards education from parents can instil the value of education in children, resulting in hard working, self-motivated students. The educational level of parents may also influence educational achievement, as some parents can assist their children with homework and assignments, enhancing their academic success.
- **Intellectual ability:** every person genetically inherits a certain level of intellectual ability. However, for a child to achieve academic success this needs to be nurtured and supported by home and school.
- **Peers:** if a child's peers are academically driven it can positively impact on educational achievement, as they may also be encouraged to work hard and succeed at school. This can also generate healthy competition, increasing a child's motivation to do well.
- **Home environment:** an overcrowded house can make it difficult for children to find a quiet study space, affecting educational progress. Inadequate furniture, e.g. no desk, can make it difficult to complete homework. Inadequate heating can cause illness, which can lead to absences from school, affecting progress in education as days are missed.

REMEMBER IT!

'**S**tudents **F**eel **P**ride **I**n **P**resenting **H**omework.'
School environment, **F**amily size, **P**arental attitude, **I**ntellectual ability, **P**eers, **H**ome environment.

? Give an account of four major factors that influence the educational achievement of students attending third-level. (20) **OL**

Analyse the principal factors that influence educational achievement. (24) **HL**

Provision of education in Ireland

The Irish education system consists of:

- pre-school education
- special needs education
- primary education
- third-level education
- second-level education
- adult and second-chance education.

Pre-school education

Although not considered formal education, pre-school education is viewed as the starting point of a child's educational development outside the home, as it provides a stimulating and interactive learning environment. A free pre-school education scheme is now available for all children from three years of age.

Types of pre-school education

Day care centres (including crèches and nurseries)	• Operate a childminding service with integrated education and socialisation development • Provide eating, sleeping, changing, washing and playing facilities • Can be community based or privately run • Cater for children up to five years of age • Run by qualified persons, with a certain ratio of carers-to-children to ensure adequate care and attention
Playgroups and playschools	• Provide a pre-school programme that involves learning-based play and 'learning by doing' to prepare children for the move to primary school • Operate for three to four hours daily (usually 9 a.m. to 1 p.m.) • Can be community based or privately run • Cater for children between three and five years of age • Run by qualified persons, with a certain ratio of carers-to-children to ensure adequate care and attention
Montessori schools	• Operate a childminding service that enables children to learn at their own pace through play. They can choose the activities they participate in from many possibilities. • Self-motivation, independence and creativity are encouraged • Cater for children up to five years of age • Generally privately run by trained Montessori teachers, with a certain ratio of carers-to-children to ensure adequate care and attention
Naíonraí	• Provide a pre-school programme through the Irish language that involves learning-based play and 'learning by doing' to prepare children for the move to primary school • Operate for three to four hours daily (usually 9 a.m. to 1 p.m.) • Often used as preparation for children to attend a primary Gaelscoil • Cater for children between three and five years of age • Run by qualified persons who are Irish speakers, with a certain ratio of carers-to-children to ensure adequate care and attention

Benefits of pre-school education

✓ Children develop their social skills, e.g. the ability to communicate, share and listen, as they mix with other children and adults.

✓ Children develop confidence, as they gain independence from their parents and form relationships outside the home.

✓ Children enhance their intellectual development through the provision of a stimulating learning environment. This can help their academic progression in primary school.

✓ Children enhance their physical development, e.g. hand–eye coordination, through playing games and completing jigsaws.

Initiatives to support equality of opportunity in pre-primary schools

Early Childhood Care and Education Scheme (ECCE)

This scheme provides three hours of free early childhood care and education for children of pre-school age five days a week to enable them to be ready for a formal learning and social environment at primary school. Children are eligible for the scheme when they reach three years of age until they transfer to primary school, provided that they are not older than five and a half years of age at the end of the pre-school year. Childcare services taking part in the ECCE scheme must provide an appropriate pre-school educational programme that follows Síolta, the national framework for early years care and education.

Early Start Pre-School Programme

This programme offers a one-year pre-primary school intervention scheme in selected primary schools in disadvantaged areas. The objective is to enhance the overall development of children aged between three and four years of age who are at risk of not reaching their potential within the education system. The curriculum focuses on language, cognition and social and personal development to provide a good foundation for future educational achievement. It is run by qualified primary school teachers, childcare workers and volunteer parents, and it runs for two and a half hours a day. After completing the Early Start Pre-School Programme, children proceed to junior infants.

? Give details of **one** government scheme that supports the provision of pre-school education. (10) **OL**

Primary education

Children generally first attend primary school between the ages of four or five, although it is not compulsory until six years of age.

Types of primary schools

National schools/ Gaelscoileanna	• Make up the majority of primary schools (96%)
	• The majority are owned by religious denominations
	• Managed by a board of management
	• Mostly denominational (90% are under the patronage of the Catholic Church)
	• Can be single-sex or co-educational
	• Receive funding from the Department of Education and Skills

Educate Together primary schools	• Managed by a board of management • Multi-denominational • Co-educational • Receive funding from the Department of Education and Skills
Private primary schools	• Managed by a board of management • Mostly denominational • Can be single-sex or co-educational • Not eligible for Department of Education and Skills funding

Primary school curriculum

- Primary education is delivered over eight years, with no formal examination at the end.
- It aims to nurture the spiritual, moral, cognitive, emotional, imaginative, social and physical needs of children so they have the ability to meet the demands of life now and in the future.
- It provides a broad learning experience by offering language (English and Irish); Mathematics; Social, Environmental and Scientific Education; ICT; Arts Music and Drama; Physical Education; Social, Personal and Health Education; and Religious Education. It also places particular emphasis on literacy and numeracy development.
- Teachers are encouraged to include a variety of teaching and learning approaches to cater for the different needs and learning styles of individual children. This helps create an inclusive learning environment.

Educational supports/resources available in primary schools

- Interactive whiteboards: enable teachers to encourage children to participate more in their learning.
- Laptops and tablets: allow access to educational apps and websites that can assist educational advancement. These also allow children to take more control of their own learning.
- Educational psychologists: work in partnership with teachers, parents and children in identifying the educational needs of children.
- The School Book Grant Scheme.
- The Home School Community Liaison Scheme (HSCL).

➜ For information on the **School Book Grant Scheme** and the **Home School Community Liaison Scheme** see pages 544 and 509.

Provisions for children with special educational needs in primary schools

For information on provisions for children with special educational needs in primary schools see page 504.

 Discuss primary level education in Ireland. Refer to:
- choice/types of primary school
- educational supports/resources
- curriculum offered
- provision for pupils with special needs. (30) **HL**

Second-level education

Children generally attend secondary school between the ages of 12 and 18. It is only compulsory up until 16 years of age, or until a child has completed three years of second-level education.

Types of secondary schools

Voluntary secondary schools	• Under the trusteeship of religious communities, boards of governors or individuals • Managed by a board of management • Mostly denominational • Can be single-sex or co-educational • Receive funding from the Department of Education and Skills
Community and comprehensive schools	• Managed by a board of management • Mostly denominational • Co-educational • Receive funding from the Department of Education and Skills
Vocational schools and community colleges	• Owned by local Education and Training Boards (ETB) • Managed by a board of management • Non-denominational • Co-educational • Receive funding from the Department of Education and Skills • The main providers of adult education and community education courses
Educate Together secondary schools	• Managed by a board of management • Multi-denominational • Co-educational • Receive funding from the Department of Education and Skills
Private secondary schools	• Managed by a board of management. • Mostly denominational • Can be single-sex or co-educational • Not eligible for Department of Education and Skills funding to assist with running costs

Did you know
The first Educate Together secondary school opened in Ireland in 2014.

Did you know
There are 55 private fee-paying secondary schools in Ireland.

Educational programmes offered in secondary schools

Junior cycle

- This is a three-year educational programme with compulsory assessment.
- It aims to extend and deepen the quality of students' knowledge, develop personal/social confidence, and prepare them for further study or employment.
- Students study a variety of subjects including English, Irish and Maths.

→ For more information on **junior cycle** see www.juniorcycle.ie

Did you know
Since 2014 a new junior cycle framework has been introduced by the Department of Education and Skills. This involves new content in established subjects, newly developed short courses and a new approach to assessment and reporting.

Transition Year (TY) programme

- An optional or mandatory broad educational programme offered between junior and senior cycle.
- It aims to provide students with an education that encourages personal development, promotes skill development with an emphasis on independent learning and incorporates adult- and working-life experiences.
- Each school designs its own Transition Year programme within set guidelines to suit the needs and interests of its students, e.g. it may include work experience or the organisation of a musical.
- There is no state examination at the end. Assessment is usually continual in the form of projects, portfolios, oral, practical and written activities.

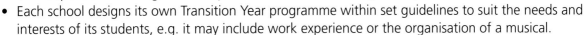

GO FIGURE 123

At present, 75% of secondary schools offer the Transition Year programme.

Leaving Certificate programme

- This is a two-year programme with a compulsory set of examinations at the end.
- It aims to equip students with the skills and knowledge necessary for further study or the world of work.
- Students study at least five subjects, including the compulsory subjects English, Irish and Maths.
- It caters for different abilities, as subjects are examined at Higher and Ordinary level. Irish and Maths are also offered at Foundation Level.
- Some subjects, e.g. Home Economics and Geography, award marks towards project work.
- Each grade received in the final exams carries points that are added together to obtain entry to third-level education.

Leaving Certificate Vocational Programme (LCVP)

- This is a two-year programme with a compulsory set of examinations at the end.
- Students study at least five subjects, one of which must be Irish and two of which must be selected from one of the designated vocational subject groupings, e.g. Home Economics and Accounting or Business or Economics. A recognised course in a modern European language must also be studied.
- In addition, students must study two compulsory link modules – enterprise education and preparation for the world of work – with the aim of introducing students to the world of work and business. The link modules are assessed by a written exam (40%) and a coursework portfolio (60%). A pass, merit or distinction certification can be attained, and these results can be converted to points and used for entry to third-level education.

Leaving Certificate Applied (LCA) programme

- This is a two-year modular-based programme, divided into four half-year sessions.
- It aims to prepare students for the requirements of further education or training, e.g. a Post-Leaving Certificate Course (PLC), and for the world of work.
- Students must participate in:
  o general education, e.g. Irish, modern languages, social education
  o vocational preparation, e.g. work experience, English and communication
  o vocational education, e.g. information and communication technology, hotel catering and tourism.
- Assessment is continual, with practical, oral and written exams at the end of the second year. A pass, merit or distinction certification can be attained.

❓ **Second level education in Ireland has undergone significant change in recent years.**

Discuss the above statement and refer to range of programmes offered in second level schools. (8) **OL**

Name and give details of **one** education initiative that helps to retain young people in school. (10) **OL**

Name **and** give details of **two** education programmes designed specifically to help retain young people in second level education. State two benefits to the student of each programme named. (30) **OL**

Educational supports/resources available in secondary schools are the same as those available in primary schools (see page 501).

> **Second level education in Ireland has undergone significant change in recent years.**
> Discuss the above statement and refer to facilities and resources provided in schools. (8) **OL**

Special needs education

HL Special needs education is the practice of educating students with special needs in a way that addresses their individual differences and unique needs. The Education for Persons with Special Educational Needs (EPSEN) Act 2004 states that children with special needs are to be educated in an inclusive classroom setting in a mainstream primary or secondary school, unless this would not be in the best interests of the child or would affect the provision of education to the other children in their class. In this instance they may attend a special school. Examples of special needs include visual and hearing impairments, Down's syndrome, autistic spectrum disorders, attention deficit hyperactivity disorder (ADHD), dyslexia and dyspraxia.

> **Did you know** ?
>
> By law, new school buildings must have disabled toilets, ramps, wide doors and a lift if the building is over one storey.

Educational supports/resources provided in mainstream primary and secondary schools for students with special educational needs

- Learning support/resource teachers provide additional support for children with special educational needs on an individual or group basis. They work with parents and teachers to ensure they are using teaching strategies to assist each child to achieve their full academic potential.
- Special needs assistants (SNAs) provide non-teaching care to students with special educational needs, e.g. help going to the toilet.
- A visiting teacher service provides advice and support to ensure that the needs of children and young people with visual or hearing impairments are met.
- Assistive technology enables students with special educational needs to maintain their independence, e.g. laptops with zoom text software for students who are visually impaired.
- Second-level schools provide reasonable accommodations in examinations to limit the impact of the student's disability on their exam performance, e.g. the provision of a reader, use of a word processor, use of a tape recorder or scribe, or a spelling and grammar waiver.
- Some primary and second-level schools provide special classes with low pupil–teacher ratios, so children with special educational needs, e.g. autistic spectrum disorders, receive more one-on-one attention than in a regular classroom.

> **Did you know** ?
>
> To be eligible for the provision of an SNA or learning support/resource teacher, students have to have undergo a psychological assessment by the National Educational Psychological Service (NEPS).

> **?** Give an account of the supports provided in second level schools for students with special education needs. (18) **HL**

Special schools

- Over 140 special schools are available throughout Ireland for students between 5 and 18 years of age with particular learning disabilities and special needs, e.g. visual or hearing impairments.
- Many provide education to Leaving Certificate level, but also offer programmes such as life skills courses for students who would not benefit from state exams.
- Some children with special needs may attend a mainstream school for part of the week and attend a special school on the other days.
- For children who live far away from special schools the Department of Education and Skills provides transport services from certain areas.

Third-level education

Third-level education in Ireland is made up of four sectors.

- **Universities**, e.g. University of Limerick (UL) and Trinity College Dublin (TCD), offer certificate, diploma, degree, masters and doctorate courses.
- **Colleges of Education**, e.g. St Patrick's College of Education, Dublin (primary education) and St Angela's College, Sligo (Home Economics teacher training), offer teacher training courses.
- **Institutes of Technology**, e.g. Dundalk Institute of Technology (DKIT) and Institute of Technology Tralee (ITT), offer certificate, diploma, degree, masters and doctorate courses.
- **Independent private colleges**, e.g. Griffith College, Dublin and Portobello Institute, Dublin, offer certificate, diploma, degree and masters courses.

> **GO FIGURE**
> 48% of Irish people between 25 and 34 years of age hold university-level qualifications (the highest rate in Europe).

Applications for undergraduate college courses in Ireland are generally made through the Central Applications Office (CAO). Each course has entry-level points. The number of entry-level points needed for any course depends on the number of places and the number of applicants, so the entry levels vary from year to year. On completion of the Leaving Certificate the CAO converts students' grades into points, based on their scores in their six best subjects, and third-level places are awarded on this basis. A certain number of places on undergraduate courses are reserved for mature students (23 years or older), students who completed a PLC course and foreign students. Application for these places vary, depending on the third-level institution.

Adult and second-chance education

Adult and second-chance education aims to promote a culture of lifelong learning by creating opportunities for adults of all ages and educational levels to go back to education and gain skills within a flexible learning system and qualifications structure.

Reasons why adults may choose to return to education

- To gain qualifications that they may not have had the opportunity to attain when younger. These may be sought to obtain a job and move away from relying on social welfare payments.
- To improve qualifications to allow for a career change or to gain an internal promotion. This may be desired to improve income, or due to the monotony of a current job.
- To keep up with technological advances in the workplace, e.g. iPad training. This up-skilling is vital to retain current employment or to increase employment prospects in the future.
- To develop literacy and numeracy skills, as some adults may be **functionally illiterate** due to leaving education early. These skills can be sought to obtain employment or to be able to complete daily tasks, e.g. reading an electricity bill.
- To interact with other people from different backgrounds and ages. This social interaction is commonly sought by those who have retired.
- To spend time on a particular interest, e.g. painting or photography, for enjoyment and relaxation.

Lit Hit

Functionally illiterate means lacking literacy skills required for everyday needs, e.g. filling in a form.

Discuss **four** factors that contribute to the increasing demand for adult and second chance education in Ireland. (16) **HL**

Analyse the possible reasons why many people return to education having concluded their initial education and/or training. (24) **HL**

Factors adults should consider when deciding to return to education

- **Cost:** adults should consider the cost of returning to education to ensure they can afford it, as course fees can be expensive. A variety of financial assistance schemes are available to assist with this, e.g. the Student Grant Scheme.
- **Supports available:** adults should research the supports available, e.g. childcare support, to make the transition back to education easier for them. The National Adult Learning Organisation (AONTAS) provides advice and support in all areas of adult education.
- **Course delivery:** adults should consider the flexibility of course-delivery options, e.g. full-time, part-time, or online, to ensure their return to education can fit in with their lifestyle and avoid causing them to experience role overload.
- **Course specifications:** adults should research course specifications to ensure they choose a course that meets their needs. If adults are considering returning to education to enhance their job prospects or gain a promotion, they need to ensure the course chosen will provide them with sufficient qualifications.

> Explain what you understand by 'second chance' education. (6) **OL**
>
> Analyse the considerations that adults may take into account when deciding to return to education. (20) **HL**

Provision/availability of adult and second-chance education

- **Third-level colleges and universities:** e.g. University College Dublin (UCD) and Institute of Technology Sligo, offer a wide variety of courses.
- **Private colleges:** e.g. Griffith College, offer an array of fee-paying courses. These fees must be paid, as private colleges are not part of the free fees scheme.
- **Distance-learning colleges:** e.g. Open University, provide a large selection of courses that can be studied at home online. This may suit those who live far away from a college or who wish to study at their own pace.
- **Education and Training Boards (ETBs):** e.g. Dublin and Dun Laoghaire ETB and Cork ETB, deliver education and training programmes, including PLC courses and adult literacy services through a national network of colleges, schools and community education centres nationwide. ETBs are also responsible for providing a wide range of traineeship courses, apprenticeship programmes and specific skills training courses.
- **Teagasc and Coillte:** Teagasc offer specific further education in agriculture, food, horticulture, forestry and equine studies in their agricultural colleges nationwide, e.g. Ballyhaise Agricultural College and Clonakilty Agricultural College. They work in conjunction with Institutes of Technology to provide some courses in these areas. Coillte offer training courses, e.g. in pesticide application and landscaping.
- **Vocational Training Opportunities Scheme (VTOS):** for information on VTOS see page 511.

> Describe the provision of education in Ireland today with regard to adult and second chance education. (20) **HL**

Post-Leaving Certificate (PLC) courses

Post-Leaving Certificate (PLC) courses take place in secondary schools, colleges and community education centres throughout Ireland, and are delivered by Education Training Boards (ETBs).

Courses offered are made up of practical work, academic work and work experience, and aim to develop technological and vocational skills needed for further education or the world of work. Courses offered include legal studies, childcare and business studies. They are full-time and last for one or two years. On completion, the qualification awarded by Quality and Qualifications Ireland (QQI) varies, depending on the duration and type of course. In some cases the qualifications obtained can be used to gain access to third-level education, such as Institutes of Technology. Specific third-level places are reserved for students progressing this way.

Factors that influence equality of opportunity in education

Gender

- Gender inequality in education is no longer as prevalent as it was in the past, when it was mainly males who advanced to third-level education. Nowadays there is an equal representation of both genders in third level.
- In recent times girls have outperformed boys in state examinations. Studies have shown that the reasons for this include the following:
  - girls tend to read more than boys
  - girls often spend more time on homework
  - girls may concentrate more and behave better in class, while boys are more likely to give in to peer pressue and be disruptive
  - girls often mature earlier than boys, which may mean that they are quicker to recognise the importance and seriousness of examinations.
- Textbooks are now more gender-neutral than in the past.
- Some inequality still lies in the lack of subject choices in single-sex schools. Traditionally male-dominated subjects, e.g. Engineering, may not be offered in all-girls schools.

HL Socio-economic status

- Children from higher socio-economic backgrounds can be afforded more opportunities to progress in education, e.g. access to resources such as laptops or grinds for subjects they find challenging. Children from lower socio-economic backgrounds may not have the same access to these types of resources, affecting equality of opportunity in education.
- Educational opportunity can also be hindered by the cost of uniforms, books and extracurricular activities. Certain children from lower socio-economic backgrounds may not be able to afford necessary resources, and this can sometimes affect their educational achievement. Financial assistance, e.g. the Back to School Clothing and Footwear Allowance, aims to reduce this inequality.
- The opportunity to attend third-level education may not be available to children from lower socio-economic backgrounds due to the cost. This may reduce their academic motivation in school. The Student Grant Scheme aims to reduce this inequality.

Place of residence

Many students in Ireland may find it difficult to reach their full potential within the education system due to their place of residence being disadvantaged. Areas are considered disadvantaged if they have:

- high unemployment levels
- low-quality housing
- low literacy and numeracy levels
- high numbers of one-parent families.

Schools in these areas are more likely to have issues with social problems, e.g. non-attendance and discipline, which creates a school environment where it may be difficult to learn. To counteract inequality of opportunity in education among these students, certain disadvantaged areas throughout Ireland have schools that are participating in the Delivering Equality of Opportunity In Schools (DEIS) Action Plan.

➔ For more information on the **DEIS Action Plan** see page 510.

> **?** Discuss **three** factors that may have contributed to girls outperforming boys in state examinations. (15) **OL**
>
> Discuss equality of opportunity in education with reference to the following: gender equality. (10) **HL**
>
> Outline the measures taken to alleviate gender inequity in education. (12) **HL**

Groups that experience inequality of opportunity in education

Early school leavers

GO FIGURE

One in six young people in Ireland leave school before getting a Leaving Certificate.

Early school leaving refers to non-participation in school before reaching 16 years of age or before completing three years of post-primary education. A variety of environmental factors, including home, school and community, can cause students to leave school early. The number of early school leavers is highest among students from disadvantaged areas.

Students who leave school early are more likely to experience social exclusion and be unemployed due to few educational qualifications. Certain programmes are now available for early school leavers to get back into education to improve their standard of living in the future.
These include:

- YouthReach
- VTOS
- Post-Leaving Certificate (PLC) courses

➔ For more information on **YouthReach, VTOS** and **PLC courses** see pages 511 and 507.

Other groups

Other groups that may not experience equality of opportunity in education include:

- **students with special educational needs**, as special schools that provide for their specific needs may not be within an accessible distance. Education supports/resources are provided in mainstream schools to overcome this

- **students of immigrant families**, as cultural differences or language barriers can make it difficult to receive an equal education. This often causes them to become **marginalised**. Educational supports/resources are provided in mainstream schools to overcome this, including:
  - an Irish language exemption if primary education was received outside Ireland up to the age of 11
  - differentiated instruction strategies, e.g. providing photos with key words to assist with comprehension
  - learning support to assist language development.

➔ For information on **education supports/ resources provided in mainstream schools for students with special educational needs** see page 504.

Lit Hit
Marginalised means left out of the mainstream or seen as unimportant

Second level education in Ireland has undergone significant change in recent years.
Discuss the above statement and refer to opportunities for early school leavers. (8) **OL**

Analyse how the supports provided in schools accommodate the educational requirements of pupils from different ethnic backgrounds. (9) **HL**

Discuss equality of opportunity in education with reference to the following: early school leavers. (10) **HL**

Initiatives for improving access to education

Many government-funded initiatives aim to improve accessibility to education for all.

Primary and second-level initiatives

Back to School Clothing and Footwear Allowance

This allowance helps low-income families meet the cost of uniforms and footwear for children going to school. To be eligible parents/guardians need to be receiving certain social welfare payments or participating in a training, employment or adult education scheme. The allowance is €100 for each child aged 4–11 and €200 for each young person aged 12–22. Young people aged between 18–22 must be in full-time second-level education to receive this allowance.

Home School Community Liaison Scheme (HSCL)

This scheme is a school-based prevention strategy targeted at students from disadvantaged areas who are at risk of not reaching their potential in the education system and becoming early school leavers. It aims to retain students in the education system past compulsory education. To achieve this, Home School Community Liaison coordinators:

* promote active co-operation between home, school and relevant community agencies in promoting the education of children
* raise awareness in parents of their own abilities to enhance their child's progress at school and to assist them in developing relevant skills.

Education welfare services of the Child and Family Agency (TUSLA)

This agency aims to encourage and support regular school attendance of students, in particular those who are at risk of early school leaving. To achieve this, education welfare officers are employed at a local level to:

An Ghníomhaireacht um
Leanaí agus an Teaghlach
Child and Family Agency

* support and provide advice to parents and children who are experiencing difficulty with school attendance
* follow up on absences and ensure problems around attendance are addressed before it becomes a crisis issue. If a child has missed 20 days or more of school, the school must inform the statutory educational welfare services of the Child and Family Agency
* monitor children being educated at home to ensure they are receiving a certain minimum education.

DEIS (Delivering Equality of Opportunity in Schools) programme

This programme aims to enable disadvantaged students to gain full benefit from the education system and reduce the number of early school leavers. Schools participating in the DEIS action programme provide:

- a school completion programme supporting children by providing initiatives such as homework clubs, after-school supports and mentoring programmes
- a school meals programme, e.g. breakfast clubs
- access to Home School Community Liaison services
- access to the School Books Grant Scheme (DEIS schools receive more funding for this scheme than non-DEIS schools).

Second-level initiatives

Examination systems

Changes in the examination system within secondary schools have improved accessibility to education. For example:

- subject-level differentiation provides exams at Higher, Ordinary and, in some cases, Foundation Level
- access to reasonable accommodations, e.g. the provision of a reader, use of a word processor, tape recorder or scribe, or a spelling and grammar waiver
- practical exams, journals, orals and reports allow for marks to be obtained before the written examination.

Leaving Certificate Applied (LCA) programme

For information on the LCA programme see page 503.

Third-level initiatives

Higher Education Access Route (HEAR)

This scheme aims to improve access to college for school leavers from lower socio-economic backgrounds. A number of places on various courses are reserved for those who qualify. Students can be eligible for these places on a reduced points basis if certain social, cultural and financial criteria are met. Applications for the scheme must be submitted through the Central Applications Office (CAO).

Disability Access Route to Education (DARE)

This scheme aims to improve access to college for school leavers with a disability or specific learning difficulty. A number of places on various courses are reserved for those who qualify. Students can be eligible for these places on a reduced points basis if they provide evidence that their disability has affected their educational performance considerably. Applications for the scheme must be submitted through the Central Applications Office (CAO).

Third-level and adult/second-chance initiatives
Student Grant Scheme

This scheme provides means-tested financial support to students completing full-time higher-education undergraduate courses and full-time Post-Leaving Certificate (PLC) courses. Student grants are divided into:

- **maintenance grants:** contribution towards living costs (this is the only grant that is available to PLC students)
- **fee grants:** contribution to cover all of or part of the student contribution fee, cost of field trips and all or part of tuition fees (if these are not covered by the free fees scheme).

For second-chance students to be eligible they must be over the age of 23, not have successfully completed an earlier course and they must be returning to pursue an approved course after a break in their studies of at least five years.

Back to Education Allowance (BTEA)

This allowance is available to individuals who wish to pursue a full-time second- or third-level course. Those eligible include people who are unemployed, parenting alone, or have a disability and are getting certain social welfare payments. They must also be over the age of 21, or 24 for a postgraduate course. The allowance received is equal to previous social welfare payments for those over 26. Those under 26 receive a payment of €160 per week (any means that they have will be deducted from this rate).

Adult/second-chance initiatives
YouthReach

YouthReach offers education and training opportunities in centres to unemployed early school leavers between 15 and 20 years of age. It aims to provide students with qualifications and skills required to progress into further education or the world of work. This programme usually runs over a two-year period. Students can obtain a range of qualifications including the Junior Certificate, Leaving Certificate subjects, Leaving Certificate Applied and QQI Further Education and Training Awards. A weekly training allowance is paid to those over 16 years of age. It is funded by the Department of Education and Skills. YouthReach centres are managed by Education and Training Boards (ETBs).

Vocational Training Opportunities Scheme (VTOS)

VTOS offers education and training opportunities to unemployed people over 21 years of age who have been in receipt of certain social welfare payments for at least six months. It aims to provide students with qualifications and skills required to progress into further education or the world of work. The courses offered run for up to two years. Students can obtain a range of qualifications including Junior Certificate, Leaving Certificate and QQI Further Education and Training Awards. A weekly VTOS training allowance equivalent to their social welfare entitlements is paid. It is funded by the Department of Education and Skills and operated through local ETBs.

Springboard

Springboard provides free places for unemployed people on a range of part-time and full-time higher education courses at certificate, degree and master's levels. In general, to be eligible a person must be unemployed, have previous history of employment and be actively seeking work and available to take up work. Participants can still receive their existing social welfare payments while completing a Springboard course.

> ❓ Name and give details of **one** contemporary initiative that has improved access for students to third level education. (10) **HL**
>
> Name and give details of **two** initiatives that have improved access to second chance education. (14) **HL**
>
> Evaluate **three** supports that are available to improve the accessibility of second-level education for all students. (15) **HL**
>
> Name and describe **two** contemporary initiatives which aim to improve the accessibility of education. (18) **HL**

Chapter 26: Work

🔗 WORK
6.3.1–
6.3.2

What you will learn:

- **Defining work**
- **Categories of work**
- **Reasons why people work**
- **Attitudes to work and work attainment**
- **Variations in working conditions**
- **Changes in patterns of work and work availability in Ireland**
- **The role of unpaid and voluntary work in the community**
- **Benefits of voluntary work for the volunteer and the community**

- **Changing patterns in gender roles within the family**
- **The impact of dual-earner families on family life**
- **Childcare facilities available to parents**
- **Factors to consider when choosing childcare**
- **Evaluation of two types of childcare options: childminders and day-care centres**

CONCEPTS OF WORK

Defining work

Work can be defined as physical or mental effort or activity directed towards the production or accomplishment of something. This definition means different things to different people, depending on their personal situation, e.g. gardening can be a person's work or leisure activity. For many people work is an economic necessity that is vital for survival.

Categories of work

Work may be categorised as paid work, unpaid work or voluntary work.

Paid work

- Paid work involves working for financial reward.
- A person can be self-employed or work for an employer.
- Work available can be full time, temporary or part time.
- The range of skills and qualifications required varies from job to job.
- Work is often carried out in a designated area, however this is changing due to technological advances, e.g. Skype, meaning that more people can work from home.

Unpaid work

- Unpaid work involves working for no financial reward, e.g. housework or caring for an elderly parent.
- People can feel undervalued in this work and bored due to its monotony, which can affect self-esteem. It also lacks the advantages associated with paid work, e.g. wages.

Voluntary work

- Voluntary work involves working in the community or for local charities, e.g. Voluntary Services Overseas (VSO) Ireland or St Vincent de Paul, with no financial reward.
- People participate in this work as it is internally rewarding and as they want to make a difference in people's lives.

> **?** Explain the difference between paid work and unpaid work. (10) **OL**
>
> Differentiate between (a) voluntary work and (b) unpaid work. (10) **HL**

Reasons why people work

- To earn money to meet their own and their family's basic needs, e.g. food and housing.
- To increase affluence, which over time can lead to an improved standard of living.
- To have a form of social contact with others who have similar interests. In some cases this may lead to friendships beyond the workplace.
- To make use of educational qualifications. More people now than ever before have attained an educational qualification at third level.
- To obtain a rewarding sense of satisfaction, e.g. a nurse caring for an ill patient. This satisfaction causes people to want to work hard and take pride in their jobs.
- To enjoy a high status or identity, e.g. Gardaí and solicitors enjoy high status. This gives a feeling of being valued, which can enhance self-esteem.

GO FIGURE 123

Over one million people in Ireland between the ages of 20 and 65 have a third-level qualification.

> **?** Identify **and** discuss **four** of the key reasons why people work. (20) **OL**

Attitudes to work and work attainment

Attitudes to work and work **attainment** are influenced by a number of factors.

Job satisfaction

Job satisfaction refers to the degree of enjoyment individuals get from their chosen area of work. The higher the job satisfaction experienced by an employee the more positive their attitude towards work. Job satisfaction can be categorised as intrinsic or extrinsic. Many people will experience both types.

- **Intrinsic satisfaction:** the satisfaction or pleasure experienced from completing a job, rather than the financial gain provided. If a person is intrinsically motivated at work they tend to have more positive feelings on the job and a higher level of self-esteem. This satisfaction is often associated with **vocations**, e.g. veterinarians or teachers.
- **Extrinsic satisfaction:** the satisfaction or pleasure experienced from the benefits associated with a job, rather than the job itself. These benefits may include high wages, bonuses, company cars and time off. Luxury items, e.g. designer clothing, can be purchased with the wages received. Many people stay in unfulfilling, monotonous jobs if they are happy with the benefits provided.

If a person is neither intrinsically nor extrinsically satisfied from their work they experience low job satisfaction.

Lit Hit
Attainment means achievement.

Lit Hit
A vocation is a strong feeling of suitability for a particular career or occupation.

Effects of low job satisfaction

When workers experience low job satisfaction it can cause them to:

- lack self-motivation and have a poor work ethic
- produce inferior work
- take unofficial or extended breaks at work
- take days off work as they do not want to face their monotonous job
- speak negatively about a business, potentially causing customer loss.

Socio-economic background

- Children from higher socio-economic backgrounds are more likely to aspire to higher-paid careers, as they tend to be given access to the supports and educational opportunities required to obtain the necessary qualifications for these professions.
- Children from lower socio-economic backgrounds are less likely to have access to the supports and educational opportunities required for higher-paid careers, and therefore may have lower expectations in terms of career opportunities.

Social contact

- Many people work for social contact, as they get to associate with others who have similar interests. In some cases this may lead to friendships outside the workplace. This interaction gives people a feeling of belonging and enhances self-esteem, which in turn can improve people's attitude to work.
- Loss of social contact due to **redundancy** or retirement can lead to feelings of loneliness or isolation.

Lit Hit
Redundancy means no longer in employment because there is no more work available.

Work ethic

- Work ethic concerns a person's attitudes, feelings and beliefs about work. It includes their attitudes to punctuality, absenteeism, loyalty and motivation.
- Workers exhibiting a good work ethic are usually more likely to attain a job, job promotion or be given more responsibility, as they exhibit qualities such as being hard-working, honest, respectful of authority and willing to learn.
- Work ethic is usually developed at home, e.g. by completing household jobs, and at school, e.g. through study habits.

Working conditions

- A safe, clean, friendly workplace influences attitudes to work, as it creates happy employees, which in turn creates a productive work environment.
- A **hostile** work environment can cause employees to be less motivated. This is especially the case if the hostility is between the employer and management.

Lit Hit
Hostile means unfriendly.

Personal identity and status

- Work gives people a personal identity and status, e.g. doctors and barristers enjoy high status in some communities.
- For many, this identity and status makes them feel valued, which enhances self-esteem. This also causes people to have a more positive attitude towards work.

REMEMBER IT!
'Julie Spent Several Weekends Working Productively.'
Job satisfaction, Socio-economic background, Social contact, Work ethic, Working conditions, Personal identity and status.

? Explain how a low level of job satisfaction might affect the individual. (12) **OL**

Discuss **three** factors that influence a person's attitude to work. (18) **OL**

Assess how intrinsic **and** extrinsic factors affect attitudes to work. (10) **HL**

Identify **and** elaborate on the factors that affect an individual's attitude to work. (15) **HL**

Variations in working conditions

Working hours

- People nowadays tend to work shorter working weeks than in previous decades, due to improved legislation which governs a legal maximum working week of 48 hours.
- Many occupations offer more flexible working hours outside of the conventional nine-to-five day, e.g. flexi-time, part-time work and job-sharing, which have changed the structure of the workplace.
- Many people also complete their working hours from home due to technological advances, e.g. Skype.

Employee participation

- The level of participation employees have in decision-making processes varies from profession to profession.
- Employee participation empowers workers, as they feel valued within a business when their input is given consideration. This benefits a business, as employees have increased confidence, productivity, loyalty and creative thinking when they know their ideas will be taken on board.
- The effectiveness of employee participation is still not valued in many work environments, as managers and business owners still feel they know what decisions are best.

Manual work

- Labour intensity varies, depending on the occupation, e.g. a bricklayer endures more physical labour than a pharmacist.
- In recent times many labour-intensive jobs, e.g. farming, have become safer and less physically strenuous due to technological advances. These advances have also reduced the number of jobs available.

> **Did you know**
>
> Despite improvements in safety, the agriculture sector represented roughly 55% of all work-related deaths in 2014.

Stress levels

- Stress levels vary greatly among professions. Although they are well paid, jobs that carry a lot of responsibility and require long working hours, e.g. jobs in the medical profession or managerial roles, can be stressful.
- Long hours can negatively impact on a person's:
  o productivity
  o physical health, increasing risk of coronary heart disease and cancer
  o mental health, increasing risk of depression
  o family relationships, as long hours prohibit bonding time with spouses and children.

Entitlements

- All employees are entitled to fair treatment and to not be exploited by employers, regardless of the occupation.
- Legislation governs this and ensures people receive legal entitlements including minimum wage, annual leave, maternity leave and sick pay.
- People need to be aware of their entitlements to avoid being exploited.

HL Changes in patterns of work and work availability in Ireland

A number of major social, economic and technological changes have altered the patterns of work and work availability in today's society.

Effect of technological development on industry

For the last fifty to sixty years, technological developments within industry have significantly increased, leading to industrial automation. Automation involves the use of a mechanical device to perform tasks that were previously completed by human beings. This has led to many areas of production only requiring employees in a supervisory capacity to ensure mechanical devices function correctly.

Impact of increased industrial automation on work and work availability

✓ Automation provides a cleaner, healthier and safer work environment, as it eliminates dangerous and physically exerting jobs, e.g. the lifting of heavy materials.

✓ Production can be more accurate, e.g. stitching on jeans.

✓ It increases productivity, as more items can be produced in a shorter time frame.

✓ It reduces working hours for employees, as machinery enhances productivity, increasing leisure time.

✓ It increases job opportunities for third-level educated workers, e.g. mechanical engineers, as they are needed to supervise automation machinery.

✓ It reduces labour costs for employers, as fewer employees are needed. However, the initial cost of automation machinery can be expensive.

✗ It reduces social interaction in the workplace due to reduced numbers of employees.

✗ It increases unemployment rates among unskilled or uneducated workers, as unskilled work is being overtaken by machines.

✗ It reduces job satisfaction, as many jobs simply require the supervising of machines, which can be mundane and repetitive.

> **Did you know** ❓
>
> Due to automation, 600,000 Creme Eggs can be made in a 12-hour shift at a Cadbury chocolate factory.

Decline in primary and secondary industries and increase in tertiary (service) industries

Industry can be divided into three main sectors: primary, secondary and tertiary (service).

Primary industry	Secondary industry	Tertiary (service) industry
Involves the extraction and collection of natural resources. Examples include: • forestry • agriculture • fishing.	Involves processing raw materials from the primary sector into finished products. Examples include: • food production • building construction • automobile construction.	Involves supplying services. Examples include: • education • retail • finance • healthcare.

Changes in the global economy and advances in technology have greatly altered the types of work available. In modern society, far fewer people are involved in jobs within primary and secondary industries, and there has been a move towards positions in the tertiary (service) industry.

Reasons for the decline in primary industry work

• Technological developments have led to fewer employees being required to work on land, as machines now carry out most of the work.

Reasons for the decline in secondary industry work

• Technological developments have led to fewer employees required in manufacturing, e.g. in car or food production.

• Global competition is causing manufacturing factories to relocate to countries where the cost of labour and equipment is low, so they can produce items cheaply, allowing them to compete on global markets.

Reasons for the increase in tertiary (service) work

• Expansion and growth of the world economy is leading to more jobs in telecommunications, education, transport and retail.

• The Irish government are providing grants to multinational companies, e.g. Google, which attracts them to Ireland and increases tertiary employment opportunities.

• More disposable income is enabling people to spend more money on goods or services. This increases the employment opportunities within the tertiary sector, as business success causes employers to need more workers.

• Increased tourism within Ireland. This raises employment in the tertiary sector, as tour guides, hotel managers, etc. are needed.

Increased educational requirements to obtain employment

• Increased educational requirements are now necessary to obtain employment, due to a movement towards jobs within the tertiary (service) industry in recent years.

• To obtain employment in this sector many companies expect employees to have a minimum of a third-level degree. In many instances this may not even be enough, with some companies requiring employees to have a postgraduate qualification. This is causing an ever-increasing number of people to advance to third level. Unfortunately this increase in educational requirements is prohibiting many unskilled workers from acquiring employment opportunities in this sector.

• The well-educated workforce in Ireland is now one of the main factors attracting multinational companies to Ireland. The Irish educational system is highly regarded globally.

 Discuss how patterns of work **and** work availability have been affected by:
  • developing technology
  • the decline in primary and secondary industries and the growth in service industries
  • increased educational requirements. (25) **HL**

Increased participation of women in the workforce

In 1961 women accounted for just 26.4% of the workforce, today this has risen to 55.9%. Many factors have attributed to this increase in women in the workforce.

- **Social acceptance:** under the Marriage Ban 1933, female civil servants, including teachers, had to resign from their jobs when they married, as they were expected to become homemakers. The lifting of this ban and the gradual introduction of anti-discrimination and equality legislation has advanced women's rights in the workplace.

- **Economic necessity:** with the increasing cost of living, it is often necessary for women to participate in paid employment, as dual incomes are needed to meet the basic needs of the family. High rates of male unemployment have also led to women becoming the breadwinners in many households, and men becoming stay-at-home parents.

> **GO FIGURE 12³**
>
> In 1986 only 445 men in Ireland were stay-at-home fathers. Nowadays this has increased, with up to 10,000 men considering themselves stay-at-home fathers.

- **Higher education attainment:** an ever-increasing number of women are advancing to third-level education. This has improved their value on the job market and boosted job prospects, causing women to shift roles from working in the home to working outside the home.

- **Childcare supports:** some workplaces offer crèche facilities. The state also runs the Early Childhood Care and Education (ECCE) scheme, which provides free early childhood care and education for children of pre-school age. This has increased the number of women entering the workforce, as they can avail of affordable childcare.

- **Part-time or job-sharing options:** increased availability of part-time work and job-sharing options has helped women balance work and family responsibilities, enabling them to stay in the workforce after the arrival of children. This can, however, affect pension entitlements on retirement, as not as many hours are worked.

Despite these advances women still experience inequalities in the workplace.

- Women tend to be concentrated in low-paid jobs with little room for promotion, e.g. 80% of clerical workers and 66% of retail workers are women. This is gradually changing, due to increased educational qualifications.

- Fewer women hold jobs with authority, e.g. in roles in government, finance and law enforcement, compared to men. At present only 33% of Irish workers at managerial level are female.

> **?**
>
> Discuss **three** reasons why there are more dual-earner households in modern Ireland. (12) **OL**
>
> Analyse the factors that have contributed to the increased participation rate of women in the Irish labour market. (20) **HL**

Increased flexibility in the workplace

Flexibility in the workplace has come about due to the introduction of flexible working hours.

- **Flexi-time:** allows employees to leave work early or come in early once a certain minimum number of hours are completed, usually over a monthly period. Employees can build up hours to earn days off.
- **Job-sharing:** enables two employees to become part-time and share the work normally fulfilled by one person working full time.
- **Part-time work:** involves employees working fewer hours per week than a full-time job.
- **Parental leave:** a leave of absence from a job for an employee to care for their child or children. 18 weeks' parental leave is available per child. Each parent has an equal separate entitlement to parental leave.
- **Career break:** a period of time where an employee chooses not to work, typically to raise children or pursue other interests, e.g. travel. A person is not paid if they take a career break.

Many people also have the option nowadays to work from home, due to increases and improvements in technology and communications, e.g. email and Skype.

> **?** Discuss, giving examples, how flexibility in working hours has impacted on work/life balance for many people. (20) **HL**

Improved working conditions

Working conditions have improved greatly in all occupations. This has occurred due to the introduction of legislation governing working conditions, minimum wage, employment equality and working hours.

Safety, Health and Welfare at Work Acts 2005 and 2010

- These acts set out the rights and obligations of both employers and employees to maintain health and safety in the workplace.
- Under these acts employers must:
  o provide instruction and training to employees on health and safety, e.g. heavy lifting training for manual workers
  o provide protective clothing and equipment to employees, e.g. eye goggles in a laboratory.
- Under these acts employees must:
  o not engage in improper conduct or behaviour likely to put the welfare of themselves or others at risk
  o not be under the influence of drink or drugs in the workplace.
- These acts stipulate fines and penalties for breaches of the health and safety legislation. The Health and Safety Authority monitors compliance with this legislation.

National Minimum Wage Act 2000

For information on the national minimum wage see page 545.

Employment Equality Acts 1998–2015

- These acts deal with promoting equality and banning discrimination within employment. Discrimination related to any of the following nine grounds is prohibited: gender, civil status, family status, age, race, religion, disability, sexual orientation or membership of the Travelling community.
- Some areas of employment that are covered by this legislation include equal pay, access to employment, promotion and dismissal.

Protection of Young Persons (Employment) Act 1996

- This act protects the health of young workers and ensures that work carried out when attending school does not impact on a young person's educational progress.
- It sets minimum age limits for employment, rest intervals and maximum working hours.

	Children (14–15 years)	**Young people (16–17 years)**
Working hours	• Employers cannot employ children aged under 16 in regular, full-time jobs • Children aged between 14 and 15 can complete up to 35 hours' light work during the school holidays per week • Children aged between 14 and 15 can complete up to 40 hours' work as part of an approved work experience per week • Children aged 15 may complete eight hours' of light work a week in school term time • Written permission from a parent is needed before taking up a job • They must provide employers with a copy of their birth certificate as proof of age	• Young people aged between 16 and 17 can complete up to 40 hours' work per week with a maximum of eight hours a day • They must provide employers with a copy of their birth certificate as proof of age
Rest intervals	• A half hour rest break after every four hours	• A half hour rest break after every four and a half hours
Times of work	• Only permitted to work between 8 a.m. and 8 p.m.	• Only permitted to work between 6 a.m. and 10 p.m.
Wage payment	• Paid the national minimum wage of €6.41 per hour (under 18 years of age)	

> **?**
>
> Explain how the rights of young people in part-time work are protected. (10) **OL**
>
> Outline the protection provided by the Protection of Young Persons (Employment) Act, (1996). (10) **OL**
>
> Give **two** examples of how legislation protects the rights of people in employment. (10) **HL**
>
> Discuss how changes in the availability of work have affected individuals and families in Ireland. (20) **HL**
>
> Discuss the impact of social, economic and technological changes on patterns of work and work availability in Ireland. (24) **HL**

The role of unpaid and voluntary work in the community

Role of unpaid work in the community

- Unpaid work that is home based, e.g. caring for an elderly parent, reduces the reliance on state resources, e.g. home nurses, freeing up supports for other people.

Role of voluntary work in the community

- Voluntary work supplies a wide range of services to various disadvantaged and underprivileged groups, e.g. older people and the homeless. Services include financial assistance, advisory assistance and material assistance, e.g. food and clothes.
- Voluntary work complements the work of government departments at a local level, but provides a more personal service, e.g. Focus Ireland provides temporary accommodation to those awaiting social housing.
- Voluntary organisations often run services that should be provided by state funding, e.g. the Ronald McDonald House provides accommodation for families whose children are seriously ill and undergoing medical treatment in hospital.
- Voluntary work creates awareness of social problems, e.g. poverty, by attracting media attention through fundraisers or protests, leading to social change and reform.
- Voluntary organisations offer advice to the government to assist with the development of effective government policies and legislation, e.g. the Simon Community provide input about reducing homelessness nationwide.

Give details of two different types of support provided by voluntary organisations to families when the main wage earner is unemployed. (14) **OL**

Discuss, giving examples, the role of voluntary work in the community. (18) **HL**

Benefits of voluntary work for the volunteer and the community

Benefits of voluntary work for the volunteer

- Voluntary work improves the mood and self-esteem of volunteers, as they participate in rewarding and fulfilling work that makes a difference.
- Volunteers develop key transferable skills, such as communication, patience and teamwork, which will benefit volunteers in paid employment.
- Voluntary work helps build friendships, improving volunteers' sense of belonging and purpose. This social contact may be important, especially for older people volunteering.
- Volunteers develop **empathy**, as they witness difficulties faced by others.

Lit Hit

Empathy is the ability to understand and share another person's feelings.

Benefits of voluntary work for the community

- Voluntary work provides services quickly to those in need in a community, reducing disadvantages for community members.
- Voluntary work improves a community, e.g. by restoring and cleaning the local landscape or by alleviating poverty and social problems.
- Voluntary work creates a sense of community spirit, as volunteers come together to achieve a common goal, e.g. organising a charity fundraiser.
- Voluntary work can create strong friendships and relationships among volunteers, which can create an increased sense of closeness within a community.

Discuss the benefits of voluntary work to:
- the individual and
- the community. (20) **OL**

Evaluate the benefits to be gained from voluntary work by the volunteer. (12) **HL**

WORK

RECONCILING EMPLOYMENT WITH FAMILY RESPONSIBILITIES

Changing patterns in gender roles within the family

A gender role is a behaviour that society expects individuals of either sex to follow. In the past, traditional roles within the family were segregated into male and female gender roles. Men were the breadwinners and worked outside the home, whereas women worked inside the home and were involved with childcare and housework.

In modern times there have been significant changes in roles, due to a growing number of women moving into the workforce and a move towards egalitarian relationships among younger couples. This has led to integrated roles being evident in homes, with parents taking joint responsibility for parenting, childcare and household jobs. A more egalitarian approach has also been taken in family decisions, e.g. financial arrangements, choice of school for children and discipline. Parents are also now more aware of gender stereotyping, so they can adopt a more open approach when dividing household jobs.

The impact of dual-earner families on family life

Dual-earner families involve both parents being engaged in paid employment. Due to a variety of personal, social and economic reasons this is becoming increasingly common among families nowadays.

Advantages and disadvantages of dual-earner households

Advantages	Disadvantages
✓ Increases disposable income available, enabling families to have a higher standard of living and increased financial security ✓ Fathers are more involved in parenting, allowing them to form a closer bond with their children ✓ Fathers are more involved in household tasks, leading to a more egalitarian household. This introduces children to gender equality from a young age. ✓ Children tend to have healthier attitudes towards work and they develop a strong work ethic, as their parents are positive, working role models	✗ Role overload can occur when parents attempt to play several roles at one time. Women, in particular, struggle to find the balance between their careers and being the main homemaker. ✗ Role conflict can occur when the expectations of a person in one role clashes with what is expected in another role. This can cause parents to feel guilty if they let family members down. ✗ Extra responsibilities can fall on older children, e.g. caring for younger siblings or making dinner. This can affect school work. ✗ Children may feel lonely and neglected if spending a lot of time in childcare due to parents working long hours. This can lead to resentment. ✗ Vulnerable family members, e.g. elderly grandparents, may need to be cared for outside the home in nursing homes. This can create friction and resentment within families.

> **?** Explain why childcare facilities are required in modern society. (15) **OL**
>
> Discuss the impact of dual-earner families on family life. Refer to:
> - role overload
> - role conflict
> - distribution of parental and home care responsibilities. (20) **OL**
>
> Discuss the impact of dual-earner families on family life. Refer to **each** of the following:
> - distribution of parental duties
> - distribution of home-care responsibilities
> - role conflict. (26) **OL**

Childcare facilities available to parents

As the number of dual-earner families has increased in recent years there is an ever-increasing number of families who need to avail of childcare facilities. Options available include:

- childminders
- day-care centres (nurseries and crèches)
- playgroups and playschools
- Montessori schools
- Naíonraí

➜ For more information on **childcare facilities available to parents** see page 499.

- after-school groups: these are offered in community-based or privately-run childcare facilities that look after primary school children until their parents finish work. During this time younger children may play and socialise, while older children complete their homework with the assistance of supervisors.

> **?** Identify **and** describe **three** child care options that a family with young children could consider. (21) **OL**

Factors to consider when choosing childcare

- **Price:** income level will determine the amount of money available to spend on childcare. Childminders tend to be the most cost-effective form of childcare. Sometimes, when parents weigh up the cost of childcare, they may decide it is more economically viable for one parent to stay at home to mind the child.
- **Environment:** parents need to consider whether they would prefer to keep their child within the home environment with a childminder, or seek childcare outside the home. If seeking childcare outside the home, parents should ensure the premises chosen are hygienic and safe.

- **Age and needs of a child:** due to their young age, babies have more physical, emotional and social requirements than toddlers, so parents need to consider this when choosing childcare. Often a childminder is a more favourable option for babies, as they can ensure more one-to-one attention than a day-care centre. Toddlers may be more suited to childcare outside the home, as they are more independent and can benefit from interacting with other children of the same age. If a child has special needs extra care should be taken when choosing childcare to ensure that their needs are met.
- **Convenience:** childcare needs to be convenient in terms of working hours and proximity to home or work. Often the most convenient option can be a childminder in the family home, as parents do not have to drop or collect their children and childminders can be more flexible if parents' work schedules change.

WORK

- **Experience and qualifications:** parents should obtain references and investigate experience and qualifications of childcare workers. Where possible, they should opt for childcare services that are **accredited**, e.g. Montessori schools are accredited by the Irish Montessori Education Board (IMEB). This will give parents peace of mind, as they will be sure that their chosen childcare option involves people who are capable of looking after their child.

Lit Hit

Accredited means given official approval.

REMEMBER IT!

'PEACE.'

Price, **E**nvironment, **A**ge and needs of a child, **C**onvenience, **E**xperience and qualifications.

Evaluation of two types of childcare options: childminders and day-care centres

Childminders

- Childminders are self-employed people who mind other people's children in their own home or the child's home.
- Specific qualifications are not required, as they can be family members.
- Childminders must be over 18 years of age.

Desirable characteristics of childminders

Childminders should:

- have a love of children and be dedicated to their job
- have the ability to promote a child's learning and development by providing activities and learning experiences suitable for the child's age
- be able to support and care for the emotional, social, intellectual and physical needs of a child
- provide a secure and happy environment in which the health, safety and welfare of the child is assured
- be in good health, free from physical or mental illness, e.g. addiction
- be willing to work in partnership with parents and maintain communication to discuss the child's developments or problems that arise

Did you know

Approximately 70% of Irish parents with a pre-school child use a childminder.

 GO FIGURE

The average national full-time fee for a childminder is €659 per child per month.

HL Advantages and disadvantages of childminders

Advantages	Disadvantages
✓ Often come to the child's home, making it easier for parents to organise their morning schedule	✗ No back-up option for childcare if the childminder is ill. This can affect the family routine
✓ Can give more one-on-one time and individual attention to a child	✗ May not have adequate training to support and care for the child's emotional, social, intellectual and physical needs
✓ A child has a reduced risk of susceptibility to illness, as they are not around large numbers of children	✗ Rearing methods, e.g. how to deal with discipline, may differ from the parents, leading to tension and confusion for the child
✓ Can be more flexible about pick-up and drop-off times if parents' work schedules change	✗ Difficult for parents to monitor and assess the attention and care provided, especially when children are young and not able to communicate with their parents
✓ Can be less expensive than other forms of childcare	

Day-care centres

- Day-care centres include crèches and nurseries.
- They aim to provide a home away from home for young babies, toddlers and children.

Desirable characteristics of day-care centres

Day-care centres should:

- have premises with sufficient indoor and outdoor space for the number of children, and efficient systems of heating, lighting, ventilation and sanitation
- be self-contained, with sleeping areas, nappy changing facilities, play areas and food preparation areas
- be easily accessible for parents and children, but still safe and secure so that children are safe
- be run by trained persons with a love of children who can support and care for their emotional, social, intellectual and physical needs. There must be the appropriate number of adults-to-children to ensure children are adequately supervised and safe.
- provide a hygienic and safe environment to keep children free from danger and illness/ infections, e.g. toys and furniture meet safety requirements
- provide premises that have a wide variety of resources, e.g. age-appropriate toys, so children can learn at their own rate through play in a fun and active environment

GO FIGURE

The national average cost of a full-time baby place in a community crèche is approximately €699 a month, while the average cost of a private crèche is approximately €780 monthly.

HL

Advantages and disadvantages of day-care centres

WORK

Advantages	Disadvantages
✓ All staff members are qualified in childhood education or childcare, so they can adequately support children's needs	✗ Children can find it challenging to settle into a bustling environment with unfamiliar faces, especially if they are used to the quiet of home
✓ Offer a stimulating environment with a variety of resources to enhance a child's development	✗ Large groups of children reduces one-on-one time and individual attention a child may receive from day-care workers
✓ Regulations set minimum health, safety and caregiver standards that must be maintained. This is monitored and inspected by the Child and Family Agency (Tusla), so parents can be assured of high standards.	✗ A child has an increased risk of susceptibility to illness, as they are around large numbers of children
✓ Reliable option, as opening hours and days of operation are known in advance and guaranteed	✗ Operate strict opening hours that may not be suitable for parents who get delayed at work
✓ Children can develop social skills, e.g. sharing and listening, due to interacting and playing in large group situations with other children of the same age	✗ Tends to be an expensive form of childcare

?

Summarise **four** factors that a parent should consider when choosing a preschool. (16) **OL**

Outline the reasons why each of the following is important in crèches / pre-schools:
- adequate levels of supervision • sufficient resources • high levels of hygiene and safety. (18) **OL**

Name **two** types of childcare available in your locality. Outline the key considerations a parent should take into account when evaluating a child care option. (14) **HL**

Chapter 27: Unemployment

UNEMPLOYMENT

6.5

What you will learn:

- **Defining unemployment**
- **Types of unemployment**
- **Unemployment in Ireland**

- **Groups at risk of unemployment**
- **Causes of unemployment**
- **Effects of unemployment**

Defining unemployment

Unemployment occurs when a person actively searching for employment is unable to find work. The term *unemployed* does not include people who make a voluntary decision to not work, e.g. a stay-at-home parent. The unemployment levels in a country reflect the state of the economy. When a country's economy is strong, unemployment figures tend to be low. During times of economic downturn unemployment figure rise.

? Define unemployment. (6) **OL**/(2) **HL**

Types of unemployment

There are two main types of unemployment:

- **short-term unemployment:** when a person is out of work for less than six months
- **long-term unemployment:** when a person is out of work for longer than six months. If long-term unemployment is prevalent in a country it is an indication that the economy is in recession.

HL Unemployment in Ireland

- During the 1980s unemployment rates reached an all-time high of 17.3% in 1985, due to an economic recession.
- Rapid economic growth between 1994 and 2007 reduced unemployment rates to a record low of 3.7% in 2001. This economic boom era became known as the Celtic Tiger.
- In 2008 Ireland's economy started to decline again, causing unemployment to increase and reach 15% in 2012. This caused mass emigration, especially among construction workers and newly qualified graduates unable to get work.

Irish Unemployment Over Time

- At present Ireland's economy is showing signs of recovery, resulting in a reduction in unemployment. However, there is still a long way for Ireland's recovery to go, as currently Ireland has:
  - o an unemployment rate of approximately 8.5%
  - o around 320,000 people currently on the live register.

? Comment on the extent of unemployment in Ireland today. (12) **HL**

Groups at risk of unemployment

Group	Possible reasons
Migrants	• May not have the level of language fluency required to obtain a job • Qualifications may not be recognised by potential employers if obtained in another country • May have sufficient qualifications to work, but experience discrimination by potential employers
Early school leavers	• May have few or no qualifications to obtain jobs • May lack literacy skills necessary to compile a CV, making it difficult to apply for jobs
People with criminal records	• May not be trusted by potential employers
People with illnesses, disabilities or special needs	• May not be physically, mentally or emotionally able to work • May have sufficient qualifications to work, but experience discrimination by potential employers
People who are homeless	• May not have access to communications, e.g. phone or email, making it difficult to apply for jobs, or for potential employers to make contact • May have sufficient qualifications to work, but experience discrimination by potential employers

 Identify **two** groups of people who have difficulty in securing employment **and** discuss reasons for high unemployment among each group named. (18) **HL**

Causes of unemployment

- **Geographical location:** rural areas tend to have higher rates of unemployment, as multinational companies tend to favour urban areas to establish businesses due to better infrastructure and telecommunications.
- **Foreign/global competition:** the increased availability of cheaper imported products has led to reduced demand for goods produced in Ireland. This affects jobs directly in the manufacturing industry and indirectly in the service industry. To compete with competitive global prices many Irish manufacturing factories have relocated to countries where the cost of labour and equipment is low, so that they can produce goods at cheaper prices.

- **Low incentive:** in some cases social welfare payments can be more financially rewarding than wages from low-paid jobs, providing little incentive for the long-term unemployed to return to work. Returning to work could also mean a loss of additional benefits, e.g. Fuel Allowance, reducing incentive even further.
- **Economic recession:** a downturn in the economy results in job losses and increases reliance on social welfare payments. This leads to lower tax revenue for the government to cover the country's running costs.

- **Seasonal factors:** some forms of employment are seasonal, e.g. tourism and fishing in the summer time and retail at Christmas time. During the off-peak season large numbers of staff are made redundant, increasing unemployment.

- **Automation/technological advances:** advances in technology have resulted in automated machines, e.g. self-service checkouts, being able to complete work previously done by people. This leads to higher unemployment rates, especially among unskilled workers.

- **Demand for products and services:** reduced disposable income, especially during times of recession, impacts on the demand for products and services, as individuals' spending power is reduced. This leads to workers being laid off, increasing unemployment. The demand for products and services is lower in rural locations, as they have smaller populations. This can result in higher unemployment rates in these areas.

REMEMBER IT!

'**G**etting **F**ired **L**eaves **E**veryone **S**ad **A**nd **D**own.'

Geographical location, **F**oreign/global competition, **L**ow incentive, **E**conomic recession, **S**easonal factors, **A**utomation/technological advances, **D**emand for products and services.

? '*There were 53,200 males and 32,400 females unemployed in the second quarter of 2005.*' (The Central Statistics Office 2005).

Why, in your opinion, are there more males than females unemployed in 2005? (10) **OL**

Analyse how **each** of the following has impacted on current rates of unemployment:
- geographical location
- the global economy
- the level of demand for products and services. (20) **HL**

Analyse the causes of unemployment. (24) **HL**

Effects of unemployment

On individuals

- **Financial insecurity:** loss of employment can leave individuals unable to pay their bills or rent/mortgage due to lack of regular income, creating financial insecurity. This can lead to mounting debt and the possibly of falling below the poverty line.

- **Loss of identity and status:** when individuals become unemployed they lose the sense of identity and status awarded by their job. This can make them feel undervalued, causing feelings of low self-worth.

- **Social isolation:** unemployment isolates individuals from the social contact that comes with working with others. This can lead to feelings of social isolation and loneliness. Unemployment can also prevent individuals from actively participating in leisure activities and social events due to limited income, further increasing social isolation from peers and family members.

- **Depression and destructive habits:** numerous job refusals and the inability to obtain work can reduce long-term unemployed individuals' self-esteem and create feelings of hopelessness and failure. This can heighten the risk of depression and participation in self-destructive habits such as alcohol and drug abuse. It can also increase suicide rates.

Did you know ?

Research on suicide rates in Ireland has shown that between 2008 and 2012, there were 476 more male suicides than would have been expected had the recession not happened.

On family units

- **Decline in standard of living:** unemployment leaves families reliant on social welfare payments, which often leads to a decline in standards of living as the provision of basic needs may become difficult. This can cause an eventual decline into poverty.

- **Repossession of the family home:** missed mortgage repayments due to loss of employment can cause homes to be repossessed. This leaves families homeless or in emergency accommodation, making it difficult to create a stable home and daily routine.

- **Relationship problems:** the relationship between couples can become strained due to financial stress and worry from unemployment, increasing the risk of relationship problems or marital breakdown. A former breadwinner may also create tension due to the resentment of being unemployed while their partner goes out to work.

- **Decline in education success:** children's school work and concentration in class may be affected due to worrying about their family's financial situation. Teenagers may not achieve their full academic potential if they have to drop out to work to support the family income.

On society

- **Emigration:** due to low levels of work availability, many people are forced to emigrate to find work. This is especially common in rural areas, leading to depopulation, lower birth rates, and isolation of older people.

- **Antisocial behaviour:** unemployment and the resulting boredom can lead to an increase in antisocial behaviour such as drug or alcohol abuse, crime and vandalism. This causes areas in society to develop bad reputations and become unemployment black spots.

- **Increase in taxes:** during times of high levels of unemployment the government must allocate a larger percentage of the budget on social welfare payments. As a result, the government must increase tax levels on those working to cover these costs.

- **Unemployment cycle:** children from unemployed households are more likely to be unemployed themselves, as they are less likely to have access to the same opportunities as a working household, e.g. educational resources. This can create an unemployment cycle in society over generations.

Did you know ?

Between April 2013 and April 2014, 81,900 people emigrated from Ireland.

? Discuss the negative effects of unemployment on **each** of the following:
  - young adults
  - families with young children. (18) **OL**

  Assess the effects of decreasing employment opportunities in Ireland today. **(10) HL**

  Discuss the effects of unemployment on:
  - the individual
  - the family
  - society. (24) **OL**

UNEMPLOYMENT

Chapter 28:
Leisure

∞ LEISURE
6.4

What you will learn:

- **Defining leisure**
- **Types of leisure activities**
- **Functions and value of leisure**
- **Factors that influence leisure activities**

- **The role of leisure in physical, social and emotional development**
- **Evaluation of leisure facilities available in a community: a fitness centre and a golf club**

Defining leisure

Leisure is the time when a person is free from the demands of work or meeting the necessities of life. This time can be spent on chosen activities that are enjoyable and relaxing.

> **?** Define leisure. (6) **OL/HL**

Types of leisure activities

Sporting activities			Entertainment activities		
• Golf	• Karate	• Yoga	• Reading	• Pottery	• Cinema
• Horse riding	• Soccer	• Basketball	• Bingo	• Guitar	• Drama

The leisure activities offered in communities vary greatly. Cities and towns offer leisure options such as cinemas or bowling that may not be available in rural areas. Leisure activities in rural areas are often linked to the natural surroundings, e.g. fishing or horse riding.

Functions and value of leisure

- Leisure helps individuals relax and unwind from the stresses of demanding daily tasks at home and work. This can benefit mental health and reduce the risk of depression.
- Active leisure pursuits improve physical well-being, e.g. fitness and muscle strength.
- Group or team leisure activities facilitate social interaction. This encourages positive relationships between people of different ages and from different backgrounds.

- Leisure assists the development of new skills, e.g. cooking or painting, which enhances emotional well-being, as people feel satisfaction and raised self-esteem when they overcome new challenges.
- Leisure encourages family bonding if activities are enjoyed with next of kin. This can improve communication and teamwork.
- Leisure alleviates feelings of boredom, as individuals are kept occupied. This may deter young people from participating in antisocial behaviours, e.g. vandalism.
- Leisure allows parents set a good example for children, encouraging them to make the best use of their leisure time.

? Evaluate the importance of leisure for all family members. (10) **OL**

Discuss the reasons why leisure is important in today's society. (15) **OL**

Discuss the function and value of leisure in today's society. (15) **HL**

Factors that influence leisure activities

There are five main factors that influence the leisure activities individuals opt to partake in: social influences, cultural influences, age, gender and occupation.

Social influences

- **Income:** individuals with little disposable income may choose leisure activities that are inexpensive or free, e.g. walking. Individuals with more disposable income may be able to participate in more costly leisure activities, e.g. attending a gym or a golf club.
- **Location:** the availability of leisure activities in a local area will influence leisure pursuits chosen. Urban areas tend to have more choice and range of leisure activities, e.g. swimming or bowling, due to larger numbers of people availing of them.

▲ TRX

- **Trends:** leisure activities chosen can follow trends, usually decided by media and celebrities. Some current popular activities include: zumba and TRX (suspension training). Trends come and go quickly and are usually replaced by a new **fad**.
- **Social division:** in the past, social division influenced leisure pursuits chosen, e.g. horse racing and cricket were mainly pursued by higher socio-economic groups. Today these activities are enjoyed across the social divide.

Lit Hit
A fad is a temporary enthusiasm or a craze.

? State the impact of the recession on family leisure activities. (10) **OL**

Cultural influences

- **Sporting culture:** certain sports and games are associated with specific countries, e.g. hurling with Ireland and American football with the United States, influencing choice of leisure activities.
- **Dance culture:** certain dancing styles are associated with specific countries, e.g. Irish dancing in Ireland and flamenco in Spain, influencing choice of leisure activities.

▲ American football

- **Family culture:** children's choice of leisure activities is often influenced by the leisure activities of their parents. For example, a child who is raised in a household where both parents play a musical instrument, may also choose to participate in music as a leisure pursuit.

Age

- Age greatly influences time available for leisure activities. Young people and retired people tend to have fewer commitments and more time to spend on leisure activities in comparison to young parents with children.
- The amount of disposable income available for leisure can vary by age. Young families tend to have less money to spend on leisure activities as they have childcare costs, which are not encountered by individuals with no children.
- Leisure interests chosen can vary depending on age. Children and teenagers tend to opt for physically active or technology-based leisure activities, e.g. basketball or playing Xbox, in comparison to adults or older people who may choose more social or sedentary-based activities, e.g. golf or crochet.
- Some leisure activities are regarded as too dangerous for children, e.g. children under the age of ten cannot scuba-dive, prohibiting their participation.

▲ Crochet

Gender

- Nowadays **stereotyping** is not permitted in leisure activities, although some are still dominated by one gender, e.g. mixed martial arts and fishing by males and ballet and embroidery by females.

> **Lit Hit**
> Stereotyping is a fixed belief about a particular group or class of people.

▲ Mixed martial arts

- The amount of time available for leisure activities is often influenced by gender. Women who are working tend to have less time for leisure than working males, as they often take on the main duties of the homemaker as well as being in full-time work.

Occupation

- The amount of time available for leisure pursuits is influenced by occupation. A person who works part-time will have more time for leisure pursuits compared to a person who completes shift work or overtime. The availability of career breaks and job-sharing has allowed more time for some people to participate in leisure activities.
- The type of work a person participates in also impacts leisure choices, as people often choose activities that contrast with their job. For example, a sedentary worker may opt for an active leisure activity to expel energy at the end of a day, in comparison to a person in a highly active job who many opt for a relaxing activity.
- Leisure pursuits chosen can be an extension of work for some, e.g. playing a round of golf could be combined with discussing a business deal.

> **?** Give an account of **three** factors that influence family leisure patterns. (15) **OL**
>
> Describe how (a) age and (b) gender impact on a person's choice of leisure activities. (12) **HL**
>
> Outline how social and cultural influences impact on a person's choice of leisure activities. (15) **HL**

REMEMBER IT!
'**S**ome **C**hoose **A**ctive **G**ames **O**nly.'
Social influences, **C**ultural influences, **A**ge, **G**ender, **O**ccupation.

The role of leisure activities in physical, social and emotional development

Physical development

- Active leisure activities can contribute to physical development, as they help to improve fitness, develop muscle strength and control weight.
- As many active leisure activities are participated in outdoors, they can aid general good health and well-being, since fresh air strengthens the immune system.

Social development

- Group or team-based leisure activities can enable individuals to:
  - meet people and make new friends. This is especially important for people who have retired as it reduces the risk of loneliness and depression
  - develop cooperation and communication skills.
- When leisure activities are completed as a family it can encourage bonding, which strengthens relationships, enhancing closeness.
- Many leisure activities require a leader, e.g. a team captain or a chairperson. This can enable individuals to develop their leadership skills and gain confidence to express and form opinions.
- Listening skills can be enhanced through leisure activities, such as the cinema or quizzes.

Emotional development

- A person's self-esteem and confidence can be improved by participating in leisure activities are that competitive or provide a challenge to overcome, e.g. a basketball match, as they feel a sense of pride in their achievement.
- Many leisure activities, e.g. yoga and listening to music, provide an opportunity to relax and unwind from a stressful day. This can benefit mental health and reduce the risk of depression.
- A sense of belonging can be obtained through group or team-based leisure pursuits. This is fundamental to an individual's sense of happiness and mental well-being.
- Winning and losing during competitive leisure activities, e.g. football, can help people cope with the successes and failures of everyday life.

> **?** Discuss the importance of leisure activities for teenagers with reference to:
> - physical development   • social development   • emotional development. (24) **OL**
>
> Discuss, giving examples, the role of leisure activities in personal development. Refer to the following factors:
> - physical   • social   • emotional. (18) **HL**

LEISURE

Evaluation of leisure facilities available in a community: a fitness centre and a golf club

	Fitness centre	Golf club

Facilities offered	• Fully equipped gym • Exercise classes, e.g. circuits and box fit • A sports hall • AstroTurf football pitches for indoor soccer • Changing facilities	• 9- or 18-hole golf course • Pitching and putting practice green • Equipment shop • Trolley and buggy hire • Changing facilities
Membership fee and ongoing costs	• Costs can range between approximately €300 and €700 for 12 months. This enables members to get free access to most facilities. • Family membership rates are available and family members and friends can attend the gym with a member for a reduced rate • Gym gear, e.g. runners and weights gloves, need to be purchased, which can be expensive	• Costs can range between approximately €150 to €8,000 for 12 months. This enables members to get free access to most facilities. • Family membership rates are available and family members and friends can play with a member for a reduced rate • Golf clubs, balls, shoes, etc. need to be purchased, which can be expensive • Competition entry may require a fee
Value for money	• Many activities are provided for in a single area, e.g. fitness classes and gym equipment • Needs to be used regularly to be financially good value • Can be very busy at peak times, e.g. 7–8 a.m. or 6–8 p.m., making it difficult to get the gym equipment desired • Can be used in all weather conditions	• Needs to be regularly used to be good value • Access may be restricted on certain days for competitions • Can be closed if weather conditions are bad

Time required	• Varies, depending on the chosen activity, e.g. exercise classes usually take one hour	• Varies, depending on the number of holes, difficulty and size of the course. On average 18 holes of golf takes four hours.
Physical benefits	• Improves fitness • Controls weight • Increases muscle development • Boosts energy levels • Promotes cardiovascular health	• Promotes cardiovascular health • Promotes muscle toning • Enhances the immune system due to fresh air • Enhances balance control and posture

Did you know ?

A fast-paced fitness class can burn approximately 570 calories per hour.

Did you know ?

Playing 18 holes of golf and carrying your clubs can burn almost 2000 calories.

Emotional benefits	• Reduces stress • Promotes relaxation • Provides a sense of achievement, e.g. a personal best on the treadmill or a hole in one
Social benefits	• Provides an opportunity to meet new people and possibly make new friends • Allows people the opportunity to set up social contacts for other leisure activities
Value to the community	• Provides employment, e.g. gym supervisor and reception staff • Only benefits those who can afford it, low-income families may not be able to avail of a membership • Creates community links, especially in rural areas, as many local people might avail of the facility

?

Name **and** evaluate **two** leisure facilities popular with retired people. (12) **HL**

Name and evaluate **two** leisure facilities available in your community. Refer to:
• cost and value for money
• the range of facilities offered. (18) **HL**

LEISURE

Chapter 29: Poverty

POVERTY

6.6.1, 6.6.2, 6.7

What you will learn:

- **Defining poverty**
- **Types of poverty**
- **Income poverty**
- **Deprivation**
- **The extent and distribution of poverty in Ireland today**
- **Causes of poverty**

- **Effects of poverty**
- **Statutory and community responses to create employment**
- **Schemes to reduce expenditure for low-income families**
- **Statutory and community/voluntary responses to eliminate poverty**

CONCEPTS OF POVERTY AND CAUSES AND EFFECTS OF POVERTY

Defining poverty

People are living in poverty if their income and resources (material, cultural and social) are so inadequate as to preclude them from having a standard of living which is regarded as acceptable by Irish society generally. As a result of inadequate income and resources people may be excluded and marginalised from participating in activities which are considered the norm for other people in society. (Government of Ireland, 1997)

At present, approximately 698,000 people are living in poverty in Ireland. Of this figure, approximately 230,000 are children.

> **?** State what you understand by poverty. (4) **OL**

Types of poverty

There are two types of poverty: absolute poverty and relative poverty.

Absolute poverty	Relative poverty
• Occurs when people are severely deprived of basic human needs, e.g. food, safe drinking water, sanitation facilities, medical care and shelter. As a result people struggle to stay alive. **Did you know ?** More than 1.3 billion people live in absolute poverty. • Some people in Ireland experience this type of poverty, e.g. those experiencing homelessness, but it is most common in developing nations	• Occurs when a person's income is less than what is needed to maintain the general standard of living expected in the society in which they live. As a result people have a low standard of living and are excluded from participating in activities that are considered normal for other people in a particular society. • Relative poverty levels vary from country to country.

> **?** Explain the difference between relative poverty **and** absolute poverty. (12) **OL**
>
> Define each of the following: • relative poverty • absolute poverty. (10) **HL**

Income poverty

Income poverty occurs when people are living below the poverty line. The poverty line is the estimated minimum level of income necessary to maintain a basic standard of living. If individuals and families are living below the poverty line they generally have a poor standard of living.

The poverty line varies from country to country. It is usually measured relative to the income levels of a country. In Ireland, the poverty line is an income of 60% of the median income (the mid-point on the scale of all incomes in the State, from the highest to the lowest). This is considered the minimum weekly disposable income that individuals or families need to be outside poverty. People whose incomes fall below this line are said to be at risk of poverty. At present 700,000 Irish people are at risk of poverty.

Minimum weekly disposable income required to avoid poverty in 2015	
Household	Weekly poverty line
1 adult	€201.74
1 adult + 1 child	€268.31
1 adult + 2 children	€334.88
2 adults	€334.88
2 adults + 1 child	€401.46
2 adults + 2 children	€468.03

Deprivation

Deprivation occurs when people fail to own items or carry out activities that are considered to be basic necessities in a society. It is measured using a deprivation index, which contains a list of items and activities that are generally taken to be the norm in a particular society. In Ireland, eleven items and activities are used to construct the deprivation index. Examples include being unable to afford:

- two pairs of strong shoes
- a meal with meat, chicken or fish every second day
- a warm, waterproof coat
- to keep the home adequately warm
- to replace worn-out furniture
- to buy presents for family or friends at least once a year.

If individuals and families are without two or more of these due to shortage of money they are said to be in deprivation. At present 1.4 million people are experiencing deprivation in Ireland.

In Ireland, when a person's income is below the poverty line and they cannot afford at least two deprivation indicators, consistent poverty occurs. At present over 376,000 people are living in consistent poverty in Ireland. Of this figure, nearly 140,000 are children.

The extent and distribution of poverty in Ireland today

Extent of poverty in Ireland

- During the 1980s the number of people living below the poverty line increased, as unemployment rates reached an all-time high of 17.3% due to an economic recession.
- Rapid economic growth between 1994 and 2007 reduced poverty rates, as unemployment rates reached a record low of 3.7% in January of 2001.
- In 2008, Ireland's economy started to decline again, causing unemployment to increase to 15% in 2012. This again increased the number of people living below the poverty line, due to a reliance on social welfare payments and high living costs.
- At present, Ireland's economy is showing signs of recovery, resulting in a reduction in poverty levels. However, there is a long way to go, as Ireland still has one of the highest poverty rates in Europe, with approximately 698,000 people living in poverty and a further 700,000 at risk of poverty of which 211,000 are children.

Distribution of poverty in Ireland

A number of groups within Irish society are more at risk of poverty than others.

Group	Possible reasons
Early school leavers	• May have few or no qualifications, prohibiting work attainment
Older people (66+)	• May be solely reliant on the State Pension as their main income, which is often not enough to meet basic needs
One-parent families	• May be unable to find a job that will provide flexible working hours • Expensive childcare may create a barrier to upskilling or obtaining a job
People with illnesses, disabilities or special needs	• May not be physically, mentally or emotionally able to work • May have sufficient qualifications but experience discrimination by potential employers, prohibiting work attainment
Migrants	• May have sufficient qualifications but experience discrimination by potential employers, prohibiting work attainment • May have to send a large amount of their wages to family in their country of origin, reducing income for themselves
Children	• May be dependent on parents who are unemployed and solely reliant on social welfare payments as their main income, which is often not enough to meet basic needs

POVERTY

> ❓ Identify **three** groups of people most at risk of poverty in Ireland today. Explain why the groups named are affected by poverty. (22) **OL**
>
> Discuss the extent and distribution of poverty in Ireland today. (20) **HL**

Causes of poverty

- **Increasing cost of housing:** increased mortgages and rental prices make it difficult for people to obtain and keep a family home, increasing their risk of poverty. A shortage in social housing is also causing many people to live in poor, overcrowded housing conditions, as this is all they can afford.

- **Family type:** large families experience greater costs and expenses, increasing their risk of poverty as their income must meet a greater number of expenditures. One-parent families also have an increased risk of poverty, due to having only one income or social welfare payments to meet basic needs.

- **Economic recession and unemployment:** high rates of unemployment occur during economic recession. This increases reliance on social welfare payments and, in turn, increases the risk of individuals and families falling below the poverty line.

- **Social problems:** individuals with alcohol, drug or gambling addictions are more likely to spend money on their addictions rather than meeting basic needs, leading to poverty.

- **Lack of education:** individuals with a low level of education are more likely to be unemployed, or employed in low-paid jobs, increasing their risk of poverty.

- **Social policy and the poverty trap:** the social welfare system provides social welfare payments to individuals and families to assist with meeting their basic needs. However, this element of social policy can **perpetuate** poverty, as social welfare payments can sometimes be more financially rewarding than wages from low-paid jobs. As returning to work would represent a financial loss, some people choose to remain dependent on welfare. This situation is known as the poverty trap.

Lit Hit
Perpetuate means to make something last indefinitely.

- **Cycle of poverty/deprivation:** children growing up in poverty are more likely to be poor when they grow up, as they are less likely to have access to certain opportunities, e.g. educational resources and high-quality housing. This can lead to these children:
  - o dropping out of school and taking low-paid jobs or being unemployed
  - o living in poor-quality housing
  - o marrying early and having children at a young age.

When they have their own children this cycle of poverty/deprivation continues to the next generation, perpetuating the problem. The cycle of poverty/deprivation tends to be concentrated in specific geographical locations including inner city areas, large social housing estates, areas of high unemployment and isolated or underdeveloped rural areas.

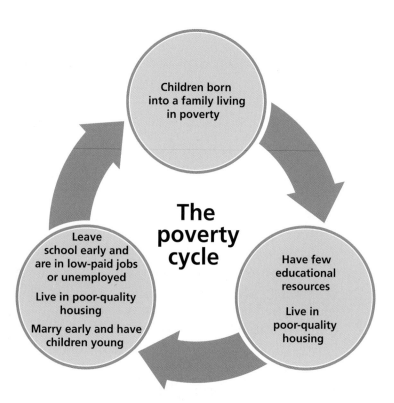

The poverty cycle

- Children born into a family living in poverty
- Have few educational resources / Live in poor-quality housing
- Leave school early and are in low-paid jobs or unemployed / Live in poor-quality housing / Marry early and have children young

REMEMBER IT!

'Irish Families Experience Some Large Scary Costs.'
Increasing cost of housing, **F**amily type, **E**conomic recession and unemployment, **S**ocial problems, **L**ack of education, **S**ocial policy and the poverty trap, **C**ycle of poverty/deprivation.

❓ Give an account of the reasons why poverty continues to be a feature of Irish society. (18) **OL**

Discuss the reasons why poverty continues to be a feature of modern society. In your answer include reference to the cycle of poverty **and** the influence of social policy on poverty. (24) **HL**

Discuss the influence of **each** of the following as a contributory factor to poverty in Ireland today:
- the economic recession   • social policy
- the cycle of deprivation in families and geographical areas. (30) **HL**

Effects of poverty

- **Debt:** many individuals in poverty do not receive enough income to cover the basic cost of living, often leading to debt. This can make access to a loan from a bank difficult, meaning they may rely on moneylenders who charge a higher rate of interest, increasing debt even further in the long term.

- **Depression and destructive habits:** poverty can reduce individuals' self-esteem, creating feelings of hopelessness and failure. This can heighten the risk of depression and participation in self-destructive habits such as alcohol and drug abuse.

- **Social isolation:** poverty can prevent individuals from participating as equals in society, e.g. in leisure and social events, leaving them isolated from families and peers. Children can also experience this at school, as they may be deprived of school extracurricular activities, e.g. school tours.

- **Relationship problems:** poverty can cause arguments over limited finances and spending. This can create tension and upset, increasing the risk of relationship problems or marital breakdown.

- **Decline in standard of living:** Individuals living in poverty are more likely to reside in sub-standard, overcrowded accommodation as this is all they can afford. Houses with damp or mould problems can impact health.

- **Educational disadvantage:** children experiencing poverty are more likely to leave school early without qualifications. This often leads to them obtaining employment in low-paid jobs or being unemployed and reliant on social welfare payments, making them more likely remain living in poverty as adults.

> **?** Describe the effects of poverty on children. (12) **OL**

POVERTY

STATUTORY AND COMMUNITY RESPONSES TO CREATE EMPLOYMENT AND ELIMINATE POVERTY

Statutory responses to create employment

Industrial Development Authority (IDA)

The IDA aims to encourage foreign investment to establish in rural and urban regions throughout Ireland, creating new employment opportunities. To achieve this it provides supports and services to potential foreign investors, including:

IDA Ireland

- information on key business sectors and locations within Ireland
- financial grants
- creating links between international businesses and third-level educational institutions and research centres.

It also encourages existing companies to expand and develop their businesses and create additional employment through the provision of grants and business support.

Why Ireland is an attractive location for foreign investment

- Offers one of the youngest and best-educated populations in Europe
- Offers an English-speaking, flexible and adaptable workforce
- Offers a low corporation tax of 12.5%. This is a tax that must be paid by a corporation based on the amount of profit generated.
- Provides a positive political and economic environment
- Provides easy access to the European market of 500 million people
- Offers grants and funding to encourage foreign investors to establish businesses in Ireland

Did you know
Ireland's corporation tax rate is low compared to other European Union countries, such as Norway at 25% and France at 33.3%.

Enterprise Ireland

For information on Enterprise Ireland see page 85.

SOLAS

SOLAS is the national further education and training authority. It is responsible for funding, planning and coordinating training and further education in Ireland. The further education and training programmes and courses offered include:

- **traineeship programmes:** integrate formal classroom training and workplace coaching with a host employer. Courses offered include childcare and software development
- **specific skills training:** provide job-related skills. Courses offered include retail skills, computer applications and office skills
- **apprenticeship programmes:** integrate formal academic training and workplace training to become craftspeople, e.g. plumbers and motor mechanics.

These programmes and courses help people to gain experience and progress into further training or employment.

Local Enterprise Offices (LEO)

Local Enterprise Offices aim to support business start-ups and develop existing microbusinesses and small businesses in order to increase job creation and sustainable jobs. To achieve this they:

- offer business information, training and grants, e.g. priming grants that are available to micro-enterprises within the first 18 months of start-up
- provide a mentor service to support business development and growth.

Did you know
A microbusiness employs ten people or fewer, compared to a small business which employs 11 to 50 people.

JobBridge

JobBridge is a national internship scheme that provides internship opportunities for unemployed people for six to nine months, enabling them to:

- gain the experience to add to their CV
- gain networking opportunities with business owners and clients
- enhance relevant knowledge and skills.

It aims to break the cycle where people require experience to get a job, but are unable to get experience because they cannot obtain a job. Interns receive an extra €52.50 per week on top of their social welfare payment.

> **?** Name and give details of any **one** organisation that helps the creation of employment in rural areas. (10) **OL**
>
> Name and give details of **one** statutory initiative aimed at creating employment. (12) **HL**
>
> Name and give details of **one** state initiative that encourages foreign investment thus creating employment. (10) **HL**

Community responses to create employment

Cottage industries

Cottages industries are small-scale industries that focus on the creation of home-based goods rather than factory-based goods. These products are often unique and of higher quality than mass-produced equivalents. Traditional Irish cottage industries include lace production and hand embroidery. Contemporary cottage industries include speciality food production, jewellery production and sculpting.

> **Did you know ?**
> There are over 750 artisan and speciality food producers across Ireland.

▲ Handmade-chocolate cottage industry

Co-operatives (co-ops)

Co-ops are farms, businesses or other organisations that are owned and run jointly by the members, who share all the profits or benefits. Members invest shares in the business to provide finances for a strong and efficient operation. All profits, after bills are paid and money is set aside for operations, are returned to co-op members. Co-ops are particularly successful in agricultural industries, e.g. horticulture, fishing and dairy. Other areas where co-ops are established include credit unions, housing and childcare.

> **Did you know ?**
> Kerry Group is one of the most successful dairy co-ops in Ireland.

POVERTY

Schemes to reduce expenditure for low-income families

Medical cards

Medical cards are issued by the Health Service Executive (HSE). Holders are entitled to a range of health services free of charge, including doctor visits, certain dental, ophthalmic (eye), and aural (ear) health services and hospital visits and they only need to pay a €2.50 charge per item dispensed on medical card prescriptions (up to a maximum charge of €25 per family per month). Parents or guardians of children with medical cards are also exempt from paying for state examination fees.

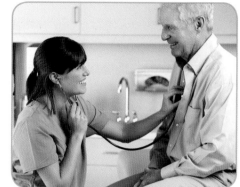

School Books Grant Scheme

This scheme is available in state primary and post-primary schools to help with the cost of school books. This scheme is mainly aimed at pupils from low-income families and families experiencing financial hardship. Funding comes from the Department of Education and Skills. Principals can use this funding to:

- establish a textbook rental scheme, whereby students can rent school books from the school each year for a small fee
- help individual students to buy books.

Fuel Allowance

This allowance helps with the cost of heating homes during the winter months. Those eligible include people dependent on long-term social welfare payments and people who are unable to provide for their own heating needs. The fuel allowance is €22.50 per week and the scheme operates for 26 weeks from October to April.

Other schemes to reduce expenditure for low-income families

- Back to School Clothing and Footwear Allowance
- Housing Assistance Payment (HAP)
- Mortgage Allowance Scheme

➜ For information on the **Back to School Clothing and Footwear Allowance**, the **Housing Assistance Payment (HAP)** and the **Mortgage Allowance Scheme** see pages 509, 304 and 304.

? Name **and** give details of **one** social welfare support/benefit paid to families with children. (9) **OL**

Name and give details of any **one** Government scheme that helps to reduce expenditure for low-income families. (10) **OL**

Name and give details of **two** government schemes that reduce expenditure for low-income families. (10) **HL**

Statutory responses to eliminate poverty

Social welfare assistance and benefits

The Department of Social Protection aims to eliminate poverty by providing the groups most vulnerable to poverty with a number of social welfare payments and benefits including:

- Jobseeker's Allowance/Benefit
- Child Benefit
- One-Parent Family Payment
- Supplementary Welfare Allowance
- Family Income Supplement.

→ For more information on **social welfare assistance and benefits** see page 273.

National minimum wage

The national minimum wage was introduced in April 2000 to ensure employees receive a minimum rate of pay for work, so employers can not exploit them and to reduce poverty. Experienced employees (those who have had an employment of any kind in any two years over the age of 18) are entitled to €9.15 per hour. Minimum wage rates can vary in accordance with the national budget.

Did you know ?

Ireland has the fifth-highest minimum wage in Europe, with Ukraine having the lowest at €0.44 per hour.

Social Inclusion and Community Activation Programme (SICAP)

This programme aims to reduce poverty and promote social inclusion and equality among the most disadvantaged individuals in society, e.g. people with disabilities and the unemployed. To achieve this it:

- increases access to formal and informal educational development activities
- increases people's work-readiness and employment prospects through advice and guidance supports and training initiatives
- provides support, advice and access to start-up funds to those wanting to set up their own business or social enterprise.

SICAP

Social Inclusion & Community Activation Programme

RAPID (Revitalising Areas by Planning, Investment and Development) programme

This programme aims to improve the quality of life and the opportunities available to residents in 51 of the most disadvantaged communities in Irish cities and towns. To achieve this it delivers additional facilities and services and/or redesigns current ones so they are more appropriate to the needs of the community, including:

- cultural, sports and recreational facilities, e.g. playgrounds
- family supports, e.g. addiction counselling
- education services, e.g. adult and second-chance education
- public safety, e.g. the installation of CCTV to address antisocial behaviour.

Other statutory responses

- Money Advice and Budgeting Service (MABS)
- SOLAS

→ For information on **MABS** and **SOLAS** see pages 281 and 542.

Write an informative note on the Family Income Supplement (FIS). (10) **OL**

Give a brief account of **three** different payments provided by the Department of Social and Family Affairs to families with children. (18) **OL**

Give an account of **two** statutory initiatives aimed specifically at eliminating poverty in Ireland. (16) **HL**

Community/voluntary responses to eliminate poverty

Society of St Vincent de Paul (SVP)

The Society of St Vincent de Paul (SVP) is the largest voluntary charitable organisation in Ireland, with over 11,000 volunteers. It works to:
- promote social justice and support the creation of a more caring society
- provide financial, material and advisory assistance to those experiencing poverty and social exclusion.

Did you know

The SVP spend in excess of €70 million per year providing assistance to individuals and families in need.

Services provided	Sources of funding
• Visits to people in nursing homes, hospitals and prisons • Hostels and social-housing projects for people who are homeless • Childcare, homework and breakfast clubs in their resource centres • Day-care services for older people so that they can continue to live independently in their own homes • Education grants to enable individuals receive equal educational opportunities	• Corporate and public donations • Government support for various projects tackling social inclusion, e.g. the building and maintenance of social housing • Contributions from volunteers at weekly meetings • Charity shops

Focus Ireland

Focus Ireland works to prevent people becoming, remaining or returning to homelessness by:
- offering advice, support, education and housing to help people to have and keep a home
- campaigning for the rights of people experiencing homelessness and the prevention of homelessness.

Services provided	Sources of funding
• Emergency short- and long-term accommodation for people out of homes • An outreach team to work with people experiencing homelessness on Dublin's streets, helping to connect them with services that will help them • A coffee shop in Temple Bar, Dublin, which provides affordable meals for people experiencing homelessness • A Preparation for Education Training and Employment (PETE) programme for people aged 18 and over to prepare them for education and training • An extension day service where people aged between 16 and 25 who are experiencing homelessness can get something to eat, do their laundry and get advice and information	• Corporate and public donations • Government funding • Sale of Christmas cards • Charity shops 

? Name and give details of **one** voluntary initiative which helps to alleviate the effects of poverty in the community. (12) **OL**

Write an informative note on one national voluntary organisation which works with individuals/families experiencing poverty. (10) **HL**

Index

A

abattoirs 255
acid rain 453
adolescents 60, 373, 378
adulteration 252
adults 61, 505–6
advertising 4, 329
Advertising Standards Authority of Ireland
    (ASAI) 341
aesthetic awareness of food 180–3
agri-food industry 82
air pollution 347
alcohol 80, 199
aluminium 195, 444
amino acids 6–10
anaemia 5, 38–41, 46, 59
Annual Percentage Rate (APR) 287
anorexia nervosa 60
anti-social behaviour 529
antibodies 58
antioxidants 202, 204
architects 409
attic insulation 472–3

B

babies 37, 58
Back to Education Allowance (BTEA) 511
Back to School Clothing and Footwear
    Allowance 509
bacteria 216–21
    advantages/disadvantages 221
    classification 219–20
    endospore-forming 218
    food spoilage 224
    food poisoning 224–7
    growth of 216–7
    reproduction of 217
    structure of 217
    toxins 218
baking 165, 175–6, 179
barcoding 201
basidiomycetes (large fungi) 214
bed linen 441
beds 438–9
Beef and Lamb Quality Assurance Scheme
    (BLQAS) 98
BER (Building Energy Rating) 400, 456
beri beri 42
beta-carotene 34–5
Better Energy Warmer Homes Scheme (BEWH) 412
Billpay 284
biomass 107
blinds 440
blood 38, 46
BMI classifications 70
BMR (basal metabolic rate) 52
bone diseases 37, 44
Bord Bia 85, 98, 116
Bord Iascaigh Mhara (BIM) 85
bowel disorders 65–6
breastfeeding 58, 62
budgeting 278–81
builders 409
Building Control Authority 411
Building Control Regulations (1997–2013) 400
Building Controls Act (1990) 412
Building Energy Rating (BER) 400, 456
Building Regulations Act (1991) 411
bulimia nervosa 60
butter 125–6

C

calcium 44–5, 76, 80–1
canning 104, 145, 237–8, 241–2
Capital Acquisitions Tax 386
carbohydrates 17–24, 59
    absorption of 24
    biological functions of 23
    classification of 18–19

and dietary disorders 23
digestion of 24
elemental composition of 17
energy value of 23
heat, effects of 23
Reference Intake (RI) 23
utilisation of 24
care labels (on textiles) 323–4
caramelisation 20, 160
carpets 429–30
central heating 469–71
centrifuge 108
cereals 133–8
    dietetic value of 134–5
    products 137–8
    types of 133
charge cards 285
cheese 126–30
    classification of 126–7
    composition/value of 127–8
    culinary uses of 130
    production 128–9
chemical preservation 235, 238, 241
cheques 282
childcare 518, 523–5
Childcare Act (1991) 385
childminders 524
children
    child-parent relationships 376–7
    energy requirements 53
    IT skills 495
    nutritional requirements 59
    and poverty 538
    rights within the family 377
    roles/responsibilities 373
Children and Family Relationships Act (2015) 359
cholesterol 70
Chorleywood processing 179
chutney 234–5
cirrhosis 61
Citizens Information Board 340
climate change 453
clothing, functions of 320
co-operative housing 402–3
co-operatives 543
coal 450, 454
coeliac disease 74
colloidal solution 30
colour/colour schemes 413–15
communications technology 495
Competition and Consumer Protection
    Commission 340
condensation 477
Consumer Credit Act (1995) 287, 300
Consumer Protection Act (2007) 336, 339
consumers
    choices 328–9
    complaints procedure 342
    impulse buying 331–2
    and information sources 335
    and online shopping 331, 333
    protection agencies 340–1
    protection legislation 338–40
    research 334–5
    responsibilities 337
    and retail psychology 332
    rights 336
    shopping patterns 333
    symbols (quality/safety/hazard) 343
Consumers' Association of Ireland (CAI) 341
convalescents 52, 64
convenience foods 190–1
convulsions 44
cook-chill food production 191–2
cooker hoods 479
cooking methods 160–7
    baking 165, 175–6, 179
    barbecuing 166
    boiling 161
    braising 163
    dry 165–6

frying 167
grilling 166
moist 161–4
poaching 161
pressure cooking 163–4
roasting 165
steaming 162
stewing 162
copper 443
coronary heart disease (CHD) 69–70
cottage industries 543
cream 123–4
cream substitutes 124
credit 284–7
credit cards 285
credit transfer/giro 284
creditors 286
crystallisation 20
culture 2, 264, 269, 353
curtains 439–40

D

dairy spreads 152
day-care centres 525
debit cards 282
deficiency diseases 5
    bone diseases 37
    neural tube defects (NTDs) 41
    pellagra 43
    scurvy 39
    see also anaemia; dietary deficiencies
deforestation 344
dehydration 145, 235, 239, 241
DEIS (Delivering Equality of Opportunity in Schools)
    508, 510
denaturation 12
dental disease 37, 39, 44, 73
Department of Agriculture, Food and the Marine 85,
    253–4
Department of Health 85, 254
Department of Housing, Planning, Community and
    Local Government 302
Department of Social Protection 273
deprivation 537
detergents 322
dextrinisation 22, 160
diabetes mellitus 71–2
dietary deficiencies 65–7
    calcium 44
    folate/folic acid 41
    iodine 48
    iron 39, 46
    potassium 49
    sodium (salt) 49
    vitamins 35–43
    zinc 48
dietary disorders 23, 32
dietary excesses 68–73
dietary guidelines see nutritional guidelines
diets
    Irish diet 77–81
    modified diets 74–6
digestive system 15
direct debits/standing orders 283
Disability Access Route to Education (DARE) 510
disaccharides 18
divorce 370
Domestic Violence Act (1996) 385
draught insulation 475
duvets 441

E

Early Childhood Care and Education Scheme
    (ECCE) 500
Early Start Pre-School Programme 500
eating disorders 60
eating patterns 3, 77–8
education 496–511
    access initiatives 509–11
    achievement 498

Acknowledgements

The Publisher wishes to thank Elaine Quinn for her work on some original chapters.

Photographs, Logos and Illustrations:

3drenderedlogos.com/Alamy Stock Photo; Accord; ACORN 1/Alamy Stock Photo; Acreagemedia | Dreamstime.com; Advertising Standards Authority for Ireland: ASAI; age fotostock/Alamy Stock; Photo; ALEX HYDE/SCIENCE PHOTO LIBRARY; Alex Segre/Alamy Stock Photo; allesalltag/Alamy Stock Photo; An Bord Pleanála; An Post; Andrew Paterson/Alamy Stock Photo; Anthony Dunn/Alamy Stock Photo; Art Directors & TRIP/Alamy Stock Photo; Art of Food/Alamy Stock Photo; ASP Food/ Alamy Stock Photo; Aurora Photos/Alamy Stock Photo; Bigstock; BIOPHOTO ASSOCIATES/SCIENCE PHOTO LIBRARY; Blend Images/Alamy Stock Photo; Bon Appetit/Alamy Stock Photo; Bord Bia; Bord Iascaigh Mhara; British Retail Photography/ Alamy Stock Photo; BSI Kitemark™; BSIP SA/Alamy Stock PhotoBubbles Photolibrary/Alamy Stock Photo; By Ian Miles-Flashpoint Pictures/Alamy Stock Photo; Camera Press Ltd/Alamy Stock Photo; CanStock; capt.digby/Alamy Stock Photo; Carolyn Jenkins/Alamy Stock Photo; CBsigns/Alamy Stock Photo; Charlie Newham/Alamy Stock Photo; Chris Pancewicz/ Alamy Stock Photo; Chris Pearsall/Alamy Stock Photo; Christopher Nash/Alamy Stock Photo; Citizens Information; Cluid Housing; Clynt Garnham Food & Drink/Alamy Stock Photo; Consumers' Association of Ireland; Cultura Creative (RF)/ Alamy Stock Photo; Cultura RM/Alamy Stock Photo; DARE; Dave G. Houser/Alamy Stock Photo; David J. Green - lifestyle themes/Alamy Stock Photo; David Lee/Alamy Stock Photo; deefish/Alamy Stock Photo; DELOCHE/SCIENCE PHOTO LIBRARY; Department of Agriculture, Food and the Marine; Department of Health; Department of the Environment, Community and Local Government; Design Pics Inc/Alamy Stock Photo; Dorling Kindersley ltd/Alamy Stock Photo; DR HAROUT TANIELIAN/ SCIENCE PHOTO LIBRARY; DR M.A. ANSARY/SCIENCE PHOTO LIBRARY; Dragomir Misina/Alamy Stock Photo; Dunca Daniel Mihai/Alamy Stock Photo; Ed Brown/Alamy Stock Photo; Edd Westmacott/Alamy Stock Photo; Educate Together; EIQA Q Mark; Elizabeth Whiting & Associates/Alamy Stock Photo; Enable Ireland; ENFO; Enterprise Ireland; EU Ecolabel; evan Hurd/Alamy Stock Photo; Everett Collection Historical/Alamy Stock Photo; FeedStock/Alamy Stock Photo; Food and Drink Photos/Alamy Stock Photo; Foodcollection.com/Alamy Stock Photo; foodfolio/Alamy Stock Photo; FORGET Patrick/ SAGAPHOTO.COM/Alamy Stock Photo; frans lemmens/Alamy Stock Photo; FRIEDRICH SAURER/SCIENCE PHOTO LIBRARY; G&D Images/Alamy Stock Photo; Gary Dermody; geogphotos/Alamy Stock Photo; GoodMood Photo/Alamy Stock Photo; Guaranteed Irish; HEAR; Helen Sessions/Alamy Stock Photo; Hero Images Inc./Alamy Stock Photo; Holmes Garden Photos/ Alamy Stock Photo; Ian Allenden/Alamy Stock Photo; Ian Dagnall/Alamy Stock Photo; IDA Ireland; imageBROKER/Alamy Stock Photo; Images & Stories/Alamy Stock Photo; incamerastock/Alamy Stock Photo; Irish Universities Nutrition Alliance; jackie ellis/Alamy Stock Photo; Janine Wiedel Photolibrary/Alamy Stock Photo; Jeff Gilbert/Alamy Stock Photo; Jochen Tack/ Alamy Stock Photo; Joe Belanger/Alamy Stock Photo; John Boud/Alamy Stock Photo; John Henshall/Alamy Stock Photo; Johnstones Trade Paints; Juice Images/Alamy Stock Photo; Justin Kase ztwoz/Alamy Stock Photo; Kathleen Ryan; keith morris/Alamy Stock Photo; Ken Welsh/Alamy Stock Photo; Kevin Wheal/Alamy Stock Photo; kris Mercer/Alamy Stock Photo; Kristoffer Tripplaar/Alamy Stock Photo; Lenscap/Alamy Stock Photo; Liam White/Alamy Stock Photo; Loop Images Ltd/ Alamy Stock Photo; Love Irish Food; MABS; macana/Alamy Stock Photo; Magimix; Malcolm Case-Green/Alamy Stock Photo; Mark Collinson/Alamy Stock Photo; Martina Nee; Matthew Taylor/Alamy Stock Photo; Maurice Savage/Alamy Stock Photo; Mediablitzimages/Alamy Stock Photo; Michael Griffin/Alamy Stock Photo; Mick Sinclair/Alamy Stock Photo; Mike Abrahams/ Alamy Stock Photo; Mike Abrahams/Alamy Stock Photo; Miriam Heppell/Alamy Stock Photo; Mode Images/Alamy Stock Photo; Nabco - Co-operative Housing Ireland; National Standards Authority of Ireland; neil hardwick/Alamy Stock Photo; Neil Overy/Alamy Stock Photo; Neil Setchfield/Alamy Stock Photo; Newscast Online/Alamy Stock Photo; Nigel Cattlin/ Alamy Stock Photo; Nobó; Oliver Ring/Alamy Stock Photo; PBimages/Alamy Stock Photo; Peter Alvey People/Alamy Stock Photo; Peter Cavanagh/Alamy Stock Photo; Phanie/Alamy Stock Photo; Phil Crean A/Alamy Stock Photo; Phil Degginger/ Alamy Stock Photo; PhotoAlto sas/Alamy Stock Photo; Picture Partners/Alamy Stock Photo; PROBAN®; Rachel Husband/ Alamy Stock Photo; Radharc Images/Alamy Stock Photo; RealFood/Alamy Stock Photo; Rehab Group; Relationships Ireland; RGB Ventures/SuperStock/Alamy Stock Photo; Richard Levine/Alamy Stock Photo; Richard Wayman/Alamy Stock Photo; Rob Wilkinson/Alamy Stock Photo; Robert Convery/Alamy Stock Photo; rumal/Alamy Stock Photo; russ witherington/Alamy Stock Photo; safefood; Science Photo Library/Alamy Stock Photo; Science Photo Library/Alamy Stock Photo; sciencephotos/ Alamy Stock Photo; sciencephotos/Alamy Stock Photo; sciencephotos/Alamy Stock Photo; ScotStock/Alamy Stock Photo; shinypix/Alamy Stock Photo; Shutterstock; SICAP; Sinéad Keogh; ST. MARY'S HOSPITAL MEDICAL SCHOOL/SCIENCE PHOTO LIBRARY; Stephen Barnes/Gluten Free/Alamy Stock Photo; Steven May/Alamy Stock Photo; Stocktrek Images, Inc./Alamy Stock Photo; Sustainable Energy Authority of Ireland; T.M.O.Buildings/Alamy Stock Photo; Teagasc; Ted Foxx/Alamy Stock Photo; The Advertising Archives/Alamy Stock Photo; The Competition and Conusmer Protection Commission; The Food Safety Authority of Ireland; The Office of the Ombudsman; Tim Gainey/Alamy Stock Photo; Tom Craig/Alamy Stock Photo; Torbjšrn Lagerwall/Alamy Stock Phot; TP/Alamy Stock Photo; Trevor Chriss/Alamy Stock Photo; Tusla; UrbanImages/Alamy Stock Photo; US NATIONAL LIBRARY OF MEDICINE/SCIENCE PHOTO LIBRARY; VHI; VTOS; WEEE Ireland; Westend61 GmbH/ Alamy Stock Photo; Wikimedia Commons; WILDLIFE GmbH/Alamy Stock Photo; WorkImages/Alamy Stock Photo; Wuu/ Alamy Stock Photo; ZUMA Press, Inc./Alamy Stock Photo

CHRIST'S HOSPITAL IN THE HORSHAM ERA

CHRIST'S HOSPITAL
IN THE HORSHAM ERA

Ken Mansell

ASHWATER
PRESS

Also by Ken Mansell

Christ's Hospital in the Victorian Era *(published 2011)*
Christ's Hospital Pupils 1552–1902 *(published 2014)*

Designed and published for Ken Mansell by
Ashwater Press
68 Tranmere Road, Whitton, Twickenham, Middlesex, TW2 7JB
in association with Christ's Hospital

www.ashwaterpress.co.uk.

Printed by The Dorset Press, Dorchester, England

ISBN 978-0-9927119-7-9

Contents

This list includes all the main headings and the more important sub-headings.

Illustrations

Tables

The Author

Ken Mansell *was born in London in 1942. He attended Burghley Road School, NW5, from where he obtained a London County Council competitive place at Christ's Hospital in 1953. Following eight wonderful years in the Horsham countryside he went to Imperial College, London, from where he emerged in 1964 with a 1st Class Degree in Mathematics, after which he obtained a Diploma there in Statistics and Operational Research.*

After university Ken joined the UK Government Statistical Service (GSS), being employed – apart from an eleven-year period from 1972 when he was at the Department of Trade and Industry – in the central departments of the Central Statistical Office and the Office for National Statistics. He left the GSS in 1996 and worked as a statistical consultant, mainly for the European Union Statistical Office, being involved with helping the then Accession Countries to establish their key economic statistics in the form required by the EU. He hung up his pen in 2003 and began learning the art of book-binding and researching his family history, whence sprang the idea for his 2011 book "Christ's Hospital in the Victorian Era".

In 2014, he published "Christ's Hospital Pupils 1552-1902" which provided a list of the names of the 46,000 pupils who had been admitted to CH over this period, together with their years at the School; the book also gave a list of over 900 'notable' Old Blues (OBs) who had entered CH before 1902, together with some brief biographical information. This third book brings the CH story up to date, presenting an account of the main events at the School across the Horsham years, as well as a list of essentially post-1902 notable OBs, with brief biographical details.

Amongst his wide-ranging involvement with CH and the Old Blue community, he is a Donation Governor with a presentee currently at the School, a member of the Amicable Society of Blues, and is one of a small team of volunteers which helps out in the School Museum.

Author's Notes

Christ's Hospital   *A variety of words will be used in this book to describe the School (or Schools) of Christ's Hospital, in particular the Bluecoat School, the Foundation, Hertford, Horsham, Housey, the Hospital, the House or Newgate Street; the meaning should be unambiguous. However, since 2007, the term Foundation has a particular significance (see para 1.258), it and the School having been made separate legal entities.*

Value of money   *It will be useful to try to put a value on the historic monetary (£ sterling) data included herein which will have some meaning in the present day. This is conventionally assessed through some measure of whole economy 'inflation', which provides a factor by which historic figures can be uprated to something approximating to values relevant to the current time, The process has a number of conceptual and data availability problems, the results being more approximate the further back in time for which they are made. The issues are well discussed on the "Measuring Worth" website which also provides the source of the inflation data used in the book. Two separate approaches are considered below.*

First, in respect of an 'item', a present-day purchasing power value may be obtained by inflating by a consumer price index. As an example, the £40 raised by the Amicable Society in support of boxing in the mid-1920s (para 1.91) has a present-day value of around £2,000. Secondly, for a 'project', some rough idea of the present-day cost of the work can be derived by inflating by an average earnings index (making the implicit assumption that earnings and costs in the construction industry have moved similarly to overall average earnings). Here, for example, the building and refurbishment work in the 1960s, estimated at £850,000 (para 1.155), would have a current cost of the order of £30 million.

The estimated present-day values are given, throughout the book, in rounded form (with 'm' denoting 'million' and 'k' 'thousand'). The purchasing power value is given in normal type, the 'construction cost' figure in italics. In a few cases, for example where a figure relates to a fund which had been established for a particular project, both values are given.

The Index   *The index is selective and is in two sections, relating essentially to 'names' and 'other'. To avoid repetition, however, the index of names does not include the 1,225 notable Old Blues given in the Annex to Chapter 2. Further, the 'other' index does not include any references to material appearing within the lists of 'Notables', while matters relevant to the individual Schools – Hertford boys and girls, Horsham and London – are most generally included under those four specific headings.*

Some abbreviations   *Conventional abbreviations have been used throughout. Some are given below, together with others which are essentially specific to the book.*

ASB	Amicable Society of Blues
b	born
BSB	Benevolent Society of Blues
CH	Christ's Hospital
CHIVE	"Christ's Hospital in the Victorian Era"
CHOBA	Christ's Hospital Old Blues' Association
d	died
DNB	"Oxford Dictionary of National Biography"
DG	Donation Governor
Names	"Christ's Hospital Pupils 1552-1902"
ng	not given
OB	Old Blue
OGB	Old Governing Body
RMS	Royal Mathematical School
W	CH Worthy
WWW	"Who Was Who"

Three symbols   *A superscript '^z' denotes a notable (generally from the Horsham era) for whom biographical details are given in the list (paras 2.22-38) in Chapter 2.*

An asterisk '*' denotes a notable (from the pre-Horsham era) whose name is included in the list in the Annex to Chapter 2.

A hash '(#)', in paras 2.22-38, denotes the existence of a commemorative plaque at Horsham or Hertford.

Introduction

Background

I.1 Christ's Hospital (CH, the Bluecoat School) opened its doors to children in 1552. Since then, around 65,000 boys and girls have been educated on the Foundation (see para 2.2) at its establishments in London, Hertfordshire and Horsham. The principal aim of this book is to present an account of the main events at the School following its move from London to Horsham in 1902, this whole period not hitherto much covered in CH literature. The book also identifies notable Old Blues (OBs, former pupils) mainly from the Horsham era, with brief biographical details given; these names have been augmented in a separate, full list by certain pre-Horsham notables. The lists do not include any person still alive.

I.2 The idea for this book flowed readily from the author's two earlier books – *Christ's Hospital in the Victorian Era* (*CHIVE*, 2011) and *Christ's Hospital Pupils, 1552-1902* (*Names*, 2014). Whilst the main purpose of the latter book was to provide a list of the names of the 46,000 plus pupils who had been admitted to CH over the pre-Horsham period, together with their years at the School, it also presented a list of notable OBs, with brief biographical information, for the period covered.

Structure of the book

I.3 The story of the Horsham era, which is given in Chapter 1, is based mainly on the School's magazine, *The Blue* (see paras A2.19-25), the author not having relevant access to, for example, material in the minutes of the ruling Council of Almoners or its sub-committees. There are two other important points about the book. First, it essentially covers developments at the boys' School at Horsham, although the main events at the girls' School at Hertford (pre the 1985 merger at Horsham) are included, insofar as they were reported in the "Hertford Letter" which appeared in *The Blue* or were identified from a quick perusal of the Hertford newsletter and School magazine. Secondly, whilst it is hoped that the key aspects of the Horsham era have been covered, there is inevitably a large element of personal preference in deciding what might be regarded as the main achievements in for example the arts or sport, or what features of School life should be mentioned, the author's choice reflecting some discussion with colleagues. Preceding the above, Chapter 1 also includes a brief, earlier history of the School, repeating some material included in *Names*. Chapter 2 then contains the information on Old Blue notables, this relating to former pupils who became eminent in later life or who contributed much to the School or OB community, the list not including any person still alive. The information given is for around 415 Horsham entrants, together with about 60 pre-Horsham notables who were not included in the list in *Names*, and includes years at CH and some brief biographical details. The Annex to Chapter 2 then provides a full list of 1,225 names (with years at CH) of Old Blue notables spanning the whole existence of the School, the 475 names above being augmented by 750 of the pre-Horsham era, most of whom appeared in *Names*. There are also two Appendices. Appendix 1 provides analyses of numbers of pupils at the School, where they came from and the cost of their education, and Appendix 2 gives information about certain Old Blue institutions.

Acknowledgements and thanks

I.4 In addition to the sources mentioned above, the author is indebted to Christ's Hospital for permitting access to the Museum's archives, including the extensive collection of photographs, engravings and paintings which have provided many of the images for the book, and also for the use of the School crest on the cover. Other acknowledgments related to content, for example to the Oxford University Press and Bloomsbury Publishing Plc, and to the National Portrait Gallery, are made at the appropriate places in the book.

Thanks

I should like to express my thanks to a number of people in particular. First, I am grateful to Greg Andrews, the Foundation's Clerk and Chief Executive, for assisting with certain administrative and other aspects of the book. Thanks also go to two colleagues with whom I work on a voluntary basis in the CH Museum: Mike Barford (Hon Curator and a master at the School, 1971-74) and Clifford Jones (CH, 1957-64), both of whom provided valuable comments on an initial draft, and assisted in a number of other ways. As with my two previous books, the tasks of proof-reading and editing were undertaken by Robert Fennell (CH, 1952-58) a near contemporary of mine at Christ's Hospital and also in the same House; while publication has again been expertly and assiduously effected by Ken Coton, the proprietor of Ashwater Press. My sincere thanks go especially to these two friends. I also wish to express my appreciation to the Museum, which has helped to finance the book. Lastly, I should like to acknowledge with thanks the work of the printers, Henry Ling Ltd (The Dorset Press). Despite all this much-welcomed assistance, the responsibility for any errors that might remain is mine.

Chapter 1
Some Historical Information

The early years

1.1   Christ's Hospital was founded in London by King Edward VI in 1552 (the event being depicted in Illustration 1), with the aim of providing care and education for poor children. The School was located in Newgate Street, in the City of London, on the site of the former Greyfriars monastery. King Edward signed the Royal Charter for the School in June 1553, not long before his death in early July at the very young age of 15.

1.2   The first children – both boys and girls – numbering 380 were taken in at the end of 1552. Some were barely out of the cradle and, in those early days, care of the children was probably a more important feature than their education. Early on, having first been seen in russet-coloured garb, the School established its distinctive boys' uniform of blue coat, yellow stockings and bands, providing the origin of its common name "The Bluecoat School". In broad terms this uniform has altered little over the years. In the very early days, although the initial focus of the Hospital had been on care, the 1560s saw an early indication of future academic success as the first scholars were sent to Oxford and Cambridge.

1.3   The development of the School over the next few decades was not without its problems, and expenditure began to run ahead of income, and reductions had to be made to the numbers of children housed by the Foundation. However, the School benefitted greatly from the splendid munificence of Dame Mary Ramsey who bequeathed various estates and money for the Writing School, and also made provision for the Foundation to have within their gift the livings of five parishes. There was also a somewhat novel and perhaps little-known source of funding which emerged around this time, with the Foundation being charged in 1582 with the task of licensing the working of cars and carts within the City, from which they were entitled to keep some or all of the monies paid for licences. The Woodmongers' Company took over the task in

1605, the work reverting in 1665 to CH, which continued the practice up to 1838.

1.4   The School could not escape the two dramatic events of the mid-1660s; a plan of CH about this time is at Illustration 2. First, the Great Plague of 1665 reportedly led to the death of some 30 children. Then in the following year, although the Great Fire claimed no casualties from the 300 or so children at the School, it destroyed most of its buildings, as well as many houses both inside and outside the site which were owned by the Foundation and from which rents accrued. The generosity of the Corporation of the City of London and its citizens and businesses enabled much essential repair and rebuilding of the School over the next four years. But this was only a temporary measure and, benefitting from a number of generous benefactions – particularly from Sir Robert Clayton, Sir John Frederick, Sir John Moore (whose statue adorns the front of Big School at Horsham) and Erasmus Smith – a major rebuilding programme, involving both Sir Christopher Wren and Nicholas Hawksmoor, was undertaken over the next 25 years. Illustration 3 shows the central part of the site after the rebuilding had been completed.

1.5   In addition to the London site, which was predominantly for boys, with only one Ward (Boarding House) given over to girls, children, particularly those who were being cared for rather than educated, were sent to nearby houses where

1. Edward VI founding Christ's Hospital.

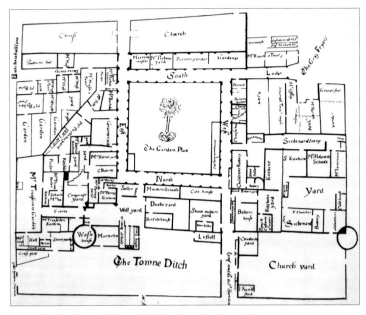

2. London – Plan of CH before the Great Fire.

'nurses' (occasionally male) were paid eight (old) pence to one shilling per week (about £10 to £15 in today's money – see Author's Notes) to care for them; the children would then go to the Newgate Street School perhaps around the age of 10. The nursing arrangements were later extended to locations at Hertford, Ware and Hoddesdon, all in the county of Hertfordshire. Educational arrangements were developed at Ware for upwards of 200 boys and at Hoddesdon for some 40 girls. Then, in the early 1680s, the acquisition of some land at Hertford led to the development of a purpose-built boarding school, the area being extended at the end of that decade to form what was to become the location of 'CH Hertford'. The establishment at Hoddesdon was closed in 1697, that in Ware in 1761.

1.6　The School was run by an elected Court of Governors, supported by an executive Committee of Almoners and, variously, sub-committees on finance and education. One key task of the Court in the 1670s was to formalise the arrangements for admission to the School, the procedure being described in Appendix 1, which also explains the system of "Donation Governors" (or just Governors) which provided the main means of entry to CH up to about 1890.

The Royal Mathematical School

1.7　A further key development took place in 1673 when the Royal Mathematical School (RMS) was founded and granted Royal Charter by King Charles II. The initial suggestion for its establishment came from Sir Robert Clayton, concern having been expressed that, despite the country's pre-eminence on the sea, improvements were needed to the quality and supply of sailors for the Royal Navy and the merchant marine and to the efficiency of officers as navigators. Various other luminaries, including Samuel Pepys, John Flamsteed (the first Astronomer Royal), Sir Isaac Newton and Sir Christopher Wren – all of whom were Governors of CH – were also involved with the early development of the RMS. A number of skilful mariners emerged from the RMS, but perhaps the main legacy was the creation of similar navigating schools in both the UK and overseas. One other notable, related event was the completion c1690 of a painting – of massive proportions, measuring about 26 metres by five metres – by Antonio Verrio, to commemorate the founder and foundation of the RMS. The painting is now in the School's Dining Hall at Horsham.

The 18th century

1.8　The 18th century saw further new buildings for the London School, while at Hertford there was improved provision for the arrival of an increasing number of girls, including further rebuilding there. However, in the eyes of many historians of the School, the 18th century would best be remembered for the era of Head Master Revd James Boyer*, himself a pupil there between 1744 and 1752. Through his hands passed, amongst others, Samuel Taylor Coleridge*, James Leigh Hunt*, and Charles Lamb*, all widely known, and providing the names for three of the Horsham School's eight House Blocks, and Thomas Fanshaw Middleton*, Bishop of Calcutta, yielding a fourth Block name. One particular event of the later 18th century might also be mentioned. In 1774 the Revd William Hetherington, a Governor, left CH £20,000 (£2.2m) to provide pensions to elderly blind persons. In the ensuing years, other benefactors also made bequests for this purpose, and by the end of the 1880s the fund for this non-educational aspect of the Hospital's activities had grown to around £250,000 (£25m) and was providing pensions for some 1,200 people, a figure in excess of the number of children being educated. For the RMS, the quality of teaching was further improved and pupils remained longer in tuition, with some degree of stability being achieved during the very long tenure of James Hodgson who was Master from 1709 to 1755. Then in 1775, William Wales, who had accompanied Captain Cook on his second voyage around the world, was appointed to the post, serving until his death in 1798. One particular feature of his teaching related to the developments taking place in the measurement of longitude; in addition he brought a degree of discipline to the role which seems previously to have been largely absent.

The 19th century

1.9　Further extensive rebuilding of the London School took place in the first thirty years of the 19th century, including the magnificent new Gothic Great Hall (Illustration 4, exterior, and Illustration 5, interior – for both see overleaf) which, at the time, was the largest unsupported (centrally) building in London, apart from Westminster Hall. There were also new Wards and a new Infirmary, staff houses and a combined Mathematical and Grammar School (which also included the Drawing School). The Hall – completed in 1829 – sadly had a life of barely 70 years. The cost of all this rebuilding work was put at around £150,000 (£120m), about a third of which was met by contributions to a special fund, with the rest coming

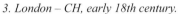

3. London – CH, early 18th century.

4. London – The Great Hall, exterior.

5. London – The Great Hall, interior.

from a variety of other sources, including reserves, rents and dividends.

1.10 Three events of the next two decades are worthy of mention, although two had unforeseen and unfortunate consequences. First, in 1837, following long-standing custom, when Her Majesty Queen Victoria, the new monarch, paid her first visit to the City of London she was welcomed by an address from a pupil of Christ's Hospital, the honour falling to the Senior Grecian, Frederick Gifford Nash*, who was but five weeks younger than the monarch. However, a few days after the address it emerged that the copy of the speech which had been presented to the Queen was in the hands of Mr William Brackstone Tarbutt, a CH Governor. The Court of Governors – aghast at Tarbutt's brazen subterfuge in acquiring the document – resolved that he surrender the copy of the speech to the Treasurer, in order that it might be returned to Her Majesty. This Tarbutt refused to do, he displaying his 'prize' in "church and reading room, in warehouse and counting-house". However, he did not bask long in this glory, dying in 1839. Secondly, also in 1837, the School was part of the Charity Commission scheme of inquiries directed at charities. The Commission's report, published in 1840, made no specific recommendations, its main impact probably being to have planted in the minds of the Governors the seeds for possible action in the future.

1.11 Thirdly, in 1845, in an historic occasion for the Foundation, Queen Victoria and Prince Albert were received by the President and Treasurer and attended a "public supper" at the School, such suppers having been introduced some time earlier to minimise the disruption caused by people wandering through the grounds. After the supper, Her Majesty agreed that two paintings – of herself and of her husband – could be commissioned; these now flank the Verrio in the Dining Hall. Sadly, a few days after the joyous occasion, the Lord Mayor complained to the Foundation that, in his role as "head of all the Royal Hospitals belonging to the City" he was "entitled to preside there upon all occasions, public or private, when he shall think fit"; and he regarded that the "taking precedence by the CH President and Treasurer" at the recent supper was an invasion of his "ancient and undoubted rights". The dispute rumbled on through the year, with the Foundation attempting to establish their rights and strongly rejecting the claims of the Mayor, and even in October locking the gates

to prevent him entering the School. Into the next year, with the matter still no nearer resolution, the (new) Mayor said that he would not attend the Easter Spital sermons (an event for which a special anthem would be written by the School's Music Master, a practice begun around 1610 and continuing until 1862) or receive the boys at the Mansion House, both annual traditions. It was only on Good Friday that some form of accord was reached, including the reinstatement of most of the arrangements for the sermons and the Mansion House visit.

1.12 Moving into the 1850s, in 1853 Revd Dr George Jacob was appointed 'Head Master' (the first non-Old Blue for about 80 years) and the School celebrated the tercentenary of its foundation, while in the following year HRH The Duke of Cambridge became the first Royal President of the School. HRH was to serve the Foundation, actively and positively, for very nearly 50 years until his death in 1904, the role, for much of the time, being carried out alongside the 'day job' as Commander-in-Chief of the British Army to which he had been appointed in 1856, a post which he held until 1895. However, his election as President had not been without controversy, the then Lord Mayor (Thomas Sidney) averring that only Aldermen of the City of London were eligible, by Statute and Charter, to be elected to this post. Despite these claims, HRH received a reasonably comprehensive endorsement, Governors at a March Court meeting voting 216 to 87 in his favour. One regrettable consequence of these events was that the Mayor refused to attend the preaching of the Spital sermons on Easter Monday and Tuesday, and said that it would be inconvenient for him to receive the Hospital pupils at the Mansion House on the Tuesday. No compromise could be found, so the Treasurer decided that Hospital funds should be used to provide the monies usually given to the boys by the Lord Mayor, but it seems that they did miss out on the traditional Mansion House treat of buns and wine.

1.13 It may be of interest to mention one perhaps little-known feature of CH for which change became necessary about this time. The School's responsibility and concern for the living continued with the burial of the departed. Generally speaking, funeral arrangements for pupils would be made

6. The CH burial area at Ilford Cemetery and the monument.

by the parents or guardian of the child, with burial probably taking place near their home. However, in some instances, for example where parents might be overseas, or there were cost or medical considerations, children were buried at or close to the School. However, in 1858, following legislation by the Home Office on burial procedures generally, the practice of interment in much of the School grounds was made illegal. As a result, in the middle of that year and with due promptness, a sum of £100 (£8k) was made available by the Governors for the purchase of a plot of burial ground in the recently opened City of London Cemetery at Ilford in east London. Later, in 1890, arrangements were put in hand to erect there a monument of polished grey granite and eight feet in height. The plot and monument exist today – see Illustration 6 – and they make for a moving visit. At Hertford, many burials during the Victorian era would have taken place at nearby All Saints church. Following the move to Horsham, nearby Itchingfield Parish Church became the final resting place of a number of masters and other staff and pupils.

1.14 In 1864 the School came under the education microscope, this time as part of the Taunton Commission Inquiry of the Endowed Schools' sector. The Commission made sundry recommendations, including the possible demise of the ruling Court of Governors. However, one Latin phrase in the final report stood out. In recognising the history of "so remarkable a school" and "the attachment which it has inspired in the hearts of many of its scholars", the report said that "Christ's Hospital is a thing without parallel in the country, and sui generis". Two other important events occurred in 1868. First, the new Head of the School (Revd George Bell*) would no longer be Head primus inter pares, but would be the first official Head Master of Christ's Hospital. He would also have a role in forming the curriculum at both London and Hertford, and have more responsibility for discipline outside the classroom. Secondly, the year marked the founding of one of the gems in CH's crown, namely the Band, its establishment and initial development owing much to the generosity of the School's Treasurer, Mr William Foster White*.

The Scheme of Administration – discussion

1.15 Deliberation over Taunton had raised again the key issue of the location of the School. The matter was discussed

in 1869 at a meeting of the Court of Governors, the vote – on a surprisingly low turnout of probably less than one-third of the total number of Governors – against a move being won by 69 (plus two tellers) to 55 (plus two tellers). The Court also set about dealing with the provisions of the 1869 Endowed Schools Act. These, which would shape the future of Christ's Hospital, were to be effected through the Endowed Schools' Commission (ESC) establishing a scheme of arrangement with individual schools. The Court – much concerned by the issues of the management of the School and the possible demise of the system of Donation Governors – took the initiative and set about preparing their own (draft) scheme of administration for the School. And so began a war – perhaps not too inappropriate a description given its nature and the length of time (20 years) over which it was to be conducted, and for which only a summary will be presented here – with the Commissioners, with the acrimonious discussion often seeming likely to threaten the whole future of the School.

1.16 In all, five main draft schemes were produced – two by the School (1870 and 1875), one by the ESC (1873), and two by the Charity Commission (CC) who took over the ESC functions when it was abolished in 1875 (1880 and 1885). The main areas of debate, which changed little over the years, were: (i) governance, where the Foundation wished to see essentially a continuance of existing practice while the ESC/CC wanted a new ruling Council of Almoners without Governor majority; (ii) the presentation privileges of the Donation Governors (which provided the main method of entry for pupils into CH), which the School wanted to retain and the ESC/CC to water down or remove; (iii) certain endowments, where the Foundation disagreed with the ESC/CC contention that they should be used for educational purposes; (iv) the number and size of the future Boarding and (proposed) Day Schools, with the Foundation arguing for a more cautious line; (v) the extent of the responsibilities of the Head Master, with the Court being more restrictive than the ESC/CC; (vi) whether the School should be removed from London; (vii) whether fees should be charged, and (viii) matters related to the possible introduction of competitive admission arrangements, the Court being generally unenthusiastic about these last three issues.

1.17 There was extensive discussion within the Foundation and with the ESC and the Charity Commission, but agreement could not be reached. The Charity Commission's offer in 1886 of some minor changes to their then draft was not acceptable to the Court, and the definitive Scheme for the future governance and administration of Christ's Hospital was approved by the national Committee of Council on Education in June 1888. The following year the Court's appeal to the Judicial Committee of the Privy Council against the Scheme was rejected, while the Court decided against an appeal to Parliament.

Some other events

1.18 Before turning to the denouement of the matters related to the Scheme, consideration should be given to a number of other important events which had occurred. First, in 1872, following an approach from the Mid-London Railway Company, the School agreed to sell the Newgate Street site (for £600,000 (£50m)) for the construction of an underground railway line, although there appeared to have been no plans for an alternative location. Fortunately, the sale did not go ahead, the company having failed to get their Bill passed in Parliament. Secondly, in 1875 the Court agreed that the girls' School at Hertford should be regenerated. The numbers of girls had declined from around 70 at the start of the Victorian era to as low as around 15 in the second half of the 1860s. The possibility of closing the girls' School had been discussed for some years. However, it emerged from legal advice that closure of the School would be against the provision of certain important Trusts which provided funds for the Foundation. So the girls' School survived and numbers were increased; amongst other changes the charity-like garb, which had been worn from the early days of the School's founding, was changed to something more fashionable and more comfortable – a dark blue skirt and matching cape or cloak. Thirdly, Revd Richard Lee* had succeeded Revd George Bell* as Head Master in 1876, seeing the School through the last quarter of the 19th century and into the end of the London era.

1.19 Fourthly, in 1877 there occurred a major and tragic event which impacted greatly on all the various deliberations about the scheme and indeed more widely. This sad episode was the death of William Arthur Gibbs*, a pupil at the London School. Gibbs was not quite 13 and had been at CH for less than two years when he was found in a side ward of the Infirmary by one of the nurses hanging by the cord of a ventilator, his feet on the floor, but dead. A coroner's inquest was held, with the verdict being returned of suicide whilst in a state of temporary insanity. The death of Gibbs generated much comment in the Press, the prime allegation being that the monitors had exercised undue levels of discipline. Responding to this and the apparent public opinion, the Home Secretary set up a Royal Commission to examine the tragedy and also certain aspects of the management of the School. Purely in relation to the circumstances of the tragic suicide, the Commission endorsed the view of the coroner's jury that no blame should be attached to the School's authorities or to the monitors. They also took the opportunity to make one other major pronouncement which had emerged from the deliberations, namely that the removal of School from London was regarded as "indispensable".

1.20 Lastly, in 1890, the School had a lucky escape when a fire broke out in the matron's room on the second floor of a building which housed a number of Wards. The School's own fire brigade had burst into action, but their effectiveness was limited by the height at which the fire was burning. The nearby Fire Brigades (including, coincidentally, a volunteer unit from Horsham which was undergoing an annual inspection

in London) soon arrived and the fire was quickly under control. However, the damage, including to nearby Wards, was considerable.

The Scheme of Administration – implementation

1.21 Parliamentary process being duly followed, the Queen gave approval to the Scheme of Administration for Christ's Hospital on 15th August 1890. Although it technically became law on that date, the Charity Commission extended the operational date until the turn of the year in order to allow the necessary appointments to be made to the Council of Almoners (the successor to the Court of Governors and the Committee of Almoners). Thus, at last, after some 20 years of deliberations, often acrimonious and immensely consuming of time and resources, the deed was done. The Scheme – running to some 150 clauses – for the future administration of Christ's Hospital was to come into effect on 1st January 1891.

1.22 So, what did the final Scheme say? In addition to matters of governance and management, it dealt, mostly beneficially and progressively it should be said, with various educational aspects, such as the roles and responsibilities of the Head Master and other teaching staff, and the curriculum. In the context of governance, the Donation Governors lost their power to govern through their ability to vote in the Court, such matters now being undertaken in the 43-strong Council of Almoners, within which Governors would be permitted to elect only 20 members. Further, the Governors would also see a reduction in their presenting rights – only one presentee could be at the School at any one time, while there was an upper limit on the total number of children who could be so presented.

1.23 However, amongst the extensive details, two key clauses, which explained the requirements for the future provision of education and the location of the Schools which were to furnish it, stood out. First, clause 65 stated: "As soon as conveniently may be after the date of the Scheme, the Council of Almoners shall provide for the Schools, upon convenient sites, buildings suitable, in the case of the boys' School for 700 boarders, in the case of the girls' School for 350 boarders, in the case of the Preparatory School for 120 boarders, in the case of the Science School for 600 scholars, and in the case of the girls' Day School for 400 scholars…." Thus, the outrageously ambitious proposals of the Scheme would involve provision of education for 2,170 children, about twice the number being educated in the years just before it came into being. Secondly, clause 63 said, in respect of the boarding schools, "The Hospital Schools should be maintained within a convenient distance of London". The uncertainty engendered by this last statement was to lead to prolonged debate over the ensuing years, and it was in sharp contrast to the precision generally existing in the other clauses of the Scheme. For example clause 64, covering the location of a proposed Day (Science) School for boys and a Day School for girls, said that these Schools were "…to be maintained in the county of Middlesex, and at a distance of not more than three miles measured in a straight line from the Royal Exchange in the City of London".

1.24 The (old) ruling Court of Governors held its last meeting on 1st December 1890, with the President in the Chair. HRH The Duke of Cambridge was strongly against many of the changes, and he considered laying down his office, but felt it would be wrong of him if he failed to do what he could to link the past with the present. The last meeting of the Committee of Almoners of the old regime was held on 18th December

1890, with Treasurer John Derby Allcroft in the Chair, he having earlier indicated that he did not wish to undertake the role for the new Council under the Scheme. Allcroft would be succeeded by Walter Vaughan Morgan*.

The new governance of the Foundation

1.25 The Scheme brought with it substantial changes in the way the Foundation was governed and managed. Indeed, this final decade or so of the 19th century was to be probably the most momentous in the long history of the School.

1.26 The main business of the Council in their early years concerned the issue of finding a new location for the School. In addition, at the end of 1891 the Treasurer, Vaughan Morgan*, prepared a financial statement for the Council. It painted a bleak picture. One interesting observation – perhaps in part a reflection of his views on what had happened – is that the President, The Duke of Cambridge, did not chair a meeting of the Council until January 1893, and then one not of great substance. In contrast, he continued to take the chair quite frequently at meetings of the old Court of Governors and the old Committee of Almoners.

Which endowments?

1.27 Another important issue to be addressed was to determine which of the Foundation's many endowments were to be used within the Scheme to fund educational purposes. The main argument here concerned those monies (now held in Trust by the Old Governing Body (OGB) and valued at around £110,000 (£11m)) which had been given within 50 years of the 1869 Endowed Schools Act, or subsequent to the Act. To put this figure in some perspective, the annual cost of running Christ's Hospital in the early 1890s was about £60,000. In mid-1892, the OGB put forward to Council two suggestions as to how these funds could be used. The first was to set up a special school, such as for mathematics, since, under the Scheme, entry to the RMS was no longer being made. The second proposal, which the OGB preferred, would have as its main purpose the return of certain privileges to the Donation Governors. Specifically, the OGB would pay over the £3,000 (£0.3m) or so per year interest from the exempt endowments for use under the Scheme on condition that Governors would receive improved presentation rights. It was to take about four years of wrangling with the Charity Commission, discussion with the Attorney General and a judgement from the Court of Chancery, before the matter was resolved. The final outcome in mid-April 1896 saw the Commission proposing that improved presentation rights would be introduced for Donation Governors on condition that the annual income of the exempted endowments would be used for the purposes of the Scheme, this arrangement being virtually identical to what the OGB had proposed four years earlier. In addition, nominations for sons of officers in the Royal Navy were introduced.

The School will be moved to...?

1.28 In considering where the new school might be located, the Foundation had interpreted the requirement of clause 63 of the Scheme that it should be "within a convenient distance of London" as an hour's rail journey; they also specified a site of 250 acres as a minimum area. Around 100 different sites were considered and about 40 places were visited, and a list of six possible locations was put forward, as follows, it not being clear whether there was any significance in the ordering:

Brickendonbury, Herts; Aylesbury Dairy Co, Horsham, Sussex; Kenwards, Haywards Heath, Sussex; Lillingstone Estate (part of), Eynesford, Kent; Wonersh Park, Bramley, Surrey; and at Sunningdale, Berks.

1.29 Following further discussions with the owners of the Aylesbury Dairy Company, in the summer of 1892 the Foundation purchased the Horsham site – of about 1,100 acres and including many buildings – for about £53,000 (£5m), replacing the five and a bit acres in Newgate Street. Later, in 1897, the School purchased an adjacent site of some 70 acres for just over £2,000 (£0.2m), thus making the familiar figure of a site of about 1,200 acres. Around 120 years on from the original much-disputed purchase, apart from the housing development at Bluecoat Pond (just south of the railway station) and a few other pieces of land which have been sold or were lost to road development, the Foundation still owns the bulk of the original site.

The financial position

1.30 The other issue of concern related to the deteriorating financial position, in part reflecting the loss of around £3,000 each year from the interest on the exempted funds. Reductions made to pupil numbers over the next couple of years did lead to lower losses. Then, in 1892, as permitted by the Scheme, the Council of Almoners took the historic but necessary step of introducing a system of fees, set, for those deemed able to pay, at levels of £10 (£1k), £15 and £20 per annum. Hitherto, education at CH had been basically free, although up to 1869 teaching staff had received some income from a very small number of private pupils (see para 2.20). However, the resulting improvement to the financial position was largely offset by the need to close the London School in the autumn of 1893 for about nine months following an outbreak of scarlet fever.

1.31 The commencement of 1894 probably represented the nadir of the Foundation's fortunes. The London School was closed, the funding position was dire, there appeared to be deadlock with the Charity Commission on reviewing the Scheme and the position of the exempted endowments, and the prospect of a new dawn at Horsham (although still some years away) was attracting widespread criticism. At a public meeting in July, the President is reported to have made the celebrated remark, in respect of the future of the School, that "I cannot for the life of me see how we can fail to end in absolute ruin". By the end of that year, the Foundation were reporting a figure of only 722 children, over 400 below the number at the end of 1890 at the start of the Scheme. Then in 1895, an increase in income, coupled with the effect of this large reduction, led to a surplus, the first positive balance for at least eight years.

1.32 The 1896 agreement with the Charity Commission on the exempted endowments meant that life at Christ's Hospital, while not quite returning to pre-Scheme stability – indeed many aspects of the way the School was administered and of the nature of the educational system had undoubtedly changed (and for the better) – could now operate on a firmer financial footing and, perhaps the necessary establishment of the element of fee-paying apart, in a way more commensurate with the original charitable nature of the Foundation. We thus come to the end of one tumultuous period in the history of the Foundation, and the beginning of another which was to see the boys' School move to Horsham and the girls' School develop at Hertford.

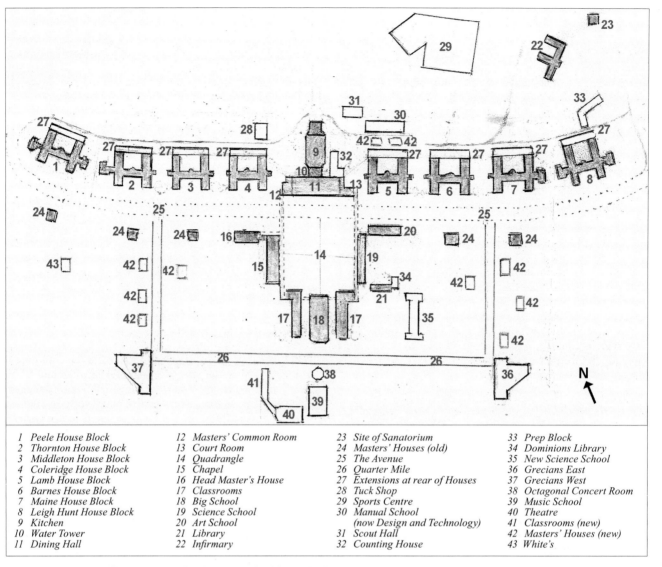

1	*Peele House Block*	*12*	*Masters' Common Room*
2	*Thornton House Block*	*13*	*Court Room*
3	*Middleton House Block*	*14*	*Quadrangle*
4	*Coleridge House Block*	*15*	*Chapel*
5	*Lamb House Block*	*16*	*Head Master's House*
6	*Barnes House Block*	*17*	*Classrooms*
7	*Maine House Block*	*18*	*Big School*
8	*Leigh Hunt House Block*	*19*	*Science School*
9	*Kitchen*	*20*	*Art School*
10	*Water Tower*	*21*	*Library*
11	*Dining Hall*	*22*	*Infirmary*

23	*Site of Sanatorium*	*33*	*Prep Block*
24	*Masters' Houses (old)*	*34*	*Dominions Library*
25	*The Avenue*	*35*	*New Science School*
26	*Quarter Mile*	*36*	*Grecians East*
27	*Extensions at rear of Houses*	*37*	*Grecians West*
28	*Tuck Shop*	*38*	*Octagonal Concert Room*
29	*Sports Centre*	*39*	*Music School*
30	*Manual School*	*40*	*Theatre*
	(now Design and Technology)	*41*	*Classrooms (new)*
31	*Scout Hall*	*42*	*Masters' Houses (new)*
32	*Counting House*	*43*	*White's*

7. Horsham – A plan of the present School (original buildings shaded).

Assessment of events

1.33 In *CHIVE*, the author made an assessment of the events related to the Scheme and its initial consequences. He thought that the move out of London just had to happen, and important and necessary changes were needed to the governance and educational nature of the School. However, it is difficult not to feel that the Charity Commission handled extremely poorly its own role in these matters, particularly concerning the position and the rights of the Donation Governors. Moreover, there seemed to be a total disregard of the sensitivities that underlay an institution which had over 300 years of history, as well as a lamentable procrastination in their modus operandi, these and other aspects proving extremely costly to the Foundation and representing a degree of ineptitude and inefficiency of which the Commission could scarcely be proud.

The building of the new School at Horsham

1.34 *CHIVE* also contained a detailed narrative about the building of the new School at Horsham from which some key points only will be reproduced here. As background to what follows here and later in the book, it will be useful to have some idea of the new School site. To this end, Illustration 7 reproduces the plan, included in *CHIVE*, showing the main buildings from 1902 to the early 21st century; also given is an aerial view of the present School (Illustration 8). Both images exclude the Language and Resources Centre which was added in 2015 (see para 1.254, which also refers to the new Mellstrom Centre (the erstwhile Library and Dominions Library)).

One important early consideration had been the location of the School within the 1,200 acre site, the initial suggestion favouring nearby Sharpenhurst Hill, to the west of the coast rail line, and which (at some 280 feet above sea level) would also provide a splendid outlook, it being said that on a clear day six counties can be seen. The idea was soon abandoned though when it became apparent that the costs of sinking foundations there would be prohibitively high, further factors being the thought that young boys might be too exposed to the winter cold, and the distance from the proposed station.

1.35 Having decided on the lower terrain, following a competition, Messrs Aston Webb and Ingress Bell were chosen as the architects for the new School, a particular feature of their design being strong use of the lateral dimension, rather than buildings set around courts. However, not everyone was happy with the new arrangements, there being concern expressed at aspects such as cost, distance from London, and the size and suitability of the new site, particularly the matter of drainage. One of the more vocal objections had come from Sir Henry Peek (whose father had founded the Peek Frean biscuit firm in the early 1860s) who proposed an alternative site (to Horsham) for the location of the School; the land was in Wimbledon, where Peek had lived, and Peek himself was the proposed seller; and he would be willing to accept the Horsham site in part payment. Peek's initial proposals did not seem to attract much support, so in 1895 he established an essay competition related to the "present condition of Christ's Hospital, the means of extricating it from its existing

8. *Horsham – An aerial view of the present School (from the south).*

difficulties, and for making the future of the Royal Foundation fully in accord with its glorious past". However, this too failed to change opinion. Sir Henry Peek was not to see the School built at Horsham, he having died in 1898.

Progress and arrangements for the tenders

1.36 Towards the end of 1896 the Council took the key decision that the building work would be contracted out in two phases, the first to cover the sub-structures, to ground level, while the second would relate to the super-structures, essentially the buildings themselves. Before this, much work needed to be undertaken to level the site on which the School would be built, the terrain being very uneven with differences in levels of up to nine feet in certain parts

1.37 The Council accepted the lowest tender (from thirteen firms) for the first, sub-structure contract – of around £22,500 (*£9m*) – from James Longley & Co of Crawley, and work began in April 1897. The initial work – aided by the construction of a new siding at the nearby existing railway halt to provide a means of receiving materials – was mostly finished by mid-October, the Council having earlier decided that the Foundation Stone for the new School should be laid on 23rd October, Founder's Day. The ceremony (see Illustration 9), strong on Masonic tradition, was held in a huge marquee and witnessed by over 2,000 people, including pupils from both London and Hertford.

1.38 About this time, discussion with the London, Brighton & South Coast Railway Co resulted in an agreement that the Company would finance (around £25,000 (*£10m*)) the building of a station, to cover both the main line and the Horsham/Guildford line, on land provided by the Foundation. Further, arrangements were made to seek tenders for the super-structure work for building the School. Here, the lowest figure – about £385,000 (*£155m*) – again came from Longley (who were awarded the contract), although this was apparently some £115,000 (*£45m*) above the architects' own estimates of cost. Possible savings were examined, essentially from the use of different materials, from modifying certain internal building work, and the omission of certain structural features, in particular the walls and railings which were to connect the fronts of the House Blocks, and the covered walkways at the rear of the Houses. The Charity Commission approved

the reduced tender for the building work (for which initially only six Boarding House Blocks were included) of £295,000 (*£120m*).

The main building work

1.39 The building work commenced around the turn of 1897/1898. Two interesting features of the work were first the construction of a Dining Hall Tower, which would house the two tanks containing the School's water supply. Water would be pumped from the much-deepened Aylesbury Dairy Co well (located at what is the present-day Bluecoat Pond housing development) to a massive (300,000 gallon) reservoir to be built on the top of Sharpenhurst Hill, from where a gravity main would provide water to the Tower (making its height an important calculation) and hence to the Houses and Kitchen and to other buildings. The Tower, which can be seen from miles around, consumed about three-quarters of a million bricks, and cost around £2,500 (*£1m*). During the Second World War it was suggested that it served as a marker for German planes en route to London from the South Coast,

9. *Horsham – The laying of the Foundation Stone, 1897.*

10. Horsham – The Tube.

this facility being deemed to provide the School with some degree of safety from bombing. The second feature was a subway – the Tube (a later image is shown at Illustration 10) – running under the Boarding Houses which would provide a passageway (initially meant for staff, but later given over to the pupils when the covered walkways at the rear of the Houses were dispensed with) and also house the utility pipes, cables and wires, enabling ready maintenance. Early in 1899, the Charity Commission approved the addition of the seventh House Block and the Preparatory School. There was, though, one important difference from the Webb/Bell plan, in that the Prep House Block, originally sited at the west end of the Avenue, was 'moved' to the east end (possibly because it would be closer to the Infirmary), with the additional House Block (Peele) being built in its place at the west end.

1.40 Work progressed generally satisfactorily, including the removal to Horsham of the 'Verrio' and 13 other paintings from the Great Hall and the main arch in the Newgate Street Grecians' Cloisters, this being 'split', with the stones from the two sides being used to form the outer faces of the Avenue arches in the Horsham Quadrangle. The splendid railway station was completed (Illustration 11) and initially named Christ's Hospital, West Horsham, later just Christ's Hospital, often without the apostrophe, although such punctuation does

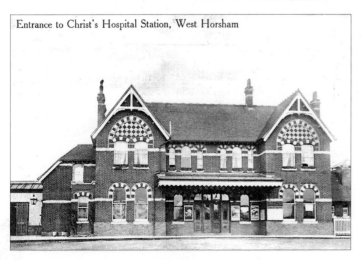

Entrance to Christ's Hospital Station, West Horsham

11. Horsham – CH Railway Station.

12. Horsham – Workers from James Longley & Co.

exist there at present. The various 'utility' issues – sewage, drainage, heating, electricity and water supply – were all satisfactorily resolved, the last requiring the employment of a diver to deal with a leak in the reservoir which had been constructed on Sharpenhurst Hill. By the spring of 1902 most of the buildings were deemed 'finished', the exceptions being the Chapel, which did not become available for use until September, services in the summer term taking place in Big School, and the Science School.

1.41 Longley had done an excellent job, transforming what were largely open cow fields into a magnificent School, and the buildings received many architectural plaudits, although perhaps inevitably there were to be some critics. Some of the Longley team which undertook the work can be seen in Illustration 12, with one of the Longley family directors in the centre. It had always been planned that, following this initial work, further buildings would be constructed and the contracts for this work were also awarded to Longley. The main buildings were: a number of additional houses for married masters and cottages for the domestic and related staff; the Cricket Pavilion; the Post Office; the Tuck Shop; the Lodge entrances; the Fountain in the Quadrangle; the Music School, and the Manual School.

Whither Hertford?

1.42 While all this activity was taking place at Horsham, a particular issue for the Council concerned the future of the girls' School, an image of the then Hertford site being shown in Illustration 13. The idea of building the girls' School at Horsham, previously rejected, had found its way back on the agenda, although there remained strong opposition to having boys and girls on the same site, including from Head Mistress Miss Robertson (who had been appointed in 1893). However, the decision on location was eventually taken in the light of the financial position, it being estimated that to construct a girls' School for some 350 pupils at Horsham would cost around £200,000 (£80m), only about one-tenth of which might be derived from the sale of the Hertford site. Such monies were just not available. Council therefore decided that the new girls' School would be developed on the existing site, once the boys had moved, the proposal being approved by the Charity Commission, who later also agreed the plans for work which would cost about £10,000 (£4m). The new School buildings are described in para 1.67.

The death of Queen Victoria

1.43 Before moving on we might note that an important event had occurred in 1901 when, on 22nd January, Queen Victoria died aged 81, after 63 years on the throne. She had

13. Hertford – The Entrance Gates and Avenue.

been a Governor of Christ's Hospital since 1843 and had been a strong supporter of the Foundation in a number of other ways. The Council asked the President to sign and present to the King (Edward VII) an address of condolence upon the passing away of her late Majesty, and of congratulations to his Majesty on his accession to the throne. Council also agreed that a presentation be issued for the admission of a child designated by her late Majesty who, had she survived until 5th February, would have been entitled to a presentation on that day. There was a further, fitting, final link with the School. On 1st February, Captain GA Broad (1852-60), as Sergeant-at-Arms to the new King, had navigated HMS *Alberta* on her memorable journey across the Solent with Her Majesty's mortal remains.

Disposal of the London site

1.44 There were to be many difficult discussions relating to the sale of the London site, of which a 'bird's-eye' view is shown in the drawing (Illustration 14) by Edwin Spencer Hartley, a pupil at CH, 1890-97. Nearby St Bartholomew's Hospital (Barts) had particular interest in an area of about one and a half acres across the northern area of the site, while a number of offers were received for the entire site. The Foundation eventually agreed on one of £720,000 (£70m) for the whole site and a draft contract was prepared, at which point it was revealed to the potential buyer that part of the site was held leasehold (the lessor being the Corporation of London), and to resolve the matter an Enabling Act of Parliament needed to be introduced for the transfer of the leases.

1.45 While the School commenced the drafting of the Bill to acquire the leases, it came to light that Barts were planning to introduce a Bill of their own enabling them to purchase, compulsorily, that portion of the CH site they had previously intimated they wished to acquire, with valuation to be decided by arbitration. The Foundation's own Bill effectively became law in the summer (of 1901), and the School began discussions for implementation with the Corporation. Barts'

Bill came into law in the late summer, and towards the end of 1901 they gave notice that they wished to exercise their rights for the purchase of the one and a half acres of the site, its value going to arbitration. Here, the Foundation proposed a figure of £340,000 (£33m), and Barts came up with £140,000 (£13m), the arbitrator decided on a 'mid-way' value of around £240,000 (£23m).

1.46 The Foundation could now address the issue of how best to dispose of the rest of the site (of around three and two-thirds acres). Initially, it was proposed that the site should be developed as a series of building plots. An offer emerged to take an 80-year building lease on the bulk of site for £20,000 (£2m) a year. Then in early 1904, His Majesty's Government, on behalf of the General Post Office, made an offer for the freehold of the site involving payment to the Foundation of an annual sum of £23,000 (£2.3m) in perpetuity. This arrangement was followed up to 1958, and apparently was then redeemed by payment of a capital sum of £430,000 (£9m). It seems that

14. London – An aerial drawing of the School (from the SE), c1900.

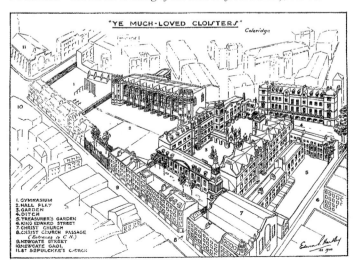

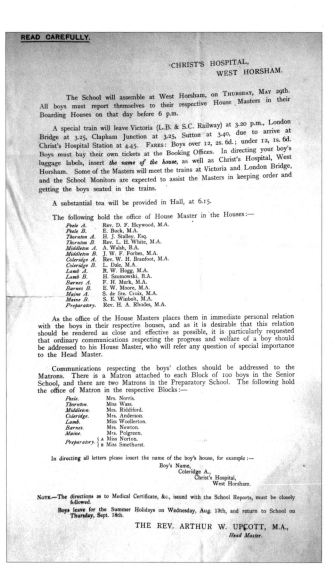

'CHRIST'S HOSPITAL,
WEST HORSHAM.

The School will assemble at West Horsham, on THURSDAY, MAY 29th. All boys must report themselves to their respective House Masters in their Boarding Houses on that day before 6 p.m.

A special train will leave Victoria (L.B. & S.C. Railway) at 3.20 p.m., London Bridge at 3.25, Clapham Junction at 3.25, Sutton at 3.40, due to arrive at Christ's Hospital Station at 4.45. FARES: Boys over 12, 2s. 6d.; under 12, 1s. 6d. Boys must buy their own tickets at the Booking Offices. In directing your boy's luggage labels, insert *the name of the house*, as well as Christ's Hospital, West Horsham. Some of the Masters will meet the trains at Victoria and London Bridge, and the School Monitors are expected to assist the Masters in keeping order and getting the boys seated in the trains.

A substantial tea will be provided in Hall, at 6.15.

The following hold the office of House Master in the Houses :—

Peele A.	Rev. D. F. Heywood, M.A.
Peele B.	E. Buck, M.A.
Thornton A.	H. J. Stalley, Esq.
Thornton B.	Rev. L. H. White, M.A.
Middleton A.	A. Walsh, B.A.
Middleton B.	J. W. F. Forbes, M.A.
Coleridge A.	Rev. W. H. Branfoot, M.A.
Coleridge B.	L. Dale, M.A.
Lamb A.	R. W. Hogg, M.A.
Lamb B.	H. Szumowski, B.A.
Barnes A.	F. H. Merk, M.A.
Barnes B.	E. W. Moore, M.A.
Maine A.	S. de Ste. Croix, M.A.
Maine B.	S. E. Winbolt, M.A.
Preparatory.	Rev. H. A. Rhodes, M.A.

As the office of the House Masters places them in immediate personal relation with the boys in their respective houses, and as it is desirable that this relation should be rendered as close and effective as possible, it is particularly requested that ordinary communications respecting the progress and welfare of a boy should be addressed to his House Master, who will refer any question of special importance to the Head Master.

Communications respecting the boys' clothes should be addressed to the Matrons. There is a Matron attached to each Block of 100 boys in the Senior School, and there are two Matrons in the Preparatory School. The following hold the office of Matron in the respective Blocks :—

Peele.	Mrs. Norris.
Thornton.	Miss Wass.
Middleton.	Mrs. Riddiford.
Coleridge.	Mrs. Anderson.
Lamb.	Miss Woollerton.
Barnes.	Mrs. Newton.
Maine.	Mrs. Polgreen.
Preparatory.	A Miss Norton. B Miss Smethurst.

In directing all letters please insert the name of the boy's house, for example :—

Boy's Name,
Coleridge A.,
Christ's Hospital,
West Horsham.

NOTE.—The directions as to Medical Certificate, &c., issued with the School Reports, must be closely followed.

Boys leave for the Summer Holidays on Wednesday, Aug. 13th, and return to School on Thursday, Sept. 18th.

THE REV. ARTHUR W. UPCOTT, M.A.,
Head Master.

15. *The Head Master's note for the assembly of the new School at Horsham.*

nothing recognisable remains there today of the old School. There is, though, a blue plaque (at eye-level) on the wall of the building in Newgate Street which the School's drum majors salute whenever the Band marches past, for example for the annual St Matthew's Day visit (around 21st September) when the School is received by the Lord Mayor.

1.47 Despite the destruction not all was lost; indeed the remains of the old Christ's Hospital were distributed far and wide. Some building features were saved and transported to the new School at Horsham, in particular the Wren Portico,

the organ from the Great Hall, the Grecians' Cloister arch, the main gates, and certain statuary, while sundry furniture and fittings were incorporated in the Dining Hall, classrooms and dormitories there. The Writing School clock found its way to Burton Bradstock in Dorset, and five of the stone pinnacles from the Great Hall were used to provide support for a memorial shelter at Beaminster in Hampshire. Further, some of the stone was used to build the Thames wall at Dagenham to resist high tides and potential flooding. And perhaps the most intriguing story of all was that four of the original Giffs Cloisters arches were transported to the garden of a country house in Los Altos Hills just above San Francisco.

What had been achieved?

1.48 In ending this part of our story, it will not be out of place to recapitulate on what had been achieved. There was at Horsham a new School, of unrivalled facilities and magnificent design, set in spacious country grounds. Its buildings, essentially Tudor in architectural style, contained (at the time of the move) some 20 million red bricks and a million and a half tiles. There were also, mixing bases of measurement, around 100,000 cubic feet of off-white Bath, Portland and York stone; over 800 cubic metres of timber in the roofs of the Dining Hall, Big School and Chapel; about 20,000 square metres of Longley's patent wood-block floor, mostly pitch pine, but some wainscot oak, spread across most buildings and constituting an area not far short of the whole London site; and 100 miles of electrical wiring and 40 miles of heating pipes, all mostly hidden in the extensive subterranean network of the Tube. Of the initial 1,200 acre site, the buildings occupied probably around 20 acres, with about another 100 plus acres given over to playing fields. The builders, Longley, were also responsible for the once-magnificent Christ's Hospital station, with its special platform for the school train. The construction of the School as it then stood had spanned about five and a half years, at a cost (including the land) of the order of £450,000-£500,000 (*£165m-£185m*). Thus, for about the pre-credit crunch price of a four-bedroom detached house at nearby Bluecoat Pond, by the old Swimming Baths, a whole school was built!

The 20th Century Onwards

The move to Horsham and settling in

The move to Horsham

1.49 One important issue needed to be resolved before the move. After much deliberation, Head Master Revd Lee*

16 and 17. Horsham – The first day.

18. Horsham – The School teaching staff, early Horsham.

decided not to go to Horsham, and Revd Arthur William Upcott, Headmaster of St Edmund's, Canterbury since 1891, was elected to the post. For other masters, 22 moved from London (mostly) or Hertford, to join the 21 new entrants at Horsham. For the pupils, following various farewell events in the spring of 1902 in both London and Hertford, and a six-week break, the new Head's Assembly Notice (Illustration 15) bade them to the new School on 29th May, this date, perhaps by coincidence but more likely by design, being the date on which the Great Hall in Newgate Street had been opened in 1829. The boys travelled by trains from London Bridge and from Victoria, these joining together at Sutton, to the then splendid Christ's Hospital station, where they were welcomed by Dr Upcott and his masters. For such an auspicious occasion it is regrettable that, so far, the Museum has only a few photographs of the arrival. Two are shown in Illustrations 16 and 17, which depict the boys – many with hand-luggage – assembling in the station yard under the watchful eye of some of the staff before undertaking the short ten-minute march to the School. In the background can be seen a number of horse-drawn carriages, presumably for masters or luggage. A short while later, the Head and his masters assembled in front of Big School for their own photograph (Illustration 18). Not all the names are known but include, as well as Upcott (centre), of those mentioned in this book: Dr Herbert Aldersmith (third row, with hat), TH Boardman (back row, third from left), CE (Chas) Browne (seated second row, furthest right), AW Lockhart* (back row, fourth from right) and RM Wilkinson (back row, furthest right).

1.50 The boys marched from the station with probably more than a modicum of apprehension, to be admitted to the splendour and spaciousness of their new home. They had been told of their new Houses but seemingly had not been informed of their location in the Avenue, so some confusion ensued.

There were reports of the boys' surprise at the School having its own station, of being greeted by the housemasters and of seeing a day-room without beds; there would have been less of a surprise, however, in seeing the dormitory, where the iron-framed beds, the boards, the mattresses, the pillows and settles (iron bedside 'lockers') were all taken from the Wards in London, these items being used well into the 20th century – see Illustration 19. The pulpit, tables and benches in the Dining Hall and some of the masters' desks in the classrooms would also be familiar, as would be some of the masters themselves. In most respects, though, the contrast with London must have been immense, and the freshness of the new environment, so full of possibilities, may have helped to alleviate for many the sadness which was likely to have resulted from the prospect of seeing parents or friends less frequently than hitherto.

19. Horsham – A Dormitory.

20 Horsham – The Science School.

1.51 It may be of interest to record (below) how the 16 Wards in London became 14 Houses in Horsham, and to give the House colours which would be used there, many of these, despite changes over the years, still in evidence in the author's time in the 1950s. There was no Horsham equivalent to Ward VI in London, while Ward XV had ceased to exist in the mid-1890s, being converted to a science laboratory.

Peele A (Ward VII) – Maroon and white	*Peele B (IV) – Green and white*
Thornton A (XII) – Red, white and blue	*Thornton B (IX) – Blue and white*
Middleton A (XVI) – Black and red	*Middleton B (VIII) – Green and black*
Coleridge A (XI) – Red, black and white	*Coleridge B (XIII) – Red, yellow and black*
Lamb A (XIV) – Chocolate and white	*Lamb B (X) – Dark blue and white*
Barnes A (V) – Red and blue	*Barnes B (II) – White and red*
Maine A (III) – Black and gold	*Maine B (I) – Black and white*

1.52 From the information in the children's registers, the author estimates that the new complement of boys numbered about 660. Four boys were discharged in mid-June after barely two weeks at the School, and a further four in July. It is hard not to feel a small sense of disappointment on their behalf at being able to spend so little time in their new pastures after the claustrophobia of London. In August, 39 were discharged, including six who had been preferred to Oxbridge. But the traffic in these initial days was not all one way, the 6th June having seen the arrival of 70 new pupils, with further admissions taking place in September. The start of the new term in 1903 would see around 730 boys at Horsham.

1.53 In reviewing the School's first few months at Horsham, Head Master Upcott said that the boys had taken very well to their new surroundings, reflecting the work of the masters, old and new having blended and bonded with tact and enthusiasm; the detailed planning by the Governors; and the legacy of previous Head Master Lee* and Warden Hay in bequeathing "an inheritance of boys admirably disciplined, hard-working and loyal". For the masters from London or Hertford, and perhaps for some of the new intake, there was, of course, the important transition to the role of housemaster. There was also a corresponding change in the role of the Grecians (senior pupils) who would now exercise greater authority over the boys in the House than they had done in London. Much credit must go to Upcott himself for guiding the School through what was one of the potentially most difficult transitional phases of its long history. Finally, despite the many changes which occurred there was one which, although widely suggested beforehand, did not happen. This concerned the distinctive School uniform which, while suitable for, and distinctly recognisable in, the City, many predicted would look completely out of place in the rural environment of Horsham and regarded a new dress as inevitable. Thankfully, such prognostications were not fulfilled.

Settling in

1.54 The pupils appear to have settled in enthusiastically. In one very early Horsham event, they marched to the top of Sharpenhurst Hill where the bonfire (which had been prepared for King Edward VII's coronation which was delayed from June to August) was lit, with the boys forming a huge ring around the fire, singing the National Anthem, Rule Britannia and Auld Lang Syne. Also early on, a Games Committee of masters and pupils was formed to establish arrangements for sport across the School, one particular area being the laws for rugby (then called football, but to avoid confusion we will refer to it as rugby), Ward matches in London having taken place on the asphalt in front of the Great Hall. The Committee was also responsible for the running of the Tuck Shop, the profits of which (these being about £200 (£20k) in 1903) being used to finance sport at the School.

1.55 As mentioned earlier, the Chapel remained to be completed, it being dedicated in June 1903 at a service conducted by Dr Wilberforce, Bishop of Chichester who, a few months earlier, had conducted the first confirmation service at the School. The Chapel was the only building for

21 Horsham – Ceremony of the unveiling of the statue on the Science School of the Duke of Cambridge, 1903.

which external funding had been sought, about 200 OBs and others raising about £4,000 (£400k), in addition to a wide range of donations for specific purposes and particular gifts. These last included the organ (for which a total cost figure of around £3,500 (£350k) was given), the reredos and the east and west windows (the north window was presented by Walter Vaughan Morgan* (Treasurer) and his brother Septimus*) and the pulpit and lectern. The installation of the organ was not without its problems, the water needed to enable it to function leading to the closure of the Swimming Baths for a few days, the inconvenience being later reversed when the filling of the Baths put the organ out of use for a while.

1.56 Final work had also been undertaken for Big School, in particular, the erection of the clock and the bell which so regularly and inescapably governed the boys' daily schedule. The new turret clock had four dials, six feet in diameter, glazed for illumination, with best gunmetal movement, and with two bells, together of nine hundredweight, the smaller to 'ting-tang' quarters and the larger to strike the hours. The tower was illuminated in April 1903. The building was used for services while the Chapel was being built, this arrangement generating the first of many complaints over the years about the poor acoustics there.

22. Horsham – Pupils in a Science Laboratory, 1905.

1.57 One other aspect of the new buildings might be mentioned. A key feature of the design of the School was the prominence given to the Science School (Illustration 20), it being one of the four central buildings surrounding the Quadrangle, sending out a strong signal of the importance which was to be accorded to the subject. Indeed, it was widely acknowledged that the facilities were amongst the finest of any science building of any school in the country. Statues of King Edward VII (centre), the Duke of Cambridge (left, north) – the ceremony of the unveiling in 1903 being shown in Illustration 21 – and Sir Walter Vaughan Morgan* adorn the front of the building. Science instruction at Horsham would now build on the start made just before the move, this having been prompted by Professor Henry Armstrong (see para 1.111) and greatly facilitated by the appointment of the first science

master, CE Browne, in 1899. Illustration 22 shows pupils at work in one of the laboratories in 1905 – but where are their safety goggles?

1.58 The first Speech Day since 1900 was held on 29th July 1903, its format – including musical and choral pieces, contributions in Latin, French and Greek, the English Oration, the glove ceremony (in which money was collected in white gloves and subsequently distributed to those with Oxbridge awards, a tradition which continued up to the Second World War) and prize-giving – being seemingly similar to what had happened in London and making for a long event. The Oration, delivered from memory, was usually received with rapt attention, this decorum being affected the following year when a report said that silence was regularly interrupted by the turning of the pages of the copy of the speech which had been given to the audience. Illustration 23 shows the Lord Mayor and his party assembled by the Fountain in the Quadrangle, en route (probably) to the 1908 Speech Day ceremony, whilst

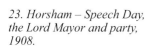

23. Horsham – Speech Day, the Lord Mayor and party, 1908.

24. Horsham – Speech Day, the Governors.

Illustration 24 depicts Governors, with their staffs of office, probably attending the same event, where they would form a guard of honour for the Mayor and the other distinguished guests.

1.59   Concerts, involving orchestral and choral pieces and the Band, and similar entertainments were quickly established, including an event principally for domestic staff, an idea which Upcott had imported from his previous school. Upcott himself frequently performed as a singer at these concerts. In 1905, the Band benefitted from the generous donation of 14 solo instruments. At the same time, the pupils had developed House plays, re-formed the Debating Society which had flourished in London, and set up the Natural History Society (NHS) embracing botany, entomology, geology, ornithology, photography (and later meteorology). With such a wide brief, and little competition, it was not surprising that membership of the NHS soon exceeded 100, including many Grecians, with about 40 masters also joining; further, a separate branch was also introduced for the Preparatory School. Illustration 25 shows pupils, possibly on an NHS venture, near the School.

1.60   In March 1904 there came the sad news of the death, at the age of 84, of the President, The Duke of Cambridge

25. Horsham – Boys on a Natural History Society trip.

26. HRH The Duke of Cambridge, CH President, 1854-1904.

(Illustration 26), who had served in that post for a few days short of 50 years – a loyal and most industrious reign. During this time and the dozen or so years he served before as a Governor, the Duke would have presented over 100 children to the School. The Head Master, Head Mistress, two Grecians and the Head Girl attended his funeral service. In May, the Prince of Wales (George, son of King Edward VII) was elected President. Barely a week later he paid a surprise visit to Horsham and requested a whole (day's) holiday for the School, perpetuating a much-valued London tradition. Half-holidays were, from time to time, also granted for academic achievement by pupils or former pupils, and for certain other events, for example, later, in celebrating the 25th birthday of Upcott's daughter.

1.61   For much of his life, as mentioned earlier, the Duke of Cambridge's day job had been as head of the Army. As such, he would surely have approved the news that, in February 1904, the School received permission from the War Office to establish a Cadet Corps which would be attached to the 1st Volunteer Battalion of the Royal Sussex Regiment. About 220 pupils enrolled, although initially finance could provide uniforms for little more than half this number. Rifles were soon provided and there was much relief that bayonet practice passed off without casualties. The Corps assembled for inspection at the end of Speech Day that year and later had a Field Day, while one of their first exercises saw them fight the "Battle of Sharpenhurst", an event repeated the following year in which a contingent from Cranleigh were charged with defending the Hill from the marauding CH attackers, the image (Illustration 27, depicting correspondent, umpire and bugler) providing little indication as to the nature of the

27. Horsham – The battle of Sharpenhurst.

battle or the result, which was seemingly deemed to be a draw. Indoor shooting was practised in a range set up in the Baths; the building was also to house the School's Armoury. Later, a purpose-built inside range was opened in 1911 and a proper outside range was built.

1.62 Away from CH, about this time there were two names on the list for the position of Lord Mayor of the City of London. Nothing unusual in that – except that both were Old Blues – with John Pound* being elected for 1904-05,

28. Horsham – The Swimming Baths, interior.

29. Horsham – The Gymnasium, interior.

and with Walter Vaughan Morgan* then elected for 1905-06, and both subsequently receiving baronetcies. Over their two years in office, the School and Old Blues were often specially involved with Mayoral events including Lord Mayor's Day (where Cadets formed a guard of honour and girls from Hertford attended), the Spital Sermon, Speech Day (a larger occasion than usual) and St Matthew's Day (which in 1904 senior girls had attended, the first time for 130 years). For the last-mentioned, in 1906 the boys attended the main ceremony, with the whole girls' School being invited to the Mansion House the following day.

1.63 On the sports field, as pupils got used to playing rugby on grass, they were also able to participate 'on campus' in cricket, athletics, swimming, fives (the Rugby version, although Eton fives had been played in London), gymnastics and chess. Rugby and cricket competitions were established by House (rather than House Block), there generally being both knock-out and league events for 1st and 2nd XVs – rugby being played in both the Michaelmas and Lent terms – and 1st and 2nd XIs. Swimming was contested by the Houses according to a seemingly complicated system of scoring points, not only for actual events, but also for the numbers of pupils who could swim a length, this procedure serving as some incentive to reduce the number of non-swimmers in the School, *The Blue* recording an increase in the proportion of 'swimmers' from two-fifths in 1903 to four-fifths in 1907. One interesting event was "swimming in coats", although winning times were not given. The Baths and adjacent Gymnasium – both built in converted barns – are shown in use, in later years, in Illustrations 28 and 29 respectively. For athletics, Houses competed across a range of events for a cup. Illustration 30 shows putting the weight in the 1909 'Games', the event seemingly causing much damage to the grass on Big Side (the sports field south of the Quarter Mile). However, one event, which did not appear to be part of the scoring system, was a "Band race" of unknown distance in which it seemed the participants ran whilst carrying their musical instrument. Regrettably, the results were given by the name of the pupil, rather than the instrument, although the author has it on good authority that the winner was probably the clarinet, with the bass drum nowhere to be seen. The steeplechase – an event which could not be run in London – was also well contested.

1.64 At the more competitive level, inter-school performances in these early years often left much to be desired. However, the quality of both coaching and playing facilities

30. Horsham – Putting the weight.

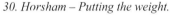

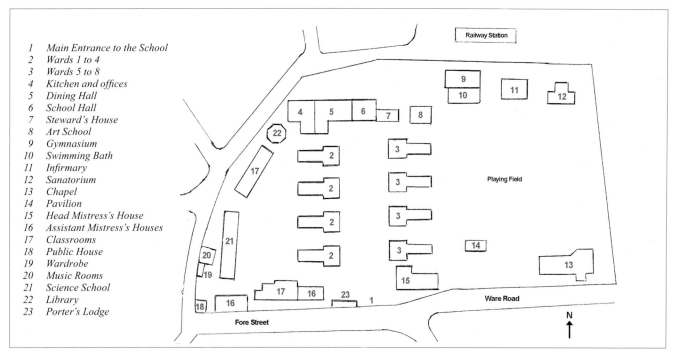

1　Main Entrance to the School
2　Wards 1 to 4
3　Wards 5 to 8
4　Kitchen and offices
5　Dining Hall
6　School Hall
7　Steward's House
8　Art School
9　Gymnasium
10　Swimming Bath
11　Infirmary
12　Sanatorium
13　Chapel
14　Pavilion
15　Head Mistress's House
16　Assistant Mistress's Houses
17　Classrooms
18　Public House
19　Wardrobe
20　Music Rooms
21　Science School
22　Library
23　Porter's Lodge

31. Hertford – A plan of the girls' School, late 1930s.

slowly improved, and an appropriate level of opposition was established. Then, on the rugby field, the XV went through the 1911/12 season with an unbeaten record, winning all their 11 games, scoring (in an era when a try was worth three points) 359 points and conceding but 28. A few months later, the cricket season was graced by an exceptional individual performance for the XI, one WJ Cullen[z] scoring four centuries and amassing 738 runs for an average of 67, followed next season by two centuries in a total of 554 runs, averaging 55; over the period 1910-1913 he scored a then record 1,579 runs for the XI. There were swimming matches against, amongst others, Lancing and the Old Blues, the latter also providing the opposition on the fives court, along with, for example, Epsom College.

1.65 The Prep School seemed to have established itself reasonably well. Although the Prep was housed at the far eastern end of the Avenue, they dined in Hall with the Senior School, their classrooms were located in the block where the senior boys were taught, while Chapel and various cultural activities were also shared. Sport was keenly contested between Prep A and Prep B with athletics including a Victor Ludorum Cup for the best performer and also featuring a Tug of War versus the Grecians, with 30 from the Prep pulling against 15 seniors, the numbers, like the outcome, often being uncertain.

1.66 In May 1910, there occurred the death of King Edward VII. A period of mourning was observed and services were held at Horsham and Hertford, and Speech Day was cancelled at both locations. He was succeeded by his second son, George, then President of Christ's Hospital. Interestingly, on becoming King George V he continued in the role of President (to 1919) at which time his son Edward, Prince of Wales, succeeded him. The new King had received the Loyal Address from the Senior Grecian, George Crofts (1903-11), in June 1911, the event being attended by six Grecians and six monitresses; Crofts was sadly killed in WW1. Amongst other notable pre-War deaths, the Revd W Haig Brown* – the author of "The Votum" – had passed away in 1907, and the Revd G Bell* (Head Master) in 1913. At the School, the year 1913 also saw

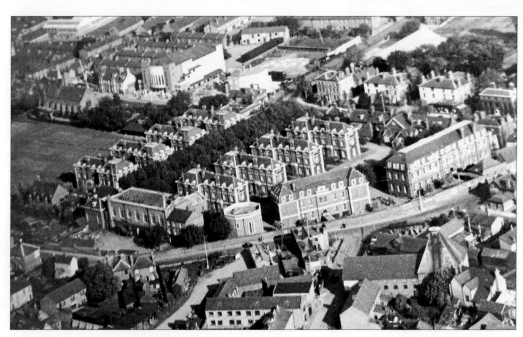

32. Hertford – An aerial view of the girls' School (from the NW).

33. Hertford – The Chapel, interior.

34. Hertford – The Swimming Baths, interior.

the retirement of the Medical Officer, Dr Aldersmith, who had been in post since 1870; he was succeeded by Dr Gerald E Friend, MO at St George's Hospital.

1.67   Now that Hertford was solely a girls' School, this independence gave added value to its presumed status as one of the oldest (if not the oldest) girls' boarding schools in the country. Brief mention was made earlier of the proposed re-development which can best be seen in Illustration 31 – a late 1930s plan of the new School – and Illustration 32 – a (possibly mid-century) aerial photograph of the School. The main improvements made in the early 1900s were the building of eight new separate three-storey Ward blocks (key 2 being numbered 1 to 4, running north, and key 3, 5 to 8, running south) in roughly the same location as the old boys' Wards; a new Chapel (13) and buildings for science (21), art (8) and music (20), as well as some additional classrooms (17), and a new Infirmary (11) and Sanatorium (12), Swimming Baths (10) and Gymnasium (9), all on a site, including playing fields, of around nine acres. In addition, various modifications were made to existing buildings. The new buildings were opened in 1906 by the President, HRH The Prince of Wales. The interiors of the Chapel and the Swimming Baths can be seen in Illustrations 33 and 34 respectively, both of unknown date. [The Public House (18) was not part of the School.]

1.68   Amongst other Hertford events, perhaps the most noteworthy was the gift, in 1904, by an anonymous donor of £20,000 (£2m) to fund places for 10 girls, the donor giving a further £10,000 (£1m) a few years later. Within the School, the girls soon established a Discussion Society and a Natural History Society, and later a Science Society. An annual "sale of work" to raise money for charities and a regular Christmas concert were established, and one of the first School plays was "Twelfth Night". In sport, hockey and tennis were developed early on, with netball and cricket soon following. Inter-school matches were organised as well as the Ward competitions, and hockey and then cricket matches were played against the Old Girls. Earlier, in 1898, a newsletter from the monitresses to the Old Girls had been started and a reunion had taken place in London the following year, with the first Old Girls' Day being held at Hertford in 1903. Then in February 1905, the Christ's Hospital Old Girls' Association was formed, the body soon attracting 200 members. For Founder's Day, Head Mistress Robertson had established the custom of her recounting

the history of the School, followed by a half-holiday in the afternoon with a dance in the evening. In 1908, reflecting the heavy burden of her office, Miss Robertson was granted leave of absence for seven months, travelling to Europe and Canada (staying with her brother in British Columbia). The first Hertford Speech Day was held in June 1909, with prize-giving taking place the following month. A Board of Education inspection in 1910 was highly satisfactory, a standard which was to be confirmed later in 1915 and 1921. One event of the time – Empire Day in 1913 – is shown in Illustration 35.

1.69   Finally, a few other features of the initial years at Horsham might be mentioned briefly. First, at the end of Speech Day in June 1904 the Cricket Pavilion was opened, it having been financed by contributions from Old Blues and others. Secondly, the Fountain in the Quad – essentially the statue of Edward VI (which had been on the Grammar School building in London) surrounded by the new statues of four Old Blues who gave their name to Houses (Coleridge, Lamb, Maine and Middleton) – was deemed completed. However, the Fountain part was never to function. Thirdly, around the turn of 1904/05, a Sub Post Office was opened just south of the present-day Bluecoat Pond buildings, the wish being

35. Hertford – Empire Day, 1913.

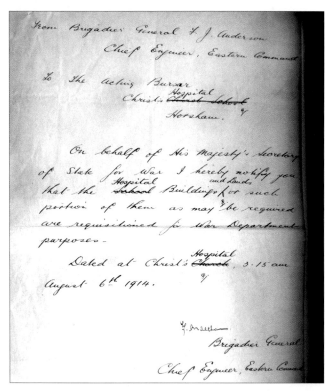

36. Horsham – WW1, the School is requisitioned.

37. Horsham – A telegram about the requisition.

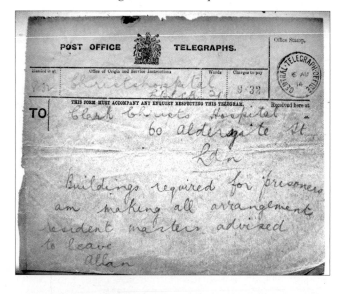

expressed that it might soon have telegraphic and telephonic communications. Fourthly, in 1907, the extensive planting of trees across the site provided a more "park-like" aspect, with the wide view being "no more than quietly broken up". Fifthly, despite occasional entreaties by the School, King Edward VII had decided not to re-instigate the practice of the Monarch receiving the RMS boys, this perhaps not all that surprising given that it had been in abeyance for some 13 years.

The First World War and the aftermath

The War years

1.70 The War started early at CH. At 3am on Thursday 6th August – two days after the declaration – a Brigadier General from Eastern Command, accompanied by the local Superintendent of Police, arrived at Horsham to inform the School that its premises were required as a prison. In the absence of Head Master Upcott (who was on a family holiday

at Wellington College, Berkshire) and the bursar, Colonel R Boyd (who had been called up for service), the deputation met the Steward, George Allan*, and left a written requisition, timed at 3.15am (Illustration 36). A telegram brought the Head from his holiday, he being met at the School gates by sentries armed with fixed bayonets. Meanwhile, Allan had arranged for furniture and movables to be cleared from the House Blocks. He also sent a telegram (Illustration 37) to the Clerk in London: "Buildings required for prisoners am making all arrangements resident masters advised to leave."

1.71 At 8.30pm that day, 85 prisoners (who were mostly reservists and were being prevented from leaving the country and returning to Germany) and an escort arrived and were billeted in Barnes House Block. Allan provided "active service rations" and said he was keeping a strict account of all outlays, while MO Dr Friend was providing medical facilities. Then on Friday, a colonel from Eastern Command arrived to take charge of the prison. Further arrivals over the next few days meant that, by the end of Monday, the strength of the prisoners and escort was 600, use now being made of other House Blocks (Lamb, Maine and Peele).

1.72 On the Monday morning (10th), Sir Joseph Savory, vice-Chairman of the Council of Almoners, visited the War Office in London to make representations on behalf of the School and to seek further information. He was told that the decision to requisition the School was essentially a local one, taken at very short notice, and it was hoped that the prisoners ("respectable types" – a view confirmed by Allan) would be removed within a week. A formal letter of explanation was sent to Savory the following day, it saying that occupation might extend until the end of the month. Savory called a special meeting of Council on Wednesday 12th August to discuss the situation, and an Advisory Committee was set up to deal with the matter; in particular there had been some concern as to whether the School would be ready to receive the pupils at the start of the Michaelmas term on 15th September. Around the third week of August the prisoners were moved out of the School and housed in a compound erected on Sharpenhurst Hill. Then towards the end of August they began to be relocated – mostly to Aldershot – and all were gone in the first week of September, the only outward indication remaining being the Sharpenhurst camp. Within the School, a large body of workmen armed with disinfectant and paint had hastily removed all traces of the occupation in the Houses, this work being costed at £620 (£50k). The pupils did return to CH on the due date for the start of term.

1.73 *The Blue* reported that the first OB casualty of the War was Lieutenant JH Drake (1889-95) who had died on 20th September. Throughout the War the publication provided details of those serving and those killed. Further, in June 1916, a Roll of Honour was included in cases on the wall of the west Cloisters, the names being added to from time to time. Although a dedicated memorial was to be established in 1920, the Roll remained there until 1936, by when time and weather had already much affected the careful penmanship of the original. Of particular note, two OBs – 2nd Lieutenant EF Baxter* and Lieutenant-Colonel W Elstob* – received the highest honour, the VC (the first such honour to an Old Blue had been awarded to Captain HW Pitcher* in 1863), these three recipients being shown in Illustrations 38, 39 and 40. Two other former pupils to perish were EW Cox* and LWP East*, both Brigadier Generals, the most senior rank amongst OBs to die. For the CH staff, the first death – of Captain William Eyre – occurred in August 1915, this being followed

38. 2nd Lieutenant Edward Felix Baxter, VC.

39. Lieutenant-Colonel Wilfrith Elstob, VC.

40. Captain Henry William Pitcher, VC.

by David Harvey, with permission of "This England"

in August 1917 by Lieutenant-Colonel TH Boardman, who had been commander of the School OTC.

1.74 From an early stage, the Head Master had the daunting task of conveying to the School the immensely sad news of the passing of Old Blues, many of whom had been under his charge. This he would do at the Sunday morning Chapel service, the announcements also having a profound effect on the pupils. One unknown Old Blue recorded: "One of the first names to be read out was PWJ Stevenson who had left at the end of the summer term in 1914, joined the Army and was a 2nd Lieutenant when he was killed in action in May 1915. He was one of the very senior boys in the School, a very good scholar and athlete, and House Captain of Coleridge B. It is very easy to imagine how we, young as we were, who remembered him felt when we heard his name read out. Of all other names that were read before the War was over, his name was the one that affected us most". [Stevenson had achieved a classical scholarship to St John's College, Oxford. The manner of his death – rescuing a wounded soldier – elicited the tribute in *The Blue* that it was a "noble sacrifice, worthy of his whole life". His elder sister, Frances, who became Countess Lloyd George, was to be a generous supporter of CH.]

1.75 Some other features of the War merit mention. First, the pupils at Horsham undertook a substantial amount of work for the War in the Manual School. Some of it – done by a team of about 25 in a full and arduous seven and a half hour working day – was high precision, for example aeroplane parts; other output included components for shells and dummy cartridges, and wooden rifles (used for training). Secondly, the OTC was reported as putting in two parades a week, with Field Days exercises seeing members of the Corps divided into attackers and defenders and using blank ammunition. As the War progressed, the value of the OTC in helping to get individuals commissioned became increasingly recognised. Elsewhere, scouts, signallers and engineers were detected in "obscurer portions of Sussex", and local Territorials were given permission to drill in the School grounds and to use the range. Thirdly, in early 1917 some land, seemingly the site of the present-day Sports Centre and to the north, was ploughed up in preparation for a crop of oats. Lastly, an interesting contribution to the stories of the War came from the pen of the then Lieutenant EC Blunden[z], who arranged to hold a meeting of five Old Blues in his battalion which became known as the "Feast of Five". The event is remembered in a poignant photograph in the School Museum, perhaps less for the meeting itself, than for the fact that two of the five were killed a few months later while a third took his life some years after the end of the War.

1.76 More generally, both Horsham and Hertford had to cope with the inevitable food rationing, personal accounts of the War at Horsham saying that both quality and quantity left much to be desired, with in one instance mention of a special implement, made of wood with nails protruding at regular intervals, which was used to divide out the loaves of bread according to the proscribed ration. In one interesting development, at the request of the Government, the School supplied information about the amount of food consumed, this helping to formulate policy on rationing across the country. At Horsham, masters who had gone to fight were replaced by those who had retired, some of whom were quite eminent, although not necessarily capable teachers or good at keeping order. But the aim was that lessons, School events and activities should continue largely unaffected. Of the two main ceremonies, first, Speech Day was mostly held, but in 'reduced' form, with the Lord Mayor, sans regalia, although measles rather than war had led to the cancellation of the 1914 event at Hertford. During this time, JHE Woods[z] – seen in Illustration 41 delivering the Oration in 1913 – was Senior Grecian for two years (1912/13 and 1913/14), the author being aware of only one previous example of this over the last 180 years, EM Field (1859-71),

41. JHE Woods delivering the Speech Day oration, 1913.

in 1869/70 and 1870/71. Secondly, for St Matthew's Day, the visit to the Mansion House was cancelled in 1914 and 1915, but arrangements were made for the pupils still to receive the traditional largesse. The ceremony resumed in 1916, with the OTC representing Horsham and, for the first time, a number of monitresses attending from Hertford (see Illustration 42, names unfortunately not known), a similar arrangement occurring the following year. Also in 1916, Founder's Day was celebrated by a lunch, a service at Christ Church and a reception by the Lord Mayor at the Mansion House, the Head Master and six Grecians also attending the day. The following year, in addition to the senior boys, for the first time a number of monitresses attended the celebrations.

1.77 On the sports field, whilst House and inter-school competitions generally continued, reports in *The Blue*, rugby and cricket apart, were few and far between, this reflecting reductions in the size of the publication. The XV and XI appeared to have mixed results, although the rugby side were said to have had a good run in matches against other schools over the period 1912 to 1917. In athletics, there was a noteworthy performance at the 1916 sports afternoon, when EV Bell^z won the Open quarter-mile, half-mile and mile, *The Blue* report adding that he had "previously won the steeplechase" (but not presumably on the same afternoon). It appears that physical training had been a casualty of the War, *The Blue* stating that it had resumed in September 1918, but not having said when it had been stopped.

1.78 At Hertford there was much War activity in the town, with drilling of troops barracked there and the "very stirring" sight of the regular passage of others through the town en route to the east coast. The School held a concert, with an invitation extended to some of the troops stationed in the town, whilst, in another example of help, when a large contingent of troops arrived – with those unable to find billets camping outside the School in their lorries – the staff rose early the following morning to provide them with breakfast. Inside the gates, life and work continued much as normal. The pupils undertook knitting for the War effort, while later, as part of a nationwide campaign, the younger girls collected conkers (these being used to make acetone, an important component of the smokeless propellant for shells and bullets). In 1914, Old Girls' Day had celebrated the 21st anniversary of the arrival at the School of Head Mistress Miss Robertson. One interesting lecture about this time had been given by a Miss Gertrude Bacon, a "practised airwoman", who was stated as being the first Englishwoman to fly an aeroplane. In 1916, Miss Robertson introduced badges for the monitresses. In July 1920, in the first summer gathering since 1914, well over 200 Old Girls and former members of staff enjoyed a convivial afternoon at the School.

Post-War

1.79 At the end of the War, there were special Thanksgiving Services for the Armistice at both Horsham and Hertford. Soon afterwards, the Head Master received a letter from the War Office thanking him for the effort rendered by the School during the War, in particular for those who had provided their support for the Officers' Training Corps and for the high quality of staff which had emerged. In 1919, as a memento of the work undertaken by the OTC, the War Office presented the School with a German field-gun and a German trench-mortar, these being placed at the ends of the Quarter Mile. It is unclear whether they were used in any (instructional) shape or form, or even looked after, probably neither, since their appearance

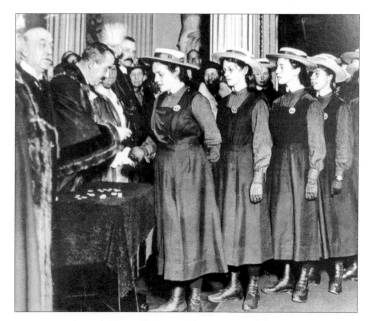

42. Hertford monitresses at St Matthew's Day, 1916.

provoked a letter in *The Blue* in early 1931 from one signing himself (or herself) as "DISGUSTED", which referred to "masses of rusty steel clambered over by small boys", one of the guns "with its barrel stuffed with mud" and concluding that German visitors to the School were distressed to find "their treasured Krupp guns here in such a state". This letter must surely have expedited their removal.

1.80 If the War had not wrought enough devastation, the whole world was now even more affected by the influenza pandemic of 1918-19. At Horsham the boys were inoculated against the disease, this action appearing to be wholly successful. However, at Hertford about two-thirds of the School succumbed, suggesting that they had not been similarly inoculated. All recovered, eventually, and the Michaelmas term was curtailed by two weeks. The War had also had a debilitating effect on the School's finances, leading to the sale of some precious volumes, including a first edition (1687) of Sir Isaac Newton's *Philosophie Naturalis Principia Mathematica*.

1.81 A Roll of Honour and Service was published in 1920. It contained the names of Governors, members of staff and Old Blues who served in the War, identifying those who had perished in the service of their country. The Roll gave the dates at CH and the House or Ward (for OBs), and the regiment in which the individuals had served. It also gave details of honours and decorations awarded, and indicated whether they were killed, died of wounds or died on active service; wounded; mentioned in despatches; prisoner of war; or missing. The Roll records details of 57 Governors (four of whom were OBs), 31 masters (11 OBs) and 2,048 other Old Blues who served their country, with 376 reported deaths (four Governors, four masters and 368 Old Blues). It was also tentatively suggested in the Roll – presumably based on numbers of OBs and their age distribution – that at least 3,000 would probably have served, noting and lamenting the absence of information on the other 1,000. The Roll also listed over 375 distinctions, including the two Victoria Crosses mentioned earlier.

1.82 In early 1919 an appeal was launched for funds to remember "our departed brothers", and a sum of £3,000 (£125k) was sought. Remembrance would take two forms: a memorial, to be designed by Sir Aston Webb, one of the architects of the School, in the form of stone tablets on the

43. Horsham – The unveiling of the WW1 Memorial, 1920.

front wall of Dining Hall, whilst the major part would seek to provide for the dependants of Old Blues who had died, and to assist those who had been maimed, blinded, wrecked in health, or temporarily ruined in business as the result of active service. In the event, some £6,000 (£250k) was raised. For the Memorial itself, the names are arrayed in two tablets of Portland stone, in each there being three 'panels' which are separated by figures of two young boys, one in School dress and the other in the uniform of the Officer Training Corps. The Memorial, which also included the laying of the three plots of grass (previously an area of asphalt and seemingly the route taken by Houses marching into Hall) just in front of the Dining Hall, was unveiled on Founder's Day (October 23rd) 1920 by the Rt Revd EH Pearce*, Bishop of Worcester, the event – shown in Illustration 43 – also being attended by senior girls from Hertford. In its original form the Memorial included the names of 364 "Sons of this House" who gave their lives in the Great War. Further names have been added across the years.

1.83 One unfortunate feature of what should have been a reverential and uniting process was the occasional criticism made of the figures on the Memorial, some saying they were "undignified" and that the Housey boy was "effeminate", and others using phrases like "grotesque toy soldier" and "stone dolls", such comments continuing well into the middle of the decade. Illustration 44 brings together the two figures at the centre of the controversy. Towards the end of 1926, seats were introduced around the Memorial, this making for a more

44. The Housey boy statues on the Memorial.

pleasing aspect. On Old Blues' Day in 1922 there had been a commemoration of those OBs who had given their lives in the First World War. The whole School paraded in the Quad in front of the Memorial and a short service was held.

1.84 The year 1923 had seen the installation in the Chapel of the last of the 16 paintings by Frank (later Sir) Brangwyn,

45. Horsham – The Chapel, interior, early Horsham.

his work having begun in 1912. The bare walls of the Chapel before the murals were installed can be seen in Illustration 45. The paintings – 14 are each about fourteen feet by eight feet, with two 'half' murals – strikingly depict the spread of the Gospel around the world, in rough chronological sequence from along the eastern wall to the organ and then returning down the western wall towards the gallery, the last depicting a scene from the slums of London. Illustration 46 is of one of the murals, the black and white image doing no justice to their subtle pastel colours. The bulk of the cost of the murals came from the residue of the fund which had been set up to furnish and decorate the Chapel as part of the building of the Horsham School. In 1930, Brangwyn generously presented seven of his original drawings to the School, these now being safely stored, and occasionally displayed, in the Museum.

1.85 There were a number of miscellaneous events during these War years worthy of mention. First, in September 1915, an Army biplane landed on Sharpenhurst, the crew apparently thinking they were at Farnborough, which was some 30 miles away. They departed, amidst much local interest, after lunch at the Head's house. Secondly, a short while later, in an event

46. A Brangwyn mural.

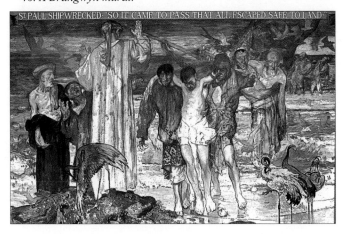

which also got much local attention, two Artillery observation balloons landed near Housey; these were "apprehended", deflated and sent back to London on the next train. Thirdly, despite having to cope with the ravages of war, Head Master Upcott found time in 1916 to pen the words of the School's evocative Foundation Hymn which begins with the line "Praise the Lord for our Foundation", the equally important music being written by RM Wilkinson, the Head of Music. Fourthly, the OTC had been photographed in 1918, this perhaps leading to a whole School photograph – probably the first at Horsham – in 1919. For the record, the Museum has whole School photographs for these early years for 1919, 1922, 1926, 1929 and 1936. There is then a gap of around 55 years, during which time it seems that such photographs were not taken, with the Museum's next image relating to 1990, then 1996, 1998, 2001, 2006, 2010, 2014 and 2016. For Hertford, the Museum holds photographs for 1919, 1981 and 1984. Others may have been taken at both locations. Lastly, around 1917, Guy Calthrop* was appointed State Controller of Mines, with a seat in Cabinet: this was thought to be the first time an Old Blue had held such a position at the centre of Government.

1.86 Of personnel, there were three notable deaths about this time. First, two Old Blues – Sir John Pound* in September 1915 (Illustration 47) and Sir Walter Vaughan Morgan*, November 1916 (Illustration 48), both Lord Mayors of London, and then, in March 1918, Dr Aldersmith, the School's long-serving MO. The year 1919 saw the resignation of Head Master Upcott, who had been in post since the move in 1902. Upcott's legacy was the successful re-establishment of Christ's Hospital in the rural environment. There was more space, more possibilities, more freedom for everyone, but these benefits still needed strong direction and guidance. In the classroom, previously dominated by classics and mathematics, science and engineering had developed rapidly, and music improved out of all recognition. And there was of course his Foundation Hymn. His successor was William Hamilton Fyfe, Fellow and Tutor, Merton College, Oxford. The new Head Master and his team, including two women, can be seen in Illustration 49, with the following people who appear elsewhere in this book being identified: 'Teddy' Edwards (front row, seated on ground, at left), CE Browne (second row, on WHF's left) and RM Wilkinson (third row from back, second from right (with mortar board)).

1.87 In May 1919, as mentioned earlier, HRH Edward Prince of Wales accepted the Presidency of Christ's Hospital, in succession to King George V who became the School's Patron. He made his first visit to Horsham in May 1921, arriving in his Rolls Royce. After lunch in Dining Hall he addressed the School from the Hall Warden's desk, signifying the conclusion of his speech – in which he had referred to CH's two wartime VCs – by banging the gavel. HRH then visited various School buildings and took tea in the Head Master's house. To say – as *The Blue* did – his farewell was greeted as enthusiastically as his arrival should not be misinterpreted.

Consolidation in the 1920s and 1930s

1.88 The year 1920 marked the 50th anniversary of *The Blue* (see paras A2.19-25), its editor taking the opportunity to encourage contributions. One regular source of material for the publication was furnished by changes in and deaths

47 and 48: Sir John Pound, Lord Mayor, 1904-05 and Sir Walter Vaughan Morgan, Lord Mayor, 1905-06, CH Treasurer.

49. Horsham – The School teaching staff, early 1920s

50. Horsham – Big School, interior, c1928.

of personnel connected with the School. Towards the end of the year, Septimus Croft*, who had been Treasurer during the difficult years of the War, resigned, the role being taken by Frederick White*, who had just turned 80; White served for only two years, being succeeded in 1922 by Mervyn Davie*. On White's 86th birthday, the Senior Grecian was sent to his Itchingfield home (Muntham) to present the greetings of the School, and on his death in 1927, the flag on the Water Tower over the Dining Hall was flown at half-mast. Also in 1920, the Clerk, Richard Franks*, retired, having served for some 30 years, to be replaced by Thomas Limmer*, who in turn gave way to George Allan* in 1922. The year 1922 also saw, within the space of three months, the passing of CH's last two Head Masters – Revd R Lee* in February 1922 and Revd AW Upcott in May. Later, memorials to each were included in the west Cloisters. The fund set up for Upcott paid for the memorial tablet, with the residue being used to establish the "Upcott Memorial Music Library" which would contain a range of books, scores and libretti. Earlier, at the end of 1921, the death had occurred of Sir Joseph Savory, sometime Lord Mayor, who had a long and close connection with the School, particularly in the difficult years following the introduction of the Scheme in 1891. Also in 1921, Head Mistress Robertson retired, to be succeeded by Miss Nora Craig, Head of Saltburn High School. Miss Robertson had been appointed in 1893 and had seen the exodus of the boys to Horsham, the building of the new School at Hertford, and the difficult years of the war. She had been at the head of a School of now around 280 pupils and had contributed greatly to its improved academic standards. And not to be forgotten was her role in founding the Old Girls' Association in 1905.

1.89 At Horsham, in music, a fairly full programme of School concerts included talented and regular performances from three pupils who were to make their names in this field in later life – Constant Lambert[z], John Hunt[z] and Percy Young[z] – and also from Cecil ('Bill') Kirby[z]. A wider form of entertainment, comprising the traditional concert, with sketches, and performed by both pupils and staff, was also very popular, one event in Big School (a rather bare-

looking image of the inside of the building c1928 is given in Illustration 50) in 1924 attracting an audience in excess of 1,200, something which present-day health and safety regulations would not permit. Further, for a while, Gilbert and Sullivan was put on every other year. Towards the end of the Michaelmas term in 1928, the School was asked to perform two concerts in the Christmas holidays, in Clerkenwell and Poplar. Despite the timing and short notice, support amongst the pupils seemed strong and, with little time for rehearsal, a programme was established and the performances were given to appreciative audiences, with proceeds going to the churches in which they were held. The success of the venture led to an annual series of such concerts over the next few years, the programmes being a mix of choral and musical performances and also sketches by a group of senior pupils who went under the name of "The Blackberries", the venues embracing churches, church halls and clubs, and with a wide range of beneficiaries. At the end of the summer term 1929 Robert Wilkinson, Head of Music since 1902, retired, his last Speech Day concert being greeted with triumphal acclaim, with the magnitude of his long-term achievements in post being reflected in the fact that over 170 people had subscribed to a farewell present and, enduringly, by the music he had composed for the Foundation Hymn.

1.90 In respect of drama, where House plays, performed in the Lent term generally in the heavily adapted day-rooms, provided staple fare, the School saw more ambitious offerings in the form of a series of French plays in the early 1920s, Gilbert and Sullivan and of course Shakespeare, including productions by the leaving Grecians. Amongst an ever-increasing number of societies there emerged a Modern Literary Society, one of whose early guests was writer and historian Hilaire Belloc, an Astronomy and Astrophysics Society, and the 1930 Society. Meanwhile, the Debating Society continued to flourish, its more prominent speakers of this time including RMM Stewart[z], AA Muir[z] and GJ Whitrow[z]. [Whitrow tutored the author at Imperial College in the early 1960s, the Mathematics Department then being located in a building which later became part of the Victoria

51. *Sir Henry Cole.*

by Lock and Whitfield, © National Portrait Gallery, London

and Albert Museum, the particular wing being named after another Old Blue, Sir Henry Cole* (Illustration 51), who had played a major role in establishing the Museum and earlier had been a key instigator of the Great Exhibition of 1851.]

1.91 On the sports fields, by and large rugby and cricket results in this decade seemed not to come up to expectations. In 1927, in an attempt to improve the standard of rugby in the School generally, House leagues were replaced by a system based on 'clubs' in which 14 sides, drawn from across the Houses, would be established on merit and games between adjacent teams would allow players to move up and down the sides. It is not clear whether the idea was deemed a success. In cricket, HWF Franklin[z] accumulated a record 131 wickets across his years playing for the XI, but elsewhere the interest was often in the review of the season, where the performance

of the players was put under the microscope, and comment, often harsh, was made. One offering which caught the author's eye said that as a batsman he (a future Head Master who shall remain anonymous) "suffers far too much from nerves to survive very long". Elsewhere, swimming seemed to have established a regular series of inter-school matches, whilst in athletics, a tri-angular match, for seniors and for juniors, with Brighton and Cranleigh was held for the first time in 1925. Other sporting snippets included the Amicable Society (see paras A2.14-15) raising £40 (£2k) in support of boxing, whilst in fives, the pupils achieved a first ever success against the Common Room. For the less organised, when weather permitted, pupils tobogganed on Sharpenhurst and skated on Doctor's Lake (to the east of Bluecoat Pond).

1.92 The Speech Day celebrations at Horsham and Hertford in 1922 saw, for the first time, a group of a dozen senior Grecians attending the Hertford event and a similar sized party of senior monitresses going to the Horsham ceremony, each group finding many aspects of life at the other place worthy of high praise and envy. In the 1925 St Matthew's Day ceremony, the Hertford girls were included in the march from Christ Church to the Mansion House for the first time; two years later they were at the head of the parade, behind the Band. At about the same time, the largesse received by the monitresses was increased to a guinea, thus achieving parity with the Grecians, and then, in the mid-1930s, the girls were to receive their largesse from the Lord Mayor before the boys. One other long-standing St Matthew's Day tradition had apparently seen its demise in 1928 when buns – so much an integral part of the Mansion House fare – were no longer provided.

1.93 Amongst other events at Hertford, in 1921 the school acquired 10 acres of land at nearby Ashbourne for use as a playing field, with a Pavilion being added in 1926. Illustration 52 shows the opening ceremony. In 1922, the first edition of an annual school magazine appeared, this being additional to the existing newsletter. At Speech Day in 1923 the glove ceremony (a long-established tradition at the boys' School which provided monies for pupils going to university) was

52. *Hertford – The opening of the Sports Pavilion.*

introduced. Then in 1925, the Governors gifted seven handsome oak Honours Boards which record the recipients of various prizes, these being transferred from the hall at Hertford to Horsham with the merger and now located on the walls of the corridor by the Court Room. (En passant, apparently there are no similar boards for boys.) The regular Christmas activities, including the "sale of work", continued, whilst a new French Society was formed. However, one of the more notable events of these years was the surprise visit by the President at the end of 1926, his short speech being particularly memorable, as was the extra holiday granted to the pupils.

1.94 The 'service' part of the Housey ethos and the Old Blue community life had been particularly evident in work at the St John's Mission, King's Cross, whose founding had been promoted by the CH Club in 1892 (see paras A2.9-11). Now, in November 1927, the Head Master chaired a meeting in London to consider possible ways in which both School and OB groups might take a more practical part in civic work in London. Various ideas were discussed, including some thoughts from the Revd 'Tubby' Clayton, founder of Toc H ("Talbot House", an international Christian movement), one suggestion being that the School should form links with a boys' club which then might benefit from attending a camp near the School. A committee was formed to establish the present position and to make proposals as to what Old Blues and the School might do. It took a while for these deliberations to bear fruit and the initial events were regarded as something of an experiment, but prosper they did. The camp in 1932, for example, saw about 60 boys from two clubs in London, with a few Housey pupils, spending 10 days staying in Barnes, enjoying fine weather, the Sussex countryside, much sport and other activities, and a camaraderie within a social environment which both groups were unlikely to have experienced before. Then the following year, about 30 boys from a different club and a slightly fewer number of Housey boys, had to forgo the luxury of a Boarding House to rough it in tents by the Tuck Shop. The arrangements appeared to continue through much of the decade with, for example, the Thameside Boys' Club visiting in 1937, with a seemingly more extensive sports day and prize-giving.

1.95 As a further example of community work, at the end of 1928 the School had 'adopted' Bronllwyn School, a village school, not in London, but in what was regarded as a 'distressed' area of the Rhondda Valley. Money was collected for the school and parents were encouraged to send parcels. Later, in early 1929, a small group, of unknown composition,

53. Horsham – The opening of the Scout Hut, 1930.

visited the school and were able to see the problems and how the CH involvement had managed to alleviate some of them, the report ending by saying that the school had produced many champion boxers, including Jimmy Wilde who became World Flyweight Champion and was one of the greatest British fighters of all time.

1.96 Back at Horsham, there were some internal changes to the buildings including expansion of the Tuck Shop and its tea room, and a reorganisation and redecoration of what had become a well-equipped Library, where opening hours were greatly increased. There were also a variety of improvements to Big School, particularly to the lighting and the panelling, both widely admired, and also to the ever-problematic acoustics where, even some time later, the jury still seemed to be out. These changes probably helped to enhance the glory of the organ which had been built and installed by Elliott and Hill in the Great Hall in London in 1830, and then carefully removed, transported and re-installed at Horsham in the summer of 1902. The cleaner air of Horsham meant that the pipes needed to be cleared of dust far less frequently than in London, although, at the time of its centenary, it was observed that cleaning was desirable. Today, over 85 years on from its centenary, the organ still stands resplendent in Big School, but, perhaps inevitably and despite periodic overall, the quality of its performance has suffered. Indeed, for some years it was deemed unplayable, but following the generosity of John Chumrow[z], it was brought back to life a few years ago, Chumrow also having provided funds for some refurbishment in the Music School.

1.97 There were two major changes to the landscape of the School in 1930. First, the New Science School (a second Science Block) was constructed, the result of many munificent contributions, the building forming the third, east side of the Garden Quad (being one building short of a second quadrangle), this hitherto open space of unused ground having been levelled and laid to lawn and landscaped with a central pool. The new Block, which included a number of laboratories (especially for biology), a science library and lecture theatre, and rooms for geography, helped to keep CH near the forefront of public schools' science facilities, and was opened by the Royal President in October, following a welcoming address by the Bishop of Worcester, EH Pearce*. HRH inspected the building, lunched in Dining Hall, where he addressed the School, had a whistle-stop tour of various buildings and a rugby match, before departing the way he had arrived – in his Gipsy Moth aeroplane. Sadly, in the eyes of the author, the building has one obvious defect, namely that the colour of the brickwork does not better match that of the other School buildings. Also built in 1930, near to the Manual School, was the Scout Hut, a most generous gift from Lord Wakefield, businessman, philanthropist and Lord Mayor of London. The building was opened by Lord Baden Powell, the Chief Scout, who shook hands with every member of the CH troop. The ceremony is shown in Illustration 53, with Lord Wakefield (centre, carrying hat) and Head Master Fyfe (on Baden Powell's left). Within the last couple of years, the Hut has been refurbished and goes by the name of the Lord Wakefield Centre, a multi-purpose building which, following the demise of the troop a few years ago, regrettably may never again see the presence of scouts.

1.98 Amongst other events of the period which might be mentioned, first the General Strike of 1926 seemed to have little impact at Horsham and Hertford, although there had been a severe reduction in the number of Governors attending the girls' sports day, this being compensated by the record numbers at Speech Day a few weeks later. Secondly, overseas travel by CH pupils around this time had seemed generally somewhat limited, reflecting lack of both opportunity and money, although the School did have an Overseas Travel fund. However, in 1928, JC Wilmot-Buxton (1920-30) joined the School Empire Tour party, numbering some 40 public schoolboys, for a 10-week tour of South Africa and Rhodesia. An education as the trip undoubtedly was, Wilmot-Buxton greatly acknowledged the enthusiastic welcome from sundry Old Blues during his travels.

1.99 Within the OB community, the early part of the 1920s had seen a severe decline in the fortunes of the CH Club, indeed it appeared near to closure, that this did not happen owing much to the efforts of Percy Giles*. More favourably, in March 1924, the centenary of the Benevolent Society of Blues was celebrated with a service at Christ Church, followed by a meeting in the Old Grammar School (which had become part of St Bartholomew's Hospital) and, for a few, including some Grecians, afternoon tea there. Then in October 1925, Housey's sons, past, present (apparently some senior boys only and not girls) and adopted, gathered, with Treasurer Davie* in the Chair, at the Connaught Rooms in London to celebrate the 100th Founder's Day Dinner. Finally, the year 1929 marked what was claimed to be the tercentenary of the founding of the Amicable Society of Blues, part of the celebrations being subsumed within the St Matthew's Day event. More information about these OB institutions is given in Appendix 2.

1.100 In 1930, Joseph Brown* succeeded to the post of Treasurer, and in the same year Head Master Fyfe, with 15 other Heads, embarked on a five-week tour of colleges and universities in Canada. Not long after his return, he announced that he would be leaving CH at the end of the summer term to take up an appointment as Principal of Queen's University, Kingston, Ontario; such shortness of notice would not be allowed in the contract today. One of his many legacies was an expansion of the range of opportunities for pupils on leaving CH, as one commentator wrote, Oxbridge and the City were enlarged into a "hydra-headed variety of openings".

1.101 The new Head Master of CH was to be Henry Lael Oswald Flecker, previously Head at Berkhamsted School. Previously might be the wrong word since, reflecting the haste with which the change had been made, he was, for a while, to continue his Berkhamsted duties as well, this double-jobbing apparently lasting a whole term. In November 1932, the Head's engagement to Miss MP Hessey was announced, and they were married in the School Chapel the following March, two girls from Hertford being invited to the ceremony which is shown in Illustration 54. The Museum has the Register of Banns and the Register of Marriage, the event constituting the sole entries in both books.

1.102 It might be of interest to see the winter week-day time-table of this era, as described in Allan's* 1937 book on Christ's Hospital, this being broadly similar to what the author can recall from his time at CH in the 1950s: 7.00, getting-up bell; 7.20, trades (preparation for meals); 7.30-8.00, breakfast; 8.40, Chapel; 9.00-10.20, school; 10.20-10.55, break for PT and biscuits; 10.55-12.15, school; 12.45, trades; 1.00-1.45, lunch; 2.15-4.00, activities; 4.10-5.50, school; 6.00-6.30, tea; 7.35, prep; 8.05, Duty (a short religious offering in the House) and bed for juniors; 9.05, bed for seniors; later, bed for monitors. For the pupil, the week-day time-table represented a sequence

Housey boys formed a guard of honour for their headmaster, HLO Flecker, and his bride, Miss Mary Hessey, after their wedding – the first to take place in the School Chapel.

54. The wedding of Head Master Oswald Flecker and Miss MP Hessey.

of moves as follows: House – Dining Hall (marching) – House – Chapel (marching) – Classrooms – House – Classrooms – House – Dining Hall (marching) – House – Classrooms – House – Dining Hall (marching) – House. The author was in Peele B, the furthest but one House in the west end of the Avenue. He has calculated that, during his eight years at the School, in respect of this week-day routine and adding in the week-end, he must have walked more than 2,500 miles further than someone in one of the central Houses.

1.103 Another new head – CS Lang, of Music – made an early mark, introducing a House instrumental competition and arranging for the London Symphony Orchestra to visit the School. Such concerts, with Lang himself conducting, continued for a few years. Also in the early 1930s, the School participated in a scheme for the interchange of concerts between public schools, CH undertaking such arrangements with Eton and Wellington. The traditional Easter, Speech Day and Christmas concerts continued to flourish, with two notable and regular performers amongst the pupils being Ivor Keys[z] and Denis Womersley[z]. In July 1932, at the invitation of the Horsham Urban District Council, the Band played an evening concert before an audience of over 1,000 in Horsham Park. In the school year 1935/36, the Band entered the School Orchestra and Junior Band Festival at London's Queen's Hall for the first time, coming away with two cups.

1.104 In sport, in 1931, H Pearson (1924-32) won the steeplechase for the third year running – see Illustration 55 (an image of his 1930 success) – he, for some reason unknown, not being able to attempt an unprecedented fourth win in 1932. His three wins were matched a few years later, I Keys (mentioned just above) winning in 1935, 1936 and 1938. Shooting was established at the School in the early 1930s, and it was certainly more than beginners' luck when, in 1932, in its first time of entering and against all the odds, the VIII finished 2nd in the Ashburton Shield (the public schools' rifle competition) out of 86 entries. Hockey had been played by a few pupils during the Lent term. Now, in 1933, it was decided to extend its scope

55. H Pearson, winning the steeplechase, 1930.

with the intention that it would become the main sport of the term, with time for rugby being reduced. Each House Block had a hockey pitch, although this was often too soft to be used. On the rugby field, across a broadly average set of annual results, an occasional theme of the season's review of the XV had been that the pack lacked bulk, a disadvantage which was only partly ameliorated by speed. In cricket, the 245 scored by R Kemp (1925-32) in the first round of the 1930 House cup-ties was probably some sort of record and seems worthy of mention here, whilst inter-school competition was extended with an under-14 XI playing neighbouring preparatory schools. A few years later, in the 1933 season, TWB Middleton (1925-33), captain of the School XI, scored 510 runs with an average of 102, the elements of this achievement being too soon to be registered on the new scoreboard which a Mr TJ McGaw gifted to the School in 1938. Down at the Baths, by the mid-1930s there had been great advances in the standard of swimming at the School, these improvements owing much to Bill Kirby[z]. In 1937, the Grecians' Tennis Club was provided with a hard court, courtesy of the Governors, the benefit being shared with other pupils and the masters. In athletics, a "Standards Cup" was introduced in 1938, competitors being awarded a point if they succeeded in achieving the 'standard' designated for the particular event in the individual competition.

1.105 The success of the Debating Society spawned the formation of a Middle School group in the early 1930s, although it was to be the main Society which benefitted a few years later from the contribution of three female speakers, their presence leading to a full attendance for the event. Amongst other new groups, there appeared a Film Society, apparently a further offspring of the seemingly ubiquitous Natural History Society, which was able to utilise the screening arrangements in Big School for films, hitherto generally used for those of an educational nature, although it did have to overcome a few seemingly misplaced criticisms which, in today's language, might be characterised by the term "dumbing down". Towards the end of 1938, five scouts were immeasurably grateful for the opportunity to cross the globe to join the Sydney Jamboree. In respect of the Corps, whether it reflected a surplus of playing space or its unsuitability, around the end of 1931 one of the fives courts was roofed in to became a room for the Signals section of the OTC.

1.106 In further rebuilding work, not far from the New Science School, and as an annex to the main Library, there was built the Dominions Library, which was opened by the Lord Mayor on Speech Day, 1932. The new Library was the gift of Thomas Henderson Whitehead, an Exchange Bank Manager, who had seen service in all parts of the globe, particularly the Far East and America; indeed, he claimed that he had travelled four times around the world. Apparently, at an early stage in his life in the eastern hemisphere, an OB friend had done him a "good turn" of inestimable value. Whitehead had then resolved that if, at a later date, it was ever in his power to do so, he would try to repay the favour to the School, which he regarded as one of the noblest institutions in the world. The resulting building, which must have been beyond any expectations, would house literature and pictures relating to each of the UK's Dominions. Sadly, Whitehead died in 1933, the year after his benefaction. Amongst other things, the Dominions Library soon became the new home of the Debating Society. Later, in 1937, a new building (the "Prep Block") appeared at the rear of the Prep Houses. The ground floor contained a hall, with a stage at one end, a library and manual and hobby rooms; upstairs were a number of classrooms. The availability of these new facilities meant that the erstwhile Prep classrooms in the main school

could now be used by the senior boys, the re-organisation providing, amongst other things, special reading rooms for the Classical Grecians and the Modern Language and History Grecians, as well as extra space for office accommodation.

1.107 In Chapel, early in 1931 the organ gave a "despairing gasp", and a Bechstein Grand piano provided the music accompaniment for the services whilst the new organ was being built; indeed for a brief while services were held in Big School as the old organ was dismantled and the new one installed, it being dedicated by Dr EC Pearce*, the Bishop of Derby, in October 1931. In the middle of the year a Housey Psalter (along the lines of the English Psalter) was brought into use. In 1936, an extended trial was being held of having Duty in Houses in the morning and Evensong (at 8.15) in the Chapel. Also in Chapel, an occasional criticism had been that the red brick pillars tended to break the artistic line of the Brangwyn murals. Now, in 1934, attempts were made to minimise this problem by covering some of the pillars with a quiet draping, it being accepted that this was but a temporary solution. Later, in 1939, the existing wood panelling was continued up the buttresses, providing a gentler framework than the erstwhile red brick. The funding for this work was provided by Sir Harry Vanderpant – a strong supporter of the School – whose knighthood had been awarded a few months earlier. The mid-1930s had also seen the introduction of a new oak staircase to the gallery, this improving the safety of the access by the Prep School as well as the appearance of the ante-Chapel.

1.108 Elsewhere, a report said that an enlargement of the Art School allowed the potter to turn his wheel "without fear of covering his neighbour's painting with dripping clay" although the author understands that such coverage was still possible. There were also internal improvements to the changing rooms within the Houses, including the installation of wash-basins with hot and cold running water. Outside, in 1935, the prospect of elm disease had resulted in the cutting down of the wych elms in the western Avenue, creating a stark, though temporary, wilderness until maples were planted; the eastern end, with its limes, was not affected. At the rear of the Houses, new asphalt provided a smoother environment for roller skating, whilst the growth in another form of transport – the car – saw garages being added to various masters' houses.

1.109 In January 1936 the death occurred of King George V, who had been Christ's Hospital's President from 1904 to 1919. A letter of "profound sympathy" on the death of his father was sent to the then President and now King, Edward VIII, also greeting His Majesty on His Accession. The King became Patron of Christ's Hospital, the role of President being taken by HRH The Duke of York. As history relates, King Edward VIII abdicated in December 1936, the Duke of York acceding to the throne as King George VI, and becoming CH Patron, and HRH Henry Duke of Gloucester succeeding his brother as CH President.

1.110 The coronation of King George VI in May 1937 was well celebrated by the two Schools. At Horsham about four-fifths of the boys did manage to get away for the two-day holiday which had been granted. For those who remained, there was a bonfire on Sharpenhurst, preceded by a torch-light procession and followed by a firework display. At Hertford, only about one-third of the School were able to go home, the celebrations, for the majority remaining, including a "Ward-decorating" competition and an immense coronation tea. A few weeks after the coronation, the Loyal Address was presented to

56. JCD Lawrance presents the Loyal Address to King George VI, 1937.

King George VI by JCD ('Jerry') Lawrance (1929-37), Senior Grecian, an uncle of a neighbour of the author, the event shown in a regrettably poor quality photograph (Illustration 56). The ceremony, at St Paul's, was attended by equal numbers of senior boys and girls.

1.111 Earlier, towards the end of 1930, the death had occurred of Bishop EH Pearce*, but a few weeks after he had led the dedication of the New Science School. Later, there was a further major loss with the death, in 1937, of Professor Henry Armstrong, a pre-eminent scientist and educationalist, who served as the Royal Society's representative on the School's ruling Council of Almoners for over 40 years. Armstrong became Chairman of the Council's Education sub-Committee, and was later Education Adviser. From his own position on Council he was to exercise great influence in the development of science and other teaching at both Horsham and Hertford, his many and inestimable achievements leading Head Master Fyfe to proclaim him the School's second founder. The appeal made to friends for a memorial was extended to Old Blues. Later in 1949, a bronze bust (Illustration 57) was presented to Council; this memorial is now in the School's Museum, having spent most of the preceding years in the New Science School.

1.112 Of miscellaneous items, in May 1938, the School was honoured with an early visit from the new President. There was a march-past, lunch in Dining Hall, and the staff were presented

57. Professor Henry Armstrong.

to him; he also visited the Art School and the Manual School. In that same year, Charles Thompson* became Treasurer. The previous year, the composer Ralph Vaughan Williams had honoured the School with his presence on Speech Day, three of his compositions being heard in the concert programme. Next, as an indication of the academic success being achieved at this time, in 1934, 27 pupils were reported to be going to Oxbridge, of which 16 had scholarships or exhibitions, while a few years earlier of the 138 boy leavers, 134 had prospects of settled employment, with many going to commercial firms or the insurance industry. Overseas travel by CH pupils seemed to be on the increase, with a camping trip to Belgium in 1930, whilst the following year about a dozen Grecians and Deputy Grecians spent a couple of weeks in Germany, attending school with their hosts, this being a reciprocal visit following time spent at CH by a party of German boys the previous summer, and another party visited Finland. Later, in 1934, 16 scouts attended a national camp in Norway. Lastly in 1933, pupils at the School were invited to view Southern Railway's recently named engine Christ's Hospital (Illustration 58), its nameplate now being housed in the Museum.

58. The Christ's Hospital locomotive.

1.113 At Hertford, in an almost parallel visit to the one undertaken by the Horsham Head a few years before, Miss Craig, with a party of 11 other Headmistresses, visited Canada on an educational tour. The Hertford letter in *The Blue*, in wishing her an enjoyable trip, went on to hope that "she will not be so much impressed as to follow Mr Fyfe's example" (see para 1.100). In 1933, Hertford was proud to record that Mabel Jones (1906-11) became the first CH girl to be called to the bar, and two years later Nancy Perrett (1925-32) was the first to be a wrangler (a Cambridge University student who has completed the third year of the mathematical tripos with first-class honours). More girls had the opportunity to go abroad: for example, in 1933, two girls attended the Junior Summer School of the League of Nations in Geneva, and then in 1937 two visited Canada with a party organised by the Overseas League. In 1933/34, the girls at Hertford were re-clothed in blue check blouses and ribless stockings, and then new short-sleeved blue summer dresses. The School benefitted from two new buildings – an Art School in 1931 and a striking octagonal Reference Library in 1935 – both identified in the plan (para 1.67). About this same time a Common Room was provided for the senior girls. On the sports field, Hertford were competing in tennis, cricket, swimming, hockey and netball.

1.114 Of other features, on a glorious June day in 1934, 380 Old Blues were reported as having attended Old Blues' Day at Horsham, the number apparently constituting a record. One particular feature of such Days was that OBs would give funds to their erstwhile Houses, the practice being gratefully acknowledged in the House notes which later appeared in *The Blue*. And the lives of two of CH's "greatest brothers" were celebrated in November that year with a lunch at the Salters' Hall, followed by a service at Christ Church graced by a 100-strong choir from the School, it being the centenary of the death of both Samuel Taylor Coleridge* and Charles Lamb*.

The Second World War and the aftermath

The War years

1.115 In the Michaelmas term of 1938, the political crisis and the possible consequences of a war led to the whole Horsham School being fitted with respirators, and a scheme of rapid evacuation to the Tube was devised. Further, the War Office had issued a revised syllabus for OTC work, putting greater emphasis on the principles of leadership and whether recruits were likely to become potential officers. In mid-August 1939, before the start of the War on 1st September, the School opened to take in boys who preferred to leave their homes in dangerous areas, some 300 apparently taking advantage of this arrangement. The pre-term time was used to put in place various preventative measures, including filling some 20,000 sandbags which were used to strengthen the Tube and the School office, and making provision, with the use of suitable shutters and blinds, so that the ground-floors of the Houses could be occupied after sunset. However, attempts to black-out Big School came to nought, whilst the cost of doing so for the Dining Hall was said to be prohibitive, it being deemed further that darkness would be too big a problem had it become necessary to evacuate the building within the two-minute target. Some girls also returned early to Hertford where similar precautionary work, especially filling and deploying sandbags and preparing for the black-out, was undertaken.

1.116 Other War efforts at Horsham saw masters and boys engaged in Local Defence work whilst, partly through the OTC, the School and neighbouring villagers were brushing up their musketry to deal with possible parachutists. Other boys were digging the land for planting crops or helping on nearby farms. Where School land was ploughed, some Houses were temporarily dispossessed of their rugby pitches. More visible precautions included the erection of various barriers on Big Side to discourage hostile aircraft from landing, these not being removed until 1944. In the Houses, beds were moved to allow all boys to sleep in the senior (lower) dormitory which had been protected by wire netting, whilst, at times, pupils slept in the far from wholesome environment of the Tube, which also provided a safe haven from the threat of bombing during the day. The School was getting increasingly used to dealing with air raids, as Chapels, meals and sports were occasionally brought to an early end. But apprehension must have been ever-present. Horsham though was safer than London, and for a while the Counting House sought refuge in the countryside.

59. Horsham – The School fire brigade, c1940.

60. Horsham – The first meeting of the Young Farmers' Club, 1943.

It is not clear whether the School fire brigade (see Illustration 59) was called into service during the War.

1.117 However, apart from these and other more obvious effects, such as rationing, life at Horsham was to proceed as best as possible, with a number of female teachers being employed in place of those masters who had gone to war. At the end of 1939, masters and boys of Westminster Abbey Choir School were housed at CH, undertaking separate class-work and music training, but living in the Houses and attending Chapel. This arrangement lasted about a year, the decision then being taken at the end of 1940 to close the Choir School for the duration of the War. The Corps was expanded in February 1941 by the creation of the Air Training Corps, the 60 cadets awaiting uniforms, but still parading three times a week. For the main body, in addition to having to cope with the loss to the War of many of its officers, early in 1941 the Officers' Training Corps suffered a change in name, becoming the Junior Training Corps, the annual inspection that year being followed by a demonstration of tank manoeuvres, after which some pupils were given the opportunity to drive the tanks. As in the First World War, the School undertook a variety of munitions and related work in the Manual School, although seemingly on a smaller and less interesting scale, beginning with producing kettles, rakes and other articles in short supply. Also, conkers were collected for use in the production of acetone. In what appeared to be the only instance of bomb damage at the School, in the early morning of 29th June 1944 a flying-bomb was shot down by a night-fighter and crashed into the trees by the masters' garages close to the Infirmary, causing much damage to the garages and to one of the Sanatorium buildings. There was minor damage to the other Sanatorium building, and many windows in the Houses were broken, although wire-netting prevented injury by flying glass.

1.118 In respect of the main School and Old Blue ceremonies, Speech Day did continue, seemingly with the presence of the Lord Mayor but otherwise in slightly reduced (regalia) form, at both Horsham and Hertford, with the event returning closer to its peace-time state in 1946 and with the

practice of Grecians attending the Hertford ceremony and monitresses going to Horsham being renewed. St Matthew's Day – a London event – was not held between 1939 and 1944, although it appears that arrangements were made for the pupils to receive their largesse at their respective locations. The visit to London was resumed in 1945, with about 300 boys and the senior girls attending the service at St Sepulchre (rather than Christ Church, which had been severely damaged by bombs) and later being received by the Mayor at the Mansion House. The Founder's Day Dinner was not held for the first four years of the War. Celebrations were resumed in some form in 1943 with a service at St Botolph and a reception in the Court Room at the School's Counting House in Great Tower Street, attended by over 100 OBs. The Dinner was resumed in 1946 at the Dorchester, although catering difficulties allowed for an attendance of only 175, rather than the 250 who had applied for tickets.

1.119 Of other aspects to mention, whilst some concerts and entertainments at Horsham were inevitably cancelled, recitals and other performances were held in the Prep Hall, where coping with the blackout was easier than in Big School. However, the latter building did prove to be a popular location for gramophone concerts, usually on a Sunday afternoon. Early in 1942, news emerged that supplies of Housey dress were to be further reduced, and pupils were soon to be seen in 'civilian' clothes, this arrangement lasting throughout the War and beyond, indeed it was not until early 1950 that all boys were again clothed in their traditional uniform. In sport, to eke out use of rubber shoes, playing of fives was limited to inter-school or inter-House games, and play on the tennis hard court was stopped completely. Amongst the School societies, a Young Farmers Club had been established in 1943, its popularity far exceeding the numbers who were permitted to join. The opening of the Club had been graced by HRH The Duke of Norfolk who can be seen in the centre of Illustration 60, with Head Master Flecker (with moustache, just behind him) and CW Thompson*, CH Treasurer (light suit, front left), with, to his right, someone who might be Bill Kirby[z].

1.120 During this period, the School was privileged to receive two important visitors. First, in October 1942 there was a surprise visit by the President, the School's Home

- 41 -

61. Horsham – The Home Guard Unit, WW2.

Guard Unit receiving just sufficient notification to greet him with a guard of honour. HRH lunched in Hall from where he addressed the School. Illustration 61 shows the Home Guard which includes its leader, Head Master Flecker, in the centre, with W Armistead (see para 1.166) on his left, PG Matthews (the author's housemaster some years later) the taller of the two behind the Head and AH Buck[z] the shorter of the two behind Matthews. The President honoured the School again with a visit in July 1947, this time also viewing a PT and gym display in the Quad and, much to the joy of the pupils, requesting two half-holidays. Secondly, around the beginning of 1944, at a time when he would have been greatly pre-occupied by events taking place elsewhere, General Montgomery paid an unexpected visit to the School, his address being straightforward and to the point, including requesting a half-holiday for the pupils.

1.121 Before we move on, perhaps the most telling, interesting and personal accounts of the School during WW2 came from the pen of Head Master Flecker. The following reminiscences are worth reporting verbatim: first, on guard duty… "Until the construction of the observation post [in the Chapel turret], six wardens were on duty every night and perambulated the buildings during alerts. During the period of night attacks in London, alerts were continuous, and the loss of half a night's sleep every other night was a serious strain. The boredom was intense." and… "During term time, a team of masters and boys was on duty every night from 6pm to 7am. They were a mixed bag – wardens, Home Guard, fire-fighting teams and first aid practitioners. Headquarters were the School Office, whose telephone was never left untended throughout the War. The party dossed down in adjacent classrooms, ready to go up to the Chapel turret in two-hour shifts during alerts. Two were always awake in the Office. Even the sleep one got seemed of inferior quality, to judge from the snores that echoed through Common Room in the afternoon after night duty." … and examples of the dangers faced .. "An alert sounded just as dinner was finishing; then came the unmistakeable drone of a German bomber. The Avenue was full of boys as the bomber broke from the mist a few feet above our roofs, so low that

the guns, markings and crew were clearly visible. It paid no attention to us, but took a heavy toll of life in Horsham." … and in other incidents "Two day schools, one about 12 miles to the east, the other about as far to the west, were machine-gunned and many children and masters killed".

1.122 At Hertford, the girls also involved themselves in various bits of War work, including preparation of ration cards, helping the Red Cross, knitting and sewing, and growing vegetables, whilst later many went potato picking in Gloucestershire in the summer holidays. Within the School, basement shelters became dormitories, the girls making use of sleeping-bags on mattresses. Two other aspects of the War were first that fewer Governors travelled to Hertford to the main events, and secondly for a while a number of boys from Battersea Grammar School had been evacuated there. In July 1942, Hertford said farewell to Miss Craig, Head Mistress since 1921, her legacy including, in particular, her assistance to pupils wishing to go to university and her fostering of the activities of the Old Girls, and her time seeing, amongst other things, the enlargement and modernisation of the Science Block, and a new Art School and Reference Library. Her successor was Miss Dorothy West from St Swithin's School, Winchester. Early the following year, Hertford mourned the death of Miss Robertson, Miss Craig's predecessor. Towards the end of that year there was a major re-organisation in the eight Hertford Wards, from an all-age structure (9-18) to two junior and six senior Wards, this being similar to the Prep and senior school arrangement at Horsham. In 1944, monitresses and certain senior girls were allowed to attend morning service in the town. Two years later, Hertford suffered its worst epidemic (fever and streptococci) since 1927, requiring one of the Wards being converted into an extra Infirmary.

Post-War

1.123 Six years of conflict came to an end as Victory in Europe (VE) Day was celebrated on 8th May 1945. Events were held at both Horsham and Hertford, with flags prominently displayed, a Thanksgiving Service, a special tea, and bonfires, with the whole School marching up Sharpenhurst

Hill at Horsham and setting fire to a condemned hayrick, and Hertford celebrating with a conflagration in the playground. Many masters made a welcome return to CH and set about re-building their lives. In 1946, the Clerk, George Allan*, retired, being succeeded by Roger Evans[z].

1.124 Shortly after the end of the War, a committee was set up to lead an appeal for funds to provide a suitable memorial to those Old Blues, and CH masters and officers, who had died for their country. It was proposed that a Book of Memory, containing the names of the fallen in the two Wars, should be placed in the Horsham Chapel, with a suitable memorial to be dedicated at Hertford. It was also suggested that a Trust Fund be established which would be used to provide accommodation for young Old Blues who were starting their careers in London. A target of £20,000 (£800k) was suggested. However, post-War austerity was biting and, despite further appeals, monies came in only slowly. By the middle of 1948, when less than £5,000 (£200k) had been raised, the committee decided that the original idea for the provision of accommodation for the young in London could not be met. The main commemoration would be Memorial Books for the Chapels at Horsham and Hertford, and other proposals would be considered for how to use the remaining monies. In 1951, Council reported that the balance (now around £4,500 (£180k) would be devoted to a much-needed extension to the Horsham Tuck Shop, work which was eventually completed in 1956. The author was struck that, unless he has missed it, the published pronouncements did not seem to include the possibility of a memorial giving the names of the fallen, as had been done for the First World War. Indeed, it was not until 1992 that such a memorial was erected (see para 1.212).

1.125 The end of the War also saw the departure of some masters and mistresses who had filled so diligently the vacancies created by those who had enlisted; there were also, for a while, continuing problems with bread rationing and laundry facilities. A moving and memorable Service of Homage to the Fallen was held at St Peter's, Cornhill, on St Matthew's Day 1946, attended by over 500 Old Blues and relatives of the fallen. A similar service was held the following year. Unlike for WW1, a formal Roll of Honour and Service booklet was not produced, *The Blue* of April 1947 listing the then about 190 known names of the fallen, but not years at CH or House. On Old Blues' Day in June 1949, in an immensely moving service in the Chapel, the Chaplain-General to the Forces, Frederick Llewelyn Hughes[z], dedicated the Book of Memory, before giving it to the Senior Grecian on behalf of the School who placed it in its resting place close by the altar. The service was attended by about 400 OBs and over 100 relatives of those whose names were enshrined in the Book.

1.126 In sport, the end of the 1940s saw success on the rugby field with the 1st XV winning all its games in 1948/49, this following an unbeaten run against other schools the previous year, the best record for around 35 years; further, the Colts (under 16) XV had ended 1947/48 with their third successive unbeaten season. Also around this time, a new cinder athletics track (Illustration 62) was constructed (on what is now the main car park), financed largely by the generous bequest of Lord Plender (accountant, public servant, CH Governor) who had died in 1946 and an anonymous donor, replacing the grass track which had been located on Big Side. However, runners had to get used not only to the different surface, but also to the tighter bends, the track being five laps to the mile. And still on running, the steeplechase was held in 1948 for the first time since 1939, one major advance noted was that training for the

event had taken place over a number of months, rather than being crammed in to the few days before the run. Shooting benefitted from the completion of the 30-yard range down beyond Doctor's Lake, although an improved standard of performance was not initially evident.

1.127 Around the end of the War, two societies were formed, first the Railway Club, founded by Ian Allan, a Governor and son of then Clerk, George. Ian Allan had earlier founded the eponymous publishing company which specialised in transport books; later, his printing arm produced the author's *CHIVE* and the first three booklets in the Museum's Heritage Series. He provided generous assistance to *The Blue* and was a long-standing member of the Amicable Society. Secondly, the School established a CH branch of the Franco-British Society, whose object was to promote good feeling and understanding between the peoples of Great Britain and France. Lord Bessborough, chairman of the umbrella body, wished to extend the Society to all English public schools, and CH had taken the lead. A Grecians' social in 1947 seemed to break new ground by hosting an evening of ballroom dancing in the Library, partners coming from the Horsham Youth Club, apparently first having to trudge through the winter snow. But it must have been successful since a further social was scheduled two weeks later, whilst the following year, at the invitation of St Catherine's, Bramley, the event was taken further afield, the Grecians returning the courtesy a few months later. On the stage, it should not go unrecorded that the performance of "Hamlet" by the Geography Deps (Deputy Grecians, then ages 15-16) in the Michaelmas term 1945 was considered by two "cantankerous critics" to be the best CH production they had seen for 20 years.

1.128 Of personnel changes, the Treasurer, Charles Thompson*, retired in 1946, having held the post through the difficult War years, although he continued as vice-Chairman of Council until 1957. He was succeeded by Reginald Oldfield*. There was one other change of note about this time, Dr GE

62. Horsham – The Athletics Track.

63. The march-past at the Thanksgiving Service, St Paul's, 1953.

Friend retiring as the School's Medical Officer in 1946. He had been in post since 1913 and had wanted to retire in 1940 but had been persuaded to remain until the end of the War; he died at the end of 1956. He was replaced by 'Tommy' Scott[z] who faced an early problem with two cases of infantile paralysis being diagnosed, as a result of which about 100 parents availed themselves of the option to remove their boys before the end of term.

1.129 As if to show the town that CH had survived the War, in October 1946 the senior School marched into Horsham, preceded by the Band, to see Laurence Olivier's famous film "Henry V"; the Prep travelled by train. The girls also saw the film at Hertford. (The story goes that, when the film was shown to the pupils in Big School during the early 1950s, the second and third reels were projected in the wrong order – but few seemed to notice!) Then in 1948, the boys returned to the town to see a film of the Olympic Games. The Schools had to cope with the particularly severe winter of 1946/47, where snow and very low temperatures were especially bad from around mid-January to mid-March; there were also problems with fuel supply. Sporting events and other activities were greatly curtailed at both Horsham and Hertford, although the latter also had to deal with the debilitating effect of influenza, the School also ruing not having the skating and tobogganing possibilities available at Horsham. Later, amongst a few overseas trips which were possible after the War, four boys visited France with a public school party of the Franco-British Society, and a small group visited places of archaeological interest in Normandy, the trip taking in Paris and Chartres.

1.130 In a miscellany of Horsham items, first, in 1947, the Head Master suggested that a film should be made about the School. The idea received general approval and the CH Club offered to seek OBs who might have an interest in the venture. Reporting on the matter about three months later, the Club said that it had found six people with experience of every aspect of film-making who would be willing to help: the future seemed bright. Regrettably, the OB who was to pursue

the project failed to deliver, and it seems that the idea just faded away. Secondly, even if CH was unable to launch its own film, it did manage to have BBC radio record a Chapel service in July for transmission to Australia, and the Carol Service later in the year also for Australia and some European services; and then in December 1950 the BBC broadcast on the Home Service about an hour of that year's Carol Service, the Head Master and Director of Music receiving many letters of praise for the performance. Thirdly, like other schools, over the years CH had developed some of its own particular form of communication, Housey slang, unintelligible to those outside and often to Blues of different vintages. To try to throw some light on this arcane world, in early 1948 GS Atkinson (1917-24) produced a booklet *Housey Slang*, one of the author's favourite entries being krug for bread. The book would have found many uses over the years, but a particular example would have occurred in the early 1960s – to understand the joke when *The Blue* reported that Thomas K Krug had been appointed NABISCO's Divisional Vice-President for Bread. Fourthly, CH was again put on the map in 1949 as nearby Sharpenhurst Hill was triangulated by the Ordnance Survey. One noteworthy Hertford matter was that in 1948 financial considerations led to the annual magazine and newsletter being combined.

1.131 At the end of the summer term 1949, the Head was taken ill with appendicitis, necessitating an urgent operation, the prizes being presented a few days later by the former Head, (now Sir) William Fyfe. Sir William later visited the School in summer 1956, this coinciding with the Grecians' annual photograph in which he was persuaded to appear. Fyfe died in 1965, and in September 1967, following a service in Chapel, a memorial tablet was unveiled in the cloisters by Lady Fyfe.

Stability in the 1950s and early 1960s

1.132 The beginning of the 1950s saw a team of 15 HM Inspectors descend on Horsham to run their rule over the whole School. A few other happenings of this time included the erstwhile English Hymnal, with CH Supplement, being replaced in Chapel by a new edition of the Public School Hymn

Book. Also in 1950, a new Science Journal was produced, its aim being to record the activities of the practitioners of the discipline and to encourage writing of technical subjects in good English. The School had to survive the Lent term without the Head, who had gone to the West Indies, at the behest of the Colonial Office, to seek to establish connections with schools there, particularly at Secondary level, his visit apparently benefitting greatly from the widespread hospitality received from Old Blues. He would have missed the precautions which were being taken at CH against the threat of an influenza epidemic, in particular, compulsory gargling, whilst Horsham and other large towns were put out of bounds, and for a month parents were asked not to visit the School. Early in 1951, arrangements were made for Christ's Hospital to admit Oliver Whitby Foundationers. Their school, founded by Whitby for the benefit of children in three parishes in or near Chichester (and located there), had been closed, and the income of their foundation would be given to the education of up to around 12 children at CH.

1.133 However, it had not been long into the decade before thoughts turned to the arrangements which would be put in place for celebrating the School's Quatercentenary in 1953 (although the School had taken its first pupils in 1552, the charter was signed in 1553). The multitude of events included (i) a "truly moving and impressive" Thanksgiving Service at St Paul's (19th May) attended by HRH the President, the Lord Mayor and others of the City, and representatives of CH, including the 1,100 pupils (this is thought to have been the first time that the girls as a School had visited the City since they left Newgate Street in 1778), with the address given by the Archbishop of Canterbury, and for which the march-past is shown in Illustration 63; (ii) four unforgettable days at Horsham – Speech Day (Friday 19th June), a special Parents' Day (20th) at which boys and girls performed the "Foundation Play" (written by David Jesson-Dibley, a CH master, and covering events from the 20 years surrounding the founding of the School), and "Recorded Time" (by Edward Malins, also a master at CH, and showing some important episodes in the life of the School over its long history), Charter Day (26th), with the President, and again the staff and girls from Hertford, and Old Blues' Day (27th) for which about 1,800

had accepted the invitation to attend, with sports events, the two plays performed at Parents' Day and ending with Beating Retreat; and (iii) also at the Horsham School, four exhibitions, covering science, art, the work of the Manual School, and historic ephemera, paintings and manuscripts, this last display eliciting regret that such material was not permanently on show in a museum. There were also three performances, at London's Fortune Theatre, of Edmund Blunden[z]'s specially written work, "The Dede of Pittie", depicting scenes of the history of the School, performed by Old Blues.

1.134 The School had also received a message from the Prime Minister, Winston Churchill, in which he said that CH had a place of its own amongst the nation's ancient foundations, mentioned the charitable ethos of the Foundation saying that throughout the centuries the School had "remained true to the objects of your Royal Founder", and ended by hoping that "the chapters of your splendid story that remain to be written in the adventurous years ahead be worthy of all that has gone before".

1.135 There was also a Quatercentenary publication, *The Christ's Hospital Book*, with contributions, from many Old Blues, assembled by a small editorial team, more a literary work than a history of the Foundation, which achieved an exceptionally high level of 3,000 sales. About this time, two appeals were launched for the Foundation with a seemingly optimistic combined target of £500,000 (£12m, *£30m*). One – the Thankoffering Fund – was aimed essentially at Old Blues and friends, the second (and larger) – the Quatercentenary Fund – was directed primarily at banks, insurance companies and financial institutions and business houses in the City of London where the name of CH needed no special recommendation. In the event, it appeared that the two funds raised about half the hoped-for amount.

1.136 There were also various specific Quatercentenary events at Hertford, beginning in 1952 with the Old Girls' Association celebrating Founder's Day Dinner (Illustration 64). Then in 1953, events included (i) the School performing "The Pattern of Charity" (written by Hilda Harding[z] and depicting incidents in the life of the girls' School), (ii) exhibitions of arts

64. The Hertford Old Girls' Association Founder's Day Dinner, 1952.

65. HBG Johnston presents the Loyal Address to Queen Elizabeth II, 1953.

and craft, needlework and historical treasures, (iii) a special Speech Day and an Old Girls' Day, and (iv) the visit of HRH The Duchess of Gloucester.

1.137 In February 1952, the School expressed great sorrow at the death of its Royal Patron, King George VI, recalling his brief term as President (before he became King) and then, in 1937, the Loyal Address presented to him, as King, by the Senior Grecian, and his reply. The following year, the coronation of Her Majesty Queen Elizabeth II took place on 2nd June, the event being celebrated with a special holiday. However, about 100 pupils at both Horsham and Hertford were unable to go home, the staff making special arrangements to allow them to watch or listen to the ceremony on TV or wireless. A week later, a CH group, including six Grecians and six monitresses, attended the Coronation Thanksgiving Service at St Paul's, the event including the presentation, on the steps of the Cathedral, of the Loyal Address to Her Majesty by the Senior Grecian, Barrie Johnston (1945-53) – see Illustration 65. In a sad coincidence, Johnston passed away (in 2015) during the writing of this book. The contents of the Address and of Her Majesty's reply are given below.

Loyal Address

To The Queen's Most Excellent Majesty.

May it please your Majesty

Since King Edward the Sixth of Blessed Memory in 1553 granted his Royal Charter to the Religious, Royal and Ancient Foundation of Christ's Hospital, the children of Christ's Hospital have from time to time been granted the gracious privilege of presenting their humble duty on the occasion of

their Sovereign's first visit to the City of London after the coronation.

In this four hundredth year of our Foundation, we offer our humble and loyal greetings to your Majesty, deeply sensible of the honour with which your Majesty has bestowed upon us by becoming our Patron and of the privileges we enjoy by virtue of the Presidency of His Royal Highness The Duke of Gloucester.

That your Majesty may have a long, happy and prosperous reign is the earnest prayer of the Sons and Daughters of this Ancient House who share the hope of all your Majesty's subjects that your Majesty and HRH The Duke of Gloucester may be blessed with many years of health and happiness.

Her Majesty's reply

I thank you for your loyal and dutiful address.

It is with great pleasure that I receive your loyal greetings in the year when you are celebrating the four hundredth anniversary of your Foundation. By its work through the years your Ancient House has won a high reputation, and as your Patron I share with you your happiness on this notable landmark in its history.

I am confident that your fine traditions will continue to inspire all who pass through your Schools to give of their best in honourable and devoted endeavour and service, as their predecessors have in the past. May God bless the work of the Schools throughout the years that lie ahead.

1.138 The major events of 1953 had prompted a review of the facilities offered by Big School for staging certain kinds of performance, leading to an extension of the stage and improved curtaining and lighting. One other wish, for a raked auditorium, remains to be achieved. Other improvements were evident in the Kitchen, including the installation of a monster dish-washing machine. Then, at the end of 1954, the generosity of an Old Blue enabled the installation of lighting to illuminate the Verrio painting in Dining Hall. If this highlighted the need for cleaning, this was not done until early in 1964, when the painting was restored. It had been a major task to have moved it from London; now there was needed the gentler touch of the picture restorer (the task apparently falling to Carey's who had been involved with work related to the re-hanging at Horsham), the work and cleaning now clearly revealing a number of new features, including various ghostly images and a two-faced man who was thought to have been a young master who had to sacrifice his head to a nobleman-benefactor who had originally been forgotten.

1.139 In sport, in 1951, the School won the Public Schools' Seven-a-Side competition, having been runners-up three years earlier. The winning team was: A Whipp (1944-51), HBG Johnston (1945-53), JC Marvin (1943-51), MA Pearey (1942-51), SR Williams (1943-51), WE Butler (1944-53), and WP Robinson (1943-52). Of these, Johnston was Senior Grecian, as mentioned above, and Pearey[z] became Clerk to the Foundation. Illustration 66 is of the programme showing how the School won the event. In that year, within the School, for the first time, rugby cup-ties were competed, by A and B sides, at Block, rather than House, level. But rugby did not have it all its own way. Two members of staff, in an interesting development, organised and coached soccer for the younger boys – "before they were big enough to enjoy rugby" – although there was some regret that House Captains did not give more support to the initiative. On the cricket field, the star

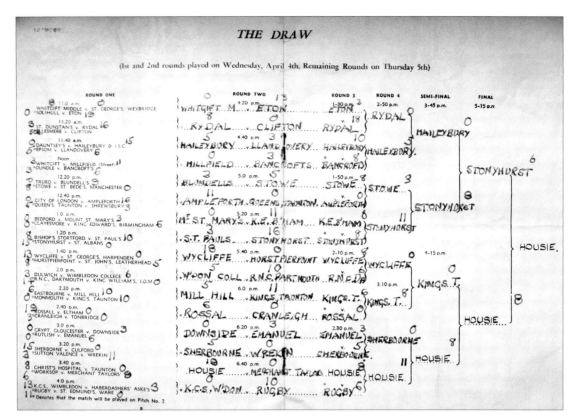

66. *How CH won the Public Schools' Seven-a-Side competition, 1951.*

of the late 1940s was undoubtedly Dennis Silk who, between 1947 and 1950, scored nearly 1,400 runs for the XI, as well as taking 120 wickets, these two achievements probably both being second in the then CH records lists. For some of this period Silk also found time to be Senior Grecian. In athletics, in 1952 Clive Hicks (1944-52) won the Schools' Challenge Shield and David Baker (1947-55) the Junior Challenge Cup in hurdles events at the White City. Other sports such as boxing, fives and gymnastics continued to be popular and well contested both intra-School and inter-school. One other achievement is worthy of mention. Rowing had been popular in the pre-Horsham era, with a number of OBs appearing in their Oxbridge College eight. However, the absence of water at Horsham led to the demise of the sport. Despite this, in 1952 JR Dingle (1940-47) gained a splendid rowing Blue in the Cambridge Boat, a unique achievement for an Old Blue.

1.140 In other miscellaneous Horsham news, the School's gramophone record of aspects of CH life in music and sound, including dinner parade (with the Band playing and the pupils marching into lunch), Grace in Dining Hall, and extracts from the Carol Service and the Leaving Service, had proved immensely popular, all 500 copies being quickly sold. Old Blues' Day 1954 was marked by a presentation to ACW ("Teddy") Edwards on completion of 50 years' service to the School; he had retired as a master just after the War, but continued at CH as the School Librarian. He died in December 1964, a memorial service being held at the School in January 1965, at which the lesson was read by Michael Stewart[z], the Foreign Secretary, who had been a former House Captain under him. Tributes to him filled eight pages of *The Blue*. Amongst overseas trips, in 1950 three historians spent a fortnight studying the fine medieval churches of Burgundy. In the summer of 1953, Montgomery – now a Field Marshal – returned to the School for the annual inspection of the CCF. The Corps were smart and passed muster, the Field Marshal saying as much in a "forthright and encouraging" speech in Big School, most of which was not reported since the Press had been denied access. Just before, the School had an RAF Day, which was attended by Barnes Wallis*, the event including

a fly-past of three Canberras of 617 Squadron and a special Service of Thanksgiving and Dedication in the Chapel. Also as part of the wider celebrations and the School's long Naval links through the Royal Mathematical School, a small group, including nine pupils, were guests aboard HMS *Perseus* at Spithead on the day of the Naval Review, the group, among other things, getting a grand view of the Royal Procession and the fly-past. Lastly, an increasing number of senior boys at the School had, from time to time, raised some concern about the lack of privacy for work and reading. In an attempt to ameliorate the position, Dr Van Praagh (Head of Science) had suggested that each House should have a Quiet Room and, putting his ideas into practice, he managed to get his proposal introduced in Peele A (where he was living) on an experimental basis. The Room had been suitably appointed and reasonably well furnished. For those who can recall the locations, it replaced the senior changing room (requiring the boys to change (for games) in the dormitory 'lav-ends' (washing areas)). The idea seemed to achieve its aim, but there was no indication at the time as to how far it was extended across the other Houses. Some 30 years later, in an article in *The Blue*, van Praagh recalled the experiment. Although not mentioning whether the idea had been adopted elsewhere, he made the more important point that the experiment had greatly interested the Council of Almoners, one of their responses being that "we must do better", the idea then seemingly being taken forward in the changes to the Houses made as part of the developments of the first half of the 1960s.

1.141 At Hertford, the early 1950s saw the School enjoying improved menus for breakfast (three courses instead of one) and tea, and the smell of paint was in the air with the Wards and Gymnasium both evoking a new freshness, and outside paths were re-surfaced. The first Hertford RAF Foundationer was admitted in 1952, although the girl had to wait a while before her badge was presented to her. In 1953, Dr Frances Page, Senior History Mistress, published her book, *Christ's Hospital, Hertford*, being only the second work (following Lempriere*'s *A History of the Girls' School of Christ's Hospital*) which dealt extensively with the girls' School. The author feels that some

67. Sir Harry Vanderpant, benefactor.

aspiring writer should update the Hertford story by covering the final 30 years there.

1.142 In July 1954, Head Master Flecker announced that he would be retiring in July 1955. He had served for 25 years, including the difficult period of World War 2, and he was now going to take the Headship at Lawrence College, Pakistan. Amongst a number of characteristics mentioned in the tributes to his long tenure, two were his administrative ability (although this not to the detriment of his scholarship) and his enthusiasm for the School. He was succeeded by CME (George) Seaman[z], previously Head at Bedford.

1.143 In March 1955, there occurred the death of Sir Harry Vanderpant, a close friend of CH and most generous benefactor – see Illustration 67. He was an Almoner serving on various committees and a Donation Governor. His main bequests were to Hertford, culminating in a donation of £30,000 (£750k, £1.9m) to the Quatercentenary Fund for the specific purpose of enlarging the School Hall there, the end-product being seen in Illustration 68, and building a new staircase to the Dining Hall. Sadly, he died just before the work was completed. A replica of a bronze bust was placed by the new staircase, this finding its way to Horsham when Hertford was closed, spending some years by the Museum staircase, until very recently when it was 'returned' to its original home in the hall of the sheltered accommodation now occupying the erstwhile Hertford School buildings at the north end of the site. In the summer, the first main event in the new Hall was Speech Day, and then, in October, the President came to Hertford to undertake the official opening. The following year, for the first time, prize-giving at Hertford was held 'in state', staff looking resplendent in their academic gowns. Of visitors to Hertford, there was Sir Mortimer Wheeler, the eminent archaeologist. In sport, the hockey XI were unbeaten in 1957. Early in 1958, Edna Howard (1916-21) became the first British-born organist to give a recital in the Festival Hall. In the same year, the Sixth Form were able to discard their tunics, these being replaced by blouses and skirts and a distinctive tie, whilst seniors generally benefitted from relaxation in the rules for

walks and shopping. An outbreak of influenza in early 1959 led to an unprecedentedly shortened six and a half week Lent term. At the end of 1960, Saturday morning became one of four lessons rather than five, the change allowing more time for walks and outings with parents, whilst the School had to survive the autumn without Miss West who had been granted a "grace term" by Council "to give me a break, to widen my horizons and to obtain new experiences", the time being spent in the United States. In 1963, the new uniform of pinafore dresses and tartan blouses was widely admired, and 'Houses' replaced 'Wards', this change in nomenclature not being to everyone's approval, particularly as the latter had been in use since the founding of the School. In 1964, with some interest in academic circles generally, CH Hertford embarked, on an experimental basis, on a four-term year. With spring term largely as was, the change essentially involved fitting in (with appropriate holidays), summer, autumn and winter terms in what had been the summer and Michaelmas terms. The arrangement continued until the merger in 1985. On the academic front, the first Natural Science Exhibition at Cambridge had been achieved in 1965.

1.144 Back at Horsham, new groups emerged alongside existing societies. In 1959, the newly formed Science Society was fortunate to have its inaugural lecture given by Barnes Wallis*, whilst an Art Society had also been recently formed. A new 1960 Society was established, on much the same lines as the 1930 Society, but for Deps; also new was a somewhat esoteric Classical Society, its membership being all those who were learning Greek, whilst in the mid-1960s there emerged the Antiquarian and Archaeological Society and a CH Mensa group. Overseas trips became increasingly frequent, including the Dramatic Society visit to Germany to perform "Julius Caesar" in 1956, and in the following year with "Twelfth Night" in Denmark. In 1959, a group of boys visited Florence, some spartan accommodation failing to affect the pleasures of the local art and architecture. In August 1960, a small party of History Grecians visited Belgium to study Flemish architecture and painting, and five History Grecians went to Northern France. Then 24 members of the Dramatic Society spent a week in Holland, on tour with "A Midsummer Night's Dream", and in 1963 a party of mostly Classical Grecians were much impressed by Rome's stately antiquity.

1.145 In music, in February 1955, soprano April Cantelo and Colin Davis[z] (then husband and wife) gave a recital in the exquisite surroundings of the Dominions Library. A few years later, in 1959, TP Cowell (1908-11) gave the School a new Steinway grand piano, its first usage being in the more than competent hands of fellow OB John Hunt[z]. In December 1962, the Big School Choir of 200 voices was invited to perform with the Royal Philharmonic Orchestra at a charity concert in the Royal Festival Hall. The importance of music at CH was further evidenced in the figure of over 300 pupils being in receipt of a weekly music lesson. A change in the 1950s saw the Carol Service being held twice so more people could attend, a practice which seemed to continue for about 10 years. Individual national success in the Arts was celebrated in 1964 with NG Jeffcoat (1958-65) becoming the first member of the School to act with the National Youth Theatre and six musicians playing with the National Youth Orchestra. Earlier, in 1958 the young musicians of the Prep School performed at a public concert for the first time in the Prep Hall.

68. Hertford – The School Hall, interior.

69. Thornton A march into Dining Hall during the 'flu epidemic, 1957.

1.146 One of the most noteworthy events of the second half of the 1950s, and one which will last long in the memory of those who experienced it, was the influenza epidemic which hit the School in the Michaelmas term of 1957. The attack (of Asian 'flu) began on Sunday 22nd September, the third day of term, and spread rapidly. Within a week, the Infirmary was full, and the healthy were evacuated, in quick succession, from Maine, Barnes, Lamb and Coleridge House Blocks, these buildings now providing emergency medical accommodation. At its worst, over 120 patients were admitted in a single day. Help had arrived from outside, including some parents, to support the efforts of CH personnel. In early October, Dr Scott[z] (MO) and his staff, in particular, must have been greatly relieved to see a decrease in the intake of patients and, almost as quickly as the epidemic had developed, matters improved, with the House Blocks discharging their convalescents, although the return of boys to their own Houses was a little more complicated than their earlier dispersion. In all, more than 630 people, mostly boys (around three-quarters of the whole School) but including masters and other estate personnel, had been affected. Interestingly, in the Prep School only about of a third of the 120 pupils succumbed, a much lower incidence than the senior school. For those who were not affected, there was much reading in class, instead of proper lessons, and a skeleton Band played greatly reduced House numbers into lunch, the iconic image (Illustration 69) being of Peter Ironmonger (1954-61) – another who passed away (in 2016) during the writing of this book – marching alone, for Thornton A, the image being included partly because the author is somewhere in the following House. Nowadays, and with fewer wards available at the Infirmary, the pupils would be sent home. Although the influenza battle had been won, in 1958 there was a short spell of illness at the very end of the summer term, this requiring a second Leaving Service. A few years later, at the other extreme, there was one night in the early 1960s when there was no in-patient in the Infirmary. The author was fortunate not to be affected by the 1957 epidemic; indeed he was one of the likely very few not to have spent a night in the Infirmary in his eight years at CH.

1.147 In the late 1950s, rugby and cricket were still the predominant School sports, while there had been success in the swimming pool in 1958 when all senior matches were won. Going into the 1960s other sports opportunities were expanding, in particular tennis and hockey were becoming better organised in the summer term. Indeed, tennis soon became the official alternative to cricket, with seven courts (on better ground than the rugby pitches of hitherto) being made available and an inter-House tournament arranged, with four hockey pitches also being marked out. About this time, rugby and cricket leagues were put on a Block, rather than a House, basis and a House rugby sevens knock-out competition was introduced. A clock appeared on the Cricket Pavilion, a bequest of HS Goodwin, a former master. In one of the more interesting sporting developments of the late 1950s, a small group of enthusiasts had established a sailing club which, with masters providing transportation, had held a number of unofficial matches with neighbouring schools which had boats and water on which to sail. Seemingly against all the odds, the team won its two matches in 1961, constituting an unbeaten season. Lastly, the bane of many generations of CH pupils, PT in the morning break, was done away with, the anxious wait for the morning bell, the ringing of which had earlier signalled its cancellation, no longer providing a classroom distraction. One statistic of interest here is that, over the period 1941 to 1957, the PT competition had been won 15 times by one of the six Houses at the east end of the Avenue, putting to shame the eight west end Houses, one of which was the author's.

1.148 Of some other events of the time, first in November 1958, there occurred the tragic, accidental death of Roger Evans[z], Clerk since 1946; he was succeeded by AE Allison[z]. Secondly, earlier that year, at a ceremony attended by many Old Blues, a tablet to the memory of John and Frances West, major benefactors to CH (see para A1.6), was unveiled at St Nicholas Church, Newbury, by the School's Treasurer, Barnes Wallis*. Thirdly, at Horsham, in 1960, the Christ's Hospital team of PA Flynn (1959-60) and JRH Thomas (1951-60) won "The Observer" Silver Mace in the Public Schools' Debating Association's annual tournament, the pair opposing the motion "That this House would bring back the birch". Fourthly, around the turn of the decade, the School entertained a party of headmasters and headmistresses from the Soviet Union. They were able to tell the visitors that Russian was now in the curriculum, but it is not clear whether they also mentioned that, in the early 18th century, two Old Blues, Richard Grice* and Stephen Gwyn*, had taught at the Moscow School of Mathematics, which was apparently modelled on the RMS. Fifthly, five new masters' houses were built on the south side of the Avenue and various improvements were made to the

70. Horsham – A Day-room.

Boarding Houses including brighter (strip) lighting, whilst scaffolding began to adorn the school buildings as a major 10-year programme of repair to the brickwork and stonework commenced, the latter involving some use of synthetic stone which, the author understands, generally has a longer life than the real thing. Sixthly, in 1964, a then record-equalling 19 awards had been gained at Oxbridge. Finally, in March 1964, the School was shaken by the noise of what was a fatal rail crash involving two goods trains at Itchingfield Junction, with some trucks being derailed onto the edge of the nearby Colts rugby pitch. Although the line was cleared within 24 hours, the wrecked trucks remained alongside the line for some weeks.

1.149 Some reduction in martial manoeuvres occurred around 1957 when marching in Houses into Chapel was abandoned; pupils now walked, a surely more dignified way. A few years later microphones were installed there for a trial period. In a further change, on an experimental basis, the two compulsory whole School Sunday services were replaced by one full service (morning or evening), with a second service, one week for seniors, the next week for juniors, these being compulsory for that part of the School for which they were intended and voluntary for the rest. At the end of 1957, HLO Flecker, the previous Head, home for a while from Pakistan, read one of the lessons at the Carol Service. Later the following year, ill health had forced a return home from Pakistan and he died in October after a brief time in an Oxford hospital. A fund was set up in his honour and on Old Blues' Day 1961, a memorial tablet was unveiled by his widow in the west Cloisters. A major development in 1964 saw each House of the Upper School having a service of Holy Communion in its day-room once on a weekday. In a comparatively infrequent quirk of the calendar, the year 1959 saw Easter celebrated at the School, there being a gigantic egg hunt for over 800 small chocolate eggs which had been hidden by staff. However, only eight years later, in 1967, Easter again occurred during term time, when a Chapel editorial in *The Blue* musing, perhaps optimistically rather than prophetically, that "…if, as seems likely, the date of Easter becomes fixed, it is probably the last

time ever that these days will occur during term". There was a full series of services during Easter week, beginning with 80 boys being confirmed on Palm Sunday. The services were very well attended, with the question being asked as to how many boys would have gone to a service had they been at home. There was a whole holiday on Good Friday, but apparently no egg hunt.

1.150 Friday afternoons were seeing an increasing range of activities for the pupils. For many years, an obligatory activity for the older boys had been the Combined Cadet Force. Now, in the mid-1960s, about 60 years after its founding, the Corps became voluntary, this change perhaps partly prompted by a Ministry of Defence edict to reduce the size of the contingent, one hoped-for virtue of this new status being that it would embrace a more committed group of boys. A few years earlier, the Corps' RAF Section had taken proud possession of a glider. As if to presage the CCF change, in 1958, a new group, called the Public Service Corps, had been set up to "do something constructive for the community", its initial work including painting posts and creosoting the bicycle sheds, and later laying paving stones and improving the changing facilities at the Gymnasium and the surface of the Grecians' hard tennis court. Other developments of the mid-1960s saw pupils involving themselves with the Duke of Edinburgh's nascent Award Scheme and community service more widely, including a group of boys visiting homes for the elderly and for disabled children; further, following a suggestion from the Chief Superintendent of the Crawley division of the Sussex Constabulary, a Police Cadet Group was introduced. For those leaving school, a still quite small, but increasing, number were taking a year's break before going to university, some working on the Voluntary Service Overseas Scheme.

1.151 We now go back a few years for a story of much relevance to the author. In April 1961, one of the School's mathematics masters, John Eric Bullard[z], died. He was a generous benefactor to the School and others, one act – proposing and funding the placing of a memorial tablet in Westminster Abbey to Sir William Herschel, the eminent astronomer who discovered the planet Uranus – being particularly noteworthy. Following a highly successful career in the Civil Service, in 1954 at the advanced age of 50, and for what reason within him unknown to most, he put aside this form of public service where, had he remained, he might well have become head of the Ministry, to come to teach at CH. He brought with him to the School not only a fine mathematical brain but also the incisive mind and an ability for administration which had so characterised his Civil Service days, such faculties being seen to excellent advantage in, for example, coping with the seemingly irreconcilable complexities of the School timetable. His age and a far from robust health limited his involvement with certain school activities, for example games, but he more than made his mark in the classroom and elsewhere. He died suddenly in 1961, at the start of the summer term. With the problems of finding a replacement at such short notice, the three senior Mathematics Grecians, of which the author was one, shared the teaching of the junior forms, with other masters taking what would have been Bullard's senior classes. It was a fascinating and fruitful experience for the author, although not fulfilling enough to see him pursue a career as a teacher. Bullard left his mark in another way, his idea for a children's playground seeing fruition in 1963 at the hands of the now ubiquitous (and slightly renamed) Public Service Group, and being used by masters' children, this scheme perhaps being regarded as a fore-runner of the present-day Bluecoat Nursery.

1.152 In an interesting experiment in early day pupil power, at the end of 1959 a Monitors' Council was created, essentially to promote knowledge about the running of the School and to provide a wider forum from which relevant ideas might be drawn. The Council, whose role was to recommend, rather than to decide, would consist of three monitors from each House and be chaired by the Senior Grecian. Initial topics discussed included sporting activities, clothing regulations and the House gardens. This development may have been of interest to the group of Her Majesty's School Inspectors who visited the School in the Lent term 1961. Always a potentially daunting time, *The Blue* reported that "we survived the ordeal", adding, rather cryptically, that "we were, in fact, "most handsomely reprieved"". Later, at the Founder's Day Dinner in October, Head Master Seaman², in his speech, said that the Inspectors had regarded Christ's Hospital as being "beyond doubt a great School".

1.153 However, the speech contained much more important content, indeed it was described by the CH Treasurer, Barnes Wallis*, as "one of the greatest ever made about the School". The academic world was seeing an expansion of the universities and other places of further education. With more children staying longer at school it was vital that the senior boys had an appropriate environment in which they could work. The facilities in the CH senior school – all age (11-19) Houses containing 50 boys in which all but two senior monitors would work, rest and play essentially in a single day-room (Illustration 70), as they had done for the past 60 years – were just not fit for purpose. For many of those at the Dinner, although not unfamiliar with the problem, the first inkling of a possible solution at CH had come in this speech. The key features of Seaman's proposals as mentioned then were to raise the minimum age of entry, to re-structure the School into senior and junior Houses, and to improve accommodation in the Houses.

1.154 These ideas were soon worked up into the following plan. First, all pupils would now enter at around age 11. Secondly, the senior school (for boys aged about 14 and over)

71. Horsham – A toyce.

would be accommodated in five House Blocks (the four in the west end of the Avenue, plus Lamb), with the junior school occupying the other three east end Blocks, this change being achieved alongside the closure of the Prep House Block. Thirdly, refurbishments would be made to the Blocks to provide an improved standard of accommodation appropriate to the two groups of pupils. In the senior Houses, the younger boys would continue to 'live' in the day-room, a middle stratum would have the benefit of toyces, these (Illustration 71) having been designed by Barnes Wallis, whilst older boys (essentially the monitors and Grecians) would have individual studies. The day-room would continue to serve as a common room for the whole House and a reading room would be provided. For the three junior House Blocks, pupils would continue to live in a day-room, but a reading room and a well-equipped hobbies room would be available. Further, the junior school would use the classrooms in the old Prep Block and have their own playing fields and spaces. Across the whole School, some improvements would be made to the drainage for the rugby pitches, and to the cricket pitches, whilst new squash courts, fives courts and hard tennis courts would be provided, this period also seeing some formal organisation for the sports of volleyball and basketball, both earlier played in spare time on the back asphalt. One interesting feature of the plans was that, looking beyond the main, immediate project, they envisaged a west quadrangle, a mirror image on the other side of Big School to the Garden (New) Quad (or east quadrangle). An appeal for funds for the main work was launched in 1962, the expected cost being "at least £500,000" (£10m. *£20m*), of which it was hoped that £200,000 would come from Old Blues, parents and Governors, with the remainder sought from other friends of the School and, for example, business organisations.

1.155 The building and refurbishment work proceeded apace, most of it being completed by mid-1965, and the re-

72. *Hertford – A Day-room.*

organisation and consequent changes occurred over the next few terms, culminating in the closure of the Prep School in summer 1966, the House Block being named Leigh Hunt. The vastly improved living and working conditions, with much more space, was widely appreciated by those who had experienced the previous accommodation, but all this still required some thoughtful adaptation by the pupils to the new environment. The initial cost of the work was well exceeded, the final figure coming in at over £850,000 (*£30m*). Around two-thirds of the total cost had been provided by Old Blues and friends of the School, including, at one important stage, some anonymous Trustees giving a donation of £50,000, the group later giving a further gift of £140,000.

1.156 At Hertford, the new minimum age was also introduced, the School reversing the senior/junior split, with the eight Houses becoming all age (11-18) again. There were many similarities with Horsham in the House living arrangements, although numbers were fewer – 35 girls to 50 boys – making for what would be a seemingly less crowded day-room (Illustration 72); generally speaking, improvements to the buildings were on a somewhat smaller scale.

1.157 Of other issues, the Horsham School had suffered, like elsewhere, the extremely cold weather of the first two months of 1963, a temperature of 29° F not being deemed low enough to prevent the return for the Lent term. Before this, Estate Office staff had spent three weeks clearing roads and paths

of snow – in all they put down some 50 tons of sand – and later had to deal with low stocks of coal. Most outside sport could not take place, although cross-country runners did brave the elements, and Big School was turned into an additional gymnasium, this function being shared, co-operatively it seems, with rehearsals for the School play. For a brief time the Infirmary was at full stretch, requiring for a while the use of Lamb A as 'overspill' medical accommodation. The weather brought some advantages, with tobogganing on Sharpenhurst and skating on Doctor's Lake, where the more enthusiastic and capable played ice-hockey. *The Blue* reported that, on 9th February, the appearance of the Band at dinner parade "strung out two abreast along a narrow path dug out in the quadrangle gave us a clear sign that we were winning through".

Change in the mid-1960s and early 1970s

1.158 So, in September 1966, the new system of senior and junior Houses replaced the previous all-age arrangement, the changes, just to remind the reader, seeing the minimum age of entry increasing from nine to about 11, the junior/senior dividing line being set at around 14, and the demise of the Preparatory School. In the new scheme, as mentioned earlier, there were six junior Houses – Leigh Hunt, Maine and Barnes, each with an A and a B House – all located at the east end of the Avenue, and 10 senior Houses – Lamb, Coleridge, Middleton, Thornton and Peele, again each with an A and a B House – with Lamb at the east end and the other four at the west end. One other important change occurred in the arrangements for meals in Dining Hall where the erstwhile long tables seating

73. Horsham – The Dining Hall, interior, c1950s.

50 boys were replaced by tables, now with formica tops, for 14 boys, each House having three and a half tables. The table configuration used hitherto for much of the time is shown in Illustration 73, although for a while, initially, tables had been set out parallel to, rather than across, the length of the Hall. The huge Verrio painting can be seen in the photograph, as can AH Buck[z], he being the master in the very foreground. The main change to the serving arrangements was the use of trolleys which heated the food and kept it hot prior to serving, this improvement having certain repercussions for the range and nature of 'trades' undertaken by the pupils. One sad loss was the replacement of the large hemispherical 'kiff' bowls by traditional cups holding less than half the volume of tea. Illustration 74 is an image of a bowl, the tea bag providing an indication of its size.

1.159 In sport, the transition to the new House structure required some modification to how games were organised. During the change, there was a need for some complicated "cutting and pasting" of the Houses to provide less unequal competition, this resulting in, for example, for 1st leagues rugby, the combining of the residue of Maine and Barnes into what was a powerful "MarsBars" team, while for 2nd leagues there emerged the likes of quasi Houses "BaLamb X" and "BaLamb Y". Later, in respect of School matches, U13, U14 and U15 rugby teams were established. In senior rugby, 'A' Cup-Ties were contested on a House basis, 'B' Cup-Ties on a Block basis and 'C' (under-15) by House. In cricket, time

was called on it as a compulsory sport in 1968, this affecting initially the number of Houses which could field teams; but the School 1st XI benefitted from a tour of Holland in 1967 and again in 1969. In soccer, a competition was organised for the under-12s in the junior Houses, and in 1968 the first proper pitch appeared on Little Side (the grounds at the north of the School). In the same year, the hockey XI played their first games against other schools, as did the squash teams, where, as an indication of its popularity, a 1st team, Colts, under-15s, under-14s and under-13s all appeared. In the 1967 senior steeplechase, G Mason (1960-67) achieved a third successive victory; he had also won the junior event in 1964, his three senior victories matching the earlier achievement of Pearson

74. A 'kiff' bowl.

75. Hertford – The Dining Hall, interior.

and Keys[z] (para 1.104). Basketball was also becoming increasingly popular, being contested at senior and U15 level, much benefit no doubt being derived from a tour to Berlin in the summer of 1967. Tennis numbers continued to grow, with up to 100 seniors and 60 juniors filling the courts (not all at the same time), and standards improved.

1.160 In music, in March 1966, the Chapel was the venue for a most worthy and enthusiastic performance by the School for the BBC "Songs of Praise" TV programme. The first junior music competition – covering instrumental and vocal performers – was introduced in 1967. The standard was deemed commendably high, and reference was made to the two Leigh Hunt Houses apparently having a greater number of instrumentalists than other Houses. Surprisingly, though, the result did not seem to be given. Amongst the societies, new activities included ballroom dancing, while the Shelter Group, in its first year of operation, raised £85 (£1.4k) for the National Campaign for the Homeless.

1.161 As for Hertford, having shown, just above, a photograph of the Horsham Dining Hall, it may be of interest to see the Hall at the girls' School (Illustration 75), one particular feature being the benefactors' shields – originally in the London School and now seen below the corbels – which the Museum had restored a few years ago before they were incorporated in the history library. Amongst events at Hertford in the mid-1960s the School became increasingly involved with the Duke of Edinburgh's Award Scheme, whilst in 1968 the Head Mistress took a party of seniors to southern France. From 1968, Council agreed that 65 girls could attend the St Matthew's Day celebrations in London, up from 25. There were also changes to the buildings with, in a major development in early 1968, the upper dormitories being converted into

double study bedrooms, and in 1969 the Sixth Form acquired a new Form Room. In respect of dress, changes were made to the Sunday uniforms, with cherry-red jackets replacing blue blazers, and straight blue pinafore dresses succeeding pleated grey ones. The year earlier, junior girls were allowed to wear jeans during week-end free-time.

1.162 Perhaps the main event of this period occurred in October 1966 when all the Horsham and Hertford pupils attended Westminster Abbey for a Service of Thanksgiving for the School's foundation. Although the founder, King Edward VI, was buried in the Abbey near his grand-father King Henry VII, his tomb was under the altar, and for many years there was no visible memorial to him there. During the service, a memorial stone (Illustration 76) given by Christ's Hospital, was dedicated by the Dean of Westminster, the Very Revd Dr Eric Abbott. Two aspects of a meticulously planned day might be mentioned. First, the pupils lunched at nearby Caxton Hall, the manager being an Old Blue. Secondly, the warm letter received a few days later from Dr Abbott offered high praise for what the School had done, referring to the inspiration which their presence had brought to the Abbey.

1.163 It is likely that there would have been more than a modicum of concern at Horsham at the beginning of 1967 when three members of the Royal Commission on Public Schools descended on the School apparently with a brief, from the Government, "to discover the best ways of integrating the public schools into the state system", while in parallel a separate study, by a team of sociologists, was taking place into the need for boarding education. However, nothing of substance appears to have emerged from all this activity. Coincidentally, this visitation had occurred in the very same year in which, within an ever-increasing number of pupils going to university, the School produced a record 23 Oxbridge awards. An interesting feature of the changing academic

76. *King Edward VI memorial stone, Westminster Abbey.*

climate was the growing tendency for many senior boys, with a university place, to leave before the end of the school year; in one year this number may have been perhaps around a third of leavers, such practice having obvious implications for sport, particularly cricket, and other activities.

1.164 In Chapel, in 1967, following authorisation by the Church of England, a new communion service was introduced at Horsham, mostly on an experimental basis, including at some of the day-room services. A key feature of the change, which was then used fully the following year, provided much greater participation by the communicants. Towards the end of 1969, major changes were made to the arrangements for Chapel services, these hitherto having long been compulsory throughout the week, although for Sunday a small voluntary element had been allowed for senior (essentially post-third year) boys, following the introduction of separate senior and junior services. Now there were to be major changes for seniors, with the degree of compulsion being further reduced, in particular that they would be required to attend Chapel on only the first and last Sunday of each term, together with some modifications for the weekday arrangements.

1.165 Of miscellaneous items, first, in a development which appeared at the time (around mid-1960s) not to get the attention it warranted, Peele A decided, as an experiment, to do away with the House punishment system. It was reported as being successful and to be continued "indefinitely", but it was unclear how far the idea was extended to the other Houses, although the author is aware of one which did try this policy, but not for long. Secondly, at the end of 1967, *The Outlook*, a publication for literary and artistic works which had been established by the pupils in 1921, appeared in new form, this benefitting much from the developments in lithography. The first issue, of 500

copies, quickly sold out, and the aim would be to try to achieve 750 copies for the second issue, with wider marketing to the OB community, not just the School. Thirdly, the year 1968 saw the introduction of an internal telephone service between Peele A and three other Houses, the six initial lines dealing with some 700 calls a week, progress being held back (only temporarily) when the supply of wire ran out. By 1973, the exchange was handling about 2,500 calls a week. On the telephone theme, the author could not resist the snippet of news proclaiming that, later in the 1970s, the Head Master had made the ten millionth long-distance call via the Horsham (town) exchange – to the previous year's Senior Grecian in Sydney. Fourthly, the editorial in *The Blue* of April 1968 contained a plea for closer links with the town. The piece mentioned sporadic music, arts and public service links, and argued for greater interest by the boys and more encouragement to them by the staff, citing a number of activities, such as films and archaeology, where useful links could be formed with the town. Lastly, in 1970 *The Blue* was 100 years old. Some information on its history is given in paras A2.19-25.

1.166 Of personnel, in 1966, Allison[z] retired as Clerk, to be succeeded by AW Robinson[z], he serving for five years being followed by RF Salisbury[z] (1940-46, sadly died in 2017). A few years after his retirement, Allison oversaw the arrangements for the transfer of the CH archives from the School's Counting House in Great Tower Street to the Guildhall. The phrases "Several tons" or "Already five lorries, with more to come" were used to describe the massive volume of material – registers, minute books, deed boxes, manuscripts, charters, maps, these all stretching back to the founding of the School and earlier. The collection is now held at the London Metropolitan Archives, the author previously (for *Names*) having the privilege of inspecting the first register of admissions dating from 1563. In 1967, the School lost one of its stalwarts with the retirement of Bill Armistead, who had joined CH in 1927. Bill was a mathematician and had become Master of the Royal Mathematical School in 1937 and Second Master in 1949. The author had the pleasure of being one of his button Grecians. Amongst visitors to CH were, in May 1969, Dr Ramsey, Archbishop of Canterbury, who addressed the whole School in Chapel and later answered questions from staff and seniors in Big School; and in the following year, Cardinal Heenan, Archbishop of Westminster, who spoke to the senior School in Chapel, being the first Cardinal to visit CH. Also in 1969, Dr Trevor Hoskins (1940-50) succeeded Dr Scott[z] as School MO, and was to hold the post for over 20 years.

1.167 In 1969, Head Master Seaman[z] announced his retirement. He had been in post since 1955, his main legacy being the far-reaching changes which created senior and junior Houses, and the accompanying improvements to accommodation and sports facilities. Most sadly, Seaman's retirement was short-lived, as he died suddenly in 1974. He had been working on a book, *Christ's Hospital: the Last Years in London*, and left a typescript of four chapters which finished in about 1880. Fortunately, for OBs and others, his wife, Peggy, had the foresight and dedication to collate the available text, incomplete as it was from the original intention, in the form of the above book, which was published in 1977. A memorial tablet to him was placed in the west Cloisters. He was succeeded as Head by David Newsome, Senior Tutor, Emmanuel College, Cambridge. The year after Seaman's announcement, came news of a second major retirement, namely Sir Barnes Wallis*, Treasurer and Chairman of the Council of Almoners. Some details of his life are given in para

77. Horsham – The Arts Centre, 1974.

1.192, but mention might be made here of his work in not only masterminding the progress of the 1960s Development Programme, but also his hands-on contribution in drawing many of the plans for the Boarding Houses, this splendid legacy of this work now residing in the School's Museum. He was succeeded by Sir Eric Riches[z], an eminent surgeon.

1.168 A plethora of strikes at the start of the 1970s – power, postal and oil tanker drivers – inevitably led to some inconvenience to life at both Horsham and Hertford. At Horsham, certain staff had to traipse around the country collecting exam scripts of potential CH pupils, while the shortage of oil reduced the length of breakfasts and the number of baths which could be taken. The School seemed to come through the national power cuts early in 1972 with few problems, use being made of a variety of different kinds of generators and with the ingenuity of physics masters much in demand, although some Chapel events which required use of the organ needed to be retimed. There were few reports of problems at either Horsham or Hertford arising from the effects of the "three-day week" in early 1974, during which commercial users of electricity were limited to three specified consecutive days' supply, this restriction having been introduced to conserve electricity, the generation of which was severely restricted by the industrial action by coal miners.

1.169 We now come to the next phase in the development of the Horsham School. Four main proposals had been agreed in Council. First, with more boys staying on at Christ's Hospital and an increasing range of subjects for them to study, there was a concomitant need for more teaching staff and additional classrooms, some with special equipment, such as a language laboratory. Secondly, one such new subject was drama, and this added to the erstwhile pressure for a theatre which could be used for dramatic productions, as well as lectures and films, for example, for which Big School, their present home, was not really suitable. Thirdly, in partly similar vein, the Music School had served CH well for over 60 years, but now really needed to be modernised and enlarged, particularly to provide more practice and teaching rooms and also more storage space for instruments. The fourth proposal was for a new indoor Sports Centre, which would replace the existing Gymnasium and Swimming Baths. A Centre would provide more facilities for sport, including basketball, circuit-training and indoor

cricket, whilst swimmers had long clamoured for a pool which was heated so that it could be used in winter. As a further benefit, the present Gymnasium and Baths could be used for storage. Initially, the total cost of the four projects was put at over £500,000 (£11m). A little later, rough costs of the first three were given as: classrooms, £130,000 (£2.8m), Theatre, £180,000 (£4m) and Music School, £120,000 (£2.6m), with the Sports Centre not apparently being costed at this stage. Indeed it was soon decided to put this project to one side for the moment. An appeal – the second in 10 years – for £500,000 (£7m, £11m) for the first three projects was launched in 1970. Architects Messrs Howell, Killick, Partridge and Amis were engaged to undertake the work.

1.170 From the start the School became strongly involved with fund-raising, for example through special events, such as markets and fairs on Parents' Day and Open Day, a Son et Lumière, an Elizabethan Banquet and a Grand Ball, Around the middle of 1972, by which time about £370,000 (£4m, £7m) had been raised in total, the Council of Almoners reviewed the plans and their costs. Inflation had already increased the costs of the three projects to about £630,000 (£7m, £12m), so Council decided that the focus should be on what was now collectively called the Arts Centre (the three projects), and to defer indefinitely the building of the Sports Centre. While the work was going ahead, inflation continued to bite – for example, the retail prices index rose by about 50 per cent between 1970 and 1974, and was to increase by around 25 per cent between 1974 and 1975. With a few additional developments, including the laying of a new gas main, the estimated costs of building the Arts Centre soon increased to over £900,000 (£15m). The appeal brought in about £400,000, the further £500,000 being met from a variety of sources including loans.

1.171 The work on the Arts Centre was completed in the summer of 1974. Illustration 77 shows the Theatre (front left), classrooms (left), and the enlarged Music School (front right) and the Octagon. In describing the functionality of the new Theatre, one of the key words used was 'versatility', the building being capable of being used "in-the-round" or as conventional proscenium, as well as all auditorium types in between. The Theatre – with the interior shown in Illustration 78 – could seat around 500 people and was readily adaptable to performances other than drama, including for films, concerts, lectures, and also for workshops and classes. For the new Music School, there were 11 teaching rooms, 40 practice rooms, two ensemble rooms, a refurbished Band room and ample storage space; there was also the new Octagon building, which could be used as a small concert room, rehearsal room or lecture theatre. And the 12 new classrooms enabled the bringing together of the History Department under one roof and the creation of a history library. Arrangements were also put in hand to landscape the area around the Centre, the architects generously deciding to provide these amenities as a memorial to Professor Howell, the designer of the buildings, who had sadly died in 1974. The Centre won the RIBA Award (South East region) in 1975, and was fourth in the national competition. At a ceremony held in the Theatre in December 1975, HRH Princess Alice, Duchess of Gloucester, widow of the School's late Royal President (see para 1.175), unveiled a plaque commemorating the occasion and presented the awards to representatives of the architects and the builders (Bovis Construction Southern Ltd) and also to the CH Treasurer, representing the Governors of Christ's Hospital. The excellent award-winning architectural features aside, there was general acclaim in its first few years of operation for the educational benefits it had brought and for how the endeavour

78. Horsham – The Theatre, interior.

(the Tree of Heaven), one of four planted in 1907 in West Gun Copse, which apparently was felled by mistake, *The Blue* claiming that it had been the victim of a myopic tree surgeon.

1.174 In Chapel, new hymn books were introduced in 1972, these omitting some favourites, such as the mournful tune of the Leaving Service, which were included in a supplement. In 1976, the main bit of Chapel news was of an event which happened outside, rather than inside, the chaplain arriving back at the School to find his way into the building blocked by red and white warning boards, a large piece of masonry having earlier fallen from the coping over one of the windows. Fortunately there were no injuries, and safe access to the Chapel was soon ensured. Also externally, there was some concern that the Chapel bell was not sounding its funereal best, and indeed might be cracked. Close investigation by a specialist, Douglas Hughes (1927-34), ruled this out, the cause being identified as the operational pulleys and cables, and the hammer. Hughes generously agreed to replace all these, at his own expense, the outcome being there for all to hear. Then in 1978, following some long-held concern that the vastness of the Chapel was not suitable for private prayer, a classroom in the Prep Block was transformed into the Chapel of St Edward the Martyr, and in May, Eric Kemp, the Lord Bishop of Chichester, in a short service based on the Communion, dedicated the new Chapel.

had improved links with the surrounding community, although JE Morpurgo[z] (in his 1984 revision of Allan (1947)) said that the delicate balance between these two often conflicting aims took a while to resolve.

1.172 As mentioned above, inflation was having a major impact on the Foundation's financial position. As an example, the average cost of educating a pupil at CH – about £640 in 1970 – had almost doubled by 1975; further details of this aspect of the School's administration are given in paras A1.21-25. As a result, in mid-1976 an Endowment Appeal was launched under the chairmanship of Fred Grant[z]. Again, the Schools gave whole-hearted commitment to the venture and sought to raise £20,000, a figure which was to be well exceeded. Moving into 1980, the Appeal had raised around £550,000 (£2m, *£3m*), with the exceptional achievements of the Horsham and Hertford Schools raising over £40,000 from a variety of School and House events, such as an antique fair, and from various sales and sponsorships. Interestingly, around this time, one of the suggestions for cost-saving which had been mooted was the closure of the Hertford School, bringing boys and girls together at Horsham, with smaller overall numbers.

1.173 Elsewhere, routine building and refurbishment work continued, including a new nurses' home in the old Sanatorium; improved lighting and new carpeting in the Library; and certain extensions to the Prep Block where, later in 1977, the hall was converted to a gymnasium for use by the junior boys. Longer-term work included the re-tiling of the roofs across the School, whilst the Dominions Library was converted into an extensive and much-needed reference library. The landscape across the estate was dramatically changed at the end of the decade by the felling of some 620 trees, including an Ailanthus Altimissa

1.175 Amongst the deaths during this time was that of the Duke of Windsor who had been President of Christ's Hospital from 1919 to 1936, in which year he had become King Edward VIII, his passing occurring on 29th May 1972, the 70th anniversary of the School's move to Horsham. On 10th June 1974, there occurred the death of the then current President, Prince Henry, Duke of Gloucester, who had been elected to the post in 1937 and who had attended many of the principal School events of his era including the Quatercentenary celebrations in 1953 and the laying of the Memorial Stone to King Edward VI in Westminster Abbey in 1966, as well as making a number of private and informal visits to the Horsham and Hertford Schools. His son, Prince Richard, succeeded him as President, HRH making an early visit to Horsham the following year. As with all such visits, much planning and organisation was needed, particularly with regard to security generally and for the landing of the helicopter. Visits to the Chapel, the Craft and Technical (ex-Manual) School, the Library and the Arts Centre were followed by dinner parade, lunch on the dais, and photographs in front of Big School, before the helicopter departure. Of two other deaths, that of George Seaman[z], in November 1974, has been mentioned above, while a few months earlier the School had lost one of its 20th century luminaries, Edmund Blunden[z], *The Blue* of June 1974 containing some moving recollections of his life by AH Buck[z].

1.176 Three anniversaries were celebrated a few years into the decade. Perhaps the main event was the tercentenary of the founding of the Royal Mathematical School for which, on 15th May 1973, the School laid a wreath on the tomb of King Charles II (who had granted the Royal Charter) at Westminster Abbey. The Thanksgiving Service – attended by Horsham and Hertford – featured a memorable fanfare composed by

79. The CH Station and railway lines, early Horsham.

the Bandmaster and an informative address by the Dean, Eric Abbott, in which he recounted the history of the RMS and spoke about the conjunction of mathematics and art. After the Service, HRH The Duchess of Gloucester took the salute outside the Great West Door as the column of marchers – first the junior boys, then the Band, followed by the girls, and finally the senior boys – headed for Waterloo Station. At CH, the main events were a week-long exhibition in the Dominions Library, with many documents and other material pertaining to the founding of the RMS and its development, and a special concert, preceded by a buffet supper in Dining Hall, to which many VIPs and past members of the RMS were invited. The Museum's current Hon Curator, Mike Barford, remembers acting as security guard for the Library exhibition, spending nights there with a hockey stick by his side. The RMS of today is, of course, much different from its past, but its history has not been lost – indeed it has been well documented by Clifford Jones (1957-64, a Museum colleague of the author) in his book *The Sea and the Sky*. Further, the author (a mathematician) hopes that he will be around to join in the celebrations for the RMS's 350th anniversary in 2023.

1.177   The other two events were bicentenaries of births, first Samuel Taylor Coleridge* in 1972, then Charles Lamb* three years later. Coleridge was remembered in a week of celebratory events including an exhibition in the Art School of some 100 items, especially books, manuscripts and letters; a series of four lectures by Coleridge experts delivered in Big School, and a service of commemoration. The celebration of Lamb's bicentenary in 1975 was on a much smaller scale, the main feature being a two-hour presentation of his life and works, in the presence of a large gathering of the Charles Lamb Society, who also enjoyed an exhibition of some of his writings.

1.178   In a major academic development in the Michaelmas term 1972, tutorial arrangements were introduced for senior boys. A further academic advance was achieved in 1973 when the School acquired a language laboratory, this greatly expanding the flexibility for teaching. The added advantage of the privacy element and the facility whereby pupils could go at their own speed were seen as two particular benefits. On a less academic, but nevertheless educational, front, Friday afternoon

activities were increasingly seeing boys in cars with L plates careering around Big Side like "the dodgem stall at the fair". Probably some of these boys would have been the beneficiaries when, in July 1973, in a momentous day in the life of Christ's Hospital, the first half pint was pulled in the newly created Grecians' Club. The purpose of the Club was to provide a place where the older boys could meet socially in the evening, away from their Houses. The Head Master and Council had approved the idea, the builders had done their bit at the back of the Scout Hut, and local magistrates had been persuaded to grant the alcohol licence. Later that year, the Club boasted a handsome bar, the front panelling of which had been made from the old Newgate Street table tops. In 1979, the Club held its first fancy dress dance, and soon afterwards draught Guinness and a pool table arrived.

1.179   On the sports field, the cricket XI of 1973, with four wins and eight draws, were only the second unbeaten XI since the move to Horsham, the previous one being in 1940, and later, in 1977, Quentin Brown (1971-77) achieved a record haul of 132 wickets in his years in the XI. Also in 1973 the Feeder Cricks cricket team, comprising boys and members of staff, was founded. The team would play Sunday and evening games against local village sides, thus meeting the main purpose of its founding, namely to improve links with the local community. Inter-school football matches were played officially for the first time early in 1972, the XI undertaking a tour to Berlin later in the summer. At the end of that year, the School played in the Annual Public Schools' Six-a-Side Tournament, topping the qualifying league, but then going out in the quarter-finals conceding their one and only goal, whilst in 1974 Iain Swalwell (1966-73) became the School's first soccer Blue, for Cambridge. In hockey, the first all-weather pitch was completed in the Lent term 1972, this allowing an earlier start to the season than hitherto. The athletics track – now around 25 years old – was renovated in early 1973, but there appeared to be greater interest in the steeplechase, where a record 250-plus boys contested the three team cups and the individual trophies. Some Judo classes were mixed, although this was probably not the reason for reports in *The Blue* appearing not under Sport but in the Societies section. The report of shooting referred to the best season for 43 years, including repeating the 1932 2nd position in the Ashburton Shield.

1.180   In 1972, the School said goodbye to an old friend, the CH station. In the days of few cars it had been constructed as an integral part of the School. It had various changes of name before it became Christ's Hospital, often without the apostrophe, although such punctuation does exist there at present. In its hey-day, as can be seen in the view (looking south) in Illustration 79, the station boasted six platforms, with the special track for the School train on the left and the Guildford branch line – which closed in the 1960s as part of the Beeching cuts – on the right. On the day before its demise a party of mourners from the School said a sad farewell on Platform 1. There remain just the two central lines and corresponding platforms, with a small building (roughly where the waiting rooms were on the old central platform area) which serves as a (limited hours) ticket office.

1.181   In drama, in 1971, Coleridge House Block and

Horsham High School for Girls combined in an immensely ambitious production, the first by Trevor Hoskins (1940-50), the School's Medical Officer, of Anouilh's "Antigone". The end-product, despite breaking much new ground and having to overcome a number of problems, including the use of the Prep Hall venue, was widely and appreciatively received. Also about this time, in a rare, indeed probably then unique, event, the School play "Twelfth Night" was produced by a Grecian, Tim Swinton (1964-72), the cast including one of the country's leading present-day thespians, Roger Allam (1964-72), in the role of Sir Toby Belch. One other memorable play of this time (1973) was "Indians", 120 of them, a gargantuan production which made full use of a massive Big School set and which elicited the comment that it was "…something new and exciting, a vision of a new dramatic territory…"

1.182 In the first half of the 1970s, Christ's Hospital, keen to display its rich heritage, began a programme of tours of the site, with visitors learning the history of the School and viewing the magnificent buildings and splendid collection of art and memorabilia, and also seeing Band Parade and the pupils marching into lunch. The tours – named after Verrio (see para 1.7) – were run by the pupils and included afternoon tea. Visitor numbers built up very quickly in these early years and by the end of the 1970s exceeded 1,500 a year. The Verrio tours continue to this day, still conducted by the pupils, but including various improvements from those early days.

1.183 At Hertford, the main change in the early 1970s was the retirement of Miss West after a long and dedicated 30 years as Head Mistress, to be succeeded by Miss Elizabeth Tucker. Soon into Miss Tucker's reign, a number of changes were made to the arrangements for Chapel services and a variety of additional privileges were introduced across the School, including a greater freedom for the pupils to wear their own clothes, and leave-weekends for monitresses, this latter soon being extended to all girls; later, senior pupils were not required to wear the uniform when travelling to and from School. One particular development which caught the author's eye and which had occurred right at the start of the decade was the need to erect barbed wire around the School to 'secure' the walls and keep out the Hertford youth. On the sporting front, there were a number of improvements to the available facilities, including a hard playing surface for hockey, and new hard tennis courts and squash courts, whilst indoors, arrangements were made for the playing of badminton and volleyball. In 1975, a new gallery was installed in the Reference Library. The following year, the new President was welcomed, whilst for the first time the girls joined the boys' choir in singing at the St Matthew's Day service. The year 1977 marked the 75th anniversary of the Hertford girls' School and the 425th anniversary of the opening of Christ's Hospital, one or both of these events perhaps leading to two monitresses being invited to the Founder's Day Dinner. One other feature of interest which happened in 1978 was the staging of a play "Time to Celebrate", written by Head Mistress Tucker and depicting scenes of life at CH, the piece having been written to commemorate the arrival of girls at Hertford in 1778.

1.184 Amongst other items at Horsham, first, the requirement to travel in full Housey uniform at the beginning and end of term was abolished in 1970, *The Blue* adding wryly that, given some of the outfits seen on the Housey Special, passengers at Victoria Station would still have cause to stand and stare. Secondly, half-term holidays were introduced in the Michaelmas term 1971. Thirdly, in October 1971, the Senior Grecian, Christopher Tremayne (1963-70), attended the Canonization Service of 40 English and Welsh Martyrs in Rome, one of the former being Saint Edmund Campion, who was thought to have been educated privately at CH (see para 2.20). At one point after the main ceremony, Tremayne was amongst a group of about 40 people presented to the Pope. Fourthly, the year 1973 marked the retirement of Arthur Rider who had been a master at the School, save for the period of the War, from 1931 to 1973, his long and loyal service, which included Head of the Modern Languages Department and Commander of the Corps, culminating in the post of Second Master. Fifthly, around 1972, in a highly imaginative and useful venture, a Thrift Shop was established, essentially an exchange for used and under-used sports or other kit. From small beginnings – it made a profit of £100 (£400) in the first year – about £450 (£1,700) was made in 1978 and, come 1981, £2,000 (£7,500) raised from the Shop and other sources provided for the purchase of a new School minibus. Lastly, 1972/73 saw Coleridge A achieve the likely unique feat of providing the Senior Grecian for the third year running.

Consolidation from the mid-1970s, and planning for the merger

1.185 Of the various societies, 1975 was the 50th year of scouting at CH, and the Scout Group celebrated with an anniversary dinner in the Court Room, the guests including Jack Hood Phillips, who had founded the Group, and the Rt Hon Michael Stewart[z], who was the Troop's first senior boy. An even more noteworthy event occurred in 1977 with the Debating Society celebrating its centenary, a worthy achievement by any yardstick. The motion at the first meeting of the Society had been "That it is not in the School's best interest to move CH into the country", and then 100 years later "That this House would put its head down and shove". The former, perhaps narrow, topic sought the mood of the pupils on what was to become a major issue for the School namely the possibility of leaving London, whilst the latter would seem to provide much more scope for the speakers' imagination. The names of a few notable debaters amongst the pupils have been given, en passant, earlier, but it should not go unmentioned that masters always played an important formative and contributory role in the conduct of the Society. Perhaps more ambitiously, there was established an Equestrian Society whose members, suitably transported, would ride in St Leonard's Forest. In mid-1977, the boys established a Computer Group, the development, coincidentally or otherwise, following closely on the heels of the acquisition by the School's administrative office of its first computer,

1.186 In the second half of the 1970s, some of the main sporting matters involved the less well-known activities, with the development of badminton and, in a move to strengthen involvement in the game, the formation of a hockey club, the initiative certainly providing an increased number of players. There was also a growing interest in golf, with some semi-official participation in schools' competitions being seen as more than moderately successful given its lack of recognition at CH as a bona fide sport and limited time for practice. Later, lessons were provided at a local driving range, with rounds being played at a nearby course, and boys took part in regular competitions. In tennis, the IV had an unbeaten season in 1980.

1.187 In music, at the end of 1976, the Band played at the opening of the new shopping precinct in Horsham, the report in *The Blue* proffering the thought, admittedly with some hesitation, that it had been the first time that the Band had

80. A model of the London School.

until over 300 years after the founding of the Royal Mathematical School; there was no news over the next few years of the activity of the new group. However, in another part of the CCF, in 1979, a contingent of eight RAF cadets made a highly instructive and enjoyable visit to RAF Laarbruch in Germany.

1.190 Amongst changes in personnel, in 1976, the Treasurer, Sir Eric Riches[z], retired, to be replaced by Alistair Alan (but known as Angus) Ross[z]. It was observed that, during his six years in post, Riches had seen into office, in chronological order, a new Head Master, a new Clerk, a new Head Mistress and a new President. Then in 1979 Head Master Newsome resigned, having been in post since 1970, his time being characterised in particular by the enthusiasm of his leadership and the appearance of the Theatre.

1.191 The new Head Master was Derek Baker[z], who had been a lecturer in history at Edinburgh University. Two of his initial manifestations were first – and evident to all – the restoration of the ringing of bells before periods and also at the end of the five minute period-break to start off the next lesson, Baker himself sometimes undertaking the ringing, and secondly – known by only a few at the time – was a trip to the top of the Water Tower to view his domain from on high.

1.192 However, Baker's period in office was to have a sad beginning. In October 1979, Sir Barnes Wallis* died. In addition to his immense work for CH, Wallis (Illustration 81) had achieved international renown by his invention of the "bouncing bomb" which he developed in WW2 as a means of destroying the erstwhile impregnable dams of Germany's Ruhr Valley. He was responsible for sundry other inventions and was reported to have had 140 patents credited to his name. He stands as one of the greatest ever creative engineers of the aviation industry. For his work connected with the Dambusters' raid he was awarded £10,000 (£400k) by the Government. However, so deeply concerned was he that so many had died delivering his weapons, he arranged for this award to be given to Christ's Hospital to help fund places for children of RAF war widows, the sum being soon matched by an equivalent amount from the RAF Benevolent Fund. The Trust so established, and supported by subsequent donations from the RAF Association and the 617 Squadron (The Dambusters) Aircrew Association, permitted the presentation of 145 children (104 boys and 41 girls) over the years 1951 to 1999. And into the new millennium, despite declining funds, children are still being presented. There was a Service of Thanksgiving for the life of Sir Barnes in St Paul's in February 1980, in the presence of HRH The Prince of Wales, attended by both the Horsham and Hertford Schools, at which an Address was delivered by Professor Jack Morpurgo[z]. Then at the end of the service, after the National Anthem, as the procession moved down the nave, the Band struck up the evocative Dambusters March, most movingly charging the Cathedral with "nostalgic feelings and associations". Nowadays, the seminar room in the CH Museum contains sundry reminders of Sir Barnes, including a painting, a bust, a geodetic structure (a triangular piece of metalwork, being his design of part of the lower fuselage of a Vickers Wellington which was recovered from Loch Ness), and, as mentioned earlier, his own hand-drawn plans of the 1960s building work.

1.193 We now come to the most important development of

marched through the town. Indeed, the next issue brought forward due correction, with the reference to the visit in 1946 to see the film "Henry V". In 1977, the Band did break new ground in its visit to the picturesque Goodwood race course, whilst the following years saw three concerts with the band of the Honourable Artillery Company, all with a minimum of rehearsal and all receiving high praise. There were two major pieces of choral news in 1977. First, the choir visited the beautiful cathedral at Chartres, singing at a service and performing at a concert in the cavernous church, and then, after a day to recuperate, appearing at a second service. A few months later, the School rejoiced in the success of Andrew March (1977-83) who became Chorister of the Year in a competition organised by the Royal School of Church Music.

1.188 One particular piece of the craftsman's ability which greatly appealed to the author was the construction of a model of the London School (Illustration 80) by Christopher Baile (1971-76), the work, including planning, being spread over three years. The model was based on a plan of the School relating to around 1795, and made use of an extensive collection of prints to provide details of the buildings' elevations; where such information was not available, walls were left blank. The model, which measures about three-quarters of a metre square, with most buildings having a height of around 10 cms, was made largely of balsa wood, with judicious use of strengthening struts and braces. It was completed in time for a Pepys Society visit to the School in 1976, and was also viewed by the Duke of Gloucester on a visit he made. Nowadays, it deservedly forms part of the Museum's exhibition.

1.189 Of two other matters, first, the School seemed to have survived the unbearably hot summer of 1976, with temperatures getting up to 95° F. Shirt-sleeve order became de rigeur, including, and rare if not unique for the time, for the Band (but not necessarily the drum majors) and for the dinner parade. Drought conditions prevailed and grass turned yellow. Apparently, much lager was drunk in the Grecians' Club. Many people could no doubt remember where they were when the drought ended, *The Blue* reminding us of an all-night thunderstorm near the end of term, the author wallowing in a downpour in Montreal where he was for the 1976 Olympic Games. Secondly, *The Blue* of November 1975 referred to the launch of a new naval section of the Corps, this seeming a little ironic that such a development should not have occurred

81. Sir Barnes Neville Wallis, CH Treasurer.

the 20th century at CH. After much deliberation, but perhaps without much surprise, in April 1980 Council announced the intention to close the School at Hertford, with the girls being moved to join the boys at Horsham. Whilst the financial position of running two schools was the key factor in the decision, particularly following the high inflation of the 1970s, much merit was seen in co-education and the inestimable social and other benefits which would ensue. As plans evolved, it was decided that about 230 girls would be admitted in September 1985, with Coleridge and Barnes designated as the first two girls' House Blocks, this choice probably already following the idea of alternate boys'/girls' Blocks along the Avenue. With about 640 boys, the initial boys/girls ratio was not too dissimilar from what had existed hitherto in the 20th century. However, this was largely a practical consideration, the aim being for equality of numbers as soon as could be achieved. The inter-regnum before the move would require detailed planning on the numbers of those admitted and leaving, and on the House location at both Horsham and Hertford. This involved, for example, the creation at Horsham of a Thornton C (Thornton B plus Coleridge A) and Middleton C (Middleton B plus Coleridge B), with some boys being accommodated in the erstwhile School Post Office, which had closed in 1981, and in one of the vacant master's houses in the Avenue. Later, for a while, the refurbished Coleridge Block was re-inhabited by boys.

1.194 In terms of the structure of the Houses, the boys would continue their senior/junior split, this now being achieved (from Michaelmas 1984) by having the 'A' Houses of the six boys' House Blocks as senior Houses, and the 'B' houses as junior Houses, this involving, for example, initially, the erstwhile junior Houses of Leigh Hunt A and Maine A being upgraded to senior Houses, and Lamb B (previously a senior House) being modified as a junior House. In contrast, the girls coming to Horsham would continue the all-age (11-18) basis which had been in use at Hertford. And problematic as these structural issues were, perhaps the main matter for decision was the uniform to be worn by the girls at Horsham. In the event, a new 'Bluecoat' uniform for the girls was created by Peter Rice, a theatrical designer, comprising an outer blue coat, pleated skirt, and with bands and yellow socks for everyday

wear (Illustration 82), with a longer skirt and lace jabot for formal occasions (Illustration 83). In the view of the author, the end-product, as worn respectively by sisters Heidi Johnson (2008-15) and Jasmine Johnson (2005-12) – the author's first two presentees – represents a perfect complement to the 460-year-old uniform of the boys.

1.195 Of more than passing interest, the contract for the refurbishment and conversion work, including improved staff accommodation, had been awarded to Longley of Crawley, who had built the Horsham School over 80 years earlier. Amongst a flurry of on-site activity in the early 1980s, there appeared new office accommodation between the Chapel and the Classics Block, three new classrooms, a new computing centre and a careers room. There were also improvements to the old biology laboratories and to the Grecians' Club, while a School monitors' room was erected by the Tuck Shop, with appeals being made for a colour television, a deep-freeze and a distillery. The Art School was redecorated, and a new quartz clock controlled the time on the four Big School clock faces. However, there was one event in 1984 which, in the mind of the author (and probably many others), was little removed from a piece of architectural vandalism, namely the insertion of a mezzanine floor in the hallowed Dominions Library, this action destroying the wonderful character and charm of the place. In his *Names* book, the author expressed the fervent wish that "some day there may be a return to its original form". Good (architectural) sense has prevailed and the Library has indeed been returned to its former elegance. Then, in 1985, the Infirmary was refurbished. Going in the other direction, as it were, the sewage farm (the School, initially, processing its own waste) was dismantled, the erstwhile pungent outfall apparently attracting a variety of interesting birds, but probably little else.

1.196 Amidst all this activity, the Band continued triumphantly, playing on successive days at the Royal Albert Hall, first the full Band at the "Festival of Youth Marching

82 and 83. The new uniform for girls.

82 – with permission of Heidi Johnson; 83 – with permission of Jasmine Johnson

84. Hertford – The Horsham band plays, 1984.

Bands Gala" and then the Show Band at the Church Army "Centenary Celebration Gala". Both performances, to audiences of over 4,000, were exhilarating and distinctly memorable. It also continued to play (often leading) at the Lord Mayor's parade, a cherished role apparently first undertaken in 1974 and essentially annually from 1981. And then, in the summer of 1984, a year before the merger, the Band gave a concert in Castle Hall in the town of Hertford, prior to which they performed at the School, as for lunch parade (Illustration 84), thus giving a foretaste of what was to become a regular feature for the girls going to Horsham.

1.197 In Chapel, from the end of 1980, a master or a group of boys took four morning services a week, while in the following February, in a special service, the organ was officially re-dedicated, it having been removed for nearly a year for a complete renovation by Rushworth and Dreaper Ltd of Liverpool, the company which had built and installed it in 1931. It was then the largest public school organ in the country. Following the re-dedication service, Mr Alistair Rushworth gave a lecture on the organ. Sad to relate, about the time (in 2016) this item was being prepared, it was reported that Mr Rushworth had died.

1.198 In sport, one of the most noteworthy features of these years was the rugby XV being unbeaten in 1981 (thought to be the first occasion since 1948), a feat which was splendidly repeated in 1982, some of this success being laid at the door of Tom Godfrey (1977-83) who captained the England Under-16 side. Earlier, in 1980, on the cricket field Nicholas Konig (1973-80) became the leading career aggregate run-scorer. Then in 1983, the football XI won all its 10 inter-school matches and had four players chosen for the Lent term Public Schools' XI. In the same year, the hockey XI were unbeaten in 11 games against other schools, winning eight and drawing three. Elsewhere, fencing had been introduced in 1984, the sport enjoying a successful start despite some potentially better performers being 'claimed' by other sports.

1.199 Involvement with the various societies and with overseas trips continued apace. The former included, perhaps not surprisingly, an ever-expanding Wine Society, and also a new Campaign for Nuclear Disarmament group and a Europa Club, this last seen as having a close link with the Modern Languages Department. The overseas trips included a thought-provoking visit to Leningrad and Moscow in 1981, followed by a similar venture two years later. Then, in 1984, one of the more ambitious trips of this period was the expedition to the Himalayas undertaken by the Mountaineering and Exploring Club, the visit, which was to see the adventurers climbing to a height of 19,000 feet, requiring three years to plan and including nine months of often intense physical preparation.

1.200 There were two notable weather features which affected the Horsham School in 1981. First, in the Lent term, a freak storm, lasting over eight hours, engulfed the town of Horsham causing record flooding there and in the surrounding areas, and cutting off CH entirely from the outside world. Secondly, those in Chapel at 8.40am one October morning felt the whole building shake with the "thud and buffet of a mighty wind"; outside, skies darkened and torrential rain fell. Emerging from Chapel some 10 minutes later when the worst was over, the first sight was of the Avenue being ankle-deep in leaves, twigs and branches. Further afield, trees had been torn asunder, including a massive oak in the middle of the running track and one which had crashed into the Head Master's garden. Many rugby posts were down. The explanation was that CH had been struck by a miniature tornado, the reading on the School's meteorological barograph showing a sudden sharp dip in pressure at that precise time in the morning.

1.201 Amongst other items at Horsham, in the early 1980s parents of pupils in the Great Erasmus form were invited to meet the masters and mistresses who were teaching their sons, this scheme later being extended across all forms and also continuing today. Secondly, in November 1980, the Theatre hosted the semi-final of the BBC TV quiz programme, "Mastermind", for which, as transmission would not be for some time, those in the audience were asked to remove

85. The commemorative plaque for the merger, 1985.

poppies. Later, in 1987, two further programmes in the series were recorded at the School. Thirdly, in May 1981, the President once again honoured the School with a visit, arriving by helicopter and being greeted by a fanfare from the Band written by Ken Naylor, a music master and Director of the Arts Centre. Fourthly, in the Lent term 1982, the School was affected by three medium-scale epidemics – influenza, vomiting and gastroenteritis – leading someone to remark that even illnesses go in threes. Fifthly, two changes to timetabling saw Parents' Day being held on a Sunday for the first time, and Speech Day on the last Saturday of term, the initial view being that both changes had been successful. Nowadays, Parents' Day does take place on a Sunday, but Speech Day, the date often depending on the diary of the Lord Mayor, is held towards the end of May. Sixthly, a team of Grecians won £2,500 (£8k) for the School and five pocket calculators for themselves as the first prize in the SEGAS Information Technology 82 Project. Lastly, another change to past practice was that the St Matthew's Day visit of 1983 involved the School being received by the Lord Mayor at the Guildhall rather than the Mansion House, this arrangement continuing to the present day.

1.202 Of events at Hertford, in 1980 the School celebrated, in the presence of the President, the 300th anniversary of the opening of CH at the Hertford location. In 1982, Miss Elizabeth Tucker resigned as Head Mistress, to be succeeded by Miss Jean Morrison. With the merger in prospect, there were regular visits of parties of Hertford girls to Horsham to see where they would be undertaking their future education, and in one particular early initiative boys and girls combined to advance their A Level geography work, such joint lessons later becoming more common and 'togetherness' being extended to meals. Amongst sporting activities, a number of pupils were involving themselves in canoeing, apparently at Clacton-on-Sea. In the Lent term 1983, an influenza epidemic affected about half the School, and then in the following year there was the final major drama production, "Noye's Fludde",

the performance, in All Saints' Church, involving every pupil in the School. Of particular note, the last pre-merger gathering of Old Girls, held in September 1984, attracted about 700 former pupils.

1.203 In mid-1984, ill-health caused the resignation of Angus Ross[z], Treasurer, he being replaced by Professor Edward Kenney (1935-43). Ross, who had been in post during the latter part of the high inflation years of the 1970s and then in the pre-merger period of the first half of the 1980s, sadly died in December 1984. In his memory, the monies subscribed to a memorial fund were used to finance an annual choral and orchestral concert at CH; this began in 1987 and is, today, a major event in the School's music calendar.

1.204 Then in 1985, just a few months before the merger, there came news of the resignation of Head Master Baker[z], this being as sudden as it was unexpected, as he had served only five years. The key issue during his era was the preparation for the merger, during which time the Block system of senior boys in A Houses and junior boys in B Houses was introduced. A particular legacy of his time was the development of the Careers Department. Most propitiously, with the merger imminent, at very short notice the School managed to entice out of retirement John Hansford[z] to serve for four terms over this most critical period, his last and most relevant position having been Headmaster at King Edward's School, Witley, a co-educational boarding school.

The merger in 1985 and developments to 2000

1.205 The girls came to Horsham in September 1985, the word 'reunited' being used in more than one description of the memorable day, it not being forgotten that boys and girls had been together before in both London and Hertford. The amalgamation of the two Schools was marked on Founder's Day 1985 with the President, HRH The Duke of Gloucester, unveiling a commemorative plaque placed in the front wall of Dining Hall above the Foundation Stone which had to be lowered to accommodate it – see Illustration 85. The day included a Chapel service, dinner parade, lunch (in Hall for the Royal Party and pupils, and in Big School for 600 guests and staff), a tour of the School, and ended with afternoon tea in the Library. To mark the occasion, every member of the School was given a commemorative plate, based on the design used at Hertford in the 18th century.

1.206 It may sound a bit glib to say that the merger seems to have gone well, indeed very well, testimony to five years of assiduous planning and the flexibility of those involved on the ground. Head Master Hansford's role did not stop with the 're-unification', he helping to formulate his vision of the future of the new School. In this work he had been greatly assisted by Miss Jean Morrison, Head Mistress at Hertford (1982-85) who had also made a major contribution to the planning process. Now, with Hertford closed, she came to Horsham for a year to assist the Head. For the pupils, their daily lives would never be the same. In addition to the more obvious features of mixed classes and dining, and mixed company generally, the composition (and sound) of the choirs and the make-up of the Band, for example, were forever changed.

1.207 As mentioned before, the girls had come from Hertford with an all-age (11-18) House structure which was continued at Horsham, while the boys had just changed from senior and junior House blocks to a senior (A House) and junior (B) arrangement. However, the girls did need to experience two

86. The effect of the great storm in the Avenue, 1987.

changes. First, they had to get used again to an academic year of three (rather than four) terms. Secondly, the girls had to sacrifice their monitress badges, no such identification existing at Horsham; such badges in future were to be awarded to the girl becoming Senior Grecian or Second Monitor. So, initially, there were to be around 230 girls in two House Blocks – Coleridge and Barnes – and about 640 boys in the other six Blocks. Leigh Hunt was to be the next Block for conversion, the work being completed in 1992, with numbers of boys and girls then becoming around 520 and 300 respectively. Later, in order to increase the number of senior girls at the School, temporary accommodation, called 'Hertford', was established in the Infirmary for about 10 Grecians.

1.208 Various other developments about the School included, in the eyes of some, the replacement of one monstrosity with another, although both had their obvious uses. The loss was the public conveniences in the Art School car park, in which place there emerged a hideous two-storeyed Portakabin classroom block. In 1987, the School's Counting House moved from its Great Tower Street premises in the City into the new buildings at the east end of Dining Hall, the Lord Mayor unveiling a commemorative plaque. Also in 1987, the Home Farm, which for many years provided the creamy raw milk at the School's breakfast table and a working venue with a difference for the pupils, was now likely to fall foul of EEC requirements on milk production and had to close. In early summer 1989, a new clock tower was hoisted into position atop Big School, but no bells were to be heard for a while. At the end of 1991, the installation of new lighting in Chapel greatly enhanced the appearance of Brangwyn's murals, as well as giving a much warmer feel to the whole Chapel. In 1996, what had been known in earlier days as the Manual School, now became the Design and Technology Department, there having been an interim change of name – to the Craft, Design and Technology Department – somewhere between 1961 and 1996.

1.209 One other development of the early 1990s, provided by a "trusted source" rather than *The Blue*, merits mention. Following the Dominions Library debacle of the 1980s (see para 1.195), it seems that "mezzanine man" was still alive and about to inflict his architectural ideology on a far more iconic building. Apparently, there was discussion – where, unknown – of the possibility of installing a 'mezzanine' floor in Big School. Now, building upwards and making better use of space are important features of architectural design, although these are generally much less controversial when practised for new, rather than existing, buildings. The design of Big School, particularly its large windows and the presence of the 1830 organ at its south end, made it difficult for the author to envisage how such an additional floor might have been introduced. Had the change been made, those seeing the building for the first time may have expressed paeans of praise for the seamless integration of the new with the old and for the improved functionalism, However, for those who knew what had been, their sadness at the change would have received scant consolation from the (presumed) unchanged appearance of the exterior. Thank goodness, nothing happened.

1.210 In 1986/87 there were changes to CH governance as James Forbes[z] succeeded Professor Edward Kenney as Treasurer, Richard Poulton took on the role of Head Master following Hansford[z]'s interim tenure, and Captain Michael Pearey[z] replaced Roy Salisbury[z] as Clerk. Salisbury had spent 40 years in all in the Counting House, 15 as Clerk. Around the end of the decade, with the millennium but ten years away, the Treasurer set up the Way Ahead Committee to provide a more formalised planning procedure for the future of the School as it moved into the 21st century.

1.211 As the 1980s ended, thoughts worldwide turned to the 50th anniversary of the start of WW2. At CH, in one particularly imaginative fund-raising venture, in the summer of 1989 the School, focussing on an iconic WW1 battlefield, organised a "Somme Walk" in aid of the World War Memorial Appeal for Disaster Relief, the Walk involving one representative from each House walking 16 miles on the Somme battlefield. Despite inclement weather, the participants saw it through, raising about £3,000 (£7k) for the fund. A few months later, a service was held in the Chapel for the School and Old Blues to honour the memory of those Old Blues and members of staff who had given their lives in WW2. The Revd Kenneth Oliver² gave an Address, this being followed by the playing of the Last Post and Reveille, remembrance being further evident in the order of service which listed the names of those who had died.

1.212 Probably encouraged by this service and given the existence of the WW1 memorial on the front of Dining Hall, a small group of Old Blues explored with the School the possibility of providing a more permanent memorial to the fallen of WW2. Council approved, provided it was financed by private subscription, and a special appeal was launched. The new memorial took the form of two panels, placed on either side of the then existing WW1 memorial on the Dining Hall, containing the names, Houses and years at CH of over 200 Old Blues whose deaths occurred in WW2. It was dedicated at a moving service, led by the Revd P Brownless (1930-37), on Old Blues' Day 1992. Included there (for WW2) are the names of six Old Girls, and recorded on a small separate tablet are two names of OBs who perished in Korea and Suez. In May 1995, the School commemorated the 50th anniversary of the end of World War 2, sharing the event with some 30 Old Blues who were at Housey during the War. Following a Chapel service, a short Service of Re-dedication to Peace was held in the Quad.

1.213 In 1988 the School began to assimilate the new GCSE exams, and soon afterwards, a prime-time prep period was introduced, the idea having emanated apparently from the

87. The Avenue, pre-storm.

previous year's School monitors. Possibly reflecting outside influences, a new Business Studies Department was created. In 1992 the Salters' Livery Company most generously gave the School £175,000 (£320k, *£360k*) to refurbish the five chemistry laboratories, with the new Department to be known as the Salters' School of Chemistry. In November the following year, with most of the work completed, the Master of the Company, Lord Porter, in the presence of CH's President, HRH The Duke of Gloucester, opened the new School. The end-product, which included new and modified support and store rooms and new central heating, was deemed to be a superb, well-equipped facility. An interesting development in the curriculum occurred in 1993 with the introduction of a 'Discovery' course for new entrants. The course, which covered the pupils' first year, would provide tutorial facilities, cross-curricular activities, including some outside the School, and scope for personal development. Individual timetables needed to be adjusted in the Michaelmas term as the School calendar moved to a 40-period week and an 8.30am start. Another aspect of CH life which bears mention relates to the Careers Department; indeed, this help with pupils' careers can be traced back to the second half of the 19th century where it was in the hands of John Wingfield*, and more recently had been a particular feature of Baker's period as Head. Now, formalised and expanded, as further education and job opportunities increased, the Department provided an extensive range of information, advice and training for those in their last few years at the School.

1.214 The School continued in the broadcasters' eye. On the morning of Remembrance Sunday, 1988, a full School Chapel service was broadcast, nationally, by ITV (South), the rehearsal, for camera and others, taking place on the previous evening, with the Band having just returned from leading the procession at the Lord Mayor's Show. Much work had gone into preparing for the service, and the School and staff could be justly proud of producing a high quality and moving event on the day. The following year, the cameras of a French company, and the microphones of BBC radio – for their flagship programme "Any Questions?" – were in evidence.

1.215 Another of those events for which most people can recall where they were when it happened, and which had a lasting impact on the School, was the great storm on the night/ morning of Thursday/Friday 15th/16th October 1987. The roll of devastation will still bring a tear to the eye of some, with about 240 trees being felled across the estate, including most of those in the Avenue (see Illustration 86) and along the Quarter Mile. The central buildings seemed mostly to have escaped the impact of the fallen trees, but some brickwork and tiling did suffer damage. A little further afield, the roof of the old Gymnasium blew off, landing on the Swimming Pool roof, this ill wind providing further argument, if any were required, for the need for a Sports Centre (finance of course permitting). As a result of the heroic efforts of the estate staff and many others, the Avenue was cleared by Friday evening, although it took about six weeks to dispose of all the fallen trees. Over the next few months, amongst other work, the Gymnasium roof was replaced and a "roof of sorts" appeared on the Pool. By January 1988, the cost of the repair work was over £40,000 (*£125k*). An unofficial appeal for funds raised in excess of this amount. The trees destroyed in the main Avenue were replaced by whitebeams which seem to have had a rather chequered growth. Now, approaching 30 years on from the storm, the author wonders whether he will ever again see the luxuriant green canopy which once ran along the axis of the School (Illustration 87), whilst some of what was lost from the

88. The Quarter Mile, pre-storm.

Quarter Mile can be seen in the wonderful winter photograph at Illustration 88.

1.216 Towards the end of the 1980s and into the next decade, the School kept the visa department of the Russian Embassy busy with a further series of visits: a group of four spending four weeks at Oriel in 1987; five Deputy Grecians (joining a group of 25 students from British universities) spending a month on an intensive language course; pupils from the Upper Fourth (Year 10) and Great Erasmus (Year 11) forms enjoying an Easter trip to Leningrad and Moscow the following year; and the Deps (Year 12) form going again to Moscow in summer, 1990, these visits continuing almost annually well into the 1990s. Also becoming regular features of these years were exchange study trips to Pleneuf in France for the Deps and to sundry places in Germany, including Berlin and Ansbach, these visits involving various of those forms.

1.217 On the sports field, the girls' first XI hockey team were unbeaten in their 1987/88 school matches, an achievement repeated in 1994/95 where they conceded but one goal; in the following year, the XI toured The Hague. About this later time, a mixed hockey club was established (or re-established), seemingly playing, initially at least, indoors. In cricket, the boys' XI of 1991 achieved the best results for many years, winning eight and drawing three of its 11 inter-school fixtures. Later, in 1997, the XI embarked on an 18-day tour of South Africa. However, the sporting highlight of the 1990s was almost certainly the rugby tour of Australia, organised by Sean Davey, Head of Rugby. The greatly memorable trip – from Perth in the west to Sydney in the east – was exceptionally well hosted, with many Old Blues contributing en route; some pupils apparently even remembered the rugby. Towards the end of the decade, rugby strategy needed to be re-thought, as

School teams were able to practise on only two, rather than three, days each week, although this change did not prevent Elijah Sobanjo (1992-99) and Andrew Higgins (1992-99) from gaining English rugby caps at U16 and U18 levels, respectively. In squash, in October 1999, the boys' team embarked on its first European tour, to Spain, some matches being played against local clubs.

1.218 In 1988, the Band united again (after a ten-year gap) with the Honourable Artillery Company to play in Big School, whilst on the road, as it were, it performed at Twickenham for the first time in 1991 at the England v France rugby international. Then in May 1997, in a memorable and possibly unique event, the Band Beat Retreat at the Tower of London, by invitation of Lieutenant-General Sir Michael Gray[z], Lieutenant of the Tower. Those fortunate to attend witnessed a spectacular performance, the author's framed print of the occasion providing but small recompense for what he had missed. Later, at the end of 1999, the Band produced a CD, "Christ's Hospital, A Century of Progress", a wonderful mix of Band and ensemble playing and vocals, which finishes with the deeply emotional music at the end of the Leaving Service and then the traditional finale, "Sussex by the Sea".

1.219 The 1988 School concert seemed to break new ground in that it was in two parts. Nothing unusual in that, but the first half was held in Big School, the second in Chapel. In early 1992, benefitting from some fund-raising, the Music School acquired a Steinway piano, its presence providing a strong stimulus to excellence. In 1994, in a particularly meritorious achievement, Tim Benjamin (1987-92) became the Lloyds Bank Young Composer of the Year, with a composition "Antagony" for two wind groups, amplified strings and percussion. In 1997, the School began a series of annual concert performances at the Purcell Room on London's South Bank, appearing there for about six years, before moving to St John's, Smith Square.

1.220 In the summer of 1990, the School held its first Open Day for 15 years, opening its doors to the local community for a very successful event, raising in the process a goodly sum for the Sports Centre Appeal (see below). The year 1991 marked the centenary of the CH Club, but unfortunately May's cold and chilly weather adversely affected the celebrations at Horsham on Old Blues' Day, although the fireworks display still took place. Also in that term, a special reunion of the CH Old Girls' Association was held at Horsham to mark the departure from the School of the last of the girls who had come from Hertford. With the School summer term becoming increasingly busy, and the not insubstantial work that goes into preparing and rehearsing for major events, it was decided that, in 1995, a combined Old Blues' Day and Parents' Day would be held. The School seemed to find the event a success, while the CH Club survey suggested a rough 2:1 OB vote in favour, with various other comments made and probably digested. The views of the parents are not known. The arrangement appeared to continue for some years afterwards. Regrettably, the date of Old Blues' Day appears to have become a very movable feast, shifting between the summer and Michaelmas terms, the date also being influenced by the existence of "x years on" and House reunions; indeed, there was no such event in 2016.

1.221 It was mentioned earlier how the development proposals of the early 1970s had included the desirability of building a Sports Centre (then going under the longer name of Sports and Social Centre, and shortened here for convenience), a project which had to be shelved on cost grounds. Now,

89. The Sports Centre.

around 1987, a working party was set up to make proposals for the building of a Centre at CH, the cost probably being in the region of £3.5 million (*£9m*). Following much effort, the key issue of funding was largely resolved (see below), and in early 1989 planning permission was obtained from Horsham District Council. Work then started in May, with the new building – comprising a 25-metre indoor swimming pool, a large sports hall, a gymnasium, six squash courts, meeting and conference rooms and a coffee bar – being completed in August 1990. The following month, the Centre – see Illustration 89 – was officially opened by the President, HRH The Duke of Gloucester. While the main use of the Centre was for CH pupils, from the early days the facilities have also been used by outside clubs and individuals. The opening of the Centre meant a nostalgic farewell to the old Swimming Baths, with particular memories of the tightly scheduled House baths providing much welcome relief on a hot summer afternoon, while the converted Prep Block gymnasium was converted again – to three classrooms.

1.222 With the Sports Centre project largely in mind, a new organisation, the Christ's Hospital Partnership (CHP), had been set up, under Ian Rodgers (1952-59), the two-fold aim being (i) to raise funds for this work and for two other major projects over the next five years, and (ii) to put in place a permanent fund-raising organisation at CH. For the Sports Centre, CHP had a target of £1.75 million (£4.0m, *£4.5m*), with the other half coming from the Foundation, and a further £1 million for each of two other projects – upgrading the boarding Houses and staff accommodation, and to improve educational facilities and buildings, again, for both, with matching funding to be provided by the Foundation. To launch CHP, the City of London had most generously given £250,000, essentially for the Sports Centre. As ever, the School engaged enthusiastically in the fund-raising process, one particularly entertaining event being a Great Handicap Steeplechase Sweepstake in which about 15 members of staff, including the Head, and 15 pupils competed in a three-mile handicap race around the School. However, more exertion was spent by a pupil, Frank Villeneuve-Smith (1983-90), who completed a London – Land's End – John O'Groats – London hitch hike in less than 70 hours, raising £350 in the process.

1.223 In 1990, under the guidance of history master Muir-John Potter, the School gave enhanced focus to the further development of its community service ethos. Amongst the initial work, fundraising had been directed at the redecoration and renovation of a sports hall at a High School in Sighisoara in Romania, and in the summer of 1992 a CH party visited the school to assist with the completion of the work and to attend the opening. As well as the obvious sporting and other benefits the hall would provide, it was readily evident that the very presence of external (Housey) pupils and the links which were forged were equally important to the Romanian children. Whilst there, Potter, who also visited a mental institution about 20 kms from the school, felt moved to try to establish a partnership between the school and Housey to see what assistance could be provided to them. So it was that in October 1993, there was a second visit to Sighisoara. *The Blue* carried a detailed account of the mission, suffice it to say here that Potter opined that "...an educational experience of the richest kind had been felt by all concerned". There were then further expeditions, it seemed almost annually, the pupils extending both the geographical and service boundaries of their work. For his achievements in Romania and also closer to home in West Sussex, Potter was awarded the MBE in 1997. When he left CH in 2006, it was estimated that around 600 CH pupils had travelled to Romania influencing the lives of many times this number of children there. Indeed, the community action programmes had, around 2004, become an optional activity within the country's national curriculum, and within a couple of years nearly 60,000 Romanian children had become involved in local projects there.

1.224 In 1991, Council introduced a new basis of financial eligibility for admission. Briefly and broadly, hitherto the upper limit of family income for conventional entry was £23,500, whilst at the lower end those with an income below £6,500 were not required to pay fees. Now, using a new concept of National Average Family Income (NAFI), which was produced by the author's erstwhile employer, the Central Statistical Office, and was set at £18,000, Council raised the upper income limit to £36,000 (twice NAFI), the change leading to a more realistic assessment of a family's ability to pay fees as well as providing a wider field of applicants for admission, with the 'no fees' level being raised to £9,000 (half NAFI).

1.225 One of the less cerebral, but still challenging, groups set up in early 1992 was the Juggling Club (Illustration 90), where not only balls were thrown into the air, but also knives and fire-sticks, these last two probably falling foul of present-day health and safety rules. Reflecting growing interest generally in conservation, a new Ecology Group was formed in 1993, its name later being changed to "The Green Blues" and comprising four sub-groups: Re-cycling, Conservation, Gardening and Campaigns. One early feature of the work was

90. The Juggling Club.

the planting of trees in a new area, to be known as "Bede's Copse", after an Old Blue, Father Bede Griffiths[z]. A second major conservation initiative involved a thorough assessment and work-plan for nearby Shelley's Wood.

1.226 One feature of the Upper Fourth and Great Erasmus forms was that it was compulsory for pupils to take part in an activity on a Friday afternoon, such involvement often extending into their other personal time. The wide choice of activities available embraced: the Combined Cadet Force (with Army, Navy and RAF sections); Scouts, leading to Venture Scouts; the Duke of Edinburgh Award Scheme; and the Community Service Group. This important and integral aspect of a child's education – part of the so-called co-curricular programme – provides not only much inherent enjoyment, but also opportunity for many facets of personal development, and indeed many pupils continue their involvement into their later years.

1.227 In March 1994, the Head Master presented new badges to the 47 Wests' Gifts children at the School, and in the following year a commemorative plaque to the Wests was unveiled in the appropriately named west Cloisters at Horsham. The event had been the idea of the Founder of the "John and Frances West Family Group", which had been set up in 1985 so that members could share their genealogy. About 180 such members attended the 1995 ceremony, the Group returning to CH in 2003 and again in 2015. Some details of the Wests' immense generosity, which dates back to around 1720, are given in para A1.6.

1.228 In October 1994, the School Museum, sited on the top floor of the Infirmary, and under its curator, Nicholas Plumley, was officially opened by Lord Montagu. Professor Jack Morpurgo[z], as Chairman of the Treasures Committee, in a brief introductory address, extolled its heritage and educational use within the School and also stressed its value beyond CH. The Museum continued to evolve for a few years, mounting various exhibitions, including one on the role played by the School in WW1, and in 1999 embracing the "Oral History Project" in which Old Blues and former members of staff, at both Horsham and Hertford, were invited to record onto tape their recollections of life at the School. Sadly, in the very early part of this century, the post of curator in the Museum was lost, although certain work was undertaken, including setting up two exhibitions. Then in 2003, the Museum was, essentially, 'mothballed' for around three years until Mike Barford (CH master, 1971-74) established a small team of volunteers to get the facility open again for one day a week, much of the initial work involving the massive task of developing and computerising the cataloguing of the vast number of items in its possession. Later, Barford was appointed the Hon Curator and the team was joined by Elizabeth Bridges as Assistant Curator, bringing much knowledge and experience, and enabling the place to be open for a second day each week. In 2016, Laura Kidner was appointed to the post of Senior Museum Officer, further enhancing the Museum's professional expertise and extending its outreach capabilities.

1.229 Over the last ten years, under Barford's energetic leadership and organisation, and supported by the Heritage Committee (the erstwhile Treasures Committee) and its two Chairmen, Peter Bloomfield (1944-51) and Bill Richards (1961-70), much has been achieved. Alongside the basic work of running the Museum, including dealing with continuing problems of storage space and getting some of the material digitised, the team has produced eight booklets covering an extensive range of the School's heritage and life, and three major books; mounted various exhibitions within the Museum, alongside the wide-ranging permanent display, and contributed to external displays, such as by the Horsham town museum and by Bank of America Merrill Lynch (for both, see para 1.263); researched and answered over 1,000 family history queries from the public (this work undertaken by Clifford Jones who also found time to produce his book *Sea and the Sky* (see para 1.176)) and dealt with a regular flow of questions from within CH. Other names of volunteers deserve mention: Trevor Hoskins (1940-50) who, in the earlier days, catalogued the many items of medical material; Brian Head (1947-55, sadly died in 2017) who sought out, across the globe, copies of the School's Easter anthems (some relating to the 17th century) and succeeded in getting some of them sung; Diana Gould (1942-51, daughter of Clerk AW Robinson[z]), the Hertford expert who continued the substantial task of transcribing the hundreds of letters written by the eminent OB explorer, John Septimus Roe*, this work – begun by Kerren Simmonds[z] – was later completed by Head. Lastly, Peter Wildey (1953-59) and the author, who were largely jacks of all trades, with the cataloguing work featuring prominently. Wildey employed his knowledge of silver and later provided a range of framed pictures of the School, whilst the author found time to write his two books *CHIVE* and *Names*, and this present one. The Museum has just recently set up a comprehensive website, a major development of the existing facility, which will provide an improved link with the School, Old Blue community and the outside world. There remains the earnest hope for a more central location for the Museum with improved access and for some extension of its opening hours.

1.230 Away from Horsham, in 1995 Richard Nichols[z] was appointed Aldermanic Sheriff, and then, two years later, in November, he became the 670th Lord Mayor of London, and the fourth Old Blue to hold the post, following in the footsteps of Thomas Johnson* (elected Mayor 1840), John Pound* (1904) and Walter Vaughan Morgan* (1905). The author has, for nearly 20 years, dined out on the story that, not only was he in the same House as Nichols, but for a while he was his swab (fag). During Nichols's term in office, the Venerable Frank Weston[z] served as his chaplain. The School and OB community featured prominently in various parts of Nichols's year. At the very start, in the Lord Mayor's Show, not only was the Band at the head of the procession, but the first float was a modification of the Orrery, showing not the motion of the planets around the sun, but the various spheres of excellence evident at the School. Then, towards the end of his term, Founder's Day Dinner was held at his City home, the Mansion House. Sadly, during the writing of this book, Sir Richard (as he later became) passed away in March 2016.

1.231 There were two important changes in personnel in 1996. First, Susan Mitchell (née Hamilton, 1947-56) became the first woman to be appointed to the post of Treasurer, succeeding James Forbes[z]. Secondly, Dr Peter Southern, Head of Bancroft's School, was appointed Head Master, replacing Richard Poulton who had seen the merger well and truly established. Two years later in September 1998, the Clerk, Captain Michael Pearey[z], passed away, his distinguished life remembered in a memorial service at the School, with moving tributes for his work in his comparatively short time in office and for the courage shown at the end of his life. He was succeeded by Michael Simpkin. Three other personnel items are worthy of mention. First, the first female Senior Grecian – Harriet Richmond (1986-93) – was appointed for the School year 1992/93. Secondly, the year 1993 was Bill

Kirby[z]'s 90th birthday, the event being celebrated by some 80 colleagues in the Court Room, with the Band earlier having played "Happy Birthday" to him in the Quad. Kirby made the new millennium, dying in February 2000, just before his 97th birthday. Thirdly, 1998 saw the retirement of Keith Fielder, an everyman who did everything (but particularly electricals) after 50 years' service at CH.

1.232 November 1997 marked the centenary of the laying of the foundation stone at Horsham, and the anniversary was widely celebrated in the Michaelmas term. The St Matthew's Day visit to London included the whole School, with the service held at St Paul's in the presence of the President. Founder's Day was celebrated on the due date (23rd October) by both pupils and Old Blues, with a Chapel service, a commemorative service in the Quad, a fly-past, a special service for Old Blues, with the Founder's Day Dinner, to which all Grecians were invited, held in Dining Hall. The day was concluded with a spectacular fireworks display. Then in November, as just mentioned, the Lord Mayor's Show had heralded the beginning of Richard Nichols[z]'s year as Mayor.

1.233 Towards the end of the decade, it emerged that the West Sussex Structure Plan might be giving consideration to the use of CH land for housing, such possibility having been on planning agendas since around the mid-1980s, and a special meeting of the Court of Governors was convened in April 1998 attended by the Horsham District Planning Officer. The view of the Council of Almoners was that, if sites at CH were deemed suitable for housing, it would wish to engage in constructive discussion, although no development was envisaged before 2004. The Treasurer later set up a working party to consider the suitability and development of the CH site and buildings. In 2000, the Horsham District Council draft housing strategy included certain CH land amongst possible sites for such development. The Council of Almoners, whilst backing the principle of the proposal, reiterated that much clarification was required before it would consider selling CH land. Whilst this planning was in abeyance, new housing did spring up on the site of Home Farm and the old Gymnasium and Swimming Pool, the development being called Bluecoat Pond. Today, in respect of the main planning issues, uncertainty and rumour seem to abound in equal measure.

1.234 The year 1998 saw the publication, under the auspices of the CH Club, of *Who's Blue*, a directory of former pupils of CH. It contained the names of nearly 5,000 Old Blues, with House and years at CH and some brief biographical details, the publication updating the earlier periodic listing of Club members which included only House and years at the School. In the following year, the School set up its own website, and was increasingly embracing many other IT and related developments. And before the new millennium, colour pages appeared in the body of *The Blue*.

1.235 At the end of the 1990s, there emerged a seeming plethora of student committees charged with influencing, in some shape or form, the running of the School, the official line being to embrace such roles as providing a more agreeable educational environment, though possibly at the expense of some functional speed and efficiency. There was then established a Monitorial Body, comprising about 20 to 25 Grecians, who would be charged with helping to represent pupils' views and undertake certain duties across the School, and who would have access to the School's Senior Management Team. One issue which may have occupied the new Body was the desirability or otherwise of the new arrangement whereby

juniors meander into lunch, before emerging to join up with their senior colleagues, thus allowing the perpetuation of the splendid, long-term tradition of "dinner parade" with the whole School marching formally into lunch, played in by the Band.

1.236 Amongst miscellaneous items of interest, first at the end of the 1980s, a firm of contract caterers took over the running of the Kitchen, the change attracting generally favourable comments on the quality of the food, although the quantity seemed not yet enough for some growing children. Process was also changed with a new cafeteria system introduced, this being further developed in 1996. Secondly, in Chapel, further changes in 1994 saw junior Chapel (for the two lowest forms) being held on Wednesdays and senior (for the rest of the School) on Tuesdays. In 1996, Sunday Chapel was changed to a full School Chapel morning or evening service.

Into the 21st century

1.237 It is appropriate to commence the final section of this part of the book with the key proposals for taking CH into the 21st century, these appearing within a so-called "Master Plan", which, with certain other likely expenditure, was expected to absorb about £60 million (£90m, *£90m*) over the medium term. The plan – prepared by architects RHWL who included Senior Partner Nick Thompson (1945-52) – comprised five projects; (i) two new Grecians' Boarding Houses at the ends of the Quarter Mile; (ii) additional classrooms to the south of the existing classroom blocks creating a new quadrangle at the back of Big School; (iii) a new 'arts' quadrangle at the back of the Science School. with appropriate developments to nearby existing buildings; (iv) a new Design and Technology building which would form part of the new arts complex; and (v) improved or new facilities for the Common Room, Reception and the Museum. A further key development was internal improvements to the existing 16 Boarding Houses. A "100 Years On Appeal" for £5 million was launched early in 2000 and reached its target in mid-2003, with an important contribution coming from efforts by the School. However, the bulk of the funding would need to be found from the School's coffers, including the reserves.

1.238 Of the Plan, first the Grecians' Houses, which contain 72 study/bedrooms in each block to accommodate the senior pupils, were completed in 2001; the previous year, the boys had reverted to an all-age (11-18) structure in the Houses, as was used for the girls, instead of the junior/senior split. Secondly, the refurbishment of the House Blocks (which involved pupils being temporarily decamped to the Prep Block while work was carried out) was finished in 2008, although financial constraints had led to some reining back in the nature of the modifications originally planned. Amongst other early work, some additional staff accommodation was built and a new, third level was installed in the Art School. However, the financial position continued to be tight, being exacerbated by a number of unforeseen problems, including with the Dining Hall windows and roof, and with the gas supply, these all causing thc other four projects in the Plan to be put on hold. More recent developments are mentioned below.

1.239 In 2002 and 2003, the School engaged in a range of events to celebrate various anniversaries associated with its opening (1552) and the granting of the charter (1553) and the move from London (1902). In March 2002, there was a Foundation Service at St Paul's which involved the School, Bridewell Hospital (now King Edward's School, Witley) and

91. The 450th Anniversary Stone, laid by HM The Queen, October 2003.

St Thomas's Hospital, these being Edward VI's three Royal Hospitals. Then in May 2002, Centenary Day marked the 100th anniversary of the move from London, there being a series of events including a Service of Re-dedication, a re-enactment of the laying of the Foundation Stone, and various music and drama productions and displays highlighting the earlier years. Later in the year, the CH Drama Department performed the "Old Wife's Tale" by George Peele (eponym of Peele Block and a private pupil at CH in the early years of the School), the performance in the splendid setting of Middle Temple being particularly memorable. Then, in March 2003, to celebrate the signing of the Royal Charter, over 300 performers were involved in a special concert at the Barbican, under the baton of Sir Colin Davis[z]. There were also two exhibitions at the CH Museum, one covering the history of the School, the other Samuel Pepys (it was the tercentenary of his death) and the Royal Mathematical School which had been founded in 1673. Later, in October, the Founder's Day Dinner was held in the Dining Hall at CH, one particular feature of the occasion being Group Captain John Veal[z] handing a 'Greetings' scroll to two pupils which was to be placed, together with a record of the anniversary events, in a time capsule which would be opened at the School's 500th anniversary in 2052.

1.240 One other such event – the most prestigious of them all – took place in October 2003 when Her Majesty The Queen, the Royal Patron, visited the School to celebrate the 450th anniversary of the receipt of the Royal Charter. Her Majesty was accompanied by HRH The Duke of Edinburgh, and HRH The Duke of Gloucester, the Royal President, and the Duchess of Gloucester. In a full programme, the Royal party saw the traditional march-past; toured the School meeting pupils and staff; and attended a Service of Commemoration in the Garden Quad, unveiling a commemorative stone on the wall of the Library there (Illustration 91). Following luncheon in Dining Hall, there were further presentations, before, at the end of a most memorable occasion, Her Majesty and the Duke of Edinburgh left by the Royal car for Horsham. One other event of the day had been the formal opening of the recently refurbished Leigh Hunt House Block by HRH the President.

1.241 HRH The Duke of Gloucester continued to make periodic visits to the School. He had visited in December 1999, and as just mentioned had accompanied Her Majesty The Queen in October 2003. Then, in March 2005, he paid a further visit to mark his 30th anniversary as President, an event which was also celebrated by his attendance at the Founder's Day Dinner in October. He made a further visit in July 2007, and also in 2012, as part of the School's 460th anniversary celebrations. In 2015, he was present at a major fund-raising event at Middle Temple, and a few months later he opened the new Language and Resources Centre at Horsham.

1.242 Moving away from main events for the moment, amongst the School's various cultural activities, perhaps the most memorable occurred in 2004 when CH agreed to provide a small group of 10 classical musicians, all aged about 13, to learn the art of rock music from Gene Simmonds, legendary front man of the American rock band "Kiss". The idea was that, under Simmonds' tuition over a period of about four weeks, the pupils would endeavour to learn how to play and perform rock music to a level which would enable them to support "Motorhead" (a very well-known rock band so the author is informed), in front of an audience of thousands of rock fans at the Hammersmith Apollo. A daunting assignment, if nothing else. However, Simmonds patiently taught rock, pupils diligently learnt a new style of music and how to perform it and to play new instruments, and they chose their own front man for the vocals on the day. The cameras rolled at Horsham and elsewhere (including Los Angeles), the whole event being shown in a series of programmes on Channel 4 the following year. The pupils were far from overawed by the occasion and performed wonderfully well, a huge credit to themselves and to the School.

1.243 Elsewhere in music, the Band continued to perform far and wide, its near regular fare of Lord's, Twickenham Stadium and the Lord Mayor's Show being augmented by appearances at the US Ambassador's London residence (2000); California's Roses Parade in Pasadena (2002); at the Sussex cricket ground at Hove in 2003 to celebrate the county's first championship title; in the Mall, as part of HM The Queen's 80th birthday celebrations in 2006; and a short while later, with the choir, charming the residents of Paris and the visitors to Disneyland. Then, in 2008, the Band played at Southampton, prior to the departure of the QE2 to Dubai where she would become a floating hotel. It was also to appear at a number of First World War commemorative events, as mentioned below. And in 2016, having played at Lord's on Saturday 11th June, the Band returned to London on the Sunday to play in the Mall at the Queen's 90th Birthday Lunch, the occasion attended by 10,000 guests. The Band – the only school band taking part – celebrated the 1990s, one of the seven decades of the Queen's reign being represented during the parade.

1.244 Other noteworthy events in music included the choir singing for Prince Charles when he visited a detention centre for illegal immigrants at Gatwick (2000); musicians performing at the Queen's Golden Jubilee celebrations (2002); and the installation of the organ, which had been in the Dining Hall at Hertford, in its new location in the Dining Hall at Horsham (2002). There were two notable individual achievements in 2010/11, with Bart Callaghan (2005-12) playing in the National Youth Orchestra, and Myrddin Rees Davies (2008-15) in the National Youth Band. In 2014, in its first year of entering, Schola Cantorum came third in the finals of the Barnardo's School Choir of the Year competition, and made the finals again the following year, in which they also visited Prague to perform in the magnificent St Vitus Cathedral. In drama, it is not easy to pick out the key productions over these years, but "West Side Story" (2003), "The Magic Flute" (2006), "The Crucible" (2010), "Fiddler on the Roof" (2012) and "Les Miserables" (2016) should all probably feature.

1.245 In respect of the School's wider programme of activities, mention was made earlier of the Community Action Programme, particularly in Romania. Also worthy of note – and with a particular international context – is the Model United Nations (MUN) programme which aims to build an understanding of current international challenges and to develop the skills required by young people in a globalised world. The events – held at different schools, including CH – involve pupils engaging as 'diplomats' in discussion on and resolution of a fictional problem, as in the UN Security Council or General Assembly. Notwithstanding the immense learning and educational benefits to the pupils, in the few years MUN has been established CH has achieved great success, winning many individual and team awards for their participation.

1.246 In sport, new ground was broken in 2000 with a combined tour to Barbados – boys (cricket) and girls (netball) – this format being repeated in 2004 with a rugby and hockey tour of South Africa, and a return to Australia in 2009 also for a rugby and hockey tour. The girls' hockey XI achieved an unbeaten season in 2005/06. In rugby, a pupil named Joe Launchbury (2002-09) represented England in a number of Association of European rugby internationals. Joe made his full England XV debut in 2012, and since then (to end-March 2017) had gained 42 caps; he is also captain of Wasps Rugby Club. In 2003, the girls' rugby team, in their first appearance in the event, were runners-up in the national Public Schools' Sevens competition, a feat repeated in 2016. There were major advances in athletics with the School coming third in the national track and field competition in 2007, and then runners-up in 2012, whilst at the individual level in 2011/12 Nick Ofonagaro (2005-12) competed for England, winning gold. In cricket, in 2002, Andries Kruger (2000-02) broke the School record for runs in a season, scoring 835 at an average of 60, whilst in 2007, a record seven pupils scored eight centuries for the XI. In 2008 the team toured Barbados, whilst in the following year, Matthew Bassett (2002-09) became the leading run-scorer in the history of CH cricket, with a total of 1,674, although this figure was then well and truly eclipsed in 2014 by Luke Hansford (2007-14), whose aggregate of 2,175 had included four centuries in five innings in the 2013 season. In football, the 2008 XI had its best season for some 25 years, winning eight, drawing four and suffering a single defeat. One sport where the School had performed exceptionally well was fives, with boys and girls winning a number of National school titles across the years, the two most successful exponents of the game being Luke Thomson (2004-11) and Louise Mathias (2008-15), the latter winning her fourth national title (at U18 level) in 2015, following success at U13, U14 and U16 levels. Amongst other more esoteric sports, in 2013 Katerina Poulios (2012-) was selected for the Hellenic National Ice Skating Team, and the following year Elliot Bayley (2013-) represented England in the Taekwondo World Cup, returning with a gold and two bronze medals. Elsewhere, other increasingly popular sports – which also would not have been played in London – included basketball and American Football.

1.247 Amongst overseas visits, musicians went to Calcutta in 2004, there was an art trip to New York in 2006 and the following year, in what must have been a particularly moving occasion, a party of 33 Grecians visited Berlin and Poland to bring to life the history of the rise of Nazism and the impact of the Holocaust. A small group of 16 pupils enjoyed a ski trip to Colorado in 2008. In 2010, 13 pupils and four members of staff undertook an expedition to the Himalayas, including climbing to the Annapurna Base camp, raising £4,500 in the process for two Nepali-based charities; a later visit, which also raised funds for charity, was made in 2013. Then further afield, in 2014 a group of pupils attended a Chinese Language Council summer camp held in that country, a second visit being made the following year.

1.248 In the media, the School featured quite prominently in two programmes in the BBC TV's "Who Do You Think You Are" series, with appearances in 2009 by Fiona Bruce (TV newsreader and presenter), whose great uncle had been admitted to CH in 1925, and in 2013 by Gary Lineker (footballer and presenter), who had an ancestor at the School in 1798-1804, Lineker engaging especially well with the pupils. However, there was one potential major media development which did not seem to see the light of day, the Disney filming in the Quad, which contained a number of replica field guns and similar armaments, for what was to be "John Carter from Mars", apparently finding its way on to the cutting room floor, along with the words "from Mars" when the film was finally released in 2012. More successfully in 2012, BBC Radio 2 recorded the choirs and whole School in Chapel for two "Sunday Half Hour" programmes, and in 2014, BS Fuji TV Japan filmed a prime-time documentary there, part of a series on the lives and aspirations of children across the globe.

1.249 Returning to major events, in 2008 the School became involved in the commemoration of the 90th anniversary of the ending of the First World War, the Band having the honour to play at the Menin Gate in October, the pupils also touring the War graves at Ypres and identifying the resting places of Old Blues buried there. In November, there was a Remembrance Service in the Chapel for all Old Blues who had lost their lives in the Great War, followed two days later, on Armistice Day, by a particularly moving service, with wreaths being laid in front of the War Memorial, the impeccable behaviour of the CH pupils, including the placing of the poppies on the grass in the Quad, leaving a lasting memory for the author.

1.250 Later, the commemoration of the centenary of the War became a major event for the School and Old Blue community. In 2014, the 120-strong School Band gave a short performance at the Menin Gate, and Old Blues laid a wreath in memory of those former pupils who lost their lives. There was also an exhibition in the Museum portraying the impact of the War on the School, while historian David Miller (1948-55) prepared a commemorative booklet "In their own words", being recollections of the War by Old Blues, some who survived, some who died, as well as an updated Roll of Honour now listing the names of 382 fallen, together with certain CH and service details. A free copy of the booklet is being made available to pupils across the years 2014-2018 through the generosity of the Amicable Foundation (the charitable arm of the Amicable Society – see paras A2.14-15). In 2015, a group of four OBs undertook a commemorative tour to the Flanders and Somme regions, visiting 11 cemeteries and memorials at which over 100 Old Blues are buried or memorialised, and at each the Revd in the group led a short act of remembrance, and a British Legion poppy wreath bearing the CH crest was laid. In 2016, a second tour took place, by three OBs, this time concentrating on the area around the Somme in northern France, the group visiting 31 cemeteries and memorials and laying wreaths as in the previous year. Further annual visits are planned.

1.251 Not long into the centenary commemorations,

92 Lance Corporal (now
Corporal) Joshua Leakey, VC.
with permission of Corporal Leakey

the School and Old Blue community were immensely proud to hear that Lance Corporal (now Corporal) Joshua Leakey (1999-2006) – Illustration 92 – had been awarded the Victoria Cross for his involvement in a joint UK-US raid in Helmand Province, Afghanistan, in August 2013.

1.252 Amongst a number of in-house developments around this time, four deserve mention. First, in 2009, the leaving Grecians introduced the idea of the "Grecians' Gift", whereby they would raise funds annually to establish a permanent feature of their time at CH. The initial choice was a sundial and plants in the Garden Quad, but the most eye-catching project has been the huge (15 metres by nearly 2 metres) mural depicting a 360 degree image of the main Quad which adorns the upside platform at Christ's Hospital station (and which has remained graffiti-free during the three years it has been there). Secondly, in 2011, Christ's Hospital introduced its first ever "Lifetime Achievement Award", the first recipient – in recognition of his work in electronic engineering and his major benefactions to the School – being Jack Doyle (1940-48). Later, the scope was extended, becoming the "Special Recognition Awards" scheme, embracing achievements in various fields, such as a chosen career; community engagement and leadership; enterprise and innovation; excellence in sports and the arts; commitment to CH; and a young achiever's award. Thirdly, around 2012, a "Peer Mentor" scheme was introduced as part of the School's pastoral support programme. Potential mentors are trained in aspects such as listening skills and problem-solving, as well as undertaking basic child protection training. Fourthly, around 2012 and to the great delight of the author and many others, CH re-introduced the singing of the School song, "The Votum", essentially at Speech Day. It had for long been sung at certain OB events, particularly the Founder's Day Dinner, but had fallen out of use at Housey, the change now providing an added incentive to the author to learn the eight Latin verses.

1.253 Returning now to bricks and mortar, away from the Master Plan, ongoing refurbishment and related work had continued apace around the turn of the century, including a number of new staff houses, such as at the rear of Lamb; the conversion of the Prep Block to accommodate the Wardrobe, Cleaning and Facilities Management Departments; new boiler installations in the Art School and Health Centre; the upgrading of the Music School's practice rooms; restoration and other work at the back of Big School, particularly the re-gilding of the statue of the Founder; and a greatly improved Cricket Pavilion. Some of this activity would have proceeded unbeknown to most of the School. However, one bit of work which could not have been missed (unless it had occurred during the holidays) was a survey of the 40 metre Water Tower undertaken using an hydraulic platform (capable of extending to 70 metres) carried by a massive 47 ton truck, the Tower housing the two massive tanks which for many years stored the School's water supply. The inspection was generally favourable although, inevitably, some repairs were needed to the brickwork, but the main work was to involve the removal of the two water tanks (empty since 1980), this permitting views through the top of the Tower. Lastly, in 2016, the School began generating electricity from a huge solar farm on land to the south of the estate, the development providing about 20 per cent of the School's current electricity usage.

1.254 Of the larger building developments, the substantial task of refurbishing the School's Kitchen began in 2008, the work including the construction of a 'temporary' kitchen (still there today but due to be replaced over the next few years) alongside Coleridge House Block; the key 'servery' part of the operation was completed in 2011. Four developments involved important Old Blue benefactions. First, a number of improvements had been made to the Design and Technology Department, particularly the provision of state-of-the-art machinery and improved facilities and working environment, these the generous gift of Jack Doyle (1940-48), the building becoming, in 2007, the Doyle Design and Technology Department. A second major initiative came from the benevolence of Chris Buggé (1956-63), this helping to fund the four-year project to refurbish and modernise the eight laboratories of the New Science School, the resulting new equipment and lay-out greatly enhancing the quality of science education. Thirdly, perhaps the most eye-catching new development is the Language and Resources Centre (LARC) which seemed to spring up from out of the ground in barely a year in 2015 on the south side of the Quarter Mile (to the east of the Music School). The new building (Illustration 93) – which includes a digital language laboratory, specially appointed language classrooms, a fully equipped library, two dedicated computer suites and new facilities for the provision of teaching and learning support skills – was opened by HRH The Duke of Gloucester, the School's President, in October 2015. The reported near £9 million cost was met mostly by the Foundation and the School, but with support from a generous benefactor, Jamie Arnell (1980-87). Lastly, Graham Mellstrom (1941-48) has provided funds which have enabled the conversion of the earlier Library and Dominions Library into the Mellstrom Careers Centre, the new building being opened in October 2016 by Mrs Susan Pryor, Lord Lieutenant of West Sussex. The project builds strongly on the initiative whereby OBs and others had provided careers advice at a series of seminars and professional gatherings. The facilities will be used by other schools, as part of CH's outreach programme. The new development has seen, as mentioned earlier, the removal of the mezzanine floor in the erstwhile Dominions Library, which is now an 80-seat lecture theatre.

1.255 In personnel, around the start of this period, David Farrington (1956-63) succeeded Susan Mitchell as Treasurer in 2002, Farrington then being followed in 2007 by Sir Garry Johnson (1948-54). Also in 2007, John Franklin, Head of Ardingly College, succeeded Dr Peter Southern as Head Master. And to make a clean sweep, as it were, that year also saw Paul Tuckwell replacing Michael Simpkin as Clerk. Tuckwell served for but two years, being succeeded by Rear-Admiral David Cooke, whose own term in office was cut short by illness, and he sadly died in 2014. Within the last few years, in 2013 Guy Perricone was appointed Treasurer and Greg Andrews, Clerk. Three notable deaths of this era were Miss Jean Morrison (Head Mistress, Hertford) in 2000, David Newsome (Head Master) in 2004, and Miss Dorothy West (Head Mistress, Hertford) in 2006. In early 2009, staff, pupils and the wider CH community were immensely saddened at the news of the death, in a climbing accident in the Alps, of Rob

93. The Language and Resources Centre.

Gauntlett[z] and James Atkinson[z]. Rob and fellow OB James Hooper (1998-2005) had earlier, in 2006, a year after leaving CH, become the youngest Britons to climb Mount Everest, and not long afterwards undertook a man-powered Pole to Pole trek. Sadly, a few years later in 2013, Jack Hutton-Potts[z] and Vaughan Holme (CH master) were also to die whilst climbing in Anglesey. Prominent visitors to the School over this period have included Rowan Williams, Archbishop of Canterbury (2007); Sir Tom Stoppard, playwright and screenwriter (2012); Al Gore, former US vice-President (2013); Baroness Scotland, barrister, Attorney General, later Secretary-General, Commonwealth (2013), and Desmond Tutu, bishop, social rights activist (2014).

1.256 One other death, which occurred in 2007, was that of Mrs Kathleen Watts, aged 104. Mrs Watts was a House Block matron from 1948 to 1965, for most of this time in Peele, and her passing brought back to the author many memories of the loving care and attention she had provided to him and others in her charge. She was the first matron who had been married and had children, two of whom – a son Martin (1947-54) and a daughter Patricia (married name Wynn, 1938-44) – had attended CH (Illustration 94). In 2002, the author was privileged to be present at a 100th birthday celebration at the School, whilst in the following year Mrs Watts joined us in the House on the occasion of the Peele B annual reunion lunch.

1.257 Across the years, the School's academic achievements were well recorded in *The Blue*, as were the regular visits by a variety of inspectorates, including in 2004, 2009, and 2012. The last had been arranged at only five days' notice, but the School came through with flying colours, all ten main aspects being classified as excellent. However, despite this fulsome praise, the School did recognise that there was still room for improvement. In respect of exam results, each year there appeared to be a plethora of multiple A*s at GCSE, AS, A2 and A level. Amongst the many fine achievements over the past decade or so one which struck the author was that of two pupils – Pascal Porcheron (1999-2006) and Joanna Poon (1999-2006) – being marked, in 2004, in the top five for GCSE French, an exam sat by over 163,000 students. One further point to be mentioned under this head is that, reflecting increases in the numbers of international students, in 2011 the School adopted the International Baccalaureate alongside the existing A level examinations, providing the sixth-form pupils with a possibly difficult, but welcome, choice of educational routes, this approach since being extended to IGCSE. The

impressive IB results have been due testimony to the success of the change. Lastly, in 2015, the erstwhile modular A Levels were phased out and replaced by a linear system with an exam at the end of a two-year course; in addition, the Cambridge pre-U syllabus has been introduced for some subjects.

1.258 Finally, it is important to say a few words about the School's governance and financial position. In 2007, Christ's Hospital was devolved into two legal entities – the School and the Foundation – the change providing clearer accountability and also protecting the CH Endowment from any major legal claim which might arise from the School's educational activities. As a consequence of the change, the School had its own Governing Body. In 2011, the School took responsibility for the Admissions, Marketing, Development, Facilities Management, Finance and Human Resources Departments, all previously under the Foundation, although a few years later the development work reverted to the Foundation. The devolved structure was soon engaged in dealing with the financial problems which emerged from the effects of the banking crisis of 2008 and relatively rapidly increasing inflation in the academic sector. These had a particularly severe effect on the School, given the unique funding arrangements in which about two-thirds of income comes from the Endowment. The Council formulated a five-year (2011-2016) financial plan for the future of the School, including a range of cost savings and proposals to increase income for example from commercial activities and from an increase in the number of full fee-payers to just over 100 (about one-eighth of the then nominal size of the School) over the period; arrangements were also made for the admission of up to 50 day pupils, these changes occurring within an increase from around 800 to 880 in total pupil numbers, and including a marked increase in the admission of international students. This was the first time day pupils had been formally admitted to Christ's Hospital, although prior to 1869 masters had been allowed to educate a small number of 'private' pupils (see para 2.20) who did not board at the School. Alongside these developments, there has been increased fund-raising activity, one key event being held in 2015 at Middle Temple in the presence of the President, HRH The Duke of Gloucester.

1.259 To bring matters right up-to-date, following wide discussion, a new financial plan, covering the years 2017

94. Mrs Kathleen Watts, CH matron.

to 2022 has been established. The need to recruit a new Head Master from 2017 has led to the decision that CH is to revert to a single governing body, reporting to the Council of Almoners, but with the Foundation and School continuing to operate as two separate charities, this arrangement, as mentioned above, providing protection for the Endowment. The new structure is being implemented in September 2017 under the new Head Master, Simon Reid (currently Principal, Gordonstoun School). On the issue of the level of full fee-payers at the School, the increase over the past few years – to around a quarter (boarding and day pupils) – had been seen by some as being at variance with the historical charitable ethos of the School. However, the School must have money to operate and, given its funding structure, Council had regarded the increase as essential to restore the finances of Christ's Hospital to a sustainable position. Further, it should be noted that the number of assisted places – these including about 14 per cent who pay no fees and between 35 and 40 per cent paying less than 10 per cent of the full fee – has been largely maintained over the last five years. The financial position, whilst improving, remains challenging, but Council hopes to increase the proportion of assisted places for needy pupils over the next five years.

1.260 Two particular fund-raising initiatives merit mention here. First, in July 2002, the Partnership Office established an Education Fund the main purpose of which would be to provide monies for a range of School activities, principally, for sports and music equipment, library and teaching resources, and for educational trips. An innovative approach to raising funds had been introduced with letters being sent to potential OB donors explaining the purpose of the Fund and saying that they were to be contacted by telephone, unless they wished not to be called. The calls were made by a small team of pupils and ex-pupils in the week or so after the end of the summer term. The arrangement was deemed an unqualified success, a report in 2006 saying that £320,000 (£450k) had been raised since 2002. This form of fund-raising continues today. One related development was the establishment in 2005 of the 1552 Society, consisting of Old Blues who have intimated that they have remembered CH in their wills, the group being invited, usually annually, to different School events, such as a concert, play or Beating Retreat, thus keeping people involved with the development work and as a small token of thanks. Secondly, there is the more recent initiative called the "Blue Fund", which invites donors to join forces and, in partnership, fund a full seven-year boarding education at the School, the total sum per pupil sought currently amounting to £190,000. The initiative was the idea of Neville Osmond[z](sadly another to pass away while this book was being written), and was introduced a few years ago following certain pilot work by the Sue Thomson Foundation which had been established in 1988 by Susan Mitchell (1947-56), former Treasurer of CH, who has for many years been a most generous benefactor to the School.

1.261 History, tradition and links with the City of London have always represented major features of the Christ's Hospital scene, three recent events being particular examples of the bringing together of the past and the present. First, in 2014, Senior Grecian James Winsbury (2008-15) and Second Monitor Olivia Walsh (2008-15) were honoured to be invited by the Worshipful Company of Carmen to its annual Cart Hiring ceremony, the link with the School, as explained in para 1.3, stretching back to 1582. Secondly, in 2016, two senior choristers, Mattie Slade (2009-16) and Max Thomas (2009-16), together with organist Catherine Ennis (1965-73),

95. The CH Christ Church sculpture.

Director of Music at St Lawrence Jewry in the City of London, were invited to perform at the unveiling of the newly restored organ in Londonderry's Guildhall, which itself had recently undergone refurbishment. Here, the CH link goes back to the early 17th century when, in 1615, 12 pupils were sent to Derry to become apprentices to work on the rebuilding of the city's walls, an event depicted in a restored stained-glass window in the Guildhall. Thirdly, at the time of writing this book, a permanent sculpture is planned for a location close to the site of the original School to mark its foundation and continued relationship with the City. The competition for the sculpture was won by Andrew Brown, a former Artist-in-Residence at CH, his winning design reflecting themes relating to past generations of pupils and the on-going vision of providing education for children of promise regardless of means. The intention is to site the sculpture – about 2.5 metres long and 1.5 metres high and depicting children marching in their famous Tudor uniform (Illustration 95) – in the Christchurch Greyfriars Church Garden, subject to the satisfactory resolution of funding and other issues.

1.262 Finally, a number of miscellaneous items of interest caught the author's eye, these being in roughly chronological order: (i) a notable contribution to the millennium celebrations came in the form a book *Christ's Hospital in the Year 2000*, which described life at the School during the academic year 2000/01; (ii) in September 2003, Old Blues' Day celebrations included recognition of 50 years of the RAF Foundationers' Trust which had been set up by Barnes Wallis* for the benefit of children of RAF personnel (see para 1.192). The following month the annual CCF Inspection was conducted by Viscount Montgomery of Alamein, his father having performed the same function 50 years earlier (see para 1.140); (iii) a noteworthy initiative of the Wests' Foundation was the preparation of a video on the life of John and Frances West (great benefactors to the School – see para A1.6), the short film including information about the past and present work of the Foundation, (iv) in 2005, the CH Club was dissolved, being replaced by the CH Association (later the CH Old Blues' Association) – see paras A2.2-8.

1.263   Continuing the miscellaneous items: (v) one of the most notable achievements by a CH pupil occurred in 2011, when Thomas Williams (2009-11) and a fellow student from Collyers VI Form College, won a Young Start-Up Talent award, worth £50,000, with the proposal for a business project to facilitate re-cycling of text books amongst students; (vi) in 2013, the whole School attended the St Matthew's Day service at St Paul's, the visit also celebrating the 460th anniversary of the School's charter, this latter event in addition being the subject of an exhibition in the Horsham town museum; (vii) also in 2013, the Bank of America Merrill Lynch hosted a special exhibition about Christ's Hospital at their City offices on the site where the School stood from 1552 to 1902; (viii) towards the end of 2015, a time capsule, containing items and ephemera from the years 2015, 1965, 1915, 1865 and 1815, was sealed (neither its location nor when it would be opened being revealed in the report in *The Blue*), and lastly (ix) in the summer of 2016, for the first time (which the author hopes will not be the last), leaving Grecians were presented with a special gift – a glass engraving containing "The Charge" (see para 2.40) and a 3D projection of the Dining Hall.

1.264   Bits of news continued to emerge right to the end of the preparation of this book. There were three items the author thought worthy of inclusion. First, in December 2016 a new (second) all-weather hockey pitch was opened by Maddie Hinch, gold medal winning goalkeeper in the Rio Olympic games. Secondly, the familiarity of the School site might lead some to overlook the fact that many of the building are Grade II* listed (the starred status applying to only about 10 per cent of all Grade II buildings). As part of the planning process for the next ten years, the School commissioned a Condition Survey of the buildings and supporting infrastructure. Reflecting work done, particularly over the last five to ten years, the Survey report was generally good, the detail providing information to assist with establishing a ten-year maintenance plan. Thirdly, in April 2017 the Hertford Memorial Plaque – in memory of the CH girls, boys and staff who dwelt at Hertford from 1682 to 1985 – was installed in the west Cloisters.

Chapter 2
Notable Old Blues

Derivation of the lists

2.1 It was mentioned earlier that about 65,000 pupils have been educated at Christ's Hospital since its foundation, this total excluding those educated privately, about which more below (para 2.20). The author's *Names* book included a list of about 900 'notable' Old Blues – those who became eminent in later life or who contributed much to the School or OB community – together with brief biographical details, derived from the 46,000 plus pupils who had been admitted to the School prior to the move to Horsham in 1902. This same kind of information is now given here for around 415 OBs who were admitted (post-1902) to the Horsham and Hertford Schools, these names being augmented by around 60 OBs who entered CH before the Horsham era but who did not feature in the list of notables given in *Names*. In addition, these 475 names are included in the Annex at the end of this chapter in a comprehensive list of 1,225 notables identified by the author across the whole life of the School, that is also including most of those admitted pre-1902 who appeared as notables in *Names*. The lists do not include any person still alive.

2.2 Some general background points need to be made about how the information presented here has been assembled. First, on coverage, the lists of notable Old Blues given in this book include only names recorded in the Admission Registers – often termed being 'on the Foundation' – thus excluding private pupils. Secondly, on sources, information about such people and their achievements tends to be less explicit the further one goes back in time; moreover, material in respect of those OBs who had gone overseas would generally be even more elusive. Thirdly, the special position of Christ's Hospital needs to be borne in mind, in particular the background and status of the children and their parents, and the fact that, certainly prior to the move to Horsham, most pupils would generally have left the School at age 15, with relatively few families having the means to enable their children to go to university, or to train for certain professions such as the law and medicine, or the Army. As GAT Allan* in his book *Christ's Hospital* (1937) put it, "…it is not in the nature of things that from a school like Christ's Hospital we can turn out men whose names are household words. We do not produce Prime Ministers, Archbishops or Lord Chancellors…"

2.3 However, as Allan also said, the School "can point to a number of Bishops, Archdeacons, Heads of Colleges, Headmasters of great schools, Lord Mayors, and merchant princes of the City, magistrates in the Indian Civil Service, writers, doctors, lawyers, and soldiers and sailors of high rank". To which may be added a plethora of authors and composers; poets and writers; professors and public servants; industrialists and scientists; diplomats and explorers. That so much was achieved against such a restricted and seemingly infertile background represents much credit on the staff of the School for the quality of education and care, as well as being an excellent example of the ethos of the School, characteristics which would be well demonstrated using an academic measurement concept based on "value-added".

2.4 Various books on Christ's Hospital – in particular Allan (1937) and *The History of Christ's Hospital* (1821) by JI Wilson*, and the author's own two earlier works – have included information about 'famous' Old Blues, with some details of their lives. Also, a list of so-called "Worthies" – 336 names, being 212 "Distinguished Blues" and 124 "Donation Governors and Benefactors", and not including any pupil who had entered the School after 1850 – was assembled by Arthur Lockhart* and William Lempriere* in 1913, this list

later being enhanced in the early 1930s by the addition of about 60 extra (still pre-1850) names. The original material produced appeared in a small booklet, with the names being included in panels in Big School. The panels – for which an example is given in Illustration 96 (gold names on a charcoal background) – were removed in 1937 when Big School was

96. A Panel of Worthies.

cleaned and were not replaced. They now reside in a storage cupboard located in the Museum, a seemingly unworthy end to the Worthies.

2.5 The earlier information assembled on famous Old Blues would have drawn on a variety of sources, including in particular the *Oxford Dictionary of National Biography* and *Who's Who*. The former – published originally in the Victorian era – appeared in its latest form from the Oxford University Press in 2004 in 60 volumes each of around 1,000 pages, its introduction referring to around 65 million words providing biographical details of some 56,000 people: an online version is available, including some updates, as is an index of the names included therein. The latter, first published in 1849, is largely and most conveniently explored through the ten volumes of *Who Was Who*, which cover the years between 1897 and 2000, and for which in 2002 the publishers – A&C Black – published an index which gives full name (by surname), year of birth and death, and volume reference, for some 80,000 names. Subsequent information appears in the annual *Who's Who* publications. Again, information is also available online.

2.6 The list of the 475 notables given in paras 2.22-38 – strictly, those who were admitted to the Horsham and Hertford Schools after 29th May 1902, together with some from the pre-Horsham era not earlier included in *Names* – has been assembled from three main sources viz: (i) the *Dictionary of National Biography* (about 40 names, and denoted by DNB at the end of the entry); (ii) *Who Was Who* (around 200, and denoted by WWW); and (iii) the "author's choice", this category, covering about 260 names, being OBs he has considered worthy of mention, the choice being based on a variety of sources and criteria, as explained below. Each entry contains very brief biographical information (with years at CH and dates of birth and death), as available from the School and OB magazine *The Blue*, in particular, and from the DNB and WWW sources, with permission from, and due acknowledgement to, respectively, the Oxford University Press and Bloomsbury Publishing Plc.

2.7 The main source of information for the author's selection of names is the obituaries section of *The Blue* (and later *The Old Blue*), and its erstwhile Hertford equivalents. Use has also been made of the ubiquitous internet which has provided access to a wide range of interesting material. Generally speaking, those recorded in *The Blue* for whom the author was aware of an obituary in the national broadsheets have been included, as have those who appeared to achieve a degree of fame which seems to have gone largely unheralded. Also included are the names of those OBs who gave good or long service to Christ's Hospital or the Old Blue community. Some names feature in both the DNB and WWW groups, the overall total of 475 being less than the sum of the three individual categories referred to above. Where the names included in the list differ from those in the Admission Registers, for example on marriage, the original form is also given, with all examples of such changes being given in para 2.43.

2.8 In presenting the list, an attempt has been made to classify the entries into 17 broad 'industry' groups, as set out in para 2.42. This is not straightforward since, as in most classifications, it will be often found that some people can be assigned to more than one group. As two examples with the categories used below, a colonel of the RAMC could be allocated to "Army" or "Medical", and a lawyer working in public service (in the UK or overseas) could be classified to "Other business/industry" or "Public service, UK" or "Public service, overseas". For the record, in these particular cases, we have used "Army" and "Public service", respectively. Where more than one career was pursued, an attempt has been made to choose the main one. In addition to the industry groups, the classification contains two further well-defined separate categories, as explained below.

2.9 First, group '(a)' (War and other deaths) relates to Old Blue deaths and covers those who died (i) in wars, (ii) at School or as young OBs, and (iii) having become centenarians. In respect of the first sub-category, in all about 600 OBs are reported as having lost their lives in WW1 and WW2, their names being honoured on the War Memorial on the front of Dining Hall and recorded in two books by historian David Miller (1948-55). For our list, 15 names have been included, these representing the wider sacrifice of all Old Blues killed in all such conflicts. For the second sub-category, the names include a number for whom plaques are included in the Horsham or Hertford Chapels. Again, the chosen names may be deemed to represent the deaths of all pupils at Horsham and Hertford, and of all young OBs. For the third sub-category – centenarians – inclusion essentially relies on knowledge of the particular event. Secondly, group '(q)' (Christ's Hospital) contains the names of those who had a particularly strong association with the School in, for example, the classroom or Counting House, or for its governance or for the OB community and its clubs and societies.

2.10 The point should be made that there are potential and obvious qualifications about the list of notable Old Blues presented here, in particular the comprehensiveness, or otherwise, of the available biographical information and the very element of choice of who is and who is not included. On the former, one of the main issues relates to information on benefactors, much of the more recent data rightly being confidential to CH, notwithstanding the desire of some donors to be anonymous. On the issue of choice – perhaps particularly relevant to the selection of the names included in groups (a) (deaths) and (q) (CH) – the author has sought informal advice from various knowledgeable colleagues. However, the final choice has been his, and his apologies are offered to anyone who feels aggrieved at the absence (or inclusion) of a particular name. Before giving the list (paras 2.22-38), two features of the notables are mentioned.

Some notable notables

2.11 In the *Names* book, an attempt was made to identify the more eminent (pre-1902) notables. Rather than just doing the same here for the post-1902 list, the text below relates to all OB notables (as included in the list in the Annex to this chapter), with those for whom biographical details are given here marked with a 'z'

2.12 Amongst the more renowned Old Blues are likely to be: scientist and inventor, Sir Barnes Wallis (also CH Treasurer and major benefactor); literary alumni – Samuel Taylor Coleridge, Charles Lamb and James Leigh Hunt (all eponyms of Houses at the School), Edmund Blunden^z, Jack Morpurgo^z and Keith Douglas^z. Elsewhere in the arts, where Sir Henry Cole was an eminent patron of the Victorian era, music embraced Sir Colin Davis^z, Sir William Glock^z, Constant Lambert^z and Percy Young^z, while also included are painters Charles Barron^z, Maurice de Sausmarez^z and Keith Vaughan^z; artist/designer Philip Youngman-Carter^z; writer and essayist John Middleton

Murry; writer Francis Clifford[z] (at CH, ALB Thompson): screenwriter Clive Exton[z]; writers/journalists Bernard Levin[z], Robert Pitman[z] and Robert Heller[z]; photographer Tony Ray-Jones[z]; songwriter Sydney Carter[z]; and leading actor Michael Wilding[z].

2.13 In the academic world, amongst many professors were Margaret Gowing[z] (history of science), Philip Hall[z] (mathematics), Sir Richard Lodge (history), Russell Meiggs[z] (ancient history), John Stevens[z] (English), Gerald Whitrow[z] (history of mathematics) and Sir Christopher Zeeman[z] (mathematics); and academic administrator Sir Henry Reichel. The Church has housed bishops Mordecai Carey, Rowley Hill, Thomas Middleton (also eponym of a CH House), brothers Edmund Pearce and Ernest Pearce, Ross Hook[z] and Frank Weston[z]; and Bede Griffiths[z] was a celebrated monk. In public service, the UK benefitted from the work of senior civil servants Sir Richard Clarke[z], Sir Eric Speed[z], Sir John Woods[z] and Sir John Hodsoll[z]; overseas, perhaps the most prominent name was Sir Louis Cavagnari, military administrator and envoy, with the diplomatic service also including Sir Edward Thornton (eponym of a CH House), Sir Donald Hopson[z], Sir Foley Newns[z] and Sir John Whitehead[z]; in addition, Sir Jenkin Coles served as Speaker, House of Assembly, S Australia, and Sir Alexander Cunningham as Director General of Survey, India. In the UK Parliament, Sir Gabriel Goldney was an MP, and Baron (Michael) Stewart[z] an MP and Peer.

2.14 From the military, which includes hero of Waterloo Field Marshal John Colborne, Air Chief Marshal Sir Hugh Constantine[z], Air Marshal Sir Reginald Emson[z], Lieutenant-General Sir Michael Gray[z], and Brigadier General Edgar Cox, OBs are particularly proud of three VCs, 2nd Lieutenant Edward Baxter, Lieutenant-Colonel Wilfrith Elstob and Captain Henry Pitcher, while WW2 saw the particularly poignant deaths of Peter McRae[z] and Michael Rennie[z]. The list also includes four Lord Mayors of London: Thomas Johnson, Sir John Pound, Sir Walter Vaughan Morgan (also CH Treasurer and major benefactor) and Sir Richard Nichols[z]; also four noteworthy Head Masters of CH – James Boyer, George Bell (also Master of Marlborough and the founder of the CH Club), Richard Lee and Clarence Seaman[z]

2.15 Then from the professions we have Lord Moynihan, Baron (Russell) Brock[z] and Sir Eric Riches[z], surgeons; James Jurin and Louis Harold Gray[z], physicians; Sir Arthur Bowley, statistician; Ida Busbridge[z], mathematician; and Sir Langham Dale (working in S Africa), and Carol Adams[z] and Michael Marland[z] (both UK), influential educationalists. From industry, there are Sir Guy Calthrop, Controller of Mines (WW1), Sir Arthur Dorman, iron and steel manufacturer, Sir Harold Harding[z], civil engineer, George Ross-Goobey[z], Pension Fund Manager, and Sir Leslie Smith[z], Chairman, British Oxygen Company; from the Press, Sir (William) Linton Andrews, Editor of the "Yorkshire Post", Thomas Barnes, Editor of "The Times", and journalist Sir Ian Trethowan[z] who became Director General of the BBC; Sir (George) Rowland Hill, President, Rugby Football Union; and the other three eponyms of CH Houses – John Henry Sumner Maine, jurist, and Joshua Barnes, academic, the third (George Peele, poet) being a private pupil.

2.16 Perhaps less well-known but worthy of mention here are: Ezekiel Cheever and Elias Corlett, early day schoolmasters in the USA; George Shelley and Charles Snell, contemporaneous, eminent calligraphers; Henry Lilly, heraldic painter; Jeremiah Markland, learned critic; Thomas Brewer and David Mason[z], celebrated exponents (though separated by centuries) of, respectively, the viol and the trumpet; William Powell, William Terriss (at CH, Lewin), Tenniel Evans[z] and Patrick Holt[z] (at CH, Parsons), actors; Terence Fisher[z], Film Director, and Peter Handford[z], Film Sound Recordist; Albany Ward, Cinema Exhibitor; Aylmer Maude, translator of Tolstoy; Edward Butler[z], librarian and translator; Sir Francis Haden, etcher; Henry Meyer, engraver, and Alan Fletcher[z], Graphic Designer. There were then: Henry and Henry Woodthorpe (father and son) Town Clerks of London; William Haig Brown, Headmaster of Charterhouse and author of "The Votum", and Elizabeth Thompson, Head Mistress of Hertford girls' School; Arthur Cooper, the "walking parson"; Edward Mallan Collick, Archdeacon of the Goldfields, Western Australia; and into the 20th century John Dymoke[z], the Queen's Champion.

2.17 Also included are: Edmund Parkes, the father of hygiene; Christopher Ounsted[z], psychiatrist and pioneer in the field of children's brain diseases; Norman Guthkelch[z], the UK's first paediatric neurosurgeon and leading authority on "shaken baby syndrome"; Thomas Clark[z], palaeontologist; Rupert Bruce-Mitford[z], archaeologist; Keith Roberts[z], theoretical physicist and early developer of large-scale computing; Frank Bruce[z], public health engineer; William Farrer, Australian agronomist; Rex Paterson[z], agricultural innovator; Patrick Rance[z], cheesemonger; Henry Durant[z], opinion pollster and market researcher; Frank Scudamore, Victorian Post Office reformer; and Edward Merewether[z], medical inspector. There were also three celebrated Australian explorers, Septimus Roe, Ernest Giles and Harry Tietkens; John Reeves, naturalist, who gave his name to the Reeves pheasant; Robert Harrild, developer of commercial printing; brothers William Reeves and Thomas Reeves, founders of the Reeves paints company; John Marston, manufacturer of cars, motor cycles and cycles, and Peter Berthon[z], BRM car designer.

2.18 In respect of CH, there were major benefactors to the School: Richard Thornton, Thomas Brown, John Thackeray, Robert Precious, Richard Le Keux, Revd Edmund Tew and Peter Clay[z], while those who served the School well in other ways included; Clerks of the Foundation Matthias Dipnall, Richard Franks, and George Allan; and others who gave long service as administrators, such as George Ludlow and John Sharpe, or in the classroom, including Henry Bowker, Frederick Merk, Francis Sykes, Henry Sharp and Bill Kirby[z]. Amongst valuable benefactions are the fascinating log-books of the voyages of Joseph Terry and Charles Shea. For the OB community, Percy Giles and Ronnie Jones[z] were stalwarts of, respectively, the CH Club and the OBRFC, with Walter Chamberlain[z] playing an influential role for the latter and more widely.

2.19 Although we have excluded from the list those individuals who are still alive, the author cannot resist mentioning here a few names of eminent Old Blues who are gratefully still with us, including: from the arts: Charles Hazlewood (at CH 1978-85), conductor; John Gale (1938-46), theatre producer; Roger Allam (1964-72) and Jason Flemyng (1978-83), actors; and Bryan Magee (1941-48), author and philosopher. From the church, the Very Revd John Arnold (1943-52), and from academia: Baroness (Ruth) Deech (also lawyer and bioethicist, 1953-61); Professors Edward Kenney (classics, 1935-43), Lance Lanyon (veterinary science, 1954-61) and Alan Ryan (politics, 1951-59); educationalist Sir John Daniel (1952-61), and headmaster and cricketer, Dennis Silk (1942-50). From public service: Anthea Case (1956-63), Elizabeth Llewellyn-

Smith (1946-53), Pamela Mason (1936-44), Sir Geoffrey Otton (1939-45) and Sir Michael Tims (1942-47). From business: Baron (David) Simon (1950-58), Sir John Wickerson (1948-54), Sir David Norgrove (1959-67), Jeremy King (restaurateur, 1964-72) and John Edmonds (Trades Unionist, 1954-62); from the legal world, Sir Rupert Jackson (1958-66) and David Green (1964-71), and journalists Roger Highfield (1968-75) and Con Coughlin (1966-73). From the Military: General Sir Garry Johnson (former CH Treasurer, 1948-54), and recent winner of the Victoria Cross, Lance Corporal (now Corporal) Joshua Leakey (1999-2006). From the sporting arena, John Snow (1951-59) and Joe Launchbury (2002-09), international cricketer and rugby player respectively. And for the OB community, Susan Mitchell (major fund-raiser and former CH Treasurer, 1947-56).

Private pupils

2.20 In respect of private pupils, for whom there is no formal record, over the years there have been many claims that particular people were educated privately at CH. The weight of evidence and opinion seems to suggest that the following were private pupils (with years of birth and death given): Edmund Campion (1540-1581, Jesuit priest and martyr); William Camden (1551-1623, historian and herald); George Peele (c1556-c1596, poet, eponym of a CH House); David Augustine Baker (1575-1641, Benedictine mystic and writer); Edward Colston (1636-1721, merchant and politician); Warren Hastings (1732-1818, first Governor-General of India), and Augustus Welby Northmore Pugin (1812-1852, architect). In addition, during the course of his earlier research using the DNB, the author came across nine other names where reference was made to the boy being educated at Christ's Hospital, 'privately' being mentioned in most instances. These were: Sir Thomas Bertie (formerly Hoar, 1758-1825, naval officer); William Higgins Coleman (c1816-1863, botanist); Edward Dubois (1774-1850, writer); Sir Henry Morland (1837-1891, naval officer and Indian civil servant); Ralph Payne, Baron Lavington (1739-1807, politician, Governor of the Leeward Islands); John Pond (1767-1836, astronomer); Charles Pritchard (1808-1893, headmaster and astronomer); John Sterling (1806-1844, writer and poet), and George William Frederick Villiers, fourth Earl of Clarendon (1800-1870, politician). The jury is out in respect of those nine boys. Of others, Allan (1937) says that Admiral Sir Cloudesley Shovel (1650-1707, naval commander, politician) may have been a private pupil; he appears to have been a Governor. However, it seems that the strength of view is that the following – often stated to have been privately educated at CH – probably did not attend the School at all: Samuel Richardson (1689-1761, writer); Sir John Frederick (1601-1685, merchant, politician, Lord Mayor of London, President of CH); and Rear-Admiral Sir Thomas Troubridge (c1758-1807, naval commander, politician).

List of Notable Old Blues, mainly post-1902

2.21 'Later' names have been used in the list below (and the one in the Annex), the main changes compared with those obtaining at CH being given in para 2.43, with the name at CH followed by the later designation; also shown (para 2.42) are the industry categories used in the listings. Biographical information relating to Christ's Hospital is given in italics; further, OBs commemorated in plaques in the Horsham Chapel, ante-Chapel or Cloisters are denoted thus (#).

97. Lieutenant Edward Vaughan Bell.

2.22 War and other deaths

War

BELL, *Edward Vaughan. 1909-1917.* b 1899. Lieutenant, RAF; earlier in Royal Naval Air Service. Shot down and killed, May 1918.

BROWNSCOMBE, *Brian. 1926-1933.* b 1915. Captain, RAMC. Commanded the Regimental Aid Post at Arnhem. Having surrendered, he was murdered by the Waffen SS in September 1944. Earlier, awarded the George Medal.

98. Captain Brian Brownscombe.

with permission of Bob Gerritsen, author of 'For No Apparent Reason: the Shooting of Captain Brian Brownscombe GM, RAMC', Sigmond Publishing, 2000

BUCHANAN, *James Richebourg. 1924-1932.* b 1915. Pilot Officer (Pilot), RAFVR. Operated with 609 Squadron from Kinloss and Northolt in early part of War, and then Nether Wallop. He was killed during the Battle of Britain in July 1940, being shot down near Weymouth.

COATES, *Daisy Catherine Elizabeth, [at CH, Katherine not Catherine]. 1908-1915.* b 1897. In 1940, was serving at the Mission House of St Peter's Church, Wapping, where the incumbent was also an Old Blue. In October of that year, at the height of the Blitz, the House suffered a direct hit and Sister Coates was killed instantly. She is commemorated in a stained-glass window in the chapel of the Church.

COBBOLD, *Peter Charles Vincent. 1907-1913.* b 1897. Served in Royal Flying Corps (later RAF) in WW1, after which he worked in Borneo. In WW2, he escaped the initial Japanese invasion in early 1942, only to be captured and murdered by the Japanese in September 1942.

CREESE, *Alfred Richard. 1910-1917.* b 1898. Lieutenant, RAF. Survived WW1, but was one of the many fit, healthy young men who died (in November 1918) in the 'Spanish flu' pandemic.

DAVIS, *Howard Leslie. 1929-1938.* b 1920. Flight Sergeant (Pilot), RAFVR. He was one of seven siblings – three boys and four girls – who went to CH, one of his brothers being Colin (para 2.27). Served with 149 Squadron, a mainstay of Bomber Command. He was killed in a raid on Essen in June 1942.

DELL, *George William. 1904-1908.* b 1891. Private, US Army. Thought to be the only Old Blue to die (in 1918) in the US Army.

EKINS, *Franklin George. 1905-1913.* b 1896. Lieutenant, Royal Irish Regiment. Severely wounded and awarded MC, September 1916, subsequently gaining two bars to his MC, a rare achievement. He died in January 1919.

ELRINGTON, *Maxwell. 1910-1915.* b 1899. Brigadier, Border Regiment, commanding 71st Infantry Brigade. Killed in action April 1945; OBE. Most senior Old Blue (by rank) to die in WW2. Had earlier served in WW1, and army posts including in Palestine (Major). DSO.

McRAE, *Foster Moverley, [usually, Peter]. 1926-1934.* b 1916. Surgeon-Lieutenant, RNVR. A brilliant all-round sportsman at CH, later playing cricket for Somerset. In February 1944, his ship – part of a convoy – was torpedoed and sank. McRae survived and clambered aboard a Carley float which soon became over-crowded. McRae reportedly remarked "There's not enough room for all of us" and slipped over the side, never to be seen again.

99. Peter McRae.

PILLOW, *Edwin Cedric Stuart. 1938-1944.* b 1928. Too young to join the Forces, Pillow was living with his widowed mother in SE London when, in March 1945, their street was hit by one of the last V2 missiles to land on English soil, killing all the occupants instantly. As far as is known, he was the youngest OB to die in WW2.

100. Michael Rennie.
with permission of Gordonstoun School

RENNIE, *Michael. 1928-1935.* b 1917. Served in WW2 as a civilian escort to children who were evacuated to the Dominions and the USA. Killed when the passenger liner, City of Benares, en route to Canada and carrying a number of such children, was torpedoed in September 1940. Rennie survived the sinking and rescued many children, but died soon afterwards.

SATCHELL, *Mary. 1925-1933.* b 1915. Sister (Major), Queen Alexandra's Imperial Military Nursing Service, serving in France, Egypt and Italy. d May 1945.

WOODHAMS, *Geoffrey. 1901-1910.* b 1891. Captain, Royal Sussex Regiment. Killed in March 1916 when rescuing one of his men who had been wounded. *At CH, "one of the best all-round fellows the School had ever had."*

School and Young OBs

ATKINSON, *James Peter Geoffrey. 1999-2006.* b 1987. Died, with Robert Gauntlett (below), whilst climbing in the Alps, 2009. Earlier, had supported Gauntlett's Everest expedition and managed the Pole to Pole trek (again see below).

101. James Peter Geoffrey Atkinson.

BLATHWAYT, *Percy. 1853-1858.* b 1843. Died 1858, being the first boy buried in the School's ground at the City of London Cemetery, Ilford, Essex, his name being inscribed on the monument there.

CONNOR, *Ernest Stephen. 1902-1905.* b 1890. Killed by lightning on the School playing fields, 1905. (#)

DEANE, *Eileen Violet Chambers. 1909-1914.* b 1897. Died 1914, *a plaque was placed in the Hertford Chapel.*

ENGELBRECHT, *Julian Ekstein. 1984-1989.* b 1972. Died in a car accident in 1991. (#)

GAUNTLETT, *Robert Douglas. 1998-2005.* b 1987. In 2006, became youngest Briton to climb Mt Everest (with James Hooper, 1998-2005). In 2007/08 journeyed (again with Hooper) from North to South Magnetic Poles using only human and natural power. Died, with James Atkinson (above), whilst climbing in the Alps, 2009.

102. Robert Douglas Gauntlett.

HALDEN, *Ian Michael. 1977-1984.* b 1966. Flying Officer. Killed in 1991 in a flying accident in the Falkland Islands. (#)

HUTTON-POTTS, *Jack Peter. 2001-2008.* b 1990. Died climbing in North Wales (with Vaughan Holme, CH staff, who also died) 2013.

JOWETT, *James Peter. 1980-1987.* b 1969. *Senior Grecian, CH.* Died of leukaemia, 1990. (#)

SMITH, *Daniel. 1988-1991.* b 1977. Died of leukaemia, 1991. (#)

STAPLES, *Kathleen Mary. 1890-1896.* b 1882. One of four children of James Staples*, CH master for nearly 40 years; she died at Hertford in 1896 and was *remembered in a memorial in the new Hertford Chapel.*

WILLIAMS, *Alistair Glenn. 1956-1963.* b 1946. Died whilst trying to rescue a work colleague who had been overcome by marsh gas, 1969.

103. James Peter Jowett.

Centenarians

ABBOTT, *Reginald James. 1912-1918.* b 1902. Employed with Marconi International Marine Radio Communication Co working on the development of radio and TV, and of broadcasting. Served WW2; Defence Medal. Later, work in Europe and for the voluntary sector. Died 2005, aged 102.

AYLETT, *Winifred Ethel, [née TAYLOR]. 1908-1913.* b 1896. Employed as a civil servant in the Public Trustee Office. Died 1998, aged 101.

104. Edward Stanley Benfield.

BENFIELD, *Edward Stanley. 1904-1908.* b 1892. On leaving CH, emigrated to USA, where he worked initially for Proctor & Gamble. Then joined Frank B Hall (insurance brokers), retiring 50 years later as President. Died 1998, aged 106.

BOMFORD, *Arthur Henry. 1884-1889.* b 1874. Worked for 57 years from apprentice to top executive with a textile wholesaler which eventually became Courtaulds. Died 1975, aged 101.

BRITTAN, *Herbert William. 1874-1880.* b 1864. Employed in the Post Office Savings Bank for 43 years. Was cycling and swimming in his 90s. Died in 1969, aged 105; with Thomas Young (below) probably the oldest pre-Horsham Old Blue.

105. Dorothy May Davey.

DAVEY, *Dorothy May. 1909-1914.* b 1897. A headmistress. *Helped foster relationships between the Old Girls and the Hertford School.* Died 1998, aged 100.

ENGLEDOW, *Gladys. 1915-1922.* b 1904. Headmistress, Godolphin School, Salisbury. Previously, Headmistress, Newark-on-Trent High School, Truro High School. Later (in 80th year), became a Lay Reader. Initially, undergraduate, Newnham College, Cambridge; then various teaching (mathematics) posts. Died 2006, aged 101.

FREEMAN, *Maggie Rentoul, [née CUTHBERTSON]. 1895-1898.* b 1882. Initially, a pupil-teacher, then attended Stockwell College. Died 1984, aged 102.

GUILLEBAUD, *Phoebe Monica, [née REYNOLDS]. 1917-1925.* b 1908. Worked initially as an assistant matron in a school. Later, much involved with local matters in Marlborough, serving on the Town Council and in the WRVS. Died 2009, aged 101.

HALL, *Frances Helena. 1893-1900.* b 1882. One of a comparatively large number of 10 girls (from one school) who were admitted from Tiffin GS near the end of the Victorian era. Died 1984, aged 102.

HILL, *Margaret Lilian Alice, [née NEAL]. 1901-1909.* b 1892. Emigrated to Australia after WW1, where she married. Became State Secretary of the Methodist Conference Women's Auxiliary of Overseas Missions. Died 1992, aged 100.

JONES, *Hannah Mabel, [née SMITH]. 1899-1904.* b 1887. On leaving Hertford, Jones was proposing to compete in the Civil Service examination. Died 1988, aged 101.

KINGSFORD, *Peter Wilfred. 1920-1925.* b 1908. Historian. Senior Research Fellow, Hatfield Polytechnic. Previously, Head of Department, Hatfield College of Technology. Author. Died 2010, aged 101.

106. Phoebe Monica Guillebaud, [née Reynolds].

MACKIE, *Joseph Millard. 1878-1885.* b 1870. Joined the Secretary's Office at Lloyd's, spending the whole of his working life (46 years) there, retiring as Superintendent of the Room. He had a collection of scrapbooks which were preserved in the Lloyd's Library. Died 1972, aged 102.

MAYNE, *Philip. 1911-1918.* b 1899. Technical Director, ICI. Previously at National Physical Laboratory. Died 2007, aged 107, one of the last, if not the last, serving officers of WW1.

107. Philip Mayne.

MORGAN, *Hilda Joyce, [née GIBBS]. 1920-1926.* b 1909. Employed as a teacher. Died 2010, aged 101.

PROCTOR, *Anne Ines Louie, [née ANGUS]. 1916-1925.* b 1907. Worked as a teacher, in the church and as a marriage guidance counsellor. *Wrote of her time at CH Hertford in "Blue Skirts into Blue Stockings (or recollections of Christ's Hospital)", 1981.* Died 2008, aged 101.

SMITH, *Bowen Eleny. 1835-1841.* b 1826. Clerk. Died 1926, aged 100.

STEWART-SMITH, *Kathleen Georgiana Maule, [née FINCH]. 1916-1924.* b 1907. Did much work assisting her Revd husband, including in his role as Warden, Brasted Place, Kent; also in Jerusalem; and later when he was Archdeacon of Bromley and of Rochester. Earlier, HM Inspector of Schools. *CH: Governor.* Died 2009, aged 102.

108. Kathleen Georgiana Maule Stewart-Smith, [née Finch].

TAYLOR, *Doris Winifred, [née PEAKE]. 1906-1915.* b 1897. Died 1997, aged 100.

VEAR, *Kenneth Charles. 1921-1929.* b 1911. Distinguished academic botanist, teaching at Seale-Hayne Agriculture College, Devon. His textbook "Agricultural Botany" became a standard reference work. Died 2012, aged 101.

WELFARE, *Freda May. 1917-1922.* b 1905. Primary school teacher. Died 2005, aged 100.

YOUNG, *Thomas. 1800-1809.* b 1793. Founded a firm of drapers at Watford, one of its major lines being the supply of clothing for navvies. Through this activity he became a friend of George Stephenson, the railway pioneer. Earlier, in sea service. Died 1898, aged 105.

2.23 *Academic (UK, universities)*

ALLAN, *Donald James. 1917-1926.* b 1907. Professor of Greek, Glasgow University; previously, Dean of the Faculty of Arts. Earlier, Fellow, Tutor, Balliol College, Oxford. Reader in Ancient Philosophy, Edinburgh University. Author. FBA. d 1978. (WWW)

ALLEN, *William Sidney. 1929-1937.* b 1918. Professor of Comparative Philology, Cambridge University. Fellow, Trinity College, Cambridge. Editor and author. FBA. *CH: Almoner.* d 2004. (WWW)

ANDERSON, *Declan John. 1932-1938.* b 1920. Professor (later Emeritus) of Oral Biology, University of Bristol. Earlier, Professor of Physiology (Dentistry), Guy's Hospital; visiting Professor of Physiology, Oregon University. Author. d 2016. (WWW)

BAKER, *Leonard Graham Derek. 1943-1950.* b 1931. Professor of History and Director posts, University of Texas;

109. Prof William Sidney Allen.

Visiting Professor, University of Houston. Previously, *Head Master of Christ's Hospital (1979-1985). President, ASB.* Earlier, Senior History Master, The Leys School; Lecturer in Medieval History, Edinburgh University. Author and editor. FRHistS. d 2015. (WWW)

BARNES, *John Arundel. 1929-1936.* b 1918. Professor (later Emeritus) of Sociology, Cambridge University. Fellow, Churchill College, Cambridge. Earlier, Professor of Anthropology in Australia; Fellow, St John's College, Cambridge. Author. Served RNVR, WW2; DSC. FBA. d 2010. (WWW)

BARRINGTON, *Ernest James William. 1919-1927.* b 1909. Professor (later Emeritus) of Zoology, Nottingham University. Earlier, Visiting Professor in New York, Buenos Aires and Sao Paulo. Editor, author. FRS. d 1985. (WWW)

110. Prof Leonard Graham Derek Baker.

BISHOP, *Terence Alan Martyn. 1920-1924.* b 1907. Reader in Palaeography, Department of History, Cambridge University. Author. FBA. d 1994. (WWW)

BROCK, *William Ranulf. 1928-1934.* b 1916. Professor of Modern History, University of Glasgow. Previously, visiting professorships, USA; Fellow, Trinity College, Cambridge and Selwyn College, Cambridge. His main work was the history of the USA, which he pursued latterly with his Selwyn Fellowship. FBA. d 2014.

BRUCE, *Frank Edward. 1926-1933.* b 1915. Professor of Public Health Engineering, Imperial College. Later, Visiting Professor, City University. Pioneered the study of public health engineering, working initially at Harvard. Practised widely as a consultant (including to WHO), advising on water supply and sewage disposal. President, Institution of Public Health Engineers. Executive Vice-President, Royal Society of Health. d 2003.

111. Prof Frank Edward Bruce.

BUSBRIDGE, *Ida. 1919-1926.* b 1908. Vice-Principal, Fellow (later Emeritus), St Hugh's College, Oxford. Previously, Lecturer in Mathematics there. Pioneered the teaching of mathematics to women undergraduates at Oxford University. Earlier, mathematical research at University College, London. FRAS. *CH: Governor.* d 1988.

DEAN, *William Reginald. 1908-1915.* b 1896. Professor of Mathematics, University College, London. Fellow, Lecturer in Mathematics, Trinity College, Cambridge. Later, Visiting Professor, University of Arizona. *CH: Almoner.* d 1973. (WWW)

Du BOULAY, *Francis Robin Houssemayne. 1931-1938.* b 1920. Professor (later Emeritus) of Medieval History,

112. Prof Philip Hall.

University of London; previously Reader. Lecturer, Bedford College. Hon Sec, Royal Historical Society. Author. FBA. *CH: Almoner, Governor.* d 2008. (WWW)

EASTON, *Malcolm Fyfe. 1919-1929.* b 1910. Reader, History of Art, Hull University; previously, Senior Lecturer there. Major role in establishing University's art collection. Initially, long spell as an artist, then art teacher. Author. d 1993.

ESCRITT, *Charles Ewart. 1917-1923.* b 1905. Secretary, Oxford University Appointments Committee. Fellow, Keble College, Oxford. OBE. d 1990. (WWW)

FRANKLIN, *Kenneth James. 1908-1916.* b 1897. Professor Emeritus of Physiology, London University; previously, Professor of Physiology, St Bartholomew's Hospital. Earlier, Fellow (later Emeritus), Tutor and Lecturer, Oriel College, Oxford; Dean, Medical School, Oxford. Author. FRS, FRCP. d 1966. (WWW)

GOWING, *Margaret Mary, [née ELLIOTT]. 1932-1938.* b 1921. Professor of the History of Science, Oxford University. Early career in Civil Service as historian, Cabinet Office, and UK Atomic Energy Authority. Reader in Contemporary History, University of Kent. Fellow of Linacre College, Oxford. Author. d 1998. (DNB, WWW)

HALL, *Philip. 1915-1922.* b 1904. Professor (later Emeritus) of Pure Mathematics, Cambridge University. Earlier, Fellow, King's College, Cambridge, and Lecturer in Mathematics, Cambridge University. Served at Bletchley Park, WW2. FRS. d 1982. (DNB, WWW)

HOLLOWAY, *Bernard John. 1929-1937.* b 1918. Head, Careers and Appointments Service, Manchester University and University's Institute of Science and Technology, developing 'Clearing House' approach and Register of Graduate Employment and Training. Earlier, schoolmaster and researcher at British Nylon Spinners. d 1995.

113. Prof Ivor Christopher Banfield Keys.

KEYS, *Ivor Christopher Banfield. 1931-1938*. b 1919. Professor (later Emeritus) of Music, Birmingham University. Previously, Professor of Music, Queen's University, Belfast, and Nottingham University. Composer. Author. CBE. FRCM, FRCO. d 1995. (WWW)

LE PAGE, *Robert Brock. 1932-1937*. b 1920. Professor of Languages, University of York. Later, Professor Emeritus in the West Indies. Earlier, worked in Jamaica on Jamaican dialects; Professor of English, Kuala Lumpur. d 2006.

MARTIN, *Rhea, [née MITCHELL]. 1939-1948*. b 1930. Pro-Vice-Chancellor, University of Hertfordshire. Previously, barrister and magistrate; Lecturer and Dean, School of Law, Hatfield Polytechnic. Later, work for Citizens Advice Bureau and employment tribunals. OBE. d 2014.

114. Rhea Martin [née Mitchell].

McNAULTY, *Norah. 1906-1912*. b 1895. Registrar, Bedford College, where she had earlier graduated, her course having a special interest in philology. When the Royal Holloway and Bedford New College was established at Egham, it was proposed to name a new building in her name. *CH: Governor.* d 1990.

MEIGGS, *Russell. 1912-1921*. b 1902. Fellow and Tutor in Ancient History, Balliol College, Oxford. Lecturer in Ancient History, Oxford University. Visiting Professor, Swarthmore College, Leeds. Author. FBA. d 1989. (DNB, WWW)

MORPURGO, *Jack Eric. 1929-1936*. b 1918. Professor (later Emeritus) of American Literature, University of Leeds. Earlier, Editor, Penguin Books; General Editor, Pelican Books. Director General (later Vice-President), National Book League. Various university appointments overseas, including The College of William and Mary, Virginia. Author of many books (including some on Christ's Hospital). *CH: Almoner; Deputy Chairmen, Council of Almoners; Governor; President, ASB.* d 2000. (WWW)

115. Prof Jack Eric Morpurgo.

MURPHY, *Neville Richard. 1902-1909*. b 1890. Principal, Hertford College, Oxford. Fellow, earlier Hon Fellow, there. d 1971. (WWW)

NORTHCOTT, *Douglas Geoffrey. 1927-1935*. b 1916. Professor (later Emeritus) of Mathematics, Sheffield University. Earlier, Research Fellow, Cambridge and Princeton Universities. Author. FRS. *CH: Almoner.* d 2005. (WWW)

ROBERTS, *Arthur Loten. 1918-1924*. b 1906. Professor (later Emeritus) of Coal, Gas and Fuel Industries, Leeds University. Earlier, Senior Lecturer, Leeds University; posts with Gas Board, Gas Council and Gas Corporation. OBE. d 2000. (WWW)

SLADE, *Edwin. 1913-1922*. b 1903. Academic lawyer. Called to the Bar. Various appointments at St John's College, Oxford, including Senior Dean, Proctor, Fellow, Tutor and Lecturer. *CH: Almoner.* d 1989.

SMAIL, *Raymond Charles. 1924-1932*. b 1913. Senior Tutor, earlier Fellow, Sidney Sussex College, Cambridge, specialising in medieval history and the Crusades. Served WW2, Major, Royal Artillery; MBE. FRHistS. d 1986.

SNELLGROVE, *David Llewelyn. 1930-1938.* b 1920. Professor, School of Oriental and African Studies, a leading scholar of the languages, history and religion of Buddhist India and Tibet. Earlier, Lecturer and Reader, SOAS. Travelled extensively in India. Author. FBA. d 2016. (WWW)

STEVENS, *John Edgar. 1932-1938.* b 1921. President, Magdalene College, Cambridge. Professor (later Emeritus), Medieval and Renaissance English, Cambridge University. Earlier, Fellow and Tutor, Magdalene College; Lecturer in English, Cambridge University. Musicologist and musician, author. CBE. FBA. d 2002. (DNB, WWW)

SWIFT, *Herbert Walker. 1907-1914.* b 1894. Professor of Engineering, Sheffield University. Previous appointments included Head of Department of Mechanical Engineering, Bradford Technical College. d 1960. (WWW)

116. Prof Gerald James Whitrow.
with permission of Natural History Wiki

WHITROW, *Gerald James. 1923-1930.* b 1912. Professor of the History and Application of Mathematics, Imperial College. Previously, Reader in Mathematics there. President, British Society for the History of Science; President, British Society for the Philosophy of Science; President (and founder), British Society for the History of Mathematics. Author. FRAS. d 2000. (DNB)

YOUNG, *Percy Marshall. 1924-1930.* b 1912. Director of Music, Wolverhampton College of Technology. Developed choral and orchestral concerts, including some for the BBC. Author, including books for young readers, and on football.

117. Percy Marshall Young.

Composer of many works, including for piano and orchestra. d 2004. (DNB)

118. Prof Sir Erik Christopher Zeeman.

ZEEMAN, *Erik Christopher. 1934-1943.* b 1925. Knight (1991). Founding Professor, Mathematics Institute, University of Warwick. Earlier, Research Fellow and Lecturer, Gonville and Caius College, Cambridge. Later, Principal, Hertford College, Oxford, and Gresham Professor of Geometry, Gresham College, London. President, London Mathematical Society and The Mathematical Association. FRS. *CH: Almoner.* d 2016. (WWW)

2.24   *Academic (UK, schools)*

CROFT, *William Bleaden. 1859-1870.* b 1851. Physics and mathematics master, Winchester College, for over 40 years, some of his experimental work featuring in the development of wireless telegraphy. d 1928.

DAVEY, *Roy Charles. 1926-1934.* b 1915. Headmaster, King's School, Bruton. Previously, Senior Master, Warden, The Village College, Impington, Cambs. FRSA. d 2007. (WWW)

FRANKLIN, *Henry William Fernehough. 1914-1920.* b 1901. Headmaster, Epsom College. Previously, master at Rugby School and Radley College. Played 92 games of first-class cricket between 1921 and 1931, for Essex, Oxford University and Surrey. d 1985. (WWW)

HANSFORD, *John Talbot. 1931-1940.* b 1922. Headmaster, King Edward's School, Witley and Bury Grammar School for Boys. Earlier, teacher and employed in aerospace industry. *Head Master of Christ's Hospital (1985-1987), being brought in at very short notice to oversee the change to co-education. Governor.* d 2012.

119. John Talbot Hansford.

HORNBY, *John. 1875-1886.* b 1867. Schoolmaster, Wellington School; previously, Denstone College. *Work for CH Club (to which he left his library), BSB (a director) and OBRFC (a Vice-President); one year as a CH master.* d 1933.

LODGE, *John. 1902-1906.* b 1890. Headmaster, Nantwich GS and Acton GS. Previously, Headmaster, Leominster GS, and teaching posts including at Kilburn GS. d 1954. (WWW)

MACINTOSH, *William Henry. 1865-1875.* b 1856. Vice-Principal (previously master) at Locker's Park Preparatory School, Herts, serving in all for nearly 40 years. d 1935.

MARLAND, *Peter Michael. 1944-1953.* b 1934. General Editor, Heinemann School Management Series. Founder, Head Teacher, North Westminster Community School; earlier, Headmaster, Woodberry Down School. Member, many educational committees and other bodies. His pioneering educational work was widely acclaimed. Author. CBE. d 2008. (DNB, WWW)

120. Peter Michael Marland.

PLUMPTRE, *Edward Vallis Cecil. 1913-1920.* b 1902. Head, Classics Department, Harrow School; previously, master there. d 1980.

PYKE, *George Frederick. 1904-1908.* b 1892. Headmaster, St Nicholas Primary School, Newbury. d 1971. (#)

RICHARDS, *Frank Roydon. 1910-1917.* b 1899. Rector, Glasgow Academy. Previously, Headmaster, Bridlington School; *master, CH.* d 1978. (WWW)

ROGERS, *Thomas Alfred. 1861-1872.* b 1853. Schoolmaster, Wellington College, for nearly 40 years. d 1931.

SEAMAN, *Clarence Milton Edwards. 1920-1927.* b 1908. *Head Master of Christ's Hospital, 1955-1970.* Previously,

Headmaster, Bedford School; Rector, Edinburgh Academy; master at Bedford and Rugby schools. CBE. *Governor; President, CH Club.* d 1974. (WWW) (#)

TAMBLING, *Christopher. 1976-1982.* b 1964. Director of Music, Downside School. Earlier, master at Sedbergh School and Glenalmond College. Conductor, Perth City Orchestra. Organist, composer and arranger (for both, in particular, masses). d 2015.

WAGNER, *Orlando Henry. 1875-1883.* b 1867. Headmaster, Wagner's Preparatory School, Kensington. Chairman, Council of Incorporated Association of Preparatory Schools. *CH: Almoner, Governor.* d 1956.

WATLING, *Edward Fairchild. 1912-1918.* b 1899. Classics master, King Edward VII School, Sheffield. Translator, particularly of Sophocles' Theban Plays; actor; sketch writer; book and theatre reviewer. d 1990.

WILLIAMS, *Thomas Brian. 1924-1933.* b 1915. Revd. Earlier, Chaplain, St Edward's School, Oxford, and King's School, Canterbury, where he also taught. Later, Incumbent, Hough on the Hill, Lincolnshire. d 1983 (#)

WILSON, *Joyce Elizabeth. 1919-1927.* b 1908. Headmistress, Gainsborough Girls' High School. Earlier, mathematics teacher, *including brief spell at CH Hertford*, and Deputy Head, County School for Girls, Dartford. d 2001.

WILSON, *Sydney Ernest. 1909-1917.* b 1898. Principal, King William's College, Isle of Man. Previously, Headmaster, schoolmaster, Burton on Trent GS. d 1973. (WWW)

2.25 *Academic (overseas)*

BULMER, *Ralph Neville Hermon. 1939-1946.* b 1928. Professor of Social Anthropology, University of Auckland, specialising in Ethnobiology. Previously, Foundation Professor of Social Anthropology, University of Papua New Guinea (the country in which he had undertaken the fieldwork for his PhD); Lecturer, University of Auckland. d 1988.

CLARK, *Thomas Henry. 1905-1910.* b 1893. Professor (later

121. Clarence Milton Edwards Seaman.

122. Prof Thomas Henry Clark.

from Geological Society of America, photo probably from McGill University

123. Prof Rupert Leo Scott Bruce-Mitford.

Emeritus) of Palaeontology, McGill University, Toronto. Adviser on geology for the University's Redpath Museum, following Director post there. Earlier, attended Harvard. Author. Had mineral – Thomasclarkite – named in his honour. Died 1996, aged 102.

HUNT, *Harold John. 1917-1923.* b 1905. Professor of Music, Tokyo Arts University. Previously, Visiting Professor, Cornell University. As a pianist, gave many recitals in London, the provinces and Europe. FRAM. *CH: master.* d 1976.

KROLL, *Richard Wilhelm Francis. 1966-1971.* b 1953. Professor of English, University of California. Earlier, academic posts including Assistant Professor, Princeton University. Author of two major studies on the literature and culture of the English Restoration period and of many related articles. d 2009.

LEACH, *Eva Frances. 1915-1923.* b 1905. Headmistress, Henrietta Barnett School, Hampstead. d 1957.

MORGAN, *Clement Yorke. 1915-1922.* b 1903. Rector, Michaelhouse, Natal. Previously, Sub-Warden, master, Radley College. d 1960. (WWW)

PEARSON, *William Burton. 1931-1940.* b 1921. Dean of Science, Professor of Physics and Chemistry, University of Waterloo, Ontario; later, Emeritus Professor. Previously, research scientist, National Research Council of Canada. Served RAF, WW2; MC. FRSC, CM. d 2005.

STONE, *Arthur Harold. 1927-1935.* b 1916. Professor of Mathematics, University of Rochester, USA. Initially, worked in USA, then UK – at Manchester University and Fellow, Trinity College, Cambridge – before returning to USA. Specialised in topology and known for his work on flexagons (flat, folded strips of paper which can be flexed in various ways). d 2000.

WOODHEAD, *William Dudley. 1895-1904.* b 1885. Professor Emeritus of Classics, McGill University, Montreal. Previously, Dean of Arts and Science there. Earlier, posts at University College, Toronto and University of Alberta. *Contributor to CH Exhibitioners' Fund.* d 1957.

2.26   *Cultural (administrators)*

BRADLEY, *Leslie Ripley. 1905-1908.* b 1892. Director, Imperial War Museum. Previously, Curator, Secretary, IWM. CB, CBE, OBE, MBE. d 1968. (WWW)

BRUCE-MITFORD, *Rupert Leo Scott. 1925-1933.* b 1914. Archaeologist. Research Keeper, British Museum. Previously, Keeper of British, Medieval and Later Antiquities. Subsequently, Slade Professor of Fine Art, Cambridge University. Author. FBA, FSA. d 1994. (DNB, WWW)

BUTLER, *Edward Dundas. 1850-1857.* b 1842. Librarian (mainly maps), British Museum. Translator, especially of Hungarian and Finnish. d 1919. (DNB)

CHEW, *Vincent Kenneth. 1926-1933.* b 1915. Research Fellow, Science Museum. Previously, various posts at Science Museum, including Keeper, Department of Physics. Earlier, schoolmaster. d 2008. (WWW)

COX, *Nicholas George. 1951-1961.* b 1942. Director of Government Services, Public Record Office (now National Archives). Helped establish procedures for release of official information, seeking to achieve as much openness as possible, his work culminating in the Freedom of Information Act. d 2004.

DAVIES, *Stephen Howard. 1956-1963.* b 1945. Associate Director, National Theatre. Earlier, Associate Director, Bristol Old Vic and the Royal Shakespeare Company, where he founded and was co-director at The Warehouse. Director for other theatres, opera, TV and film. Winner of three Olivier awards. CBE. FRSA. d 2016. (WWW)

GLOCK, *William Frederick. 1919-1926.* b 1908. Knight (1970). Controller of Music, BBC. Director, School of Music, Dartington Hall, Later, Artistic Director, Bath Festival, and administrative posts at, for example, Covent Garden and Arts Council (also Lecturer in music). Earlier, journalist, music critic and editor. CBE. d 2000. (DNB, WWW)

124. Sir William Frederick Glock.

PARKER, *Hampton Wildman. 1909-1914.* b 1897. Keeper (previously Deputy Keeper), Department of Zoology, British Museum (Natural History). Earlier, Assistant Keeper, NH Museum. CBE. d 1968. (WWW)

THORNTON, *James Cholmondeley. 1918-1926.* b 1906. Director (previously Secretary), UK and British Commonwealth Branch, Calouste Gulbenkian Foundation. Earlier, an assistant controller and deputy secretary, BBC. d 1969. (WWW)

TICKNER, *Martin. 1952-1958.* b 1941. Theatrical manager. Initially, worked in various theatres, including Lyric, Hammersmith, and for John Gale Productions. Much work for charity events and arranging theatrical memorial services. d 1992.

125. Sir James Ian Raley Trethowan.

TRETHOWAN, *James Ian Raley. 1933-1938.* b 1922. Knight (1980). Chairman, Director, Thames Television Ltd. Director, Consultant, Thorn EMI. Earlier, journalist; Deputy Editor, ITN; Managing Director, BBC Radio, TV. Director General, BBC. Various other appointments, including Chairman, Horserace Betting Levy Board. *CH: Vice-President, OBRFC.* d 1990. (WWW)

WOON, *Peter. 1942-1949.* b 1931. Editor, BBC TV news, introducing journalists as newsreaders. Oversaw the launch of "The Six O'Clock News". Initially, a journalist and reporter, then an editor. Controller of BBC's radio news service, introducing permanent female presenters on the Radio's "Today" programme. Later, Head of BBC's publicity and their representative in the USA. d 2014.

2.27 *Cultural (individuals)*

BARRON, *Charles Howard Washington. 1910-1916.* b 1900. Portrait painter and landscape artist, with works in many galleries and private collections worldwide. Major works include HM Queen and Sir Winston Churchill and for 50th anniversary of the RAF. Initially, art teacher and practised in London, Europe and Australia. d 1991.

BATE, *Henry Francis. 1868-1874.* b 1858. Artist, painter. Exhibitor at principal art exhibitions. JP. OBE. d 1950. (WWW)

BLUNDEN, *Edmund Charles. 1909-1915.* b 1896. Poet, author and critic. Professor of Poetry, Oxford University. Earlier, Professor of English Literature, Tokyo University; Fellow, Tutor, Merton College, Oxford, where Keith Douglas (below) came under his wing; Emeritus Professor, University of Hong Kong. Extensive range of poetry and prose, including "Undertones of War", *"Life of Leigh Hunt"* and *"Christ's*

Hospital: a Retrospect". Served WW1; MC. CBE. FRSL. d 1974. (DNB, WWW)

126. Prof Edmund Charles Blunden.

BOLDER, *Robert. [at CH, Robert Joseph EDNEY]. 1868-1874.* b 1859. Actor. Began career as a stage actor, then appeared in many American silent films, including "Beyond the Rocks". Died, Beverley Hills, California, 1937.

BOX, *Harold Elton, [at CH, Harold BOX]. 1912-1918.* b 1903. Tried many jobs before becoming a songwriter, being particularly successful in his work for radio. Perhaps best known for collaboration on the song "I've got a lovely bunch of coconuts". d 1981.

BROWN, *Wilfred Henry. 1933-1939.* b 1921. Singer (tenor). Performed widely in Europe and Canada, particularly works of Gerald Finzi, and including with the English Chamber Orchestra. Many solo broadcasts for BBC and commercial recordings. Earlier, schoolmaster. d 1971.

CARTER, *Sydney Bertram. 1926-1933.* b 1915. Songwriter and journalist. Amongst many earlier collaborations was a musical partnership with composer Donald Swann; prolific songwriter covering many genres, including folk. Best known for "Lord of the Dance". Various journalist and editor roles. d 2004. (DNB)

127. Sydney Bertram Carter.
with permission of Stainer & Bell Ltd

CAVENDISH, *Richard. 1940-1949.* b 1930. Writer, particularly on the occult, his works including "The Black Arts" and the encyclopaedic "Man, Myth and Magic" which he also edited. Wrote also for "History Today". Worked originally in the City, briefly, and in the USA. d 2016.

128. Sir Colin Rex Davis.

DAVIS, *Colin Rex. 1938-1944.* b 1927. Knight (1980). Principal Conductor (earlier Conductor), President, London Symphony Orchestra. Previously, many conductor appointments, including BBC Symphony Orchestra; Bavarian Radio Symphony Orchestra (guest); Boston Symphony Orchestra (principal guest), and Musical Director, Royal Opera House. Many international concert awards. CH, CBE. *CH: Special Recognition Award.* d 2013. (WWW) Brother of Howard Leslie (para 2.22).

de SAUSMAREZ, *Lionel Maurice. 1926-1932.* b 1915. Painter, lecturer and writer on the visual arts. Principal, Byam Shaw School of Drawing and Painting. Exhibited at Royal Academy and widely with works in many major galleries and museums, and portraits for many organisations. RBA. d 1969. (DNB, WWW)

DIX, *Joshua Airlie. 1880-1887.* b 1872. Organist, composer, best known for the popular songs "The Trumpeter" and "A Jolly Old Cavalier"; also music for light opera. d 1911.

DOUGLAS, *Keith Castellain. 1931-1938.* b 1920. Poet. Served WW2, writing in the desert campaign (including "Alamein to Zem Zem") and in England to where he returned when wounded. Earlier, tutored at Merton College, Oxford by Edmund Blunden (above). Killed a few days after D-Day invasion, 1944, robbing English literature of "one of the most individual and accomplished poets of his generation". (DNB)

EVANS, *Walter Tenniel. 1937-1944.* b 1926. Revd. Actor. Trained initially at RADA. Acted in repertory, then many popular and successful radio and TV appearances, including "The Navy Lark", all spanning about 45 years. Latterly, with

129. Keith Castellain Douglas.

the National Theatre. Amidst the acting, found time to get ordained, ministering at a church in Bucks. d 2009.

EXTON, *Clive, [at CH, Clive Jack Montague BROOKS]. 1941-1945.* b 1930. Screenwriter. Initially, actor and stage manager. Wrote for theatre and (mainly adaptations) for cinema and TV, including for "Armchair Theatre", and latterly as lead writer for the "Hercule Poirot" series and for "Rosemary and Thyme". d 2007. (DNB)

FARRELL, *Nigel George. 1963-1970.* b 1953. Producer, presenter, maker of documentaries for TV and radio. Worked initially for local press and radio; later BBC, pioneering the 'docu-soap' and creating the series "The Village" (Radio 4, later TV) and "An Island Parish" (BBC2). Later, programmes for Channel 4. d 2011.

FISHER, *Terence Roland. 1913-1919.* b 1904. Film director. Early film career as editor; director work (including some for TV) principally for Hammer Films, where he extended characterisation beyond the basic horror genre. His film "The Mummy" was a particular success. d 1980. (DNB)

130. Revd Walter Tenniel Evans.

131. Clive Exton [Clive Jack Montague Brooks].

132. Alan Gerard Fletcher.

133. Leonard Constant Lambert.
by Bassano Ltd, © National Portrait Gallery, London

FLETCHER, *Alan Gerard. 1941-1948.* b 1931. Graphic designer. Early work in USA, later in London for Penguin. Helped to establish a major design studio (Pentagram), later working independently with many corporate clients. A prolific and highly regarded graphic designer. FRCA. d 2006. (DNB)

GODDEN, *James. 1889-1896.* b 1879. Actor, as Jimmy Godden, performed in a number of West End comedies and reviews, then films. Earlier, a civil servant and concert pianist. d 1955.

GREEN, *John Kenneth. 1918-1922.* b 1905. Artist, best known for landscape and portrait paintings, but also undertook costume and set designs for opera. Exhibited widely, including in New York and in London at Royal Academy. d 1986.

HANDFORD, *Peter Thomas. 1929-1935.* b 1919. Film sound recordist. Early training with Denham Film Studios; some camera work in WW2. Later, freelance, including work for Alfred Hitchcock and Boulting Brothers; sound recordist for many films, including "Murder on the Orient Express" and "The Entertainer"; also work for TV. d 2007. (DNB)

134. Henry Bernard Levin.

HAVINDEN, *Ashley Eldrid. 1912-1919.* b 1903. Designer, typographer, painter. Director, WS Crawford Ltd, Advertising Agents; Director, Design International Ltd. Exhibited posters and advertising design worldwide, and specific exhibitions of paintings, rugs and textiles. OBE. d 1973. (WWW)

HAWES, *Stanley Gilbert. 1916-1922.* b 1905. Producer-in-Chief, Australian Government's film-making body. Earlier, film work in Birmingham and London. Then, employed with National Film Boards in Canada and Australia. Initially, clerk with Birmingham Corporation. MBE. d 1991.

LAMBERT, *Leonard Constant. 1915-1922.* b 1905. Composer, conductor and critic. Initially, wrote "Romeo and Juliet" (commissioned by Diaghileff) and "Pomona" for the Russian Ballet. Many other ballet, orchestral and choral compositions, including for Covent Garden and Sadler's Wells; best-known for concert work "The Rio Grande". Critic, contributor for various publications, including "New Statesman". d 1951. (DNB, WWW)

LEVIN, *Henry Bernard. 1939-1945.* b 1928. Journalist, author. Prolific contributor to many UK and international newspapers and magazines, principally "The Times", "The Sunday Times", "Observer" and "International Herald Tribune". TV and radio writer and broadcaster. CBE. d 2004. (DNB, WWW)

LONGMATE, *Norman Richard. 1936-1943.* b 1925. Author, much of his work being produced whilst employed at the BBC. Formerly, a leader and feature writer, then a BBC producer and part of the secretariat. Initially, wrote detective novels, then works of social history, including "How We Lived Then". *Published an autobiography, mostly his life at CH.* d 2016.

135. Norman Richard Longmate.
by Bryan Harris, with permission of Jill Longmate

MARSHALL, *Austin John. 1947-1953.* b 1937. Record producer and songwriter. Initially, worked as a graphic designer. Later, joined the record industry, writing many songs, his folk music being widely acclaimed, and producing many albums. Latterly, worked in New York, including as a poet. d 2013.

MASON, *David Frederick. 1936-1942.* b 1926. Professor of Music (Trumpet), Royal College of Music. Played principal trumpet in the Royal Philharmonic and Philharmonia Orchestras and many solo pieces including for Beatles songs such as "Penny Lane". *CH: Governor.* d 2011.

136. Prof David Frederick Mason.

MITCHELL, *Charlotte, [at CH, Edna Winifred MITCHELL]. 1935-1942.* b 1926. Actress and poet. Appeared in repertory theatre; radio (including "The Goon Show" and "Waggoners Walk"); TV (including "The Adventures of Black Beauty"); and films (including "The French Lieutenant's Woman"). Also wrote for TV. Produced a number of collections of poetry. d 2012.

PARSONS, *Patrick George. 1922-1929.* b 1912. As Patrick Holt, leading "second features" actor; "The Dennis Price of the B film". Later, more a character actor, and appearing on stage and TV. Earlier, in repertory theatre. Served Far East, WW2, often on secret missions; later Lieutenant-Colonel. *Contemporary of and in same CH Boarding House as Michael Wilding (below).* d 1993.

PIPPETT, *Roger Samuel. 1907-1912.* b 1895. Literary critic and adviser. Reader for the Book of the Month Club. Previously, Book Editor, "PM" (a New York daily). Sundry dramatic and literary reviews for the "Daily Herald", "PM" and the "New York Times". d 1962. (WWW)

PITMAN, *Robert Percy. 1934-1943.* b 1924. Journalist and author. Began journalism as book critic for the "Sunday Express", then weekly 'pungent' column for the "Daily Express"; later appeared regularly on TV and radio. In his

137. Robert Percy Pitman.
with permission of Alice Pitman

memory, the Express established an annual award for the best first book by a British author. Initially, an English teacher. d 1969. (DNB)

ROSS, *Eric Arthur. 1905-1909.* b 1894. Young actor who was playing Hamlet at the Old Vic just before his death in 1919. Earlier, in repertory theatre and a successful American tour.

SWAN, *Michael Lancelot. 1933-1940.* b 1923. Traveller and writer. Employed earlier with Faber and Faber. Travel books covered Europe, Mexico and South America. Essayist on art and literature, book reviewer, editor and broadcaster. d 1967.

THOMPSON, *Arthur Leonard Bell. 1928-1935.* b 1917. Writer, as Francis Clifford, especially thrillers. Two of his better-known works are "The Naked Runner" (subsequently made into a feature film starring Frank Sinatra) and "Act of Mercy". Served WW2, Burma; DSO: later with Special Operations Executive. d 1975.

TODD, *Herbert Eatton. 1919-1925.* b 1908. Writer of children's fiction, best known for his "Bobby Brewster" books. Lectured at over 6,000 schools and libraries. d 1988.

VAUGHAN, *John Keith. 1921-1929.* b 1912. Painter, designer and illustrator. Tutor, Slade School of Art. Many one-man shows in galleries and works in public collections in London and around the world. CBE. d 1977. (DNB, WWW)

138. John Keith Vaughan.

139. Michael Charles Gauntlett Wilding.

WILDING, *Michael Charles Gauntlett. 1922-1928.* b 1912. Stage and film actor. Extensive range of appearances on the stage (initially) and TV (later), but particularly for film, including "An Ideal Husband" in UK and Hitchcock's "Stage Fright" in Hollywood. One-time husband of legendary film actress Elizabeth Taylor. Initially, portrait painter and commercial artist. d 1979. *Contemporary of and in same CH Boarding House as Patrick Parsons (above).* (DNB, WWW)

WILSON, *Joyce, [née FORRINGTON]. 1938-1945.* b 1927. Author of over a dozen books, including "Magnificent Failures". Work included for BBC and as a freelance journalist and teacher of handicapped children. d 2003.

YOUNGMAN-CARTER, *Philip. 1917-1921.* b. 1904. Author, artist, designer of book jackets. Initially, worked as an illustrator and graphic artist. Served WW2, founder and co-editor of "Soldier" the first army magazine. Post-War, editorial posts at the "Daily Express" and the "Tatler". Later, artist, author and illustrator, expanding his work as a designer of book jackets to some 2,000 covers. d 1969.

140. Philip Youngman-Carter.

2.28 *Ecclesiastical*

ARNOLD, *Audrey Joyce. 1935-1943.* b 1925. Sister Columbia, Order of Saint Benedict (OSB). After graduating from Newnham College, Cambridge, joined the OSB at St Mary's Abbey, West Malling, Kent. Later, at the invitation of the bishop, moved to Maine, USA, where she died in 1992.

BARTLETT, *Charles Oldfield. 1866-1873.* b 1858. Revd. Public Preacher, Diocese of Gloucester; Hon Canon, Gloucester Cathedral. Previously, curacies in Weston-Super-Mare and Gloucestershire. Rural Dean, New Forest. d 1937. (WWW)

BAZIRE, *Reginald Victor. 1913-1916.* b 1900. Revd Canon. Archdeacon and Borough Dean, Wandsworth; previously, Archdeacon, Hon Canon, Southwark. Earlier, missionary, China Inland Mission; Rural Dean, Battersea. d 1990. (WWW)

BIRT, *William Raymond. 1921-1928.* b 1911. Ven Canon. Archdeacon (later Emeritus) of Berkshire. Hon Canon, Christ Church Cathedral, Oxford. Earlier, ecclesiastical posts including vicar and Rural Dean of Newbury. d 2002. (WWW)

BOYLE, *Noel Stuart Stirling. 1901-1905.* b 1888. Revd. Various ecclesiastical appointments, including as an Army chaplain in WW1 and at parishes in Hampshire, Birmingham and Somerset. He died in 1988, a few days before his 100th birthday and the 75th anniversary of his ordination.

141. Revd Noel Stuart Stirling Boyle.

BRYAN, *Frank Colin. 1903-1910.* b 1891. Revd. Chairman, Baptist Missionary Society and Baptist Ministers' Fellowship; President, Baptist Union, GB and Ireland. Earlier, various curacies; Superintendent of the Eastern Area of England. Author. A passionate advocate of Church unity. d 1972.

DELIGHT, *John David. 1936-1943.* b 1925. Ven. Archdeacon (later Emeritus) of Stoke. Previous ecclesiastical appointments including Hon Canon, All Souls Cathedral, Machakos, Kenya. Prebendary, Lichfield Cathedral, and posts in Leicester and Walsall. d 2013. Brother of Paul Charles (below).

DELIGHT, *Paul Charles. 1940-1949.* b 1931. Revd. Various ecclesiastical posts including Macclesfield, Guernsey (also Prison Chaplain) and lastly Stodden (Bedfordshire). Did much work in approved schools. England rugby triallist. d 1995. Brother of John David (above).

GREENSLADE, *Stanley Lawrence. 1916-1923*. b 1905. Revd. Canon, Christ Church, and Regius Professor of Ecclesiastical History, Oxford University. Professor of Divinity, Durham and Cambridge Universities. Fellow, Chaplain, Tutor, St John's College, Oxford; Fellow, Selwyn College, Cambridge. Examining Chaplain to various bishops; Canon, Durham. Author. FBA. *CH: Almoner*. d 1977. (WWW)

GRIFFITHS, *Alan Richard 1919-1926*. b 1906. Bede Griffiths. Monastic superior at an ashram (spiritual heritage), Shantivanam, India. Became Benedictine monk following conversion to Roman Catholicism soon after graduating, spending time at various UK abbeys. Moved to India, pursuing monastic life there and travelling. d 1993. (DNB)

142. Bede Alan Richard Griffiths.

HOLBROW, *Thomas. 1837-1849*. b 1829. Revd. Ecclesiastical appointments covering nearly 70 years, including Hardwicke, Coleford and Sandhurst (all Gloucestershire) and finally Stagshaw, Newcastle-on-Tyne. d 1923.

HOOK, *Ross Sydney. 1928-1936*. b 1917. Rt Revd. Bishop of Bradford. Later, Chief of Staff to Archbishop of Canterbury.

143. Bishop Ross Sydney Hook.

Previously, various ecclesiastical appointments, including chaplain, RNVR (Royal Marine Commandos) in WW2; MC. Rector and Rural Dean, Chelsea; Bishop Suffragan of Grantham; Examining Chaplain to Bishops of Rochester and Lincoln. *CH: Almoner*. d 1996. (WWW)

HORSTEAD, *James Lawrence Cecil. 1910-1915*. b 1898. Rt Revd. Canon Emeritus, Leicester Cathedral; previously, Assistant Bishop, Diocese of Leicester. Earlier ecclesiastical appointments including Bishop of Sierra Leone and Archbishop of West Africa. Principal, Fourah Bay College, Sierra Leone. CMG, CBE. d 1989. (WWW)

144. Bishop James Lawrence Cecil Horstead.

HUGHES, *Frederick Llewelyn. 1904-1913*. b 1894. Very Revd. Dean of Ripon. Ecclesiastical appointments initially in London and Mansfield; later Hon Canon, Southwell and Canterbury Cathedrals. Served WWI, WW2 (latterly, Chaplain-General to the Forces; MC, TD). Chaplain to King George V1. CB, CBE. d 1967. (WWW)

KING, *Philip David. 1946-1954*. b 1935. Revd Canon. Secretary, Church of England's Board of Mission in the "Decade of Evangelism" (essentially the 1990s). Initially, curacies in Surrey and Fulham; then General Secretary, South American Mission Society. Later roles included for the Partnership for World Mission, and establishing the National College for Evangelists. Author. d 2006.

KNIGHT, *Marcus. 1915-1920*. b 1903. Very Revd. Dean of Exeter. Earlier, ecclesiastical appointments in London and Warwickshire. Hon Sec, Church of England Council for Education. Canon, Precentor, Chapter Treasurer, St Paul's. d 1988. (WWW)

MILLBOURN, *Arthur Russell. 1904-1911*. b 1892. Revd. Canon Emeritus, Canon Residentiary, Bristol Cathedral. Earlier, Headmaster, Colston's School, Bristol. d 1973. (WWW)

MORRIS, *David Freestone. 1915-1923*. b 1905. Revd Dom, Benedictine Order. Abbot, Nashdom Abbey, Bucks; later, served at Elmore Abbey, Berks. d 1997.

145. Seven Peele A OBs: Revd Kenneth Cyril Oliver, Wilfred Leslie Binns, [EEG Street], Louis Reginald Fradin, Cecil Francis [usually Bill] Kirby, Albert Wilson Robinson, John Farrant Bunford.

OLIVER, *Kenneth Cyril. 1918-1926.* b 1908. Revd. Various ecclesiastical posts including curacies in Yorkshire and Birmingham, Chaplain HAC, and work for Toc H. Served WW2, Senior Chaplain, North Africa, and Assistant Chaplain General, Middle East. Later, Assistant Chaplain General, Far East; Hon Chaplain to the Queen; priest at Climping. OBE. *CH: Governor.* d 1990.

RANDOLPH, *Thomas Berkeley. 1913-1923.* b 1904. Ven Archdeacon (later Emeritus) of Hereford. Canon Residentiary, Hereford Cathedral. Earlier, various ecclesiastical posts, including in Calcutta, Reading and Oxford. d 1987. (WWW) Brother of Cyril George (para 2.33).

SINGERS-DAVIES, *Richard William Frederick, [at CH, Richard William Frederick DAVIES]. 1868-1875.* b 1859. Revd Canon. Ecclesiastical appointments including Canon of St David's Cathedral and at Llandriddod Wells, Brecon, and at Bristol. Chaplain, RAMC and Hon Chaplain to Invalid Soldiers. d 1936. (WWW)

SULLIVAN, *Edward Godfrey. 1886-1892.* b 1876. Ven Archdeacon of Dublin. Vicar, St Ann's Dublin. Earlier, in commerce. d 1954.

USHER-WILSON, *Lucian Charles. 1912-1919.* b 1903. Rt Revd. Bishop of Upper Nile; then Bishop, Mbale, Uganda. Previously, missionary, Rural Dean, Uganda. Later, Assistant Bishop, Hon Canon, Guildford. Earlier, schoolmaster. CBE. d 1984. (WWW)

VINE, *Marshall George. 1859-1865.* b 1850. Revd. Warden and Chaplain, Philanthropic Society's Farm School. Previously, ecclesiastical appointments at Steyning, Sussex, and Leeds; Hon Diocesan Inspector of Schools, Rochester; Hon Canon, Southwark Cathedral. d 1918. (WWW)

WAGNER, *Peter Edward. 1945-1950.* b 1933. Ven Canon. Archdeacon of Masvingo, Rhodesia (now Zimbabwe). Initially, two ecclesiastical appointments in Birmingham. He then moved to Rhodesia, where posts included Warden, St Barnabas Centre, Mashonaland and Dean of Gweru Cathedral, Masvingo. In this latter post he was reportedly murdered in 2001 whilst praying in his church.

WESTON, *Frank Valentine. 1945-1954.* b 1935. Rt Revd. Bishop Suffragan of Knaresborough, North Yorkshire. Previously, various ecclesiastical posts including Archdeacon of Oxford and Canon of Christ Church, Oxford. Principal/

146. Bishop Frank Valentine Weston.

Professor, Edinburgh Theological College. *CH: Almoner, Governor.* d 2003. (WWW)

2.29 Royal Air Force

BEARDSWORTH, *George Braithwaite. 1916-1922.* b 1904. Air Vice-Marshal. Senior Air Staff Officer, Technical Training Command. Served WW2, Far East, Canada, Middle East. CB. FRAeS. d 1959. (WWW)

CONSTANTINE, *Hugh Alex. 1917-1925.* b 1908. Knight (1958). Air Chief Marshal. Co-ordinator, Anglo-American Relations, Ministry of Defence (Air). Served Bomber Command WW2; DSO. Later appointments including Commandant, Imperial Defence College, and at NATO. England rugby triallist. *CH: Almoner, Governor.* CB, CBE. d 1992. (WWW)

147. Air Chief Marshal Sir Hugh Alex Constantine.
by Walter Bird, © National Portrait Gallery, London

DONALDSON, *Arthur Hay. 1924-1932.* b 1915. Group Captain. RAF service, including WW2: Commanding Officer, 263 Squadron (succeeding his brother, John William (below)) and Wing Leader in Malta; DSO, DFC and bar, AFC. Later, Deputy Director, Air Defence, Air Ministry. d 1980. Brother of Edward Mortlock (below) and John William (below).

DONALDSON, *Edward Mortlock. 1922-1928.* b 1912. Air Commodore. Air correspondent, Daily Telegraph. Previously, RAF service, including Commander of first jet station in WW2; DSO, AFC and bar. Post-War, Commander, RAF High Speed Flight and holder of world speed record. Station Commander, Germany; Commandant, Royal Air Force Flying College. CB, CBE. d 1992. (WWW) Brother of Arthur Hay (above) and John William (below).

148. Air Commodore Edward Mortlock Donaldson.

DONALDSON, *John William. 1920-1927.* b 1910. Squadron Leader (Pilot). RAF service, including WW2: Commander, 263 Squadron (where he was succeeded by his brother Arthur Hay (above)), serving in Norway; DSO, AFC. Killed in action at sea, June 1940. Brother of Arthur Hay (above) and Edward Mortlock (above).

[Four Donaldson brothers were educated at CH. The oldest, Donald, emigrated to New Zealand. As shown above, the other three all received the DSO (likely to be the only set of three brothers to be so decorated) and various other honours, one report saying that this involved their widowed mother making 13 visits to Buckingham Palace.]

EMSON, *Reginald Herbert Embleton. 1922-1929.* b 1912. Knight (1966). Air Marshal. Inspector-General of the RAF. Served WW2, including at Fighter Command HQ; AFC. Later, Director, Ministry of Supply; Air Attaché post, Washington, and Deputy Chief, Air Staff. CB, CBE. d 1995. (WWW)

MEARS, *Cuthbert Vincent. 1912-1919.* b 1903. Air Commodore. Director of Intelligence (Security), Air Ministry. Command Accountant, Far East. Earlier, accounting and auditing roles with RAF in Cairo, and served WW2. Later, work for RAF Benevolent Fund. CBE. d 1992.

MOTT, *Arnold John. 1926-1933.* b 1916. Squadron Leader. Served WW2, including in bombing operations and with the SOE; MBE. Later, employed with Inland Revenue and Grant Thornton (tax accountants). d 2002.

OLIVER, *John Oliver William. 1921-1929.* b 1911. Assistant Chief of Staff, Allied Forces, Northern Europe. Served Fighter Command (Group Captain), WW2; DSO, DFC; later in Germany, Egypt and Iraq. Latterly, various personnel and training posts with the Thorn Group. CB. d 1997. (WWW)

PARRY, *Rey Griffith. 1899-1905.* b 1889. Air Vice-Marshal. Initially, in RN, serving in Dardanelles in WW1, becoming a Lieutenant-Commander; DSO. Then joined RAF, progressing through the ranks, including WW2 service: CB. d 1969. (WWW)

RIXSON, *Dennis Fenn. 1930-1936.* b 1918. Air Commodore. Commandant, Royal Observer Corps. Initially, RAF service including WW2 in Egypt and Sudan; OBE, DFC, AFC. Post-RAF, major charitable work for Royal Hospital and Home for Incurables and for the Development Trust for the Young Disabled. Founder member, Forces Retirement Association. CVO. d 1994.

SAKER, *Harold John. 1910-1913.* b 1897. Served RAF in WW1, then various Signals Officer posts, including with Fighter Command. Left (then rejoined) RAF, serving WW2, Group Captain, Chief Signals Officer, Fighter Command, an expert in his field. Post-RAF, Head, Aviation Department with firm of civil engineers. Lost his life in mysterious disappearance of the plane "Star Ariel" in which he was flying over the Atlantic in 1949. MVO.

SEYMOUR, *Roland George. 1915-1922.* b 1905. Air Commodore. Deputy Assistant Chief of Staff (Logistics), SHAPE. Served variously including as Deputy to Air Officer (Administration) Mediterranean Allied Forces, and in Iraq, Africa, Italy and Singapore. CB, CBE. d 1983. (WWW)

SINCLAIR, *Laurence Frank. 1919-1924.* b 1908. Knight (1957). Air Vice-Marshal. Controller, National Air Traffic Control Services. RAF service including WW2, Commander, Tactical Light Bomber Force, North Africa and Italy; GC, DSO and bar, CBE. ADC to King George VI. Post-War appointments included Commandant, RAF, Cranwell and Joint Services Staff College. CB. d 2002. (WWW)

2.30 *Army*

ALBAN, *Clifton Edward Rawdon Grant. 1900-1905.* b 1889. Major-General. Earlier, Colonel, The King's Regiment. Served WW1, Adjutant; DSO with two bars. Later, posts included General Staff Officer, War Office; ADC to King George VI. CBE. d 1964.

AMERS, *John Henry. 1917-1922.* b 1904. Major-General, Royal Engineers. Director of Fortification and Works, BAOR. Served RE, WW2, Africa, Middle East and Italy; OBE. Post-War service including in Japan. d 1990. (WWW)

CAVENDISH, *Henry Patrick. 1913-1919.* b 1901. Brigadier, Royal Engineers. Chief Engineer, Northern Command, York. Served initially in India, then in WW2 in desert campaign; OBE, DSO. Returned to India, then served in UK, and later became Chief Engineer, Land Forces, Hong Kong. CBE. d 1971.

CHATTERTON, *Frank William. 1847-1854.* b 1839. Colonel. Served Indian Army; Commander, Calcutta Volunteers. Later, Chief Commissioner, Andeman Islands. CIE. d 1924. (WWW)

ERSKINE-TULLOCH, *Piers Hector. 1939-1947.* b 1929. Major, HQ, 2nd Armoured Division, BAOR. Earlier, Army service including in Austria, Italy, Korea and Malaya (with Gurkha Rifles, MC); various UK and overseas staff appointments. Later, second-in-command of Sultan of Brunei's Gurkha Reserve Unit. d 2013.

149. Major Piers Hector Erskine-Tulloch.

EVANS, *James Morgan. 1932-1940.* b 1922. Colonel. Served Gurkha Rifles, WW2; MC. Post-War, various Army appointments, including as a Defence Attaché. Later, founder and Managing Director of an export company. Chairman, Vice-President, British Nepal Society; trustee, the Gurkha Museum. d 2017.

FLETCHER, *Henry Clyde. 1837-1843.* b 1828. Major-General. Served Madras Staff Corps. d 1913.

GERRARD-WRIGHT, *Richard Eustace John. 1942-1947.* b 1930. Major-General. Director, Territorial Army and Cadets. Army service worldwide, in particular in Egypt, Germany and Malaya, including Colonel Commandant, Queen's Division. Deputy Lieutenant, Cambridgeshire and Lincolnshire. CB, CBE, OBE, MBE. d 2012. (WWW)

GRAY, *Michael Stuart. 1942-1950.* b 1932. Knight (1986). Lieutenant-General. Colonel Commandant, Parachute Regiment. Served in various theatres of war, including Cyprus, Suez and Northern Ireland; Military Attaché, Washington. Lieutenant, Tower of London; Deputy Lieutenant, East Riding of Yorkshire. Various company President and Chairman appointments. OBE. *CH: President, ASB.* d 2011. (WWW)

HUNTER, *Robert Dow. 1929-1936.* b 1919. Colonel. Served in Royal Artillery in WW2; MC. Post-War, re-enlisted in the HAC, becoming Regimental Colonel. Chairman, PJ Hunter & Co, the first company in Britain to produce muesli. President, 323 Air Cadet Squadron. *CH: Governor.* d 2016.

LANE, *William Byam. 1874-1881.* b 1866. Lieutenant-Colonel. Served Indian Medical Service. Acting Director of Health Services, Mesopotamia. Previous posts included

150. Lieutenant-General Sir Michael Stuart Gray.

Inspector-General, Civil Jails (Mesopotamia) and Inspector-General of Prisons (Central Provinces, India). CBE, CIE. d 1945. (WWW)

LONGDEN, *Harry Leicester. 1913-1917.* b 1900. Major-General. Army service including WW2 in France and North West Europe; CB, CBE, OBE. d 1981. (WWW)

MORRIS, *George Mortimer. 1876-1883.* b 1868. Brigadier. Served Indian Army in WW1 in Mesopotamia; CB, DSO. d 1954. (WWW)

NORTH, *Thomas. 1904-1909.* b 1893. Major-General (US). Served (US Army) WW1 in France; work for American Battle Monuments Commission in France and Belgium; WW2, Section Head, Operations Staff. Later, Secretary-Executive of the Monuments Commission. d 1990.

151. Major-General Thomas North.

PASLEY, *Joseph Montagu Sabine. 1911-1913.* b 1898. Major-General. Commanded 1st Anti-Aircraft Group. Served WW1 and WW2; CBE. CB, MVO. d 1978. (WWW)

PIERCE, *Thomas. 1836-1842.* b 1827. Major-General. Served in the Bengal Army (1844-1876), fighting in the 1st and 2nd Sikh Wars. d 1885.

PRYNNE, *Harold Vernon. 1878-1885.* b 1869. Colonel. Army service including in China: in WW1, RAMC; CBE, DSO. Later, Chief Medical Officer, GPO. FRCS. d 1954. (WWW)

SPRINGHALL, *Robert John. 1910-1917*. b 1900. Brigadier. Army service, including in Egypt, North China and India; WW2, Middle East and Malta. Later, Commander, East and West Riding Areas, and Colonel, East Yorkshire Regiment and Prince of Wales's Own Regiment of Yorkshire. CB, OBE. d 1965. (WWW)

TIGHE, *Patrick Anthony Macartan. 1933-1939*. b 1923. Major-General. Colonel Commandant, Royal Signals. Served WW2 in RAF, then Royal Signals. Post-War, served Malaya (MBE) and Hong Kong; other posts in Royal Signals, including Signals Office-in-Chief, Army. Later, Chairman, Ex-Services Mental Welfare Society. CB. d 1989. (WWW)

TREMLETT, *Erroll Arthur Edwin. 1905-1909*. b 1893. Major-General. Army service in WW1 and in WW2, including command of various Ack-Ack defence groups and flying bomb deployment; CB, TD. Post-War, appointments included Hon Colonel, 656 Light Ack-Ack Regiment; Gold Staff Officer, coronation of Her Majesty the Queen. d 1982. (WWW)

TULLET, *Graham Beverley. 1953-1959.* b 1941. Lieutenant-Colonel, including service in Middle East. Post-Army, worked in Bombay where he became the last English President of the Bombay Yacht Club. Later, council member of the Royal Commonwealth Ex-Services League. OBE, MBE. d 2015.

WHITE, *Gilbert Anthony. 1925-1933*. b 1916. Major-General. Served WW2, N Africa and Italy; MBE. Later, military posts including on Earl Mountbatten's personal staff, Ministry of Defence, with BAOR, and Chief, Joint Services Liaison Organisation, Bonn. d 2003. (WWW)

152. Major-General Gilbert Anthony White.

WIGHT, *Ian Lyttleton. 1916-1922*. b 1905. Brigadier. Commandant, 1st Suffolks, Malaya. Previously, served WW2 in Abyssinia and Burma; DSO. Later, active role in Territorial Army. OBE. d 1989.

WILSON-HAFFENDEN, *Donald James. 1911-1916*. b 1900. Major-General. Served WW1, Washington; WW2, including quartermaster (Dunkirk) and deputy adjutant and quartermaster posts in India. In retirement, various Church Missionary Society posts. CBE. d 1986. (WWW)

2.31 *Royal Navy*

ADAMS, *William Leslie Graham. 1913-1919*. b 1901. Rear-Admiral. Director of Civil Defence, Southern Region. CB, OBE. d 1963. (WWW)

ALSTON, *Alfred Gilmore. 1877-1884*. b 1867. Captain, RN. Served WW1, including as Naval Transport Officer in Egypt; CMG. Initially, in Merchant Service. d 1954.

ARMSTRONG, *Douglas Henry Fyfe. 1916-1921*. b 1905. Captain, RN. Served for 38 years, including in WW2 commanding HMS *Marsdale* (DSC) and Commodore of Mediterranean convoys; RD. Later, public service in Sussex, including as Councillor and Alderman. Younger Brother, Trinity House; Master, Warden, Hon Company of Master Mariners. d 1976.

BARNARD, *John James. 1836-1841*. b 1826. Lieutenant, Royal Navy. Killed by Indians in 1851 at the Yukon River when searching for the lost expedition of Sir John Franklin. (#)

BOCKETT-PUGH, *Ian Hamilton. 1910-1917*. b 1900. Captain, RN. Naval service from 1920, serving in WW2 in HMS *Westcott* and HMS *Philoctetes*, being awarded DSO (1942), bar (1943), second bar (1944). d 1982.

CARTER, *Bernard. 1898-1900*. b 1885. Captain (S), RN. Served WW1, Paymaster Lieutenant-Commander; WW2 (post retirement), Base Accountant Officer, Alexandria. CBE. d 1954. (WWW)

CLEMITSON, *Francis Edward. 1912-1917*. b 1899. Rear-Admiral. Served WW2; later Deputy Engineer-in-Chief of the Fleet (Administration). CB. d 1981. (WWW)

ELLIOTT, *Harry Manly Casely. 1880-1887*. b 1872. Paymaster Rear-Admiral. Served WW1, HMS *Collingwood*. d 1946.

FORREST, *William Ivon Norman. 1923-1931*. b 1914. Surgeon Rear-Admiral (D). Director of Naval Dental Services, Ministry of Defence. Earlier, Dental House Surgeon, Guy's Hospital; then dental posts in the RN. CB. d 2002. (WWW)

HENDERSON, *Geoffrey Archer. 1924-1930*. b 1913. Rear-Admiral. Naval appointments included Secretary to Chief of Naval Staff in WW2; post-War, Director, Naval Office Appointments; and Director, Management and Support Intelligence, MoD. Later, Administration Manager, National Mutual Life Assurance Society. CB. d 1985. (WWW)

HEWLETT, *Graham. 1874-1879*. b 1864. Paymaster Captain. Naval service in Egyptian War; Secretary to Second in Command, North China; Secretary to Vice-Admiral commanding 2nd battle squadron. Served WW1; CB. Later, Anglican Church Commissioner, Malta. d 1937. (WWW)

JOHNSON, *Martin Challenor Page. 1921-1926*. b 1911. Lieutenant-Commander. During RNR service in WW2 was awarded the George Medal for making safe four torpedoes in the only German submarine to be captured and brought to Britain. Initially, in Merchant Service and the Prison and Borstal Commission, to which he returned, post-War; then senior seamanship instructor, National Nautical School. d 2004.

LAYBOURNE, *Alan Watson. 1911-1915.* b 1898. Rear-Admiral. Naval service, WW1, including Jutland; WW2 (including in USA); CBE. Later, Clerk to Dean and Chapter, Durham Cathedral. CB. *CH: Almoner, Governor.* d 1977. (WWW)

LEAHY, *James Palmer. 1881-1886.* b 1871. Engineer Rear-Admiral. Engineer Manager, Chatham Dockyard. Previously, Chief Engineer, Haulbowline (Cork) and Malta Dockyards. RN service WW1, including Battle of Jutland; OBE. CB. d 1940. (WWW)

OMMANNEY, *Henry Mortlock. 1879-1885.* b 1870. Paymaster Rear-Admiral. Served WW1, HMS *Ganges.* d 1935.

PEAREY, *Michael Alan. 1942-1951.* b 1933. Captain, RN. Naval service in many parts of the world, 1951-1986. President, Rugby Football Union. England rugby triallist (playing opposite WPC Davies, a CH master); captain, Royal Navy Rugby Union. *Clerk of CH (1986-1998); Governor.* d 1998. (#)

153. Lieutenant-Commander (later Captain) Michael Alan Pearey, RN.
with permission of Richard Pearey

SOLFLEET, *Gerald. 1885-1891.* b 1876. Paymaster Rear-Admiral. Served RN, including WW1, Paymaster Commander, HMS *Maidstone.* d 1942.

SUTTON, *Alan William Frank. 1923-1930.* b 1912. Captain, RN. Service including in WW2, being the last survivor of 42 young Naval airmen whose attack in 1940 on the Italian fleet changed the balance of power in the Mediterranean; DSC, later, bar; Post-War, various RN appointments worldwide; ADC to the Queen; Director, Royal Navy Staff College. Latterly, worked for Distillers Company and BP. CBE. d 2008.

TURNER, *Bradwell Talbot. 1917-1920.* b 1907. Commander, RN. Served WW2, DSO; Naval Attaché, Oslo. Barrister-at-law. Later, employed with Marconi Co. JP. CVO, OBE. d 1990. (WWW)

VINCENT, *Patrick Michael Causabon. 1934-1942.* b 1925. Captain, RN. Served WW2 in Far East, later including on Royal Yacht Britannia. Post-RN, worked for Institute of Chartered Accountants and as a fund-raiser for Great Ormond Street Children's Hospital. Chairman, Falkland Islands (where he had been born) Trust and Burma Star Association. CBE. d 2012.

WOOLLEY, *Charles Edward Allen. 1870-1878.* b 1863. Paymaster Rear-Admiral. RN service including Egyptian War, and in Boer War as Secretary to Commander-in-Chief, Cape Station. In WW1, Paymaster Captain, HMS *Attention;* CMG. d 1940. (WWW)

2.32 *Medical*

BAKER, *Charles Gaffney. 1920-1925.* b 1907. Physician (Cardiac), Guy's Hospital. Consultant Cardiologist, King Edward Convalescent Home for Officers. Served WW2, Lieutenant-Colonel RAMC; OBE. FRCP. d 1969. (WWW)

BROCK, *Russell Claude. 1915-1920.* b 1903. Baron (of Wimbledon), Life Peer (1965). Director, Department of Surgical Science, Royal College of Surgeons. Surgeon, Guy's Hospital and Brompton Hospital. Earlier, medical appointments, including Surgeon to LCC and Queen Mary's Hospital, Roehampton. Recipient of many medals for medical work. Author. Knight (1954). FRCS, FRCP. *CH: Almoner; Governor; President, ASB.* d 1980. (DNB, WWW)

154. Baron Russell Claude Brock.
by Elliott & Fry, © National Portrait Gallery, London

CREAMER, *Brian. 1938-1943.* b 1926. Consultant Physician (earlier Physician), St Thomas's Hospital; previously, Senior Lecturer in Medicine there. Other medical appointments included Visiting Professor, Iran; Hon Consultant in Gastroenterology to the Army. FRCP. *CH: Almoner, Governor.* d 2005. (WWW)

DOLMAN, *Claude Ernest. 1916-1925.* b 1906. Professor, Department of Bacteriology, University of British Columbia.

Previously, Professor, Department of Nursing and Health there. Later, Research Professor, Professor Emeritus of Microbiology, UBC. Earlier, work at University of Toronto, and trained in London under Sir Alexander Fleming. FRCP, FRSC, serving as President. d 1994.

FORD, *Leslie. 1924-1929.* b 1913. Consultant Physician, Fairfield Hospital, Beds. Previously, Physician Superintendent, Three Counties Hospital, Beds. Psychiatrist, earlier at St George's Hospital and then for Home Office. Called to the Bar. Initially in banking. d 1987.

GILBERTSON, *Moyna Patricia. 1942-1948.* b 1931. Physio-therapist. Executive Director, Association for Spina Bifida and Hydrocephalus. Chairman, Association of Paediatric Physiotherapists. OBE. *CH: Almoner, Governor; Special Recognition Award.* d 2016.

155. Moyna Patricia Gilbertson.

GUTHKELCH, *Arthur Norman. 1924-1933.* b 1915. Pro-fessor of Neurosurgery, Pittsburgh Children's Hospital and University Medical Centre, Tucson. Earlier, neurosurgeon posts at hospitals in UK, including in Manchester, Salford and Hull. Pioneering work related to "shaken baby syndrome". Served RAMC, WW2. Died 2016, aged 100.

HANSELL, *Peter. 1931-1938.* b 1921. Physician. Pioneer of medical photography. Founder, London School of Medical Photography. Founder Chairman, Institute of Medical and Biological Illustration. Chairman, Medical Group, Royal Photographic Society (which administers a scholarship in his memory). Various medical appointments, including Hon Consultant Physician, Westminster Hospital and Moorfields Eye Hospital. Author, editor. FRCP. d 2002.

OUNSTED, *Christopher. 1930-1940.* b 1921. Consultant Psychiatrist, Director, Human Development Research Unit (which he had established), Park Hospital for Children, Oxford. Pioneer in the field of children's brain diseases, the Hospital being a centre for international research on such diseases, especially epilepsy and meningitis. d 1992.

PEMBERTON, *John. 1922-1930.* b 1912. Professor of Social and Preventative Medicine, Queen's University, Belfast. Earlier, medical career at University College Hospital and Reader in Social Medicine, Sheffield University. FRCP. d 2010. (WWW)

PERRY, *Kenneth Murray Allan. 1920-1927.* b 1909. Physician, Royal Masonic Hospital; Consultant Physician, London Hospital, and Physician, London, Brentwood District and Warley Hospitals. Medical Adviser, Council for Training for the Ministry of the Church of England. FRCP. d 1984. (WWW)

PHILPS, *Frank Richard. 1924-1931.* b 1914. Consultant in Exfoliative Cytology, University College Hospital, London. Later, Director, Department of Cytology, Royal Free/UCH. Served RAF Medical Service, WW2; MBE. Nature film maker. d 1995. (WWW)

RAINS, *Anthony John Harding. 1930-1938.* b 1920. Professor of Surgery and Hon Consultant Surgeon, Charing Cross Hospital. Other medical appointments, including Lecturer and Senior Lecturer, University of Birmingham; Hon Consultant Surgeon to the Army; Chairman, Medical Commission on Accident Prevention. FRCS. CBE. d 2014. (WWW)

RICHES, *Eric William. 1909-1915.* b 1897. Knight (1958). Emeritus Surgeon and Urologist, Middlesex Hospital. Previously, various consultant urologist or urologist posts, including with the Army and Royal Masonic Hospital. Earlier, professorships in Texas and Toronto. Served WW1, Captain and Adjutant; MC. FRCS. *Treasurer of Christ's Hospital (1970-1976); Chairman, Council of Almoners; Governor; President, ASB; President, BSB.* d 1987. (DNB, WWW)

156. Sir Eric William Riches.

SAVIN, *Lewis Herbert. 1913-1918.* b 1901. Consultant (previously Senior) Surgeon, King's College Hospital. Earlier, various ophthalmic surgeon and consultant posts including to LCC General Hospitals and Whipps Cross Hospital; Senior Surgeon at Royal Eye Hospital. FRCS. d 1983. (WWW)

SEARS, *William Gordon. 1910-1918.* b 1901. Consultant Physician and Superintendent, Mile End Hospital, earlier coping with many casualties of the WW2 air raids in east London. President, Hunterian Society. Chairman, Board of Examiners, General Nursing Council. Author. MRCP. *CH: President, ASB, for which he is reported to have attended over 100 consecutive dinners (three a year).* d 1983.

WYLIE, *John Anthony Hamilton. 1928-1936.* b 1919. Bacteriologist, Brompton Hospital for Diseases of the Chest. Later, Urologist in charge of tissue culture, Royal Cancer

Hospital. Earlier, bacteriologist in Oxford and Surgeon Lieutenant-Commander, RN. d 1987.

2.33 Other business/industry (managerial)

BAND, *Edward George Underwood. 1936-1944.* b 1926. President (earlier founder), Band, Lavis & Associates (marine vehicles research), Washington. Previously, Research Professor, Webb Institute of Naval Architecture, New York; marine engineer and related work in England, Toronto and USA. d 2008.

157. Edward George Underwood Band.

BARBER, *Donald. 1915-1923.* b 1905. Director, Retail Distributors' Association. CBE, OBE. *Founded the publication "The Outlook" at CH.* d 1957. (WWW)

BARNETT, *Ben Lewis. 1906-1913.* b 1894. Knight (1952). Chairman, Commonwealth Telecommunications Board; Deputy Director General, GPO; Director, Pye Ltd; Adviser, ATV Ltd. Served WW1; MC. CB. *Almoner; Governor; President, CH Club.* d 1979. (WWW)

BRODIE, *Douglas Campbell. 1915-1918.* b 1902. President, CI Gardner Johnson Ltd (Vancouver, shipping). Earlier, shipping posts with Butterfield & Swire, China, and later in Japan. Died in 2006, aged 104.

BRUCE, *Robert Elton Spencer. 1945-1954.* b 1936. Editor, "Woman's Own". Previously, Editor "Literary Quarterly" and "New Chapter". d 1971. (WWW)

BUCKLEY, *James Arthur. 1928-1934.* b 1917. Chairman, East Midlands Gas Board. President, Institution of Gas Engineers. Member, British Gas Corporation. CBE. d 2004. (WWW)

BUNCH, *Austin Wyeth. 1929-1935.* b 1918. Knight (1983). Deputy Chairman, Electricity Council. Previously, Chairman, Southern Electricity Board. Chairman, British Electricity Internat Ltd. Later, Vice-Patron, National President, British Limbless Ex-Servicemen's Association. CBE, MBE. d 2008. (WWW)

BUNFORD, *John Farrant. 1912-1920.* b 1901. Chief Executive, National Provident Institution. Previously, Manager, Actuary, NPI. Later, a non-executive director there. Initially, with Scottish Amicable and Royal Exchange Assurance. Chairman, Life Offices' Association. President, Institute of Actuaries. FIA. *CH: Governor.* d 1992. (WWW) *(See illustration 145 on page 95.)*

CAVENDISH, *Edward Patrick James. 1951-1957.* b 1939. Publisher, specialising in partwork publications (periodicals). Initially, worked for British Printing Corporation, then co-founder Marshall Cavendish, which had a number of successes, including "Mind Alive". Left the company and founded Eaglemoss, again being successful with a range of magazine titles. A major supporter of children's education in Kenya. d 2000.

CHAMBERLAIN, *Walter Ernest. 1907-1910.* b 1894. Founder, with brother, Chamberlain Group of Companies (including construction and engineering). Previously, the brothers founded an Estate Agents and Surveyors. *Major benefactor to CH; Almoner; Governor; important role in improving the School's approach to property investment; President, OBRFC; President, ASB.* d 1959.

CLAY, *Harold Peter. 1915-1922.* b 1904. President, Metropolitan Pensions Association Group. Previously, undertook pioneering work on occupational pensions with MPA. Earlier, employed with Metropolitan Life Insurance Co, New York. FIA. *Major benefactor to CH; Governor; President, ASB; Secretary, OBRFC; Master, CH Lodge.* d 1970. (#)

COOKE, *Stanley Jack. 1917-1922.* b 1905. Chairman, Managing Director, Gilman & Co Ltd (trading), Hong Kong. Other appointments in HK including Deputy Chairman, HKSB. Various directorships in Far East. Initially, worked in banking and stockbroking. *Generous benefactor to the CH Development Appeal in the 1960s, and supporter of OBRFC and BSB (Life Director).* d 1972.

DURANT, *Henry William. 1914-1919.* b 1902. Opinion pollster and market researcher. Established the British Institute of Public Opinion (later Social Survey Ltd). Developed and improved statistical techniques for public and commercial surveys. Established the Market Research Society and its European counterpart. d 1982. (DNB)

FLETCHER, *Winston. 1948-1949.* b 1937. President, Institute of Practitioners in Advertising; Chairman, Advertising Association. Influential figure in advertising industry; established (and sold on) two advertising companies. CBE. d 2012.

FORBES, *James. 1934-1941.* b 1923. Chairman, Tate & Lyle Group Pension Fund. Various finance and director appointments, including Cadbury Schweppes, British Transport Hotels, Steetley plc and Compass Hotels. Forestry Commissioner. *Treasurer of Christ's Hospital (1987-1996); Chairman, Council of Almoners; Governor; President, BSB.* d 2011. (WWW)

158. James Forbes.

FORDE, *Ivo Mathew Leopold Dieskan. 1917-1925.* b 1906. Non-Executive Director, Kleinwort Benson. Previously, director and broker roles with the bank. Earlier, employed at Guaranty Trust Company, New York. Served WW2 with Royal Artillery; OBE. *CH: Almoner, Governor.* d 1989.

159. Louis Harold Gray.

GRAY, *Louis Harold. 1918-1924.* b 1905. Nuffield Fellow and Director, British Empire Cancer Campaign Research Unit in Radiobiology. The 'gray', a unit of radiation dosage, is named after him. Previously, various senior physicist posts. Earlier, Fellow, Trinity College, Cambridge. FRS. d 1965. (DNB, WWW)

GREEN, *Violet Evelyn Ivy Suzanne, [née GOODING]. 1922-1928.* b 1911. Owner and Chairman, "West Sussex County Times" for 45 years. When she died in 1987 she left around £1 million in trust to help the elderly in the Horsham District, one product of her legacy being the Suzanne Green Day Centre in Horsham.

HARDING, *Harold John Boyer. 1909-1917.* b 1900. Knight (1968). Consulting Civil Engineer. Earlier, joined John Mowlem & Co Ltd, becoming a director. Later, established own company; consultant to Channel Tunnel Study Group. Fellow, Imperial College, London. d 1986. (DNB, WWW)

HELLER, *Robert Gordon Barry. 1942-1950.* b 1932. Founder, Editor, business magazine "Management Today". Oversaw launch of similar magazines, including "Computing" and "Accountancy Age". Previously, Business Editor, "The Observer"; employed at "Financial Times", including as US Correspondent. Author. d 2012.

160. Robert Gordon Barry Heller.

HUNTER-JOHNSON, *David Alan. 1926-1933.* b 1915. Managing Director, J Henry Schroder Wagg & Co, and other appointments in company. Director of various Investment Trust Companies. Earlier, posts in Civil Service and for Church of England. Author. d 2011. (WWW)

KINGDON, *Roger Taylor. 1940-1949.* b 1930. Chief executive, Davy Corporation (engineering). Earlier, various appointments including in companies in Davy Group. CBE. *CH: Governor.* d 2015. (WWW)

KNOWLES, *William Charles Goddard. 1920-1926.* b 1908. Executive Director, Lloyd's Register of Shipping. Earlier, Manager, Butterfield & Swire (shipping) and Chairman, Taikoo Dockyard and Engineering Co Ltd, both Hong Kong. Various board posts in HK and Vice-Chancellor, HK University. CBE. d 1969.

MARLOW, *Roger Douglas Frederick. 1923-1929.* b 1912. Deputy Director-General, Institute of Directors. Earlier, Secretary and Chief Executive roles with trade bodies, including London Chamber of Commerce and Sino-British Trade Council. Served RNVR (Lieutenant Commander), WW2; DSC. JP. *CH: Governor.* d 1986. (WWW)

MAYER, *John. 1916-1921.* b 1904. Chairman, International Combustion Ltd. Previously, Joint Managing-Director, IC (Holdings) Ltd. Earlier, Chief Engineer, IC. CBE. d 1967. (WWW)

MENZIES, *Alexander Charles George. 1911-1917.* b 1897. Director of Research, Hilger & Watts (makers of optical measurement instruments). Previously, Professor of Physics, Southampton University; earlier, inaugurated Physics Department, Leicester University. d 1974.

MESSENGER, *William Aubrey. 1909-1915.* b 1898. Chairman, Saward, Baker & Co Ltd (Advertising Agency); previously, Director and Joint Managing Director there. President, Institute of Practitioners in Advertising, which he had helped to found. Leading role in National Advertising Benevolent Society. Served WW1, Royal Fusiliers; MC. *CH: Governor.* d 1975.

MORRELL, *James George. 1933-1939.* b 1923. Author, business forecaster. Founder Director, Henley Centre for Forecasting. Founder, James Morrell & Associates, economic consultants. Visiting Professor, Bradford University. Economic Adviser, Charterhouse Group. Publications include annual forecasts for the UK economy and the housing market. d 2000. (WWW)

NICHOLS, *Richard Everard. 1947-1955.* b 1938. Knight (1998). Lord Mayor of London, 1997-1998. Later, Chancellor, University of Ulster; co-founder and later Chairman of Board of Trustees of Cure Parkinson's Trust. Master, Worshipful Company of Salters. Solicitor, senior Partner and later Chairman, Sedgwick Kelly LLP. *CH: Almoner, Governor; Special Recognition Award.* d 2016. (WWW)

161. Sir Richard Everard Nichols.

O'CONNOR, *William Leslie Maurice. 1917-1923.* b 1905. Chairman, Calor Gas Holding Co. Previously, Deputy Chairman and Director, British Coking Association. Director of Carbonisation, National Coal Board. Chairman, British Coke Research Association. CBE. d 1959.

PATERSON, *Rex Munro. 1912-1918.* b 1902. Agricultural innovator and farmer. Initially farmed in Canada. In UK, developed grass-based system of dairy production. Became largest farmer in Hampshire. Later, developed farm mechanisation; work for NFU. OBE. d 1978. (DNB)

PHELAN, *Daniel John. 1968-1975.* b 1956. Founder, editor, Civil Society Media, a publishing company providing magazines for the charity sector, including "Charity Finance". Developed charity audit data and launched "Governance", a magazine for charity trustees. Helped to create the annual Charity Awards. Initially, worked in the record industry. d 2015.

PICKARD, *Michael John. 1950-1957.* b 1939. Chairman and Chief Executive, Royal London Mutual Insurance Society. Various senior appointments with financial, professional and charitable organisations, including Master, Worshipful Company of Insurers. *Governor; long-term involvement with many aspects of CH life, particularly OBRFC.* d 2014.

162. *Michael John Pickard.*
with permission of Russell Pickard

RANDOLPH, *Cyril George. 1910-1916.* b 1899. Chairman, Director, Sun Life Assurance Society and General Funds Investment Trust. Previously, a managing director, Glynn Mills & Co. *CH: Almoner; Governor; President, ASB.* d 1985. (WWW) Brother of Thomas Berkeley (para 2.28).

RECKNELL, *George Hugh. 1906-1909.* b 1893. Actuary, Manager, Director, National Mutual Life Assurance Society. Previously, Chairman, First Irish Investments Ltd; investment adviser to BOAC/BEA joint pension fund. FIA. d 1975. (WWW)

ROSS, *Alan Alistair [usually Angus]. 1930-1937.* b 1920. President, Chairman, Ogilvy, Benson & Mather (advertising);

163. *Alan Alistair Ross.*

President, Institute of Practitioners in Advertising; Chairman, Advertising Association. OBE. *Treasurer of Christ's Hospital (1976-1984); Almoner; Governor; President, BSB.* d 1984.

ROSS-GOOBEY, *George Henry. 1922-1928.* b 1911. Pension Fund Manager. Director, Investment Manager, Imperial Tobacco. At IT, initiated switch of investments from gilts to shares, beginning new approach to investing. President, National Association of Pension Funds. Earlier, employed in various insurance companies. *CH: Almoner; Governor; President, ASB.* d 1999. (DNB)

164. *George Henry Ross-Goobey.*

SELLERS, *Robert Firth. 1934-1943.* b 1924. Director (previously Deputy Director), Animal Virus Research Institute. Earlier, related work in England and Venezuela. Later, consultant on foreign animal diseases. FRSE. d 2011. (WWW)

SMITH, *Frank Ewart. 1909-1919.* b 1897. Knight (1946). Deputy Chairman, ICI. Earlier, various engineering and managerial posts, ICI, including Technical Director and

165. Piers Ashworth.

Chief Engineer. Various Government adviser posts. FRS. *CH: Almoner.* d 1995. (WWW)

SMITH, *Leslie Edward George. 1930-1935.* b 1919. Knight (1977). Chairman, Director, BOC Group plc. Previously, Director, British Gas plc and Chairman, British Oxygen and other posts in the company, including Group Managing Director and Accountant. d 2006. (DNB, WWW)

SPRAGG, *Cyril Douglas. 1907-1910.* b 1894. Secretary (previously Assistant Secretary), Royal Institute of British Architects. Later, various honorary appointments in international institutes of architecture. CBE. *CH: Governor.* d 1986. (WWW)

STEEL, *Joseph Lincoln Spedding. 1911-1918.* b 1900. Knight (1965). Director, ICI Ltd, Charterhouse Investment Trust. Chairman, Triplex Holdings Ltd. Earlier, posts at ICI including Chairman, Alkali Division. President, International Chamber of Commerce; Chairman, Overseas Committee, Federation of British Industries. JP. d 1985. (WWW)

STEPHENS, *Wilson Treeve. 1922-1928.* b 1912. Editor of "The Field"; later consultant. Earlier, consultant, "Country Illustrated"; newspaper editorial and staff posts. Author. d 2012, aged 100. (WWW)

STEPHENSON, *John Robin. 1940-1948.* b 1931. Secretary, Marylebone Cricket Club, International Cricket Council. Previously, Assistant Secretary, MCC, managing various overseas tours. Earlier, military service, including in Egypt and Korea, Commanding Officer, 5 Queen's Regiment, Lieutenant-Colonel; OBE. CBE. d 2003. (WWW)

TEMPLE, *Richmond. 1903-1908.* b 1893. Director, Dorchester Hotel Company; previously, Director, Savoy Hotel Company. Earlier, public relations adviser and business consultant to many large companies, following employment in Canada and India. *CH: Almoner, Governor.* d 1958.

THORNTON, *Michael James. 1930-1937.* b 1919. Chief of Economic Intelligence Department, Bank of England. Earlier,

Deputy Chief Cashier. Employed for 40 years at the Bank. Served WW2, Major; MC. CBE. d 1989. (WWW)

TRINDER, *Arthur William. 1912-1918.* b 1901. Bond dealer. Manager, Union Discount Company of London Ltd which he had joined soon after leaving school. Chairman, London District Markets Association. d 1959. (DNB)

WARING, *Henry William Allen. 1915-1923.* b 1906. Director, Guest, Keen & Nettlefold Ltd. Deputy Chairman, Director, GKN companies. Chairman, Steel Committee, Economic Commission for Europe. Earlier, a chartered accountant; British Consular work in Europe and Control Commissioner for Germany. CMG. d 1962. (WWW)

WHEBLE, *Bernard Spencer. 1916-1921.* b 1904. Chairman, International Chamber of Commerce Commission and International Chamber of Commerce Banking Commission. A founding father of electronic data interchange, by which commercial transactions, such as invoices and receipts, pass automatically between companies, and adviser on its benefits. Author. CBE. d 1998.

2.34 *Other business/industry (professions)*

ASHWORTH, *Piers. 1943-1950.* b 1931. Queen's Counsel, a Recorder of the Crown Court. Chairman, Bar Mutual Indemnity Fund Ltd. *CH: Almoner, Governor.* d 2004. (WWW)

BARR, *Reginald Alfred. 1932-1939.* b 1920. Circuit Judge; formerly Judge of County Courts. Standing Counsel for the Registrar of Restrictive Trading Agreements. d 2007. (WWW)

BERTHON, *Peter Lorraine Ashton. 1916-1922.* b 1906. Designer of racing cars and engines. Co-founder, English Racing Automobiles. Co-Designer of BRM racing car, his V8 engine winning the 1962 World Championship for BRM and Graham Hill. d 1971.

166. Peter Lorraine Ashton Berthon.

BOOTH, *David. 1919-1925.* b 1908. Architect, establishing his own practice, also a furniture designer. President, Berks, Bucks and Oxon Architectural Association. FRIBA. d 1962.

CARRINGTON, *Jack Herbert. 1921-1926.* b 1909. Table tennis player and coach, particularly to Johnny Leach, with whom he won an English doubles championship, the pair also being runners up in the World championships. On retiring as a player, he continued work as a coach. d 1984.

CHILDS-CLARKE, *Arthur William. 1916-1922.* b 1905. Played 66 games of first-class cricket between 1923 and 1948, for Middlesex and Northants (Captain). Employed variously in insurance, banking, sales and as a publican. d 1980.

CHRIST, *George Elgie. 1916-1921.* b 1904. Parliamentary Liaison Officer, Conservative Party; Editor, "Weekly News Letter". Previously, political correspondent, "Daily Telegraph". CBE. *CH: Almoner; Governor; Vice-President, BSB.* d 1972. (WWW)

DAVIS, *William. 1831-1836.* b 1821. Emigrated to Australia shortly after leaving CH. Initially, worked in banking and at a cattle station. Inherited an estate, farming wheat. Introduced cricket locally, with much success. JP. d 1910.

GAINSBOROUGH, *George Fotheringham. 1926-1933.* b 1915. Barrister-at-law. Secretary, Institution of Electrical Engineers. Earlier, on scientific staff, National Physical Laboratory, and employment at Ministries of Supply and Aviation. Hon Sec, Commonwealth Engineering Conference and World Federation of Engineering Organisations. CBE. *CH: Governor; President, ASB.* d 2008. (WWW)

GURNEY, *Norah Kathleen May, [née DEWAR]. 1933-1939.* b 1921. Director, Borthwick Institute of Historical Research, York University, mainly concerned with church records. Previously, Chief Archivist and researcher there. Earlier, with Sheffield City Library. Served WW1 in Naval Intelligence. d 1974.

HEISELER, *Patricia Joy, [née PAGET]. 1929-1936.* b 1919. Deputy Director, National Book League. Previously, Personnel Manager and Senior Administrative Assistant to the Director (JE Morpurgo, para 2.23). Earlier, War service with ATS and employment in Inland Waterways. d 1996.

HUTTON, *David Graham. 1916-1920.* b 1904. Economist; author. Barrister-at-law. Earlier, posts at London School of Economics, "The Economist", the Foreign Office and the Ministry of Information. OBE. d 1988. (WWW)

JOHNSON, *George Arthur. 1915-1922.* b 1903. Editor, "The Statesman", Calcutta and Delhi. Previously, Assistant Editor, "The Statesman" and "The Mail", Madras. d 1972. (WWW)

KING, *Mark Howard Robert. 1926-1934.* b 1915. Chairman, National Employers' Mutual Assurance Association. Previously, with Commercial Union for over 40 years. International rugby referee; President, London Society of Rugby Referees. CBE. d 2003.

LING, *Arthur George. 1924-1931.* b 1913. Architect and Town Planner, Arthur Ling & Associates. Previously, various related posts, including Chief Planning Officer, LCC, and City Architect and Planning Officer, Coventry; Professor of Architecture and Civic Planning, Nottingham University;

and visiting Professor in Chile, Australia and New Zealand. FRIBA. d 1995. (WWW)

LYNAM, *Charles. 1836-1843.* b 1829. Architect, receiving many commissions for public buildings in Stoke; also Borough Surveyor. Much local work as an archaeologist. Mayor, magistrate in Stoke. FRIBA, FSA. d 1921.

MOOTE, *Margaret Louise, [née TUTT]. 1934-1942.* b 1923. Following Bachelor's and PhD degrees at Oxford University, worked initially in England in nuclear chemistry, then for Atomic Energy, Canada. Later, studied psychology and computer science, and undertook much local voluntary work. d 2005.

PALEY, *Edward Graham. 1832-1838.* b 1823. Architect, working mainly on the design of new churches, including St Peter's (later Lancaster Cathedral), and also the Royal Albert Asylum in the city. *His was one of four unsuccessful firms contesting the final stage of the competition to build CH, Horsham.* FRIBA. d 1895.

PEARCE, *Thomas Neill. 1917-1922.* b 1905. Cricketer: captain of Essex, playing 250 first-class games between 1929 and 1950, later President; test selector; manager of MCC tours. Rugby player and international referee. Initially, banker; later Director of a distillery company. Served WW2; TD. OBE. *CH: Governor; strong supporter of OBRFC (including President); President, ASB.* d 1994.

167. Thomas Neill Pearce.

PEWTRESS, *Alfred William. 1904-1907.* b 1891. Played 50 games of first-class cricket between 1919 and 1925, for Lancashire. Served WW1, Captain, Royal Field Artillery; MC. d 1960.

PHILLIPS, *Francis Hugh Addison. 1911-1917.* b 1901. Revered BBC announcer (generally known as "Frank"), making a particular contribution during WW2: "The voice of the Establishment at its best". Other broadcasting work for BBC. Appeared as the BBC announcer in the film "The Dam Busters". Earlier, engineer then professional singer, touring widely. d 1980.

RANCE, *Patrick Lowry Cole Holwell. 1927-1936.* b 1918. Cheesemonger and writer on cheese. Following military career, including WW2 (Major), and various jobs, became a shopkeeper, stocking a range of some 200 cheeses, including the Dorset blue vinny which was thought to be extinct. Later, continued his work in France. d 1999. (DNB)

RAY-JONES, *Holroyd Anthony. 1950-1957.* b 1941. Photographer. Initially, studied graphic design, including at Yale University. Focussed on photography and returned to England, undertaking commercial work, then a major project (in black/white) on the British in their leisure time, published as "A Day Off: an English Journal". Returned to USA, then back to England where he died in 1972. (DNB)

SAWYER, *Henry George. 1851-1856.* b 1841. Head Keeper, Richmond Park, for nearly 40 years, where he was involved with arranging shooting parties for royalty, his house being used to entertain them for luncheon. d 1916.

SCHOOLING, *Anthony John Marshall. 1930-1937.* b 1920. Broadcaster. Senior Lecturer in Radio, Polytechnic of Central London. Earlier, established broadcasting system for schools in Singapore; scriptwriter, presenter, BBC. d 1991.

SHEARS, *David John Arthur. 1935-1944.* b 1926. Served as a foreign correspondent with the "Daily Telegraph", particularly in Washington and in Germany, where he helped to expose an espionage ring. Earlier, employed with Reuters in Pakistan, Holland and Washington. d 2013.

SIMON, *Noel Murray. 1931-1939.* b 1921. Pioneer of conservation in East Africa. Served WW2, including in Kenya. Returned there post-War, becoming Chairman, Kenya Wildlife Society; then worked at World Conservation Union, Switzerland. Returned to UK, where he wrote many books on conservation and some for children. d 2008.

SMITH, *Geoffrey. 1937-1944.* b 1925. Played 42 games of first-class cricket between 1951 and 1958, for Kent, being, at his death (in 2016), the county's oldest living capped player. *CH: Governor; Editor, Old Blues section of "The Blue".*

STEPHENS, *Olive, [née VOYSEY-MARTIN]. 1930-1935.* b 1918. After being runner-up in the BBC Radio's "Brain of Britain" quiz programme, she became a regular member of the panel in the popular "Ask Me Another" TV series. d 1987.

STONE, *Leslie Charles. 1945-1952.* b 1934. Political journalist. Initially, worked in USA and then for the Westminster Press in the UK. Joined BBC, becoming head of the current affairs talks section in the World Service, and then chief commentator, his particular expertise being with American politics. Post-BBC, lectured in the USA. d 2001.

STUBBS, *Peter Hugh Satow. 1939-1946.* b 1928. Deputy Editor, "New Scientist", writing on challenging scientific matters, particularly geophysics and space exploration. d 1994.

WILLIAMS, *Evan Clifford. 1905-1911.* b 1892. Industrial scientist. Professor of Chemical Engineering, University College, London. Research Director and Vice-President, Shell Development Co, California; later, other Research Director posts in USA. Initially, a research chemist. d 1973. (WWW)

YATES, *Ivan Michael. 1936-1944.* b 1926. Assistant Editor, Chief Leader Writer, "The Observer". Previously, posts on "The Observer" and with other newspapers, covering topics such as politics and church affairs. Earlier, researcher. d 1975.

2.35 *Public service (UK)*

ADAMS, *Carol. 1959-1965.* b 1948. Educationalist. Chief

168. Carol Adams.

Executive, General Teaching Council for England. Previously, Director of Education for Wolverhampton and Chief Education Officer for Shropshire. Earlier, Chief Inspector for Equal Opportunities, ILEA. d 2007. (DNB)

BAVIN, *Alfred Robert Walter. 1928-1935.* b 1917. Deputy Secretary, Department of Health and Social Security, Ministry of Health. Previously, postings in MoH (including Principal Private Secretary to the Minister) and Cabinet Office. CB. d 2006. (WWW)

BELCHER, *Ronald Harry. 1925-1934.* b 1916. Under Secretary, Ministry of Overseas Development. Previously, Indian Civil Service, Commonwealth Relations Office. Deputy High Commissioner, South Africa, Delhi. CMG. d 2002. (WWW)

BELL, *Robert Donald Murray. 1926-1935.* b 1916. Under Secretary, Scottish Department. Earlier Civil Service posts included Private Secretary to the Secretary of State for Scotland. CB. d 2001. (WWW)

BLUNDUN, *Percy Young. 1895-1902.* b 1882. Civil servant. Principal Assistant Secretary, Ministry of Labour and National Service. Served also in Board of Trade and, initially, in Estates Duty Office, Dublin. Linguist. d 1951.

BULLARD, *John Eric. 1915-1922.* b 1903. Under Secretary, National Assistance Board. Previously, Civil Service posts in Treasury and Unemployment Assistance Board. Initially, first place in CS examinations in his year. *Later, master, Christ's Hospital; Governor.* CB. d 1961. (WWW)

CLARKE, *Richard William Barnes. 1922-1928.* b 1910. Knight (1964). Permanent Secretary, Ministry of Technology, Ministry of Aviation. Later, various industry appointments, including Chairman, Stothert & Pitt (engineering); Director, Courtaulds, EMI, GKN, Guinness Peat Group and Orion Insurance Co. CB, OBE. d 1975. (DNB, WWW)

COLEMAN, *Herbert Cecil. 1905-1909.* b 1893. Under Secretary, Ministry of Pensions; previously, Accountant-General and other posts in the Ministry. Served WW1, Captain; MC. CBE. d 1956. (WWW)

DREW, *Arthur Charles Walter. 1922-1931.* b 1912. Knight (1964). Public servant. Chairman, Museum of Empire and Commonwealth. Previously, Permanent Under Secretary of

169. Sir Richard William Barnes Clarke.
by Walter Bird, © National Portrait Gallery, London

State at the War Office and at the Ministry of Defence. Later, appointments at British Museum, Imperial War and RAF Museums; Chairman, Museum and Galleries Commission. JP. CB. *CH: President, ASB.* d 1993. (WWW)

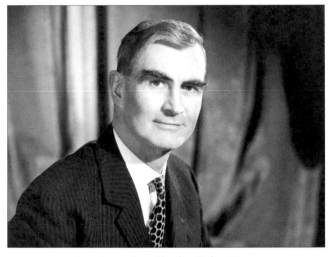

170. Sir Arthur Charles Walter Drew.
by Walter Bird, © National Portrait Gallery, London

DYMOKE, *John Lindley Marmion. 1937-1943.* b 1926. Vice Lord-Lieutenant of Lincolnshire; High Sheriff of Lincolnshire. The 34th Hereditary Queen's Champion, serving as bearer of the Union Standard at the coronation in 1953. Military service (Lieutenant-Colonel), Far East, Middle East, Europe and USA. Later, farmer and landowner. MBE. d 2015. (WWW)

171. John Lindley Marmion Dymoke.

FRANKLIN, *Reginald Hector. 1906-1909.* b 1893. Knight (1950). Civil servant. Deputy Secretary, Ministry of Agriculture, Fisheries and Food. Previous posts there included Private Secretary to successive Ministers. CB, CBE. *President, CH Club.* d 1957. (WWW)

FRASER, *William Robert. 1903-1910.* b 1891. Knight (1944). Civil servant. Deputy Chairman and Permanent Secretary, Central Land Board and War Damage Commission. Served previously in Department of Health and HM Treasury. KCB; KBE; CB. d 1985. (WWW)

GENTRY, *Jack Sydney Bates. 1911-1916.* b 1899. Public Servant, UK and India. General Manager, Tees Conservancy Commission. Earlier, Deputy Regional Port Director, Calcutta. JP. CBE, OBE, CIE. *CH: Governor.* d 1978. (WWW)

GOODMAN, *Vyvian Edwin. 1902-1905.* b 1889. Public Servant. Deputy Lieutenant and High Sheriff of Bedfordshire. Chairman, Bedfordshire Education Committee. JP. MBE. *CH: President, ASB.* d 1961. (WWW)

GRANT, *Gordon. 1918-1924.* b 1907. Secretary, Trade Marks, Patents and Designs Federation. Previously, Under Secretary, and Comptroller-General, Patents, Designs and Trade Marks. both Board of Trade; and Principal Private Secretary to Minister of Labour. CB. d 1979. (WWW)

HERZIG, *Christopher. 1936-1945.* b 1926. Civil servant. Director, External Relations, International Atomic Energy Agency. Previously, Under Secretary, Departments of Trade and Industry, and Energy; earlier, Private Secretary to Lord President of Council and Minister of Technology. Served at Bletchley Park, WW2. CBE. d 1993. (WWW)

HODSOLL, *Eric John. 1904-1911.* b 1894. Knight (1944). Wing Commander. Civil servant, Home Office. Inspector General, Air Raid Precautions Department and Civil Defence and Emergency Planning Departments, WW2. Served RAF, WW1, including commanding a seaplane base, and later in India. CB. d 1971. (DNB, WWW)

172. Sir Eric John Hodsoll.
by EJ Elliott & Fry, © National Portrait Gallery, London

KING, *Edward John Boswell. 1904-1907*. b 1891. Public servant. Served variously in London County Council, including as Chief Officer of Supplies. First President, Institute of Public Supplies. Served WW1, Lieutenant, RGA; MC. CBE. d 1975. (WWW)

KIRKMAN, *Charles Alfred. 1933-1941*. b 1922. Under Secretary, Medical Research Council, his work there as a scientific administrator being much concerned with the financing of research. Earlier, served in Colonial Office. CBE. d 2009.

LEWIS, *Eric William Charles. 1926-1933*. b 1914. Controller of Death Duties, Board of Inland Revenue. Previously, posts in Estate Duty Office, IR. Later, member, Civil Service Appeals Board. CB. d 1981. (WWW)

LIVESEY, *Robert Cowburn. 1940-1946*. b 1928. Director, National Ports Council. Later, Manager, Port of Milford Haven; consultant on legal aspects of ports and harbours. Earlier, civil servant, Ministry of Transport, then with NPC. CBE. d 2005.

MANNING, *Frederick Edwin Alfred. 1908-1911*. b 1897. Director of the Post Office in Wales and Border Counties. Previously, Civil Service posts in Home Office and Foreign Office; various appointments for University of London. Served Tank Corps, WW1; MC, TD. CBE. d 1987. (WWW)

MARRIOTT, *Patrick Arthur. 1908-1916*. b 1899. Governor, HM Prison, Parkhurst, Isle of Wight. Previously, Governor at Lincoln, Brixton and Pentonville. d 1980. (WWW)

MEREWETHER, *Edward Rowland Alworth. 1902-1908*. b 1892. Consultant in Industrial Health, Admiralty; Senior Medical Inspector of Factories, Ministry of Labour and National Service. Chief Medical Adviser, Ministry of Agriculture Fisheries and Food. Earlier, barrister-at-law. Hon Physician to King George VI. CB, CBE. FRSE, FRCP. d 1970. (DNB, WWW)

MUIR, *Alec Andrew. 1919-1928*. b 1909. Chief Constable, Durham Constabulary. Earlier, with Metropolitan Police. Deputy Lieutenant, County Durham. CBE. QPM. d 1997. (WWW)

REED, *Michael. 1923-1930*. b 1912. Registrar General; Director, Office of Population Censuses and Surveys. Previously, Under Secretary, Ministry of Health; Private Secretary to the Minister. CB. d 1985. (WWW)

RICKS, *John Plowman. 1922-1928*. b 1910. Knight (1964). Solicitor to the Post Office. Earlier, various appointments in the PO, including Assistant Solicitor. *CH: Governor*. d 1991. (WWW)

RIDGE, *Anthony Hubert. 1925-1932*. b 1913. Director General (previously Deputy DG), International Bureau, Universal Postal Union. Earlier, Director and other posts in GPO, including Private Secretary to Postmaster General. *CH: Governor*. d 2010. (WWW)

ROBERTS, *Keith Varnden. 1936-1943*. b 1925. Head, Theoretical Physics Division, UK Atomic Energy Authority. Major contributor to UK post-War research on thermonuclear weapons and later to the development of large-scale computing. Earlier, Research Fellow, King's College, Cambridge. d 1985.

ROOT, *Frederick James. 1917-1924*. b 1906. Deputy Secretary, Ministry of Public Buildings and Works. Previously, Civil Service posts, including Private Secretary to successive Ministers of Works. CB. d 1982. (WWW)

SPEED, *Eric Bourne Bentinck. 1904-1914*. b 1895. Knight (1943). Permanent Under Secretary of State for War. Previously, various Civil Service posts, including in War Office and Treasury, and as Private Secretary to Stanley Baldwin. Served WW1 (Captain); MC. KCB, KBE. *CH: Governor; President, ASB*. d 1971. (WWW)

STEWART, *Robert Michael Maitland. 1918-1925*. b 1906. Baron (of Fulham) (1979). Life Peer. Served two spells as Secretary of State for Foreign Affairs. Also, Secretary of State for Education and Science and for Economic Affairs. MP, Fulham East, Fulham and Hammersmith, Fulham. Later, Member of the European Parliament. Initially, a schoolmaster. PC, CH. d 1990. (DNB, WWW)

173. Baron Robert Michael Maitland Stewart.
by Bassano Ltd, © National Portrait Gallery, London

STOTESBURY, *Herbert Wentworth. 1927-1935*. b 1916. Assistant Under Secretary of State, Probation and Aftercare Department, Home Office. Earlier, various Civil Service appointments in Home Office. d 1988. (WWW)

SUTHERLAND, *Anthony Frederic Arthur. 1926-1935*. b 1916. Under Secretary, Department of Employment. Previously, served in Ministry of Labour, including as Principal Private Secretary to various Ministers; Counsellor (Labour), British Embassy, Rome. d 1996. (WWW)

SYMONS, *Ronald Stuart. 1917-1923*. b 1904. Minister in UK Delegation to OECD. Initially, Indian Civil Service, with posts in the Departments of Government, including Deputy Secretary and Joint Secretary, Finance Department. Then, Home Civil Service, serving as Assistant Secretary in Treasury. CMG, CIE. d 1977. (WWW)

TUCKER, *Brian George. 1932-1939*. b 1922. Deputy

Secretary, Department of Energy. Member, UK Atomic Energy Authority. Earlier, various Civil Service posts, then Ministry of Power, including Principal Private Secretary to the Minister; Ministry of Technology and Cabinet Office. CB, OBE. *CH: Governor.* d 2005. (WWW)

VEAL, *John Bartholomew. 1920-1926.* b 1909. Civil Aviation Safety Adviser, DTI. Previously, various air training and safety roles in Government departments, including Chief Inspector of Accidents (Board of Trade) and Director General of Safety and Operations (DTI). Initially, RAF service, then Reserve. Commanded navigation and flying training schools in WW2; AFC. CBE. *CH: Governor.* Died 2009, aged 99. (WWW)

WILLIAMS, *Henry Jameson Middleton. 1908-1913.* b 1897. Lieutenant-Colonel. Served WW1, France. Then work for War Graves Commission including co-ordinating burial arrangements and helping to choose five unknown soldiers one of whom was buried at Westminster Abbey. Employed with Lewis Group, Liverpool, but returned to help the WGC post-WW2. d 1993.

WILLIAMSON, *William Henry. 1861-1867.* b 1852. Leading member of the Corporation of London, including a Deputy Alderman; a lieutenant for the City; Chairman, Port Sanitary Committee. Liveryman, Fishmongers' Company. An oyster salesman who gave much support to the Billingsgate Mission. d 1911.

WOODS, *John Harold Edmund. 1906-1914.* b 1895. Knight (1945). Permanent Secretary, Board of Trade. Previously, Permanent Secretary, Ministry of Production. Earlier, posts in Treasury. Later, various Board appointments with official organisations and companies, including English Electric Co Ltd and Marconi. GCB, CB, MVO. *CH: Almoner, Governor; President, ASB.* d 1962. (DNB, WWW)

2.36 *Public service (overseas)*

BATES, *William Stanley. 1932-1939.* b 1920. Ambassador to Korea. Previously, High Commissioner, Guyana; Head, Communications Department, FCO. CMG. d 1993. (WWW)

BRANT, *Colin Trevor. 1939-1948.* b 1929. Diplomatic Service. Ambassador to Qatar. Later, Consul General, South Africa; international business consultant. Earlier posts including in Middle East and Counsellor, Washington. CMG, CVO. *CH: Almoner, Governor.* d 2015. (WWW)

CUMMINGS, *Henry Reginald. 1896-1902.* b 1886. Director, Information Division, European Office, United Nations Relief and Rehabilitation Association. Earlier, worked on various newspapers; for League of Nations Secretariat; adviser, BBC; freelance broadcaster. d 1970.

CUSDEN, *Victor Vincent. 1905-1909.* b 1893. Diplomat. Consul-General, Izmir, Turkey; previously CG and acting-CG posts mainly in Europe. OBE. d 1980. (WWW)

DAVIDSON, *James Alfred. 1933-1939.* b 1922. Diplomat. FCO posts including Governor, British Virgin Islands, and High Commissioner, Brunei. Earlier, served in Royal Navy, Commander; and called to the Bar. OBE. d 2004. (WWW)

EDMONDS, *Cecil John. 1902-1906.* b 1889. Diplomat. Various appointments in Middle East, including work for the League of Nations, and Adviser to Ministry of Interior, Iraq.

Later, Minister in HM Foreign Service and Lecturer, SOAS. CMG, CBE, OBE. d 1979. (WWW)

EDMUNDS, *Percy James. 1902-1909.* b 1890. Knight (1946). Chief Engineer, Indian Posts and Telegraph Department; previously, Director of Wireless there. CIE. d 1959. (WWW)

FRAMPTON, *Algernon de Kewer. 1913-1920.* b 1904. Colonial Service. Director of Agriculture, Barbados. Previously, Professor of Agriculture, Trinidad; agricultural adviser, British West Indies, and related work there and in Nigeria, British Guiana and Malaya. CMG. d 1974. (WWW)

FRAMPTON, *Henry James. 1910-1916.* b 1897. Indian Civil Service. Served WW1, Acting Captain; MC. CSI, CIE. d 1980. (WWW)

HEATH, *Andrew. 1964-1971.* b 1953. Diplomat. Deputy High Commissioner to New Zealand. Previously, various FCO posts, including in Kuwait and Washington. d 1996. (WWW)

HOPSON, *Donald Charles. 1926-1934.* b 1915. Knight (1968). Diplomat. Ambassador to Argentina. Previously, Ambassador to Venezuela, Mongolia and Laos. Earlier, consular posts in Saigon, Budapest and Buenos Aires. Served WW2, major (Commandos); DSO, MC, TD. CMG. d 1974. (WWW)

174. Sir Donald Charles Hopson.
by Walter Bird, © National Portrait Gallery, London

JENNINGS, *Percival Henry. 1914-1920.* b 1903. Director-General, Overseas Audit Service. Previously, Auditor and Director of Audit in Gold Coast, Nigeria and Hong Kong. CBE. d 1995. (WWW)

KEMP, *Charles. 1910-1914.* b 1897. UK Senior Trade Commissioner and Economic Adviser to the High Commissioner, South Africa. Previously, various Trade Commissioner roles in East Africa, South Africa and Canada. CMG, CBE. d 1983. (WWW)

LEWEN, *John Henry. 1931-1939*. b 1920. Ambassador to the People's Republic of Mozambique. Previously, Diplomatic Service posts including for Council of Ministers of the European Communities; Consul-General, Jerusalem and Head of Chancery, Rabat. CMG. d 2008. (WWW)

MIDGLEY, *Eric Atkinson. 1924-1932*. b 1913. Ambassador to Switzerland. Previously, Diplomatic Service posts in The Hague and Washington. Earlier, Indian Civil Service; Trade Commissioner. Delhi. CMG, MBE. d 2000. (WWW)

MITCHELL, *Leslie Herbert. 1925-1932*. b 1914. Diplomat. Various appointments including First Secretary, Bonn and Washington, and Second Secretary, Copenhagen. CBE, OBE. d 1989. (WWW)

NEWNS, *Alfred Foley Francis Polden. 1919-1928*. b 1909. Knight (1963). Secretary to Cabinet, Government of Bahamas. Previously, Deputy/Acting Governor, Sierra Leone; Adviser to Government there post-independence. Colonial Service posts in Nigeria. Consultant to several governments on internal political procedure. CMG, CVO. FRSA. d 1998. (WWW)

175. Sir Alfred Foley Francis Polden Newns.

OWEN, *John Simpson. 1922-1932*. b 1912. Conservationist. Director of National Parks, Tanzania. Previously, political service in Sudan. Later, consultant on National Parks in Eastern and Central Africa. OBE. d 1995. (WWW)

SANDFORD, *George Ritchie. 1904-1911*. b 1892. Knight (1947). Governor, Commander-in-Chief, Bahamas. Previously, Administrator, East Africa High Commission; Chief Secretary, East African Governors' Conference. Earlier, barrister-at-law; various Colonial Office posts, including in Kenya, Tanganyika and Palestine. CMG, OBE. d 1950. (WWW) (#)

SHELDON-WILLIAMS, *Inglis Patrick. 1918-1926*. b 1908. Worked for British Council in various countries. Best known for his work (unfinished at his death) on the magnum opus of the philosopher, Johannes Scottus Eriugena. d 1973.

SMITH, *Lawrence Delpré. 1915-1924*. b 1905. Senior Puisne Judge, Supreme Court, Sarawak, North Borneo and Brunei. Earlier, various Colonial Service and legal posts, including in Tanganyika, Palestine and Gambia. *CH: Hon Treasurer, BSB.* d 1996. (WWW)

STEIL, *John Wellesley. 1908-1912*. b 1899. Secretary for African Affairs, Uganda. Earlier, Colonial Service roles in Uganda, including District Officer and Senior Provincial Commissioner. Later, farmer in Australia. CMG, MBE. d 1983. (WWW)

TANDY, *Arthur Harry. 1915-1922*. b 1903. Knight (1962). Diplomat. Ambassador to the European Communities. Previously, Minister, British Embassy, Buenos Aires; Consul and Counsellor postings in Europe and USA. CBE. d 1964. (WWW)

WARD, *Wilfrid Arthur. 1904-1908*. b 1892. Commissioner for Malaya in the UK. Previously, Resident Commissioner, Selangor; Under Secretary, Straits Settlement. Served WW1, Captain; MC. Then Malayan Civil Service. CMG. d 1981. (WWW)

WHITEHEAD, *John Stainton. 1943-1950*. b 1932. Knight (1986). Ambassador to Japan. Previously, various Diplomatic Service posts including First Secretary, Washington and Tokyo; Counsellor, Bonn, and Minister, Tokyo. Later, various board appointments with official organisations and companies particularly related to Japan; Chairman, Daiwa Anglo-Japanese Foundation. GCMG, CVO. *CH: Almoner.* d 2013. (WWW)

WISE, *John Humphrey. 1902-1909*. b 1890. Knight (1943). Secretary to Governor, Borneo. Counsellor to Governor and Adviser to Secretary of State, Burma. Earlier, various posts in Indian Civil Service. Later, Deputy Chairman, Raw Cotton Commission. CBE. d 1984. (WWW)

WITHERS-GILL, *Joseph, [at CH, Joseph GILL]. 1866-1874*. b 1858. Colonial Service, including Political Resident in Northern Nigeria. Earlier, worked in South Africa. Later, served in Ministry of Munitions, WW1; OBE. d 1931.

WOMERSLEY, *Denis Keith. 1931-1938*. b 1920. Diplomat. Foreign Office appointments in Middle East and Europe, including Bonn. CBE. *CH: Governor.* d 2010. (WWW)

WOODWARD, *Denys Cuthbert. 1911-1917*. b 1902. General Manager, Nigerian Railways. Previously, with London & North Western Railways. Later, Chairman, Nigeria Hotels Ltd. CMG. d 1972. (WWW)

2.37 *"Worthies" and Benefactors.*

See para 2.39

2.38 *Christ's Hospital*

ALLISON, *Alan Evan. 1916-1922*. b 1905. *Clerk of CH (1958-1966), serving in the Counting House for over 40 years; Governor.* d 1985.

BARNES, *Sidney. 1898-1904*. b 1887. *Various posts over many years for OBRFC and for BSB (including Vice-President and Secretary).* Employed with Holt & Co (banking) for 44 years, becoming Chief Cashier. Served WW2, Secret Service; MBE. d 1962.

BINNS, *Wilfred Leslie. 1917-1922*. b 1906. *Governor, close involvement with the OBRFC and with many aspects of CH – "one of the most loyal of Old Blues"; President, ASB.* Accountant, in the wine trade. d 1992. *(See illustration 145 on page 95.)*

BIRD, *James Derek. 1940-1948.* b 1930. *Governor; President, Treasurer, ASB; long-serving director and trustee, BSB. He amassed a magnificent collection of CH memorabilia which he bequeathed to the CH Museum.* Accountant with Ernst & Young. d 2012.

BOSTOCK, *Lilian Ada. 1907-1911.* b 1895. *Awarded BEM in WW1, the only known Old Blue girl to receive a decoration in the War.* Chief Supervisor, London Telecommunications Region. ISM. d 1988.

BUCK, *Archibald Hector. 1910-1919.* b 1900. *Classics master, CH, 1928-1956; benefactor.* Later, reader with the Oxford University Press. Initially, master at Oakham School. d 1987. (#)

176. Archibald Hector Buck.

CHUMROW, *Ernest John, [at CH, CHMUROW]. 1939-1946.* b 1928. *Governor; benefactor to BSB and to CH music; Special Recognition Award.* Chairman, Waltham Forest Housing Action Trust. Previously, Director, Wiggins Teape Group. OBE. d 2015

COSTIN, *Maurice Olaf. 1918-1923.* b 1906. *CH: Governor; involvement with OBRFC (including as Team Secretary); BSB (Director); CH Club (including as President); President, Hon Sec, ASB.* Director, Price & Pierce (timber merchants) where he had been employed since leaving School. d 1974.

CROSS, *Arthur, [at CH, KRAUSS]. 1896-1899.* b 1883. *CH: major role (including as Treasurer) with Herbert Moody (below) in rebuilding and running OBRFC after WW1, and obtaining and developing the ground at Fairlop, the club then often fielding eight sides each week. Resided at the ground.* Worked in banking. MBE. d 1961.

CULLEN, *William John. 1907-1913.* b 1894. *Eminent CH athlete and sportsman (including four centuries for School XI in 1912).* Ireland rugby cap; earlier, England triallist. Served WW1, Leinster Regiment; MBE. Later, employed Bombay Company Ltd, East India. d 1960.

DADSON, *Eric Fulton. 1913-1919.* b 1903. *CH benefactor, establishing a prize fund to assist pupils with travel to the*

Low Countries; Governor. Previously, President, Chairman, Imperial Continental Gas Association. Served WW2, SOE. d 1995.

DAVIES, *Eric Charles. 1910-1916.* b 1899. *Long-term enthusiastic Old Blue, active particularly in OBRFC, BSB, the CH Club and the Votum Lodge; reported to have attended every Founder's Day dinner held between 1917 and 1990.* d 1993.

DRAKE, *Colin Stuart. 1939-1947.* b 1928. *Editor, Old Blues section of "The Blue", bringing in many new elements.* Initially, in Army, then Territorial Army; TD. Post-Army, worked in personnel and management, becoming Group Personnel Manager, Harrison & Crosfield plc (conglomerate). FSA. d 2005.

EVANS, *Eric Bertram. 1910-1917.* b 1901. *Served as an auditor of the BSB for 30 years and joint auditor of the OBRFC for 40 years; Hon Sec, CH Club.* Chartered Accountant. d 1975.

EVANS, *Roger Courtenay. 1912-1917.* b 1901. *Clerk of CH (1946-1958), Receiver (1932-1946), having joined the Counting House direct from School.* d 1958.

EWAN, *Robert Wilson. 1918-1924.* b 1907. *Governor. With his strong Christian beliefs, he gave much assistance to pupils in the CH Christian Union.* Senior Partner in a firm of City Accountants. Treasurer, Church Army. d 1973.

FIRMIN, *Percy Judge. 1899-1903.* b 1887. *Served BSB (Director and Vice-President); CH Club (Vice-President); editor of the Old Blues section of "The Blue" for many years; Masonic work for CH Lodges, and voluntary work in the CH Offices.* Managing Director, Oxo Ltd; earlier, with parent company Liebig. d 1967.

FRADIN, *Louis Reginald. 1914-1919.* b 1902. *Governor; much involvement with BSB, including Treasurer and a director for nearly 55 years; Vice-President, OBRFC.* Partner in an accountancy firm. d 1985. *(See illustration 145 on page 95.)*

GIBBINS, *Charles George. 1920-1926.* b 1909. *Served CH and OBs widely, including as a Governor; OBRFC; President, CH Club; President, ASB; and Masonic activities.* Partner, Colegrave & Co (stockbrokers). d 1985.

GILBERT, *William. 1852-1860.* b 1845. *"One of the staunchest sons of CH", his involvement including: President, CH Club; Treasurer, BSB; President, ASB; and with the OBRFC.* Lifelong employment in the linen trade. d 1926.

GILLHAM, *John Moor. 1928-1935.* b 1918. *Long-term association with CH, including: Almoner; chairman of two construction committees; Governor; President, ASB; with CH Club and BSB; trustee of the Sue Thomson Foundation.* Long career with Bovis (construction), where he became a director. d 2009.

177. John Moor Gillham.

GRANT, *Frederick. 1936-1942.* b 1925. *Almoner; Governor; President, ASB; Chairman, 1976 Endowment Appeal Committee; other CH involvement including with OBRFC; Special Recognition Award.* Managing director, Metropolitan Pensions Association. d 2015.

178. Frederick Grant.

GREEN, *Donald Richard. 1910-1917.* b 1901. *Co-founder (with Percy Giles*, para 1.99) of the Old Blues Dramatic Society, being an active member throughout most of the 36 years of its existence, acting as secretary as well as producing and starring in many plays.* Employed in the leather trade. d 1979.

HANKIN, *Barclay Dundas. 1927-1936.* b 1918. *Governor; benefactor; author of idiosyncratic book on CH "In this Place, 1927-2004", (published 2005).* Head of Operational Research, London Transport. Later, worked on staff satisfaction in the Civil Service. Earlier had served in the Army, including in WW2, Major. d 2007.

179. Barclay Dundas Hankin.

HARVEY, *Cyril. 1914-1919.* b 1903. *Almoner; Vice-Chairman, Council of Almoners; Chairman, Finance Committee; Governor; President, CH Club; President, ASB.* d 1992.

HOBDEN, *Herbert John. 1920-1926.* b 1909. *Receiver (1958-1966), having served in Counting House from 1928 (save for wartime break); Governor; Secretary, Stewards of Founder's Day Dinner for over 35 years; Fixture Secretary, OBRFC.* d 1985.

HUBBARD, *Roy. 1930-1935.* b 1918. *Active member of the CH Club, including President and Secretary.* Assistant Secretary, the Cunard Steamship Co plc. Earlier had been imprisoned for five years during WW2. d 1998.

HUBBLE, *Harry Denniss. 1911-1917.* b 1902. *Almoner; Governor; benefactor; much involved with developments at Horsham.* Fruit farmer. d 1965.

JACOBS, *Norman Nathaniel. 1941-1949.* b 1930. *Almoner; Governor; President, ASB; work for CH Club.* Partner, Slaughter & May. Later, Chairman, Football Licensing Authority. OBE. ERD, FRSA. d 2003.

JONES, *Ronald Austin. 1919-1926.* b 1909. *Major role in holding together Old Blues Rugby Football Club in WW2 and then re-establishing it as the pre-eminent Old Boys side, including serving as Treasurer and Secretary. Secretary, CH Endowment Appeal (1976); Governor; Hon Sec, Peter Clay Trust (para 2.33).* Bank manager. d 1991.

180. Ronald Austin Jones.

KIRBY, *Cecil Francis, [usually Bill]. 1914-1922.* b 1903. *Biology master at CH from 1925-1963, with break for War service, residing at the School until 1999. Generous benefactor to CH; Governor.* Served WW2, Major, Royal Signals (TD), his post-War involvement at CH influencing the service careers of many pupils. MBE. d 2000. (#) *(See illustration 145 on page 95.)*

LEGATE, *Pamela. 1955-1962.* b 1944. *Co-author, "Christ's Hospital in the Year 2000".* Freelance writer and journalist, particularly for the travel industry. Earlier work included as a bilingual secretary in Paris and Vienna. d 2001.

181. Pamela Legate.

LORD, *Freda Marjorie Edith. 1913-1918.* b 1901. *Founder member Old Blues Dramatic Society, serving as Secretary for some 30 years and appearing in most of the Society's productions.* Employed in the Post Office. d 1987.

MACKNESS, *Leslie Edward. 1893-1898.* b 1880. *Much involved with OBRFC, particularly as Hon Sec and Chairman, and with BSB, including as Secretary.* d 1971.

MACKRILL, *Frank Henry Arthur. 1907-1911.* b 1895. *CH: Governor; work for BSB (Director) and OBRFC (Vice-President); President, ASB.* Managing Director, Glynwed. Chairman of various engineering trade associations. Initially, with PLA. d 1980.

MOODY, *Lewis Herbert. 1895-1899.* b 1883. *Major role (including as Secretary) with Arthur Cross (above) in rebuilding and running OBRFC after WW1, and obtaining and developing the ground at Fairlop, the club then often fielding eight sides each week.* Worked in banking. d 1953.

NEWALL, *Joan, [née BUTLER]. 1930-1936.* b 1919. *Governor. Long service to CH, including in the Counting House; as Secretary for the Old Girls' Association and for the BSB and the CH Club.* Earlier, a civil servant and a meteorologist in the WAAF. d 2009.

NEWSTEAD, *Charles William. 1910-1915.* b 1898. *Active member of the Old Blues Dramatic Society throughout the 36 years of its existence, producing and starring in many plays. Vice-President, OBRFC.* Long service with Tate & Lyle, where he was the voice of "Mr Cube" in the company's anti-nationalisation campaign. d 1984.

NORMAN, *Eric Glynn. 1916-1922.* b 1906. *Taught 'craftmanship' in CH's Manual School (now Design and Technology) for around 35 years.* d 1981.

OSMOND, *Christopher Neville. 1944-1951.* b 1932. *Much work for CH, particularly in the area of fund-raising, and for the CH Club (Chairman and Secretary); ran CH Career Network; Governor; Special Recognition Award.* Management, organisation and personnel consultant. d 2016.

OVERALL, *Florence. 1912-1920.* b 1903. *Served in the CH Counting House for 40 years, her role during the period of WW2 being particularly important. Her work included writing up the elegantly scribed admission registers and minute books.* d 1987.

RASINI, *Charles Luigi Domenico. 1925-1931.* b 1914. *Governor; Governor-Auditor; President, ASB; President, CH Club.* Chartered Accountant; FCA. Director of an asphalting company. d 1998.

READ, *Ewart Kingsley. 1909-1915.* b 1898. *Established a Trust Fund for Christ's Hospital; Almoner; Governor. Amongst his other CH activities, President, CH Club; major work for the BSB (including Treasurer for 20 years).* An actuary. FIA. d 1967.

ROBINSON, *Albert Wilson. 1917-1922.* b 1905. *Clerk of CH (1966-1971); Steward, Hertford (1939-1959, with wartime break); Steward, Horsham (1959-1966); served the Foundation for around 45 years; Governor; work for CH Club and BSB (Vice-President); President, ASB.* d 1991. (#) *(See illustration 145 on page 95.)*

SALISBURY, *Roy Fortescue. 1940-1946.* b 1929. *Clerk of CH (1971-1986), serving in the Counting House for 40 years. Governor; President, ASB.* Later, Charity Administrator. d 2017.

SCOTT, *Thomas Lamb. 1917-1924.* b 1905. *CH Medical Officer, 1946-1969, reorganising the Infirmary after the War and coping with major changes in medicine and medical practice. President, ASB. Pillar of the Masonic brotherhood.* Earlier, work in Nigeria and as Medical Officer of Health in Somerset. Secretary, Medical Officers of Schools Association. LRCP. d 1972.

182. Thomas Lamb Scott.

SIMMONDS, *Kerren. 1957-1966.* b 1948. *Long association with CH, including Chairman, Old Girls' Association, and with the CH Club and the Old Blues' Association; CH Museum volunteer.* Worked for many years in academic management, University of Chichester. d 2013.

183. Kerren Simmonds.

SMITH, *Francis Henry. 1919-1926.* b 1909. *Editor, Old Blues section of "The Blue" for 28 years; Vice-President, CH Club.* Librarian, Archivist, British Transport Staff College. Previously, Librarian, Royal Aeronautical Society. Earlier, Assistant Librarian, Institute of Civil Engineering. d 1995.

STEVENS, *Carol, [née RAYSON]. 1959-1965. b 1947. Almoner; Governor; various contributions to the CH Club, the CH Old Blues' Association and the BSB (Director).* Director, Government Relations, The Prince's Trust; previously, planning policy work in the Department of the Environment. d 2010.

STIFF, *William James. 1913-1919. b 1900. Almoner; Governor; other CH involvement including, in particular, arranging special trips for the girls at Hertford.* d 1989.

STRIPP, *Herbert Francis Edward. 1909-1914. b 1898. Major involvement with the OBRFC, including as Hon Sec, and particularly during WW2, and also work with cricket club (especially during war years) and the swimming and athletic clubs.* A chartered accountant. d 1976.

TAYLOR, *William George. 1914-1921. b 1902. Almoner; Governor; and active in various clubs and societies, including Vice-President, CH Club.* Manager, Shell, joining company after graduating and working initially in Far East and later in Africa. d 1954.

THACKSTON, *Hazel, [née CRAIG]. 1938-1944. b 1927. Many contributions to CH including Governor; for the Old Girls' Association, the CH Club, the BSB (including as Chairman) and Chief Steward, Founder's Day Dinner.* Private Secretary to senior management in a number of major companies. d. 2007.

WALES, *Charles Douglas. 1911-1917. b 1900.* Branch Manager, Union Insurance Society of Canton Ltd, Calcutta; previously, in Bombay. Earlier, with the Company in Hong Kong, Shanghai and Japan. d 1984.

WALES, *Frank Vernon. 1920-1925. b 1908.* Worked in insurance. d 1961.

184. Five Wales brothers: Sydney Herbert Thomas, Hubert Edward Robert, Charles Douglas, Frederick William and Frank Vernon.

WALES, *Frederick William. 1910-1915.* b 1899. Employed at Port of London Authority. d 1962.

WALES, *Hubert Edward Robert. 1918-1923.* b 1907. Worked as Librarian at ICI. d 1967.

WALES, *Sydney Herbert Thomas. 1914-1918.* b 1902. Employed at Port of London Authority. d 1956.

[The five WALES brothers' time at Horsham spanned the period 1910 to 1925. Over these years there was always at least one brother at the School; in two years there were three. After CH, they were fully engaged with Old Blues rugby, indeed in one game in 1926 against Woodford all five played in the same team. Three played at County level. Variously, they played other sports for the OBs, including cricket, swimming and fives, Similarly, they involved themselves with the administration of the clubs, particularly rugby, Sydney living in a converted pavilion at Fairlop and undertaking certain ground secretary functions. And they had a sister, Mary Hilda, who went to Hertford (1916-1921).]

WATT, *Jack. 1930-1936. b 1919. Extensive activity with CH and OBs including: Almoner; Governor; President, ASB; President, OBRFC.* Director, Imperial Continental Gas Association; previously, Managing Director. Served WW2; DSO, MC: later, Major. d 1996.

WEBB, *Stephen Richard. 1960-1969. b 1951. Long-term involvement with many aspects of CH and OB life, including OBRFC, BSB (also Chairman), CH Club and later CHOBA (including Chairman); Governor; Member, School Board; Special Recognition Award.* Divisional Director, Cap Gemini plc (IT consultants). d 2014.

185. Stephen Richard Webb.

WICKHAM, *Harry Temple. 1895-1904.* b 1884. *A devoted and loyal supporter of CH. President, ASB.* Supervisor, BBC Persian Services; previously, school principal and service in Indian Police. d 1979.

Postscript

2.39   The author would like to conclude with two postscripts. First, the life of the School is very much guided by its ethos and driven by its Head, the staff and the children. Various names – particularly of Treasurers, Clerks, Head Masters and Head Mistresses – have been mentioned throughout the book. The author would now wish to add that, during the course of his research, he identified about 50 people who had served Christ's Hospital at Horsham for more than 30 years. Of these, the author associates most closely with his mathematics master Bill Armistead (served CH 1927-67, see also para 1.166), his housemaster Peter Matthews (science, 1940-77, see also para 1.120), and three other masters: Harry Spurrier (history, 1950-87), Tom Keeley (classics, 1956-92) and Norman Fryer (mathematics, 1949-84), for their instruction on the rugby and cricket fields. These five can perhaps also represent the long service of others.

2.40   Secondly, as with his two previous books, *CHIVE* and *Names*, the author would like to recall the Foundation's Charge which is delivered at the School's immensely moving Leaving Service:

"I charge you never to forget the great benefits that you have received in this place, and in time to come according to your means to do all that you can to enable others to enjoy the same advantages; and remember that you carry with you, wherever you go, the good name of Christ's Hospital. May God Almighty bless you in your ways and keep you in the knowledge of his love."

Annex: List of Notable Old Blues, all

Introduction

2.41 As mentioned earlier, for completeness this Annex gives an alphabetical list of around 1,225 names of **all** notable Old Blues identified by the author spanning the whole existence of the School, the 475 post-1902 (mainly) names above being augmented by some 750 from the pre-Horsham era. The latter – derived largely in the same way as the later names – are essentially an update and slight revision of what was included in *Names*, the main changes being (i) the inclusion of about 60 new pre-Horsham names, the result of further research, for whom biographical information has been given in the details above; (ii) the inclusion (in group (a)) of a small (representative) number of names only, rather than all (about 160) Newgate Street names who died in WW1, and (iii) the exclusion (from group (p)) of those individuals from the list of Worthies (see para 2.4) whose sole reason for inclusion there appeared to be that they were Donation Governors. In the list of notables included in *Names*, group (p) was made up entirely of Worthies; as these relate to pre-1850 admissions, there are no entries in this group for the post-1902 notables. In the list below, which also gives years at CH, the bracketed letter (eg (a)) at the end of the name refers to a particular 'industry' group (as in para 2.42); further, a superscript '*z*' denotes a notable (generally from the Horsham era) for whom biographical details have been given in paras 2.22-38.

2.42 The industry categories (see paras 2.8-10) used in paras 2.22-38 and below are:

(a) *War and other deaths* – para 2.22 [for pre-Horsham, includes War deaths only – see para 2.9]
(b) *Academic (UK, universities)* – para 2.23
(c) *Academic (UK, schools)* – para 2.24
(d) *Academic (overseas)* – para 2.25
(e) *Cultural (administrators)* – para 2.26
(f) *Cultural (individuals)* – para 2.27
(g) *Ecclesiastical* – para 2.28
(h) *RAF service* – para 2.29
(i) *Army service* – para 2.30
(j) *Naval service* – para 2.31
(k) *Medical* – para 2.32
(l) *Other business/industry (managerial)* – para 2.33
(m) *Other business/industry (professions)* – para 2.34
(n) *Public service (UK)* – para 2.35
(o) *Public service (overseas)* – para 2.36
(p) *Benefactors and Donation Governors* – para 2.37 [pre-Horsham only – see para 2.41]
(q) *Christ's Hospital* – para 2.38

2.43 As mentioned in para 2.21, the lists of notables use 'later' names. The main changes compared with those obtaining at CH are given below, with the name at CH followed by the later designation.

ANGUS, Anne Ines Louie. PROCTOR.
BANKS, Henry Collingwood. Henry COLLINGWOOD BANKS.
BARON, Charles William. Charles William BARON-SUCKLING.
BONNOR, Hannam Edward. Albany WARD.
BROOKS, Clive Jack Montague. Clive EXTON.
BROWN, William Haig. William HAIG BROWN.
BUTLER, Joan. NEWALL.
CARPENTER, Charles Howard. Charles Howard ISDELL-CARPENTER.
CHMUROW, Ernest John. CHUMROW.
CRAIG, Algernon Tudor. Algernon TUDOR-CRAIG.
CRAIG, Hazel. THACKSTON.
CUTHBERTSON, Maggie Rentoul. FREEMAN.
DAVIES, Richard William Frederick. Richard William Frederick SINGERS-DAVIES.
DENNISS, Edmund Robert Bartley. Edmund Robert Bartley BARTLEY-DENNISS.

DEWAR, Norah Kathleen May. GURNEY.
EDNEY, Robert Joseph. Robert BOLDER.
ELLIOTT, Margaret Mary. GOWING.
FINCH, Kathleen Georgiana Maule. STEWART-SMITH.
FORRINGTON, Joyce. WILSON.
GIBBS, Hilda Joyce. MORGAN.
GILL, Joseph. Joseph WITHERS-GILL.
GOODING, Violet Evelyn Ivy Suzanne. GREEN.
GRAMMOR, John. VICARS.
GREEN, Charles William Tandy. Charles William TANDY-GREEN.
GREENE, Hugh. Ferdinand BROOKS.
HALE, John Richard Westgarth. HILDYARD.
JONES, Charles Mark Jenkin. Charles Mark JENKIN-JONES.
JONES, John Archibald Rupert. John Archibald RUPERT-JONES.
KINNESMAN, Arthur. KYNNESMAN.
KRAUSS, Arthur. CROSS.
LEWIN, William Charles James. William TERRISS.
MITCHELL, Rhea. MARTIN.
MORGAN, Septimus Vaughan. Septimus VAUGHAN MORGAN.
MORGAN, Walter Vaughan. Walter VAUGHAN MORGAN.
NEAL, Margaret Lilian Alice. HILL.
PAGET, Patricia Joy. HEISELER.
PARINCHAFFE, Richard. PERRINCHIEF.
PARSONS, Patrick George. Patrick HOLT.
PEAKE, Doris Winifred. TAYLOR.
RAYSON, Carol. STEVENS.
REYNOLDS, Phoebe Monica. GUILLEBAUD.
SMITH, Hannah Mabel. JONES.
TAYLOR, Winifred Ethel. AYLETT.
TUTT, Margaret Louise. MOOTE.
VOYSEY-MARTIN, Olive. STEPHENS.
WHITE, Joseph (at CH 1784-89). James WHITE.
YOW, George. YEO.

The full list of all notable Old Blues begins on the facing page.

ABBOTT, Herbert Edward Stacy. 1824-1829. (i)
ABBOTT, Reginald James. 1912-1918. (a)^z
ADAMS, Carol. 1959-1965. (n)^z
ADAMS, Richard Newton. 1802-1810. (b)
ADAMS, William Leslie Graham. 1913-1919. (j)^z
AIREY, John Alfred Lumb. 1831-1841. (c)
AIREY, Robert Berkeley. 1884-1889. (i)
ALBAN, Clifton Edward Rawdon Grant. 1900-1905. (i)^z
ALLAN, Donald James. 1917-1926. (b)^z
ALLAN, George Albert Thomas. 1890-1896. (q)
ALLCOCK, William Plaxton. 1784-1792. (p)
ALLEN, Bertram Cowles. 1886-1891. (j)
ALLEN, Frederick Charles. 1875-1880. (l)
ALLEN, Henry Ross. 1882-1888. (j)
ALLEN, Robert. 1784-1792. (m)
ALLEN, William Sidney. 1929-1937. (b)^z
ALLISON, Alan Evan. 1916-1922. (q)^z
ALLPRESS, Edward Whetham. 1831-1839. (p)
ALLUM, William. 1717-1726. (p)
ALSTON, Alfred Gilmore. 1877-1884. (j)^z
ALT, Just Henry. 1805-1815. (d)
AMERS, John Henry. 1917-1922. (i)^z
AMERY, William Bankes. 1896-1899. (n)
AMOS, John. 1789-1796. (p)
ANDERSON, Alfred. 1851-1857. (i)
ANDERSON, Declan John. 1932-1938. (b)^z
ANDREWS, Robert. 1829-1839. (b)
ANDREWS, William Linton. 1898-1902. (l)
APPLETON, Richard. 1858-1867. (b)
ARMBRUSTER, Carl Hubert Joseph Hans Richter. 1883-1893. (o)
ARMSTRONG, Douglas Henry Fyfe. 1916-1921. (j)^z
ARNOLD, Audrey Joyce. 1935-1943. (g)^z
ASHWORTH, Piers. 1943-1950. (m)^z
ASKWITH, Edward Harrison. 1874-1883. (g)
ATKINSON, James Peter Geoffrey. 1999-2006. (a)^z
AUDLEY, Matthew. 1686-1696. (q)
AVELING, Thomas Butts. 1791-1797. (p)
AVORY, Henry. 1834-1840. (n)
AYLETT, Winifred Ethel. 1908-1913. (a)^z
AYNGE, William. 1758-1764. (p)
BABER, Edward Colborne. 1853-1862. (o)
BACK, William Henry. 1816-1822. (q)
BAKER, Charles Gaffney. 1920-1925. (k)^z
BAKER, John Alfred. 1890-1897. (o)
BAKER, Leonard Graham Derek. 1943-1950. (b)^z
BAKER, William. 1700-1707. (p)
BALSTON, William. 1769-1774. (m)
BAND, Edward George Underwood. 1936-1944. (l)^z
BANNISTER, John. 1573-1592. (q)
BARBER, Donald. 1915-1923. (l)^z
BARKER, Thomas Richard. 1808-1813. (c)
BARNARD, John James. 1836-1841. (j)^z
BARNES, John Arundel. 1929-1936. (b)^z
BARNES, Joshua. c1657-1670. (b)
BARNES, Sidney. 1898-1904. (q)^z
BARNES, Thomas. 1796-1804. (l)
BARNETT, Ben Lewis. 1906-1913. (l)^z
BARON-SUCKLING, Charles William. 1869-1881. (g)
BARR, Reginald Alfred. 1932-1939. (m)^z
BARRINGTON, Ernest James William. 1919-1927. (b)^z
BARRON, Charles Howard Washington. 1910-1916. (f)^z
BARTLETT, Charles Oldfield. 1866-1873. (g)^z
BARTLEY-DENNISS, Edmund Robert Bartley. 1861-1869. (n)
BASKCOMB, Archibald William Berry. 1888-1895. (f)
BASKCOMB, Lawrence Ward. 1895-1899. (f)
BATE, Henry Francis. 1868-1874. (f)^z
BATES, George William. 1876-1883. (q)

BATES, William Stanley. 1932-1939. (o)^z
BATT, Charles Ernest. 1883-1890. (j)
BAVIN, Alfred Robert Walter. 1928-1935. (n)^z
BAXTER, Edward Felix. 1896-1901. (a)
BAZIRE, Reginald Victor. 1913-1916. (g)^z
BEARDSWORTH, George Braithwaite. 1916-1922. (h)^z
BEAUCHAMP, Henry King. 1875-1882. (m)
BEAUMONT, John. 1847-1855. (l)
BEAZLEY, John Davidson. 1898-1903. (b)
BEGBIE, Francis Richard. 1818-1829. (b)
BEIOLEY, Joseph. 1793-1800. (p)
BELCHER, Ronald Harry. 1925-1934. (n)^z
BELL, Bernard Humphrey. 1894-1903. (o)
BELL, Edward Vaughan. 1909-1917. (a)^z
BELL, Francis Jeffrey. 1862-1873. (e)
BELL, George Charles. 1842-1851. (c)
BELL, John Thomas. 1855-1867. (q)
BELL, Robert Donald Murray. 1926-1935. (n)^z
BELLASIS, Edward. 1808-1815. (m)
BENFIELD, Edward Stanley. 1904-1908. (a)^z
BENSON, Walmsley John. 1897-1902. (a)
BENT, John. 1783-1790. (n)
BERTHON, Peter Lorraine Ashton. 1916-1922. (m)^z
BILLINGSLEY, Samuell. 1685-1692. (g)
BINFIELD, Henry. 1745-1753. (g)
BINNS, Wilfred Leslie. 1917-1922. (q)^z
BIRD, James Derek. 1940-1948. (q)^z
BIRT, William Raymond. 1921-1928. (g)^z
BISHOP, Terence Alan Martyn. 1920-1924. (b)^z
BISSELL, William. 1772-1780. (p)
BLACK, John Reddie. 1833-1841. (m)
BLACK, Robert. 1837-1848. (m)
BLAKE, John Frederick. 1848-1855. (b)
BLANCH, William Harnett. 1843-1851. (f)
BLATHWAYT, Percy. 1853-1858. (a)^z
BLUNDEN, Edmund Charles. 1909-1915. (f)^z
BLUNDUN, Percy Young. 1895-1902. (n)^z
BOCKETT-PUGH, Ian Hamilton. 1910-1917. (j)^z
BOILEAU, Guy Hamilton. 1880-1885. (i)
BOLDER, Robert. 1868-1874. (f)^z
BOMFORD, Arthur Henry. 1884-1889. (a)^z
BOOR, Leonard George. 1833-1840. (k)
BOOTH, David. 1919-1925. (m)^z
BOSTOCK, Lilian Ada. 1907-1911. (q)^z
BOSTOCK, Robert Chignell. 1839-1844. (m)
BOWDEN, John. 1710-1717. (q)
BOWKER, Henry Francis. 1820-1825. (q)
BOWLEY, Arthur Lyon. 1879-1888. (b)
BOWRA, William. 1756-1763. (q)
BOX, Harold Elton. 1912-1918. (f)^z
BOYER, James. 1744-1752. (q)
BOYLE, Noel Stuart Stirling. 1901-1905. (g)^z
BRADFORD, William Vincent. 1896-1902. (n)
BRADLEY, Leslie Ripley. 1905-1908. (e)^z
BRANFOOT, Walter Haigh. 1863-1872. (q)
BRANT, Colin Trevor. 1939-1948. (o)^z
BREWER, Thomas. 1614-1626. (f)
BRIGGS, Samuel. 1785-1791. (p)
BRISCOE, William Richard Brunskill. 1862-1873. (n)
BRITTAN, Herbert William. 1874-1880. (a)^z
BROCK, Russell Claude. 1915-1920. (k)^z
BROCK, William Ranulf. 1928-1934. (b)^z
BROCKBANK, Thomas Henry. 1850-1857. (p)
BRODIE, Douglas Campbell. 1915-1918. (l)^z
BROOKES, George John. 1808-1818. (q)
BROOKS, Ferdinand. 1592-1601^2. (g)
BROOKS, George. 1750-1756. (p)

BROOKS, John. 1746-1756. (p)
BROWN, Gilbert Wilson. 1842-1851. (o)
BROWN, James. 1716-1726. (b)
BROWN, John. 1809-1813. (p)
BROWN, Joseph James. 1873-1878. (q)
BROWN, Thomas. 1785-1792. (q)
BROWN, Wilfred Henry. 1933-1939. (f)[z]
BROWNING, Colin Arrott Robertson. 1840-1848. (o)
BROWNING, Robert Jardine. 1860-1872. (o)
BROWNSCOMBE, Brian. 1926-1933. (a)[z]
BRUCE, Frank Edward. 1926-1933. (b)[z]
BRUCE, Robert Elton Spencer. 1945-1954. (l)[z]
BRUCE-MITFORD, Rupert Leo Scott. 1925-1933. (e)[z]
BRUNSKILL, Gerald FitzGibbon. 1874-1881. (n)
BRYAN, Frank Colin. 1903-1910. (g)[z]
BUCHANAN, James Courtney. 1886-1896. (n)
BUCHANAN, James Richebourg. 1924-1932. (a)[z]
BUCK, Archibald Hector. 1910-1919. (q)[z]
BUCKLE, George. 1828-1838. (g)
BUCKLEY, James Arthur. 1928-1934. (l)[z]
BUCKMASTER, George Alfred. 1867-1874. (b)
BULLARD, John Eric. 1915-1922. (n)[z]
BULMER, Ralph Neville Hermon. 1939-1946. (d)[z]
BUNCH, Austin Wyeth. 1929-1935. (l)[z]
BUNCHER, Llewellyn Edward. 1890-1900. (m)
BUNFORD, John Farrant. 1912-1920. (l)[z]
BUNKER, Percy Edwin. 1896-1899. (o)
BUNN, Robert. 1745-1751. (p)
BURGESS, Herbert Edward. 1872-1878. (n)
BURNABY, Robert. 1837-1843. (o)
BURNS, James Glencairn. 1802-1809. (o)
BURNSIDE, William. 1860-1871. (b)
BURR, William. 1735-1743. (p)
BURT, Cyril Lodowic. 1895-1902. (b)
BURTON, James. 1788-1793. (p)
BUSBRIDGE, Ida. 1919-1926. (b)[z]
BUSHNAN, Joseph. 1754-1758. (n)
BUTLER, Alfred Joshua. 1860-1869. (b)
BUTLER, Edward Dundas. 1850-1857. (e)[z]
CALTHROP, Calthrop Guy Spencer. 1879-1885. (l)
CANNON, Richard. 1789-1794. (n)
CARAJANAKI, George Demetrius. 1871-1878. (a)
CAREY, Mordecai. 1695-1705. (g)
CARLOS, Edward Stafford. 1849-1861. (c)
CARRINGTON, Jack Herbert. 1921-1926. (m)[z]
CARTER, Bernard. 1898-1900. (j)[z]
CARTER, Robert Markham. 1885-1890. (i)
CARTER, Sydney Bertram. 1926-1933. (f)[z]
CARUER, Jonathan. 1639-ng. (p)
CASS, Thomas. 1827-1834. (o)
CAUTLEY, William Grainger. 1790-1801. (g)
CAVAGNARI, Pierre Louis Napoleon. 1851-1856. (o)
CAVE BROWNE CAVE, Bernard. 1877-1883. (a)
CAVENDISH, Edward Patrick James. 1951-1957. (l)[z]
CAVENDISH, Henry Patrick. 1913-1919. (i)[z]
CAVENDISH, Richard. 1940-1949. (f)[z]
CAWSTON, Samuel William. 1829-1835. (p)
CHAMBERLAIN, Walter Ernest. 1907-1910. (l)[z]
CHATTERTON, Frank William. 1847-1854. (i)[z]
CHEEVER, Ezechiell. 1626-1633. (d)
CHESTER, Henry Marjoribanks. 1840-1849. (o)
CHEW, Vincent Kenneth. 1926-1933. (e)[z]
CHEYNE, Charles. 1812-1818. (p)
CHILDS-CLARKE, Arthur William. 1916-1922. (m)[z]
CHILTON, Arthur. 1873-1883. (c)
CHRIST, George Elgie. 1916-1921. (m)[z]
CHRISTIAN, Ewan. 1823-1829. (m)

CHRISTIAN, Robert Bertram Keough. 1879-1889. (l)
CHUMROW, Ernest John. 1939-1946. (q)[z]
CHURCHILL, Smith Wild. 1845-1857. (c)
CLARK, Thomas Henry. 1905-1910. (d)[z]
CLARKE, Arthur Gurdon. 1900-1904. (q)
CLARKE, Richard William Barnes. 1922-1928. (n)[z]
CLARKE, William. 1597-c1613. (g)
CLAY, Harold Peter. 1915-1922. (l)[z]
CLAYSON, David Saxton. 1896-1902. (o)
CLEMITSON, Francis Edward. 1912-1917. (j)[z]
COATES, Daisy Catherine Elizabeth. 1908-1915. (a)[z]
COBB, Samuel. 1683-1695. (f)
COBBOLD, Peter Charles Vincent. 1907-1913. (a)[z]
COETLOGON, Charles Edward. 1755-1766. (g)
COHEN, James. 1823-1834. (g)
COLBORNE, John. 1785-1789. (i)
COLE, Henry. 1817-1823. (e)
COLE, James. 1639-1653. (p)
COLE, Robert. 1810-1818. (k)
COLE, Thomas. 1753-1760. (p)
COLEMAN, Everard Home Roberts. 1827-1834. (n)
COLEMAN, Herbert Cecil. 1905-1909. (n)[z]
COLERIDGE, Samuel Taylor. 1782-1791. (f)
COLES, Jenkin. 1850-1854. (o)
COLFE, Richard (major). 1559-1569. (g)
COLLICK, Edward Mallan. 1878-1884. (g)
COLLINGWOOD BANKS, Henry. 1869-1877. (q)
COMB, Robert. 1843-1849. (p)
CONNOR, Ernest Stephen. 1902-1905. (a)[z]
CONSTANTINE, Hugh Alex. 1917-1925. (h)[z]
COOKE, Stanley Jack. 1917-1922. (l)[z]
COOKE, William. 1719-1726. (f)
COOPER, Arthur Nevile. 1858-1865. (g)
CORBET, Cyril. 1858-1862. (a)
CORDEROY, John. 1758-1765 (p)
CORLETT, Elias. 1619-1626. (d)
CORNELL, George. 1794-1800. (p)
CORP, James. 1766-1769. (p)
CORP, Richard. 1773-1775. (q)
COSTIN, Eric Boyd. 1899-1905. (i)
COSTIN, Maurice Olaf. 1918-1923. (q)[z]
COTTON, Charles. 1811-1823. (q)
COTTON, Matthew. 1781-1788. (q)
COURTNEY, Frederick. 1845-1851. (g)
COWDEROY, Benjamin Thomas. 1821-1826. (o)
COX, Edgar William. 1890-1900. (i)
COX, Edward John Owen. 1875-1881. (o)
COX, Frederick. 1818-1823. (q)
COX, Nicholas George. 1951-1961. (e)[z]
CRAVEN, Laurence. 1839-1849. (m)
CRAWFORD, Lawrence Hugh. 1863-1870. (j)
CREAMER, Brian. 1938-1943. (k)[z]
CREESE, Alfred Richard. 1910-1917. (a)[z]
CREW, Isaac. 1693-1701. (g)
CROAD, George Hector. 1838-1849. (n)
CROFT, Septimus. 1862-1869. (q)
CROFT, William Bleaden. 1859-1870. (c)[z]
CROSBY, Thomas Frederick Gordon. 1898-1900. (m)
CROSS Arthur. 1896-1899. (q)[z]
CROSS, William Henry. 1844-1851. (m)
CROUCH, William. 1775-1782. (p)
CULLEN, William John. 1907-1913. (q)[z]
CUMMINGS, Henry Reginald. 1896-1902. (o)[z]
CUNNINGHAM, Alexander. 1823-1826. (o)
CUNNINGHAM, Peter. 1825-1831. (f)
CURTIS, Alfred Barwick. 1863-1869. (a)
CUSDEN, Victor Vincent. 1905-1909. (o)[z]

DADSON, Eric Fulton. 1913-1919. (q)[z]
DAGLEY, Richard. 1770-1777. (f)
DALE, Langham. 1834-1844. (d)
DALE, Thomas. 1805-1812. (g)
DALE, Thomas Aquila. 1798-1809. (c)
DALLY, Frederick. 1847-1853. (m)
DANTER, Harold Walter Phillips. 1896-1902. (g)
DAVEY, Dorothy May. 1909-1914. (a)[z]
DAVEY, Roy Charles. 1926-1934. (c)[z]
DAVIDSON, James Alfred. 1933-1939. (o)[z]
DAVIDSON, John Wallace Ord. 1899-1906. (o)
DAVIDSON-HOUSTON, Charles Elrington Duncan. 1881-1888. (i)
DAVIE, Mervyn Bowcher. 1885-1892. (q)
DAVIES, Eric Charles. 1910-1916. (q)[z]
DAVIES, Spencer Howard. 1956-1963. (e)[z]
DAVIS, Colin Rex. 1938-1944. (f)[z]
DAVIS, Howard Leslie. 1929-1938. (a)[z]
DAVIS, William. 1831-1836. (m)[z]
de SAUSMAREZ, Lionel Maurice. 1926-1932. (f)[z]
DEAN, William Reginald. 1908-1915. (b)[z]
DEANE, Eileen Violet Chambers. 1909-1914. (a)[z]
DEAR, Lawrence Hart. 1874-1881. (q)
DELIGHT, John David. 1936-1943. (g)[z]
DELIGHT, Paul Charles. 1940-1949. (g)[z]
DELL, George William. 1904-1908. (a)[z]
DESHON, Henry Fitz-gibbon. 1868-1874. (o)
DICKINSON, George Cockburn. 1846-1854. (p)
DIPNALL, James Fairlie Thomas. 1827-1834. (p)
DIPNALL, Matthias Sidney Smith. 1829-1835. (q)
DISTURNELL, Josiah. 1751-1762. (g)
DIX, Joshua Airlie. 1880-1887. (f)[z]
DIXON, Kennett. 1879-1884. (j)
DOLMAN, Claude Ernest. 1916-1925. (k)[z]
DONALDSON, Arthur Hay. 1924-1932. (h)[z]
DONALDSON, Edward Mortlock. 1922-1928. (h)[z]
DONALDSON, John William. 1920-1927. (h)[z]
DONNITHORNE, Vyvyan Henry. 1896-1902. (g)
DORMAN, Arthur John. 1856-1863. (l)
DOUGLAS, Keith Castellain. 1931-1938. (f)[z]
DOUNE, George, 1583-ng. (p)
DOVEY, William Thomas. 1802-1809. (p)
DOWNIE, Harold Frederick. 1901-1908. (n)
DRAKE, Colin Stuart. 1939-1947. (q)[z]
DRAKE, John Harold. 1889-1895. (a)
DRAYSON, Alfred Cecil. 1897-1902. (a)
DRAYSON, Edwin Howard. 1901-1906. (j)
DRAYSON, Fitz Alan George. 1898-1905. (i)
DREW, Arthur Charles Walter. 1922-1931. (n)[z]
DREW, William Leworthy Good. 1834-1842. (o)
Du BOULAY, Francis Robin Houssemayne. 1931-1938. (b)[z]
DUNCAN, Patrick. 1835-1841. (i)
DUNFORD, Benjamin. 1701-1705. (p)
DUNLOP, James Craufurd. 1874-1880. (n)
DURANT, Henry William. 1914-1919. (l)[z]
DYER, George. 1762-1774. (f)
DYMOKE, John Lindley Marmion. 1937-1943. (n)[z]
EARNSHAW, Edwin. 1848-1854. (p)
EAST, Lionel William Pellew. 1874-1882. (i)
EASTON, Malcolm Fyfe. 1919-1929. (b)[z]
EDGAR, William Harold. 1896-1901. (j)
EDMONDS, Cecil John. 1902-1906. (o)[z]
EDMUNDS, Percy James. 1902-1909. (o)[z]
EDWARDS, Herbert Edward Osman. 1872-1883. (c)
EDWARDS, William Frederick Savery. 1881-1887. (i)
EKINS, Franklin George. 1905-1913. (a)[z]
ELLIOTT, Edward Casselton. 1893-1898. (l)
ELLIOTT, Harry Manly Casely. 1880-1887. (j)[z]

ELRINGTON, Maxwell. 1910-1915. (a)[z]
ELSTOB, Wilfrith. 1898-1905. (i)
ELWALL, Alfred. 1826-1834. (d)
EMSON, Reginald Herbert Embleton. 1922-1929. (h)[z]
ENGELBACH, Lewis William. 1845-1852. (n)
ENGELBRECHT, Julian Ekstein. 1984-1989. (a)[z]
ENGLEDOW, Gladys. 1915-1922. (a)[z]
ENGLEHEART, Francis. 1784-1790. (m)
ERSKINE-TULLOCH, Piers Hector. 1939-1947. (i)[z]
ESCRITT, Charles Ewart. 1917-1923. (b)[z]
ESSERY, William Joseph. 1871-1875. (k)
EVANS, Eric Bertram. 1910-1917. (q)[z]
EVANS, James Morgan. 1932-1940. (i)[z]
EVANS, Roger Courtenay. 1912-1917. (q)[z]
EVANS, Walter Tenniel. 1937-1944. (f)[z]
EVERARD, Thomas. 1730-1735. (o)
EVERITT, Michael. 1726-1732. (j)
EWAN, Robert Wilson. 1918-1924. (q)[z]
EXTON, Clive. 1941-1945. (f)[z]
FARR, George Henry. 1827-1839. (d)
FARRELL, Nigel George. 1963-1970. (f)[z]
FARRER, William James. 1853-1864. (m)
FEW, Charles. 1786-1793. (p)
FFINCH, Benjamin Traill. 1847-1855. (o)
FFINCH, Matthew Mortimer. 1847-1857. (g)
FIELD, Matthew. 1756-1767. (q)
FILDER, Edward. 1801-1809. (p)
FIRMIN, Percy Judge. 1899-1903. (q)[z]
FISHER, Terence Roland. 1913-1919. (f)[z]
FLETCHER, Alan Gerard. 1941-1948. (f)[z]
FLETCHER, Henry Clyde. 1837-1843. (i)[z]
FLETCHER, Samuel. 1819-1830. (b)
FLETCHER, Winston. 1948-1949. (l)[z]
FLEW, Robert Newton. 1897-1905. (b)
FOORD, Henry Stilles. 1807-1812. (i)
FORBES, James. 1934-1941. (l)[z]
FORD, Leslie. 1924-1929. (k)[z]
FORDE, Ivo Mathew Leopold Dieskan. 1917-1925. (l)[z]
FORDHAM, John. 1622-1628. (p)
FORREST, William Ivon Norman. 1923-1931. (j)[z]
FORSDYKE, Edgar John. 1895-1902. (e)
FOSTER, William Shrubsole. 1846-1856. (o)
FOX, Cyril Fred. 1895-1899. (e)
FOX, William Tilbury. 1844-1851. (k)
FOXELL, Maurice Frederic. 1901-1905. (g)
FRADIN, Louis Reginald. 1914-1919. (q)[z]
FRAMPTON, Algernon de Kewer. 1913-1920. (o)[z]
FRAMPTON, Henry James. 1910-1916. (o)[z]
FRANCIS, Augustus Lawrence. 1857-1866. (c)
FRANCIS, Edward Nattali. 1830-1836. (p)
FRANCIS, Samuel. 1766-1771. (p)
FRANKLIN, Frederick William. 1783-1793. (q)
FRANKLIN, Henry William Fernehough. 1914-1920. (c)[z]
FRANKLIN, Kenneth James. 1908-1916. (b)[z]
FRANKLIN, Reginald Hector. 1906-1909. (n)[z]
FRANKS, Richard Lee. 1865-1871. (q)
FRASER, William Robert. 1903-1910. (n)[z]
FREEMAN, John. 1741-1747. (p)
FREEMAN, Maggie Rentoul. 1895-1898. (a)[z]
FULLER, Franklin Bland. 1871-1878. (a)
FULLER, Walter William. 1846-1852. (p)
FURRELL, James Wyburd. 1846-1864. (o)
FYFFE, Charles Allen, 1854-1864. (f)
FYNN, Henry Francis. 1810-1816. (o)
GAINSBOROUGH, George Fotheringham. 1926-1933. (m)[z]
GARDINER, William James. 1816-1822. (p)
GARDNER, Charles James Hookham. 1883-1891. (i)

GARDNER, Henry. 1840-1847. (p)
GARLING, Daniel Burr. 1795-1799. (p)
GAUNTLETT, John George. 1842-1852. (g)
GAUNTLETT, Robert Douglas. 1998-2005. (a)[z]
GEARY, Frederick Charles. 1897-1905. (b)
GENTRY, Jack Sydney Bates. 1911-1916. (n)[z]
GERRARD-WRIGHT, Richard Eustace John. 1942-1947. (i)[z]
GERTY, Francis Hamilton. 1885-1892. (j)
GIBBINS, Charles George. 1920-1926. (q)[z]
GIBBS, Henry Charles Beaumont. 1843-1850. (m)
GIBBS, William Arthur. 1875-1877. (q)
GILBERT, Richard. 1802-1808. (p)
GILBERT, William. 1721-1731. (b)
GILBERT, William. 1852-1860. (q)[z]
GILBERTSON, Moyna Patricia. 1942-1948. (k)[z]
GILBEY, Henry Parry. 1832-1839. (p)
GILES, Percy Albert. 1902-1906. (q)
GILES, William Ernest Powell. 1845-1850. (m)
GILL, James. 1839-1850. (d)
GILLHAM, John Moor. 1928-1935. (q)[z]
GILLY, William. 1769-1780. (g)
GILLY, William Stephen. 1797-1808. (g)
GLENN, Robert George. 1849-1861. (n)
GLOCK, William Frederick. 1919-1926. (e)[z]
GODDEN, James. 1889-1896. (f)[z]
GODWIN, George. 1747-1753. (p)
GOLDNEY, Gabriel. 1820-1828. (n)
GOODMAN, Vyvian Edwin. 1902-1905. (n)[z]
GOODRICH, Edmund Richard. 1831-1838. (p)
GOWING, Margaret Mary. 1932-1938. (b)[z]
GOWLLAND, Edward Lake. 1886-1892. (i)
GRANT, Frederick. 1936-1942. (q)[z]
GRANT, Gordon. 1918-1924. (n)[z]
GRANT, John. 1784-1791. (f)
GRAY, Louis Harold. 1918-1924. (l)[z]
GRAY, Michael Stuart. 1942-1950. (i)[z]
GREEN, Donald Richard. 1910-1917. (q)[z]
GREEN, John Kenneth. 1918-1922. (f)[z]
GREEN, Melvill. 1846-1851. (p)
GREEN, Sebert Francis Saint Davids. 1877-1883. (i)
GREEN, Violet Evelyn Ivy Suzanne. 1922-1928. (l)[z]
GREENE, Hugh. 1592-c1601. (g)
GREENFIELD, William Frederick. 1834-1845. (c)
GREENHILL, Alfred George. 1856-1866. (b)
GREENSLADE, Stanley Lawrence. 1916-1923. (g)[z]
GREENWOOD, John. 1795-1805. (q)
GREY, William Sollory. 1812-1818. (p)
GRICE, Richard. 1689-1698. (d)
GRIER, John Arthur Bolton. 1890-1897. (l)
GRIFFITH, William Saint Bodfan. 1886-1892. (c)
GRIFFITHS, Alan Richard 1919-1926. (g)[z]
GRIGGS, Richard. 1819-1826. (q)
GRINLING, Henry. 1844-1848. (p)
GROVER, Thomas. 1706-1714. (b)
GUILLEBAUD, Phoebe Monica. 1917-1925. (a)[z]
GUILLEMARD, William Henry. 1823-1834. (c)
GURNEY, Norah Kathleen May. 1933-1939. (m)[z]
GUTCH, John Matthew. 1785-1790. (m)
GUTCH, Robert. 1784-1797. (g)
GUTHKELCH, Arthur Norman. 1924-1933. (k)[z]
GUY, William Augustus. 1818-1825. (k)
GWYN, Stephen. 1691-1698. (d)
HADEN, Francis Seymour. 1826-1833. (f)
HAIG BROWN, William. 1833-1842. (c)
HAKE, Guy Donne Gordon. 1898-1902. (m)
HAKE, Thomas Gordon. 1816-1824. (k)
HALDEN, Ian Michael. 1977-1984. (a)[z]

HALL, Frances Helena. 1893-1900. (a)[z]
HALL, Henry Armstrong. 1862-1868. (g)
HALL, Lewis Montgomery Murray. 1865-1871. (i)
HALL, Philip. 1915-1922. (b)[z]
HALLORAN, Laurence Hynes. 1774-1781. (m)
HAMERTON, Charles. 1747-1753. (p)
HAMILTON, Henry. 1835-1840. (m)
HAMILTON, Henry. 1864-1870. (f)
HAMILTON, John Angus Lushington Moore. 1883-1887. (m)
HAMILTON, Robert Henry. 1877-1883. (q)
HAMMOND, James Lempriere. 1838-1848. (b)
HANDFORD, Peter Thomas. 1929-1935. (f)[z]
HANKIN, Barclay Dundas. 1927-1936. (q)[z]
HANNUM, James Thomas. 1822-1828. (q)
HANSELL, Peter. 1931-1938. (k)[z]
HANSFORD, John Talbot. 1931-1940. (c)[z]
HARDING, Edwin Elmer. 1867-1875. (b)
HARDING, Harold John Boyer. 1909-1917. (l)[z]
HARDING, Hilda Blanche. 1899-1906. (q)
HARDY, Thomas Duffus. 1811-1819. (n)
HARPER, Hugo Daniel. 1832-1840. (c)
HARRILD, Robert. 1787-1793. (m)
HARRIS, Etta Grace. 1898-1903. (a)
HARRIS, Joseph. 1827-1836. (q)
HARRISON, Augustus Spiller. 1832-1843. (d)
HARVEY, Cyril. 1914-1919. (q)[z]
HARVEY, John. 1680-1687. (o)
HARWARD, Francis Edward. 1881-1888. (a)
HASKELL, Harold Noad. 1899-1906. (d)
HAVINDEN, Ashley Eldrid. 1912-1919. (f)[z]
HAWES, Stanley Gilbert. 1916-1922. (f)[z]
HAWKE, John. 1854-1861. (l)
HAWKINS, Caesar Henry. 1807-1813. (k)
HEARN, James. 1882-1892. (f)
HEATH, Andrew. 1964-1971. (o)[z]
HEATHERLY, Sawell. 1706-1718. (q)
HEISELER, Patricia Joy. 1929-1936. (m)[z]
HELLER, Robert Gordon Barry. 1942-1950. (l)[z]
HENDERSON, Geoffrey Archer. 1924-1930. (j)[z]
HENDRIKS, Augustus. 1843-1849. (l)
HENN, Charles Cooper. 1871-1882. (q)
HENN, Percy Umfreville. 1873-1883. (d)
HERZIG, Christopher. 1936-1945. (n)[z]
HEWLETT, Donald Graham. 1885-1892. (a)
HEWLETT, Graham. 1874-1879. (j)[z]
HEWLETT, James. 1647-1661. (b)
HEYWOOD, Daniel Frederick. 1865-1877. (q)
HICKS, Edward Barry. 1868-1875. (g)
HIGHTON, Edward Gilbert. 1840-1845. (m)
HILDYARD, John Richard Westgarth. 1823-1828. (p)
HILL, Edward. 1735-1744. (p)
HILL, George Rowland. 1865-1869. (n)
HILL, Margaret Lilian Alice. 1901-1909. (a)[z]
HILL, Rowley. 1845-1855. (g)
HIME, Henry Charles Rupert. 1887-1893. (i)
HIND, Charles Lewis. 1872-1878. (f)
HIPWOOD, Charles. 1877-1888. (n)
HOBDEN, Herbert John. 1920-1926. (q)[z]
HODGSON, William. 1762-1767. (p)
HODSOLL, Eric John. 1904-1911. (n)[z]
HODSON, Thomas Callan. 1880-1890. (b)
HOLBROW, Thomas. 1837-1849. (g)[z]
HOLLOWAY, Bernard John. 1929-1937. (b)[z]
HOLMES, Edward. 1792-1800. (p)
HOLMES, John Dickonson. 1883-1890. (j)
HOLMES, Susannah. 1826-1832. (q)
HOOD, Arthur. 1872-1879. (q)

HOOK, Ross Sydney. 1928-1936. (g)^z
HOPKINS, Samuel. 1709-1715. (m)
HOPSON, Donald Charles. 1926-1934. (o)^z
HORNBY, John. 1875-1886. (c)^z
HORNCASTLE, Edgar. 1889-1895. (q)
HORNE, Thomas Hartwell. 1789-1795. (e)
HORNIMAN, Henry. 1878-1885. (j)
HORSTEAD, James Lawrence Cecil. 1910-1915. (g)^z
HOUGH, James. 1827-1833. (k)
HOUGH, Sydney Samuel. 1879-1889. (o)
HOWELL, Mortimer Sloper. 1848-1859. (o)
HUBBARD, Roy. 1930-1935. (q)^z
HUBBLE, Harry Denniss. 1911-1917. (q)^z
HUDSON, Leslie Sewell. 1882-1888. (l)
HUGHES, Frederick Llewelyn. 1904-1913. (g)^z
HULL, Thomas Arthur. 1838-1845. (j)
HUMFREY, Lebbeus Charles. 1807-1816. (m)
HUMPHREYS, David. 1704-1708. (b)
HUNT, Harold John. 1917-1923. (d)^z
HUNT, James Henry Leigh. 1791-1799. (f)
HUNTER, Robert Dow. 1929-1936. (i)^z
HUNTER-JOHNSON, David Alan. 1926-1933. (l)^z
HUTTON, David Graham. 1916-1920. (m)^z
HUTTON-POTTS, Jack Peter. 2001-2008. (a)^z
HUXHAM, Harold James. 1899-1908. (o)
ILIFF, Frederick. 1809-1819. (b)
IRVING, Edward Arthur. 1859-1865. (g)
ISDELL-CARPENTER, Charles Howard. 1887-1894. (q)
JACKSON, John. 1757-1763. (p)
JACKSON, Rowland Bower. 1887-1892. (q)
JACOB, Philip. 1811-1818. (g)
JACOBS, Norman Nathaniel. 1941-1949. (q)^z
JAMES, Philip. 1749-1754. (p)
JAMES, Thomas. 1763-1769. (p)
JELFE, William. 1731-1739. (p)
JENKIN-JONES, Charles Mark. 1896-1901. (l)
JENNINGS, Percival Henry. 1914-1920. (o)^z
JOHNSON, George Arthur. 1915-1922. (m)^z
JOHNSON, Martin Challenor Page. 1921-1926. (j)^z
JOHNSON, Robert. 1750-1753. (p)
JOHNSON, Thomas. 1802-1808. (l)
JOHNSTONE, Hope. 1878-1881. (i)
JONES, Gabriel. 1732-1739. (o)
JONES, George Hugh. 1847-1854. (c)
JONES, Hannah Mabel. 1899-1904. (a)^z
JONES, Percy Herbert. 1874-1884. (j)
JONES, Ronald Austin. 1919-1926. (q)^z
JOWETT, James Peter. 1980-1987. (a)^z
JURIN, James. 1692-1702. (k)
KEANE, Edward Vivian Harvey. 1853-1859. (l)
KEBLE, John. 1757-1759. (p)
KEELEY, John. 1694-1702. (p)
KEMP, Charles. 1910-1914. (o)^z
KEMP, Frederick James. 1898-1904. (c)
KEMP, George. 1818-1827. (p)
KENDALL, Franklin Richardson. 1848-1855. (l)
KEYMER, Nathaniel. 1821-1832. (q)
KEYMER, Nathaniel. 1853-1860. (g)
KEYS, Ivor Christopher Banfield. 1931-1938. (b)^z
KIDD, Beresford James. 1872-1882. (b)
KINDER, William. 1735-1740. (p)
KING, Edward John Boswell. 1904-1907. (n)^z
KING, George Kemp. 1893-1899. (n)
KING, Henry Douglas. 1886-1890. (n)
KING, Joseph. 1783-1789. (p)
KING, Mark Howard Robert. 1926-1934. (m)^z
KING, Philip David. 1946-1954. (g)^z

KINGDON, Roger Taylor. 1940-1949. (l)^z
KINGSBURY, William. 1755-1758. (g)
KINGSFORD, Peter Wilfred. 1920-1925. (a)^z
KIRBY, Cecil Francis. 1914-1922. (q)^z
KIRKMAN, Charles Alfred. 1933-1941. (n)^z
KIRKPATRICK, Randolph. 1872-1879. (e)
KNAPP, Valentine. 1868-1876. (m)
KNIGHT, Marcus. 1915-1920. (g)^z
KNOWLES, William Charles Goddard. 1920-1926. (l)^z
KRABBE, Frederick James. 1869-1875. (j)
KROLL, Richard Wilhelm Francis. 1966-1971. (d)^z
KYNNESMAN, Arthur. 1694-1702. (p)
La TOUCHE, William Martin Digges. 1864-1869. (q)
LAING, Malcolm. 1836-1846. (q)
LAMB, Charles. 1782-1789. (f)
LAMBERT, Leonard Constant. 1915-1922. (f)^z
LANE, Michael. 1749-1757. (o)
LANE, Thomas. 1744-1753. (m)
LANE, William Byam. 1874-1881. (i)^z
LANG, William Dickson. 1887-1894. (e)
LANGLEY, Alexander. 1881-1890. (o)
LATHAM, Richard. 1778-1785. (p)
LATHAM, Thomas. 1753-1760. (p)
LAWRENCE, Roger. 1679-1688. (g)
LAXTON, William. 1809-1815. (m)
LAYBOURNE, Alan Watson. 1911-1915. (j)^z
LE GRICE, Charles Valentine. 1781-1792. (f)
Le KEUX, Richard. 1766-1770. (p)
LE PAGE, Robert Brock. 1932-1937. (b)^z
LEA, Richard. 1758-1761. (p)
LEACH, Eva Frances. 1915-1923. (d)^z
LEAHY, James Palmer. 1881-1886. (j)^z
LEDGER, Claude Kirwood. 1899-1903. (o)
LEE, Richard. 1853-1865. (q)
LEE, William. 1681-1687. (p)
LEGATE, Pamela. 1955-1962. (q)^z
LEIGH, Henry Sambrooke. 1846-1852. (f)
LEMPRIERE, William 1866-1873. (q)
LEVIN, Henry Bernard. 1939-1945. (f)^z
LEWEN, John Henry. 1931-1939. (o)^z
LEWIS, Arthur King. 1877-1886. (o)
LEWIS, Eric William Charles. 1926-1933. (n)^z
LILLY, Henry. 1595-1605. (m)
LIMMER, Thomas Edward. 1872-1878. (q)
LING, Arthur George. 1924-1931. (m)^z
LINTON, Robert George. 1890-1896. (k)
LITTLE, Robert. 1853-1860. (q)
LIVESEY, Robert Cowburn. 1940-1946. (n)^z
LLOYD, Richard Alfred. 1839-1852. (o)
LOADER, Thomas. 1837-1845. (l)
LOCKHART, Arthur William. 1859-1866. (q)
LODGE, Jeremiah. 1820-1825. (p)
LODGE, John. 1902-1906. (c)^z
LODGE, Richard. 1865-1874. (b)
LONGDEN, Harry Leicester. 1913-1917. (i)^z
LONGMATE, Norman Richard. 1936-1943. (f)^z
LORD, Freda Marjorie Edith. 1913-1918. (q)^z
LOW, Charles Ernest. 1879-1885. (o)
LUDLOW, George. 1804-1811. (q)
LUDLOW, Harvey. 1836-1842. (k)
LUDLOW, Henry. 1843-1853. (o)
LUMBY, John. 1716-1724. (g)
LYNAM, Charles. 1836-1843. (m)^z
LYNAM, Robert. 1806-1814. (f)
MACINTOSH, William Henry. 1865-1875. (c)^z
MACIRONE, George Augustus. 1843-1849. (n)
MACKELCAN, John. 1769-1773. (i)

MACKENZIE, Stephen. 1853-1859. (k)

MACKIE, Joseph Millard. 1878-1885. (a)[z]

MACKIE, Mark. 1842-1847. (q)

MACKNESS, Leslie Edward. 1893-1898. (q)[z]

MACKRILL, Frank Henry Arthur. 1907-1911. (q)[z]

MACLEAN, James Mackenzie. 1844-1854. (n)

MACLEAN, William Edward. 1882-1889. (q)

MACLEANE, Douglas. 1863-1875. (g)

MAINE, Henry James Sumner. 1829-1840. (b)

MALLESON, Herbert Cecil. 1890-1896. (k)

MALLINSON, James Elliott. 1874-1881. (q)

MANNING, Frederick Edwin Alfred. 1908-1911. (n)[z]

MAPLESTON, Thomas. 1722-1728. (p)

MARCHANT, Edgar Cardew. 1873-1883. (b)

MARILLIER, Henry Currie. 1875-1884. (l)

MARKLAND, Jeremiah. 1704-1710. (b)

MARLAND, Peter Michael. 1944-1953. (c)[z]

MARLOW, Roger Douglas Frederick. 1923-1929. (l)[z]

MARRIOT, Robert. ng-1563. (p)

MARRIOTT, George Robert Laxon. 1861-1872. (m)

MARRIOTT, Patrick Arthur. 1908-1916. (n)[z]

MARSHALL, Anthony. 1834-1840. (l)

MARSHALL, Austin John. 1947-1953. (f)[z]

MARSTON, John. 1845-1851. (l)

MARTIN, James. 1869-1877. (l)

MARTIN, Rhea. 1939-1948. (b)[z]

MASON, David Frederick. 1936-1942. (f)[z]

MASSEY, Edmond. 1701-1708. (f)

MASSEY, Robert. 1711-1717. (p)

MATHEWS, Charles Stephens. 1807-1820. (d)

MAUDE, Aylmer.1868-1874. (f)

MAURICE, Thomas. 1762-1767. (e)

MAYER, John. 1916-1921. (l)[z]

MAYNE, Philip. 1911-1918. (a)[z]

MAYOR, John Eyton Bickersteth. 1832-1836. (b)

McCALLUM, Duncan. 1900-1904. (n)

McKAY, Henry Kellock. 1859-1865. (k)

McNAULTY, Norah. 1906-1912. (b)[z]

McRAE, Foster Moverley. 1926-1934. (a)[z]

MEARD, George. 1719-1726. (p)

MEARS, Cuthbert Vincent. 1912-1919. (h)[z]

MEIGGS, Russell. 1912-1921. (b)[z]

MENZIES, Alexander Charles George. 1911-1917. (l)[z]

MEREWETHER, Edward Rowland Alworth. 1902-1908. (n)[z]

MERK, Frederick Holland. 1874-1882. (q)

MERRIMAN, Charles Victor. 1849-1860. (g)

MESSENGER, William Aubrey. 1909-1915. (l)[z]

MEYER, Henry. 1791-1794. (f)

MIALL, William George. 1875-1881. (q)

MICHELL, Lewis Loyd. 1852-1857. (l)

MIDDLETON, Ralph. 1828-1835. (p)

MIDDLETON, Thomas Fanshaw. 1779-1788. (g)

MIDGLEY, Eric Atkinson. 1924-1932. (o)[z]

MILLBOURN, Arthur Russell. 1904-1911. (g)[z]

MILLETT, Arthur Fenning. 1848-1860. (o)

MITCHELL, Charlotte. 1935-1942. (f)[z]

MITCHELL, Edward. 1647-1652. (p)

MITCHELL, Leslie Herbert. 1925-1932. (o)[z]

MITCHELL, Thomas. 1790-1802. (b)

MONK, Henry Wentworth. 1834-1842. (g)

MOODY, Lewis Herbert. 1895-1899. (q)[z]

MOOR, Ralph Denham Rayment. 1868-1875. (o)

MOORE, Robert Frank. 1899-1905. (a)

MOOREY, John. 1715-1723. (p)

MOOTE, Margaret Louise. 1934-1942. (m)[z]

MORGAN, Clement Yorke. 1915-1922. (d)[z]

MORGAN, Hilda Joyce. 1920-1926. (a)[z]

MORPURGO, Jack Eric. 1929-1936. (b)[z]

MORRELL, James George. 1933-1939. (l)[z]

MORRIS, David Freestone. 1915-1923. (g)[z]

MORRIS, George Mortimer. 1876-1883. (i)[z]

MORRIS, John. 1841-1848. (q)

MORRIS, Samuel Sheppard Oakley. 1857-1866. (j)

MORSON, James Collin Francis. 1849-1861. (c)

MOSELEY, Edward. 1690-1697. (o)

MOSES, William. 1632-1639. (b)

MOTT, Arnold John. 1926-1933. (h)[z]

MOTT, Charles. 1798-1803. (n)

MOYNIHAN, Berkeley George Andrew. 1875-1881. (k)

MUIR, Alec Andrew. 1919-1928. (n)[z]

MURGATROYD, Frederic. 1805-1809. (q)

MURIEL, Hugh Evans. 1841-1847. (g)

MURPHY, Neville Richard. 1902-1909. (b)[z]

MURRY, John Middleton. 1901-1908. (f)

NASH, Frederick Gifford. 1826-1838. (g)

NATTALI, Benjamin. 1850-1857. (m)

NEALE, James. 1731-1739. (f)

NEALE, William Henry. 1793-1803. (f)

NESBITT, Allan James. 1848-1855. (g)

NEWALL, Joan. 1930-1936. (q)[z]

NEWCOMB, Charles George. 1826-1831. (p)

NEWCOMBE, Stewart Francis. 1887-1893. (i)

NEWNS, Alfred Foley Francis Polden. 1919-1928. (o)[z]

NEWNUM, John Henry, 1852-1863. (q)

NEWPORT, Henry. 1830-1841. (c)

NEWSTEAD, Charles William. 1910-1915. (q)[z]

NEWTE, Horace Wickham. 1879-1885. (f)

NEWTON, James Williams. 1749-1758. (g)

NEWTON, William. 1743-1750. (m)

NICHOLS, Richard Everard. 1947-1955. (l)[z]

NIXSON, Thomas. 1766-1772. (l)

NORMAN, Eric Glynn. 1916-1922. (q)[z]

NORTH, Thomas. 1904-1909. (i)[z]

NORTHCOTT, Douglas Geoffrey. 1927-1935. (b)[z]

NORTON, George. 1801-1806. (m)

NOSWORTHY, Richard. 1869-1876. (o)

O'CONNOR, William Leslie Maurice. 1917-1923. (l)[z]

OLDFIELD, Reginald Edgeley. 1895-1903. (q)

OLIVER, John Oliver William. 1921-1929. (h)[z]

OLIVER, Kenneth Cyril. 1918-1926. (g)[z]

OMMANNEY, Henry Mortlock. 1879-1885. (j)[z]

ONYON, William. 1869-1877. (j)

OSMOND, Christopher Neville, 1944-1951. (q)[z]

OSTLER, Henry Hubert. 1886-1892. (o)

OUNSTED, Christopher. 1930-1940. (k)[z]

OVERALL, Florence. 1912-1920. (q)[z]

OWEN, John Simpson. 1922-1932. (o)[z]

OWEN, William Henry. 1864-1872. (j)

OWEN, William. 1799-1811. (b)

OZELL, John. 1687-1694. (f)

PAGE, Robert. 1786-1789. (p)

PAINE, William. 1626-1635. (p)

PALEY, Edward Graham. 1832-1838. (m)[z]

PALMER, John. 1741-1748. (p)

PALMER, Joseph Blades. 1858-1867. (g)

PANTON, Richard. 1733-1742. (p)

PAREZ, Claude Herbert. 1842-1853. (n)

PARK, William Robert. 1888-1895. (g)

PARKER, Hampton Wildman. 1909-1914. (e)[z]

PARKER, John. 1653-1664. (b)

PARKES, Edmund Alexander. 1829-1834. (k)

PARLBY, Joshua. 1864-1870. (m)

PARR, Thomas. 1727-1734. (p)

PARREY, William. 1639-1644. (q)

PARRY, Rey Griffith. 1899-1905. (h)[z]
PARSONS, Patrick George. 1922-1929. (f)[z]
PASLEY, Joseph Montagu Sabine. 1911-1913. (i)[z]
PATERSON, Rex Munro. 1912-1918. (l)[z]
PATTENDEN, George Edwin. 1830-1842. (c)
PAYNE, William. 1829-1836. (n)
PEACEY, Basil William. 1898-1905. (g)
PEACOCKE, Thomas. 1637-1642. (p)
PEARCE, Edmund Courtenay. 1879-1889. (g)
PEARCE, Ernest Harold. 1874-1884. (g)
PEARCE, Thomas Neill. 1917-1922. (m)[z]
PEAREY, Michael Alan. 1942-1951. (j)[z]
PEARSON, William Burton. 1931-1940. (d)[z]
PEMBERTON, Augustus Charles. 1883-1889. (q)
PEMBERTON, John. 1922-1930. (k)[z]
PENN, James. 1736-1745. (g)
PENNYCUICK, Charles Edward Ducat. 1852-1855. (o)
PENNYCUICK, John. 1850-1856. (o)
PERKINS, George. 1616-1629. (q)
PERRINCHIEF, Richard. 1625-1641. (g)
PERROTT, Sir Edward Bindloss, Bart. 1797-1799. (i)
PERRY, Kenneth Murray Allan. 1920-1927. (k)[z]
PETERS, Arthur Edward George. 1874-1883. (g)
PETLEY, Eaton Wallace. 1860-1865. (o)
PEWTRESS, Alfred William. 1904-1907. (m)[z]
PHELAN, Daniel John. 1968-1975. (l)[z]
PHILLIPS, Francis Hugh Addison. 1911-1917. (m)[z]
PHILLIPS, Samuel John. 1829-1841. (c)
PHILPS, Frank Richard. 1924-1931. (k)[z]
PHIPPS, Albert Edmund. 1883-1887. (l)
PICKARD, Michael John. 1950-1957. (l)[z]
PICKERING, William. 1751-1760. (b)
PIERCE, Thomas. 1836-1842. (i)[z]
PILKINGTON, Henry Seymour Hoyle. 1879-1884. (o)
PILLOW, Edwin Cedric Stuart. 1938-1944. (a)[z]
PINCHBACK, William. 1756-1762. (p)
PINHEY, Hamnett Kirkes. 1792-1799. (p)
PIPPETT, Roger Samuel. 1907-1912. (f)[z]
PITCHER, Duncan George. 1847-1854. (i)
PITCHER, Henry Jones. 1788-1794. (p)
PITCHER, Henry William. 1848-1856. (i)
PITMAN, John Rogers. 1792-1800. (g)
PITMAN, Robert Percy. 1934-1943. (f)[z]
PLATT, Thomas. 1763-1770. (p)
PLUMPTRE, Edward Vallis Cecil. 1913-1920. (c)[z]
POCOCK, Robert John. 1898-1908. (m)
POLEHAMPTON, Thomas Stedman. 1834-1846. (g)
POORE, Francis Harwood. 1849-1853. (j)
POTTER, Thomas Johnson. 1834-1846. (q)
POUND, John. 1838-1844. (l)
POWELL, William. 1748-1750. (f)
PRECIOUS, Robert. 1743-1749. (p)
PRENTIS, William. 1708-1714. (l)
PRICE, Thomas. 1811-1816. (p)
PRINCE, Thomas. 1795-1806. (b)
PRISTON, Stewart Browne. 1893-1896. (g)
PROCTOR, Anne Ines Louie. 1916-1925. (a)[z]
PROWSE, Richard Thomas. 1843-1850. (n)
PRYNNE, Harold Vernon. 1878-1885. (i)[z]
PULLAN, Richard Popplewell. 1833-1840. (m)
PULLEN, William Le Geyt. 1864-1871. (j)
PULLER, Christopher. 1729-1738. (p)
PULLINGER, Henry Robert. 1897-1903. (c)
PYKE, George Frederick. 1904-1908. (c)[z]
PYNE, Alexander. 1858-1870. (d)
PYNE, Percy Rivington. 1828-1835. (l)
QUENNELL, Sidney Metcalfe. 1850-1855. (m)

RAINS, Anthony John Harding. 1930-1938. (k)[z]
RANCE, Patrick Lowry Cole Holwell. 1927-1936. (m)[z]
RANDOLPH, Cyril George. 1910-1916. (l)[z]
RANDOLPH, Thomas Berkeley. 1913-1923. (g)[z]
RASHLEIGH, Vernon Stanhope. 1889-1894. (j)
RASINI, Charles Luigi Domenico. 1925-1931. (q)[z]
RAY-JONES, Holroyd Anthony. 1950-1957. (m)[z]
READ, Ewart Kingsley. 1909-1915. (q)[z]
RECKNELL, George Hugh. 1906-1909. (l)[z]
REDHOUSE, James William. 1819-1826. (o)
REED, Michael. 1923-1930. (n)[z]
REEVES, John. 1781-1789. (m)
REEVES, Thomas. 1744-1750. (m)
REEVES, William. 1748-1754. (m)
REICHEL, Henry Rudolf. 1866-1875. (b)
REILLY, William Edmund Moyses. 1835-1841. (i)
RENNIE, Michael. 1928-1935. (a)[z]
REYNOLDS, Shirley. 1881-1888. (m)
RICE, Edward. 1802-1813. (q)
RICHARDS, Edward Windsor. 1840-1846. (l)
RICHARDS, Frank Roydon. 1910-1917. (c)[z]
RICHARDS, George. 1776-1785. (f)
RICHARDS, Thomas. 1809-1815. (m)
RICHARDSON, William. 1742-1750. (p)
RICHES, Eric William. 1909-1915. (k)[z]
RICKS, John Plowman. 1922-1928. (n)[z]
RIDGE, Anthony Hubert. 1925-1932. (n)[z]
RIDGE, Lacy William. 1847-1854. (m)
RIDOUT, Dudley Howard. 1874-1880. (i)
RIX, William. 1745-1749. (n)
RIXSON, Dennis Fenn. 1930-1936. (h)[z]
ROBERTS, Arthur Loten. 1918-1924. (b)[z]
ROBERTS, Herbert Ainslie. 1874-1883. (b)
ROBERTS, Keith Varnden. 1936-1943. (n)[z]
ROBERTS, Thomas. 1805-1811. (p)
ROBERTS, William. 1826-1837. (o)
ROBERTSON, Thomas Dixon Marr Trotter. 1864-1872. (n)
ROBINSON, Albert Wilson. 1917-1922. (q)[z]
ROBINSON, Gregory. 1884-1891. (f)
ROBISON, Samuel. 1792-1798. (p)
ROBSON, Alan. 1898-1907. (c)
ROCHE, John Knatchbull. 1824-1834. (o)
ROCK, William Frederick. 1811-1817. (m)
ROE, John Septimus. 1807-1813. (m)
ROE, Reginald Heber. 1860-1869. (d)
ROGERS, James. 1833-1839. (p)
ROGERS, Philip Graham. 1886-1896. (o)
ROGERS, Thomas Alfred. 1861-1872. (c)[z]
ROLFE, Alfred James. 1879-1887. (d)
ROMANIS, William. 1833-1842. (f)
ROOT, Frederick James. 1917-1924. (n)[z]
ROSS, Alan Alistair. 1930-1937. (l)[z]
ROSS, Eric Arthur. 1905-1909. (f)[z]
ROSS, William Alston. 1885-1887. (o)
ROSS-GOOBEY, George Henry. 1922-1928. (l)[z]
ROWED, William Edward. 1831-1836. (p)
RUPERT-JONES, John Archibald. 1883-1888. (m)
RUSSELL, Frederick Vernon. 1879-1886. (l)
RUSSELL, William Allan. 1837-1847. (o)
SACHS, Roy Tessier Seaver. 1898-1903. (a)
SAKER, Harold John. 1910-1913. (h)[z]
SALISBURY, Roy Fortescue. 1940-1946. (q)[z]
SANDFORD, George Ritchie. 1904-1911. (o)[z]
SANDWITH, Thomas Backhouse. 1838-1844. (o)
SANGSTER, Robert. 1758-1764. (p)
SATCHELL, Mary. 1925-1933. (a)[z]
SAUNDERS, Alan Frederic. 1896-1902. (i)

SAVIN, Lewis Herbert. 1913-1918. (k)[z]
SAWYER, Henry George. 1851-1856. (m)[z]
SCHOLEFIELD, James. 1797-1809. (b)
SCHOOLING, Anthony John Marshall. 1930-1937. (m)[z]
SCOTT, Melville Horne. 1836-1837. (g)
SCOTT, Thomas Lamb. 1917-1924. (q)[z]
SCOTT, Walter. 1865-1874. (d)
SCUDAMORE, Frank Ives. 1832-1838. (n)
SEAMAN, Clarence Milton Edwards. 1920-1927. (c)[z]
SEARLE, Charles Edward. 1837-1847. (b)
SEARS, William Gordon. 1910-1918. (k)[z]
SELBY, Peter. 1702-1711. (q)
SELLERS, Robert Firth. 1934-1943. (l)[z]
SENIOR, Bernard. 1875-1879. (o)
SEYMOUR, Roland George. 1915-1922. (h)[z]
SHARKEY, Seymour John. 1855-1866. (k)
SHARP, Henry. 1825-1832. (q)
SHARPE, John Francis Baxter. 1854-1861. (q)
SHAW, Arthur Barnsley. 1868-1880. (q)
SHEA, Charles. 1797-1802. (q)
SHEARMAN, Henry Palmer. 1839-1847. (p)
SHEARS, David John Arthur. 1935-1944. (m)[z]
SHELDON-WILLIAMS, Inglis Patrick. 1918-1926. (o)[z]
SHELLEY, George. 1677-1682. (m)
SHEPPARD, Stuart Colquhoun. 1879-1886. (q)
SHILLITO. James. 1796-1803. (p)
SHIPTON, Peter. 1721-1728. (b)
SILCOCK, Joseph. 1840-1847. (p)
SIMMONDS, Kerren. 1957-1966. (q)[z]
SIMON, Maximilian Frank. 1855-1865. (k)
SIMON, Noel Murray. 1931-1939. (m)[z]
SIMONS, William Charles. 1854-1859. (g)
SIMPSON, Wilfred Levick, 1872-1877. (m)
SINCLAIR, Laurence Frank. 1919-1924. (h)[z]
SINGERS-DAVIES, Richard William Frederick. 1868-1875. (g)[z]
SLADE, Edwin. 1913-1922. (b)[z]
SLATER, Richard. 1687-1693. (p)
SLOPER, Charles William Edmund. 1880-1886. (q)
SMAIL, Raymond Charles. 1924-1932. (b)[z]
SMART, William. 1773-1778. (p)
SMITH, Arthur Lionel. 1858-1869. (b)
SMITH, Bowen Eleny. 1835-1841. (a)[z]
SMITH, Charles Robert. 1898-1904. (o)
SMITH, Daniel. 1988-1991. (a)[z]
SMITH, Francis Henry. 1919-1926. (q)[z]
SMITH, Frank Ewart. 1909-1919. (l)[z]
SMITH, Frederick John. 1867-1876. (k)
SMITH, Geoffrey. 1937-1944. (m)[z]
SMITH, John. 1715-1720. (p)
SMITH, John. 1811-1819. (c)
SMITH, Lawrence Delpré. 1915-1924. (o)[z]
SMITH, Leslie Edward George. 1930-1935. (l)[z]
SMITH, Owen Maurice. 1901-1907. (n)
SMITH, Reginald Allender. 1881-1891. (e)
SMYTH, James. 1725-1737. (g)
SNELL, Charles. 1675-1681. (m)
SNELLGROVE, David Llewelyn. 1930-1938. (b)[z]
SOLFLEET, Gerald. 1885-1891. (j)[z]
SPARROW, John William. 1828-1834. (p)
SPEED, Eric Bourne Bentinck. 1904-1914. (n)[z]
SPELSWORTH, Samuel. 1635-1648. (p)
SPENCE, Reginald Arthur. 1888-1895. (o)
SPILSBURY, Alfred John. 1883-1893. (c)
SPRAGG, Cyril Douglas. 1907-1910. (l)[z]
SPRATT, Thomas Abel Brimage. 1819-1827. (j)
SPRINGHALL, Robert John. 1910-1917. (i)[z]
SQUIRE, John Franklin. 1749-1758. (b)

STALLEY, Henry John. 1857-1864. (q)
STAPLES, James. 1854-1862. (q)
STAPLES, Kathleen Mary. 1890-1896. (a)[z]
STEEL, Joseph Lincoln Spedding. 1911-1918. (l)[z]
STEIL, John Wellesley. 1908-1912. (o)[z]
STEPHENS, James Francis. 1800-1807. (m)
STEPHENS, John James. 1756-1762. (p)
STEPHENS, Lancelot Pepys. 1774-1784. (q)
STEPHENS, Olive. 1930-1935. (m)[z]
STEPHENS, Wilson Treeve. 1922-1928. (l)[z]
STEPHENSON, John Robin. 1940-1948. (l)[z]
STEPHENSON, Thomas. 1595-ng. (q)
STEVENS, Carol. 1959-1965. (q)[z]
STEVENS, John Edgar. 1932-1938. (b)[z]
STEWART, Francis William. 1896-1904. (o)
STEWART, Robert Michael Maitland. 1918-1925. (n)[z]
STEWART-SMITH, Kathleen Georgiana Maule. 1916-1924. (a)[z]
STIFF, William James. 1913-1919. (q)[z]
STODDART, Albert. 1853-1859. (q)
STODDART, Charles John. 1848-1854. (l)
STOE, Harry. 1762-1767. (p)
STONE, Arthur Harold. 1927-1935. (d)[z]
STONE, Leslie Charles. 1945-1952. (m)[z]
STOTESBURY, Herbert Wentworth. 1927-1935. (n)[z]
STRACEY, John. 1775-1780. (p)
STRACEY, Randolph. 1768-1772. (p)
STRANGE, William Allder. 1821-1827. (c)
STRIPP, Herbert Francis Edward. 1909-1914. (q)[z]
STRONG, Thomas Banks. 1833-1840. (n)
STRUTT, Joseph. 1785-1790. (e)
STUBBS, Peter Hugh Satow. 1939-1946. (m)[z]
SULLIVAN, Edward Godfrey, 1886-1892. (g)[z]
SURR, Thomas Skinner. 1778-1785. (n)
SUTHERLAND, Anthony Frederic Arthur. 1926-1935. (n)[z]
SUTTON, Alan William Frank. 1923-1930. (j)[z]
SWAN, Lionel Maynard. 1896-1904. (o)
SWAN, Michael Lancelot. 1933-1940. (f)[z]
SWEETING, Alfred. 1838-1850. (g)
SWEETING, Henry Dove. 1841-1852. (o)
SWIFT, Herbert Walker. 1907-1914. (b)[z]
SYKES, Francis. 1847-1852. (q)
SYMONS, Ronald Stuart. 1917-1923. (n)[z]
TAMBLING, Christopher. 1976-1982. (c)[z]
TANDY, Arthur Harry. 1915-1922. (o)[z]
TANDY-GREEN, Charles William. 1898-1903. (m)
TAYLOR, Doris Winifred. 1906-1915. (a)[z]
TAYLOR, Frederick Beatson. 1860-1870. (o)
TAYLOR, Henry. 1819-1824. (p)
TAYLOR, William. 1757-1768. (g)
TAYLOR, William George. 1914-1921. (q)[z]
TEBBUTT, Henry Jemson. 1843-1855. (g)
TEMPLE, Richmond. 1903-1908. (l)[z]
TERRISS, William. 1854-1857. (f)
TERRY, Joseph. 1670-1677. (q)
TEW, Edmund. 1711-1716. (q)
THACKERAY, John. 1788-1791. (q)
THACKSTON, Hazel. 1938-1944. (q)[z]
THOMAS, Edgar William. 1888-1895. (n)
THOMPSON, Arthur Leonard Bell. 1928-1935. (f)[z]
THOMPSON, Charles Wilfred. 1883-1890. (q)
THOMPSON, D'Arcy Wentworth. 1836-1848. (b)
THOMPSON, Elizabeth. 1804-1809. (q)
THOMPSON, Marmaduke. 1784-1796. (g)
THOMPSON, Samuel. 1774-1780. (g)
THORNTON, Edward. 1773-1785. (o)
THORNTON, James Cholmondeley. 1918-1926. (e)[z]
THORNTON, Michael James. 1930-1937. (l)[z]

THORNTON, Richard. 1785-1791. (m)
THORP, John Brown. 1870-1877. (m)
TICKNER, Martin. 1952-1958. (e)^z
TIETKENS, William Harry. 1853-1859. (m)
TIGHE, Patrick Anthony Macartan. 1933-1939. (i)^z
TILSON, Robert. 1716-1722. (b)
TODD, Herbert Eatton. 1919-1925. (f)^z
TODD, Robert Henry. 1867-1878. (k)
TOMLINSON, Charles. 1743-1750. (p)
TOWNSEND, Charles Spread. 1841-1850. (b)
TOWNSEND, John. 1766-1771. (g)
TREMLETT, Erroll Arthur Edwin. 1905-1909. (i)^z
TRETHOWAN, James Ian Raley. 1933-1938. (e)^z
TRIGG, Thomas. 1702-1713. (p)
TRIMBLE, Charles John Agnew, 1896-1902. (q)
TRINDER, Arthur William. 1912-1918. (l)^z
TROLLOPE, Arthur William. 1775-1787. (q)
TROLLOPE, George. 1809-1817. (q)
TROLLOPE, William. 1809-1817. (q)
TRUMAN, Egerton Danford Hampshire. 1888-1894. (i)
TUBBY, Alfred Herbert. 1870-1878. (k)
TUCKER, Brian George. 1932-1939. (n)^z
TUDOR-CRAIG, Algernon. 1881-1887. (i)
TULLET, Graham Beverley, 1953-1959. (i)^z
TURING, Harvey Doria. 1886-1891. (f)
TURNER, Bradwell Talbot. 1917-1920. (j)^z
TURNER, Frederick Charles. 1880-1891. (o)
TUSON, Henry Brasnell. 1843-1848. (j)
TUTTIETT, Lawrence. 1833-1840. (f)
TYERS, Charles James. 1815-1820. (o)
TYLER, John. 1775-1781. (p)
USHER-WILSON, Lucian Charles. 1912-1919. (g)^z
VANDERZEE, Francis Henry. 1848-1851. (i)
VAUGHAN MORGAN, Septimus. 1841-1847. (l)
VAUGHAN MORGAN, Walter. 1840-1846. (l)
VAUGHAN, John Keith. 1921-1929. (f)^z
VEAL, John Bartholomew. 1920-1926. (n)^z
VEAR, Kenneth Charles. 1921-1929. (a)^z
VICARS, John. 1589-1604. (f)
VIDAL, Alexander. 1828-1834. (o)
VINCENT, Patrick Michael Causabon. 1934-1942. (j)^z
VINE, Marshall George. 1859-1865. (g)^z
VOIGT, George. 1836-1845. (c)
WAGNER, Orlando Henry. 1875-1883. (c)^z
WAGNER, Peter Edward. 1945-1950. (g)^z
WALES, Charles Douglas. 1911-1917. (q)^z
WALES, Frank Vernon. 1920-1925. (q)^z
WALES, Frederick William. 1910-1915. (q)^z
WALES, Hubert Edward Robert. 1918-1923. (q)^z
WALES, Sydney Herbert Thomas. 1914-1918. (q)^z
WALLIS, Barnes Neville. 1900-1904. (m)
WALLIS, John Eyre Winstanley. 1899-1905. (g)
WALMISLEY, Herbert William. 1874-1881. (q)
WALTERS, William Charles Flamstead. 1867-1878. (b)
WARD, Albany. 1888-1894. (m)
WARD, Arthur Blackwood. 1878-1889. (k)
WARD, Arthur Hawkins. 1840-1848. (g)
WARD, Cecil Arthur. 1889-1896. (j)
WARD, Ebenezer. 1827-1832. (l)
WARD, Walter Reginald. 1878-1885. (i)
WARD, Wilfrid Arthur. 1904-1908. (o)^z
WARING, Henry William Allen. 1915-1923. (l)^z
WARNER, George Frederic. 1854-1864. (e)
WARNER, George Townsend. 1824-1833. (c)
WARNER, Thomas Courtenay. 1778-1784. (p)
WATKINS, Charles Frederick. 1804-1810. (m)
WATLING, Edward Fairchild. 1912-1918. (c)^z

WATSON, Alfred Edward Thomas. 1855-1863. (f)
WATSON, Edward. 1798-1806. (p)
WATT, Jack. 1930-1936. (q)^z
WATTS, Charles William Paxton. 1843-1854. (o)
WAUGH, Arthur Thornhill. 1851-1861. (g)
WAY, Nowell FitzUpton. 1847-1851. (j)
WEBB, Stephen Richard. 1960-1969. (q)^z
WEBB, William Spencer. 1794-1799. (p)
WEBSTER, Alphonsus. 1833-1840. (p)
WEBSTER, William Henry Albert. 1895-1900. (o)
WEEDING, Thomas. 1783-1789. (p)
WELFARE, Freda May. 1917-1922. (a)^z
WESTLAKE, Herbert Francis. 1888-1898. (g)
WESTON, Frank Valentine. 1945-1954. (g)^z
WESTON, Thomas. 1799-1806. (p)
WHEBLE, Bernard Spencer. 1916-1921. (l)^z
WHEELER, Joseph Bishop. 1842-1849. (p)
WHEELHOUSE, Claudius Galen. 1834-1842. (k)
WHITBY, Nicholas. 1633-1639. (p)
WHITE, Frederick Augustus. 1848-1855. (q)
WHITE, Gilbert Anthony. 1925-1933. (i)^z
WHITE, James. 1784-1789. (m)
WHITE, John Tahourdin. 1818-1830. (q)
WHITE, William Foster. 1818-1822. (q)
WHITE, William George. 1808-1812. (i)
WHITEHEAD, John Stainton. 1943-1950. (o)^z
WHITROW, Gerald James. 1923-1930. (b)^z
WHITTINGHAM, Harold Edward. 1898-1902. (k)
WICKHAM, Harry Temple. 1895-1904. (q)^z
WIGHT, Ian Lyttleton. 1916-1922. (i)^z
WILBY, Thomas. 1778-1783. (q)
WILBY, William Henry. 1783-1789. (p)
WILDING, Michael Charles Gauntlett. 1922-1928. (f)^z
WILKINS, George. 1847-1853. (m)
WILKINSON, Charles Nelson. 1828-1833. (p)
WILLCOX, Walter Temple. 1878-1885. (i)
WILLIAMS, Alistair Glenn. 1956-1963. (a)^z
WILLIAMS, Evan Clifford. 1905-1911. (m)^z
WILLIAMS, Henry Jameson Middleton. 1908-1913. (n)^z
WILLIAMS, John, [early19th C]. (p)
WILLIAMS, John Daniel. 1836-1847. (c)
WILLIAMS, Thomas Brian. 1924-1933. (c)^z
WILLIAMS, William. 1580-1589. (n)
WILLIAMSON, William Henry. 1861-1867. (n)^z
WILLIS, Arthur. 1751-1756. (b)
WILLIS, Arthur. 1814-1824. (c)
WILLIS, Charles Hope. 1868-1875. (j)
WILLIS, William. 1830-1837. (n)
WILSON, Christopher. 1797-1807. (g)
WILSON, Francis. 1747-1752. (p)
WILSON, John Iliff. 1801-1806. (q)
WILSON, Joyce. 1938-1945. (f)^z
WILSON, Joyce Elizabeth. 1919-1927. (c)^z
WILSON, Sydney Ernest. 1909-1917. (c)^z
WILSON-HAFFENDEN, Donald James. 1911-1916. (i)^z
WINBOLT, Samuel Edward. 1876-1887. (q)
WINGFIELD, John. 1839-1846. (q)
WINGFIELD, Richard. 1832-1838. (p)
WISE, John Humphrey. 1902-1909. (o)^z
WITHERS, Henry. 1850-1855. (p)
WITHERS, Thomas. 1779-1785. (j)
WITHERS-GILL, Joseph. 1866-1874. (o)^z
WOMERSLEY, Denis Keith. 1931-1938. (o)^z
WONHAM, Charles Scrivener. 1880-1885. (j)
WOOD, Alfred Maitland. 1848-1859. (g)
WOOD, Cecil Denyer. 1899-1907. (k)
WOOD, John. 1790-1799. (b)

WOODHAMS, Geoffrey. 1901-1910. (a)[z]
WOODHEAD, William Dudley. 1895-1904. (d)[z]
WOODS, John Harold Edmund. 1906-1914. (n)[z]
WOODTHORPE, Henry. 1764-1770. (n)
WOODTHORPE, Henry. 1787-1795. (n)
WOODWARD, Denys Cuthbert. 1911-1917. (o)[z]
WOODWARD, Frank Lee. 1879-1890. (d)
WOOLLEY, Charles Edward Allen. 1870-1878. (j)[z]
WOON, Peter. 1942-1949. (e)[z]
WORTING, Joseph. 1660-1670. (p)
WRIGHT, Paul. 1728-1735. (g)
WRIGHT, Thomas. 1754-1758. (o)
WYLIE, James Hamilton. 1852-1863. (n)
WYLIE, John Anthony Hamilton. 1928-1936. (k)[z]
YATES, Ivan Michael. 1936-1944. (m)[z]
YEO, George. 1675-1682. (q)
YOUNG, Percy Marshall. 1924-1930. (b)[z]
YOUNG, Thomas. 1800-1809. (a)[z]
YOUNGMAN-CARTER, Philip. 1917-1921. (f)[z]
ZEEMAN, Erik Christopher. 1934-1943. (b)[z]

Appendix 1
Some aspects of education at CH

A1.1 This appendix will look at some aspects of education at Christ's Hospital across the years: pupil numbers; where pupils were admitted from; and the cost of their education. As background to the three areas of analysis, it will be useful first to provide some information about the arrangements for the admission of children to the School. Much of the information provided reflects the position existing for boys, although arrangements will generally have applied pari passu to girls.

Admission

Arrangements

A1.2 In the early days of the School, two broad categories of children were admitted. The first group covered children of freemen (essentially, those with the right to trade, and usually associated with a Guild or Livery Company), the second comprised younger 'suckling' children, where care was more relevant than education, these generally being put out to be looked after by 'nurses' before entering the Newgate Street School perhaps at around the age of 10. Various ad hoc modifications to age of entry and parental requirements were made across the years, with a specific set of rules being established in 1676. The main requirements then were that children should be at least seven years old, be sons or daughters of freemen, be living in the City or its Liberties (areas outwith manorial rule or obligations to the Crown), and were orphans, wanting father or mother or both; those not permitted entry included foundlings, those with a sibling already at the School, and those who were lame or otherwise infirm. A few years later, the rule that children should be living in the City was abolished, thus increasing the geographical spread of admissions.

A1.3 The rules were further amended in later years. First, a maximum age of 10 on entry was introduced in 1809, this being raised to 11 at the end of the 1860s, at the same time the minimum age was increased to eight. Following the introduction of the Scheme in 1891, most admissions occurred at age 10 and over, including some at 12 and 13. At Horsham, with the Prep School taking children aged nine and 10, the senior School continued to take children aged 11 to 13, although by the late 1920s it appears that the bulk of entries there was at age 11. Then, as we have seen (para 1.154), in 1966 the age of entry was raised to about 11 at both Horsham and Hertford. Later, although entry at age 11 (Year 7) remained the main admission route into the School, some pupils were admitted at age 13 (the more common age for admission to public schools generally), while the completion of the two Grecians' Houses in 2001 permitted entry at age 16. Secondly, in respect of the requirement that children be sons or daughters of freemen, in 1745 Governors (see below) were allowed to present one non-free child in four, and then, over subsequent years, one in three (in 1765) and then one in two (in 1828), before the eventual abolition of the requirement in 1839. Thirdly, apart from where permitted by the special provisions of a Trust, the sibling criterion was relaxed to allow two children of the same family to be in the Hospital at the same time. However, there were occasional exceptions to all these rules.

Donation Governors

A1.4 One other important change had been made in 1676.

Hitherto, it appeared that eminent persons (such as the Lord Mayor and Aldermen) and benefactors could send, or receive preference to send, children to CH. In that year, such arrangements were formalised permitting the ex-officio City Governors the right of presentation, with similar rights being granted to benefactors in proportion to their gifts, this being the beginning of the Donation Governor (usually referred to as Governor) system of presentations. From 1677 (when the name of the presenter – Governor or Trust – was first included in the admission register) up to the introduction of the Scheme in 1891, aside from around one-sixth of total entry made through Trusts or on the Royal Mathematical School, Governor presentations provided the definitive route into CH.

A1.5 In the early years of the new arrangements for presentations, election as a Governor required a minimum donation of £200, this being doubled to £400 in 1790, and increased to £500 in 1841. (To provide some context for this last figure, the annual cost of running Christ's Hospital in 1840 was around £70,000.) Up to the introduction of the Scheme in 1891, a single donation permitted Governors to present children in rotation for life, after which time presentation rights were curtailed, these later changing to requiring a qualifying donation for each presentation. Given various financial problems at the School, perhaps surprisingly, the minimum donation remained at £500 until rising to £1,000 in 1947 (at which time annual running costs were around £150,000). Today, the minimum qualifying donation for a presentation, of £30,000, part-funds a pupil's education, with Governors being encouraged to make a higher donation to meet the full cost (estimated in 2016 as £190,000, against the School's total current and capital expenditure in that year of £28 million). Women become eligible for appointment as Governors from 1878, although Queen Victoria had been elected in 1843. In broad terms, it is estimated that around 4,500 Governors – Monarchs, Princes, Dukes, Marquesses, Earls, Viscounts, Barons, Lords, Knights, Bishops, the Military and MPs and others – were elected over the years 1676 to the present day. Pre-Horsham, the peak figure for the number of Governors was probably around 470 in 1860, this number then falling back sharply, with the uncertainties surrounding the Scheme, to about 180 just before the move from London. Numbers increased during the 20th century with, nowadays, there being around 630 Governors who have made a presentation or presentations across the years.

Trusts

A1.6 As mentioned above, aside from Governor presentations, the other route for admission into the School was provided by Trusts which had been established by various individuals or organisations, some as far back as the mid-17th century. The largest source of presentations, made from around the early 1720s, came from the immense generosity of John and Frances West. The Wests had been born in the early 1640s, John being an eminent scrivener who went on to become Master of the Clothworkers' Company and a Governor of CH; en passant, he was witness to the will of Samuel Pepys, whose role in the early days of the Royal Mathematical School has been mentioned earlier. The Wests amassed a considerable fortune, and even before they died – both in their early 80s – they transferred much of it, including land in Westminster and in certain central London parishes, to the School. Such monies were to be used for the maintenance and education, at CH, of boys and girls from Reading (16, from three different parishes), Newbury (16) and Twickenham (8), with preference to be given to those whose parents could establish consanguinity with the Wests, and for six girls born in "London or the Liberties thereof", in practice this being essentially the City. There are still Wests' presentations today, and the author estimates an overall total of some 2,100 presentees who have been educated at CH from this source. Pre-Scheme, there were also major levels of presentation from Thomas Guy, founder of Guy's Hospital, and from a number of City of London Livery Companies, such as Cooks, Drapers, Fishmongers, Grocers, Ironmongers, Mercers and Skinners. Into the 20th century and beyond, many of these are still supporting Christ's Hospital, being joined by other Companies such as Carmen, Carpenters, Clothworkers, Founders, Salters, and Tylers and Bricklayers. Of the other earlier individual benefactors, William Stoddard, Giles Russell, Walter Woodward, John Lock and John Fowke were all responsible for large numbers of presentations. Mention should also be made of the major levels of RMS presentations made from its founding in 1673, these owing much to Samuel Travers and his nephew, Samuel Holditch, and also John Stock and Henry Stone. Finally, in the 20th century, two notable sources of presentation have been the RAF Foundationers' Trust (see para 1.262) and the Sue Thomson Foundation (see para 1.260).

A1.7 One precious theme evident from most of the benefactions is the close link the School had with the City of London. This has been not only the people – the Mayor and Aldermen, the merchants, traders and financiers – but also the Corporation of the City itself (which provides for a number of presentations). Some examples of the generosity which has flowed from these sources have been given in this book. Though not quite a quid pro quo, during the London era the very location of the School and the nature of the education provided to its pupils furnished a ready source of employees for a growing number of City firms. Nowadays, although the geographical link has long been lost, the strength of the relationship between the City and the School seems barely diminished.

Other arrangements for admission

A1.8 We have seen that, in the early days, children would go to the London School or be sent out to a nurse. Following the establishment in the early 1680s of a purpose-built boarding school at Hertford, most boys on being admitted would first go there, transferring to London a few years later, but those of proven academic ability did go directly to Newgate Street. However, from 1839 it was decided that all boys would be admitted first to Hertford, although a few exceptions were made. After the introduction of the Scheme in 1891, children entering from the two new channels of Endowed Schools and Public Elementary Schools would go direct to the London establishment, with the younger boys, admitted through the Governor system or Trusts, still going first to Hertford. For girls, once the Hertford school had been established, entry would be there, where they would remain.

A1.9 It seems that, until around the middle of the 19th century, although some form of pre-admission interview existed, there had been no formal assessment of academic ability, with some children not being able to read or spell, this placing increasing demands on the Hertford teaching staff. From 1861, prospective pupils were required to show some reading ability, while in 1870 a grade scale of attainment was brought in, and then with a more formal examination system being introduced following the Scheme. Into the 20th century, improvements have been made across the years, with a major development occurring in 1980 when a two-stage admission procedure was introduced: an initial computer-based assessment of verbal, quantitative, non-verbal and spatial reasoning and, for those that pass, a residential assessment with further academic testing, during which time a child could obtain a brief experience of boarding life while his or her suitability for boarding can be assessed. This excellent arrangement continues to the present day.

A1.10 Of greater concern to the School, though, apart from the early years, was that children should be medically fit to enter, and they had to undergo a rigorous medical examination by the Hospital's medical staff with, again from around the 1860s, parents providing detailed information about the child's health and agreeing, if a physical defect was evident, that the child might be removed if any worsening occurred. The health of the children continues to be of utmost importance to the School, with a Medical Centre, located in the original Infirmary building, open 24 hours a day during term time.

A1.11 The rules of 1676 also contained reference to age at discharge – boys mostly "just before or after the age of 15", with age 14 for girls. There were certain exceptions for boys, essentially those who might go to university or who were in the RMS. This arrangement continued for most of the pre-Horsham period, there being some small extensions in the early 1870s, while following the introduction of the Scheme most children left after their 15th birthday, although a minority only – those who were likely to go to university or enter certain professions – remained at School beyond the age of 17, this practice largely continuing well into the first half of the 20th century. A small number of pupils remained at CH until reaching the age of 19, having spent eight years in the senior School. With the increase nationally in the provision of further education in the 1960s, a growing number of pupils continued at CH after reaching 17. A further development then saw the length of time a pupil spent at CH being standardised at seven years (essentially Year 7 through to Year 13).

Pupil numbers

A1.12 For *Names*, the author provided some information on the number of pupils at the School, with annual figures, separately for boys and girls, being given for intervals of 10 years, for the period 1650 to 1900. Data on numbers had been given from time to time in sources such as Court/Committee minutes, Treasurer's Accounts and the Discharge Register, but there was no consistent, long-run series. Thus, the author made certain estimates based on the year of admission and discharge as given in the registers. However, as the year of discharge is not recorded for about a quarter of those admitted in the first 100 years (mainly prior to 1600), the estimates start at 1650, with a small uncertainty for this year and for

1660 and 1670, but data are firm from 1680. He has now also provided figures for every ten years from 1900 to the present (with numbers also given for the merger year of 1985 and for 2016), this additional information coming mainly from the published annual reports.

A1.13 The information is given in Table 1. Before looking at the figures, two points should be made. First, for much of the pre-Horsham (mostly pre-fees) era, pupil numbers very much reflected the position on accommodation (at both London and Hertford) and the likely income which would be available for a given year. Although information on investment returns was largely known, the Governors had limited control over annual income. Even when fees were introduced in 1892, these initially made but a small contribution to total income. As a consequence, reflecting these two factors, pupil numbers in the pre-Horsham era fluctuated rather more than in later years. Secondly, while the pre-Horsham data relate to the beginning of the period shown, the subsequent figures, from the annual reports, appear to be for different times in the year, the numbers perhaps reflecting, therefore, the timing of admissions and discharge, although this does not appear to affect the overall trends in the post-London data.

A1.14 For boys, there were between 500 and 600 pupils on the School books in the mid-17th century. However, numbers were already beginning to decline in the 1660s when, as mentioned earlier, about 30 children died in the plague (1665), while in the following year, the Great Fire, although not claiming any of the 300 or so pupils reported as being at the London School, destroyed many school buildings. Despite temporary building work over the next four years, the number of boys was below 200 in 1670. Numbers then recovered strongly, exceeding 600 around 1690, but fell sharply in the second half of the 1690s, as the funding position deteriorated, to about 300 in 1700. However, with the Hertford school now established and taking the younger boys, there was a marked increase in the first decade of the 18th century to some 750 in 1710, with further increases to a figure of over 900 by 1740. The rest of the century saw the level fluctuate broadly between 700 and 900, with a rise to over 1,000 in 1800. Numbers were broadly flat for a while before rising again (as additional accommodation was built in London) in the 1830s to around 1,150 in 1840 and over 1,350 in 1850. Around these peak level years, there were about 950 boys in London and 400 at Hertford. The overall level then fell back and was maintained mostly between 1,000 and 1,100, before declining in the 1890s, as the financial position deteriorated, later recovering a little, in advance of the move to Horsham, to around 730 at the start of 1900. For the Horsham era, between 1902 and the merger in 1985, the number of boys can be regarded as being broadly constant – at around 820 (reflecting accommodation in 14 Houses of 50 and two Prep Houses of 60) up to 1965, and around 800 (16 Houses of 50) between 1965 and 1985 – although across the years there were clearly small movements about these figures, while numbers were run down in the few years before the merger.

A1.15 For girls, the mid-1600s levels were around 250. As with the boys, numbers then reduced in the 1660s and were down markedly to 35 at the start of 1670. Numbers picked up again and it was decided that they would be kept at around 100, although the figure came down to about 40 in 1700, reflecting the financial position. The level recovered, continuing at about the 100 mark, but was reduced to around 70 in 1760 at which it remained (save for a few further dips in the 1770s and 1780s) to the 1850s. It was decided that, rather than undertaking a

Table 1	Numbers of pupils at CH, by selected years		
	Boys	**Girls**	**All**
1650	450	240	690
1660	550	270	820
1670	175	35	210
1680	435	100	535
1690	635	120	755
1700	290	41	331
1710	757	108	865
1720	742	100	842
1730	796	115	911
1740	916	111	1027
1750	890	103	993
1760	708	72	780
1770	687	48	735
1780	922	39	961
1790	950	64	1014
1800	1009	65	1074
1810	1015	65	1080
1820	1003	70	1073
1830	1076	69	1145
1840	1150	68	1218
1850	1373	74	1447
1860	1034	48	1082
1870	1161	16	1177
1880	1050	74	1124
1890	1008	85	1093
1900	730	130	860
1910	820	240	1060
1920	831	276	1107
1930	817	285	1102
1940	797	275	1072
1950	822	276	1098
1960	823	283	1106
1970	777	279	1056
1980	805	295	1100
1985	640	230	870
1990	580	265	845
2000	470	335	805
2010	415	405	820
2016	446	436	882

major rebuilding programme at Hertford, numbers should be allowed to drop to about 20, and indeed they fell to just 16 in 1870. Then, reversing the previous decision, a rebuilding (and expansion) scheme at the girls' School was introduced a few years later, and numbers increased progressively to reach around 130 in 1900, in advance of the Horsham move, as Hertford was re-established solely as a girls' School. Numbers were then increased to an effective School size during the 20th century of 280 (eight Wards of 35), again with small annual fluctuations and some decline in the pre-merger years.

A1.16 Coming to 1985, in the first year of the merged School at Horsham, there were around 640 boys and 230 girls (in Coleridge and Barnes). Then in 1992, with a third House Block (Leigh Hunt) being given over to girls, numbers were about 520 boys and 300 girls, and finally, with changes to Thornton, in 2008 numbers were equalised at about 415.

Table 2   CH admissions, by region and year of entry

	1700-1749	1750-1799	1800-1849	1850-1902	1905-1909	1928-1932	*percentages* 2004/05	2015/16
BOYS							**BOYS AND GIRLS**	
North	0	1	4	6	6	2	2)	
Midlands	1	5	6	8	5	4	1)	4
South West	1	4	9	9	6	8	7)	
East Anglia	3	8	8	7	9	11	2)	
City of London	59	31	12	6)	41	38	27	24
Other London	32	39	41	36)				
Rest of South East	4	12	17	22	27	34	58	57
(of which Sussex)				(3)	(6)	(8)	(29)	(28)
Other	0	1	4	7	6	3	3	15
(of which Overseas)							(2)	(15)
Total (numbers)	6268	7460	8994	8328	730	610		
GIRLS								
North	0	0	1	4	5	3		
Midlands	1	2	3	5	3	1		
South West	1	1	3	4	5	5		
East Anglia	1	6	7	6	5	11		
City of London	64	40	17	9)	54	51		
Other London	30	35	48	40)				
Rest of South East	3	16	20	29	23	26		
Other	0	0	1	3	5	3		
Total (numbers)	952	575	581	684	240	225		

Figures for 2004/05 and 2015/16 relate to numbers at the School rather than admissions.

Since 2010, the School has admitted a certain number of day-pupils, the aim being for an overall pupil total of around 880 to 900, this level apparently being a likely ceiling, the figure, along with the numbers of masters and certain other staff, being the maximum which can be accommodated in Chapel or Big School.

Where pupils came from

A1.17   For both *CHIVE* and *Names*, the author gave figures relating to the geographical locations from where pupils entered CH, based on a comprehensive analysis of data in the admission registers. For this book, the author has summarised the earlier data and added certain figures for the 20th century and into the 21st. However, for the Horsham era, the author has not had access to the register details for other than the earlier years and no geographical breakdown seems to be available in the public domain until around the turn of the millennium. Thus, limited information only can be provided for this period. As background, first and as mentioned earlier, it was only from 1678 that children could be admitted from outside the City of London or its environs, the register recording about 110 children being admitted from outside this area between 1650 and 1699, out of a total for these years of some 4,800. Thus, the analysis starts from 1700. Secondly, prior to the end of the 1890s, many present-day London boroughs were not classified as London, for example Islington and Fulham were in Middlesex; Southwark and Wimbledon in Surrey; Deptford and Greenwich in Kent; and East and West Ham and Leyton in Essex. For the figures below, such data have been re-classified to reflect modern-day geography. Figures, for boys and girls separately, are presented in Table 2.

A1.18   For boys, the main geographical features during the London era were the decline in the importance of the City (from around 60 per cent of all admissions in 1700-49 to six per cent in 1850-1902), as entry requirements on location were relaxed, this change being mirrored in increases for the other regions, including for the rest of the South-East (excl London), where the share rose from four per cent to 22 per cent. Also of note, at a time when transportation was still in its infancy, are the perhaps larger than expected shares (all between six and nine per cent) relating to entries from the North, Midlands and South West Regions. Into the 20th century, with the boys' School now at Horsham, the figures – assembled for 1905-09 and 1928-32 – suggest a small geographical effect with increased admissions from Rest of South East (which includes Sussex) and a decline for the North.

A1.19   For girls, the pre-1902 analysis shows a broadly similar pattern as for the boys, viz, the decline for the City and an increase for the rest of the South-East (excl London), this latter group being more important for girls than boys, reflecting the higher incidence of admissions on the Wests'

Gift. Post-1902, when Hertford became solely a girls' School, the data (again for 1905-09 and 1928-32, but based on comparatively small numbers) suggest a possible small locational effect in the increased figure for East Anglia (which includes Hertfordshire).

A1.20 For the post-merger era, the final set of figures have been taken from the published Annual Reports for 2004/05 and 2015/16. There are two key features. First, nearly 30 per cent of all pupils now come from Sussex; this figure was already evident in 2004/05 and is thus not a consequence of the admission of day pupils in 2010. The increase for Sussex across the Horsham years perhaps reflects a policy to recruit locally. The second obvious aspect is the 15 per cent figure for overseas pupils in 2015/16, this resulting from, as explained before, a decision taken a few years ago to increase the number of such students at the School. In contrast, the lower proportion coming from London, compared with the earlier Horsham days, may reflect, in part, policy changes by the LCC and the GLC across the years. Finally, the share now coming from the "Rest of the UK" at little more than five per cent is markedly down from the high figure (of the order of 20 per cent) at the start of the Horsham era. In both cases, a greater availability of local and other schools will probably have been contributory factors.

Cost of education

A1.21 This final section provides information on how the average cost of educating a child at Christ's Hospital has changed over the last 100 or so years. The figures have been extracted or derived from the published accounts. There are some qualifications and uncertainties on the consistency of the data across the years. First, for the numerator (cost), there is the accounting definition of 'expenditure', which appears now to relate to "direct charitable expenditure", this excluding the full figures of capital expenditure but including depreciation which spreads this spending over the expected lives of the assets; also, the accounting year has changed over time. Secondly, for the denominator (numbers of pupils), it appears that the figures used are generally a notional rather than actual level. However, these various issues will not affect the broad conclusions which can be drawn about the profile shown by the data.

A1.22 Figures of average cost per pupil are given in Table 3 for intervals of five years for the period 1900 to the present day. Over this time, the estimated average cost of £60 in 1900 has rocketed to over £27,000 in 2016, a 450-fold plus rise. However, it needs to be recognised that, over this period, average UK earnings were up by a factor of around 380 and prices were nearly 100 times higher. (The greater growth in the former reflects the general effect of the availability of a substantially wider range of goods and services for consumption leading to a higher standard of living.) It is also of interest to mention one feature of the CH cost figures namely that whilst in 1900 staff costs accounted for barely a quarter of total costs, in 2015 the figure was around three-fifths.

A1.23 A second obvious feature is that we have a story of two halves. Between 1900 and 1950, the average education cost grew by a factor of just over three (an average annual increase of about two and half per cent). Over these years, the effects of two World Wars and the depression of the 1930s had a debilitating effect on the UK economy, with prices and earnings both moving erratically, with average annual growth rates of around three per cent for the latter and a little less for

Table 3 CH Education costs per child, by selected year	
Cost per year	
	£
1900	60
1905	70
1910	80
1915	70
1920	105
1925	110
1930	110
1935	110
1940	130
1945	130
1950	200
1955	250
1960	330
1965	460
1970	640
1975	1270
1980	2750
1985	5550
1990	7750
1995	10260
2000	13100
2005	17700
2010	21700
2016	27300

prices. Most of the CH spending was on current items, with very little new building work requiring new expenditure.

A1.24 Then between 1950 and 2016, the average cost of a CH education increased by a factor of 135 (an average annual rise of nearly eight per cent), with the corresponding figures for retail prices and earnings being around 30 (five and a half per cent per year) and 85 (seven per cent), respectively. The main contribution to these substantial increases came in the 1970s, where the cost of education virtually doubled between 1970 and 1975 and then more than doubled over the next five years to 1980. Over the decade as a whole, the fourfold increase in cost (an annual average rise of 16 per cent), occurred at a time of broadly similar growth for earnings with retail price increases being only marginally slower, these very strong increases in the national economy being largely due to the effect of rising oil prices. The new millennium has seen an approximate doubling in the cost of education (an average annual rate of around four and a half per cent), a period during which prices and earnings both showed average annual increases of less than three per cent.

A1.25 As we have seen earlier, there has been a substantial amount of capital expenditure on new development over this second (65-year) period, including in the 1960s and 1970s, and then related to the 1985 merger, and later including the Sports Centre, the Kitchen and the LARC. However, as mentioned just above, the full annual cost figures are spread over the expected lives of the assets rather than being recorded in full in the year in which the expenditure is incurred.

Appendix 2
Some Old Blue Institutions

A2.1   This Appendix provides some further information about a number of important Old Blue Institutions (and including the School magazine *The Blue*) which have been mentioned from time to time in the main part of the book.

The CH Club

A2.2   The Christ's Hospital Club was founded in 1891, the idea having been the subject of much discussion in Old Blue circles for some time, particularly as an increasing number of other public schools were establishing such bodies. Much of the work for its foundation was undertaken by the Revd George Bell*, then Master of Marlborough College but previously the Head at CH (1868-76), Bell linking the idea to the possibility of OBs undertaking some kind of mission work. In February 1891, about 100 Old Blues, masters and officers attended the initial meeting to discuss the proposal and the Christ's Hospital Club was born. Bell was elected the first President and a committee was formed to consider the scope of the Club and the important question of whether it should have its own premises.

A2.3   Three key members of this committee were people mentioned elsewhere in this book – Revd Richard Lee*, Walter (later Sir) Vaughan Morgan* and Arthur Lockhart* (who was to be Secretary of the Club for 21 years). The committee established a set of rules for the Club (including the need that applicants should have a formal proposer and a seconder), and the President of the Foundation, HRH The Duke of Cambridge, agreed to become Patron. Membership had reached 300 by the end of the first year, although disappointment was expressed at the small numbers of young Old Blues. An inaugural dinner had been held in May 1891, while early 1892 saw the Club promote the founding of the St John's Mission at King's Cross where OBs would work among the poor (see paras A2.9-11). In May 1901, the Duke of Cambridge, now in his 83rd year, attended the Club's spring dinner.

A2.4   The history of the Club, for all but the past 25 years, is well documented in *The Christ's Hospital Club, the first hundred years* (1992). The first part, covering the years 1891 to 1939, was based on material which appeared in *The Blue* from 1970 to 1975 under the pseudonym 'Anon' (the writer later identified – though probably recognised at the time – as PA Giles*, Hon Sec 1923-1937), the later years (1940-1990) being covered by someone else also called 'Anon'. A few important matters across the years will be mentioned here.

A2.5   One of the more dramatic events occurred shortly after WW1, when a cloud of pessimism seemed to descend on the Club, with some of those at the centre questioning whether it served any useful purpose and averring that the costs involved in its running were out of all proportion to the benefits accruing to members; indeed, there was a suggestion that the Club be wound up. A sub-committee was appointed to consider its destiny. While its remit embraced arrangements for a possible demise of the Club, there was a certain degree of optimism, led principally by Hon Sec JHE (later Sir John) Woods², in the sub-committee's deliberations, and it was a minority report from him which eventually won the day. Woods's report proposed certain administrative and financial improvements, recommended the establishment of an entertainment sub-committee, and made a plea for a room in central London where the Secretaries could undertake their work, these changes to be introduced alongside a revised set of Club rules. However, Woods, an "up-and-coming Treasury official", was unable to devote time to carry through his suggestions, and in 1923 the burden of the office of Hon Sec fell on the shoulders of Giles. And it was Giles who, in this role over the next 14 years, made a major contribution to resuscitating the Club, raising its membership from less than 500 to around 2,200, increasing the scope of OB links, particularly overseas, and strengthening its finances. Two other developments of Giles's tenure were first, in the mid-1920s, the granting of associate status to the former girl pupils of Hertford (who had established an Association in 1905), and secondly, in 1928, the Club obtained premises (an erstwhile "suite of offices"), within the School's Counting House in London at 26 Great Tower Street, the facilities later including the provision of lunches.

A2.6   Across the years, the Club was active in a number of fields, in particular: the development of the links with the regions and the universities, and also overseas, where "Le Cordon Bleu" evolved in Africa, Australia, Canada, France, Germany, Hong Kong, Malaysia, New Zealand, the United States of America and the West Indies; arranging events, such as entertainments and 'conversaziones' and being involved with the Founder's Day Dinner and Old Blues' Day; supporting Old Blue groups such as the Rugby Club and the Dramatic Society, and the magazine *The Blue*; and establishing employment and appointments registers, and later careers networks. Further, at the Club itself, the daily lunches were enjoyed by upwards of 50 people. Periodically, the Club also produced rolls of membership, with numbers topping 2,000 in the mid-1930s, and reaching 3,000 around 1950. In between these years, the Club had battened down the hatches in 1939 as WW2 started, re-opening in 1945.

A2.7   Amongst later events worthy of mention, the mid-1960s saw signs of financial problems, essentially with the in-house catering and the cost of producing *The Blue*, this being shared with the School, the solution here being an increase in the annual Club subscription to £1 (£17). Later, increased costs were to lead to the ending of the provision of daily lunches, whilst the inflation of the 1970s pushed the annual sub in the middle of the decade to £4 (£30). Then the proposed merger of 1985 led to OB girls being permitted full membership of the CH Club, the arrangement allowing them to continue as members of the CH Old Girls' Association. When the Counting House moved from London to Horsham in 1987, the Club initially sought new premises in the capital, but cost considerations led it to accept the offer of office accommodation at the School site. Then in 1998, as mentioned in the main text, the Club published *Who's Blue*, a directory of former pupils of CH, containing the names of nearly 5,000 Old Blues, with brief biographical details. It was reported that, about this time, there were some 4,000 Club members, this figure being said to be just over half of the overall OB population.

A2.8 It was not long into the new millennium when, reflecting problems in sustaining membership levels, particularly amongst the young, the Club President set up a working party to examine the meaning of the CH Club for Old Blues today. Following widespread consultation and discussion, one of the recommendations of the working party was that the Club should transform itself into an alumni association in which all those eligible would be members de facto (they could, of course, opt out), and there would no longer be an annual membership fee. The proposal – there really did not seem to be a viable alternative – was put to a postal ballot where it was "overwhelmingly accepted", the vote being confirmed at the moving final meeting of the Club in April 2005. The new body initially took the name Christ's Hospital Association, this being changed to Christ's Hospital Old Blues' Association. In 2016, there was a major survey of OB views on how they would like to engage with Christ's Hospital and on the often fraught issue of communications. A working group's report – which included recommendations for a more transparent and segmented (by age and gender) approach to communications strategy – was endorsed by Council. The School and CHOBA are considering proposals for its implementation.

The CH Mission

A2.9 One special, formal arrangement by which the charitable ethos of Christ's Hospital could be carried forward into later life came about in 1892, with the establishment of an "Association of Blues for Work amongst the Poor in London". This group, an off-shoot from the CH Club which had been founded the previous year, worked in a Mission, near King's Cross, north London, where many inhabitants were railway employees who were living in lodgings. The progenitors of the scheme, which became known as the CH Mission, were a group of Old Blues, supported by the Revd Richard Lee*, Head of the London School. Revd George Bell* was elected the first President, and the Mission was formally declared open in February 1893 by the Bishop of Bedford.

A2.10 The initial work of the Mission was directed at establishing and assisting with a Working Men's Club, and volunteers, seemingly never enough in numbers, were encouraged to give an evening a week to help out in the Club, or with the wider organisational aspects. A Men's Bible Class was established, later a children's Sunday School and a Boys' Club, and later still a Mothers' Group and a Girls' Friendly Society. OBs helped out in a variety of ways, such as making addresses at services, with Sunday School teaching, with the choir, performing in and arranging concerts, and with football coaching, as well as providing general administrative and financial assistance.

A2.11 The Mission did survive the various consequences of the move of the School from London to Horsham; indeed, not long after the move, Head Master Revd Upcott delivered an address about the Mission, and for a while it seemed that there was renewed support from pupils and staff at both Horsham and Hertford, as well as the Old Blue community. As the years passed, though, the numbers of supporters declined, despite frequent appeals, while later the War was to take away some of the more earnest workers. In the 1920s, the Mission was disestablished as a CH organisation, essentially, as TE Limmer* (Clerk) said, not because of inadequate support, but more as a result of the way the Mission had changed its approach, in the process becoming too political.

The Benevolent Society of Blues

A2.12 The Benevolent Society of Blues (BSB) was founded in 1824, probably through the Amicable Society of Blues (see below), with the object of affording relief to distressed Old Blues and the widows and orphans of Blues. In those early days, to help its charitable work, fund-raising dinners were held every three or four years, these including the School's tercentenary dinner in 1853 from which it benefitted to the tune of nearly £3,000 (£270k), adding substantially to its existing level of capital of around £8,000. Then in 1874, the Society celebrated its Golden Jubilee with a dinner chaired by the Duke of Cambridge. It had come a long way in those 50 years and although then blessed with assets now of over £20,000 (£1.7m), greatly helped by a legacy of £5,000 from Thomas Brown* in 1869 and a regular flow of annual subscriptions, a special appeal for funding produced a further £1,000. During those initial 50 years, the Society had helped over 1,000 people by gift, loan or pension, but the demands on its services were always increasing. However, it continued to flourish and by 1900 its assets had grown to over £25,000 (£2.4m), and it was providing pensions to over 40 beneficiaries and ad hoc gifts to others, in all totalling over £1,100 each year.

A2.13 The Society, through its dedicated team of directors who assess individual cases and now with a full-time secretariat based at the School, has continued its benevolent work through the 20th century and beyond, indeed its scope has been increased, in particular by presenting children of Old Blues to the School (this process beginning around 1917, with recent years having seen as many as nine BSB presentees at CH), and providing support for those pupils who are about to go to university or to study for a professional qualification. While a not insignificant part of the Society's work takes the form of advice and counselling, the funding position remains crucial to its activities. Today, the asset base, although affected by the financial crisis of 2008, stands in excess of £2.5 million, this, together with subscriptions (from a membership of over 600), donations and legacies, providing a seemingly comparatively healthy income. But the demand on the Society's benevolence remains strong, and this worthy cause will never be over-funded.

The Amicable Society of Blues

A2.14 The present-day Amicable Society of Blues was established in 1775, its previous incarnation as a dining club being traced back certainly to 1678 and possibly to 1629, and is thus thought to be one of the oldest such groups in the world. Dining remains the outward manifestation of the Society with three dinners a year – in February (the Audit Night Dinner), April (St George's Day, at which the Founder is commemorated) and November (the anniversary of the Accession of Queen Elizabeth I on 17 November, 1558). The venue was initially a City pub, but in recent years has been the Innholders' Hall. Many guests, including representatives from the School (both staff and pupils), are invited to the dinners where 'brawling' (ribbing, verbal rather than physical) has long been an idiosyncratic feature of the evening, the guilty members being fined by the President, with the monies going to the Amicable Foundation which provides funds for a variety of educational and social activities at CH. Two particular, recent examples of such benevolence have been support for the School's Model United Nations activities (see para 1.245) and an ad hoc donation enabling copies of David Miller's WW1 booklet to be given to all pupils at the School between 2014 and 2018 (see para 1.250).

A2.15 In 2012, at a time when the Society was endeavouring to recruit new, younger blood, the author was admitted to its ranks, at once increasing the average age of the membership. Nowadays, the Society numbers some 40 'Brethren' and 14 Honorary Brethren, largely but not exclusively Old Blues, and since 2013 it has extended membership to women, although by unanimous choice the use of the terms Brethren and Brother remain. It is possible that the Society may have played some role in establishing the first annual Founder's Day Dinner in 1826. On another matter, in early 1903 the Society had the rare experience of being a recipient rather than a giver, being presented with two massive carved oak chairs made from a timber beam from one of the old School buildings, such furniture, now rarely and reverently used, being housed in the Museum. The Society's motto – "Let brotherly love continue" – encapsulates well its caring and beneficent role.

The OBRFC

A2.16 No mention of Old Blue activities would be complete without reference to the Rugby Club. The Old Blues Rugby Football Club – initially called the Old Blues Football Club – was founded in 1873, and is one of the oldest of the Old Boys Rugby Clubs. The first President was the Revd George Bell*, then Head Master of the London School, with John Wingfield*, a master at the School as Treasurer, and Henry Armstrong Hall* as the first captain. One almost immediate consequence of its founding was that the boys at Newgate Street cast aside what rules had previously existed for the asphalt playground version of their game and adopted properly the new laws, making at the same time some small modification to the architecture of the buildings surrounding the pitch to furnish the appropriate facilities. However, it should not go unmentioned that, whilst the asphalt games may have had an adverse impact on skills, it brought a hardness to the tackle that many an opponent felt.

A2.17 In the initial years, the OBRFC played against the likes of Rob Roys, Selbourne, Colville Grasshoppers, Angell Town and the Arabs, some of these names probably having been lost in the passage of time. In 1881/82, there occurred a tragic event, the captain, SF Welsh (1867-75), collapsing and dying during a fixture. Although one or two games were played over the next two seasons, the Club then essentially closed down until it was re-constituted in 1893. However, much success followed quickly, with, by the end of the decade, three teams being fielded, and the 1st XV of season 1898/99 winning 17 and drawing one of its 19 games, scoring 344 points and conceding only 20; later, the 1st XV had an unbeaten run of nearly two years between November 1903 and October 1905. Two other names of the earlier years are worthy of mention – Shirley Reynolds*, who played for England, achieving two international caps in 1900 and 1901, and WJ Cullen[z] (see para 1.64) who gained a cap for Ireland in 1920.

A2.18 The Club was closed during the period of the First World War. The golden years were probably in the 1920s and 1930s with the Club, following the move, in 1921, to Fairlop (in Essex), fielding eight or nine teams and playing (and occasionally beating) many of the top club sides such Gloucester, Leicester and Bath. Four other key names of this time should be mentioned: Sir George Rowland Hill* who did much for the Club over a long period, but particularly at the time of the move to Fairlop; H Moody[z] and A Cross[z] for the great and unselfish service they had given to the Club, The Blue having said that never were two people so inaptly named: and RA Jones[z] who held the Club together during WW2,

borrowing pitches since Fairlop had apparently gone under the plough and managing to arrange fixtures over this time for at least two XVs. In 1959, a new pavilion – then thought to be one of the best in the country – was opened at Fairlop. However, recruitment became an increasing problem, and the Club, seemingly close to extinction on more than one occasion, became selectively open in 1968 (later becoming fully open). Its centenary was well celebrated in 1973, and then in the early 1980s it moved from Fairlop, where it had had its home for 60 years, to Motspur Park in South West London. The 1st XV now plays in the Surrey Leagues, with the Club having a 2nd XV and occasionally other XVs, including a Vets side. Touring remains a strong tradition. The Club's 150th anniversary is but a few years away in 2023.

"The Blue"

A2.19 In 1870, Christ's Hospital started out to produce a monthly school magazine, the intention being that any profit would go to the Boys' Charitable Fund, for its five "good causes". The magazine was to be produced by the pupils and for the pupils, with a Grecian (FJ Bell*) as editor and minimal help from the masters. The first edition, for March 1870, entitled The 'Blue' Budget, contained 16 pages and was priced at three pence (just over one penny today (£1)); 500 copies were printed. The slightly unusual name lasted only one edition, that for April being called the familiar The Blue. The early content included school, academic and sporting news, some literary and scientific articles, correspondence and a puzzle page. Interestingly, Bell's editorial had said that they hoped to include articles on science, but that religion would be omitted. The first few months of the venture augured well, the size was soon increased first to 24 then 32 pages, and roughly half the School were deemed to be regular subscribers. However, the initial euphoria was sadly short-lived, as the number of subscriptions declined and income failed to match costs. Gaps of three and four months began to appear between successive issues, and then one of 18 months before a re-launch of the magazine took place in January 1874. The target of a punctual and regular monthly publication was again proposed. The number of pages was back at 32, but the cover price had now been increased to sixpence (although probably less for the boys), and attempts were made to increase sales outside the School, with the introduction of an annual subscription of five shillings (now 25 pence (£25)), post free.

A2.20 But the problems were to continue. Barely a year after the re-launch, the financial difficulties had returned and the publication was down to 16 pages again. However, as a result of the generosity of Septimus Vaughan Morgan* who guaranteed the continuation of the publication, a further revival occurred and, by 1876, with a little more cost-cutting, the base was established from which at least parity in the battle of costs might be achieved. From this relaunch up to about the mid-1880s there had been a near monthly publication schedule. However, for the remaining 15 or so years of the century, this was reduced to nine copies each year, fitting in more sensibly with the term and holiday times.

A2.21 So much for quantity; what was the quality like? A fairly random trawl through the publications in the early years suggested a quite impressive range of content covering literary material (essays and poems); reports on school events, such as Speech Day and concerts, and on a wide range of sporting activities; school notes, which embraced obituaries and some Old Blue news; separate Oxford and Cambridge letters; and correspondence. The standard of writing, particularly the leading article, seemed high. Having said that, as anonymity generally prevailed it was not clear whether the authors were masters or boys; in practice it was probably a mixture of both. There were erudite, well-balanced discussions on matters such as the merits and demerits of the School dress; the town or country issue (the possibility of a move out of London had been considered by the Court of Governors a short while earlier); on the raising of the leaving age into the 16th year (which had been implemented in the early 1870s); and on the "public suppers" which were held at the School. There were also two articles which contained within them eerily prophetic comments. First, in the piece on the School dress, penned in February 1874, the writer had included, in the context of some musing on the future, the following few lines "....when there looms in prospect a day in which the cloisters of Grey Friars will be changed for some modern but more salubrious fabric of red brick …". Secondly, later that same year, in an article entitled "Extract from the Note Book of a Russian Traveller in England, anno 1953", the writer referred to the ancient institution of Christ's Hospital having been "reorganised some fifty years ago". The author wonders whether either of the writers was alive to see these events becoming reality in 1902. By and large, the generally good quality of the writing in *The Blue* was mostly continued beyond these initial years.

A2.22 As mentioned above, the high standard of the publication, and its maintenance, and the general administrative and financial arrangements needed to get it into print, could not have been achieved by the boys alone. While it is likely that a number of masters would have provided assistance, it seems that the main contribution came from the Revd James Fraser Cornish, a classics master who, for much of the final two decades or so of the 19th century, took over the management of the publication – to which he himself was a regular contributor. He cut the price of the magazine and greatly increased its circulation, these actions helping to put the operation on a sound financial footing, and he saw the issue of two books – *Gleanings*, in 1881 and *More Gleanings*, in 1895 – containing prose and verse, culled from the early years of the magazine. By the time of the School's move to Horsham he had established a surplus of £70 (£7k).

A2.23 Coming into the Horsham era, the initial 10 years saw a near doubling in the print run (from 700 to 1,350), whilst the first House notes – across the years for many of those still at School a staple part of the publication – to be limited initially to 50 words, had been introduced towards the end of 1903, although to begin with contributions were rather patchy. The rest of the format continued very much as before, but the number of literary contributions declined as *The Outlook* (a "literary magazine") was established in 1921. Photography began to be used as pictures of those who had fallen in WW1 were included. Then in 1929 ideas were requested for a new design for the cover, with a few suggestions being used the following year, although none was considered good enough to replace the existing design permanently. The number of issues produced each year varied over the first four Horsham decades, with the six issues of the 1930s being reduced to three during WW2, this "one per term" frequency then being continued subsequently. On lay-out, School material appeared in the first half of the publication, with Old Blue details following, but it was not until 1949 that an Old Blues section was given a formal heading, this containing, inter alia, "50 years ago", "25 years ago" and "letters" sections, and over the years an increasing volume of overseas news as former pupils established groups outside the UK. One other key feature of these earlier years was the inclusion of an index.

A2.24 In 1981 the dimensions of the magazine were increased and in 1999 desk-top publishing greatly facilitated the production process and the introduction of colour, the year also seeing further changes to dimensions (and arrangements for binding). Then in 2005, the thrice-yearly combined publication was changed to an annual publication for the School called *The Blue*, covering School matters with initially a few pages given over to Old Blue news, and a bi-annual publication, called *The Old Blue*, embracing material related to the Old Blue community. *The Blue* continued to grow in size, with nearly 250 pages appearing in the 2012/13 issue, these 18 square metres of paper being about three times the size of a typical three-term publication of the author's era which had also included the Old Blues section, photographs obviously making up much of the increase. For 2013/14 the issue was about one-half of the size of the previous year. In contrast, *The Old Blue* is now about a third of its 2005 size. Technology has also been embraced with news being disseminated via the School and CHOBA websites, and with the two publications available online. Social media, including the CH Forum (an unofficial website for discussion of CH and Old Blue matters), have also played their part. One other development which should be mentioned was the introduction in 1994 of a bi-annual newsletter – Housey! – which contained a range of news on, for example, current initiatives and developments, financial matters and forthcoming events, and complemented *The Blue*, but now focuses more on fundraising initiatives and School highlights.

A2.25 As a footnote, glossy and full of news as recent publications have been, over the years the infrequent use of surnames and the absence of captions to many of the photographs inevitably lessen the value of *The Blue* as a document of historic record. The author is not alone amongst the Museum volunteers to have some sympathy for our successors who might, in one hundred years' time, be asked for information about someone who was thought to be at the School around, say, the start of the 21st century. For the record, the Museum has assembled a number of complete sets of *The Blue* (one of which is in LARC) and several near-complete sets, missing only a few issues.

Index of Names

General Index

As explained in page 8, the index is selective. This second part relates to entries other than specific names.

PREVIOUS BOOKS ABOUT CHRIST'S HOSPITAL BY KEN MANSELL

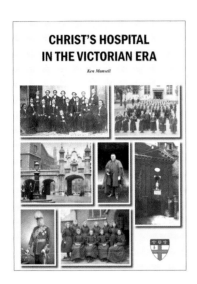

This meticulously researched book tells the story of the 11,632 boys and girls who were admitted to Christ's Hospital during the reign of Queen Victoria and chronicles the rich history of the School during the period.

Among the subjects covered:
*   *history prior to the Victorian era*
*   *admissions*
*   *the presentation process*
*   *benefactions*
*   *life and traditions at the School*
*   *the officials and teachers*
*   *famous and other Victorian Old Blues*
*   *directory of pupils' names*
*   *building the Horsham School*

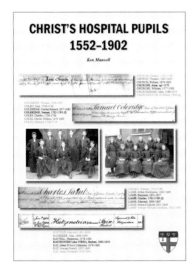

This book gives the names of over 46,500 pupils admitted to the School between 1552 and 1902, together with their years of admission and discharge. The period extends from the founding of CH to the move of the London School to Horsham.

Also covered:
*   *brief history of CH*
*   *admission arrangements*
*   *historical fluctuations in pupil numbers*
*   *life at the School*
*   *illustrated list of over 900 notable former pupils who were admitted pre-1902, with brief biographical details*

Further details of these books may be obtained as follows:
email – ken.mansell@btinternet.com
website – www.ashwaterpress.co.uk
phone (Ken Mansell) – 020 8668 5075

ASHWATER
PRESS